The Social Services

D1369966

Third edition

The Social Services
An Introduction

H. Wayne Johnson *University of Iowa*

and contributors

F. E. PEACOCK PUBLISHERS, INC.   Itasca, Illinois

Contents

Contributors

H. Wayne Johnson (Chapters 1, 2, 3, 4, 11, 14, 15, 25, Epilogue) is Coordinator of the undergraduate program of the School of Social Work of the University of Iowa. Teaching, research, and interest areas include the introductory course, juvenile/criminal justice, field experience, and rural social work. He serves on the boards of two national social work education organizations and as an accreditation site visitor for the Council on Social Work Education.

Ralph Anderson (Chapter 7) is University of Iowa Professor Emeritus and former director of the School of Social Work. He has extensive experience consulting with schools and school social workers. He is coauthor of *Human Behavior in the Social Environment: A Social Systems Approach.*

B. Eleanor Anstey (Chapter 22) is a member of the faculty of the University of Iowa, School of Social Work. She teaches courses about women in national and international social welfare, social development, and human behavior. Her publications focus on women in rural areas and international settings.

Gary Askerooth (Chapter 23) is Field Services Officer for the National Neighborhood Reinvestment Corporation in Denver, helping communities in the western United States develop nonprofit community revitalization organizations and low-income housing. He has published articles on social welfare policy and social development. Formerly a university instructor, he taught community organizing and development, and international social development.

Nancee S. Blum (Chapter 26) is a research assistant in psychiatry at the University of Iowa and teaches workshops on gerontology topics and psychiatry. She is a professional writer who has edited and authored articles in social work and medicine. Her current research is in the area of mental health and personality disorders.

Judith Burke (Chapter 24) is a professor in the School of Social Work at the University of Missouri-Columbia. She has written about women's participation in development programs, in community development, and in family therapy. Her international research experience is in Mexico and South Vietnam.

Irl Carter (Chapter 13) is Associate Professor, School of Social Work, University of Minnesota, and directs the Center for Youth Development and Research. He is coauthor of *Human Behavior in the Social Environment: A Social Systems Approach.* His research is on American Indians and youth development.

John L. Craft (Chapter 20) is director of the School of Social Work research center at the University of Iowa. He teaches beginning and advanced social work research and conducts numerous research projects. He has edited and authored books including *Statistics and Data Analysis for Social Workers,* many articles, chapters, and other publications.

W. Stanley Good (Chapter 19) is retired from the University of Iowa social work faculty where he taught administration, consultation, community organization, and social welfare policy. He was engaged in administration of public and private social work agencies. He writes on public policy, economics of the elderly, and holistic health services.

Gilbert J. Greene (Chapters 5, 6) is Associate Professor at Michigan State University School of Social Work where he teaches courses in the Clinical Social Work concentration. He has extensive professional experience working with families and has published a number of articles on this topic in social work and family therapy journals.

Michael Jacobsen (Chapter 18) chairs the social work program at Niagara University in New York State. He has published on rural human services, community change and development, as well as the sociology of professional organizations. He is currently Vice President of the National Rural Social Work Caucus.

Nancy J. Johnston (Chapter 13) is Associate Director and Coordinator of Field Instruction, School of Social Work, University of Minnesota. She teaches supervision, consultation, and social work in the workplace. Her current research is on the effect of personality types and learning styles on supervision and work styles.

Patricia Kelley (Chapter 17) is associate professor in the School of Social Work at the University of Iowa where she chairs the clinical concentration. She has published in the areas of therapy with individuals, families, and groups, and she maintains a private therapy practice.

Verne R. Kelley (Chapter 9) is Executive Director of the Mid-Eastern Iowa Community Mental Health Center. He serves on accreditation teams for the Council of Social Work Education, and is former president in Iowa of the National Association of Social Workers. His publication topics include civil liberties, rural mental health delivery, natural helpers, and treatment outcome of adolescents.

Katherine A. Kruse (Chapter 8) is on the faculty of the University of Iowa School of Social Work where she has taught courses in health care and social work practice. Her professional experience includes child welfare and medical and psychiatric social work. She has published articles on social work practice in family medicine and book chapters on discharge planning theory.

Janet Johnson Laube (Chapter 16) has been affiliated with the Iowa faculty teaching social work practice. Currently she has a clinical position in a mental health center working with individuals, families, and groups and is in private practice. She publishes articles on group therapy.

Gary R. Lowe (Chapter 21) is Associate Professor and BSW Coordinator, Indiana University, Bloomington. He has extensive experience in cross-cultural and intercultural education and professional activity and has published in the area of racism, recently focusing on South Africa.

Marilyn Southard (Chapter 22) has a clinical practice at the Northeast Iowa Community Mental Health Center specializing in women and their relationships. She is frequently a guest lecturer on feminist therapy. She writes on the subject of women's psychological development.

Marlyn Staudt (Chapter 7) has been a school social worker in Iowa for ten years and is presently employed by Great River Area Education Agency, Burlington, Iowa. She has authored several articles on the subject of school social work and is on the editorial board of the *Iowa School Social Work Journal.*

Thomas Walz (Chapter 26) is a Professor and former Director of the University of Iowa School of Social Work. He teaches in the areas of aging and public policy and has written over seventy-five articles and six books on a variety of social welfare topics. His interests include the future of social services.

Frank H. Ware (Chapter 10) is Executive Director of the Janet Wattles Community Mental Health Center in Rockford, Illinois. Formerly he directed a therapeutic community for substance abusers. He has published, lectured, and taught on substance abuse and dual diagnosis of mental illness and substance abuse.

Emma Jean Williams (Chapter 12) is semiretired from the University of Iowa School of Social Work. She came to the school after eleven years' experience in public welfare including administering a large agency in an urban community. Her interests include services for the elderly and international issues.

Preface

The theme of this text as we move now into a third edition continues to be *change*. As a pervasive fact of modern life change is clearly seen both in our social problems and in the services/programs designed as responses to such problems. Many have expanded or emerged just in the last three and a half years since we prepared the second edition. When change occurs at such a rapid pace, academic tools such as textbooks for describing and analyzing the phenomena cannot stand still. They too must evolve. Hence this new edition.

Like the two previous editions, this revised text is intended for the first course in an undergraduate social work program, whether in a four-year program or a two-year community or junior college. In some institutions, this will be the only social work course available to students, and it will most likely be offered within a sociology department or other social or behavioral science area. In other schools, this will be the first in a series of courses constituting a program, and it will probably come at the freshman/sophomore level. Some of these courses enroll students of various levels, most of whom are taking the course as an elective, whereas in others a majority are taking the first course required for a major in social work, the human services, or some similar designation.

Some schools have a two-semester or three-quarter introductory course. Patterns vary, but in such cases, one term is often devoted essentially to social welfare as a social institution and another to social work as a profession. This text could be used for either or both, but it is designed more for the institutions approach. Instructors and students will need to decide how to make best use of the book given particular needs, objectives, and patterns.

Why produce a text revision when books already exist? The fields of social work and social work education are in infinitely better shape today than fifteen years ago relative to available texts for the introductory course. Although several options exist now for instructors of this course, and some are of good quality, there remain deficiencies that many perceive to be important and that I attempted to remedy in the first two editions and do so now again. For example, the issue of substance abuse, a major contemporary problem, is updated and retained, and is not ignored as it has been in some other texts. Social work in business and industry, an emerging field, continues to be given a chapter, and there is also new content on other nontraditional settings and innovative services. Examples of totally new content are the material on social justice in Chapter 1, AIDS in Chapter 8 and elsewhere, prevention in Chapter 9, and generalist practice, case management, networking, and information and referral in Chapter 15. Material on refugees and homelessness has been expanded considerably. Rural content has been retained. The chapters in Part Three on social work practice have been rearranged, starting with a chapter on newer approaches in practice that emphasizes the generalist. Entire chapters are again devoted to social work research and administration, and housing and social development. Minorities, an extremely important subject in this era, are separated from women/sexism and are conceptualized as human diversity to include racism, ageism, handicaps, and so forth. New content on sexual orientation has been added to this part of the book. There are other new thrusts along with a real concern for trends and the future.

At the same time that we are careful to include contemporary concerns, in an introductory text we have the responsibility to cover thoroughly the large, traditional, commonplace social services, and we have done so. In fact, the only field allowed more than one chapter is services to families and children, the core of social work for decades. Similarly, social services are examined in the context of public welfare, schools, health, mental health, criminal justice, and the elderly.

Virtually every chapter could be a book in itself in view of the scope of the topics. Obviously there is much that must be omitted in each chapter in order to prevent the book as a totality from being a tome of thousands of pages. This necessitates making judgments, setting priorities, emphasizing the important (recognizing that notions of what is important vary from person to person), and at the same time including material for breadth and balance. An ever-present challenge in the introductory course is the vast territory to be covered. Hence, a text for the course is faced with the same challenge.

The chapters individually can be read as independent entities, if the reader wishes, because each can stand alone at the same time that each is an integral part of the whole. Although the order and sequence of chapters and parts is always arbitrary, there is a logical flow. Content does not have to be read in the order presented, and instructors may desire to assign reading in a different pattern. This is particularly true with regard to Parts Two and Three, which are often reversed in other books and can easily be shifted here. Clearly this book should be adapted to one's own uses, preferences, and style.

A suggestion about supplementing the text may be called for. Each instructor and many students will have ideas from their own reading and experience on appropriate supplementation. Examples I find useful are a book(s) on history of social welfare/social work and such writings as *Welfare Mother, Blaming the Victim*, and *The Color Purple*. Over the years I have also used Michael Harrington's books, most recently *The New American Poverty.*

A word about the title is in order. The title is different from that of most more-or-less comparable texts in its use of "social services" rather than "welfare" or "social work," all terms defined in Chapter 2. Most such books end up dealing with both social welfare and social work but do not reflect this fact in their titles. Hence, there is a degree of inaccuracy in many titles. This is one reason to use other phraseology. I see social services as relating to both welfare and social work, and therefore it is an acceptable term. Second, "welfare" is an emotion-laden term in the United States, and there may be value in promoting a more neutral concept. In addition, "social work" is an awkward term; physicians are not medical workers nor are attorneys legal workers. The terms "work" and "worker" are not generally used in occupational labels except for social work/er, and therefore it may be preferable to cultivate another way of thinking, at least in the title. The traditional terms are used frequently throughout the book, but the title carries a different one.

More vignettes are included in this edition for purposes of illustration. A major effort has been made to use realistic portrayals. Therefore, not all persons or situations described in the vignettes change in desired directions; not all consumers of social services are transformed and "live happily ever after." Such is life in the human services and in the real world.

We continue to place at the end of each chapter the "selected references and notes" including citations, comments, and various pieces of hopefully pertinent information that we did not want to include in the body of the chapter. These and the following "additional suggested readings" have all been updated. The latter are for the reader who would like to pursue a particular subject further. The two listings do not duplicate each other, so readers should consult both lists in determining what one might wish to read.

A genuine effort has again been made throughout to avoid sexist language. In spite of such endeavors, the reader may find that occasionally we still say "he" or "she" when there is no intention to refer to one sex more than the other. It is sometimes awkward to use language that is not sexist, but a serious attempt has been made.

Acknowledgments

It is humbling to consider how much is owed to so many. As was true of the first two editions, this book would, in all probability, not exist were it not for the generous and thoughtful contributions of chapter authors. Their interest continues, and their revised work appears again in this new version. Each author is an expert on the respective topics and each continues to be willing to subject her or his work to my editing, so that the final product is my responsibility.

Faculty from around the country were especially helpful with their constructive criticisms and suggestions. Some of these had used previous editions of the text extensively and others had not, but they took time to review the book and provide feedback. Their scholarly, penetrating observations and ideas are greatly appreciated, and some of these people will recognize their thoughts and comments incorporated into the new edition. Of course, it is not possible to be totally responsive to all suggestions, partly because there is no unanimity among them. But every idea was considered, and many were used.

A special word of thanks to the ultimate consumers, the students, who read and work with the book. It is gratifying to have feedback and reactions, both from our own students here at the University of Iowa and from others all around the country. These students are in colleges and universities, large and small, public and private, in a wide range of situations. It is especially for them that I first became interested in undertaking this endeavor and it is still for them that I continue with another edition.

Typing is a large part of this task and not very exciting for those who do all of the tedious work. Always with efficiency and good humor, the job has been done so well by Jo Conroy and Carolyn Tappan. University of Iowa librarians have been most helpful. Publishers play a special role in producing a text book. I have found all of those associated with F. E. Peacock Publishers, Inc., with whom I have dealt to be consistently competent, cordial, and supportive. This is true from Ted Peacock through the entire staff.

Finally, as always, the person who is my greatest source of assistance, inspiration, and support is my wife, Donna. It is to her and to all of my students—past, present, and future—that the book is dedicated.

H. Wayne Johnson
Iowa City, January 1989

Part One

Background

1 Introduction

H. Wayne Johnson

Welcome to the study of the social services or, more accurately, contemporary American social services. While in this book we do concern ourselves both with the historical development and future trends relative to social work and welfare, the emphasis is on current social problems, services, and methods of practice. Further, despite some consideration of international social welfare, we are most concerned with the United States.

It is important to understand that the social services constitute an extremely broad and diverse collection of endeavors. In comparison with most professions, social work is a more expansive umbrella covering a tremendous array of activities and dealing with a wide variety of problems. While all of this will be examined at greater length later, here we can note that most, though not all, of social work has in the past been divisible into one of three categories that traditionally were termed "methods" and now are often described as practice approaches. These are social casework, social groupwork, and community organization. Later we will suggest modification and refinement of this threefold construct reflecting the trend toward generalist practice, but it will suffice for now. Much social work is direct or personal service, one-to-one or in families or other small groups, with persons variously labeled clients, patients, residents, members, and so on. This "micro" activity is casework and/or to a considerable degree group-work, some of which is clinical. On the other side is indirect "macro"-level, community-oriented activity involving social planning, organizing, social action, and other related efforts.

Both of these major aspects are aimed at helping people, either individually or collectively, and both are directed at bringing about change. When change in a positive direction is not possible, as is sometimes the situation, the goal in the human services is to preserve or maintain the status quo. More about purposes and objectives later. For now it is well to keep in mind the idea of the social worker as an enabler generally, a person who empowers and who helps others to make desired things happen. Any way it is conceptualized, social workers are helpers—helping people in myriad ways to help themselves.

To be a helper requires understanding people's psychosocial situations and humans as bio-psycho-social creatures. It necessitates developing the ability to intervene in people's lives and situations in constructive ways and to build strategies for such intervention. To become this kind of a professional requires a combination of certain knowledge, skill, and attitudes/values. Much of the remainder of the book deals with these.

To illustrate the kind of knowledge required to work competently with people in a helping capacity, two aspects of human motivation and human development will be noted. The psychologist Abraham Maslow and others have postulated the idea that humans are motivated by certain basic needs. According to Maslow there is a hierarchy beginning with physiological needs and progressing to the need for safety, belongingness and love, esteem, and self-actualization or self-fulfillment (and potential). As the more basic ones are satisfied, subsequent needs replace them in importance. If the needs go unsatisfied, they remain a major force in the personality and behavior of the person in typically negative ways just as their gratification tends to have positive consequences for the person.[1]

Erik Erikson, a neo-Freudian, has contributed to our understanding of human development in important ways. He conceptualizes "eight ages of man" from infancy through old age. Each developmental stage builds on and moves forward from all previous life stages. Erikson also suggests that there are major issues of living to be resolved at each developmental level. For example, in infancy the issue is "basic trust versus mistrust," in adolescence "identity versus role confusion," and in old age "ego integrity versus despair."[2] This notion of human development acknowledges the biological realities of humankind and places these within a cultural and historical context.

Important understandings of human behavior are derived from integrating the contributions of social and behavioral scientists. In the case of Maslow and Erikson, for example, relating the idea of a hierarchy of basic needs to the notion of stages of development produces an image of the human as dynamic and changing and as possessing potential for further accomplishments. The work of Maslow, Erikson, and many others furthers the comprehension of human service workers and others dealing with people in the context of social problems.

SOCIAL CHANGE

A central theme in this book is *social change*, which is ever present in society and, in the latter part of the twentieth century, comes at a breathtaking pace. The change is multifaceted and exists on several levels. Perhaps the most conspicuous change is technological as illustrated by the information/computer revolution, to cite just one of many developments. But change is not restricted to tangibles in this age of technology that has been termed the "postindustrial" era. Just as striking are some of the modifications taking place in social institutions such as the family where, to mention only a few aspects of this phenomenon, we are experiencing much higher rates of cohabitation, divorce, single parenthood, employment of women outside the home, and early retirement than was traditionally the case. In addition, such movements as children's rights and women's rights, while not new historically, have new impetus and implications.

Long ago the sociologist William Ogburn spoke of a tendency toward what he called "culture lag" in societies in which the various cultural elements do not change at the same rate; the intangible components often tend to lag behind the material.[3] A classic illustration is our sophisticated instruments of warfare that are so far in advance (or at least seem to be) of our methods of peace keeping and international relations. The concept of culture lag is a useful one in considering social change as it relates to social work. One reason is that social work itself is changing just as are the problems and conditions with which it attempts to cope. Some facets of the helping disciplines are advanced while others are relatively primitive. For example, technologically, medicine is a highly advanced and sophisticated field; yet, much is unknown about mental illness or about how to pay the physician's bill for treatment.

That there would be value conflicts at such a time should not be surprising. Perhaps no field of endeavor is more enmeshed in these than are the social services. One need merely mention abortion, national health insurance, crime and delinquency penalties, and guaranteed annual income to suggest how extremely complex and value-conflict-laden problems and services involving social work are.

A specific example warrants mention. World population is viewed by some as an out-of-control "explosion" and potential disaster whereas others apparently see little reason for concern. The population of the earth doubled from 2.5 billion in 1950 to 5 billion in 1987 and is projected to double again to 10 billion in a few decades in the twenty-first century.[4] This has implications for food supply, water, natural resources, ecology and the environment, along with sheer space. A report in July 1984 optimistically noted that there is evidence that the number of people dying of hunger in the world has recently decreased, that the infant mortality rate is down, and that world hunger may be eradicated by the turn of the century.[5] But at the same time a UN conference in Africa ("the hungriest continent") called on nations there to spend more on agriculture or face "mass starvation."[6] The Worldwatch Institute believes that 7 million children could be saved yearly through relatively inexpensive primary care procedures—clean drinking water and sanitation. One-quarter of the 55 million deaths in the world each year occur in developing countries among children under age five. This source declares that one-third of the world's population lacks clean water, sanitation, and basic health services.[7] Regardless of what one accepts among these divergent views, value conflicts abound, and the implications for social work, both here and abroad, are profound. Chapter 24 deals further with the international realm.

Social work can be conceptualized as helping people to cope with change.[8] One advantage of this view is that it assumes that everyone is influenced by, and is an integral part of, change. Furthermore, since many social problems result from change and because it is human to have such problems, the idea that any of us may be potential users of social services becomes more acceptable. Any of us, then, might have occasion to need a social worker, not just the "poor," the people from the "wrong side of the tracks," or of some particular age, ethnic, or other group. This concept of social work may tend to bring about more humility and realism in our thinking, for troubles can, indeed, "happen to any of us."[9]

At the same time that there is pervasive change, there is also, on the other hand, a simultaneous force toward stability. While tomorrow is never exactly like yesterday, neither is it entirely different. Such continuities make a good deal of prediction possible, but the likelihood of change requires that various qualifications and caveats frequently must accompany the predictions. We will be noting in a number of ways that social work is a relatively young field (as professions go) and that it is very much in ferment, which is part and parcel of this social change.

BUREAUCRACY

Today, in this country and in much of the world we experience industrial, urban, mass society. These qualities tend to make for bureaucracy. We use the term "bureaucracy" not in a negative judgmental sense as is the case when it is so often used in conjunction with government. Rather we use it in the dictionary, neutral sense to mean "a body of officials and administrators," each of whom is responsible to his or her superiors.[10] Characteristics attributed to bureaucracy typically have a negative hue: devotion to routine, inflexibility of rules, red tape, procrastination, and reluctance to assume responsibility and to experiment.[11]

Instead of emphasizing these and other undesirable attributes of bureaucracy, it is useful to understand this phenomenon as a function of bigness. It is not just government that is bureaucratic; so also are large business, industry, labor, education, religion, and social welfare institutions. Such is the almost inevitable nature of mass organizations and social institutions.

From a human services point of view, one of the most bothersome and problematic aspects of bureaucracy is the insensitivity it may bring on the part of some personnel who are supposed to be serving others and facilitating the meeting of human needs. This should, however, be related to a larger, more generalized societal insensitivity toward people in need generally. Large cross sections of the United States population are ready and waiting to engage in what has been termed "victim blaming."[12]

BLAMING THE VICTIM

Blaming the victim takes place in connection with the poor, minorities, the elderly, children, and people with assorted problems. To delineate a group of people as problematic and then to place responsibility and criticism on them for the conditions(s) that lead to their labeling is all too commonplace. As Ira Glasser notes, "private trouble become a reason for public punishment."[13] William Ryan popularized the concept of victim blaming with his 1971 book. He demonstrated the usefulness of the concept in such diverse areas as racial and ethnic minority groups, schools/education, medical care/health, illegitimacy, housing, and crime/justice.[14] Actually it goes far beyond these broad considerations in that in a deep and profound sense, we tend to condemn those who are the products of forces and practices over which they have little or no control such as racism, discrimination, sexism, unemployment, poverty, poor health and inadequate medical care, and so on.

In view of these developments, it is not particularly surprising that we come to issues of social control, of "regulating the poor," to cite one consequence of victim blaming.[15] Such activity is not limited to the poor but includes other recipient groups as well. But we do much more than openly, conspicuously, and all too often destructively regulate some of the people we "serve." In less visible ways, many social welfare programs serve social-control functions. This is often subtle but nonetheless real. That this is a fact is not necessarily bad; social control is inherent in much of what social work is and does. The corrections and mental health fields are significant examples; both are dealt with in later chapters. What is important is that this fact be recognized and that those of us working in such fields acknowledge the power and potential we have for destructiveness as well as for constructiveness. This is one of the reasons that self-awareness is stressed so much in social work education.

SOCIAL JUSTICE

Since the responsibility of a profession like social work is to further social justice, it becomes necessary to consider this concept. Beverly and McSweeney define justice as "fairness in the relationships between people as these relate to the possession and/or acquisition of resources based on some kind of valid claim to a share of those resources."[16] They adopt from Perelman the "formal principle of justice," which holds that "all human beings, because they belong to the category of being human, must be treated in the same way."[17] In order for this rather abstract and nebulous concept of social justice to become more meaningful, it may be useful to continue on a bit further with the three Beverly/McSweeney "concrete principles" of justice:[18]

1. The allocation of resources by government must give priority to meeting basic human needs in the areas of food, clothing, and shelter for all people within the jurisdiction of that government.
2. All demands or claims on resources are valid and just if and only if they satisfy either of the following conditions:
   a. Those demands serve to enhance the conditions of humanness required in terms of providing for food, clothing, shelter.
   b. The quantity of resources available is such that additional resources are available to meet demands beyond those postulated to maintain humanness.
3. It is the responsibility of our national government to ensure that fairness prevails in the allocation of resources, and that resources are allocated in accord with Principles 1 and 2.

These basic ideas are central to what social work is all about, and we will have opportunity to examine them in numerous contexts as we move along in our subject matter.

A LOOK AHEAD

What can be accomplished in a single volume is limited in a number of ways. Much information is provided here, but it can go only so far. No book can be all things to all its readers. For example, we do not attempt to include an in-depth treatment of the how-to-do-its of working with people who have problems. Rather, this content is covered largely in a descriptive way. With other content more oriented to social policy matters, for example, we often do more than describe, analyze, and explain. Sometimes we take a position, making it clear, hopefully, that we are doing so. We do have views on many matters of public concern as far as human social well-being is concerned, and to deny this fact or to act as though this were not the case would be counterproductive when there are areas of genuine controversy and divided opinion.

Because of these limitations in almost any one book, students reading this text who believe they may want to move toward social work as a career are invited to test their interest by going beyond the book. One way to do so is to engage in volunteer work in the community, in its agencies and organizations. Spend some time volunteering (paid employment is fine, of course) with children or the elderly, for example. Work in a hospital or some other institution. Help out in a day-care center, crisis hotline, group home, or any one of the numerous possibilities in communities. In the introductory social work course with which the author is most familiar, students do forty-five hours of volunteer work. There is nothing sacred about this figure. What is important is acquiring experience and, if possible, working at a variety of things over a period of time. By the time they graduate, some students have accumulated a rich background of experiences. The more the better. Talking to social workers about their work, visiting agencies, and spending a day observing one or more professionals can all be worthwhile and valuable.

No assumption is made by the author or contributors that all readers will or should ultimately become social workers. But all can gain an understanding of social work and take it with them into other fields where the knowledge is useful and can be shared. It is essential that people be informed, so that we can all work together in our communities and society toward shared goals. Partly as a result of taking courses like the one for which this book was planned, students will someday have decision-making and leadership responsibilities greater than could have been imagined during student days. The fact of holding a degree (associate, baccalaureate, or graduate) almost inevitably makes for larger community roles, often even in the absence of college degrees. Certainly it is important to be informed taxpayers, voters, and citizens. This, at a minimum, we have a right to expect of ourselves and of each other. The author hopes the time together will be fruitful in these respects.

SUMMARY AND CONCLUSIONS

In this first rather short chapter we have initiated some preliminary exploration of what the study of social work/social welfare is all about and what this may mean for the interests and goals of at least some readers. The presence of social change has been noted, and it was suggested that social work attempts to help people to cope with change. The fact of bureaucracy and the phenomenon of blaming the victim were discussed briefly. Finally, the idea of social justice as a responsibility of social work has been introduced. Some of what has been discussed in this chapter is rather abstract. It will take on more meaning as we move along. May your journey through the remainder of the book be a pleasant and rewarding voyage.

NOTES

1. A. H. Maslow, *Motivation and Personality* (New York: Harper & Row, 1954), pp. 80–106.
2. Erik H. Erikson, *Childhood and Society,* 2nd ed. (New York: W. W. Norton & Co., 1963), p. 273.
3. William F. Ogburn, *Social Change* (New York: Viking Press, 1922), pp. 200–201.
4. My T. Vu, *World Population Projections 1985* (Baltimore: Johns Hopkins University Press for the World Bank, 1985), pp. ix–xiv.
5. "A Shift in the Wind 18" (San Francisco: "The Hunger Project," 1984).
6. "African Nations Urged To Learn To Feed Themselves," *Des Moines Register,* July 23, 1984, p. 5A.
7. "Primary Health Care Seen Big Third World Lifesaver," *Des Moines Register,* July 30, 1984, p. 5A.
8. H. Wayne Johnson, *Rural Human Services* (Itasca, Ill.: F. E. Peacock Publishers, 1980), pp. 5–6.
9. For example, see Joseph Boskin, *Issues in American Society* (Encino, Calif.: Glencoe Publishing Co., 1978).

10. *The Random House Dictionary of the English Language* (New York: Random House, 1969), p. 180.

11. Henry Pratt Fairchild, *Dictionary of Sociology* (Paterson, N.J.: Littlefield, Adams & Co., 1964), p. 29.

12. William Ryan, *Blaming the Victim*, 2nd ed. (New York: Vintage Books, 1976).

13. Ira Glasser, "Prisoners of Benevolence," in *Doing Good* by Willard Gaylin, Ira Glasser, Steven Marcus, and David Rothman (New York: Pantheon Books, 1978), p. 114.

14. Ryan, *Blaming the Victim*.

15. Frances Fox Piven and Richard A. Cloward. *Regulating the Poor* (New York: Vintage Books, 1971).

16. David P. Beverly and Edward A. McSweeney, *Social Welfare and Social Justice* (Englewood Cliffs, N.J.: Prentice-Hall, Inc., 1987), p. 5.

17. Ibid., p. 7.

18. Ibid., pp. 8–10.

ADDITIONAL SUGGESTED READINGS

Anderson, Ralph E., and Irl Carter, *Human Behavior in the Social Environment*, 3rd ed. New York: Aldine Publishing Co., 1984.

Brieland, Donald, Lela B. Costin, and Charles R. Atherton, *Contemporary Social Work*, 3rd ed. New York: McGraw-Hill Book Co., 1985.

Chess, Wayne A., and Julia Norlin, *Human Behavior and the Social Environment*. Needham Heights, Mass.: Allyn & Bacon, 1988.

Dolgoff, Ralph, and Donald Feldstein, *Understanding Social Welfare*, 2nd ed. New York: Longman, 1984.

Eitzen, D.S., *Social Problems*, 2nd ed. Newton, Mass.: Allyn & Bacon, 1983.

Federico, Ronald C., *The Social Welfare Institution*, 3rd ed. Lexington, Mass.: D.C. Heath & Co., 1980.

Ford, Jill, *Human Behavior*. Boston: Routledge & Kegan Paul, 1982.

Lipsky, Michael, *Street-Level Bureaucracy*. New York: Russell Sage Foundation, 1980.

Ogburn, W.F., and M.F. Nimkoff, *Technology and the Changing Family*. Boston: Houghton Mifflin, 1955.

Perrucie, Robert, and Marc Pilisuk, *The Triple Revolution Emerging*. Boston: Little, Brown & Co., 1971.

Specht, Riva, and Grace Craig, *Human Development: A Social Work Perspective*, 2nd ed. Englewood Cliffs, N.J.: Prentice-Hall, 1987.

Zastrow, Charles, and Karen Kirst-Ashman, *Understanding Human Behavior and the Social Environment*. Chicago: Nelson-Hall, 1987.

2 Basic Concepts: Social Welfare, Social Work, and Social Services

H. Wayne Johnson

Three terms are basic for this discussion and for the entire book: social welfare, social work, and social services. Numerous definitions of *social welfare* are found in the literature, but they tend not to differ from each other substantively. For our purposes social welfare refers to societally organized activities aimed at maintaining or improving human well-being. This very broad concept involves a number of professions, including, but not restricted to, social work. Among other occupations involved are those having to do with health, education, recreation, and public safety, to mention only a few. Social welfare encompasses both governmental and voluntary sectors and cuts across all levels of each. Since these activities are organized, it should be noted that this means both those formally and those informally organized. For example, in the United States we find rural social welfare in general less formally organized than its urban counterpart.[1]

Explicit in this definition of social welfare is the goal of human well-being. That this is a highly relative purpose is seen in the statement about the activities aiming at *maintaining* or *improving* social functioning. While improvement is the ideal, in the real world it is not always possible. Often one must settle for maintenance. The dying patient, for example, is probably not going to improve; yet, increasingly

13

there is the notion of death with dignity. In other words, much can often be done to be helpful to people in the sense of maintaining them and thus enhancing their well-being.

A second term, *social work*, requires definition, and as with social welfare, various definitive statements exist. Boehm's, developed in the late 1950s, follows:

> Social work seeks to enhance the social functioning of individuals, singly and in groups, by activities focused upon their social relationships which constitute the interaction between man and his environment.[2]

Twenty years later Baer and Federico defined social work,[3]

> Social work is concerned and involved with the interactions between people and the institutions of society that affect the ability of people to accomplish life tasks, realize aspirations and values, and alleviate distress.

In this book social work is taken to mean a profession concerned with the relationships between people and their environments and the influencing of these relationships toward maximal social functioning. Boehm found social work's "distinguishing characteristic" to be its focus on social relationships.[4] Here we take a similar position. This means that social work is concerned with human interactions and the interchange between people and their surroundings, their psycho-social situations. That this is still central to social work is seen in current developments having to do with refinement of Council on Social Work Education (CSWE) accreditation standards for undergraduate and graduate programs in colleges and universities. The analytic model for social work practice is seen to be the "person at the interface with the environment."[5] What this means is that the social worker focuses on the points at which the various levels of social systems come together and their effect on the person: individual, family, other groups, community, organizations, and society. These are the major social systems.[6] This is why, with the move to more of a social systems approach in this profession, social work is being seen as "boundary work," that is, the boundaries between the systems and/or their component parts. Social work tends to deal with exchanges between the components of these systems, for example, between family members, between an individual and a person(s) in other systems such as education or employment, between two or more groups in a community, or between several organizations.[7]

The distinction between social welfare and social work is one between social institution or system (social welfare) and occupation or profession (social work). Social welfare, a far broader concept than social work, is what sociologists call a social institution.[8] It encompasses a number of occupational endeavors including social work. On the other hand, social work refers to professional activities—what certain people do as their practice in their vocational roles.

Social services is the last concept for analysis. It is defined here as the programs or measures employing social workers or related professionals and directed toward social welfare goals. Social workers operate in many different fields: in the corrections services the worker may be a probation officer; in family social services a marriage counselor; in the field of the elderly the worker is perhaps a planner of programs, an advocate, or an organizer.

SOCIAL WORK AND SOCIOLOGY

Partly because social work courses in colleges and universities are often offered within sociology departments, but for other reasons as well, a question frequently arises as to the relationship between sociology and social work. Sociology is basically an academic discipline, a social science, with a body of scientific knowledge, while social work is professional practice.[9] Whereas sociology is a theoretically based and research-oriented study of human groups, social work represents technology or social engineering and the application of knowledge, sociological as well as other. Berger puts it well: "Social work . . . is a certain *practice* in society. Sociology is not a practice, but an attempt to understand."[10]

A rough analogy may help to make the point. Sociology is to social work approximately what biology is to medicine. Biology and sociology are bodies of knowledge, while the other two are professional services or practices. Of course, the physician must study and know more than biology; so also the social worker's sources of knowledge include, but go beyond, sociology. Other important parts of the knowledge base are psychology, human development, political science, and economics.

One difference between sociology and social work has to do with values. The sociologist, like any scientist, is committed to the "search for truth" and thus attempts to be objective and practice "value neutrality" apart from devotion to knowledge (which, incidentally, is a value in itself). The social worker functions from a different value base, one that reflects the Judeo-Christian heritage and the American and Western world humanitarian and democratic influences.

VALUES

Like any profession, social work practice entails knowledge, skills, and attitudes or values. The core values are those having to do with human

---

CODE OF ETHICS[12]
Summary of Major Principles

I. THE SOCIAL WORKER'S CONDUCT AND COMPORTMENT
   AS A SOCIAL WORKER

   A. *Propriety*
      The social worker should maintain high standards of personal conduct in the capacity or identity as social worker.

   B. *Competence and Professional Development*
      The social worker should strive to become and remain proficient in professional practice and the performance of professional functions.

   C. *Service*
      The social worker should regard as primary the service obligation of the social work profession.

   D. *Integrity*
      The social worker should act in accordance with the highest standards of professional integrity.

   E. *Scholarship and Research*
      The social worker engaged in study and research should be guided by the conventions of scholarly inquiry.

II. THE SOCIAL WORKER'S ETHICAL RESPONSIBILITY TO CLIENTS

   F. *Primacy of Clients' Interests*
      The social worker's primary responsibility is to clients.

   G. *Rights and Prerogatives of Clients*
      The social worker should make every effort to foster maximum self-determination on the part of clients.

   H. *Confidentiality and Privacy*
      The social worker should respect the privacy of clients and hold in confidence all information obtained in the course of professional service.

   I. *Fees*
      When setting fees, the social worker should ensure that they are fair, reasonable, considerate, and commensurate with the service performed and with due regard for the clients' ability to pay.

---

worth and dignity. Social workers generally deal with people experiencing problems of one kind or another and often see people who are not at their best. This makes commitment to humanitarian values especially important. Take the intoxicated person as an example; the inebriate in the gutter, untidy, irrational, uncooperative, is still a human being, and this quality gives him or her worth. The drunk is important not because of the drunkenness but because of the humanness. We are all fallible and capable of falling short of our potential. The social worker's professional values acknowledge both the strengths and weaknesses of humankind.

What are the other philosophical values upon which modern social work stands? Friedlander categorized these into a fourfold scheme, simplified as follows:[11]

III. THE SOCIAL WORKER'S ETHICAL RESPONSIBILITY TO COLLEAGUES

J. *Respect, Fairness, and Courtesy*
The social worker should treat colleagues with respect, courtesy, fairness, and good faith.

K. *Dealing with Colleagues' Clients*
The social worker has the responsibility to relate to the clients of colleagues with full professional consideration.

IV. THE SOCIAL WORKER'S ETHICAL RESPONSIBILITY TO EMPLOYERS AND EMPLOYING ORGANIZATIONS

L. *Commitments to Employing Organizations*
The social worker should adhere to commitments made to the employing organizations.

V. THE SOCIAL WORKER'S ETHICAL RESPONSIBILITY TO THE SOCIAL WORK PROFESSION

M. *Maintaining the Integrity of the Profession*
The social worker should uphold and advance the values, ethics, knowledge, and mission of the profession.

N. *Community Service*
The social worker should assist the profession in making social services available to the general public.

O. *Development of Knowledge*
The social worker should take responsibility for identifying, developing, and fully utilizing knowledge for professional practice.

VI. THE SOCIAL WORKER'S ETHICAL RESPONSIBILITY TO SOCIETY

P. *Promoting the General Welfare*
The social worker should promote the general welfare of society.

1. The humanistic values having to do with the dignity, integrity, and worth of the individual human being just alluded to.
2. The right of self-determination—the idea that the individual has the right to determine his or her own needs and how to meet them.
3. Equality of opportunity, limited only by the innate capacities of the individual.
4. People's social responsibilities toward themselves, their families, their community, and society.

The value orientation of a profession can be understood in many ways. One is to examine some of the formalized statements, creeds, and documents that are developed by organizations. In the case of social work the Code of Ethics of the National Association of Social

Workers (NASW) is perhaps the best example. Reprinted on pages 16 and 17 is a 1980 revision and expansion of the code in summary form, in which the democratic humanistic core of social work values appears rather conspicuously.

SOCIAL WORK: ART OR SCIENCE?

Another question that sometimes surfaces has to do with whether social work is an art or a science. Much of the rest of this book addresses this question, at least implicitly, but we will deal with it briefly now simply to say that the only possible answer is that it is both. To the extent that there is a transmittable body of verifiable relevant information and knowledge integrated within a subject, it is a "science."

The scientific aspect of social work is real and growing, especially as the social and behavioral sciences, on which it so heavily depends, mature. But just as the field of medicine has its individual, subjective, "bedside manner" nonscience components, so social work is partially an "art." It is an art in that some people appear to be "naturals" or possess a "knack" or talent for working with people in a helping capacity. Whatever qualities these terms are used to characterize—warmth of personality, dedication to a helping goal, empathy, and so forth—the fact remains that social work is not all science. Ideally a person possessing the personality qualities and motivation so important to this profession (art) is able to capitalize on formal education and profit from present knowledge (science).

RESIDUAL AND INSTITUTIONAL SOCIAL WELFARE

Wilensky and Lebeaux presented two useful conceptions of social welfare which they termed the "residual" and the "institutional."[13] The older residual view sees a place for social welfare services only after the breakdown of the family or the market, the proper sources for meeting needs. The newer institutional position, looking at contemporary industrial society, calls for these services as a regular societal function. These two views are philosophically at opposite ends of a scale, but in actual practice social work today is somewhere between them, mixing elements of each. Powerful social forces are at play impacting on individuals and families: population growth, industrialization, urbanization, the human rights "revolution," mobility, changes in the structure of the family, scarcity of natural resources and energy among others. From all this, the long-term historical trend appears to be from the residual toward the institutional. Some components of each conception are as follows:

Residual	*Institutional*
The needs are seen as abnormal	The needs are expected, given industrialization
Problematic situations are an emergency, a crisis	Problems are inherent in the complexity of modern life
People are helped only after the exhaustion of their resources	Help is provided before a breakdown
The problem and the service carry a stigma	There is no stigma in either the problem or the service
Help tends to take the form of temporary amelioration, a reluctant, last-resort dole or charity and is terminated as early as possible	Service is institutionalized to emphasize prevention and rehabilitation and may be permanent
Philosophy of rugged individualism	Emphasis on security, humanitarianism

Wilensky and Lebeaux conclude their discussion with this prediction, "The 'welfare state' will become the 'welfare society,' and both will be more reality than epithet."[14] At this writing, with conservatives having been in power nationally in the United States for eight years, it may be difficult to accept this historical assessment. Over the long haul, however, this does seem to be the direction in which we are moving. The thrust of modern societies is toward viewing social services as what Kahn called "social utilities," an investment in people to meet their normal needs "arising from their situations and roles in modern social life" in industrial communities.[15]

Some people find this trend disconcerting and bemoan our movement toward "socialism" or some other "ism" seen as threatening to free enterprise, capitalism, and freedom. For example, former U.S. Senator Barry Goldwater, the Republican candidate for president in 1964 and a person with unquestionable conservative credentials, devoted a chapter to "The Welfare State" in *The Conscience of a Conservative*.[16] He wrote that the welfare state is now preferred over socializing the means of production as a method of "collectivization." According to Goldwater, "Socialism-through-Welfarism poses a far greater danger to freedom than Socialism-through-Nationalization." He added, "The effect of welfarism on freedom will be felt later on— after its beneficiaries have become its victims, after dependence on government has turned into bondage and it is too late to unlock the jail." After arguing for making the helping of people in need a private matter or a concern of state and local government rather than federal, Goldwater writes, "But let us do this in a way that is conducive to the spiritual as well as the material well-being of our citizens—and in a way that will preserve their freedom."

Since Goldwater's views may be reflected in those of millions of Americans (evidence for this is the conservative administration of Ronald Reagan), it is well to examine them further, following a discussion of "welfare." The word "welfare," as we use it, connotes the general well-being of people collectively. In our society, to attain general well-being, mass (federal governmental) action is often necessary. Why do we have federal highways and a postal system, among the many other measures, except for the common good? On other governmental levels we seldom deplore our use of public educational systems, either primary/secondary or college/university. Nor do we seem distressed over our "socialized" municipal fire and police protection or water supply, sewage disposal, and garbage removal. All represent accepted general needs and expected collective governmental actions. Why should it be different in such areas as income maintenance and health, for example? Many other industrial nations do not understand the American preoccupation and obsession with the evils of socialism. They seem to understand far better than we do that such programs, in part, make capitalism and free enterprise workable by, among other things, providing a framework of protection for vulnerable individuals in mass societies. The "victims" and slaves that Goldwater refers to are such only when ignored by the communities and societies for which, incidentally, they perform much of the dirty work through typically low-wage and high-risk, but essential, occupations. Goldwater's concern for the "spiritual" well-being of people and their freedom seems strange; where is the spirituality and freedom in hunger, poverty, illness, and all the other threats to human decency? Where is the human dignity in this? Finally, Goldwater naively suggests that all money not appropriated by government for welfare is available potentially for private charity. This assumes a pervasive altruism, evidence for which appears lacking. Even if such altruism existed, private charities are generally designed to meet narrower, specific needs, not mass problems.

SOCIAL AGENCIES

Most social work is carried out within the context of an agency or organization of some kind. Collectively these are usually thought of as social agencies. A growing amount of social work is done outside the framework of an agency, in the form of private practice.[17] Social workers in private practice are generally engaged in such activities as counseling, psychotherapy in some form, consultation, or educational/training endeavors. While social workers in industry and some other contexts are in nontraditional settings, these are organizations. They influence the activities of professionals and are influenced by them as do agencies in general.

Agency settings can be classified into various categories with regard to social work practice. In some settings social workers are the principal professionals present and social work is of the essence—no social work, no agency. These are termed *primary* agencies. Examples are a welfare department, family service agency, and children's program offering adoption and foster care services. In other agencies the social work role is subordinate to that of other professionals from such fields as medicine, education, or law, and these agencies are called *secondary* or *host* settings. They are hosts to social work and can operate without this profession although we, of course, would argue that the service is of better quality when social work is present. Examples of these are hospitals (medical and psychiatric social workers), courts (probation officers), and schools (school social workers).

One of the most basic distinctions made relative to social work programs is whether they are *public* (tax-supported) or *private* (voluntary). In an earlier era this separation was clear and distinct. Now, however, it is much less so in that governmental (public) funds permeate many, if not most, formerly private agencies. This is so extensive, in fact, that some so-called private services could not exist today without public funding.[18] A common form that this takes is for public organizations such as a state department of public welfare, social services, or human services to purchase needed defined services from private providers such as a day-care center, group home, or rehabilitation program. This enables the provision of services that the department is not equipped to provide or could offer only at great expense. Once in existence, the service is available not only to the government department but often to other community entities as well.

Public agencies may be funded by local governmental units such as municipalities, counties, school districts; by regional bodies or states; by the federal government; or by some combination. The sources of funds for private agencies are often many and complex. Some combination of the following may be found: United Way money, fees, purchase-of-service charges, church or other contributions, bequests and annuities, interest from endowments, and others.

Private or voluntary agencies are of two types, sectarian (that is, church- or religious-related), and nonsectarian. Examples of the former are Lutheran Social Services, Catholic Charities, Jewish Community Centers, and many others, sometimes bearing a denominational name, but often not. Some private agencies, particularly organizations serving groups and communities, but also family and children's services, are not church-related. In view of the ecumenical movement of recent decades, the distinction between church-related and non-church-related agencies is not necessarily terribly significant. Many denominational agencies serve numerous clients, sometimes actually a majority, from outside their own groups. The infusion of public funds into private agencies noted above includes church-connected organizations, so this tends to diminish the importance of the sectarian/nonsectarian line further.

Social agencies also differ in age and size. Some go back to the beginning of the century or earlier, and others may reflect in their programs the factors and forces from the 1960s, 1970s, or 1980s that led to their creation. In size, some agencies are so small that the director may also be heavily involved in direct service. On the other end of the scale are large organizations with more than one administrative person, several supervisors, and numerous direct service workers in addition to a sizable clerical staff and perhaps others.

A social agency is often more than a single local entity; many are part of a network of organizations, stretching across a state, the nation,

American Red Cross

Saragosa, a small Texas town, was severely damaged by a tornado in 1987. Volunteer labor, primarily from the Texas Baptist Men and their families, helped rebuild most of the sixty-one homes destroyed. The Red Cross canteened the construction effort, illustrating combined sectarian and nonsectarian voluntary effort.

or even several countries. Local welfare or public social service departments, for example, are units of similar state agencies. Some states have two or more intermediate district or regional offices encompassing several counties each. Outside of a single state we next encounter the federal regional unit of this system. There are ten such multistate regions with headquarters in Boston, New York City, Philadelphia, Atlanta, Chicago, Dallas, Kansas City, Denver, San Francisco, and Seattle. Finally, at the top of the pyramid there is in Washington, D.C., the U.S. Department of Health and Human Services (HHS) or what until 1980 was the Department of Health, Education and Welfare (HEW).

Another example, this one from the private sector, is Family Service America (FSA) in Milwaukee. Some 280 local mostly private family service agencies across the nation are affiliated with FSA, which provides various supports to the local units. The Child Welfare League of America (CWLA) is a further illustration. This Washington, D.C.–based organization accredits agencies serving children. Organizations like these two set standards for agencies in their fields and engage in publication, education, information assembly and distribution, program development, research, and advocacy. Within a state an agency may have several branch operations, each offering some or all of the agency's services.

DIMENSIONS

A number of dimensions can be delineated in social work that facilitate our understanding. Included are fields, age groups, populations, and social problems. It is true that there is considerable overlapping and interrelatedness among these, but they are nonetheless useful constructs.

Bartlett points out that "field" may refer to either programs/settings/services on one hand or different kinds of social work practice in these contexts on the other.[19] In examining the so-called "fields of practice" it is advantageous to differentiate further between settings and fields. "Settings" refer to the agencies or organizations themselves rather than the larger fields of which the settings are a part. To illustrate, health and mental health are fields, whereas a hospital and a mental health center are settings. In both cases the context (setting and field) is important.

Another dimension in the social service results from categorizing people served by *ages*. Some programs focus on a single age group and others on several or even all ages. The usual groups when separating by age are infants, preschoolers, children, adolescents, young adults, middle aged, and elderly or some variation of these. A day-care center for youngsters and a nursing home for the aged point up the importance social welfare attaches to age factors.

A related and somewhat overlapping approach is concerned with *populations*. Examples are single parents, college students, widows, and the handicapped. Programming often revolves around a particular population(s) and is directed toward meeting needs and problem resolution within this context. Some problems are unique to one population whereas others are characteristic of several groups.

Finally, one way to look at social welfare measures which also relates to those just described is in terms of *social problems*. The list is long but includes crime, poverty, alcoholism, and mental illness, to cite a few. Social work may be thought of as a profession concerned with social problems, their remedy and control. The interrelatedness of these various dimensions or levels is seen if we take the case of crime (social problem), consider for example victims of offenders (populations), the youth or young adults who commit much of our crime (ages), corrections (a field of service), and a prison (a specific setting). Similar relationships exist with many, but not all, social service areas.

OTHER CONCEPTS, PRINCIPLES, TRENDS

There are a number of developments in social welfare and the broad field of human services at this time, some of which have profound implications for a field like social work. Some of these are further along than others and are far beyond the idea stage; others are still emerging. Many are interrelated with others. The order in which these principles and concepts are presented here is of no particular importance. They all are important themes, thrusts, and issues in social work currently.

1. *Least drastic or restrictive alternative.*[20] Developments of the last couple of decades have given many Americans pause as we have become increasingly aware that too much of our past programming for people in the name of helping has had damaging consequences or side effects. Hence it is now being perceived that the general principle should be followed of always using the least drastic or restrictive alternative available. Historically we have passed through a series of eras in our notions of proper treatment. Clearly from the present view some of these were harmful.

Child care is a good example. Today's view is that children should be kept at home if at all possible and supports provided to keep the family intact. If part-time arrangements such as day care do not suffice and a youngster cannot remain at home for whatever reason and if relatives are not available, foster family care may be the next possibility, a less drastic alternative than institutional care of the kind associated with the orphanage era at the turn of the century.

Another example is corrections. Incarceration of offenders is a drastic and restrictive action. There is clear evidence that most offenders do not require such severe handling and that there can and should be a variety of ways of keeping the offender in the community with less cost to the taxpayers, adequate protection for the public, potential help for the victim, and a better prognosis for the perpetrator of the illegal act. This will be discussed in greater detail in Chapter 11.

2. *Community-based services and deinstitutionalization.* A closely related trend is that of developing programs in the community that often, but not always, bring services out of distant institutions and place them closer to home. Not only does this mean that newly created programs today are more likely to be in the open community than in the more closed environment of a physical institution, but it also implies a reduced need for institutions. There is therefore a move toward reduction in size and numbers. Deinstitutionalization is happening in mental health, retardation, corrections, and child welfare, among other fields, but is uneven around the country both geographically and in the social problem being addressed. In general, community-based programs are perceived as less drastic and less restrictive than institutional programs.

It should be noted that the picture is complex, that "everything is relative," and definitions are required. For example, what about day care; are not such centers in effect institutions? The answer must be no if we recognize that day-care centers are typically community-based, often actually serving local neighborhoods. Furthermore, day care can keep some children out of institutions. A sizable number of children in day care are from single-parent families, and historically it was youngsters such as a portion of these who could not be cared for at home and were living in orphanages (institutions) with their regimentation, anonymity, depersonalization, and other limitations. Another complication is correctional institutions; many states are building more rather than deinstitutionalizing. At the same time, there has been significant deinstitutionalization of juvenile delinquents and although more institutions are being erected for adult offenders, these are often smaller and more widely dispersed. There also are some highly important community measures for both youth and adult deviants.

Sometimes the view is advanced that deinstitutionalization has gone too far, especially in such areas as mental health.[21] It is alleged that parts of our large cities have become "psychiatric ghettos" where formerly hospitalized patients idle away their time, at best unproductively, if not destructively, in neighborhoods, flophouses, and nursing homes. This view seems an exaggeration of a genuine problem and concern. Rather than being taken as an argument for more institutionalization/hospitalization, it can be seen as the case for more adequate, efficient, and creative locally based services and facilities such as mental health centers, sheltered workshops, and structured housing.

Intertwined with community-based services is the recent emergence of home-based services, sometimes termed in-home care.[22] There is striking evidence that heavy social service input into families in their own homes can substantially reduce the need for substitute care for family members, including the need for institutionalization.

3. *Permanence.*[23] In the 1970s there was a thrust in child welfare toward greater permanence in the care of children. All too often children have gone from natural home to foster home, back to natural home, and through a whole series of foster homes and other substitute care arrangements such as group homes and institutions. There is a variety of reasons for this, but the experience is generally and understandably not a positive one for the child or for other persons involved. As there has come to be more awareness of the problem, more professionals are devoting themselves to solutions. An example of the problem is children who, in adoption circles, have traditionally been labeled "hard to place." Now some agencies are having success placing youngsters for adoption who formerly would never have had the continuity of growing up in one family. Permanence is a relative concept that goes beyond children. The elderly are another example. It is now quite clear that the day of institutional care such as a nursing home or other out-of-home arrangements can be delayed or prevented altogether for large numbers of older persons if supportive services are offered in communities. The result may not be complete permanence but certainly continuity can be attained.

4. *Comprehensiveness of services and continuity of care.* Closely related to permanence are the further interrelated yet separate ideas of continuity of "care" and comprehensiveness of services. These are goals rather than accomplished facts in the social services, and there is anything but a steady progression toward these ends. Social welfare programs are in many respects a hodgepodge, a collection of pieces that do not always mesh together well. Examples of some movement toward comprehensiveness, even if not total attainment, are some of the types of public assistances that are now more integrated and less categorical, and some mental health centers that have broadened their services beyond those that are strictly clinical.

A field in which continuity of care is essential but does not currently exist for millions of Americans is health. A high price is paid for what has often been referred to as our health nonsystem. One of the products of this nonsystem is that significant numbers of people needing health care are falling between the cracks, receiving no medical services or only piecemeal ones, and lacking continuity. Still another concept is *prevention*, which in part may be an outgrowth of quality services that are comprehensive in nature and provide for continuity. While prevention, continuity, and comprehensiveness are not synonymous, they are highly interrelated. Collectively they go hand in hand with the *holistic* notion of viewing persons and situations in their entirety as totalities.

5. *Right to treatment and to refuse treatment.* Implicit in the act of becoming a "client," "patient," "resident," or whatever else a social welfare "consumer" may be termed is the idea of such person's right to treatment. All too often, for example, people have been hospitalized, incarcerated, or institutionalized in the name of care, rehabilitation, or some other facet of treatment only to find that actual treatment is nonexistent or of inferior quality. Certain mental hospitals and correctional institutions in the United States have, in recent years, been reprimanded by courts for failing to provide treatment and have been mandated to institute programs to provide it.

And as the right to receive treatment has received the attention of the courts, the individual's right to refuse treatment is also coming to be recognized. Such refusal can be an issue in a variety of settings and situations. With offenders, for example, a strong case can be made that, while the state can incarcerate as punishment, the prisoner should be free to decline "treatment" in prison and that participation in various institutional programs should be voluntary rather than mandatory.

6. *Do no harm.* It may appear contradictory that social workers who are sometimes referred to as "do gooders" by unsympathetic elements of the public should be cautioned to avoid doing harm. But this is an important idea given the extent to which some of the social worker's actions and programs contain at least the potential for damage. The sociologist Robert Merton suggested that behavioral practices have both "manifest" (intended and recognized) and "latent" (unintended and unrecognized) functions.[24] For example, young people go to college to attain an education and gain entry into certain kinds of life pursuits (manifest functions). But there may also be latent functions such as keeping them out of the labor market for a time and finding spouses.

Some of the latent functions may actually be dysfunctional, that is, they may be harmful or destructive. In medicine there is the phenomenon of iatrogenic illness, that is, illness caused by the treatment.[25] Loeb and Slosar described "sociatrogenic dysfunctions" as negative consequences resulting from social intervention activities.[26] Among the various instances of sociatrogenic dysfunctions are those they discussed, grouped under psychotherapy, corrections, mental hospitals, school dropouts, and urban renewal. In each of these contexts the destructive potential is real. Obvious examples are the stigmatizing labels used in corrections and mental hospitals. A principal point of the Loeb and Slosar article is that it is unwise to proceed as "though doing anything is better than doing nothing." In some situations, taking no action is actually preferable. And so we conclude that the idea and admonition to do no harm is important for social work.

7. *Accountability.* There can be little doubt that we are now in an era of significant demands for accountability. Various segments of the public are questioning social welfare programs and services. Funding, of course, is a central issue and concern. People understandably want to know what they are receiving for their money, whether tax funds or private contributions. But it is far more complex than this. Often it is not enough for an agency to demonstrate that it provided a certain number of units of service in a specified time period. They must also document quality and effectiveness of services. There may be skepticism about efficiency in program administration and about effectiveness. While this trend may complicate the lives of social workers and present demands that are difficult to meet, it is generally healthy, if appropriate and reasonable.

The human services should be accountable, especially in such inflationary times. But the general public may also need to be educated to understand some of the problems and limitations of this field and what can realistically be expected. Accountability is not a one-way street but one of reciprocity and mutuality. Communities, too, have accountability responsibilities. Social welfare institutions cannot be fully productive and effective without support from the society and communities of which they are a part and to whose problems they are addressed. Sometimes the obvious must be restated and stressed. Social work does not make social problems—communities and societies do, and they must provide the solutions and pay the costs. For example, one price of industrialization is unemployment; hence, there is a societal responsibility to provide some sort of income maintenance protection. These dynamics must be spelled out as often as necessary to build public understanding and support.

SUMMARY AND CONCLUSIONS

In this chapter we have considered some of the key concepts and principles in the field under study. Basic terminology is important in coming to grips with the fundamentals of any field, and this one is no exception. We have also examined a few of the dimensions and issues of social welfare/work/services today. There will be ample opportunity throughout much of the remainder of the book to flesh these out, to illustrate and explore them in greater depth and detail. In the next chapter we will take an historical look at our subject and, hopefully, gain a better understanding of how all this came to be.

NOTES

1. H. Wayne Johnson, ed., *Rural Human Services* (Itasca, Ill.: F. E. Peacock Publishers, 1980), pp. 50, 144–145. See also Leon Ginsberg, ed., *Social Work in Rural Communities: A Book of Readings* (New York: Council on Social Work Education, 1976).
2. Werner W. Boehm, "The Nature of Social Work," *Social Work* 3, no. 2 (April 1958): 18.
3. Betty L. Baer and Ronald Federico, *Educating the Baccalaureate Social Worker* (Cambridge, Mass.: Ballinger Publishing Co., 1978), p. 61.
4. Boehm, "Nature of Social Work."
5. *NASW News* 25, no. 10 (November 1980): 10.
6. Ralph E. Anderson and Irl Carter, *Human Behavior in the Social Environment*, 3rd ed. (New York: Aldine Publishing Co., 1984).
7. Gordon Hearn, "General Systems Theory and Social Work," pp. 333–359 in *Social Work Treatment*, 2nd ed., ed. Francis J. Turner (New York: Free Press, 1979). See also William E. Gordon, *The General Systems Approach: Contributions Toward an Holistic Conception of Social Work* (New York: Council on Social Work Education, 1969) and Robert Jackson and John Else, "Social Work as Boundary Work: Implications for Clinical Practice," a presentation (Washington, D.C.: NASW Professional Symposium, 1983).
8. Institutions are defined as "a stable cluster of values, norms, statuses, roles and groups that develops around a basic social need" by Ian Robertson, *Sociology*, 3rd ed. (New York: Worth Publishers, 1987), p. 93.
9. One definition of sociology is "the study of society, groups, and the social side of human nature." R.C. Wallace and W.D. Wallace, *Sociology* (Boston: Allyn & Bacon, 1985), p. 13.
10. Peter L. Berger, *Invitation to Sociology: A Humanistic Perspective* (Garden City, N.Y.: Anchor Books, 1963), p. 4.
11. Walter Friedlander, ed., *Concepts and Methods of Social Work*, 2nd ed. (Englewood Cliffs, N.J.: Prentice-Hall, 1976), pp. 2–6.
12. Effective July 1, 1980, as adopted by the 1979 NASW Delegate Assembly. The complete text, including preamble and expanded definition of principles, is available on request from the National Association of Social Workers, 7981 Eastern Avenue, Silver Spring, MD 20910.
13. Harold L. Wilensky and Charles N. Lebeaux, *Industrial Society and Social Welfare* (New York: Free Press, 1965), pp. 138–140.

14. Ibid., p. 147.
15. Alfred J. Kahn and Sheila B. Kamerman, *Social Services in International Perspective* (Washington, D.C.: U.S. Department of Health, Education and Welfare, 1976), pp. 6–7.
16. Barry Goldwater, *The Conscience of a Conservative* (New York: Macfadden Books, 1961).
17. Robert L. Barker, *Social Work in Private Practice* (Silver Spring, Md.: NASW, 1984). *NASW News*, October 1987, p. 5, indicates that about one-third of NASW members have part-time or full-time private practice.
18. Ralph M. Kramer, *Voluntary Agencies in the Welfare State* (Berkeley: University of California Press, 1981).
19. Harriet M. Bartlett, "Social Work Fields of Practice," *Encyclopedia of Social Work*, 16th ed. (New York: NASW, 1971), p. 1477.
20. Joseph Goldstein, Anna Freud, and Albert J. Solnit, *Beyond the Best Interests of the Child* (New York: Free Press, 1973).
21. "Mentally Ill Homeless Moved Into Hospitals in New York City," *Des Moines Register*, October 30, 1987, p. 3A.
22. Marvin Bryce and June C. Lloyd, eds., *Treating Families in the Home* (Springfield, Ill.: Charles C Thomas, 1981).
23. See, for example, "Case Record: A Bulletin about Permanency Planning" published by the Regional Research Institute for Human Services, Portland State University, Portland, Oregon. Another center for permanency planning is the University of Michigan.
24. Robert K. Merton, *Social Theory and Social Structure* (New York: Free Press, 1957).
25. Peter C. Loeb and John A. Slosar, Jr., "Sociatrogenic Dysfunctions: A Concern for Social Work Education," *Journal of Education for Social Work* 10, no. 2 (Spring 1974): 52.
26. Ibid, pp. 51–58.

ADDITIONAL SUGGESTED READINGS

Bailey, Roy, and Mike Brake, eds., *Radical Social Work*. New York: Pantheon Books, 1975.

Billups, James O., "Unifying Social Work: Importance of Center-Moving Ideas," *Social Work* 29, no. 2 (March–April 1984): 173–180.

Briar, Scott, "Needed: A Simple Definition of Social Work," *Social Work* 26, no. 1 (January 1981): 83–84.

Federico, Ronald C., *The Social Welfare Institution*, 3rd ed. Lexington, Mass.: D. C. Heath & Co., 1980.

Galper, Jeffrey H., *The Politics of Social Services*. Englewood Cliffs, N.J.: Prentice-Hall, 1975.

Gaylin, Willard, Ira Glasser, Steven Marcus, and David Rothman, *Doing Good*.

New York: Pantheon Books, 1978.

Gilbert, Neil, and Harry Specht, *The Emergence of Social Welfare and Social Work*, 2nd ed. Itasca, Ill.: F. E. Peacock Publishers, 1981.

Haynes, Karen S., and James S. Mickelson, *Affecting Change*. White Plains, N.Y.: Longman, 1986.

Heraud, Brian J., *Sociology and Social Work*. Oxford: Pergamon Press, 1970.

Loewenberg, Frank, and Ralph Dolgoff, *Ethical Decisions for Social Work Practice*, 3rd ed. Itasca, Ill.: F. E. Peacock Publishers, 1988.

Reamer, Frederic C., *Ethical Dilemmas in Social Service*. New York: Columbia University Press, 1983.

Rosenfeld, Jona M., "The Domain and Expertise of Social Work: A Conceptualization," *Social Work* 28, no. 3 (May–June 1983): 186–191.

Schodek, Kay, "Adjuncts to Social Casework in the 1980's," *Social Casework* 62, no. 4 (April 1981): 195–200.

Steiner, J. R., T. L. Briggs, and G. M. Gross, "Emerging Social Work Traditions, Profession Building, and Curriculum Policy Statements," *Journal of Education for Social Work* 20, no. 1 (Winter 1984): 23–31.

Tomlison, Ray J., "Something Works: Evidence from Practice Effectiveness Studies," *Social Work* 29, no. 1 (January–February 1984): 51–56.

Wells, Carolyn Cressy, and M. Kathleen Masch, *Social Work Ethics Day to Day*. New York: Longman, 1986.

3 Historical Development

H. Wayne Johnson

To understand the contemporary social welfare/social work scene in this country, it is necessary to examine the record of the historical evolution of these fields in the United States and elsewhere. Not surprisingly, the present situation has been influenced substantially by earlier events and forces here and in various parts of the world, particularly in Europe and especially in England. This chapter gives a brief summary of this historical development. The subject is vast, and for those who want to delve into it in greater depth or detail additional sources are suggested at the end of the chapter.

ENGLISH BACKGROUNDS

The development of social welfare as a social institution and social work as a profession needs to be seen in the broad context of social change. There are always various social, economic, and political factors and processes relative to social welfare activities whether the time under consideration is now or several centuries ago. Hence, there is no actual "beginning point" except as an arbitrary selection.

Karl de Schweinitz initiates his discussion of the English situation with the year 1349, because he saw an interlinked set of events tying that time in English history to the present.[1] In 1348–1349, an extremely severe epidemic of bubonic plague (the so-called Black Death) swept England, killing one-fourth of the populace. Through the balance of the century, in a period of labor shortage resulting from the plague, attitudes toward the needy changed and hardened. The Church had played a large part in caring for the poor, handicapped, and disadvantaged in earlier times. There was considerable benevolence growing out of religious motives and the desire for salvation.[2] Following the plague, however, a distinction came to be made between the able-bodied poor and those seen as unable to work, including pregnant women, young children, the handicapped, elderly, and ill. With the labor shortage, mobile needy persons, particularly those perceived as able to work, came to be viewed negatively. As Coll states, "for more than two hundred years the problem of poverty was intimately and formally linked to the problem of vagrancy."[3]

Social changes underlying and accompanying these developments were the decline of feudalism, the enclosure of land, and the Reformation.[4] While from a contemporary viewpoint feudalism may be thought of as a kind of servitude, it provided a great deal of security and met the needs of the workers. With the gradual disappearance of feudalism, new needs arose. Similarly, the Reformation brought a reduction in church organizations such as monasteries and hospitals that previously provided extensive aid for paupers.

The Statute of Laborers of 1349 was designed to curb mobility. It prohibited giving alms to able-bodied beggars; required that able-bodied persons accept any employment offered; and prohibited such persons from leaving their parish. A restrictive negative stance was replacing the earlier more positive and benevolent views of the indigent.

The next significant development came in the reign of Henry VIII in 1531 in what paradoxically is a more positive development even though it provided for licensing of begging. From a twentieth-century perspective, such a change would hardly seem constructive. But it was an effort to impose some control on a situation at that time of indiscriminate begging. Beggars unable to work were registered and assigned specific areas in which to seek alms. Since this function was a task of mayors and justices of the peace, Friedlander and Apte note this as the "beginning of a recognition of public responsibility for the poor."[5]

From this point on through the rest of the 1500s came a number of important developments that culminated in the famous Elizabethan Poor Law of 1601. From the 1530s through the rest of the century, various measures provided a plan of public relief, labor regulation, public taxation to provide funds for poor relief, and appointment of overseers of the poor to administer the law. The 1601 statute, following a major economic depression and widespread unemployment, was largely a codification and restatement of existing measures and contained little that was actually new. For the first time the poor law was entirely secular, and it was comprehensive.[6] It affected social welfare practices in the American colonies as well as in England, and our public welfare system today is still influenced by this legislation.

Elizabethan Poor Law

The principal provisions of the Elizabethan Poor Law, or the Great Poor Law as it is sometimes known, were: (1) local public responsibility, (2) relative responsibility, (3) administration by the "overseer of the poor," and (4) classification of the poor into three categories. Although this measure was a far cry from a federal system, which did not emerge in most nations until near or in the twentieth century, it did provide for public (governmental) responsibility on the local level for the poor. Relief could come from tax sources. This was a clear departure from using largely voluntary sectarian funding and personnel as had been done earlier.

Relative responsibility was the doctrine that parents were responsible for the support of their children and grandchildren, and similarly children must care for their dependent parents and grandparents. The overseer of the poor was a local public official appointed by magistrates or justices of the peace. The term "overseer of the poor" is still used in some American communities and, like "relative responsibility," is problematic as implemented. Coll makes the point that the Elizabethan Poor Law was actually intended to be "standby" legislation.[7] The preference still was for voluntary charity, and the Elizabethan plan afforded a backup if and when necessary.

Three groups of poor were delineated by the Elizabethan Poor Law:

1. The able-bodied poor or "sturdy beggars" were dealt with punitively and repressively, being forced to work in the workhouse or house of correction. Giving alms to such people was prohibited. Anyone refusing to work in the house of correction was to be jailed or put in stocks. The problem of vagrants was handled by providing that indigents who came into a community from other parishes were to be returned to the last place where they had lived for a year.

2. The impotent poor were those unable to work. Two forms of care were possible for them. They could be cared for in the poorhouse or almshouse where they were expected to work within their capacities. On the other hand, if the impotent poor had a place to live and it was felt to be less expensive to keep them there, they were given "outdoor

relief" (that is, aid in their homes rather than in institutions). This was nonmonetary aid or relief-in-kind in such forms as fuel, food, or clothing.

3. Dependent children were children whose parents were absent or were too poor to support them. They were to be placed with an adult who would take them without a charge or to the lowest bidder, that is, the person charging the least for their care. Boys were to learn a trade through apprenticeship, and girls were brought up as domestic servants.

Separating the poor into "deserving" and "undeserving" becomes quite pointed with the Elizabethan Poor Law, making it clear that to be poor is no longer acceptable; it is a sign of immorality or criminality, at least for the able-bodied. This profound development still impacts upon us centuries later in the United States and other parts of the world.

Post-Elizabethan Era

Two-thirds of a century later, in 1662, the Law of Settlement and Removal was enacted, dealing with the matter of residency, which is still an issue today.[8] Under this statute, it was possible to eject from the parish persons who it was thought might become dependent upon the community in the future. This legislation was a reaction to the view of officials and lay people of the time, often mistaken, that indigent people entered certain geographical areas in order to receive more generous aid. Removal proved to be more of a problem than a solution, and it was often easier to grant assistance than to send individuals and families to their place of legal residence.

During the 1600s and 1700s, the workhouse became a major center of activity. Conditions in these facilities were often deplorable, and reformers called for improvements. The workhouse was essentially a punitive place. To receive even this punitive help, needy people were required to give up their homes and enter the workhouse for employment. This is often termed the "workhouse test"; one had to demonstrate willingness to work.

An interesting development occurred in 1795 with the passage of the Speenhamland Act, which provided for partial outdoor relief or wage supplementation. Without entering an almshouse or workhouse, a poor person's earnings could be supplemented using a formula. The "bread scale" was used to determine what a family needed for sustenance based on the local cost of bread. Since there was no minimum wage as we are accustomed to today, employers had no reason to pay a living wage, and the Speenhamland Act had the self-defeating effect of increasing taxes for poor relief and encouraging substandard wages. That parallels in social welfare exist over the centuries is seen in the title of an article published in 1969 at the time of the Nixon administration's proposal for a family assistance plan: "Mr. Nixon's Speenhamland."[9]

The seventeenth through the nineteenth centuries were dynamic times of social change impacting significantly on human well-being and social welfare arrangements. Protestantism, the Industrial Revolution, and capitalism all became intermeshed to emphasize the work ethic and laissez-faire economic ideas. Individuals and families were exploited by mass business/industrial enterprises in an era of urbanization. Child labor was one social problem illustrative of many others as wealth was amassed at the expense of common citizens who often experienced alienation in the process. Help given to persons in distress through this era was generally handled by volunteers.

Coal mining youngster in the early 1900s, when child labor was a rampant condition. Social legislation has greatly reduced such problems although aspects still remain such as the children of migrant farm laborers working in fields and orchards.

Historical Pictures Service, Inc., Chicago.

The pendulum swung again in England with the 1834 poor law "reform." Reform is a relative term; in this case most of the change was backward-looking and repressive rather than progressive and forward-moving. Based on a biased investigation of the Poor Law, it was concluded that the existent system was "a bounty on indolence and vice."[10] Hence, the core of the new poor law was the prohibition of partial home or outdoor relief to the able-bodied. Thus, it was an undoing of the Speenhamland provisions. All able-bodied needy were to be aided only in workhouses. Only the elderly, the ill, the invalid, and widows with young children could receive outdoor relief. Finally, a new principle was added to the poor law, known as *less eligibility*, which holds that no recipient of relief could be as well off as the lowest-paid worker in the community.[11] This was an effort to make relief unattractive and uncomfortable. The reader may profit from reflecting on whether such philosophy exists in any way in the United States today.

With all this negativism, there was one respect in which the new poor law was progressive, that is, more efficient. This had to do with organization and administration. Several parishes were to be combined for purposes of relief administration into a "poor law union," and a central board of control was to be appointed by the king.[12] For the time this centralization represented progress, but today, in an era of mass organization, we often desire the opposite—decentralization.

England and other parts of Europe saw various reforms in the nineteenth century in such areas as public health, child labor, prisons, housing, charity organization, and settlement houses, among others. Not until the twentieth century, however, were income maintenance programs generally instituted. Germany became a pioneer in this field in the 1800s, preceding parallel developments of the Great Depression in the United States by a number of years. Among the famous pioneers who contributed to the growing reforms early in the century in England were Beatrice and Sidney Webb. The Beveridge Report of 1941 led, later in the decade, to the elements of the welfare state found in England today.

AMERICAN DEVELOPMENTS

Early settlers brought to our eastern seaboard social welfare ideas and practices that had taken centuries to evolve in Europe. There was much hardship in the colonial period because many people were poor when they arrived and conditions were often harsh. The Elizabethan Poor Law and the Law of Settlement were adopted here, and from the beginning there was present the notion of public aid as a "right."[13]

Forms of aid included almshouses, relief in the home, contracting out the needy as a group, and auctioning off to the lowest bidder. There were arguments for and against use of the almshouse, and its role varied over time, but there were almshouses for those unable to work and workhouses for the ablebodied. Concern about indiscriminate grouping of people into almshouses with deplorable conditions eventually led to the removal from these facilities of certain groups, such as children, and to making more specialized provisions for them.[14] There was also public outdoor relief as well as assistance from voluntary sources. Residency requirements to be eligible for aid were an early practice. Persons who were thought likely to become dependent upon the community were "warned out," that is, given notice to leave or, failing to do so, did not gain eligibility for assistance by remaining.

Prior to the twentieth century in the United States, voluntary or private social welfare activities were more extensive and generally significant than those of the public sector. One major movement was the Charity Organization Society (COS), starting in London in 1869, and based on the earlier ideas of the Rev. Thomas Chalmers. Chalmers advocated dividing the community into districts and meeting the poor personally, on a friendly basis, but he held to the notion that individual failure was the reason for poverty. The COS moved quickly to numerous American communities by way of Buffalo, New York, in 1877, where S. H. Gurteen was the founder. But in spite of all its effort to constitute a new approach to charity, the COS continued judgmental attitudes toward the poor. Paupers were seen as being to blame for their condition (victim blaming), and the COS held relief (or aid) in low esteem. Such attitudes were expressed by Josephine Shaw Lowell, a leader in the New York City COS and a nationally known figure in their movement.

Initially the COS stayed out of the relief-giving business. Central in its approach was the idea of organizing and coordinating existing relief-giving units, developing a central register of the needy, and using "friendly visitors," volunteers to visit applicants for help. In these activities, the COS represented early roots of two modern social work methods: friendly visiting was a forerunner of social casework with the idea of working with people one-to-one, and the coordinating function was an early form of what is now called community organization.

As the COS gained experience with human need and suffering in various communities, it felt a growing awareness that social problems were more complex than simply results of immorality and lack of initiative and thrift on the part of individuals, as had been the view. Hence, COS workers joined social action efforts to obtain legislation for improving conditions in such areas as housing, health, and prisons. They also played a part in bringing about the first formalized training program for social work in 1898.[15] In some communities, the COS also began to dispense relief itself rather than restrict itself to the coordination of other relief-giving bodies.

Other significant social welfare/social work developments appeared in the mid-1800s with the founding of a number of group-serving agencies, often focused on youth work. All were voluntary and became national movements. Included were the Young Men's Christian Association (YMCA), Boy's Clubs, Jewish Centers, and Young Women's Christian Association (YWCA). After the turn of the century the scouting movement emerged, for both boys and girls, Campfire Girls, Junior Red Cross, and the 4-H Clubs. Some of these organizations had European forerunners. The purpose and focus differed somewhat among these movements, but all came to be important voluntary resources and remain so today.

One of the most fascinating social innovations in urban centers on both sides of the Atlantic was the settlement house. This movement started with the work of Samuel Barnett and others at Toynbee Hall in London and spread quickly to the United States in the 1880s. One of the best known was Hull House in Chicago, established in 1889 by Jane Addams, one of the striking early personalities in American social work. Settlement houses were typically located in the inner city in areas populated by working people and immigrants. The staff of the settlements were often well-to-do people like Jane Addams who lived in the facility and set about becoming neighbors to those who lived in their neighborhoods. These dedicated leaders offered a variety of services as well as friendship and counsel, helping to acclimate foreigners as well as people who had moved into the cities from smaller communities for jobs in mushrooming industries.

The settlements provided educational and cultural programs. Naturalization activities for immigrants and training in English were important as were recreational opportunities for people of all ages. Day nurseries and kindergartens were developed. Because the social problems related to poverty were so massive and oppressive at that time, settlement house personnel became active in promoting social legislation for improved housing, factory regulation, labor laws, and health and sanitation control. Urban slums were almost indescribable in their misery; water and milk were impure; streets were unpaved and filthy; and deplorable conditions abounded. In this context settlements worked—directly serving people and also attempting to improve social conditions affecting them. Settlements also impacted upon other social movements like the juvenile court that started in Chicago in 1899. The term settlement house is no longer very common, and such facilities today are more often known as neighborhood or community centers. They are still private (voluntary) as they were originally, and many are affiliated with the National Federation of Settlements and Neighborhood Centers. Other community centers have developed under public, often municipal, auspices and often focus mainly on recreation.

The two decades preceding U.S. involvement in World War I make up the Progressive Era. As Robert Bremner observes, it was a hopeful time of confronting social problems with social workers taking leading roles in the reform efforts.[16] Many of these workers were active in the COS, settlements, and other movements. Social justice became a clear goal in this dynamic period.

Governmental Social Welfare Activities

While government, especially on the federal level, did not play a significant role in social welfare in this country until the Great Depression of the 1930s, there were some beginnings prior to this century that served as important precedents for what was to come later. On the state level, specialized facilities, usually hospitals, "asylums," schools, and prisons appeared as early as the late 1700s but expanded particularly in the nineteenth century. These represented efforts to remove certain groups of needy people from the almshouses and to provide separate treatment for them. Included in these groups were the mentally ill and retarded; the blind, deaf, and deaf-mute; and offenders.[17] In parallel developments the federal government took responsibility for certain programs for American Indians, immigrants, health, veterans, and federal offenders.[18] All these endeavors collectively were a far cry from the kind of governmental responsibility to be seen later, but they did constitute a beginning.

After the turn of the century mothers' or widows' pensions appeared in some states. They were an early form of assistance that later was to be incorporated into the nation's Social Security framework as Aid to Dependent Children and in the form principally of survivor insurance benefits.

Although the colonists had brought to America some notion of local public responsibility toward the poor, not until the severe economic crisis of the Great Depression in the 1930s, following the stock market crash in 1929, did the federal government come to assume a large role in social welfare matters. Some of this change originated in the Herbert Hoover administration as it grappled with the horrendous problems of the depression from 1929 to 1933. Hoover's conservatism, however, left his proposals unsuited to cope with the seriousness of the problems confronting the nation. The major changes came with the administration of President Franklin D. Roosevelt and his New Deal beginning in 1933. Roosevelt was determined to meet the crises of massive unemployment, poverty, and an immobilized economy and immediately instituted a series of reforms. Collectively these often were experimental trial-and-error efforts, and some were abandoned after relatively short periods of time. An alphabet soup era of new programs: FERA (Federal Emergency Relief Administration), CWA (Civil Works Administration), WPA (Works Progress Administration), CCC (Civilian Conservation Corps), NYA (National Youth Administration), and others focused on work relief, employment, conservation, help for youth and rural dwellers, and related activities. Conspicuous in the administration of some of these federal efforts was Harry Hopkins, a professional social work administrator. His participation symbolized a move toward using educationally qualified persons to staff social welfare programs.

It should also be noted that the New Deal was sympathetic with and supportive of the organized labor movement. This movement is perhaps as significant historically as any single factor in an improved standard of living and better conditions for workers generally. For this reason the current situation relative to organized labor is of interest to social work.

Not only was the role of government in social welfare transformed by the depression of the 1930s, so also was that of the private agencies. Until that time, a major function of private agencies was the provision of relief to those in financial need. Because of the broad scope of the depression, funds were exhausted in the voluntary sector, and it was not possible to raise more money to assist those in distress. With the passage of the Social Security Act in 1935, private agencies generally reduced or ended their relief-giving role, which was taken over by the public sector. In the next chapter we will examine the income maintenance programs that have evolved since 1935.

War and the Postwar Era

In the twentieth century, two world wars and other conflicts, especially that in Vietnam, have affected human needs and social services. Military service placed individuals and families in stress.[19] Disequilibrium results from war-created mobility as people move to work in defense industries, and numerous other social problems arise when nations are at war. In this country both public and private agencies have been involved in the response to such problems.

For social welfare purposes, the World War II era, the immediate postwar years, and the Korean conflict of the early 1950s constituted a relatively quiet period. When the nation is embroiled in major warfare,

priorities tend to emphasize matters other than social welfare considerations. This is not to say that there are no social problems or services
at these times. Obviously war is disruptive to a nation even when
bombs do not fall on its territory, and social programs reflect these national tensions. But significant social welfare legislation is less likely
to be enacted in this context.

Dwight Eisenhower (1953 to 1960) was a moderate Republican
president. While this administration was not associated with major federal social welfare developments, some striking social movements had
their roots in this decade. For example, the bus boycott in
Birmingham, Alabama, in 1955 initiated the civil rights movement that
was to expand nationally in the 1960s.

The 1960s to the 1980s

The 1960s and early 1970s constituted a time of great ferment in
this country with a number of powerful social movements, including
what collectively may be termed the human rights revolution. Some
aspects of this were still very much present in the late 1980s. Few of
these movements were actually new but were reappearing with new
emphases and impetus. The civil rights movement sought equal
rights for racial minorities. The "war on poverty" attempted to bring
millions of deprived Americans into the economic mainstream, and
with it came the welfare rights movement. As the 1960s progressed,
the antiwar movement expanded, aimed at terminating the involvement of the United States in the Southeast Asian conflict. New chapters were written in the decades-old women's rights activities. At
various times, attention has been and is being focused on rights of
children, prisoners, veterans, mental and other patients, those favoring access to abortion, nursing home residents, homosexuals, the
handicapped, aged, and others.[20] The children's rights movement illustrates the complexity of these controversies, since increased rights
for children may also have the effect of increasing their vulnerability.
This kind of value conflict often accompanies social change. Collectively what all of these developments tend to do is to increase the visibility of certain groups and their needs, often fairly invisible
otherwise, and the injustices experienced by large numbers of persons who are all too often discriminated against, exploited, or otherwise abused through stereotyping and scapegoating prejudice.
Generally, these groups are made up of people at risk in varying degree. Social work has an important part to play in helping people secure their rights and to safeguard these rights against infringement.
Social justice is a primary concern of social work.

By comparison with their immediate predecessors, the administrations of Gerald Ford and Jimmy Carter in the 1970s were somewhat quiescent. In 1981, a profoundly more conservative administration came into office in Washington. Federal expenditures for military defense have been greatly expanded (to a budget of almost $300 billion for 1989), and human service funds have been reduced substantially. There is general agreement that a major problem confronting most Americans is inflation, but there is disagreement on what should be done about it and what the role of the federal government should be. Once again, it is being said or implied that the poor should work; that welfare programs are too generous; and that if the economy can just become more healthy (which some may say translates into the rich becoming richer), something is bound to trickle down to the less well-off. This development demonstrates convincingly that these centuries-old issues were not settled for all time with the humanitarianism of the New Deal in the 1930s, but the pendulum continues to swing. The most certain thing about the remainder of the century appears to be uncertainty as Alvin Toffler describes in *Future Shock*, with continuing rapid technological change and profound modifications in our social institutions.[21]

Chapter 26 considers the future of social services. But at this juncture a general observation can be made. In some respects it made little difference which political party prevailed in the 1988 elections and who occupies the White House as the nation moves into the 1990s. The reason in part is the enormous national debt and federal deficit, casting a shadow over the financing of many (but not all) social welfare measures. Even the ever-present debt and deficit are not written in stone, however, and change may make the picture appear quite different in years to come.

SUMMARY AND CONCLUSIONS

To understand the present and to have some reasonable notions about the future, one must turn to the past for enlightenment. This is what we have attempted to do in this chapter. Social welfare history is a vast subject with an extensive literature of its own. Because we are so limited in the amount of space we can devote to the subject, it has been necessary to present a highly summarized portrayal.

Without subscribing to the "few great persons" theory of history, we have included the role and contributions of such figures as the Webbs, Thomas Chalmers, S. H. Gurteen, Josephine Lowell, Samuel Barnett, Jane Addams, and Harry Hopkins. These people, of course, were products of their times, but they also made a difference in those times and what followed.

More important than most of the specific events sprinkled through-out the centuries are the ongoing themes, developments, and evolution of social welfare and human services broadly. Always occurring within some context and never in a vacuum, these social problems and helping measures are usually very much bound up in and influenced by wider political, economic, and other processes, and institutions. For this reason, in order to be a student of the social services, one's study must cover a wide horizon of information and knowledge.

NOTES

1. Karl de Schweinitz, *England's Road to Social Security* (New York: A. S. Barnes & Co., 1961, Perpetua Edition), p. 2.
2. Walter A. Friedlander and Robert Z. Apte, *Introduction to Social Welfare*, 5th ed. (Englewood Cliffs, N.J.: Prentice-Hall, 1980).
3. U.S. Department of Health, Education and Welfare, *Perspectives in Public Welfare* by Blanche D. Coll (Washington, D.C.: U.S. Government Printing Office, 1969), p. 4.
4. Lucy Komisar, *Down and Out in the U.S.A.*, 2nd ed. (New York: New Viewpoints, 1977), pp. 2–4.
5. Friedlander and Apte, *Introduction*, p. 13.
6. Coll, *Perspectives*, p. 5.
7. Ibid., pp. 6–7.
8. Ralph E. Pumphrey and Muriel W. Pumphrey, eds., *The Heritage of American Social Work* (New York: Columbia University Press, 1961), pp. 17–18.
9. Edith G. Levi, "Mr. Nixon's 'Speenhamland,'" *Social Work* 15, no. 1 (January 1970): 7–11.
10. Coll, *Perspectives*, pp. 10–11.
11. Friedlander and Apte, *Introduction*, p. 21.
12. Ibid.
13. Coll, *Perspectives*, p. 19.
14. Friedlander and Apte, *Introduction*, pp. 61–62.
15. Ibid., p. 75.
16. Robert H. Bremner, *From the Depths: The Discovery of Poverty in the United States* (New York: New York University Press, 1956), pp. 201–203.
17. Friedlander and Apte, *Introduction*, pp. 63–71.
18. Ibid., p. 82–90.
19. "Military Counsels Families," *Des Moines Register,* March 22, 1981, p. 7E.
20. Donald Brieland et al., *Contemporary Social Work: An Introduction to Social Work and Social Welfare*, 3rd ed. (New York: McGraw-Hill Book Co., 1985), pp. 8–13.
21. Charles Zastrow, *Introduction to Social Welfare Institutions*, 3rd ed. (Chicago: Dorsey Press, 1986), p. 26.

ADDITIONAL SUGGESTED READINGS

Abbott, Edith, *Public Assistance*. Chicago: University of Chicago Press, 1940.

Abbott, Grace, *From Relief to Social Security*. Chicago: University of Chicago Press, 1941.

Addams, Jane, *Twenty Years at Hull House*. New York: Macmillan Co., 1922.

_____. *Second Twenty Years at Hull House*. New York: Macmillan Co., 1930.

Axinn, June, and H. Levine, *Social Welfare: A History of the American Response to Need* New York: Harper & Row, 1975.

Breckinridge, Sophonisba P., *Public Welfare Administration in the United States*. Chicago: University of Chicago Press, 1927.

Bremner, Robert H., *American Philanthropy*. Chicago: University of Chicago Press, 1960.

Chambers, Clarke, *Seedtime of Reform*. Minneapolis: University of Minnesota Press, 1963.

Devine, Edward T., *When Social Work Was Young*. New York: Macmillan Co., 1939.

Ehrenreich, John, *The Altruistic Imagination: A History of Social Work and Social Welfare Policy in the U.S.* Ithaca, N.Y.: Cornell University Press, 1985.

Feagin, Joe R., *Subordinating the Poor*. Englewood Cliffs, N.J.: Prentice-Hall, 1975, pp. 15–47.

Klein, Phillip, *From Philanthropy to Social Welfare*. San Francisco: Jossey-Bass, 1968.

Leiby, James, *A History of Social Welfare and Social Work in the United States*. New York: Columbia University Press, 1978.

Lubove, Roy, *The Professional Altruist*. Cambridge, Mass.: Harvard University Press, 1965.

Morris, Robert, *Rethinking Social Welfare*. New York: Longman, 1986.

Trattner, Walter I., *From Poor Law to Welfare State*, 3rd ed. New York: Free Press, 1984.

_____, ed., *Social Welfare or Social Control? Historical Reflections on Regulating the Poor*. Knoxville: University of Tennessee Press, 1983.

Part Two

Social Problems and Social Services

We come now to the largest part of our endeavor—the study of the major provisions made in response to our principal social problems. What we have covered so far lays a foundation for this next ambitious undertaking.

In the historical overview in the last chapter, we saw that much of the history over the centuries had to do with poverty and attempts to deal with it. This is still a primary concern as will be seen in the next chapter, which addresses public welfare and income maintenance. As will become apparent, considerable unfinished business remains on this matter. Other chapters deal with social work in relation to families and children, schools, physical and mental health, substance abuse, and criminal justice. Still others cover the elderly, social services in industry, and various emerging and nontraditional settings of social work practice.

As was noted in the Preface, you may wish to read Part Three on methods of social work practice before Part Two dealing with programs and services. This will not be necessary if you keep in mind that most social work encountered in the various settings described in Part Two is with individuals and families, groups, or communities.

4 Public Welfare and Income Maintenance

H. Wayne Johnson

In this chapter we are concerned with the basic social problem of poverty and with public welfare, the constellation of services created in response to poverty. Actually, we will examine some programs that are outside the federal-state-local tax-supported measures usually termed "public welfare," but all are collectively concerned with poverty and its alleviation or prevention. Not all are income maintenance programs in the usual sense, but all contribute, directly or indirectly, to economic betterment of individuals and families. In some cases this is through a positive impact on purchasing power, in others through increasing employability, and in still others by improvements in health, housing, nutrition, or other major aspects of life.

It may facilitate our understanding to examine poverty in terms of its *nature, causes, extent*, and *solutions*—important considerations in any social problem. On the nature of contemporary American poverty, what Michael Harrington wrote in *The Other America* in 1962 is still essentially accurate today.[1] Poor people in this country tend to fall into certain groups and possess discernible attributes. Among these are migratory agricultural laborers, Appalachian hill people (farmers, miners), racial and ethnic minorities, the elderly, the physically and/or psychologically handicapped, children, alcoholics and addicts, the poor who have migrated to the city from rural areas, and the only group that, according to Harrington, is voluntarily poor—intellectuals, bohemians, beats.[2] Some modifications in Harrington's categories must be made to update the picture (for example, adding other addicts to alcoholics), but the basic scene is essentially unchanged—millions of Americans continue to be poor in a land of affluence. This is not to say that all people occupying any one or several of these groups are poor but that most poverty-stricken Americans possess one or some of these qualities and that a disproportionately large number of people who are elderly, to cite one example, are poor. It is also true that one child in five is born into poverty today.

John K. Galbraith has made an important distinction between what he calls *case* poverty and *insular* poverty. Case poverty refers to those situations in which individuals or families remain poor, unlike most of the people in their surroundings. Certain attributes of the individuals involved relate to their poverty-stricken status. They may be intellectually, physically, or emotionally limited, undereducated, or alcoholic to cite some examples. Insular poverty, on the other hand, Galbraith compares to an island, a situation in which "everyone or nearly everyone is poor." Individual characteristics or inadequacies do not explain such poverty. Both kinds of poverty, or sets of causative factors, are found today. Both present obstacles to alleviation of the condition.[3]

Cause and effect is often a difficult matter and certainly is here. Is a person alcoholic because he is poor or poor as a result of the alcoholism? Often such conditions go hand-in-hand, aggravating and reinforcing each other. It is clear that many people who suffer poverty were born into it and had greatly constricted opportunities and lives from the beginning. For such persons, poverty is the only way of life they have ever known or probably ever will, given our present economic and social welfare systems.

Listing some of these most pronounced features of poverty reveals a good bit not only about its nature but also about its causation. Some people are poor *because* of their racial or ethnic minority status in a racist society. Obviously not all minority persons are in poverty but, again, a disproportionately high number are. The existing discrimination that works to the marked disadvantage of such persons is significant in their general well-being or lack thereof.

Harrington correctly emphasized that much poverty in this nation is invisible. Modern highways often go through urban slums above or below ground level, and the motorist sees little of the shambles along the way. Rural poverty is frequently tucked away in out-of-sight locations and may even be viewed as quaint and picturesque. The beauty of the landscape may conceal the human suffering. The elderly poor are often restricted to cheap hotel rooms, boardinghouses, and store fronts where they live out their days and years in fear, loneliness, and misery. Skid rows containing some of our alcoholics and inner-city jungles, and their junkies are not part of the experience of most Americans. Skin-and-bones starvation is fortunately not characteristic of American poverty although the poor may frequently be hungry. Rather, our poor are often obese as the result of cheap starchy foods, and the fat may go unrecognized as a sign of poverty. Finally, the fact that many of America's poor are not dressed in rags as is true in some countries makes our poverty inconspicuous.[4] Out of sight and out of mind is certainly an aspect of modern poverty and a factor contributing to its persistence. If more Americans were aware of its existence and prevalence there would possibly be greater sensitization to poverty and more interest in its reduction. This is not a certainty by any means, however, in view of the general apathy and indifference toward many social problems.

As far as poverty causation is concerned, then, we are talking about people, many of whom are too young, too old, or too disabled to work. This is important to know when we see victim-blaming bumper stickers and placards announcing, "I fight poverty—I work." Some could work if employment were available, but given the rates of unemployment we have frequently experienced in recent decades, it is obvious that there often are not enough jobs to go around or the jobs are unevenly distributed geographically or people are automated out of work. Other chronically poor people work hard, sometimes full time year after year. But the jobs they are able to obtain pay so poorly they are chronically impoverished. Many poor people have limited education, skills, and sophistication and hence bring little to an industrialized urban labor market. Lack of experience or ability in planning one's life is an element in poverty. The large families sometimes seen in the homes of poor people testify to the absence of a future orientation. Why delay gratification when tomorrow is so uncertain or is almost certain to be as empty and unrewarding as yesterday and today? Some poor people are single parents struggling to raise a family alone. Most of these are women, and they often have had little or no work experience outside the home. And women are not well paid generally in this sexist society. Hence considerable attention is being given at this time to the feminization of poverty. Similarly blacks, chicanos, American Indians and other minorities face multifaceted discrimination—in obtaining jobs, in getting promotions on the job, in procuring training or education required for certain employment, in gaining membership in unions, and so forth. Finally, some people simply do not share work-ethic values. Poverty then has many causes and contributing factors. It is a complex phenomenon. For the people experiencing it, poverty is anguish, pain, and defeat.

Unemployment and underemployment are highly related to poverty and have a profound impact on the well-being of individuals and families. This was most recently made painfully clear in the recession of the early 1980s when millions were without work. In 1988 the unemployment rate was down to below 6 percent, but it is too easy to ignore the fact that this figure represents approximately 7 million people. There is also a wide variation in joblessness among states, from a high of 10 percent in Louisiana to a low of 1.7 percent in Vermont.[5] Furthermore, the official jobless statistics do not reflect the many more who exhaust their unemployment benefits and are no longer counted. In August 1983 it was estimated that there were 1.7 million "discouraged" workers who had given up and stopped looking for jobs.[6] Part-time workers are counted as employed even though many of them want full-time work.

Formerly, economists considered a 4 percent unemployment rate "full employment," since there are always some people between jobs or in other situations without jobs currently. Now the trend is to think of full employment as approximating 6 percent unemployment. In other words people are being conditioned to expect unemployment and to see it as normal. This is not reassuring to a family facing joblessness. In recent decades there has often been an unemployment rate of 7 percent or higher.

With automation and the various technological changes displacing workers, the question is whether there will ever be enough jobs for everyone. Will work, as it has been known traditionally, become obsolete? Various job-creation programs have been proposed including the idea of shortening the workweek to 4.5 days in order to increase the number of jobs.[7] But whether any of these schemes can be adequate is an open question. In the meantime wealthy people in high places continue to say that there is an abundance of jobs; that everyone who wants work can find it; and that newspaper ads list plenty of positions. What goes unrecognized, however, is that the vacancies listed in such areas as computer specialists and technical fields requiring advanced training do little for the average person seeking work.

Accompanying the loss of employment and income for many is the loss of such benefits as insurance programs. It was estimated that in January 1983, 11 million jobless workers and their families lacked health coverage as a result of layoffs. In July 1986 the Associated Press reported that almost 80,000 retirees of LTV Corporation lost their health and insurance benefits when the company filed for bankruptcy reorganization.[8] When a family is without health and/or life insurance, it is terribly vulnerable. Studies indicate a variety of negative personal consequences for the unemployed and their families. Brenner's data show for each 1 percent increase in unemployment a 4.1 percent rise in suicides; 5.7 percent in homicides; 1.9 percent in stress-related disorders, heart disease, and cirrhosis of the liver; and an increase in mental hospital admissions of 2.3 percent for women and 4.3 percent for men. Another study showed that there are 318 additional suicides among American men when unemployment increases 1 percent. Various other studies show increases in alcohol and drug abuse, wife and child abuse, and mental illness accompanying joblessness. Research at Boston College found wives of unemployed men experiencing more anxiety and depression, and a Michigan study found children manifesting retarded physical and mental development, irritability, and digestive problems following parental unemployment.[9] The recession of the early 1980s brought a new class of "affluent poor," those who cannot pay their house mortgages or car loans because of job losses, but have too many assets to be eligible for welfare.[10]

Poverty is relative, and its occurrence varies with time and place. In the United States we have moved in this century from a nation of general poverty to one in which the poor constitute a minority for the first time. Even as recently as when Harrington wrote, perhaps one-fourth of Americans were poor: in 1986 it was 13.6 percent.[11] Such progress is encouraging and commendable; yet, the amount of poverty remaining in this country of tremendous wealth is shocking and disgraceful. The National Advisory Council on Economic Opportunity, a presidential and congressional advisory council, reported in 1980 that, in addition to the nearly 25 million Americans living in poverty, "another 40 million are near poor, so that one-third of our citizens are materially deprived."[12]

That we cannot count on the inevitability of decline in poverty is seen in developments of the 1980s. The recession and high unemployment took a heavy toll in the early 1980s, making a bad poverty situation worse. In this period there was a growth of 10 million poor people in four years. In 1987, 32.2 million Americans received less than poverty-level income ($11,611 a year for a family of four).[13] (The "poverty income guidelines" are updated each February by the Department of Health and Human Services. In 1988 the poverty line was set at $11,650 for a family of four, except in Alaska and Hawaii where it is higher.[14]) A few years ago the late British historian Arnold Toynbee spent some time in the United States. Upon leaving this country he observed that, of all the places in which to be poor, America was the worst because of its vast wealth. To be poor when everyone around you is similarly afflicted is hard, but to be poor when most are comfortable and many are rich can be unbearable.

America is a land of "private wealth and public poverty." In 1986 salary, cash and stock bonuses, and stock options for Chrysler Corporation's executive Lee Iacocca were $17.9 million. In 1983 salary and bonuses for General Motors chairman were $1.5 million and for Ford's $1.4 million—this at a time that many auto workers were laid off and some plants were closed. At the same time the Reagan administration deeply cut one social program after another in the name of economy. Yet, as the economist Lester Thurow, pointed out in 1980, welfare represents less than 1 percent of the gross national product.[15]

As is true of some other social problems, poverty is functional, that is, it serves some social purposes. From certain perspectives it is useful. Herbert Gans delineated fifteen functions served by poverty as follows: (1) Assuring that society's "dirty work" is done, (2) subsidizing through low wages many activities of the affluent, freeing up money for investments and time/energy for other pursuits, (3) creating jobs for occupations dealing with the poor, (4) prolonging the economic usefulness of goods others do not want that the poor buy and providing incomes for professionals unappealing to more affluent clients, (5) maintaining the legitimacy of dominant norms by identifying the poor as deviants, (6) providing the affluent with emotional gratification by identifying certain groups of poor as deserving, (7) providing vicarious participation for the affluent in the supposed sexual, alcoholic, and drug behavior of the poor, (8) guaranteeing the status of the nonpoor, (9) furthering the upward mobility of the nonpoor, (10) occupying the time and energies of the affluent, hence giving the latter meaning, (11) making "high" culture possible by providing labor and creating surplus capital, (12) providing "low" culture which is frequently adopted by the affluent, (13) acting as symbolic constituencies or needed opponents for some political groups, (14) absorbing the political and economic costs of societal growth and change by providing the foot soldiers for wars, land for urban renewal, and other activities, and (15) since the poor participate less in the political process, adding to political stability and a more centrist politics.[16] Gans's article helps one understand that poverty persists partly because it serves the remainder of the society. Hence, it will be difficult to remove from the societal scene.

We are sometimes told of the biblical pronouncement, "The poor you shall have with you always," and it is suggested that poverty is inevitable.[17] The question is not whether there will always be a bottom rung on the income ladder; there clearly will be in the American economic system. Rather the issue is what this means. Does it necessarily have to mean lack of human decency and dignity in housing, health, education, nutrition, and other primary life areas, or can relatively low income and human dignity be reconciled? It is the author's position that they can be. There should be no place in a wealthy advanced society for a permanent underclass.

ANTIPOVERTY PROGRAMS

We turn our attention now to those social services that have been devised as antipoverty measures. Prior to the Great Depression of the 1930s, public relief programs in this country were very modest and piecemeal. They were generally local or state in funding and structure as we saw in Chapter 3. Such arrangements proved to be grossly inadequate for the massive unemployment and misery of the 1930s. At the peak of the depression as many as 15 million—between one quarter and one third of the adult labor force—were out of work.[18] The older notions of poverty as the result of personal immorality or character defect could no longer be sustained. It is not surprising, then, that more and more people came to believe that what was required to keep the nation on an even keel economically was broad-scope income maintenance programs stressing (1) prevention, (2) permanence, and (3) federal leadership. The federal Social Security Act of 1935 was the outcome. It has been amended numerous times since then, generally in the direction of covering (protecting) a greater proportion of Americans and doing so at a more adequate economic level, although there were exceptions to this in the 1980s. Much unfinished work remains, however, as we will see.

Originally the Social Security Act encompassed three groups of provisions: (1) social insurances, (2) public assistances, and (3) health and welfare services.[19] Only the first two of these programs are directly concerned with maintaining income.

Social Insurances

Social Security. Under insurances two programs were originally included: retirement insurance, which the general public has come to equate with "social security," and unemployment compensation. Through the amending process the first of these insurances has been expanded to protect covered people from loss of income due to retirement, disability, and death leaving survivors. The acronym OASDHI is used now in reference to the social insurances with "OA" representing old age (retirement), "S" equaling survivors, "D" disability, and "H" standing for health (Medicare), which we will discuss shortly. These insurances are entirely federal and hence uniform among all states. The contributions to the federal trust funds are money withheld from workers' earnings and matched by the employer or paid by self-employed persons at a rate double the employee rate. Starting in 1988, the first $45,000 earned in a year is taxed at 7.51 percent and matched by the employer, and self-employed persons pay 15.02 percent.[20] In 1990 the tax rate goes up from 7.51 to 7.65 percent. These funds are used to pay benefits to covered persons in the case of any of the three exigencies mentioned, which otherwise generally reduce or eliminate one's income and may create great hardship.

The approximate monthly benefits for workers retiring at age sixty-five in 1988 who had maximum coverage were as follows:

Retired worker alone	$ 838
Aged couple	1,257
Spouse and two children (survivors)	1,468
Disabled worker, spouse, and child	1,280 [21]

Retirement can come at a younger age, as early as sixty-two, with reduced monthly benefits.

Numerous technicalities affect the exact benefits received, and these approximations are not actual figures of beneficiaries. The contributions to the trust funds have increased significantly between 1935 and the present, both in the amount of earnings taxed (from $3,000 in 1937 to $45,000 in 1988) and the rate at which they are taxed (1 percent in 1935 to 7.51 percent in 1988). So, also, have the benefits increased substantially during this time, reflecting the greater cost of living.

OASDHI is administered on the local level through some 1,300 offices staffed by 74,500 federal employees, who are essentially similar to private insurance claims representatives and are not social workers. The offices are often in post offices and other federal facilities and are separate from county welfare departments. The terminology of this program is that of the insurance field, that is, claims, benefits, and so forth. Herein lie some of the controversies surrounding Social Security. Unlike some private insurance, benefits received today by a Social Security beneficiary do not come directly from trust funds accumulated by that specific person who earlier was a contributor to the fund. Rather they come from monies being received in the trust funds currently from other (mainly younger) contributors. The system is one of transfer payments rather than a trust insurance. However, it does use the insurance idea of spreading the risk and does pay beneficiaries regardless of need, another concern of some critics who oppose what they perceive as the high cost of the program.

Clearly its cost, whether termed a "tax" or a "contribution," has increased substantially. In fact, this is now one of the largest taxes paid by the ordinary working individual. As of 1988, a person with an income of $45,000 or more has $3,379.50 withheld. As a flat percentage withholding from a designated portion of an employee's earnings, it is not a progressive tax; that is, a person earning $45,000 in 1988 and a person earning $1,000,000 pay exactly the same amount and, if their ages are the same and they retire at the same time, will receive the same benefits. One answer to the increasing costs of such protection is to finance the program, at least partially, through general revenues rather than entirely through wage and salary deductions. The critic of this idea argues that this would convert an "insurance" program into a "welfare" program. But as John Romanyshyn notes, there is considerable mythology in Social Security as social insurance.[22] Other countries use general revenues, and it would be a more equitable program with some reliance on a more progressive tax. Another criticism by some is that participation in the Social Security program is mandatory. This would seem necessary if the program is to accomplish its broad purpose of assuring a minimum level of living for most people. To require that all people obey traffic signs is an infringement on individual freedom, but it does prevent the chaos that could result from a voluntary compliance system.

A concern about Social Security is the low level of the benefits for some people. To expect an elderly individual to live on a few dollars monthly, as some must do, is unrealistic. It is not enough to say that Social Security was not intended to be the sole source of income and that it should supplement other monies. Given the high costs of living in an inflationary era and the modest earnings of millions of Americans, it seems unlikely that many can rely on sources of income other than Social Security in their later years. A serious limitation in the law is the lack of survivors' benefits for widows under age sixty who have no children under eighteen. A person widowed at say fifty-six who has not worked outside the home for a long time or perhaps ever may experience great difficulty in obtaining a job and hence face grave problems financially.

Still another weakness is the penalty imposed on paid employment if the Social Security beneficiary works. Between the age of retirement and age seventy, benefits are penalized one dollar for every two dollars earned over $8,400 for people sixty-five or over and $6,120 for people under sixty-five. Starting in 1990, one dollar in benefits is withheld for each three dollars in earnings over the limit. After age seventy there is no penalty. This penalty reflects the Great Depression era during which Social Security was created. At that time, an overriding concern was unemployment, so that the program was designed to discourage older people from working in order to make more jobs available for younger people needing them. Many observers today believe that it is unwise to maintain this stipulation.

One controversy in the Reagan administration era has been focused on Social Security disability beneficiaries. In order to reduce costs Congress in 1981 instructed Social Security to review the 2.7 million people receiving disability benefits. By March 1984 more than 1 million cases had been investigated and almost half a million people ordered removed from the rolls.[23] Thousands of totally disabled persons lost their sole means of support and Medicare as a result of this action. The repercussions were so severe that, starting in December 1982, beneficiaries were allowed to continue receiving benefits while they appealed cutoff notices. Interestingly almost two-thirds of the persons who appealed were reinstated.[24] Finally a federal judge ruled in July 1984, that disability payments must be reinstated to 15,000 to 20,000 persons whose denial of benefits had been appealed to federal court.[25]

As of 1988 more than nine out of every ten workers were earning protection under Social Security. When the program was initiated, only workers in industry and commerce were covered. In the 1950s, coverage was expanded to include most self-employed persons, most state and local employees, household and farm workers, members of the armed forces, and clergy. About one out of every six persons in the country received monthly benefits in 1988.[26] These 38 million people are divided thusly:

- 23.0 million retirees
- 3.5 million retirees' family members
- 7.2 million survivors
- 2.8 million disabled
- 1.3 million spouses and children of disabled

Social Security is a massive "entitlement" program. Like any large system, it has its deficiencies, but for millions of Americans it provides a much greater degree of security than would otherwise exist.

1983 Social Security Changes.   In 1983 Congress amended the Social Security Act in some significant ways. Some of these represented major retrenchment rather than the usual liberalizing direction of modifications in Social Security. (1) The retirement age of sixty-five will rise to sixty-six by the year 2009 and to sixty-seven in 2027. (2) For people retiring earlier than this, such as at age sixty-two, the present 20 percent penalty on benefits will be increased to 25 percent in 2009 and 30 percent in 2027. (3) The July cost-of-living increase was delayed until January. (4) The mechanism for determining amounts of cost-of-living increases to beneficiaries in the future was modified to reduce increases. (5) Retirees for the first time will have half of their Social Security benefits taxed if their income plus half their benefit exceeds $25,000 for individuals or $32,000 for couples.

The rationale for such tightening was that the Social Security trust funds were inadequate. As more people become elderly and the birth rate remains low, the burden on young workers to contribute to the support of the retired does increase, given this system. But it also should be noted that the trust funds would have been in better condition in the early 1980s had it not been for the nation's worst recession in forty years with extremely high unemployment.

Seemingly small changes in Social Security in order to conserve funds can have major repercussions for people. The American Association of Retired Persons reports that a Social Security cost-of-living adjustment (COLA) freeze for one year would move over 300,000 people into poverty. COLA was created to tie Social Security benefits to the cost of living. To deny such raises in an inflationary period is tantamount to cutting benefits.[27]

In the 1980s there has been growing concern about the federal deficit and debt. There is much controversy surrounding the part Social Security costs play in the deficit and whether this program too should be subject to federal cuts or be immune. Over $70 billion has been cut from Social Security mainly as a result of the 1983 amendments. In recent years $30 billion more has been cut from Medicare.[28]

Actually the federal deficit has nothing to do with Social Security, which, until 1969, was not even included in the budget because of the program's independent funding through payroll deductions. It has no connection to the general revenues and expenditures and hence is unrelated to a balanced or unbalanced budget. It may be that the only reason for the 1969 change was to create the appearance of a more balanced budget by including Social Security surpluses. Since Social Security was running a $46 billion surplus in 1987, it is unlikely that these funds will be removed from the unified budget as recommended by the National Commission on Social Security. To do so would make the federal deficit even larger.

Medicare. Medicare (Title XVIII of the Social Security Act) was designed to provide for an unmet need. Becoming effective in 1966, it provided compulsory hospital insurance and supplementary voluntary medical benefits to persons over age sixty-five and, more recently, to younger people in certain other specified situations, such as those with serious kidney disorder requiring dialysis or a transplant. The latter is an interesting development that points out the piecemeal nature of publicly supported health measures in the United States. Medicare was created for a particular age group, the elderly, and not for all people, although people of all ages have unmet health care needs. A sixty-five-year-old is covered; a sixty-four-year-old with a similar health problem or equally high medical costs has to somehow struggle along without assistance. Of the 7.51 percent Social Security payroll tax, 1.45 percent is for Medicare hospital payments. The medical insurance part of Medicare, which pays primarily doctors' fees, is paid for by the in-sured person at the monthly rate of $24.80 in 1988.

Congress became aware of the immense financial costs for kidney disease patients and amended Medicare to cover this hazard. But what of persons with cancer, heart disease, or many other financially costly conditions? Unless such persons have been entitled to Social Security disability benefits for twenty-four or more consecutive months or have been disabled since childhood, there is no help for them under this social insurance program. Serious illnesses and injuries have a way of not complying with the legislators' pigeon holes and definitions. If a particular health problem has sufficient visibility to gain political clout, provisions may be made to offset its financial consequences. Otherwise the victim must rely on his or her own resources, inade-quate though they may be in relation to the costs of treatment. The cur-rent horror stories about costs seem endless. On September 28, 1980, the CBS television program "Sixty Minutes" carried the story of a man who had died in a Florida hospital after twenty-three days in intensive care. The hospital bill was over $77,000.[29] That Medicare faces decline rather than needed increase is seen in the 1984 federal governmental action to trim $13 billion in social spending, $8 billion of which was from Medicare.

Although only 70 percent of Americans have any health insurance coverage from private or public programs, some people argue that pri-vate hospital and medical insurance such as Blue Cross-Blue Shield are the solution to this problem. This appears to be a naive position in view of the heavy costs of such coverage. Even if one is in a group pack-age plan, the costs are steep. Some people do not have access to such plans and simply cannot afford the premiums independently. For ex-ample, costs in one state in 1988 were $100 monthly for an individual (age sixty) and $230 for a family. Even with these high premiums there were substantial deductibles to be paid by the patient. Furthermore, most private insurance coverage contains limitations. What happens with massive costs of treatment, which are commonplace currently, when the insurance benefits are exhausted? Still another difficulty is that companies will not insure some people with problematic health histories or conditions. Other modern industrial nations have long since provided institutionalized public health care programs, but the United States still debates "socialized medicine" and devises partial Band-Aid responses rather than comprehensive answers.

1988 Medicare Changes.   As a result of escalating health care costs, Congress passed and on July 1, 1988, the president signed the most ex-tensive expansion of federal health benefits in a quarter century. The essence of these Medicare changes is protection against costs of care for so-called catastrophic conditions. The increased hospital benefits start in 1989, and those for physicians' fees begin in 1990.

Under the new arrangement, beneficiaries are entitled to free hospital care after an initial deductible, estimated to be approximately $560 annually. Each year this deductible will increase. Prior to this legislation the number of free days and covered days in the hospital were limited. In doctors' bills, beneficiaries will pay no more than $1,370 per year out of pocket, with this amount rising each year. Under the prior plan there was no limit on what the Medicare-covered elderly person might have to pay for physicians' services. Finally, for the first time starting in 1991 Medicare will pay for up to half the drug costs in excess of $600 yearly whereas prior to the 1988 changes there were no medication benefits.

Costs of these increased protections are steep and are to be born by elderly Americans eligible for Medicare. A tax increase for this purpose commences in 1989 along with a rise in the monthly rate to pay for the services of doctors. This significant legislation leaves unplugged the gap in long-term nursing home costs, currently some $22,000 a year. But, for the at-home spouse of a nursing-home resident under Medicare, it does increase the amount of income and assets permitted. Another basic weakness is that Medicare continues to be a program for only one age group rather than a universal, across-the-board health program for all people, which is the need.

Unemployment Insurance.   The other social insurance under the Social Security Act provides protection for the unemployed. Unemployment insurance is a federal-state cooperative program, which varies among the states. Originally in 1935 it covered persons whose employers had eight or more workers for more than twenty weeks a year and paid wages up to $3,000 a year, excluding certain types of employment. Later firms with four or more workers were included. Now states generally cover employment with only one worker twenty weeks per year. Although more groups have been included over the years, in some states one or more of the following remain excluded: agriculture labor; domestic; homemaking; work with educational, scientific, charitable, and religious organizations.

The money in the trust fund comes from a tax ranging from 1 to 4 percent on employers' payrolls; in only a few states do employees contribute. A small portion of the payroll tax is used by the federal government for administrative costs, and the balance goes to the states. States must meet the following requirements to receive federal support: (1) public employment services must handle the benefits, (2) the unemployment trust fund must receive the taxes, (3) the funds must be used only for unemployment compensation, (4) beneficiaries cannot be required to join a company union or join or resign from a labor union, and (5) there can be no denial of benefits for refusal to work where there is a strike, lockout, or labor dispute, or where substandard wages are paid.

To be eligible for unemployment compensation a worker must: (1) have worked in covered employment a stipulated period of time, (2) be out of work through no fault of his or her own, (3) be registered for work in the public employment service and apply for benefits in the same system, (4) be able to work and available for employment, and (5) serve a "waiting period," usually one week, which is not reimbursed.

In June 1988, the average weekly number of beneficiaries of unemployment insurance was approximately 2 million. The average weekly benefit for total unemployment was $141.34. At the same time, over 173,500 claimants exhausted their benefits, pointing up unmet need.[30] Benefits generally can be received for only thirty-nine weeks in one year, depending on the state, with extended benefits in certain circumstances. The latter are financed by both federal and state funds.

A major issue in unemployment insurance is whether it encourages people not to work. In addition to the fact that there are various requirements to be met before one is eligible to receive these benefits and therefore the program is not an open cash drawer, it should also be noted that employment pays much better than this insurance. Generally unemployment compensation is only one-third to one-half of the usual earnings before the loss of the job.[31] In an inflationary, high-cost-of-living era especially, few would voluntarily choose to live on these benefits rather than have their much larger usual incomes. Some such program appears essential in an industrialized society in which unemployment is an impersonal event that strikes capriciously and often harshly and over which people have little control. In any program of this size, there are bound to be certain abuses, but the need to provide some degree of financial protection for individuals and families against losses from involuntary unemployment is urgent and would seem to offset any problems. Unemployment insurance is a smaller program than OASDHI but performs an important function in the United States.

Worker's Compensation.   One public insurance program predated Social Security by a quarter of a century, but is still today less well known and understood. Formerly workmen's compensation, this plan first appeared in 1908 as a program for federal employees who were injured on the job to help with some of their medical expenses. States individually followed the federal example and, by 1920, all but six states had such legislation assisting with hospital and physician fees and paying disability and death benefits. A law and an adequate program are not the same, however, and it was 1948 before all states had coverage approaching adequacy. Worker's compensation is not uniform among the states. Funds for this protection are derived from employers.

The workplace is dangerous, more so in some fields of endeavor than others, but in certain occupations extremely hazardous. Prior to worker's compensation the only recourse an injured employee had was to sue the employer. This often had unsatisfactory results for the plaintiff for several reasons including the fact that employers frequently argued successfully either (1) that the injury was not their fault but due to the carelessness of a coworker, and/or (2) that when the employee took the job, he/she accepted all of the risks inherent in the employment. This kind of situation calls for collective remedy through public (governmental) intervention. An insurance approach spreads the risks, and the costs are shared broadly by employers, consumers, and the general public. Worker's compensation is an important resource and avenue for meeting need.

Public Assistance

The Social Security Act also provided a supplementary system of categorical public assistances (PA). These are not insurances or "entitlement" programs, and there are no contributions to trust funds as previously described for OASDHI. These cash grants come from general tax revenues through a tripartite system with federal, state, and local levels. Unlike the insurances, there is a means test, that is, to be a recipient one must prove one's eligibility by demonstrating a need. Public assistances vary among the states in specific content. The terms "aid" and "assistance" are synonymous in these programs. Originally there were three categories with a fourth for disability added in 1950:

- Old Age Assistance (OAA)
- Blind Assistance (BA)
- Aid to Dependent Children (ADC); later Aid to Families with Dependent Children (AFDC)
- Aid to the Permanently and Totally Disabled (APTD)

Beyond that of need, the major eligibility requirement for each type of assistance is implicit in each label, that is, old age (over sixty-five), a visual handicap of a defined degree, one or more children under age eighteen, a disability. Additional requirements for eligibility characterize each program.

The purpose of public assistance is to supplement the insurances under the Social Security Act. An example is a person who is in need, is not covered by Social Security, but meets the eligibility requirements for one of the types of public assistance. Another example is a person who receives some OASDHI benefits but in such a limited amount that he or she is eligible in that state for some public assistance to supplement the insurance and bring the total up to what is allowed. Generally a person may receive both an assistance and an insurance but not two types of assistance. As more and more people were covered by OASDHI and at higher levels, fewer were eligible for public assistance, and for those that continued to be eligible, the amounts were often reduced. The best example is the relationship between Social Security retirement benefits and old age assistance; as the former (OASDHI) increased, the latter (OAA) declined.

Assistance for the disabled illustrates how a program can be designed and/or administered so restrictively that it is self-defeating. To be eligible, one had to be permanently and totally disabled. One recipient of APTD was so severely handicapped from crippling arthritis that he had to wear a girdle-like appliance on the trunk of the body. It was necessary to have the help of another person to put on and remove this device daily and it was this dependency, in part, that qualified the man for APTD. But the recipient was determined to become free of this reliance on others for physical care and worked day after day for months. Finally he was successful at getting into and out of the device single-handedly without help. The result of this courageous and excruciating effort was that he lost his eligibility for APTD though nothing had changed in his economic situation![32]

Supplemental Security Income.   An important change occurred in public assistance when, in 1974, all but AFDC were federalized and consolidated into Supplemental Security Income (SSI). The Social Security Administration, not state and county welfare departments, handles SSI through the same federal offices administering OASDHI. This change raises an interesting question as to whether SSI is actually public assistance or is more of a social insurance. In addition, there is the issue of supplements in SSI available in some states and not in others.

Table 4.1 shows the numbers of SSI recipients and average payment for June 1988.[33]

AFDC.   Aid to Families with Dependent Children continues as the only remaining major cash-grant public assistance program that has not been federalized. Hence, it is not uniform among the states. It is a large program both in numbers of recipients and expenditures but small compared to the rest of the social welfare system. It is also the most controversial of the programs we have examined so far.

The nation's AFDC March 1988 statistics[34] are shown in Tables 4.2 and 4.3

Table 4.1 Supplemental Security Income

Type of Payment	Total Recipients
Total	4,412,525
Aged	1,434,042
Blind[a]	83,122
Disabled[b]	2,895,361

[a]Includes approximately 23,000 persons aged 65 or older.
[b]Includes approximately 546,000 persons aged 65 or older.

Table 4.2 Recipients of Aid to Families with Dependent Children

Families	3,791,000
Recipients	11,069,000
Children	approx. 7,400,000

Table 4.3 Average Monthly Cash Payments, AFDC

Average per family	$371.99
Average per recipient	127.41

One problem with AFDC, a program serving over 7 million children, is the great diversity of payments among states. In March 1988 the range was from a low of $114 family monthly payment in Alabama to a high of $662 in Alaska.[35] Hence the national average of about $364 does not very well reflect the wide range. While the cost of living does vary considerably around the country, this factor does not justify the extremely low payments in southern states. It is unreasonable to expect a family of approximately three people (usually one adult and two children) to live anywhere in this country, including Alabama, on $114 a month.

In half of the states there is now an unemployed parent addition to AFDC. This relatively small but important program is an acknowledgment that families are in economic need when the bread winner is out of work. It reduces the likelihood that father will desert his family or create the appearance of desertion in order that they may receive AFDC to survive.

No program for the needy in this country is more myth-filled than AFDC. As a group, AFDC mothers (most adult recipients are women) are stereotyped and scapegoated. A pamphlet published by the U.S. Department of Health, Education and Welfare in 1971 which addressed some of these issues is updated with information for 1979 and the 1980s.[36]

Myth	*Fact*
AFDC families are large.	The typical family is a mother and two children, and the trend is toward smaller families. Almost 68 percent have only one or two children. Only 8 percent have five or more children.[37]
Women have more children just to get more money.	The typical payment for an additional child on AFDC is some $75 a month, not much incentive to cover the cost of rearing an additional child when it is estimated that $70,000 is required to raise a child from birth to age eighteen. Almost half of the states place ceilings on grants that do not increase above a certain point regardless of family size.[38]
Most AFDC families are black.	Blacks constitute a minority of recipients (43 percent). Whites comprise 41 percent.[39]
Why work when you can live it up on welfare?	As noted earlier, the average grant in 1988 was about $4,450 a year for a family of three, thousands of dollars below the poverty line.
More money will be spent on alcohol and large cars, i.e., recipients are poor managers.	Studies show that recipients would spend any extra money received on essentials like food, clothing, and better housing. Many AFDC adults are excellent managers—they have to be to survive! They buy used clothing and use donated goods to make ends meet.
Once on welfare, always on welfare.	Two-thirds of welfare families have been receiving aid less than three years at any given time, half for twenty months or less. The number of long-term cases is relatively small; only 10 percent are recipients for ten years or longer.[40] It is painful to be on welfare; hence, for many it is a last resort.
Welfare families cheat.	Repeated studies show tiny numbers of recipients committing fraud. Honest errors by staff and recipients do occur largely because of the complexity of the program. Families are monitored. When individual, publicized cases of actual fraud are detected (often highly publicized), they should be prosecuted as crime and not cast millions of honest recipients under a cloud of suspicion.
Welfare rolls are full of able-bodied loafers.	Only 1 percent of welfare recipients are able-bodied males free to work and most of these want work.[41] Most adults on AFDC are mothers, many of whom work part or full time or are in training. More would work if adequate affordable day care for children were available and if decently paying jobs existed for women. It must be remembered

that some of these mothers have extremely limited marketable skills and experience. Many women go to work when the youngest child enters school full time.

Most welfare children are illegitimate.

The majority were born in wedlock.[42] It also should be recognized that some mothers of out-of-wedlock children are excellent mothers. Only recently has the government helped poor people with family planning and still not very adequately.

What all of this means is that to be a public assistance recipient is to subject oneself to a kind of second-class citizenship. There is another kind of ADC in this country that seemingly raises few eyebrows but costs billions—aid to dependent corporations, for example, Lockheed, Pennsylvania Central, Chrysler, Continental Illinois (a 1984 "bailout" of $4.5 billion), and others. Such governmental largess is replete with abuse; some question the appropriateness of paying $600,000 yearly salaries each to the two new top executive officers of Continental Illinois, for example. But apparently the large scale adds a social acceptability missing in individual victim-blaming situations.

Another issue in public assistance has to do with the separation of financial aid from the social services, which occurred in 1972. Until that time, caseworkers in public welfare handled both eligibility determination for money assistance and the provision of other nonmonetary services such as counseling, information and referral, and family management help. At least partly because of the unhappy results of the 1962 "service amendments" to the Social Security Act providing federal funds for social services to public assistance recipients, former recipients, and persons likely to become recipients, this change took place.[43] The "welfare rolls" did not decline in the 1960s as had been the hope, the result of a complex set of factors. So a $2.5 billion limitation was placed on federal payments for social services in 1975 (Title XX), and the separation was ordered. This was increased later, then cut, and in the mid 1980s set at about $2.7 billion.[44]

There are arguments on both sides of this debate. In some respects, offering services is an integral part of providing financial aid. But the two functions differ, and the contention is that they require different types of staff, nonprofessionals with investigative functions to determine eligibility for money assistance and professional social workers to deal with personal and family problems. Further, it is argued that service should be voluntary, that one's right to money assistance should not be influenced by service requirements, and that for services to be available to a broader population than public assistance recipients, dissociation of services from money programs for the poor is necessary.

Thanks to this development and the enactment of Title XX in the Social Security Act in 1975, there is an array of services for children, families, and adults in public welfare agencies apart from money grants. States determine what services are to be offered with federal funding under Title XX. Service possibilities include both concrete provisions such as day care, residential care, and meals on wheels, and less tangible activities like counseling and casework. A variety of professions and occupations are represented in these services. In this country such services are still to be systematized and institutionalized. While still restricted to serving a lower-income population, services can be provided to public assistance recipients and to others up to a stipulated percentage of the state's median income.[45] Fees can be charged for others based on a sliding scale related to ability to pay. The potential exists for public welfare agencies to become our first line of defense as good-quality public family and children's agencies. Large caseloads, heavy paperwork responsibilities, ever-changing bureaucratic regulations, and mixed policies regarding qualifications of persons to staff these programs are problems today just as in the 1960s. Such problems are obstacles to fulfillment of the potential of the services.

The fact that public welfare agencies offer protective services for both children and adults (handicapped and elderly) and deal with problems such as child abuse points out some of the magnitude of the tasks going far beyond the image of the agency as "the welfare," meaning only money grants. Today's social worker in public welfare may be carrying out tasks with individuals and families in the personal services that are very similar to those in private agencies.

Medicaid.   Medicaid, like Medicare, was enacted in 1965 and took effect the following year as Title XIX of the Social Security Act. It is now the largest federal welfare program for the poor. In the main, it provides medical care for persons who receive public assistance, that is, AFDC and SSI. There are state-to-state variations in benefits and, as is true with public assistance, federal and state governments share the cost of the program, on a fifty-five federal forty-five state formula. Expenses covered include costs of a physician, surgeon, and dentist; nursing services at home or elsewhere; drugs, laboratory fees, and medical supplies.

Originally Medicaid was designed with the intention that states would define "medically indigent" broadly to cover many low-income people in addition to public assistance receipients. But narrower definitions have tended to prevail, thus depriving a large portion of low-income medically needy people of health care. Medical indigence is an important concept. Great numbers of people in modern America are able to make ends meet financially as long as illness or injury do not strike. But when medical care is required, they reach an impasse economically. In fact, people may be destroyed financially in a short time given the present inflation in health care costs.

An actual example may help to make the point. In the 1980s a middle-class couple in their mid-twenties had their first child. The baby was born with an abdominal defect and had to remain in the hospital for special care. Because of the seriousness of the problem, the baby never left the hospital where it died three months later. The costs in this tragedy were almost $1,000 daily or a total approaching $100,000![46]

It should not be necessary to argue for a *right* to health care in the United States. Nor should health care costs be allowed to bankrupt families. Medicaid has not fulfilled its promise and potential in these kinds of situations because of its cautious implementation. Medicaid and Medicare are discussed further in Chapter 8, which deals with the subject of health.

General Assistance.   Closest to and a direct descendant of the historic poor relief is general assistance (GA) or relief, also known as temporary, emergency, or home relief. It is entirely nonfederal, being either state, local, or a combination, and is not a provision of the Social Security Act. General assistance often is relief-in-kind such as grocery, clothing, or utility orders. This program aids people who are in need and are not eligible for more institutionalized measures, or as a stop-gap while awaiting receipt of other benefits for which they are eligible. Some persons who receive other aid that is inadequate for their need may receive general assistance as a supplement.

A problem with general assistance in some states is lack of uniformity in its administration even within one state. It is sometimes granted capriciously without written standards, and the personnel administering this program may be political appointees without qualifications for the job. In at least one state,[47] the administrator of general assistance still has the title of "overseer of the poor," a term from sixteenth-century England!

Veterans Assistance.   Another welfare fragment in some states is veterans assistance, a program entirely separate from the various federal veterans benefits in medical care, education, housing, and so forth. As with general relief, it is local relief-in-kind and has the same limitations including, commonly, a "tight purse strings" administration. Examples of the demeaning "less eligibility" ways in which this program is conducted may be useful. In one midwestern agency, it is the practice to keep better quality clothing apart from less desirable goods for, in the words of the staff person, "the better people." What subjective means are used to determine who is more deserving are unknown, but obviously such a system (or nonsystem) is ripe with potential for abuse.[48]

As a veteran approaches the office of veterans assistance in one county court house, the sign on the door says, "The helping hand you are always looking for is at the end of your wrist."[49] So the very program to help veterans demeans and dehumanizes them in one more example of blaming the victim and trampling on the rights and dignity of poor people because they are poor.

Food and Housing Programs

Food is an obvious basic human need; no one can live without it. There is an abundance of evidence indicating that one aspect of poverty is poor nutrition. Food and nutrition are two different matters, of course, in that one may have enough food but poor nutrition as is seen with some nonpoor people.[50] Studies of individual cases of poverty often reveal that the poor person must set painful priorities. For example, many poor people who live on small monthly incomes such as from Social Security first pay their rent because they must have a place to live. Whatever is left over is budgeted to get through the month as well as possible. Some months food is meager, and generally there is little meat, fresh fruit, dairy products, or other items necessary to a balanced diet. Little wonder that elderly persons are sometimes observed at supermarket checkout counters purchasing canned pet food when they have no pets. Their pride and feelings of shame may even lead them to say something to the clerk about the nonexistent cat to conceal the unpleasant truth of their source of protein. Such conditions in a land of affluence are shocking to say the least. Two major programs of food distribution are food stamps and school lunches.[51]

Food Stamps. Between 1939 and 1943 there was a food stamp program, and it was reinstituted in 1961, growing rapidly since that time.[52] The distribution of surplus food commodities to institutions, schools, and needy families, which began in the 1930s, has declined in more recent years. Both of these programs are administered by the U.S. Department of Agriculture (USDA) and originally both had as a major purpose providing an outlet for surplus agricultural produce. More recently, growing emphasis has been placed on the food and nutrition needs of people, especially poor people. But the program still suffers from multiple ambiguous goals, and it can be argued that such

Food stamps are used by poor people and those of limited income to purchase food items. These stamps are substitutes for money in order to increase the purchasing power of the needy.

Stock, Boston/Bryce Flynn

programs more appropriately belong in the Department of Health and Human Services where they can be integrated with other human welfare measures rather than in the USDA where the poor's need for food may be subordinated to the farmer's need to make larger profits.

Food stamps are purchased by eligible persons for a portion of their face value or are received without payment, depending upon family size and income, and then are used like cash to purchase food in supermarkets and grocery stores. The idea is to increase the food purchasing power of the poor.

Of course, in-kind assistance is given to some individuals and families by churches, service clubs, and other groups in the form of food baskets and comparable items. The problems in this ancient charity approach include the fact that the gifts are given when the giver determines rather than when most needed so, for example, there is the

December generosity syndrome of such altruism centering around holidays like Thanksgiving and Christmas. Another shortcoming is the hit-and-miss nature of who is targeted to be the receiver and who is overlooked. Still another limitation of this alms-like activity is that while it may contribute to feelings of goodness on the part of the distributor of the largess, an ambivalent mix of happiness and humiliation may result for the recipient. A further concern is that the nature of the goods given may be questionable and inappropriate for the persons receiving them. This kind of fragmentary giving would be unnecessary if there were an adequate, institutionalized, comprehensive income maintenance system. And some of the basket carriers, in contrast to holiday generosity, take political and economic positions in opposition to more fundamental help for the needy.

Other Food Programs.   Lunches provided at school assure children one good meal a day, five days a week, nine months a year. While this is obviously limited, its impact on nutrition should not be underestimated. These services are uneven and spotty, sometimes being free or charged on a sliding scale. Many states have not implemented free lunches, and many schools do not provide them, so that once again there is unmet need and unfilled potential. Surplus foods distributed to schools can play an important role in the program in terms of nutrition, but they are unpredictable.

The Women's, Infants,' and Children's Supplementary Food Program (WIC) assists persons of certain status with such nutritionally important substances as milk.[53] Other measures focus on the food needs of the elderly such as congregate meals and meals on wheels. Again, we see fragmentary approaches rather than comprehensive services directed toward adequate nutrition for all.

Housing.   A more extensive discussion of public housing comes in a later chapter. What should be pointed out here is that housing is another fundamental requisite for all humans. Poor people have difficulty obtaining and retaining adequate housing just as they do in meeting other primary needs. Therefore subsidization of housing, as with health and nutrition, can be extremely important even in making survival possible. Generally the United States has not gone as far as have some other modern nations in providing public housing. The reasons are complex but do not minimize the human suffering resulting from lack of decent affordable living quarters for individuals and families.

It should be noted that food and housing programs are forms of assistance in kind, that is nonmonetary aid. Many people, including frequent critics of public welfare and social insurance, look with favor upon in-kind arrangements. But if there were an adequate income maintenance system, people could make their own decisions about food, shelter, and so on, and these residual programs would either be unnecessary or less needed. It may be that for various reasons, some political and economic, a mix of programs is desirable. A more comprehensive income system is slow in evolving, and even if it comes, in-kind assistance may persist.

The War on Poverty of the 1960s

In the administration of Lyndon Johnson, a new "war on poverty" was declared and, in 1964, the Economic Opportunity Act (EOA) created the Office of Economic Opportunity (OEO) and initiated a new attack on an old problem unlike the direct income maintenance approach of the Social Security Act. The EOA, amended the following year, contained major provisions that can be briefly outlined as follows, using the format and much of the language of the act itself:[54]

1. *Youth Programs*
   a. Job Corps—In residential centers, to provide youth between sixteen and twenty-one with the education, vocational training, and work experience necessary to increase their employability.
   b. Work-Training Programs—To provide useful work experience opportunities for unemployed young men and women through state and community work-training programs to increase their employability or the possibility of resumption or continuation of their education.
   c. Work-Study Programs—"The purpose . . . is to stimulate and promote the part-time employment of students of institutions of higher education who are from low-income families and are in need of the earnings from such employment to pursue courses of study at such institutions."
2. *Urban and Rural Community Action Programs*
   a. General Community Action Programs (CAP)—"To provide stimulation and incentive for urban and rural communities to mobilize their resources to combat poverty through community action programs."
   b. Adult Basic Education Programs—To provide illiterates over the age of eighteen the opportunity to learn to read and write the English language in order to increase their independence.
   c. Voluntary Assistance Program for needy children.
3. *Special Programs to Combat Poverty in Rural Areas*
   "To meet some of the special problems of rural poverty and thereby to raise and maintain the income and living standards of low-

income rural families and migrant agricultural employers and their families."

4. *Employment and Investment Incentives*

"To assist in the establishment, preservation, and strengthening of small business concerns and improve the managerial skills employed in such enterprises; and to mobilize for these objectives private as well as public managerial skills and resources."

5. *Work Experience Programs*

"To expand the opportunities for constructive work experience and other needed training available to persons who are unable to support or care for themselves or their families. In carrying out this purpose, the Director shall make maximum use of the programs available under the Manpower Development and Training Act of 1962, as amended, and Vocational Education Act of 1963."

6. *Administration and Coordination*

   a. Creates in the Executive Office of the President of the United States the Office of Economic Opportunity, etc.

   b. Establishes Volunteers in Service to America (VISTA)— commonly referred to as the domestic Peace Corps.

   c. Provides for coordination of all antipoverty programs.

The Economic Opportunity Act opened with a statement of findings and declaration of purpose as follows:

Sec. 2. Although the economic well-being and prosperity of the United States have progressed to a level surpassing any achieved in world history, and although these benefits are widely shared throughout the Nation, poverty continues to be the lot of a substantial number of our people. The United States can achieve its full economic and social potential as a nation only if every individual has the opportunity to contribute to the full extent of his capabilities and to participate in the workings of our society. It is, therefore, the policy of the United States to eliminate the paradox of poverty in the midst of plenty in this Nation by opening to everyone the opportunity for education and training, the opportunity to work, and the opportunity to live in decency and dignity. It is the purpose of this Act to strengthen, supplement, and coordinate efforts in furtherance of that policy.

This statement set the tone for a piece of legislation that did attempt to take a new approach to the problem of poverty. In some ways, it was a more basic and preventive focus than that of the Social Security Act because it attempted to bring an underprivileged portion of the population back into the mainstream of the culture via such fundamentals as employability, rather than simply providing economic maintenance.

In most respects, the war on poverty never materialized. The nation appeared unable to deal seriously with a war on poverty at home when it was enmeshed in the Vietnam conflict. The poverty war was under-funded, never receiving more than $2 billion in a single year, and withered in the Nixon-Ford-Carter era of the late 1960s and the 1970s. In the Reagan years it was dealt with even more harshly. Although the original idea was a federal unit separate from all existing governmental agencies, so that it could concentrate on poverty, bit by bit the OEO programs were dismantled, abandoned, or moved. OEO became the Community Services Administration in 1975. Later this organization was eliminated. Some examples of how much difference programs can make locally around the nation in spite of dwindling federal commitment are such remaining successful antipoverty efforts as Head Start, legal services, and community action programs. Head Start serves only about one in five preschool children from families who meet income guidelines.[55]

Tax Reform of 1986

Within the context of income maintenance, the subject of taxes may not be considered as relevant, but a system of taxation can play a large role in income distribution and in human well-being. For years the United States has had a system of progressive income taxation that in theory taxed high-income persons at a higher rate than low-income people who paid not only less taxes but a lower percentage of their incomes in taxes. Over the years various loopholes and devices were built into the tax structure to benefit the wealthier classes, hence diluting the "progressive" quality. The same is true for corporate taxes. Various strategies served to protect moneyed special interests.

In 1986 federal tax "reform" finally came but in the name of tax "simplification." While the result was a simplified federal income tax in certain respects (such as reducing the number of loopholes and tax brackets), the system continues to be extremely complex. More important for social welfare purposes was increasing corporate taxes (generated more revenues) and removing 6 million low-wage workers from the tax rolls. Still more important was a major setback for the idea of progressive income taxation; the wealthiest taxpayers are now taxed at a greatly reduced rate that is only slightly higher than that paid by the middle class. These changes did little to reduce the massive federal deficit, the existence of which is frequently used as an argument for reducing programs for the poor.

PROPOSALS FOR INCOME MAINTENANCE REFORM

Criticisms of the programs discussed here abound, but solutions are not easy. Reforms could be either small-scale or large systemic changes. Beginning with the smaller and more local and moving upward, the following can be noted:

1. The residual welfare fragments like general assistance and veterans assistance should be incorporated into broader jurisdictions, at least state level, for purposes of funding and administration. These programs should be administered by the same county/state offices handling public assistance and by qualified personnel who work from objective written standards. The aid given should be monetary rather than relief-in-kind.

2. Categorical approaches in public assistance should be dropped in favor of comprehensive, universal programs. SSI is a step in this direction, but AFDC remains problematic. The latter should be replaced with some form of guaranteed annual income. Possibilities include:

    a. The Family Assistance Plan (FAP) proposed in the Richard Nixon administration but not enacted. Originally it proposed $1,600 per year for a family of four, an extremely inadequate level. It did have the virtue of helping the working poor, an important feature. Had this plan been adopted, weak as it was, it is possible that it would subsequently have been expanded and improved as has happened with Social Security.

    b. Children's allowances are found in all Western industrialized nations except the United States. Families are paid based on the number of children. Limitations of this scheme are its cost, its possible encouragement of larger families in the face of overpopulation, and its failure to help needy childless couples and single adults, a weakness shared with FAP.

    c. Negative income tax in one proposed form of many possibilities would have the Internal Revenue Service paying families below a stipulated income considering family size. If the income cut-off figure used were too low in relation to the cost of living, this would greatly hamper the effectiveness of the program. A major advantage of this approach is that it helps everyone who is poor, single or married, with or without children. The cost of such a program is a major concern as is protection of the incentive to work. Several experiments with negative income taxes have been conducted by the federal government in both rural and urban communities in Iowa; New Jersey; North Carolina; Pennsylvania; Denver; Gary, Indiana; and Seattle, Washington. But, as Winifred Bell observes, interest in these possibilities has largely disappeared.

    d. The Jimmy Carter proposal would have replaced AFDC, SSI, and food stamps with a single federal cash grant for families, childless couples, and single adults. Public service jobs would have been provided by state and local governments, and tax credits would encourage employment of low-income workers in the private sector. It was not enacted.

3. Whatever form an income maintenance program takes, it should provide an adequate level of income in relation to the cost of living then current. "Adequate" must be defined, of course, but some minimum level assuring human dignity is required as a base.

4. Whatever welfare reform plan is eventually put in place, if any, it would be useful to move from public assistance toward social insurance as a general approach. This would represent a move from "means tested" programs to "entitlement" programs, which have the limitation of being more expensive. Means-tested programs serve the poor, whereas entitlement programs especially assist the middle class. If a program in nature and administration can come closer to treating the poor as middle-class people, it is a major gain for the needy.

5. Financing Social Security (OASDHI) in part through general revenues[56] rather than entirely by payroll taxes would strengthen the program actuarially and make it less expensive for ordinary workers. Through some means more progressive taxes should be used for financing Social Security. Income maintenance fragments like Railroad Retirement should be dropped and consolidated into OASDHI.

6. Comprehensive public health insurance is absolutely essential in any system.

Much of the problem of enacting welfare reform in the country derives from the immense difficulty in bringing about legislative compromises in this field. Proposals are often overly generous from the viewpoint of conservatives and inadequate for liberals, so that no action is taken.

Changes in 1988. A significant development did occur in 1988. On October 13, 1988, President Reagan signed welfare reform legislation (Family Support Act), which represents the most extensive change in the system's fifty-three-year history. Essentially the changes include (1) a work-for-benefits provision or "workfare" in AFDC, (2) a requirement that employers withhold from absent parents' wages court-ordered child support payments, (3) a requirement that all states offer AFDC to two-parent families at least six months of the year, and (4) an extension of Medicaid and child care subsidies to one year to assist the working poor who are trying to get off welfare. These measures are hardly generous, but they may constitute a step toward a more adequate system.

The Future

What the future holds for income maintenance is uncertain. The need for reform is real, but changes have been slow in coming and as piecemeal as the programs themselves. Present programs are helpful within their limitations. In fact, most of the reduction in poverty between the mid-1960s and 1980 was due to welfare, food stamps, and antipoverty programs, most of them federal. But what is needed is a fundamental national commitment to removing poverty and its attendant problems from this affluent society. What is most lacking is not money or know-how but will.

As this chapter has shown, a large part of the problem is public attitudes. Not only are the poor stereotyped and scapegoated, but so are programs aimed at alleviating poverty. Perhaps it should not be surprising that 40 percent of people with incomes below the poverty line receive no public help, that is, Social Security, SSI or public assistance. There appears to be little recognition of the fact that, as Mimi Abramovitz notes, we are all on welfare at one point or another. There are really three "welfare" systems—(1) programs of the welfare state, (2) tax code provisions, and (3) fringe benefits—and the welfare-state measures are a small part of the whole.[57] The latter two benefit tremendously the middle class. The other development that goes largely unnoticed is how much redistribution of resources there has been in the Reagan administration, shifting money from the poor (budget cuts) toward the wealthy (tax relief).[58] For the present we are left with the realization that ours is a meagre, reluctant welfare state, as Bruce Jansson terms it, one seemingly aimed more at maintaining a supply of cheap labor than adequately meeting human needs.

SUMMARY AND CONCLUSIONS

In this chapter we have examined the problem of poverty and what has been done and could be done in response to it. Social insurances, public assistances, and other program fragments have been described and evaluated and a need for a more comprehensive approach has been noted. The chance that these changes will occur soon seems doubtful.

NOTES

1. Micheal Harrington, *The Other America* (New York: Macmillan Co., 1962).
2. Ibid., pp. 39–138.
3. John K. Galbraith, *The Affluent Society*, 3rd ed. (Boston: Houghton Mifflin, 1976), pp. 244–254.
4. Harrington, *Other America*, pp. 1–18.
5. U.S. Department of Labor, Bureau of Labor Statistics, *Monthly Labor Review*, November 1988, p. 66.
6. "Laid-off Workers Return With Changed Attitudes," *Des Moines Register*, August 22, 1983, p. 85.
7. Barbara Bergmann, "How to Create Jobs by Shortening Work Week," *Des Moines Register*, July 7, 1984, p. 6A.
8. "Nearly 80,000 LTV Retirees Lose Benefits," *Des Moines Register*, July 19, 1986, p. 5S.
9. Jane E. Brody, "Unemployment: Consequences and Damages," *New York Times*, November 3, 1982, pp. C1, C12.
10. *U.S.A. Today*, October 19, 1983, p. 7A.
11. U.S. Department of Commerce, Bureau of the Census, *Statistical Abstract of the United States: 1988* (Washington, D.C.: U.S. Government Printing Office, 1987), p. 433.
12. "Poverty Crisis Seen in Cuts in Programs," *Des Moines Register*, October 19, 1980, p. 6A.
13. U.S. Department of Commerce, Bureau of the Census, "Money Income and Poverty Statistics in the United States, 1987," *Current Population Reports*, Series P-60, no. 161 (Washington, D.C.: U.S. Government Printing Office, 1988), pp. 7, 41.
14. *Federal Register* 53, no. 29 (February 12, 1988): 4214.
15. Lester Thurow, "Whose Income Will Be Cut to Get U.S. Going Again?" *Des Moines Register*, August 17, 1980, p. 1C.
16. Herbert J. Gans, "The Positive Functions of Poverty," *American Journal of Sociology* 78, no. 2 (September 1976): 275–289.
17. Matthew 26:11, Mark 14:7, John 12:8. All of these the statements are often taken out of context.
18. William Trattner, *From Poor Laws to Welfare State: A History of Social Welfare in America*, 2nd ed. (New York: Free Press, 1979), p. 223.
19. Of the many discussions of these provisions, a particularly useful one is by Walter Friedlander and Robert Z. Apte, *Introduction to Social Welfare*, 5th ed. (Englewood Cliffs, N.J.: Prentice-Hall, 1980), p. 105.
20. Social Security Administration, "Social Security," SSA Publication No. 05-10006, January 1988, p. 4.
21. Ibid., pp. 14–19.
22. John M. Romanyshyn, *Social Welfare: Charity to Justice* (New York: Random House, 1971), pp. 205–209.
23. "Social Security Halts Cutoffs of Disability Pay," *Des Moines Register*, December 10, 1983, p. 4A.

24. "New Disability Rules Seek to Ease Inequities in Reviews, Termination," *AARP News Bulletin*, July–August 1984, p. 1.
25. "Judge: Social Security Must Reinstate Benefits," *Des Moines Register*, July 11, 1984, p. 4a.
26. "Social Security," p. 10.
27. Jack Carlson, "Executive Director's Report," *AARP News Bulletin*, January 1988, p. 3.
28. Ibid.
29. Health care costs have risen so much that in 1983 they took 10.8 percent of the gross national product. They continue to rise at a rapid rate.
30. *Social Security Bulletin* no. 10 (October 1988), Table M-32, p. 84.
31. Friedlander and Apte, *Introduction*, p. 296.
32. From author's files.
33. U.S. Department of Health and Human Services, Social Security Administration, *Monthly Benefit Statistics*, no. 5 (October 1988), Table 4, p. 4.
34. Ibid., Table 13, p. 12.
35. Ibid.
36. U.S. Department of Health, Education and Welfare, "Welfare Myths vs. Facts," 1971.
37. Diana M. Dinitto and Thomas R. Dye, *Social Welfare: Politics and Public Policy*, 2nd ed. (Englewood Cliffs, N.J.: Prentice-Hall, 1987), p. 118.
38. Winifred Bell, *Contemporary Social Welfare*, 2nd ed. (New York: Macmillan, 1987), p. 149.
39. Dinitto and Dye, *Social Welfare*, p. 119.
40. Zastrow, *Introduction*, p. 97.
41. Ibid.
42. Ibid, p. 96.
43. George Hoshino, "Public Welfare," in Arthur E. Fink, ed., *The Field of Social Work*, 7th ed. (New York: Holt, Rinehart & Winston, 1978), pp. 96–97.
44. Bell, *Contemporary Social Welfare*, p. 231.
45. Ibid., p. 229.
46. From author's files.
47. Iowa.
48. From author's files.
49. Ibid.
50. Marilyn Flynn, "Poverty and Income Security," in *Contemporary Social Work* by Donald Brieland et al. (New York: McGraw-Hill Book Co., 1975), pp. 102–103.
51. Ibid.
52. Ellen M. Wells, "Food Stamp Program", *Encyclopedia of Social Work*, 18th ed. (Silver Spring, Md.: NASW, 1987), I: 629.
53. Iowa State Department of Health, "Special Supplemental Food Program for Women, Infants, Children" (a pamphlet), Des Moines, no date.
54. Economic Opportunity Act of 1964.
55. "Head Start Center to Get Additional Funds," *Des Moines Register*, July 7, 1984.

56. Martha N. Ozawa, "The 1983 Amendments to the Social Security Act: The Issue of Intergenerational Equity," *Social Work* 29, no. 2 (March–April 1984): 131–137.

57. Mimi Abramovitz, "Everyone Is on Welfare: 'The Role of Redistribution in Social Policy' Revisited," *Social Work* 28, no. 6 (November–December 1983): 440–445.

58. Winifred Bell, *Contemporary Social Welfare* (New York: Macmillan, 1983), pp. 235–251.

ADDITIONAL SUGGESTED READINGS

Bailey, Roy, and Mike Brake, *Radical Social Work* (New York: Pantheon Books, 1975).

Ball, Robert M., *Social Security: Today and Tomorrow* (New York: Columbia University Press, 1978).

Beverly, David P., and Edward A. McSweeney, *Social Welfare and Social Justice* (Englewood Cliffs, N.J.: Prentice-Hall, 1987), Chap. 3, 4.

Block, Fred, et al., *The Mean Season* (New York: Pantheon, 1987).

Brown, J. Larry, *Living Hungry in America* (New York: Macmillan, 1987).

DiNitto, Diane M., and Thomas R. Dye, *Social Welfare: Politics and Public Policy* (Englewood Cliffs, N.J.: Prentice-Hall, 1983).

Galper, Jeffrey H., *The Politics of Social Services* (Englewood Cliffs, N.J.: Prentice-Hall, 1975).

Ginsberg, Leon H., *The Practice of Social Work in Public Welfare* (New York: Free Press, 1983).

Harrington, Michael, *The New American Poverty* (New York: Holt, Rinehart & Winston, 1984).

Horejsi, John, Thomas Walz, and Patrick R. Connolly, *Working in Welfare: Survival Through Positive Action* (Iowa City: University of Iowa School of Social Work, 1977).

Jansson, Bruce S., *Theory and Practice of Social Welfare Policy* (Belmont, Calif.: Wadsworth, 1984).

Levitan, Sar A., *Programs in Aid of the Poor*, 5th ed. (Baltimore: Johns Hopkins University Press, 1985).

Morris, Robert, *Rethinking Social Welfare* (New York: Longman, 1986).

Reischauer, Robert W., "America's Underclass," *Public Welfare* 45, No. 4 (Fall 1987): 27–31.

Sheehan, Susan, *A Welfare Mother* (New York: New American Library, 1975).

Walz, Thomas H., and Gary Askerooth, *Upside Down Welfare State* (Minneapolis: Advocate Services, 1973).

5 Services to Families and Children in the Home

Gilbert J. Greene

The concern for the well-being of children and families has been a major part of the social work tradition and present-day social work practice. From the early days of the "friendly visitors" of the Charity Organization Societies (COS) and workers in settlement houses, the enhancement of family functioning and childhood development have been major goals of social work.

Social work's primary focus is on the social functioning of clients, and since one's basic level of social functioning is acquired within the family context, or a substitute family situation, it is only fitting that family and child welfare are of major importance to the profession. The dual concerns of strengthening family life and enhancing the welfare of children are inextricably interwoven. This relationship is indicated by Lela Costin and Ruppert Downing's definition of child welfare, which they state is "concerned with the well-being of individual children, the strengths of family life, and the rights of all children and young persons."[1] Therefore, family and child welfare are inseparable. Though most social programs and policies (for example, tax laws) affect the family in some way, only those social services that are directly oriented to the enhancement of social functioning of families and children will be discussed in this and the next chapter.

THE NEED FOR SOCIAL SERVICES TO
FAMILIES AND CHILDREN

In the United States, the responsibility for the welfare of children has traditionally been the primary concern of the family. Families tended to rely on friends, the church, the labor union, neighbors, or relatives when they needed help, rather than seek assistance from the government or formal voluntary agencies. However, in today's complex and mobile society, informal voluntary sources of assistance frequently are not available, and reliance on formal social agencies for assistance is necessary. In addition, laws and policies have been established in more recent times pertaining to child and family welfare.[2] This has led to the creation of more social services for families and may allow for families' involuntary involvement in such programs.

There have been corresponding changes in the makeup of families and their life circumstances. These changes have resulted in families needing the support provided by social services more than ever.[3] First, in any one year, there is now one divorce for every two marriages. Only 9 percent of all families with children consist of a father working outside the home, a mother in the home full time, and two children. In 1984, of all children under the age of eighteen, 20 percent lived with their mothers only while 2 percent lived with their fathers. Approximately 25 percent of the homeless population are families most often consisting of a single mother with two or three children. The number of one-parent families has been steadily increasing from 13 percent of all families in 1970 to 26 percent in 1984. In 1987, 51 percent of all new mothers were employed outside the home. The rate of labor-force participation for women with children under age eighteen increased from 18 percent in 1950 to 54 percent in 1980. In 1985, 53.2 percent of all mothers with children under the age of six were in the work force. In 1983, 85.2 percent of young black female-headed families and 72.1 percent of young white female-headed families lived below the official poverty level.

It is obvious that families and children in the United States, especially those with low incomes, are under increasing pressure. This stress has increased with the federal budget cuts of the last several years. In 1980, per capita spending for low-income programs was almost $508; however, by 1986 that figure dropped to $431.[4] Thus, it can be seen that as the need for services to families and children has increased, the funding for these services has decreased. One recent social policy change was the reduction of rates for low-income taxpayers as a result of the Tax Reform Act in 1986. In 1986, a family of four who had an income at the poverty line paid almost 11 percent of its income in federal taxes. The 1986 Tax Reform reduces this figure to 2 percent, which was the tax rate of such a family in 1979.[5] This should provide some extra money for low-income families, but it does not restore the funds cut in recent years from social and child welfare services.

When, then, are families and children seen as needing social services? Alfred Kadushin, referring to a position of the Child Welfare League of America (CWLA), states that child welfare services are provided when parents are unable to fulfill their child-rearing responsibilities or when communities fail to provide the resources and protection required by families and children. He states further:

> Child welfare services are designed to reinforce, supplant, or substitute the functions that parents have difficulty in performing and to improve conditions for children and their families by modifying existing social institutions or organizing new ones.[6]

American society tends to be oriented to change and future growth. Consequently, the position of children has become more important, so that now one can say we are a child-oriented society. If the children in our society can maximize the use of their skills and abilities, then so much the better for society. There are, however, many conditions necessary for successful growth and development. Children need to have proper nutrition and clothing, the nurturance and security of caring parents, adequate housing in safe neighborhoods, regular access to quality education, and so forth. Society has a vested interest in attempting to meet these needs.

Society has sanctioned social work to help remove many of the barriers children and families encounter in trying to carry out their tasks. The rest of this and the next chapter will discuss the major social services that have been created as means of overcoming barriers to adequate social functioning of families and children, and social work's role in the provision of such services. These services have been designed either to *support* parents in caring for their children at home, to *supplement* the care of children in their homes by their parents, or to provide *substitute* care for children outside the home when parents are deemed unable to do so, temporarily or permanently. Such a classification scheme—supportive, supplemental, substitute—will be used for the discussion of the family and social services, with supportive and supplemental services discussed in this chapter and substitute arrangements in the next chapter.

SUPPORTIVE SOCIAL SERVICES

The assumption that whenever possible, the best policy is to provide services to children in their own homes, cared for by their own parents, is the basis for supportive services. These services may be to help problematic children and families or to enhance and strengthen the functioning of nonproblematic families; however, the former services are more prevalent. The programs include (1) various types of casework and groupwork services, both therapeutic and educational, provided by family service agencies and child guidance clinics, and (2) protective services that focus on safeguarding the lives of children from the detrimental effects of abuse and neglect. Protective services may involve the temporary removal of a child or the provision of intensive casework services in the home through home-based child-care services. Supportive services are usually the first to be used when a parent-child problem develops in a family, while at the same time these services remain outside the family structure. The ultimate goal is to allow the child to continue living in his/her own home.

Family Agencies and Child Clinics

Two of the principal agencies providing casework and groupwork services are the family service agency and the child guidance clinic. These two types of agencies have many similarities and some differences. Both attempt to help problematic families by direct intervention with the child; however, the family service agency is more apt to help the child through helping the parents. Basically, there are no major differences in the cases coming to these agencies; however, more severly disturbed children tend to be referred more often to child guidance clinics primarily because they have psychiatrists on their staffs who can prescribe medication. Regardless of any differences, both types of agencies share the same goal of enhancing social functioning of the family and its individual members.

Family Service Agencies.   The origin of the family service agency was in the Charity Organization Societies that developed in the United States in the late 1880s. Before the Great Depression of the 1930s, these agencies provided economic aid and some counseling services to the economically deprived. With the federal government assuming primary responsibility for economic relief during the depression, family service agencies began to put their energies into providing casework counseling services to help clients deal with noneconomic problems. Consequently, these agencies began helping clients from all socioeconomic groups. The bulk of the noneconomic problems consisted of emotional and interpersonal concerns, parent-child conflict, and marital problems. The workers in the early days were primarily untrained volunteers. Gradually more workers were added to the payrolls of these agencies, and more training for the job was requested and provided. Thus, professional social work began. The bulk of the services provided by these agencies continues to focus on problems in marriages and parent-child interactions.[7]

The major coordinating and standard-setting organization in the family service field is the Family Service America (FSA), called the Family Service Association of America (FSAA) until 1983. FSAA was organized in 1946 after going through several previous name changes and reorganizations beginning in 1911. In 1984, FSA had 268 member agencies.[8] There are more than 700 additional voluntary family agencies in this country that do not belong to FSA, many of them sectarian.[9]

Child Guidance Clinics. The origins of the child guidance clinic lie in the efforts in 1909 of Dr. William Healy, a psychiatrist, to deal with juvenile delinquency. In his work on this problem, Healy attempted to apply the concepts of Freudian psychology. He took into consideration physical, psychological, and social factors together with parent-child interactions as contributing to the delinquent behavior of children. The basis for this approach was the premise that delinquent behavior arose out of problems in parent-child interactions and that not only did the child's behavior, but also the behavior of the parents, had to be changed.[10] Of 2,300 mental health clinics in the United States in 1976, it was estimated that only 200 provided services for children and youth.[11]

Treatment Services by Family Agencies and Guidance Clinics

Casework Services. Counseling tends to be the principal service that clients of both agencies request. Initially, a psychosocial assessment is done by conducting interviews with the child, the parents, and significant others. In this assessment phase, child guidance clinics are more likely to use psychological tests and psychiatric consultation. From all the data gathered in the assessment, a treatment plan is formulated.

Because of differential staffing patterns—family services headed by and predominantly staffed with social workers and the child guidance clinics being headed by and heavily staffed with psychiatrists—treatment may be implemented differently while maintaining similar goals. Family service is more likely to see both parents and children together routinely, at least part of the time, while in the clinic the psychiatrist may interview only the child and the social workers only the parents.[12]

Traditionally, both family service and child guidance agencies based their treatment approaches on psychoanalytic principles. In re-

cent years, however, there has been an increasing use of behavior modification techniques based on learning theory and techniques derived
from family systems theory. Another trend is the use of short-term,
problem-focused casework services as opposed to long-term psychotherapy, which has personality change of the client(s) as the primary
outcome goal. The provision of sex therapy for the treatment of any
sexual problems couples may be having is another trend. Sex therapy
is most likely to be provided in family service agencies, rather than
child guidance clinics, with children being excluded during the therapy sessions.

Groupwork Services.   A group approach in working with families
has been employed by both family service agencies and child guidance clinics. At times a group experience is used in conjunction with
casework services, and at other times it is the only service provided.
Two different types of group services are used, one with an educational focus and the other a treatment focus.[13]

The first type of group is called *family-life education.* This approach uses group discussion and/or lecture to strengthen the functioning of "nonproblematic" families and thus prevent serious family
disturbance in the future. The discussions and lectures center around
such topics as improving child-rearing practices, parent-child interactions, and marital communication in order to enhance the participants
in their roles of parents and spouses. Family life education is based on
the belief that problems may frequently arise in family relationships
due to a lack of knowledge or skills. In these types of groups, the
leader is more concerned with the participants learning content and
skills rather than dealing with the interactional processes among the
participants; therefore, she/he serves in the role of educator-expert on
family relationships.[14]

Group counseling services in family service agencies often deal
more with the needs of parents, usually those with some type of personal disturbance. Growing areas of group counseling are groups for
adult women who experienced sexual abuse as children and groups
for adult children of alcoholics. Child guidance clinics, on the other
hand, frequently provide group counseling services only for children.
Unlike family-life educators, the group counselor is not task-oriented
but sees the processes of interaction among group members as the primary means of effecting change. The counselor must help create an
environment within the group that results in high levels of trust, cohesiveness, and openness about feelings. In contrast to family-life education, group counseling has a rehabilitative, rather than preventive,
purpose. Various treatment approaches such as transactional analysis,
Gestalt therapy, and encounter/sensitivity groups may be used with

adults; play therapy or behavior modification are often used with children.

Family Therapy. Family therapy has its origin in the early 1950s in the work of Nathan Ackerman, Gregory Bateson, Jay Haley, Donald Jackson, Murray Bowen, and Virginia Satir, who studied the interactional patterns of families having one member who had been diagnosed as schizophrenic. Therapeutic techniques have been developed by these researchers and other family therapists and have been used with other types of problematic families.[15] The major theoretical premise of family therapy is that the "problematic" family member, who is the "identified patient" and can be either a child or an adult, is symptomatic of deeper relationship problems within the family. For example, there may be marital problems that if openly dealt with, could threaten continuation of the marriage, or the symptomatic behavior of the identified patient "protects" another family member from confronting his/her inadequacies or unresolved problems. The family finds it "preferable" to allow the problems of the symptom-bearer than to confront the real problems in the family. The pain and misery of the family's present problematic situation is "preferable" to the possible pain and anxiety of making changes in the family system, which would mean venturing into the unknown. Further, the problematic behavior of the individual patient serves to divert attention from other problems. Therefore, the problem of the identified patient must be viewed within the family context, leading to defining the family rather than just the identified patient as having "the problem." Just as the identified patient did not get "sick" alone, neither can she/he get "well" alone. Family therapy then involves the social worker seeing the family together for interviews rather than the problematic family member alone. The worker can observe the interactional patterns of the family that reinforce the identified patient for engaging in symptomatic behavior; the worker can then intervene directly in the family system in a way that will facilitate the development of more functional interactional patterns.

Family Advocacy. Traditionally, family service agencies and child guidance clinics provided only clinically oriented treatment services. However, in the late 1960s and early 1970s many of these agencies, especially family service agencies, broadened their scope to consider the impact of community conditions on families and children. "Family advocacy" describes "the variety of techniques social workers employ to help clients having difficulty obtaining necessary assistance from community resources."[16] Whether the social worker is advocating for an individual family (case advocacy) or groups of families (called community advocacy), the community is included in the problem definition.[17] When community conditions are identified as having a detrimental effect on the social functioning of families and family members, these agencies attempt to create new community resources and to mobilize present ones to correct these situations.

Family advocacy may involve active intervention on behalf of families who do not receive needed social, economic, emotional, or psychological services due to social problems such as racism.[18] Family advocacy "requires gathering data to document unjust policies or serious gaps in institutional programs and developing advocacy actions in concert with both the families affected and other available resources."[19]

Advocacy, however, is a minor activity of family service agencies. In 1976, 28 percent of such agencies responding to a questionnaire reported being actively involved in advocacy with only 8 percent having a full-time advocate.[20] The low participation rate of social workers in advocacy may be the result of certain conflicts inherent in such activities (for example, conflicts with funding sources and professional values).[21] Gerald Erickson, however, recently noted that there is a renewed emphasis on *empowering* clients through the provision of services, so that clients themselves competently seek changes in organizations that impact on their lives.[22]

Community Mental Health

Almost all services provided by family service agencies and child guidance clinics are also provided by Community Mental Health Centers (CMHC). As mentioned in Chapter 9, CMHCs were established as a result of federal legislation in 1963. Special provisions for children are made in section 271 of this legislation.[23] Family therapy, family life education, and group counseling are primary services provided. Prevention is emphasized with CMHC staff frequently giving presentations and classes to various community groups on topics such as parenting skills and stress management.

Protective Services

The primary purpose of protective services is to deal with situations in which a child has been neglected, abused, or exploited. Protection of children from such treatment is provided by state statutes; however, this has not always been the case. The origin of child protective services can be traced back to an incident in 1875 in New York City. A child named Mary Ellen was discovered by neighbors to have been beaten and neglected by her foster parents. Since there were no laws protecting children from such treatment, some concerned citizens worked with the Society for the Prevention of Cruelty to Animals to bring Mary Ellen's case to court as a mistreated animal. There were laws at the time protecting animals from mistreatment, and the case was successfully adjudicated with Mary Ellen being removed from the foster home. As a consequence, the New York City Society for the Prevention of Cruelty to Children (SPCC) was created that same year, and soon afterwards several states formed similar societies.[24]

As of 1966, forty-seven states provided protective services as part of their public welfare systems; however, the quality of these services varied considerably. By 1978 all fifty states provided protective services as a result of Title XX of the Social Security Act, which mandated such services. The provision of protective services is primarily the responsibility of state agencies variously called Department of Social Services, Department of Human Services, or Department of Children and Family Services.

Despite the passage of child protection laws, cases of serious abuse went unreported. Frequently neighbors, relatives, school teachers, physicians, and others did not want to become involved and risk litigation by the parents, or did not want to believe that abuse of a child was occurring within a certain family. Consequently, various statutes were instituted in some states mandating the reporting of suspected child maltreatment. The passage of the Child Abuse Prevention and Treatment Act by Congress in 1974 was the catalyst for all states to pass such reporting laws. These statutes pertain primarily to professionals such as physicians, nurses, dentists, day-care workers, social workers, and school teachers, who are likely to have contact with children and to be the first ones to become aware of suspected maltreatment. A report of child maltreatment is usually sent to the state department of social services or the local legal authorities, who have the responsibility for investigating the report further. While in most states the reporting of suspected child maltreatment is compulsory, these professionals are also protected from litigation by the parents when the maltreatment is unfounded.[25] Reports of child maltreatment can be made anonymously, but anonymous reports have a much higher rate of being unfounded than non-anonymous reports.[26]

The Child Abuse Prevention and Treatment Act also provides financial assistance to states that comply with guidelines stipulated in the legislation. The purpose of this act is to allow states to develop demonstration programs that will prevent, identify, and treat child abuse and neglect. This availability of federal funds facilitates the development of treatment facilities for children and their parents, which are necessary to fulfill the intent and purposes of all child abuse and neglect laws.[27]

Defining and differentiating neglect and abuse has been difficult. Some sources have tended to see them as one entity,[28] while others make a clear distinction between them.[29] Despite differences in definition, Sheila Kamerman and Alfred Kahn state that both include three basic characteristics:

(1) The behavior violates a norm or standard of parental conduct—for instance, of the parents' obligation to the child. This includes the child's right to have his basic needs met, not violated. ... (2) The infliction is deliberate—that is, a nonaccidental injury. (3) The abuse or neglect is severe enough to warrant intervention of some type, whether that intervention be medical, social, legal, or a combination.[30]

In such situations, the parent is unable and/or unwilling to be an effective parent. This situation is then a threat to a child's physical, emotional, and social development and well-being. Some specific situations in which intervention would be appropriate are:

1. Physical abuse.
2. Malnourishment; poor clothing; lack of proper shelter, sleeping arrangements, attendance, or supervision. Includes "failure to thrive" syndrome, which describes infants who fail to grow and develop at a normal rate.
3. Denial of essential medical care.
4. Failure to attend school regularly.
5. Exploitation, overwork.
6. Exposure to unwholesome or demoralizing circumstances.
7. Sexual abuse.
8. Somewhat less frequently the definitions include emotional abuse and neglect involving denial of the normal experiences that permit a child to feel loved, wanted, secure, and worthy.[31]

A very simple but helpful distinction between abuse and neglect to be used here is that abuse is an act of commission and neglect is an act of omission by the parents.

Child Abuse

The number of reported cases of child abuse and neglect has been steadily increasing in recent years: from 416,000 in 1976 to almost 2 million in 1985.[32] The increase in reported cases could be due to either an increase in the actual number of abuse and neglect cases and/or an increase in reporting; many cases of child maltreatment go unreported. Approximately half of all reported cases are found after investigation to be genuine cases of maltreatment. Physical abuse comprised 33 percent of all reported cases.[33] While it has been found that

72 percent of physically abused children do not require medical treatment,[34] it has been estimated that as many as 5,000 children may die each year as a result of maltreatment by parents.[35]

Maltreating families are disproportionately low-income (47.7 percent), single-parent (40.3 percent), and nonwhite (28.5 percent). More than half (59.6 percent) of all maltreating parents are female, but this may be due to the fact that females in families spend more time with children than males.[36]

A major contributing factor in child maltreatment cases is the experience of stress by the perpetrator. The fact that a disproportionate number of perpetrators are low-income, single-parent, and nonwhite points to the importance of economic distress, sexism, and racism as stressors and contributing factors.

In addition to socioeconomic factors, there are several personal characteristics that child abusers frequently, but not always, are found to have:[37]

1. A history of abuse and/or rejection in childhood.
2. Low self-esteem.
3. A rigid, domineering, impulsive personality.
4. Social isolation.
5. A record of inadequate coping behavior.
6. Poor interpersonal relationships.
7. High, unrealistic expectations of children.
8. Lack of ability to empathize with children.

It has been noted that abusers tend to have a limited ability to tolerate frustration and delays in gratification. They become angry very easily, which, together with low self-esteem, contributes to their reacting impulsively and intensely to even minor provocation. Though only about 10 percent of all abusers are actually psychotic or sociopathic, research has found that abusive parents suffer from considerably more psychological dysfunction than control groups.[38]

There is a growing awareness that the actual abuse incident is the outcome of parent-child interaction. That is, the event is not just the result of unilateral parental behavior, but the idiosyncratic behavior of the child is a contributing factor. Some children are more difficult to care for and therefore may provoke more aggressive reactions than others. Not only is the child's behavior shaped by parental response, but the reverse can also be true in that the child may selectively reject some parental interventions and reinforce others.[39] In a study of 830 substantiated reports of physical abuse it was found in a majority of the cases that the abuse event began when the parents responded to behavior of children the parents found to be noxious and aversive: "Persistent disobedience, prolonged crying and nagging, persistent negativism, destructiveness, lying, stealing, sassing, aggressive behavior toward parents, siblings, and peers, failure to perform chores, school failure and truancy, precocious or atypical sexual behavior, pot smoking, drinking, etc."[40] The parents abused the children in the process of disciplining them and thus did not see what they were doing as abuse. The authors of the study concluded, "Most instances of child abuse encountered in this study were, in effect, extensions of disciplinary actions."[41]

The event of child abuse, therefore, can be seen to be the result of the interaction among three sets of variables:[42]

1. A parent who has the potential for abuse.
2. A child who may be somewhat different and/or difficult and who fails to respond in a manner expected by his parents.
3. A crisis situation, which triggers the abusive act.

The probability of abuse is increased by social isolation, which reduces the ready availability of help and support from other people; cumulative situational tensions that lower tolerance for stress; and a community context that sanctions interpersonal violence.

A Case of Child Abuse

Jane, age twenty-one, was the youngest of four children, and her siblings were all boys. Her parents were both well educated and led very active lives. The responsibility for her upbringing was left largely to her older brothers, who alternated between ignoring her and "picking on" her. Jane felt that she was the result of an unwanted pregnancy. Her parents were both emotionally distant, with her father frequently criticizing her and using her as a scapegoat for other problems within the family. She has feelings of dislike and hostility toward men in general and her father, brothers, and husband in particular. She admits to feeling inadequate and worthless as a person and especially as a mother.

Jane was married at the age of twenty as the result of an unwanted pregnancy. She had strong ambivalent feelings about having an abortion and put off making a decision until it was unsafe to have one. She admits that she does not even like her son Bobby, age one and a half, much less love him. She feels that he is the cause of her not having "her own life" and resents that he is helpless and cries so much. She thinks that Bobby often does things to irritate her and refuses to learn how to do things for himself just to make her do them for him. She states that she wishes she never had him. She is left at home all day with Bobby while her husband is at work and receives no help from her husband when he is home. Since Bobby's birth, Jane has slapped and shaken him many times resulting in bruises and cuts. This case of child abuse was reported by a physician in a hospital emergency room who treated Bobby for a concussion and broken arm. This was Jane's worst attack on Bobby and appears to have been precipitated by the discovery of her husband's involvement in an extramarital affair.

Neglect

Of all reports of child maltreatment made in 1985, 55.7 percent were for child neglect.[43] Polansky and his associates define child neglect as:

a condition in which a caretaker responsible for the child either deliberately or by extraordinary inattentiveness permits the child to experience avoidable present suffering and/or fails to provide one or more of the ingredients generally deemed essential for developing a person's physical, intellectual and emotional capacities.[44]

Child neglect tends to be a chronic, long-term problem that can, like child abuse, sometimes be fatal. As mentioned previously, neglect is more frequently a matter of omission in child care. It involves a lack of action by and the indifference of the parents. The failure in parenting may then result in "poor feeding, uncleanliness, extremely bad housing, filthy circumstances which make the children prone to infections, lack of medical care, inadequate supervision and protection from danger, lack of intellectual stimulation, inattentiveness to the children bordering on rejection—one could go on."[45]

In one study of child neglect, the following factors were often found: poverty, poor housing, alcoholism, mental illness, and large numbers of children per family.[46] Parents who neglect their children have often been found to be immature and narcissistic, emotionally dependent in relationships, fearful of taking responsibility and making decisions, unable to tolerate anxiety, low in self-esteem, verbally inaccessible to other people, concrete and all-or-nothing in their thinking, passive and withdrawn, convinced that nothing is worth doing, emotionally depressed and numb, incompetent, and disorganized in many areas of living. These neglectful parents were usually neglected and/or abused as children and thus still very emotionally needy themselves. Such parents need "reparenting," set limits, and instruction on how to structure and organize their lives.[47]

Emotional Maltreatment

Though parents may provide adequate physical care for children, they may do serious harm by starving or abusing children emotionally.

Dealing with emotional and psychological maltreatment receives support from the Child Abuse Prevention and Treatment Act in 1974, which addresses mental as well as physical injury. Emotional and psychological maltreatment can be difficult to define and establish. Emotional neglect may include the parent scapegoating, criticizing, rejecting, ridiculing, humiliating, ostracizing the child, undermining the child's self-esteem through perfectionist expectations, being emotionally detached or indifferent, uninvolved or disinterested, or emotionally cold toward the child. Directly insulting and verbally assaulting a child's sense of self and self-esteem is considered to be emotional and psychological abuse.[48]

One of the more recent and comprehensive definitions of emotional and psychological maltreatment has been provided by James Garbarino and his associates. According to their definition, psychological maltreatment is:[49]

> a concerted attack by an adult on a child's development of self and social competence, *pattern* of psychically destructive behavior, and it takes five forms:
>> *Rejecting* (the adult refuses to acknowledge the child's worth and the legitimacy of the child's needs).
>> *Isolating* (the adult cuts the child off from normal social experiences, prevents the child from forming friendships, and makes the child believe that he or she is alone in the world).
>> *Terrorizing* (the adult verbally assaults the child, creates a climate of fear, bullies and frightens the child, and makes the child believe that the world is capricious and hostile).
>> *Ignoring* (the adult deprives the child of essential stimulation and responsiveness, stifling emotional growth and intellectual development).
>> *Corrupting* (the adult "mis-socializes" the child, stimulates the child to engage in destructive antisocial behavior, reinforces that deviance, and makes the child unfit for normal social experience).

Occasional punitive parental behavior is not thought to cause emotional and psychological damage if it occurs within an otherwise positive parent-child relationship. For emotional and psychological harm to the child to be likely, a pattern of aberrant parental behavior toward the child needs to be "persistent, continuous, and cumulative."[50] In addition, for authorities to intervene in cases of emotional and psychological maltreatment, the child must exhibit some behavior indicating emotional problems that can clearly be linked to parental behavior toward the child, and the parent must be unwilling to take corrective action or seek professional help for the child or him/herself.[51] Emotional and psychological maltreatment of children is often found to occur when children are exposed to unwholesome or demoralizing conditions or are exploited by their parents.

Sexual Abuse

Sexual abuse is sexually stimulating contact between a child and an adult; the child is someone under the age of eighteen and the adult is at least five years older than the victim. Sexual contacts may include exhibiting sex organs, genital fondling, mouth-genital contact, and actual intercourse. The sexual contacts can also be inappropriate verbal interaction that may be sexually stimulating such as the use of pornography and verbal sexual stimulation.

The incidence of child sexual abuse in the general population of the United States is difficult to determine. One recent and well-designed study found that 38 percent of 930 women respondents in a random survey had been sexually abused before the age of eighteen.[52] The vast majority of victims are female, but it has been estimated that 9 to 20 percent of all males have been victims of child sexual abuse.[53] Most experts in the field do agree that the incidence of child sexual abuse is underreported.

Stock, Boston/Michael Weisbrot

Play therapy is used by social workers and others to detect and treat child abuse and sexual abuse.

In about 90 percent of cases the perpetrator is someone the victim knows.[54] In almost 75 percent of the reported cases of child sexual abuse, the perpetrator is the father or stepfather.[55] The majority of intrafamilial sexual abuse (incest) occurs in intact families with marital problems.[56] The dynamics of incestuous families are very complex. As of 1981 there were over 300 programs nationwide specifically focused on the treatment of sexual abuse.[57] Because of the complexity of the problem, treatment is multifaceted, usually involving some combination of individual therapy, group therapy, marital therapy, and family therapy.

Social Work Intervention in Cases of Child Abuse and Neglect

As mentioned previously, cases of child neglect and abuse may be reported to law enforcement or social agencies. Robert Mulford states, "There is almost unanimous agreement that a treatment-oriented approach is more successful for the child and more beneficial to the family than a punitive approach."[58] However, despite social work's preference for a treatment approach, the legal aspects of dealing with abuse and neglect cannot be ignored. First of all, it is through the establishment of laws concerning this problem that social workers receive their sanction to provide child protection services against the wishes of parents. Child protection laws provide social workers with the necessary leverage to gain the cooperation of parents. Social workers must clearly understand this authority, given to them by the law, in order to be effective. The social worker must understand its nature and source, and convey it clearly and objectively. In turn, parents must be able to accept to some degree this authority if their functioning as parents is to improve. To provide support to social workers and to treat parents fairly, the protective service agency must establish clear and objective criteria and guidelines as a basis for intervention into the privacy of a family's life. The development of clear standards and rules, as a basis for agency intervention, and the proper observance of legal provisions will help to insure that decision making is reasoned and based upon relevant criteria, thus safeguarding the rights of all involved parties.[59]

Since neglecting and abusing parents are usually involuntary clients, they may vigorously resist and reject any attempts by social workers to help them. They may become hostile, guilty, and defensive, since their adequacy as parents is being questioned and the autonomy of the family is being threatened. However, regardless of their initial responses, the basic approach should combine empathy and understanding with firm expectations of improvement. It is very important for child protective service workers to be trained and skilled in developing and maintaining effective worker-client relationships.

The protection and safety of the maltreated child is the first priority in working with abusing and neglecting families. Treatment of the parents should also be a priority, since many of them will become jealous of their child's receiving help while they do not. Since in most cases they experienced neglect and rejection in their own childhoods, they are in great need of nurturance and protection as adults. Therefore, social services must be available at all times in response to crisis situations, and the social worker must be a stable, consistent, and reliable force for the family. The social worker must be able to respond to and help the family deal with everyday, tangible problems, behaviors, and reality needs.[60]

Families in which child maltreatment occurs often have many problems and needs. Consequently, a multiservice, multidisciplinary team approach is indicated. A number of services and interventions have been developed for meeting the needs of such families. The following is a brief list and description of some of them:[61]

1. *The hotline.* Parents may find it easier to cope with problems when emergency treatment for crises is available. They may find it reassuring to know that there is someone to talk to twenty-four hours a day, every day, if they begin to feel overwhelmed. The workers on the hotline are usually lay people who are supervised by a social worker. The hotline worker has specific training in crisis intervention and may also provide information and referral services to other facilities if needed.

2. *Crisis nurseries.* These are facilities where children may be taken when parents are unable to cope or while they themselves go for treatment. The maximum stay should be only seventy-two hours. This type of service allows parents to have a few needed hours of relief from child-care responsibilities.

3. *Social service homemakers.* These are people who can help in the home with housekeeping and family care. This may be full-time service for a few days or weeks or for a few hours a week or a period of several months. The homemaker may be a role model and a source of information for the parent(s). However, the homemaker must know how to deal with the parent tactfully, and supervision from a social worker will be helpful in doing this.

4. *Lay therapist.* These are individuals who act as supportive and concerned friends to the abusive and neglectful parents. If at all possible, these "parent aids" should be from the same ethnic and socioeconomic background as the parents. They must be recruited and carefully screened by social service agencies and readily accessible

to the parents. This availability of time makes them more of an asset in daily care than social workers. A lay therapist should have ready access to a professional social worker if the safety of the children becomes a concern. Due to the nonprofessional role of the lay therapist, the relationship with the client may not have a formal termination but will vary according to need.

5. *Psychotherapy.* Considering the extensive deprivation maltreating parents have usually experienced throughout their lives, they usually do not respond favorably to a traditional "talking therapy" approach that has "personality change" as the overall goal. Treatment should have limited and specifically defined goals in order to avoid uncovering long-standing and deeply buried needs that the therapist can do little to meet. One appropriate practical goal would be to help the parents improve interpersonal skills, so that they can develop satisfying relationships with other adults rather than looking to the children for support and comfort.

6. *Marriage and family therapy.* With two-parent families, involving the parents in conjoint therapy is usually useful, since both parents are usually involved in some way in the maltreatment of their children. Involving both parents allows them to learn to express their feelings to each other, to listen and respond openly, and to learn joint problem solving. With a single-parent family, it may be helpful to include noncustodial parents and or grandparents for some of the same reasons. Involving the children can also be helpful, provided they are old enough, the family is sufficiently verbal, and the anger level is not too high.

7. *Parent-child interaction.* One of the better ways of intervening with parents with young children, usually less than three years old, is to observe directly and change, when needed, the interactions between parent and child. In the process, the social worker can serve as a model for the parents. Sometimes, interactions are videotaped and later analyzed by the worker and parents together. Successful intervention is usually accomplished through a combination of observation, modeling, discussion, and teaching with the social worker reinforcing the parents' positive interactions with their children.

8. *Treatment in groups.* This approach can be successful by itself or as a supplement to individual treatment. Parents Anonymous, a self-help group of abusive parents, was founded along the same lines as Alcoholics Anonymous and has proven to be very effective. Group members are able to confront each other and are more open about their feelings, which they once assumed were unique, since other group members have experienced the same problems. There are many other types of groups available for mothers, fathers, or couples that are educational or therapeutic, or both.

Home-Based, Family-Centered Services

One possible response to child maltreatment is the removal of the child from the home and placement in foster care, either temporarily or permanently. This kind of placement is costly and disruptive to the family and community and should be the last resort. In recent years many programs have been established that focus on providing intensive social services in the homes of families who have children at risk for neglect, abuse, or acting-out and delinquent behavior.

Home-based, family-centered (HBFC) services "are intended to strengthen and maintain client families and to prevent family dissolution and out-of-home placement of children by providing an optimal level of services over a limited period of time."[62] HBFC services have a commitment to maintaining intact families, especially since experience has shown that it is too easy for out-of-home care, even on an emergency basis, to lead to long-term or permanent breakup of the family.[63]

HBFC programs are quite varied but tend to have the following in common:[64]

■ A primary worker or case manager establishes and maintains a nurturing, supportive relationship with the family.

■ One or more associates serve as team members or provide backup for the primary worker and may meet regularly with the worker and the family.

■ Workers are generally available in emergencies. Sometimes the family-centered staff serves as a kind of extended family for clients.

■ Family-centered programs offer reduced caseloads, staff availability, and the use of a wide variety of helping options.

■ The home is the service setting, and service includes problem-solving efforts in the family's ecological system (including school, police, employers, etc.).

■ Maximum use is made of family resources, extended family, and community. Workers quickly discover and build on strengths in families, even the most problematic families.

■ Parents remain in charge of their families as educators, nurturers, and primary care providers. They participate actively in setting program priorities, planning, and decision making.

■ Help is provided with any problem presented by the family. If the team does not have the expertise or resources needed, it arranges for or creates them.

■ Family-centered service becomes as complete and as intensive as is necessary to maintain and strengthen families and bring about needed change.

The recipients of HBFC services are usually multiproblem families that require a variety of services from several sources. These services may be found in the network of established and sanctioned institutions such as the educational and legal systems, health and welfare systems, political and industrial institutions, and religious and recreational complexes. Such services may serve either a preventive, supportive, or therapeutic function. They may include such services and interventions as instruction on proper child-rearing practices, homemaker services, day care, twenty-four-hour crisis intervention, or intensive family therapy.[65]

Whether the services provided involve case management or therapeutic interventions, the family problems and their resolution are viewed from an ecological/social systems perspective. This perspective holds that the family is a complex whole that cannot be adequately understood by understanding only its individual members; a change in one family member requires that other family members make compensatory changes, and thus the entire system is changed. A family, like any other system, has an innate tendency to seek a balanced state (homeostasis) and will resist change.[66] The ecological/systems view also considers "the complex interdependence of child, family, school, peers, neighborhood and other systemic components."[67] Consequently, social work interventions can occur anywhere within the family's social context, which must also take into consideration factors of culture, ethnicity, class, religious affiliation, and values.[68] HBFC services from an ecological/systems perspective, therefore, facilitate the development and implementation of a coherent action plan with well-coordinated services. This is very important in preventing multiproblem families from "falling between the cracks" in the system.

HBFC services have been found to be cost-effective. In 1982, HBFC services were found to average $3,800 per year per family. Foster home care, on the other hand, cost anywhere from $5,000 to $12,000 per year, and the expenditure for institutionalizing a child ranged from $11,000 to $50,000 per year.[69] In addition, HBFC services have been found to reduce out-of-home placement in 75 to 95 percent of all cases.[70]

SUPPLEMENTAL SERVICES

Services that compensate for certain inadequacies in parental care or are necessary additions to such care are considered to be *supplemental*. Ideally these services help facilitate the normal growth and development of children in their own homes. The most widely used supplemental programs, which will be discussed here, are home-maker and day-care services.

Homemaker Services

An important aspect of services to families in which a child has been maltreated is the provision of homemaker services. These services were provided on a small scale as early as 1903 in New York City. The first organized program was established by the Jewish Welfare Society of Philadelphia in 1923. The provision of housekeeper services and child care to families during the temporary absence of the mother was the primary purpose of the program. In succeeding years, homemaker services were established in many other cities. A national committee was organized in 1939 to promote these services, and it eventually became the National Council for Homemaker-Home Health Aid Services, which later changed its name to the National Homecaring Council.[71]

Homemaker services are provided by a variety of public or voluntary health or welfare agencies. The homemakers themselves are professionally supervised paraprofessionals who are trained to help the sick, aged, developmentally disabled, mentally ill, physically disabled, and those who are feeling too overwhelmed to maintain themselves and their children in their own homes. The homemaker may go beyond just performing housekeeping duties and may have some responsibility for meeting the emotional and security needs of the children. When appropriate, the homemaker may serve as a model to the parent(s) for for good parenting and housekeeping skills. The primary purpose of the homemaker is not to replace the parent(s) but to work with them to enhance their functioning.[72]

Homemaker services can be provided in a variety of situations, generally as part of an overall casework treatment plan. These services are most often provided when the mother is absent from the home or when she is present but, for whatever reason, is unable to meet her full responsibilities. The mother may be hospitalized for physical illness or psychological problems. She may need to be away from home temporarily to tend to a sick relative, or she may have deserted her family due to marital problems. Homemakers have also made important contributions to a family when the mother dies, thus allowing the father and children to stay together especially during the difficult period of adjustment and mourning. In addition, a homemaker may provide needed relief to a parent feeling overwhelmed by raising a problematic child who, for instance, may have a physical handicap or be developmentally disabled.[73]

Problems may be encountered when a homemaker enters a family system. The homemaker and the parent(s) may have different ideas about the role of the homemaker and/or child rearing and housekeeping. Homemakers might also encounter parents who feel in competition with them. In addition, homemakers must be sensitive to cultural aspects of the family's functioning.[74]

> The homemaker's relationship with the family must be predicated on the knowledge and acceptance of their cultural values and lifestyles. So much of what occurs in a household is bound by culture. Whatever new ideas are introduced to the family must be consistent with this reality. . . . If the homemaker ignores culturally determined patterns of relationship or insists on changes which are incongruent with the family's values, the homemaker's help will surely be rejected either overtly or passively.

A homemaker may be part of a professional team that may include a nurse, a nutritionist, or a physician in addition to a social worker. Usually the social worker is responsible for the training and supervision of the homemakers. A crucial aspect of this supervision is to ensure the initial and ongoing acceptance of the family and homemaker of each other, so that the homemaker services have maximum effectiveness.

Though homemaker services initially focused on helping families with children, in 1976 approximately three-fourths of all such services were going to the elderly.[75] Though this indicates that homemaker services are playing a smaller part in child welfare, they are still an important family social service. Homemaker services are sometimes essential in allowing an elderly individual or couple to continue living in their own home rather than becoming residents in a nursing home. This not only is psychologically advantageous to the aged but may also be beneficial to other family members who would be otherwise financially strained to cover the expenses of nursing-home care.

The most recent national survey of homemaker services was for 1976. At that time, there were 3,732 agency units offering homemaker services, employing approximately 82,000 people. In 1976 in the United States there were 29 homemakers per 100,000 population. This puts the United States far behind other countries such as Sweden with 923, Norway with 840, and the Netherlands with 599 per 100,000 population.[76] As a result of government budget constraints in recent years, some homemaker services have been cut, and some agencies are helping their clients to obtain these services from profit-making private enterprises. Though the homemakers provided by proprietary agencies frequently have a reference check and are insured and bonded, there are no guarantees of professional assessment, recruiting, and special training of the homemakers. Quality control of these services, therefore, is difficult to monitor.[77]

Day-Care Services

Day care is a social welfare service that usually provides child care for some part of the day. It is primarily a supplemental service that is sought out by families in which the mother is employed. Like home-maker services, day-care services allow the home and family to continue to remain the central focus of a child's life while the parents retain the primary responsibility for child rearing.

Day-care services for children have been in existence in this country since 1854 when a day nursery was established at the Nursery and Child's Hospital in New York City. Day-care services continued to grow, and in 1898 the National Federation of Day Nurseries was founded. From 1900 to 1960 federal legislation supporting day care fluctuated with the crises of the times.[78] Federal legislation supporting day care began to expand with the 1962 and 1967 amendments to the Social Security Act, which provided some funding for these services to welfare recipients. As of the end of the 1970s, according to Arthur Emlen, "the major federal child care programs—including Title XX, AFDC, Head Start, the Department of Agriculture's Child Care Food Program, federally supported preschool programs, and work-related income tax deductions—had reached estimated expenditures of $3 billion."[79] Most day care in the United States, however, is still paid by the parents of the children receiving such services.

The need for child day-care services is considerable. In addition to the previously mentioned data on working mothers in the labor force, it has also been estimated that 7 million children thirteen years old and younger are going without adult supervision for part of each day, and waiting lists for these services are long.[80]

The types of day-care programs and the auspices under which they operate are quite variable. Services may be provided by public agencies, private nonprofit programs, proprietary or profit-making operations, parent-run cooperatives, employers in the workplace, and others. With so many mothers of all income levels in the work force, day-care services have become varied and multifaceted.

Day care is an important service for families at risk of having a child removed from the home. Day care provided by drop-in centers and crisis nurseries may be helpful for such families under stress. For at-risk families, day care goes beyond the daily care and supervision of children, but also becomes an important part of an individualized case plan that helps to meet the developmental, educational, and health needs of children as well as enhance the total functioning of the family. A type of day-care service that might be a part of a case plan is family day care.

Family day care is the most used resource for care outside the home for infants and toddlers and is a significant one for school-age children.[81] Family day care is usually provided by mothers in their own homes who either have small children of their own and provide care for a few more, or whose children are grown, and they want to earn extra income. Between five and twelve children at a time are cared for in such arrangements, which may or may not require a license, depending on the state in which the home is located.[82] Family day care as part of a case plan for families with children at risk of placement is usually provided by a licensed home in the same community as the family needing the service. The mother providing the day care, in addition to relieving the social isolation of the mother of the at-risk child, can also serve as a role model and a source of useful information on parenting and use of community resources.[83]

Day-care services are also provided for children not at risk of removal from the home, which includes most children, in a variety of settings. There are day-care centers providing care for between five and one hundred children at a time in churches, recreation centers, housing projects, schools, homes, or for-profit day-care centers. In the United States in the past few years, there has been a tremendous growth of chains of large centers run by profit-seeking companies that provide day-care services to families of all income levels.[84] In addition, day-care services are frequently provided for just part of the day in a group setting with an educational focus—nursery schools for three- and four-year-old children and kindergartens for five-year-old preschoolers.

Regardless of whether child care is provided in a day-care center or an educational setting, day-care programs should provide high-quality services that include:

> (1) a strong educational program geared to the age, ability, interests, and temperamental organization of each child, (2) adequate nutrition, (3) a health program and health services when needed, (4) an opportunity for social and emotional growth, including a balance between affectional support, control, and the joy of meeting new challenges and between group experiences and appropriate time for solitude and internalization of ideas and experiences, (5) opportunities for parent education, participation, and involvement, (6) social services as needed by the child and his/her family.[85]

It is apparent that a good day-care program requires an interdisciplinary team approach involving education, health, and social work.

A mother starting a job and placing a child in day care has many implications for the family, and a social worker can help in dealing with them. The mother may welcome the opportunity to talk to a social worker about any feelings of ambivalence, doubt, fear, or guilt she may have about going to work and leaving her child in day care. The worker may help the mother become sensitive to the changes her working may have on the life of her child and family. The family may need help in exploring ways they can accommodate their daily activities to the employment demands placed on the mother. If the mother's employment is considered a necessary solution to family economic problems, the worker may help her explore the viability of other possible solutions. Mother's employment and the consequent request for day care may be a response to other problems the family is facing such as divorce, low income, illness, inadequate housing, or death, and the worker can help the family in dealing with these problems.

A child entering day care may be experiencing his or her first prolonged separation from the family. Therefore, the social worker can help the parents prepare for and deal with the child's reactions during the adjustment period. Later, if a child's behavior becomes problematic in day care, it may be a response to stressful changes at home, such as a recent job loss by the father, and the social worker in a day-care facility may help the family deal with this situation or refer them to other social agencies for needed services. In addition, the worker may act as consultant to the day-care staff on dealing with problematic children and/or parents.

Though the need for social work services in day-care facilities is obvious, only a small percentage of day-care centers employ social workers. Only 6 to 8 percent of all staff working in child care are employed exclusively to provide social work services.[86] In day care, social work is seen as an adjunct service and therefore many day-care providers find it to be dispensible. Day-care workers and teachers end up doing a considerable amount of informal social work with families. Consequently, many families go without the benefit of needed social work intervention and other services provided by social agencies in the community.

SUMMARY AND CONCLUSIONS

The discussion in this chapter has focused on services to families and children with a variety of problems and needs in varying degrees of severity. The primary goal of these programs is to reduce the various stresses impinging on families and children, so that the families may remain intact and their social functioning will hopefully be enhanced. If these services are at least minimally successful, all family members will be able to continue living in the home. Keeping families intact is not, however, always possible because of the nature and severity of their problems and needs. The next chapter discusses services to families and children in which one or more of the family members must live out of the home, either temporarily or permanently.

NOTES

1. Lela B. Costin and Ruppert Downing, "Child and Family Welfare," in Donald Brieland et al., *Contemporary Social Work: An Introduction to Social Work and Social Welfare*, 2nd ed. (New York: McGraw-Hill Book Co., 1980), p. 197.
2. For example the Child Abuse Prevention and Treatment Act, 1974; the Community Mental Health Centers Act, 1963: Title XX of the Social Security Act, 1974; the Adoption Assistance and Child Welfare Act, 1980.
3. These statistics were culled from: U.S. Congress, House, Select Committee on Children, Youth and Families, *Demographic and Social Trends: Implications for Federal Support of Dependent-Care Services for Children and the Elderly*, 98th Cong., 1st sess., Comm. Print 1984; U.S. Congress, House, Hearings Before the Select Committee on Children, Youth and Families, *Children, Youth and Families: Beginning the Assessment*, 98th Cong., 1st sess. 1983; Sheila B. Kamerman, "Family: Nuclear," *Encyclopedia of Social Work*, 18th ed. (Silver Spring, Md.: NASW, 1987); Ellen Bassuk and Lenore Rubin, "Homeless Children: A Neglected Population," *American Journal of Orthopsychiatry* 57 (1987); Esther Wattenberg, "Family: One Parent," *Encyclopedia of Social Work*, 18th ed. (Silver Spring, Md.: NASW, 1987); Marian Wright Edelman, *Families in Peril: An Agenda for Social Change* (Cambridge, Mass.: Harvard University Press, 1987).
4. Edelman, *Families in Peril*, p. 44.
5. Ibid., p. 39.
6. Alfred Kadushin, *Child Welfare Services*, 3rd ed. (New York: Macmillan Co., 1980), p. 5.
7. Salvatore Ambrosino, "Family Services: Family Service Agencies," *Encyclopedia of Social Work*, 17th ed. (Washington, D.C.: NASW, 1977), p. 429.
8. A. Gerald Erickson, "Family Services," *Encyclopedia of Social Work*, 18th ed. (Silver Spring, Md.: NASW, 1987), p. 589.
9. Alfred J. Kahn and Sheila B. Kamerman, *Helping America's Families*, (Philadelphia: Temple University Press, 1982).
10. Alfred Kadushin and Judith A. Martin, *Child Welfare Services*, 4th ed. (New York: Macmillan, 1988), p. 88.
11. Jerome M. Goldsmith, "Mental Health Services for Children," *Encyclopedia of Social Work*, 17th ed., pp. 891–897.
12. Kadushin and Martin, *Child Welfare Services*, pp. 78–91.
13. Ibid., p. 91.

14. For more on family life education see Herbert A. Otto, ed., *Marriage and Family Enrichment: New Perspectives and Programs* (Nashville, Tenn.: Abingdon Press, 1976), and Luciano L'Abate, "Skill Training Programs for Couples and Families," in Alan S. Gurman and David P. Kniskern, eds., *Handbook of Family Therapy* (New York: Brunner/Mazel, 1981), pp. 631–661.

15. For example, see Nathan W. Ackerman, *The Psychodynamics of Family Life* (New York: Basic Books, 1958); Gregory Bateson, Donald D. Jackson, Jay Haley, and John Weakland, "Toward a Theory of Schizophrenia," *Behavioral Science* 1, no. 4 (1956); Jay Haley, "Marriage Therapy," *Archives of General Psychiatry* 8 (1963); Don D. Jackson, "Family Therapy in the Family of the Schizophrenic," in Morris I. Stein, ed., *Contemporary Psychotherapies* (New York: Free Press of Glencoe, 1961); Murray Bowen, "Family Relationships in Schizophrenia," in Alfred Auerback, ed., *Schizophrenia—An Integrated Approach* (New York: Ronald Press, 1959); Virginia Satir, *Conjoint Family Therapy* (Palo Alto, Calif.: Science and Behavior Books, 1964).

16. Salvatore Ambrosino, "Integrating Counseling, Family Life Education and Family Advocacy," *Social Casework* 60 (1979): 581.

17. Jon Conte, "Service Provision to Enhance Family Functioning," in Brenda G. McGowan and William Meezan, *Child Welfare: Current Dilemmas—Future Directions* (Itasca, Ill.: Peacock Publishers, 1983).

18. Ambrosino, "Family Services," p. 431.

19. Ambrosino, "Integrating Counseling," p. 581.

20. *Agency Program and Funding—1976* (New York: Family Service Association of America, 1977).

21. Conte, "Service Provision," p. 179.

22. Erickson, "Family Services," p. 592.

23. U.S. Congress, Senate, Committee on Labor and Public Welfare, *Community Mental Health Centers Act: History of the Program and Current Problems and Issues*, 93rd Cong., 1st sess., Comm. Print, 1973.

24. Kadushin and Martin, *Child Welfare Services*, pp. 221–222.

25. MaryLee Allen and Jane Knitzer, "Child Welfare: Examining the Policy Framework," in McGowan and Meezan, *Child Welfare*, p. 99.

26. Kadushin and Martin, *Child Welfare Services*, pp. 252 & 257.

27. McGowan and Meezan, *Child Welfare*, p. 99.

28. U.S. Congress, House, "The Child Abuse Prevention and Treatment Act," *Congressional Record*, 93rd Cong., 1st sess., December 21, 1973, pp. 43201–43202; Vincent Fontana, *The Maltreated Child* (New York: Macmillan, 1973); Ruth Kempe and Henry Kempe, *Child Abuse* (Cambridge, Mass.: Harvard University Press, 1978).

29. David Gil, *Violence Against Children: Physical Abuse in the United States* (Cambridge, Mass.: Harvard University Press, 1973).

30. Sheila B. Kamerman and Alfred J. Kahn, *Social Services in the United States: Policies and Programs* (Philadelphia: Temple University Press, 1976), p. 146.

31. Sanford Katz, Ruth-Arlene W. Howe, and Mella McGrath, "Child Neglect

Laws in America," *Family Law Quarterly* 9, no. 1 (Spring 1975), cited in Kadushin and Martin, *Child Welfare Services*, p. 226.

32. American Humane Association, *Highlights of Official Child Neglect and Abuse Reporting 1985* (Denver: American Humane Association, 1987).

33. Kadushin and Martin, *Child Welfare Services*, p. 244.

34. Alfred Kadushin and Judith A. Martin, *Child Abuse: An Interactional Event* (New York: Columbia University Press, 1981), p. 9.

35. Children's Defense Fund, *A Children's Defense Budget: An Analysis of the President's 1984 Budget and Children* (Washington, D.C.: Author, 1983).

36. Kadushin and Martin, *Child Welfare Services*, pp. 245 & 246.

37. Alfred Kadushin, *Child Welfare Services*, 3rd ed. (New York: Macmillan Co., 1980), p. 178.

38. Ibid.

39. Kadushin and Martin, *Child Abuse*.

40. Ibid., p. 256.

41. Ibid., p. 263.

42. Kadushin, *Child Welfare Services*, 3rd ed., p. 184.

43. Kadushin and Martin, *Child Welfare Services*, p. 244.

44. Norman A. Polansky, Carolyn Hally, and Nancy F. Polansky, *Profile of Neglect* (Washington, D.C.: Public Services Administration, Department of H.E.W., 1975), pp. 3–5.

45. Norman A. Polansky, Mary Ann Chalmers, David P. Williams, and Elizabeth Werthan Buttenwieser, *Damaged Parents: An Anatomy of Child Neglect* (New York: University of Chicago Press, 1981), p. 5.

46. L. Young, *Wednesday's Children: A Study of Child Neglect and Abuse* (New York: McGraw-Hill, 1964).

47. Polansky et al., *Damaged Parents*.

48. Kadushin and Martin, *Child Welfare Services*, p. 236.

49. James Garbarino, Edna Guttman, and Janis Wilson Seeley, *The Psychologically Battered Child*, (San Francisco: Jossey-Bass, 1986), p. 8.

50. Kudushin and Martin, *Child Welfare Services*, p. 239.

51. Ibid., pp. 237–238.

52. Diana Russell, *Sexual Exploitation: Rape, Child Sexual Abuse and Work Harassment* (Beverly Hills, Calif.: Sage Publications, 1983).

53. Jon R. Conte, "Child Sexual Abuse," *Encyclopedia of Social Work*, 18th ed. (Silver Spring, Md.: NASW, 1987), pp. 255–260; David Finkelhor, *Sexually Victimized Children* (New York: Free Press, 1979).

54. J. R. Conte and L. Berliner, "Sexual Abuse of Children: Implications for Practice," *Social Casework* 62 (1981): 601–606.

55. Ruth S. Kempe and Henry Kempe, *The Common Secret: Sexual Abuse of Children and Adolescents* (New York: W.H. Freeman and Co., 1984).

56. K. Gruber and R. Jones, "Identifying Determinants of Risk of Sexual Victimization of Youth: A Multivariant Approach," *Child Abuse and Neglect* 7 (1983): 17–24.

57. National Center on Child Abuse and Neglect, *Study Findings: National Study of the Incidence and Severity of Child Abuse and Neglect* (Wash-

ington, D.C.: U.S. Department of Health and Human Services DHHS Publication No. (OHDS) 81-30325, 1981).

58. Robert M. Mulford, "Protective Services for Children," *Encyclopedia of Social Work*, 17th ed. (Washington, D.C.: NASW, 1977), p. 1117.

59. Lela B. Costin and Charles A. Rapp, *Child Welfare Services, Policies and Practices* (New York: McGraw-Hill, 1984).

60. Ruth S. Kempe and C. Henry Kempe, *Child Abuse* (Cambridge, Mass.: Harvard University Press, 1978); Carmine J. Magazino, "Services to Children and Families at Risk of Separation," in McGowan and Meezan, *Child Welfare*, pp. 211–254.

61. Kempe and Kempe, *Child Abuse*, pp. 19–20.

62. Janet R. Hutchinson and Kristine E. Nelson, "How Public Agencies Can Provide Family-Centered Services," *Social Casework* 66 (June 1985): 367.

63. Marvin E. Bryce, "Home-Based Care: Development and Rationale," in Sheila Maybanks and Marvin Bryce, eds., *Home-Based Services for Children and Families* (Springfield, Ill.: Charles C Thomas, 1979), pp. 15–19.

64. June C. Lloyd and Marvin E. Bryce, *Placement Prevention and Family Reunification: A Handbook for the Family-Centered Service Practitioner* (Iowa City: National Resource Center on Family Based Services, University of Iowa School of Social Work, 1984).

65. Bryce, "Home-Based Care," pp. 19–20.

66. April D. Reiss, "Family Systems: Training for Assessment," in *Treating Families in the Home: An Alternative to Placement*, ed. Marvin E. Bryce and June C. Lloyd (Springfield, Ill.: Charles C Thomas, 1980), pp. 98–107.

67. Lloyd and Bryce, *Placement Prevention and Family Reunification*, p. 6.

68. Ibid., pp. 7 & 25.

69. Marvin E. Bryce and June C. Lloyd, "Placement Prevention—Family Reunification: A View From the Child Welfare Sector," unpublished manuscript (Iowa City: National Resource Center for Family-Based Services, University of Iowa School of Social Work, 1982).

70. Kristine Nelson, "Research in Family Based Services," *Prevention Report*, Winter 1987/88, p. 11.

71. Kadushin and Martin, *Child Welfare Services.*

72. Costin and Rapp, *Child Welfare.*

73. Ibid., pp. 255–258.

74. Majorie Ziefert, "Homemaker and Day-Care Services," in *A Handbook of Child Welfare: Context, Knowledge, and Practice*, ed. Joan Laird and Ann Hartman (New York: Free Press, 1985), p. 428.

75. Florence M. Moore, "New Issues for In-Home Service," *Public Welfare*, Spring 1977, pp. 26–37.

76. Kadushin and Martin, *Child Welfare Services.*

77. Robert Hunt, "Homemaker-Home Health Aide Service," *Encyclopedia of Social Work*, 17th ed. (Washington, D.C.: NASW, 1977), p. 637.

78. Arthur C. Emlen, "Child Care Services," *Encyclopedia of Social Work*, 18th ed. (Silver Spring, Md.: NASW, 1987), p. 232.

79. Ibid., p. 234.

80. Children's Defense Fund, *A Children's Defense Budget: An Analysis of the*

President's FY 1985 Budget and Children, (Washington, D.C.: Authur, 1984).

81. Emlen, "Child Care Services," p. 237.
82. Therese W. Lansburgh, "Child Welfare: Day Care of Children," *Encyclopedia of Social Work*, 17th ed. (Washington, D.C.: NASW, 1977), p. 138.
83. Carmine J. Magazino, "Services to Children and Families at Risk of Separation," in *Child Welfare Services*, ed. McGowan and Meezan, pp. 211–254.
84. Emlen, "Child Care Services," p. 237.
85. Lansburgh, "Day Care," p. 134.
86. T. F. Baily and W. H. Baily, *Child Welfare Practice* (San Francisco: Jossey-Bass, 1983).

ADDITIONAL SUGGESTED READINGS

Blum, Marian, *The Day Care Dilemma* (Lexington, Mass.: Lexington Books, 1983.

Daro, Deborah, *Confronting Child Abuse: Research for Effective Program Design* (New York: Free Press, 1988).

Dexter, Margaret, and Wally Harbert, *The Home-Help Service* (New York: Tavistock Publications, 1983).

McAdoo, Harriette, and T. M. Jim Parham, eds., *Services to Young Families: Program Review and Policy Recommendations* (Washington, D.C.: American Public Welfare Association, 1985).

MacFarlane, Kee, and Jill Waterman, and Associates, *Sexual Abuse of Young Children: Evaluation and Treatment* (New York: Guilford Press, 1986).

Sunley, R., *Advocating Today: A Human Service Practitioner's Handbook* (New York: Family Service Association of America, 1983).

6 Services to Families and Children Outside the Home

Gilbert J. Greene

The thrust of supportive and supplemental services is to help problematic children and families in their own homes, so that families can remain permanently intact. When supportive and supplemental services are not sufficiently effective and/or available, it may be necessary to rely on substitute care services that are designed to replace the biological parents, either temporarily or permanently, by a surrogate parent(s) or a group home living arrangement. Though there has been some contention that the availability of adequate supportive and supplemental services can practically eliminate the need for substitute services, several studies show that a majority of substitute care placements are necessary, appropriate, and in all probability, unavoidable.[1] The implication, then, is that supportive and supplemental services cannot eliminate or replace substitute services. The services usually considered to be substitute care services are adoption, foster care, and institutional care, which will be discussed in this chapter. Also to be briefly discussed will be certain miscellaneous services that, though not substitute, are usually provided to families and children outside their homes. Afterwards, a listing of some present and future trends in programs for families and children will be included. The chapter concludes with a general discussion of family policy.

SUBSTITUTE SERVICES

Foster Care

Foster care provides noninstitutional substitute family care to a child for a planned period, either temporary or long-term, when his/her own family cannot care for him/her and when adoption is neither desirable nor possible.[2] Children in foster care are placed either with foster families in their own homes or in group home living situations. Foster care has been provided in one form or another for so long that it is impossible to specify when it first began.

The placing of a child in a family as an indentured servant or apprentice was extensive in the United States from its earliest days. This practice was imported from Britain and lasted in this country until the first decade of the twentieth century. The origin of modern foster-family care is attributed to Charles Loring Brace, a minister and the first secretary of the New York Children's Aid Society, which was founded in 1853. His approach involved moving "needful" children from the cities to rural areas, usually the Midwest, where the environment was considered to be "more moral." This procedure, never universally popular, was abandoned in 1929. Charles Birtwell, the leader of the Boston Children's Aid Society from 1886 to 1911, further refined foster care. He was very systematic and planned carefully, viewing foster family care as long-term and usually replacing the biological parents in a "pseudo-adoptive" situation.[3]

Foster family care is still in use with varying degrees of careful planning and systemization. There has been, however, a trend toward decreasing use of foster care. In 1984 there was an estimated total of 275,756 children in all types of foster care; a decrease of 9.2 percent from 1980.[4] Of this total, approximately 68 percent were residing in family foster homes and 32 percent in group residential settings.[5] The median length of time in such living situations has been decreasing, to approximately eighteen months in 1983 from twenty-nine months in 1977.[6]

Children are most likely to enter foster care as a result of family breakdown. A large percentage of these children are from lower-class families that suffer from chronic deprivation and environmental stress. The physical or mental illness of parents, neglect or abuse of children, broken homes, extremely low income, or behavioral problems of the child are some of the more frequent situations that lead to placement in foster care. The family problems behind foster care are usually multiple, making it difficult to locate one primary reason for each individual placement. In more recent years, unemployment, economic stress, and cutbacks in supportive social programs have made it even more difficult for such families to remain intact. Generally speaking, the vast majority of foster care placememts are due to problems in the social functioning of parents as opposed to some problematic behavior of the child.[7]

Usually a specific crisis precipitates the need for foster care placement, but many of these families had been functioning marginally, trying to deal with multiple problems and high levels of stress for some time prior to the crisis. Other resources, such as friends and relatives, are unavailable, unwilling, or unable to provide care. Supplemental social services such as homemaker service may be unavailable or inadequate.[8]

A social worker who works in a foster care situation needs to be highly competent in skills of diagnosis and assessment, counseling and psychotherapy, and case management and advocacy.[9] The foster care worker's primary duties involve supervising and working with the foster parents, working closely with the biological parents, coordinating services, and working with the legal system.[10]

In most cases the goal of foster care services is the eventual return of the child to the biological parents. Since the removal of a child from his/her own home is such a serious step, it is important for the social worker to develop, as soon as possible, a good working relationship with the biological parent(s). Once a decision has been made for foster care placement, the social worker develops with the parents a realistic service plan for improving conditions and making necessary changes for the return of the child(ren). According to Karen Blumenthal, the essential components of a service plan include:

- The specific circumstances/problems that necessitated child's placement in foster care.
- The changes that must take place before the child can return home; these must be specific, realistic, measurable, and/or observable.
- The anticipated length of the placement.
- The specific actions to be taken and/or services to be provided by the agency in correcting the conditions that led to placement.
- The specific actions to be taken by the parents in correcting the conditions that led to placement.
- The specific actions to be taken by the child in correcting the conditions that led to placement.
- The services to be provided by other community resources to help bring about the necessary changes.
- The parent-child visiting arrangements including frequency, location, length, timing, and participants.
- The approximate duration of services and the dates by which it is reasonable to expect the necessary changes to occur. (This sets the

parameters for the service program and insures that all concerned parties are cognizant of these time frames).
- A time schedule for periodic assessment of the progress toward established goals.[11]

The selection of foster parents and subsequent agency supervision are important ingredients in successful foster care. A social study of people who apply to be foster parents serves as the primary basis for selection. Then, preferably, they receive training from the agency to help them prepare to deal with the problems of foster parenting as well as to learn effective ways of performing this role. Foster parents receive payment for the child's board as well as payments for his/her needed medical and dental expenses and clothing. Usually, foster parenting is not a financially rewarding occupation especially considering its high level of demands.[12]

The social agency responsible for the child in foster care has an ongoing obligation to supervise the foster care situation to insure that adequate child care is being given. This involves the social worker consulting with the foster parents and aiding them in effectively performing their roles. Foster parents should be considered service providers and thus extensions of the professional staff.[13] Need for agency supervision and consultation is further supported by the fact that the average foster home often has special needs. Most foster parents are from lower socioeconomic groups. They tend to have limited education and are older than the foster child's own parents. They often have ambivalent feelings toward the foster child and may be unable to deal with the frequent aggressive behavior of foster children.[14]

Group Foster Home Care

Foster home care, in spite of its shortcomings, is the preferred type of placement for children who can form family ties and actively participate in it as well as live in the community without major disruptions. However, this is not the only type of foster care. Group home care, another type of foster care, may be seen as standing between foster family and institutional care. It is primarily for children who are not appropriate for foster homes or institutional care. It provides some of the closeness of family living while allowing some of the interpersonal distance, especially from adults, that is possible in institutional care. This type of setting is usually better suited to adolescents of all ages, particularly those that have continuing conflicts with parental figures. It is also well suited for adolescents because the primary developmental tasks at this stage involve establishing independence from parents and parent figures. In addition, it may serve as a "halfway house" for children who are making the transition from institutional care to returning to their own homes.[15]

The group home, which is usually agency operated, is generally a single dwelling located in a residential area of the community in a house or apartment and provides care for four to twelve children at a time. The child-care staff members may be considered either as foster parents or counselors. The staff are salaried employees, and at least one staff member is present in the home at all times. Each home has certain rules for daily living, but overall the atmosphere should be relaxed and informal. The residents of the group home, if able, are allowed to participate in the usual community social activities and attend local schools and religious services.[16]

Institutional Care

Another type of substitute care that is sometimes considered a form of foster care is the children's institution. An institution differs from a group foster home in that it is larger, caring for fifteen or more residents at a time. It may consist of more than one building; it may provide formal education on its premises, and it may or may not be in a residential part of a community.

Modern child-care institutions have their roots in the almshouses of England, which housed dependent children together with needy adults. There was little, if any, effort to provide separate services and facilities for children. This was also the case in the United States, which adopted the almshouse system. However, by the end of the eighteenth century there were a few institutions just for children. During the nineteenth century, some citizens periodically expressed concern about mixed almshouses and their effects on children, and toward the end of the century many states began to prohibit the care of children in almshouses. This trend gave rise to the development of more orphanages and foster care for children under both private and public auspices.[17]

Institutions take on various forms, serving different kinds of children. Among them are institutions for:

1. Normal but dependent and neglected children. This is the closest modern analogy to the old "orphan asylum."
2. Physically handicapped children. These are separate institutions for children who are blind, deaf, crippled, asthmatic, and so forth.
3. Mentally retarded or mentally defective children.
4. The confinement and rehabilitation of juvenile delinquents. These are often called *training schools.*

5. Emotionally disturbed children. These are known as *residential treatment centers.*[18]

The juvenile justice system is responsible for children in correctional institutions; physically and mentally handicapped children are usually the responsibility of the health care system; and dependent children in institutions and emotionally disturbed children in residential treatment centers are the responsibility of the child welfare system. Though social workers deal with all types of problematic children in various institutions, the primary concern here is with dependent and/or emotionally disturbed children, since the focus in this chapter is family and child welfare services.

At the beginning of 1980, there were more than 20,000 beds available in 368 residential treatment centers for children eighteen years old and younger. Most of these centers had approximately fifty-four beds. For the year 1979–1980, the average length of stay was 196 days.[19]

The primary reason for institutional placement tends to be the problematic behavior of the child. The child may be unable to develop a satisfactory emotional relationship with parental figures, remaining indifferent to affection that is expressed by foster parents. Or the child might be very aggressive and/or destructive to the extent that she/he would be unable to develop reciprocal relationships that are characteristic of "normal" families. Therefore, the institution seems best suited for (1) adolescents, (2) highly disturbed and potentially violent children, and (3) children who are extremely uncomfortable in close relationships.[20]

Social workers are involved in institutional care services in a variety of ways. In the decision-making process, a psychosocial study of the child and family performed by the social worker is necessary. Once institutional placement is made, the worker may need to help the parents cope with feelings of loss, guilt, and failure. For treatment to be effective, ties between the parents and child need to be maintained, and the social worker may help facilitate this. The social worker may counsel the parents and help them plan for making changes that are necessary for the child's permanent return home. The worker may also work individually with the child and conduct family therapy with the entire family together. In addition, she/he will consult closely with the institutional staff on an ongoing basis to insure that all aspects of the daily activities and institutional environment are therapeutic. This may require regular inservice education with the staff. A further aspect of social work in an institutional setting may involve liaison with other community agencies to insure that the child and family have the community supports needed to allow the child to return home permanently.

Adoption

Adoption is the legal and social process that establishes a parent-child relationship between persons unrelated by birth. This involves a child born to one set of parents, the biological parents, becoming the child of a different set of parents, the adoptive parents, and thus having the same rights and responsibilities as if they were biologically related. Adoption means a permanent family change, allowing children to have the benefits of long-term, intense family ties that they otherwise would not have. It is an appropriate step when a child's biological parent(s) cannot or will not care for him/her and other adults are capable and willing to assume, for various personal reasons, the legal responsibility of parenthood. For a child to be eligible for adoption, the parental rights of the natural parents must be legally terminated. Therefore, adoption requires cooperation between social workers and the legal system.

Adoption has a long history, dating back to the ancient Egyptians, Greeks, and Romans. It was used to provide family heirs to assure the continuity of a family name and to enhance a family's political power. Therefore, adoption was frequently for the benefit of the adopter rather than the adoptee. In the early history of the United States, adoption was not common. English common law, which was the basis for the laws in this country, did not provide for adoption. The use of indentured servants and the relation between master and apprentice further hindered the development of legal adoptions. Massachusetts in 1851 was the first state to pass an adoption law, which became the model for adoption legislation in other states. This legislation made the welfare of the child the primary concern.[21]

Though the welfare of the child was foremost in state laws, legal provisions for investigation and control of adoption by unsuitable parents varied considerably. In 1891, a Michigan law began requiring that an investigation by a judge be made before an adoption became final. Minnesota, in 1917, was the first state to require a detailed investigation and recommendation by a social welfare agency concerning the suitability of adoption.[22] Over the last several decades, social welfare agencies, the Child Welfare League of America, and the social work profession in general have worked to develop professional guidelines and standards for adoption agencies.

Adoptions can be categorized in different ways. One method of classification is to divide them into adoptions by *relatives* and by *nonrelatives*. Social agencies are seldom involved with the former but are highly involved with the latter. In 1982, a national survey estimated that 50,720 nonrelative adoptions occurred that year with 67 percent of them placed by social agencies.[23] In addition to relative and nonrelative, there are several other types of adoptions.

Independent Adoption.   In this type of adoption a social agency is not involved. Most independent adoptions are relative adoptions, most of which involve a stepparent adopting a spouse's child(ren). A second type of independent adoption involves the *direct placement* of the child with someone known by the biological parent. Two other types are *intermediary—not for profit* and *intermediary—for profit*; these are usually arranged by a physician or attorney and involve adoptive parents not known to the biological parent(s). The intermediary—not for profit is legal in forty-six states, and the intermediary—for profit is illegal in every state.[24] These three types are frequently used by adoptive parents frustrated with the formal adoptive process. There is a shortage of white, nonhandicapped infants—the most sought-after type of prospective adoptive child—and therefore agencies can be more selective in choosing adoptive parents. In 1982 it was estimated that 33 percent of all nonrelative adoptions were independent.[25] Lack of involvement of a social service agency in independent adoptions, it is generally agreed, can be risky for the child and the success of the adoption, but it has been found that such arrangements do not necessarily have serious problems.[26]

Agency Adoption.   As noted previously, most adoptions are under the auspices of a social service agency. Therefore, the responsibility of the majority of adoptions in this country belongs to the social work profession. The social worker carries out society's responsibility to children in need of an adequate, permanent home. This involves ensuring that society's responsibilities to the child, the biological parent(s), and the adopting parent(s) are met.

The selection of adoptive parents is important. The social worker is actively involved in assessing their personal qualities and the kind of home they will provide to the child and also preparing the adoptive parents to meet their new responsibilities. In the screening process the social worker assesses the suitability of prospective adoptive parents by means of several individual interviews, visits to their homes, and checking references. A number of variables are considered: age, physical and emotional health, motivation, marital adjustment, financial stability, and others. Once the agency approves applicants for adoption, the next task is to select a child appropriate for that couple/parent.[27]

After a child is selected as a possible adoptee for a couple/parent, the social worker is very active in preparing them and the child for the initial meeting. The social worker provides information about one to the other and any support and/or counseling needed during this sometimes anxious and exciting period. Older children being adopted may have more conflicts and questions about adoption, thus requiring more skills and time from the social worker.

A "trial" period of approximately six months follows placement of the child in the home. During this time, the social worker maintains some contact with the adoptive parents and the child, making home visits approximately once every three months. This contact serves a protective function for both the child and the parents, for it ensures that the child has been placed in a desirable home and is developing normally. If there are serious problems, the child may be removed before adoption is final, which has been found to occur in 3 percent of infant adoptions and up to 15 percent of adoptions involving children with special needs.[28] The emphasis during this period should be on helping the parents and the adopted child develop "a sense of kinship" and to help them with the problems that are sure to occur during this period of dramatic change in their lives.[29]

As stated previously, the type of child most in demand as an adoptee tends to be a Caucasian infant. Though there has been a shortage of this type of child for adoption, other types of children who have traditionally been harder to place are in more than adequate supply. To deal with the situation, agencies and potential adoptive parents have made some changes.

Children with Special Needs

There are many children who are free for adoption but because they are not healthy, white infants are not in great demand by most prospective adoptive parents. These children include those who are members of minority groups, are older, or are handicapped. In more recent years, adoption agencies have been involved in outreach to the community to recruit adoptive parents and have been willing to relax standards and procedures to increase the attractiveness of adopting children with special needs.

The Nonwhite Child.   The demand for minority children for adoption has not been proportionate to the numbers available for adoption. For example, black children make up 14 percent of the child population but are 25 percent of the foster care population and 33 percent of the children free for adoption.[30] It has also been found that 17 percent of black handicapped children free for adoption are placed compared to 38 percent of white handicapped children.[31] It has been much easier for agencies to find homes for white children than for black children. Efforts have been made to recruit minority adoptive parents but without great success. The primary reason appears to be economic in that minorities have proportionately lower incomes and less adequate housing than whites. Nonwhite couples who are financially able to adopt do so proportionately as much as whites.[32] Some agencies have been successful in increasing the number of placements of black children in black homes by taking steps to involve the black community actively and to make the agency more accessible to them.

Transracial Adoptions.   One way that has developed to help meet the adoptive needs of minority children is the transracial adoption, which is usually the placement of nonwhite children in white adoptive homes. Transracial adoption began in the 1950s and increased considerably in the late 1960s, peaking in 1972 when 468 agencies made 2,574 placements.[33] It has been estimated that by 1983, almost 20,000 black children had been adopted by white parents.[34]

This trend, however, was not widely supported by everyone and eventually met considerable opposition from minority groups. The opposition centered on the potential problems in the development of racial identity by the minority child being reared by white parents. The child might be considered an outcast by both the white community and his/her own minority group. It was argued that white parents, no matter how well-intentioned, could not raise a minority child in a way that would give him/her a clear sense of racial identity.

In 1972 the National Association of Black Social Workers issued a strong protest against transracial adoptions involving black children, fearing that the practice threatened the integrity and preservation of the black family. There was considerable controversy and discussion about this issue among social work professionals. Consequently, there was a consistent decline in the number of black children adopted by white parents with 831 such adoptions occurring in 1975.[35] Though there has been a sharp decline in transracial adoptions, such placements are still occurring. A rationale is that there are not enough minority families wanting to adopt. It has been pointed out, however, that potential adoptive minority families exist, but social agencies have not made enough efforts to recruit them.[36] In a review of several studies of the effects of transracial adoptions, Meezan states, "Many in the field believe that even if every effort is made to find minority homes, there will still be children who cannot be placed in the minority community and that transracial adoptions still represent an important alternative to foster care."[37] Meezan summarized guidelines for social workers involved in transracial adoptions:

- Children whenever possible should be placed with parents of the same race.

- Permanent care in an adoptive home is preferable to long-term foster care or institutionalization of minority children.
- Placing a child in a home of another race should be based on the needs of the child, not the desire of parents for a child or an expedience of the agency.
- Motivating factors for transracial adoption must be explored thoroughly with adoptive parents to insure that their expectations are realistic.
- Any parent adopting transracially must be able to accept racial and cultural differences between themselves and their child on more than an intellectual level. Such couples must be sensitive to their own prejudice and racism and the way it affects the child.
- Adoptive couples must be committed to imparting a sense of racial or ethnic identification to their child. This means that they must demonstrate ability and desire for sustained contact with members of the child's ethnic/racial group. They must relate to the cultural milieu with which the child will need to identify.

Stock Boston/Steve Hansen

Finding adoptive homes for minority and racially mixed children is difficult. Multi-racial families with adopted children have become more common, though not without controversy.

- Transracial adopting parents must be able to confront the racist nature of society and be committed on all levels to combatting this situation. They must prepare their child to face discrimination when it occurs and help diffuse its impact.[38]

Older Children.   Since most adopting families tend to prefer infants, it is not surprising to find that children over the age of two are hard to place. The placement of older children requires more services, time, and effort and is therefore more costly. However, in the long run, the savings are substantial, considering the costs of foster care and other maintenance costs. Therefore, because of the financial savings and the shortage of infants for adoption, older children are increasingly being placed for adoption.[39]

The older child can play an active role in the adoption process. As a result, the role of the social worker is important in making the adoption as problem-free as possible. The older child is likely to have been legally removed from his/her biological parents as a result of neglect and/or abuse and consequently may have suffered psychological/emotional damage. The child may anticipate rejection and be overly cautious in forming an emotional bond with the adoptive parents. All along the adoptive process the social worker needs to be sensitive to these issues and intervene when appropriate.

Adoptive parents may prefer an older child in order not to contend with the amount of care required for an infant. In addition, an older child can more immediately be an active participant in the family's life. One study of the outcome of placements of older children found them to be almost as successful as infant adoptions.[40]

Handicapped Children.   There have always been children with physical and/or mental problems in need of adoption. However, finding an adoption placement for them is extremely difficult. Such children require considerable time and energy from the parents in addition to extra expenses for medical care and other specialized treatment.

One study found that children with all types of physical handicaps of varying degrees can be placed and reared successfully in adoptive homes.[41] In this study, some of the adoptive parents had first been the foster parents of the handicapped child. In a study involving mentally handicapped children, it was found that the parents' previous experience with the handicap was a helpful factor.[42] Regardless of the disability, close cooperation among the agency, the parents, and medical personnel and facilities is required as well as knowledge of rehabilitative, educational, and counseling services in the community.

An Adoption Case

At the age of two, John Stevens was placed in foster care after his father was killed in a building construction accident and his mother, who has a severe drinking problem, became unable to provide adequate care. John was placed in foster care after neighbors reported Ms. Stevens to the Department of Social Services for neglect. For a year after placement, Ms. Stevens visited John periodically, but her living conditions did not change, primarily because she refused treatment for her drinking problem. Eventually her visits stopped, and she could not be found by department social workers. John was able to live in the foster home for the next four years, and the relationship with his foster parents was very close. The agency sought termination of parental rights after the foster parents indicated a desire to adopt John.

In the process Ms. Stevens was found living in a nearby city, and she expressed an interest in caring for John again. A social study found that Ms. Stevens no longer was drinking heavily and held a steady job. As a preliminary step, visitation was again arranged for Ms. Stevens to see John on a regular basis. However, Ms. Stevens soon afterwards began drinking again, became sporadic in her visits, and lost her job. The Department of Social Services then petitioned the court for termination of parental rights. The agency argued that John had been deserted by his mother, who had become a stranger to him, and therefore should permanently remain with the people who he perceived as his "real" parents. The petition was granted, and John was adopted by his foster parents.

Subsidized Adoptions

To help increase the adoptability of children with special needs, most states have passed legislation that provides financial assistance to adoptive parents beyond the traditional legal responsibilities. New York passed the first adoption subsidy legislation in 1968. Presently, all states provide some type of adoption subsidy. Funding for adoption subsidies has been further aided by passage of the Adoption Assistance and Child Welfare Act (P.L. 96–272) in 1980. This legislation provides federal involvement in adoption for the first time.[43]

Subsidies can be provided for a variety of purposes, such as specialized medical care and/or special education to offset increased expenses of child care and other costs. Such payments have made it possible for many special-needs children to be adopted who otherwise would have remained in foster care. In addition, it allows for some families to adopt who otherwise would not be financially able to do so. Most states have an income eligibility criterion, and a yearly review of income is required. The majority of these adoptions consist of children who are adopted by their foster parents. Previously, foster parents would lose necessary financial assistance that was available for foster care but ceased after adoption; this situation discouraged adoption of such children by their foster parents. Adoption subsidy programs help in the recruitment of adoptive parents for special-needs children and encourage foster parents to adopt such children already in their care. In addition to providing the child a permanent home, subsidized adoptions have been shown to be more cost-effective than long-term foster care. A primary reason for its cost-effectiveness is stipulation that adoption subsidies cannot be greater than the expense of keeping a child in foster care.[44]

As of 1982, it was estimated that 19,000 children were receiving adoption subsidies nationally. Although the provision of adoption subsidies is relatively new and is not yet very well researched, all indications thus far indicate that it is accomplishing its goals.[45] Though the legal status of some children in foster care is changed as a result of subsidized adoption, there is little empirical data on any resultant psychological changes; further research is needed in this area.[46]

Single-Parent Adoption

Since children with special needs are harder to place for adoption, many agencies now consider unmarried applicants as a way of providing permanent homes for these children. Single adults—never married, divorced, widowed—tend to be accepted as adoptive parents only when two-parent homes are unavailable. In most cases the adoptive parent is a single woman, but occasionally single males also adopt.

Studies have found that children who are placed with single parents tend to be those with special needs and thus difficult to place with a two-parent family.[47] The results of such adoptions, however, have tended to be quite positive. Single-parent adopters have been found to be older than other adoptive parents with many also having better incomes and more education. In addition, single-parent adopters tend to be self-aware and child-oriented, with strong connections with relatives and friends.[48] Consequently, single parents have been able to provide stable, nurturing environments for adoptive children that allow for their positive growth and development.

Some single-parent adoptive families might benefit from social work intervention in dealing with the child's feelings about not having the benefit of a two-parent family. However, sometimes this type of adoption is seen as the placement of choice, since the single adopter does not have to give support and attention to a spouse and instead can devote his/her energies to meeting the needs of the adopted child. Despite the good success rate of single-parent adoptions, they are seen as the second choice to two-parent adoptions and make up only a small percentage of all adoptions.[49]

International Adoptions

Since the end of World War II, there has been an interest in the United States in adopting orphan children from other countries. Many prospective adoptive parents in this country who are unable to adopt American children turn to this option. In one study, 87 percent of white families in the United States who adopted children from Colombia said that they did so because they were unable to adopt an American child.[50] Other contributing factors involved in the adoption of children from other countries by citizens in the United States are: "the mobility of families around the world; the increase in international marriages; the greater ease of communication between countries; the continuing large numbers of American servicemen stationed abroad . . . ; and a humanitarian concern . . . for the plight of refugee and other homeless children."[51]

International adoption is not without its controversy. Some people view it as "class, race, and national exploitation" of the countries supplying the children.[52] International adoption can be seen as depriving such countries of their "most valuable resource, its future citizens."[53] Since some children in the 1970s were removed from their home countries before they were legally available for adoption, most countries have made efforts to insure that certain guidelines are followed.[54]

Since the movement of a child from one country to begin living with a "strange" family in another has potential difficulties, such an adoption should be planned very carefully. An in-depth assessment of the prospective adopters by a recognized child welfare agency in this country must first be completed. The potential problems of adopting a child from another country must be presented to the adopters and explored with them. As with transracial adoption it is important to assess the parents' commitment to helping the child develop and maintain a racial, ethnic, and cultural identity. In addition, all necessary steps must be taken to insure that the adoption is legal in both countries. Even though an international adoption will very likely be motivated by humanitarian concerns, the child welfare agency must be actively involved in all phases of the process, including followup, to insure that the needs of the child are primary. A recent extensive review of the literature on the outcomes of both transracial and international adoptions found that these adoptions are quite successful.[55]

Sealed Records and Open Adoptions

Adoption in the United States is highly developed with tightly structured legal safeguards. After the adoption of a child has become a legal fact, the original birth certificate is sealed and replaced by an amended one. Thereafter, papers and records are unavailable for examination except by court order for good cause, such as health problems.[56]

Confidentially and anonymity have long been a part of the adoption process. Hearings are held in closed court, restricting admission to the concerned parties only, after which the birth record is permanently sealed. It is assumed that confidentiality and anonymity are required in order to encourage both birth and adoptive parents to participate in the adoptive process. There may be potentially embarrassing personal facts that these parents would never want to be available to the public or the adopted child.

This long-established practice is now being challenged in two ways. (1) Some adult adoptees are seeking to have their sealed birth records legally opened in order to learn information about their genealogical heritage. Some adoptees want to meet their birth parents. (2) Open adoptions have taken place; an open adoption is:

> a process in which the birth parents and the adoptive parents meet and exchange identifying information. The birth parents relinquish legal and basic child rearing rights to the adoptive parents. Both sets of parents retain the right to continuing contact and access to knowledge on behalf of the child.[57]

Unsealing the Record.   Adult adoptees seeking to have their birth records opened claim they have a constitutional right to know the identities of their birth parents. Adoptees argue that knowing their hereditary background is necessary for further development of their sense of identity. Others, however, believe that the rights of the birth and adoptive parents should also be protected. To open the record, according to opponents of searching adoptees, would violate the adoption agency's agreement to confidentiality and may discourage future unmarried mothers and prospective adoptive parents from pursuing adoption as an option. There are many good arguments for and against allowing the unsealing of the adoption record and letting the adult who was adopted as a child learn the identities of his/her biological parents.[58]

In recent years there has been a growing adoptee activist movement in this country to change policies and laws to allow adult adoptees access to their birth records. As of 1985, thirty-five states has passed laws allowing adult adoptees access to some identifying information about their birth parents. Some states have a reunion registry and a mutual consent procedure, which allow adoptive and biological parents to record their openness to meet if contacted. Other states allow the use of third-party intermediaries, usually social service agencies, to mediate between children and biological parents.[59]

Experience has shown that the vast majority of adult adoptees do not have or want contact with their birth parents. A survey of adoptive parents found that 15 percent of their adopted children had asked to see their birth records, and 4 percent had actually contacted their birth parents.[60] A study of adoptees in England, which has allowed the unsealing of adoption records since 1975, found that only 22 percent wanted to have contact with their birth parents.[61]

Open Adoptions. In open adoptions the birth record is not only open from the beginning, but the birth parent(s) and the adopted child may have periodic contact with each other with the consent of the adoptive parents. Such an arrangement is usually agreed upon from the beginning and often conducted independent of any social service agency.

Open adoption of older children is not very controversial, because older children tend to have a past history of contact with birth parents and extended family. Therefore, it is not realistic and usually not advisable for the adopted child to sever contact unless he or she strongly wants to.

Open adoption of infants is more controversial. Supporters of closed adoption argue that anonymity and confidentiality are necessary to safeguard the noninterference necessary for permanent attachment and bonding between the adoptive parents and child. In addition, adoptive parents have the additional security that the adopted child will not leave them for his/her birth parents.[62] Proponents of open adoption argue that there would be a decrease in the child's tendency to feel rejected by the birth parent. The birth parent benefits in that she is less likely to experience severe feelings of loss and guilt. The adoptive parents' acquaintance with the birth parent can help diminish troubling fears and fantasies they may have and allow for their relationship to the child to be more natural and honest.[63]

In addressing the controversies of unsealing adoption records and open adoption, Meezan states that experience has found that adoptees who have had contact with their birth parents usually reported satisfaction. He states further that if adoption is "truly a child-centered service, then the rights of the child are paramount."[64] Curtis believes that before adoption is ever considered, both the adoptive and biological parents should choose whether they wish to participate in an open adoption and that these choices could then be used as one of the criteria for matching children and adoptive parents. According to Curtis, it is already common for both sets of parents to use criteria in deciding who is appropriate for adoption. This process allows decisions about open versus closed adoption that are not based on outcomes that are impossible to predict.[65]

Permanency Planning

For many children placed in foster care, a goal of temporary placement will be clear from the beginning. However, for many others, the length of time to be spent in foster care will be unclear. A number of children in foster care never know when they might be returned to their biological parents or moved to another set of foster parents. It has not been uncommon for such children to spend many years in continuous foster care experiencing placement with several different families without the benefit of a plan for a permanent living situation.[66] Children in such situations are said to be experiencing "foster care drift." One study found that those children in foster care for more than eighteen months were not likely to be returned home or adopted, and thus temporary foster care became a permanent living situation by default.[67] Only in recent years have the detrimental effects of foster care drift been acknowledged and efforts made to deal with this situation. With the need for permanency planning acknowledged, specific efforts have been and are being made to deal with children adrift in foster care. One such effort with a preventive focus is home-based, family-center treatment, which was discussed in the previous chapter. This section focuses on services to families and children once a child has been removed.

Permanency planning in child welfare has been defined as:

> the systematic process of carrying out, within a brief time-limited period, a set of goal-directed activities designed to help children live in families that offer continuity of relationships with nurturing parents or caretakers and the opportunity to establish lifetime relationships.[68]

Permanence describes intent in that a permanent home is not guaranteed to last forever but is intended to be indefinite. A temporary placement may be long-term and appear to be permanent, but the all-important intent of permanence will still be absent. Even if a child lives in the same foster placement until adulthood, it is not considered to be permanent unless there is a case plan specifying the intent of permanence. A child in this situation may still experience doubt, uncertainty, and hesitancy.[69] Thus, it could be said that a child's living situation is not considered permanent until an adult has committed to take responsibility for raising the child to adulthood.[70] The perception of permanence has been found to be more important to the child's well-being than the formal legal status of the placement.[71]

The current emphasis in child welfare is on making reasonable efforts to prevent out-of-home placements. Permanency planning means that when such placements are deemed necessary, they should be in the "most family-like" setting available and in close proximity to the parent's home. Every effort should be made to rehabilitate the home of the biological parent(s) and return the child as soon as possible. If rehabilitation and reunification are not possible, parental rights should be terminated and subsequent adoption of the child should be pursued. When neither option is possible, then the child should be placed in long-term foster care with one family.[72]

Continuity and nurturance in relationships are important for the healthy development of a child. She/he needs to know that regardless of crises and problems the family may encounter, its integrity is assured. Some scholars have advocated that the "best interests of the child" should take precedence. This may then necessitate termination of the rights of the biological parents and the permanent placement of the child with parents who may or may not adopt him/her but will then become the "psychological parents." The intent is that the ultimate plan will be the "least detrimental alternative."[73]

Permanency planning can be done at any time a child is in foster care, but the sooner the better. The initial thrust is toward working with the child and his/her parents, using a structured treatment plan that will eventually allow the return of the child to the parents. Only after intensive treatment efforts have failed are alternative permanent living arrangements considered.[74]

The permanency planning process requires input from many people who share in the decision making. The social worker, however, is the key person who performs the following roles:

1. Case planning—involves the development and maintenance of fairly long-range plans (e.g., for the next four to six months).
2. Therapeutic—the worker provides the necessary clinical services to increase the chances of a successful placement in line with a preferred plan.
3. Case management—involves tasks such as keeping services coordinated among multiple providers and bringing clients into contact with various community and social resources.
4. Client advocate—workers may need to advocate within the legal

and service systems to be certain that the rights of parents and children are maintained.

5. Role of court witness—workers are called on to provide testimony as a result of their working with cases involving custody issues.[75]

Though research has shown that foster care, in general, has not been successful in achieving its ultimate goal of reuniting children with their parents or providing them with another permanent family following temporary placement, it is not clear whether permanency planning is a more successful alternative. One review of research on the success of several demonstration projects indicates that the number of children in foster care can be reduced. Success, however, required additional funding, programming, training of caseworkers, and reduced caseloads.[76] More recent reviews of research on this topic conclude that there is more to child welfare than just reducing the number of children in foster care. Marsha Seltzer and Leonard Bloksberg found that there is a low rate of unsuccessful adoptions following foster care, but there is a much higher disruption rate when foster children are returned to their biological families. In addition, they concluded from their review of studies that children who were placed in permanent homes after foster care were not any better adjusted than those who remained in foster care.[77] Richard Barth and Marianne Berry come to similar conclusions in their review of studies and state, "Of all placement options, in-home services or reunification with birth families, as it presently operates, fails most often to be free from abuse and to yield developmental well-being."[78]

The problem may not be in the concept of permanency planning itself but in its implementation. Many agencies have changed their structures to achieve permanency planning but in practice have been able to change very little. Social workers in these settings are still carrying very large caseloads. For family reunification to be successful, more intensive and longer-term services are required.[79] Social workers providing such services need to be better trained.[80] In addition, it appears that services are too often geared toward facilitating the adoption process rather than providing what is needed to allow the child to return home.[81]

Though there is still considerable progress to be made, passage of the Adoptions Assistance and Child Welfare Act in 1980 has made it possible to implement more comprehensive services to children at risk and their families. This legislation provides for several important reforms: an increase in federal funding for preventive and reunification services; the requirement that states provide safeguards and due process for children and families in order to receive funding; a system of independent monitoring of quality of treatment and care; required inventories for better information on children in foster care; and greater efforts in the adoption of hard-to-place children. Hopefully, this legislation will lead to success in foster care and adoption that is more widespread than just a few demonstration projects.

MISCELLANEOUS SERVICES

A variety of other agencies and services provide assistance of one kind or another to families and children. Some of these use social workers; others do not. Some do not use trained professionals at all but instead are guided by lay workers and the self-help philosophy. Space permits a discussion of only a few of the better-known service providers that regularly use social workers to some extent.

Services to Battered Women

Women have been physically beaten and psychologically abused throughout history, but only since the mid-1970s has domestic violence against women been recognized as a social problem of major importance.[82] Between 16 and 17 percent of all households in the United States have been found to experience some kind of violence between spouses in any one year.[83] Other studies have found that between 10 and 12 percent of married women have been raped by their husbands.[84] Some writers on the topic estimate that approximately 50 percent of all women will be battering victims at some point in their lives.[85]

The definition of battering has been problematic because it has traditionally been restricted to physical violence resulting in bodily harm. The following definition, however, broadens how this syndrome is to be perceived:

> A battered woman is a woman who is repeatedly subjected to any forceful physical or psychological behavior by a man in order to coerce her to do something he wants her to do without any concern for her rights. . . . Any woman may find herself in an abusive relationship with a man once. If it occurs a second time, and she remains in the situation, she is defined as a battered woman.[86]

Presently, there are no federal or state laws mandating the reporting of spouse abuse or providing guidelines for the protection of victims.[87]

A battered woman seeking help usually requires a variety of services. Because this problem has been ignored for so long, needed services are frequently nonexistent, inaccessible, or fragmented. The misconception that the woman is somehow responsible for being battered is an attitude that has long prevailed in society. This blaming the victim is still done subtly and not so subtly by traditional service providers. Such an attitude is counterproductive to helping a woman create a new life-style free of battering.

To help battered women effectively, it has been necessary to create a service that traditional social agencies have not provided—safe houses, which are also called emergency shelters. These "have become the cornerstone of treatment for battered women who do not wish to return home."[88] The first such residence was established in England in 1971 by Erin Pizzey. The growth of domestic violence shelters in the United States has been phenomenal. In 1978 there were 128 shelters,[89] and by 1985 there were approximately 700 shelters throughout the country.[90] These programs tend to have three purposes in common:

1. To provide a safe, secure environment for battered women and their children for a limited period of time.
2. To provide emotional support and counseling for battered women.
3. To provide information on women's legal rights, assist with court appearances, discuss housing options, and explore future life goals and directions.[91]

The average length of stay in a shelter may range from a few days to several weeks. During the initial part of her stay a woman may need crisis counseling and emergency health care. Later she may want counseling in making a decision as to whether she wants to return to live with her husband. If she decides not to return, then she may need help in obtaining continued medical care, legal and/or financial assistance, housing, transportation, vocational counseling and/or training, employment, and child care. As many as one-third of women leave shelters and return to their husbands.[92] The woman's economic dependence on her husband appears to be the primary reason for returning.[93]

Help from the shelter staff is necessary to obtain and coordinate needed services. Nonprofessionals and volunteer workers make up the majority of the staff in shelters in this country. However, approximately one-third of the shelters employ full-time social workers; a small percentage employ other professionals, full or part time, such as attorneys, psychologists, nurses, and vocational counselors.[94] Given the complexity and severity of battering and the wide array of needed services, social work services could obviously be used in each emergency shelter. Despite a variety of funding sources, many of these shelters operate "on a shoe string." The need, however, is not only the continued operation of shelters presently opened, but the creation of new ones in communities that lack them, especially since battering is not relegated to any specific geographic area, socioeconomic class, ethnic group, or religious group but is a ubiquitous problem.

Not all services to battered women are provided by women's shelters. Many social service agencies now provide support groups for victims, treatment groups for abusers, family life education, and conjoint counseling. Much still needs to be done. Barbara Star states that in addition to supporting state and local legislation, social service agencies can help by "upgrading professional staff's knowledge base and skills regarding the dynamics of and intervention in family violence through in-service training; establishing a legal aide position to keep staff apprised of court rulings and clients aware of their legal rights; . . . and maintaining positive relationships with community agencies to ensure timely and coordinated referrals."[95]

Given the seriousness and complexity of the problem of men battering women and the fact that the majority of women who leave shelters return to their husbands, it follows that separate services should be provided for these men; otherwise the cycle of violence may just continue. As of 1984, it was estimated that 220 programs had been established in the United States to help these men to stop battering. It has been suggested that more of these programs are needed but have not been developed because men do not seek help to the extent that women do.[96] Perhaps if there were more programs for men, the additional visibility, with the help of adequate marketing and public relations, would encourage more men to make use of them.

The American Red Cross

The American Red Cross was begun in 1881 by Clara Barton. It is part of an international system that attempts to prevent and ameliorate human suffering. The improvement of the quality of life and the enhancement of individual and family self-reliance are two of its major concerns. This agency's services help individuals and families to avoid, prepare for, and cope with crises and emergencies. It is financed primarily by private contributions, making it a voluntary social service organization.[97]

To achieve its goals, the Red Cross provides a variety of services, relying heavily on volunteers but also on employment of full-time professional social workers. Initially it was involved primarily in disaster relief, and it still aids in approximately 300 disasters each year, providing food and medical care as well as grants of money for rebuilding and restoring homes and businesses.[98] The American Red Cross spent $63.1 million for disaster relief in the 1982–1983 fiscal year, aiding 485,601 persons and 104,226 families.[99]

The Red Cross also provides many other community services such as operating volunteer blood services; training volunteers to work in local chapters, hospitals, and other community agencies; and transporting medical patients to and from hospitals as well as instructing them in handicrafts and hobbies. In addition, it helps military service personnel, veterans, and their families in obtaining government benefits, and provides them grants and loans in emergency situations. In 1983, there were 2,963 chapters of the Red Cross in this country staffed by 20,704 career staff and 1.46 million volunteers.[100]

Social workers, serving as volunteers or full-time staff, provide short-term casework services and crisis intervention in the performance of both community services and disaster relief. The Red Cross has been a leader in the development and application of social work methods in such situations. This may involve the provision of information, referral, outreach, and case advocacy, as well as individual, family, and group counseling. Social workers can contribute to planning, programming, and research on disaster relief at the national, state, and local levels. Though they participate at this level to some extent, social workers need to do more than they have in the past.

Travelers Aid

This voluntary social agency was begun in 1851 in St. Louis to help people moving to the West who had problems. Today it continues to focus on assisting people in difficulty away from their homes and those who are new to the community. It helps clients by providing casework services, information, and other needed special services.[101] More specifically, it strives to help individuals and families with problems related to traveling or relocation, and it works for the alleviation of social conditions that contribute to such problems. Travelers Aid serves individuals and families who experience economic, social, or personal difficulties in a new environment; are in flight due to behavioral disorders or intolerable physical and/or emotional situations; are met with unexpected illness, accidents or incompetence to complete a trip without planned, protective support; are concerned about the welfare of relatives living elsewhere; must contact people or resources not directly available to them but important in completing their move; or are local residents in crisis and no other resource is available.[102]

As of 1980, there were ninety-three Travelers Aid agencies in the United States, Canada, and Puerto Rico. In addition, 1,000 cooperating social agencies in the United States and other countries provide supplemental services by complying with requests for service from Travelers Aid societies. All these agencies form a network of services through the National Travelers Aid Association located in New York City. The local societies are autonomous and receive financial support from local private sources. The services of Travelers Aid agencies are requested more than ever due to the mobility of individuals and families in our society.[103]

Present and Future Trends in Services to Families and Children

Due to experience, research, political forces, and so forth, services to families and children do not remain static. There is a variety of trends in this service area, some of which are more developed than others.

1. The roles of case manager and therapist are interrelated and overlap.
2. Family systems theory and therapy (the ecosystemic perspective) will increasingly be used in assessment and intervention in case management and treatment.
3. The use of home-based, family-centered services by public agencies will increase.
4. Emphasis on providing services that have documented effectiveness will continue. This means that the use of brief, problem-focused treatment approaches will be emphasized.
5. Employers will increase the provision of day care for employees' children as a fringe benefit.
6. For-profit day-care franchises will increase in popularity and numbers.
7. Concern for emotional maltreatment of children will increase.
8. Subsidies for foster care and adoption services will continue.
9. More foster families will adopt, especially children with special needs.
10. Open adoptions will find increased acceptance and use.
11. Need for outreach and case-finding involving black, Hispanic, and Southeast Asian families and children will grow.

FAMILY POLICY

Most of the programs and services discussed above are the result of decisions about how to best meet the needs of client groups with specific problems. Policy and program decisions about one problem do not always take into consideration existing or proposed policies and programs designed for other target groups but which may have some bearing on and relevance to the former. This, therefore, has resulted in a fragmented system of government programs, policies, and services which impacts in a variety of ways on families and individual family members.

That such a situation exists is indicated by the fact that in 1976 there were 268 federal programs, out of 1,044, with financial commitments totaling $818 billion, which had proven or possible impact on the functioning of families. There were many other federal government activities such as tax policies and court decisions not considered in this analysis. Over one-half of the 268 programs were administered by sixteen governmental agencies other than the then Department of Health, Education and Welfare. Not all these programs were limited to the poor. There are strong indications that because of the great diversity of families in this country, the effects on families are quite variable with some families affected positively and others negatively by the same program.[104]

Awareness of such fragmentation and its varied effects on families has contributed to a call for a national comprehensive family policy. In response to such a call, some social scientists have asked the question "a comprehensive family policy for what and for whom?" Some proponents of such a policy point to the "decline of the American family," and in support of this proposition, they refer to some recent societal trends mentioned in the previous chapter.

For some people, therefore, family policy is synonymous with "pro-family" in that keeping families intact should be its primary goal. Others object to such a narrow focus, since there is such a diversity of family types in this country. The former group is supporting the integrity of the "typical" American family; however, a family consisting of a working father, homemaker mother, and two minor children makes up a very small minority of the country's population. Therefore, a narrowly focused family policy would tend to give less attention to many children and families whose needs are great. Before there is a major national investment in family policy development, it would appear that a consensus on the meaning of "family" and "family policy" is needed.

Obviously, there are many government programs that impact directly on families and others do so indirectly. Therefore, it could be said that this country does have a family policy. In this sense "'family policy' means everything government does to or for the family."[105] Since almost every government action, even building highways or providing farm subsidies, affects families somehow, the above definition does not really differentiate family policy from other social policy. What most family policy supporters want is a deliberate policy with specific intended consequences. What these specific consequences should be and for whom, however, is controversial. Many supporters state that the major objective should be "strengthening" families; others believe that government should leave families alone and not "interfere" with their functioning, and still others say that we should have programs that strengthen *all* forms of family living.

The purpose of family policies and the definition of "family" are strongly related. The "traditional" perspective holds family policy to be a means of strengthening the nuclear family. At the other end of the spectrum is the perspective that all types of significant human relationships should be treated equally. The traditionalist view implies that family types other than the nuclear family are "deviant," which means they might be stigmatized and discriminated against.[106] The "egalitarian" perspective validates the diversity and pluralism of our society and the idea of self-determination. This perspective, then, would also include single-parent families, two unrelated people living at the same address, communal families, homosexual relationships, and perhaps two people living apart.[107]

The position of Kamerman and Kahn in their review of family policies in fourteen countries is there tends to be uniform acceptance that any family type with at least one minor in residence may need special attention.[108] Elsewhere they state "there is need for *specific* attention to the needs, problems, and circumstances that especially affect families with young children."[109] This situation is what they find unique about family policy.

Despite the existence of many policies and programs that provide direct benefits to families, a comprehensive national family policy with a coherent set of principles guiding deliberate and reasoned choices does not exist in this country. To have such a family policy would require the existence of some consensus about values and goals for "strengthening" families, and such a consensus does not exist and probably never will.[110] Indeed, one writer on the subject states that "family policy is an unmanageable and potentially dangerous concept,"[111] while another states that "such a unified, comprehensive policy is unachievable and undesirable."[112] This is so because governmental intervention in this area could possibly encourage the imposition of one single standard of family life and thus prescribed behavior for families.[113] This would then result in discrimination against nontraditional families and living arrangements.[114]

Family policy supporters generally advocate a family policy that provides benefits to all families and not just "problematic" ones. This would tend to receive wide support as long as the definition of "family" and the goals of family policy are broad. If this were to occur, there would then be the problem of how to allocate dwindling resources in support of these family policy goals. The benefits of having broadly defined family policy and goals would be mediated by having to do less for families with greater need.[115]

To operationalize a "profamily" ideal into programs requires dealing with specifics. Given the limited resources now available for social programs and the increasing demands on the social welfare system, operating on a specific level would result in benefiting some families while implicitly requiring others to wait. Therefore, "what starts as comprehensive family policy inevitably becomes selective policy after all."[116]

One way to deal with the choice dilemmas of family policy is to support programs and services designed to help the families most in need—poor families and dysfunctional families. These are at least identifiable goals as opposed to "strengthening the family."[117] But if this course is followed, then we are back to the status quo, which, according to the White House Conference on Families, is a fragmented system of family social services that is not satisfactorily helping those most in need.

It is widely accepted that people require certain physical and psychological needs to be met in order to become and remain healthy, well-functioning individuals. This is not only necessary in one's early childhood but also throughout the life cycle. Such healthy and well-functioning people are an asset to society, and therefore, society has an investment in facilitating their development. Kamerman and Kahn state that family well-being should be a criterion of social policy and family policy should be a perspective on achieving this goal.[118] Elsewhere they state that their concern is with all children and families with children, not just those that are problematic.[119]

There is still the matter of reconciling the disagreement over defining family policy and its goals. This dilemma, however, should not deter us from continually striving for bettering the psychosocial worlds of children and families. Perhaps what we should focus on, rather than "enhancing family well-being," is the "enhancement of human development." There is a considerable body of scientific knowledge about this topic and it should be less controversial. Therefore, the concept of a "human development policy" could replace the concept of family policy and hopefully with more success. This may not be as difficult a shift to make as it may seem when it is realized that the source of one's identity, self-esteem, and competencies for dealing with life is the family, be it a nuclear family, single-parent family or foster family. The idea put forth here is that family development and individual development are inseparable. This idea is supported by Ooms who states that lifespan development is "a thinly disguised label for a family perspective."[120]

Since families may encounter problems for the first time during any part of the family life cycle, social services need to be available to nonproblematic families as well as problematic ones. Providing social services to nonproblematic families may help to prevent these families from becoming problematic. Kamerman and Kahn advocate that certain family policies should be provided to all families with children in order to provide a base for building adequate special services for those children who need them.[121] To this end they advocate the following be provided as a minimum: (1) a universal child or family benefit for families with children; (2) maternity or parental leaves for working parents for a period of several months; (3) personal supportive social services such as counseling, therapy, rehabilitation, child care, information and referral, housekeeping, and so on; (4) health care; (5) housing allowances.[122]

This, therefore, calls for a "life model" of policy and practice rather than a "breakdown model."[123] A preventive orientation like this should be cost-effective as was discovered to be true with home-based family services. Edelman points out that by cutting preventive programs to save money, society ends up paying more in the end for rehabilitative services. In this discussion she cites several examples:[124]

- It costs $47 for a complete set of immunizations for a child. It costs an estimated $25,000 per year to keep a mentally retarded child in an institution. The nation saved an estimated $1 billion in the first decade of measles immunization efforts. It is poor fiscal policy to have less than half of black preschoolers fully immunized.
- It costs $600 to provide a mother with comprehensive prenatal care and thus to grow healthier babies; it costs more than $1,000 per day to keep low-birth-weight babies alive through neonatal intensive care.
- It costs an average of $40 to provide a child the needed preventive checkups for an entire year under Medicaid; it averages $600 per day to hospitalize a child for an illness that could have been diagnosed and treated without hospitalization if there had been a routine preventive checkup.
- It costs $68 to provide family-planning services to a sexually active teen; it costs $3,000 to provide that teen and her baby prenatal care and delivery costs under Medicaid.
- It costs $600 to provide a year of compensatory education services to a teen; it costs more than $2,400 to finance a repeated grade for a disadvantaged student.
- It costs $7,300 to provide a mother and two children with AFDC, housing assistance, food stamps, and energy-assistance benefits at 80 percent of the poverty level; it costs $8,000 to fund those two children in foster care when that mother becomes homeless or her apartment heatless.
- It costs $1,100 to provide a summer job for a teen; it costs $20,000 to keep that teen in a juvenile institution for a year.

Policy and programs oriented toward facilitating human development should provide services needed not only by children but also their primary caretakers—their parent(s). It goes without saying that parents have profound effects on their children.[125] In advocating for preventive and remedial social policy that will enhance quality of life for children, Garbarino states: "If children are to have first claim, their parents and the conditions of parenthood must be in the forefront of our consciousness . . . it is foolhardy to think of children apart from the conditions of life for their parents . . . the evidence is clear that when the quality of life for adults suffers, children suffer."[126] Human development–oriented policies and programs should thus focus on the interrelationship between the quality of life for both children and their parents unlike family (social) policies and programs of the present, which focus primarily on problematic children. The well-being of parents has been hard to assure given recent trends such as two-parent families in which both parents are employed outside the home, single-parent families especially those in which the parent is employed outside the home, unemployment and low wages, racism and sexism just to name a few family stessors. Another recent trend affecting the quality of life for parents, and thus their children, is the increasing proportion of the population that is elderly. Parents of children under age eighteen often have elderly parents that have needs that put increased stress, financial and/or emotional, on them. This in turn can have a detrimental effect on their children.

In order to provide for the basic needs of children, parents need supportive communities and neighborhoods. Just as the well-being of children and parents is inseparable, so is the well-being of families and communities.[127] This does not necessarily mean "throwing tax dollars at problems," though there will always be need for public support in this area. As much as anything else it is a change in the way we think about the needs of families and children and thus society.

The relabeling of social policies and programs as advocated here may seem like a simple game of semantics but language and words do shape our conceptions of reality and thus social policy.[128] This notion is supported by the words of Don D. Jackson who states: "Our thoughts, research efforts and even what Benjamin Worf called 'our view of the cosmos' are limited or facilitated by the language we use."[129]

SUMMARY AND CONCLUSIONS

In the previous two chapters supportive, supplemental, and substitute services to families and children have been discussed as well as several miscellaneous family and children services. Finally some of the complexities and implications of family policy were briefly considered.

Social work has a long tradition of providing services to families and children, and such programs still are a major focus of the profession today. The need for such services is as great as ever; however, increasingly resources are becoming scarce. It is therefore imperative that social work as a profession and individual social workers remain committed to increasing the quantity and quality of such services.

NOTES

1. See, for example, Shirley Jenkins and Souber Mignon, *Paths to Child Placement* (New York: Community Council of Greater New York, 1966); Edward Mech, *Public Welfare Service for Children and Youth in Arizona* (Phoenix; State of Arizona, 1970); B. Bernstein et al., *Foster Care Needs and Alternatives to Placement—A Projection for 1975–1985* (Albany: New York State Board of Social Welfare, 1975).
2. Child Welfare League of America, *Standards for Foster Care* (New York: Author, 1959), p. 5.
3. Alfred Kadushin, *Child Welfare Services*, 3rd. ed. (New York: Macmillan Co., 1980), pp. 314–319.
4. Sumner M. Rosen, David Fanshel, and Mary E. Lutz, eds., *Face of the Nation 1987: Statistical Supplement to the 18th Edition of the Encyclopedia of Social Work* (Silver Spring, Md.: NASW, 1987), p. 97.
5. Jake Terpstra, "The Rich and Exacting Role of the Social Worker in Family Foster Care," *Child and Adolescent Social Work Journal* 4 (1987): 12.
6. Theodore J. Stein, "Foster Care for Children," *Encyclopedia of Social Work*, 18th ed. (Silver Spring, Md.: NASW, 1987), p. 641.
7. Ann W. Shyne and Anita G. Schroeder, *National Study of Social Services to Children and Their Families* (Rockville, Md.: Westat, 1978), p. 34.
8. Children's Defense Fund, *Children Without Homes* (Washington, D.C.: Author, 1978), p. 5.
9. Terpstra, "Role of the Social Worker in Family Foster Care," p. 13.
10. Ibid.
11. Karen Blumenthal, "Making Foster Family Care Responsive," in *Child Welfare: Current Dilemmas—Future Directions*, ed. Brenda G. McGowan and William Meezan, (Itasca, Ill.: Peacock, 1983), pp. 302–303.
12. Lela B. Costin and Charles A. Rapp, *Child Welfare: Policies & Practice* (New York: McGraw-Hill, 1984), pp. 325–384.
13. Ibid., p. 349.
14. Lela B. Costin and Ruppert Downing, "Child and Family Welfare," in Donald Brieland et al., *Contemporary Social Work: An Introduction to Social Work and Social Welfare* (New York: McGraw-Hill, 1980), p. 212.
15. Alfred Kadushin and Judith A. Martin, *Child Welfare Services*, 4th ed. (New York: Macmillan, 1987), pp. 670–672.

16. Costin and Rapp, *Child Welfare*, pp. 360–361.
17. Kadushin, *Child Welfare Services*, pp. 584–587.
18. Ibid., p. 583.
19. Richard Redick and Michael Witkin, "Residential Treatment Centers for Emotionally Disturbed Children, United States, 1977–1978 and 1979–1980," *Mental Health Statistical Note No. 162* (Washington, D.C.: Department of Health and Human Services, 1983), pp. 3 & 16.
20. Martin Wolins and Irving Piliavin, *Institutions or Foster Homes: A Century of Debate* (New York: Child Welfare League of America, 1964), cited in Kamerman and Kahn, *Social Services in the United States*, pp. 201 & 202.
21. Kadushin, *Child Welfare Services*, pp. 465 & 466.
22. Ibid., p. 467.
23. National Committee for Adoption, *Adoption Fact Book: United States Data Issues, Regulations and Resources* (Washington, D.C.: National Committee for Adoption, 1985).
24. Elizabeth S. Cole, "Adoption: History, Policy, and Program," in *A Handbook of Child Welfare; Context, Knowledge, and Practice*, ed. Joan Laird and Ann Hartman (New York: Free Press, 1985).
25. National Committee for Adoption, *Adoption Fact Book*.
26. William Meezan et al., *Adoption Without Agencies* (New York: Child Welfare League of America, 1978).
27. Costin, *Child Welfare*, p. 292.
28. William Meezan, "Toward an Expanded Role for Adoption Services," in McGowan and Meezan, *Child Welfare*, p. 462.
29. Kadushin, *Child Welfare Services*, p. 484.
30. Penelope Maza, *Child Welfare Research Note 2* (Washington, D.C.: Administration for Children, Youth, and Families), p. 2.
31. Elizabeth S. Cole, "Adoption," in *Encyclopedia of Social Work*, 18th ed., p. 70.
32. Costin and Rapp, *Child Welfare*, p. 427.
33. Dawn Day, *The Adoption of Black Children* (Lexington, Mass.: D.C. Heath & Co., 1979).
34. Rita J. Simon, "Adoption of Black Children by White Parents in the U.S.A.," in *Adoption: Essays in Social Policy, Law, and Sociology*, ed. Philip Bean (New York: Tavistock Publications, 1984), p. 229.
35. Opportunity, *National Survey of Black Children Adopted in 1975* (Portland, Ore.: Boys and Girls Society of Oregon, 1976), cited in Kadushin and Martin, *Child Welfare Services*, p. 597.
36. "Transracial Adoption Controversy Grows," *NASW News* 29, no. 9 (October 1984): 3, 4.
37. Meezan, "Toward an Expanded Role."
38. Ibid., p. 442.
39. Costin and Rapp, *Child Welfare*, p. 424.
40. Alfred Kadushin, *Adopting Older Children* (New York: Columbia University Press, 1970).
41. D. S. Franklin and Fred Massarik, "The Adoption of Children with Medi-

cal Conditions, Part I: Process and Outcome," *Child Welfare*, October 1969, pp. 459–467; Franklin and Massarik, "Adoption of Children with Medical Conditions, Part II: The Family Today," *Child Welfare*, November 1969, pp. 533–539; Franklin and Massarik, "The Adoption of Children with Medical Conditions, Part III: Discussion and Conclusion," *Child Welfare*, December 1969, pp. 595–601.

42. Laraine M. Glidden, "Adopting Mentally Handicapped Children," *Adoption and Fostering* 9 (1985): 53–56.

43. G. Waldinger, "Subsidized Adoption: How Paid Parents View It," *Social Work* 27 (November 1982): 516–521.

44. *Subsidized Adoption: A Study of Use and Need in Four Agencies* (Springfield, Ill.: Child Care Association, 1969).

45. Waldinger, "Subsidized Adoption."

46. Costin and Rapp, *Child Welfare*.

47. William Feigalman and Arnold Silverman, "Single Parent Adoptions," *Social Casework* 58 (July 1977): 418–425; Joan Shireman and Penny Johnson, *Adoption: Three Alternatives—Part II* (Chicago: Chicago Child Care Society, 1980).

48. Ethel Brahm, "One Parent Adoptions," *Children*, May/June 1970, p. 17; Joan Shireman and Penny Johnson, "Single Parents as Adoptive Parents," *Social Service Review*, March 1976, p. 50.

49. Meezan, "Toward an Expanded Role."

50. William Feigelman and Arnold R. Silverman, *Chosen Children: New Patterns of Adoptive Relationships* (New York: Praeger, 1983).

51. Rapp and Costin, *Child Welfare*, pp. 410, 411.

52. Cole, "Adoption: History, Policy, and Program," p, 658.

53. Kadushin and Martin, *Child Welfare Services*, p. 602.

54. Ibid., pp. 600, 601.

55. Ibid., pp. 626–632.

56. Annetee Baran, Reuben Pannor, and Arthur D. Sorosky, "Open Adoption," *Social Work* 21 (March 1976): 97–100.

57. Reuban Pannor and Annette Baran, "Open Adoption as Standard Practice," *Child Welfare* 63 (1984): 246.

58. Patick A. Curtis, "The Dialectics of Open Versus Closed Adoption of Infants," *Child Welfare* 65 (1986): 437–445.

59. Kadushin and Martin, *Child Welfare Services*, pp. 581, 582.

60. William Feigelman and Arnold Silverman, *Chosen Children*.

61. Lois Raynor, *The Adopted Child Comes of Age*, (London: George Allen and Unwin, 1980).

62. C. Wilson Anderson, "The Sealed Record in Adoption Controversy," *Social Service Review*, March 1977, pp. 141–154.

63. Pannor and Baron, "Open Adoption as Standard Practice"; Curtis, "The Dialectics of Open Versus Closed Adoption of Infants."

64. Meezan, "Toward an Expanded Role," p. 466.

65. Curtis, "The Dialectics of Open Versus Closed Adoption of Infants."

66. Henry Maas and Richard E. Engler, *Children in Need of Parents* (New York: Columbia University Press, 1959); Henry S. Maas, "Children in

Long Term Foster Care," *Child Welfare* 48 (1969): 331–334; Martin E. Bryce and Roger C. Ehlert, "144 Foster Children," *Child Welfare* 50 (1971): 449–503; Kermit T. Wiltse and Eileen Gambrill, "Foster Care, 1973: A Reappraisal," *Public Welfare* 32 (1974): 7–15; Ann M. Rothchild, "An Agency Evaluates Its Foster Care Services," *Child Welfare* 53 (1974): 42–50.

67. Maas and Engler, *Children in Need of Parents.*
68. Anthony N. Maluccio and Edith Fein, "Permanency Planning: A Redefinition," *Child Welfare* 63 (1983): 197.
69. Victor Pike, Susan Downs, Arthur Emlen, Glen Downs, and Denise Case, *Permanent Planning for Children in Foster Care: A Handbook for Social Workers.* Publication No. (OHDS) 78-30124. (Washington, D.C.: Department of Health, Education and Welfare, 1977).
70. Marsha Mailick Seltzer and Leonard M. Bloksberg, "Permanency Planning and Its Effects on Foster Children: A Review of the Literature," *Social Work* 32 (January–February 1987): 65–68.
71. Anthony N. Maluccio, Edith Fein, Jane Hamilton, Jo Lynn Klier, and Darryl Ward, "Beyond Permanency Planning," *Child Welfare* 59 (1980): 515–530.
72. Ibid.; Joan Shireman, "Achieving Permanence After Placement," in Brenda G. McGowan and William Meezan, *Child Welfare*, p. 379; Richard P. Barth and Marianne Berry, "Outcomes of Child Welfare Services under Permanency Planning," *Social Services Review*, March 1987, p. 72.
73. Joseph Goldstein, Anna Freud, and Albert J. Solnit, *Beyond the Best Interests of the Child* (New York: Free Press, 1973).
74. Pike et al., *Permanent Planning*, p. 4.
75. Edith Fein, Katherine Miller, Kathleen A. Olmstead, and George W. Howe, "The Roles of the Social Worker in Permanency Planning", *Child Welfare* 63 (1984): 353–356.
76. Duncan Lindsey, "Achievements for Children in Foster Care," *Social Work*, November 1982, pp. 491–496.
77. Seltzer and Bloksberg, "Permanency Planning and Its Effects."
78. Barth and Berry, "Outcomes of Child Welfare Services," p. 82.
79. Ibid.
80. Shireman, "Achieving Permanence."
81. Maluccio et al., "Beyond Permanency Planning"; Michael R. Sosin, "Delivering Services under Permanency Planning," *Social Service Review*, June 1987, pp. 272–290.
82. Liane V. Davis, "Battered Women: The Transformation of a Social Problem," *Social Work* 32 (July–August 1987): 306–311.
83. Murray A. Straus, Richard J. Gelles, and Suzanne K. Steinmetz, *Behind Closed Doors: Violence in the American Family* (Garden City, N.Y.: Anchor Press, 1980); U.S. Department of Justice, *Intimate Victims: A Study of Violence Among Friends and Relatives* (Washington, D.C.: Government Printing Office, 1980).
84. David Finkelhor and K. Yllo, "Forced Sex in Marriage: A Preliminary Re-

port," *Crime and Delinquency* 28 (1982): 459–478; D. Russell, "The Prevalence and Impact of Marital Rape in San Francisco," paper presented at the Annual Meeting of the American Sociological Association, New York, 1980.

85. Lenore E. Walker, *The Battered Woman* (New York: Harper & Row, 1979).
86. Ibid., p. xv.
87. Barbara Star, "Domestic Violence," in *Encyclopedia of Social Work*, 18th ed., pp. 463–476.
88. Walker, *The Battered Woman*, p. 192.
89. Albert R. Roberts and Beverly J. Roberts, *Sheltering Battered Women: A National Study and Service Guide* (New York: Springer Publishing Co., 1981).
90. Star, "Domestic Violence," p. 472.
91. Roberts and Roberts, *Sheltering Battered Women*.
92. Richare J. Gelles and Claire Pedrick Cornell, *Intimate Violence in Families* (Beverly Hills, Calif.: Sage Publications, 1985), p. 142.
93. B. E. Aguirre, "Why Do They Return? Abused Wives in Shelters," *Social Work* 30 (1985): 350–354.
94. Roberts and Roberts, *Sheltering Battered Women*, p. 42.
95. Star, "Domestic Violence," p. 474.
96. Albert R. Roberts, "Intervention with the Abusive Partner," in *Battered Women and Their Families: Intervention Strategies and Treatment Programs*, ed. Albert R. Roberts (New York: Springer, 1984).
97. *The Encyclopedia Americana*, International Edition, s.v. "Red Cross," 1980.
98. *Collier's Encyclopedia*, s.v., "Red Cross," 1980.
99. American Red Cross, *Annual Report, 1983* (Washington, D.C.: Author, 1983).
100. Ibid.
101. *The Encyclopedia Americana*, International Edition, s.v. "Travelers Aid."
102. *Encyclopedia of Associations*, 15th ed., s.v. "Travelers Aid Association of America."
103. *The Encyclopedia Americana*, s.v. "Travelers Aid."
104. White House Conference on Families, "Families and Major Institutions," 1980 Delegate Workbook (Washington, D.C.: Government Printing Office, 1980), p. 10.
105. Sheila B. Kamerman and Alfred J. Kahn, "Explorations in Family Policy," *Social Work* 21 (May 1976): 183.
106. Neil Gilbert, "An Initial Agenda for Family Policy," *Social Work* 24 (1979): 447.
107. Ibid.
108. Sheila B. Kamerman and Alfred J. Kahn, *Family Policy: Government and Family in Fourteen Countries* (New York: Columbia University Press, 1978).
109. Sheila B. Kamerman and Alfred J. Kahn, "'Child Welfare' and the Welfare

of Families with Children: A Child and Family Policy Agenda," in McGowan and Meezan, *Child Welfare.*

110. William H. Padberg, "Complexities of Family Policy: What Can Be Done?" *Social Work* 24 (1979): 451–453; A. Cherlin, "Family Policy and Family Professionals," *Journal of Family Issues* 5 (1984): 155–159.

111. Fred Barbaro, "The Case Against Family Policy," *Social Work* 6 (1979): 155–158.

112. Cherlin, "Family Policy and Family Professionals," p. 157.

113. T. Ooms, "The Necessity of a Family Perspective," *Journal of Family Issues* 5 (1984): 160–181.

114. Barbaro, "The Case Against Family Policy," p. 457.

115. Padberg, "Complexities," p. 453.

116. Steiner, *Futility of Family Policy,* p. 196.

117. Ibid., p. 198.

118. Kamerman and Kahn, "Explorations in Family Policy," p. 184.

119. Kamerman and Kahn, "'Child Welfare,'" p. 152.

120. Ooms, "The Necessity of a Family Perspective," p. 163.

121. Kamerman and Kahn, "'Child Welfare,'" p. 152.

122. Ibid., pp. 152–165.

123. C. Meyer, "Practice and Policy: A Family Focus," *Social Casework* 5 (1980): 259–265.

124. Marian Wright Edelman, *Families in Peril: An Agenda for Social Change* (Cambridge, Mass.: Harvard University Press, 1987), pp. 31, 32.

125. J. Scanzoni, "Reconsidering Family Policy: Status Quo or Force for Change?" *Journal of Family Issues* 3 (1983): 277–300.

126. J. Garbarino, "The Issue Is Human Quality: In Praise of Children," *Children and Youth Services Review* 1 (1979): 355–356.

127. Ibid., p. 30.

128. Meyer, "Practice and Policy," p. 260; Ooms, "The Necessity of a Family Perspective," p. 166.

129. Don D. Jackson, "Family Rules: Marital Quid Pro Quo," *Archives of General Psychiatry* 12 (1965): 589–594.

ADDITIONAL SUGGESTED READINGS

Children's Defense Fund. *Black and White Children in America—Key Facts* (Washington, D.C.: Children's Defense Fund, 1985).

Brekke, John S., "Detecting Wife and Child Abuse in Clinical Settings," *Social Casework* 68 (June 1987): 332–338.

Deutsch, Francine, *Child Services on Behalf of Children* (Monterey, Calif.: Brooks/Cole Publishing Co., 1983).

Edleson, Jeffrey L., "Working with Men Who Batter," *Social Work* 29 (1984): 237–242.

Moynihan, Daniel Patrick, *Family and Nation* (San Diego: Harvest/HBJ, 1987).

Moroney, Robert M., *Shared Responsibility: Families and Social Policy* (New York: Aldine DeGruyter, 1986).

Peden, Joseph R., and Fred R. Glahe (eds.), *The American Family and the State* (San Francisco: Pacific Research Institute for Public Policy, 1986).

Simon, Rita J., and Howard Altstein, *Transracial Adoptees and Their Families* (New York: Praeger, 1987).

Spakes, Patricia, *Family Policy and Family Impact Analysis* (Cambridge, Mass.: Schenkman Publishing Co., 1983).

7 Social Work in the Schools

Ralph Anderson
Marlys Staudt

Social work and the public schools are closely intertwined. All social workers dealing with children find that they must understand and work with the schools. Elementary and secondary schools have evolved into the preponderant socializing institution in American society. Virtually every citizen has spent significant formative years in these institutions. The fact that you are reading this book indicates that your own schooling experience was successful; you have accommodated to the ways of the school, which are the ways of our society. Many persons, though, have difficulty in this developmental arena, and social work is one of the professions that has proved helpful in a wide range of school-related difficulties.

By 1970 the usefulness of social work within public education was well established. Social work in education had become a field of practice, analogous to mental health, health, and corrections. In each of these settings social work is not the primary profession but works in close cooperation with one or more other professions in a multi-disciplinary team. In schools other team members include speech therapists, psychologists, guidance counselors, and teachers, but the primary profession is education and the central mission is education of youth.

School social work tends to attract those who are interested in primary prevention and in assuring developmental opportunities for children. The school provides a unique and comprehensive opportunity for early intervention into the full range of developmental issues.

HISTORICAL PERSPECTIVE

The first recorded instances of school social workers appear in 1906 and 1907 in Boston, Hartford, and New York. Interestingly, these first social workers in the schools were financed by community agencies and derived from the burgeoning conviction that the public school was the logical place for early intervention. Not until 1914 did Rochester, New York, become the first city to initiate a program totally funded from public sources. The simple yet elegant justification provided by the Rochester Board of Education continues to be the valid rationale for school social work.

> [This is] the first step in an attempt to meet a need of which the school system has been conscious for some time. It is an undisputed fact that in the environment of the child outside of school are to be found forces which will often times thwart the school in its endeavors. . . . The appointment of a visiting teacher is an attempt on the part of the school to meet its responsibility for the whole welfare of the child . . . [and] to secure maximum cooperation between the home and the school.[1]

The title "Visiting Teacher" continued in vogue for decades and connoted an official school representative who left the school building on behalf of the child, to deal with the child's parents and community agencies. Such activity was consistent with the philosophy of the Progressive Era that the public school was the key to developing the informed citizenry that is so necessary to a democracy. Education was seen as the agent of social reform; child labor laws (1916) protected children from exploitation and assured their availability for attending school, and the elaboration of compulsory school attendance assured they would attend. A major function of the early visiting teacher was to attempt to ameliorate situations contributing to school nonattendance.

In 1918 the Harkness family established the Commonwealth Fund to "do something for the welfare of mankind." One of the fund's major emphases was delinquency prevention, and to further that goal, in 1921, they funded thirty visiting teacher demonstration projects at various sites throughout the United States. These projects provided much input to the development of school social work.

From these early beginnings school social work slowly developed its acknowledged competence as an integral part of pupil personnel services. The patterns of development varied from state to state, and even school district to school district. This variation still exists today despite the goal of all school social work practice to facilitate optimal learning opportunities for children and youth. Student needs vary from district to district and even within districts. Needs also change over time. The current "social era" affects needs. For example, Lela Costin stated that the Great Depression affected the daily activity of school social workers because much emphasis was placed on locating and supplying resources to meet the physical needs of the students.[2] More recently school social workers have offered groups to students and inservice to teachers on the changing family structure and coping with loss and change. In the mid-1980s school social workers in rural areas and small towns needed to be aware of the "farm crisis" and its implications for the students they served.

Public policy and the political "arena" also affect school social work. There have been two occasions of rapid expansion in recent years, both resulting from federal initiatives. The first followed from the passage of Title I of the American Education Act in 1965, which recognized the plight of the educationally disadvantaged where the disadvantage is associated with low economic capability and low educational aspirations (later grouped under the rubric of "culturally disadvantaged"). The legislation authorized funding to be "targeted" to schools that had a preponderance of such children, mostly inner-city schools, and provided for social services to concentrate especially on home-school relationships.

The second federal initiative having major impact on social work in the schools was Public Law 94–142, the Education for All Handicapped Children Act, which was signed into law by President Gerald Ford on November 25, 1975. The primary purpose of this law is to ensure that a free appropriate public education be available to all handicapped children aged three through twenty-one. This culminated a series of court decisions, which had established a firm constitutional basis for full educational opportunity regardless of other considerations. Under the provisions of P.L. 94–142 social work services in the schools include but are not limited to:

1. Preparing a social or developmental history on a handicapped child
2. Group and individual counseling with the child and family
3. Working with those problems in the child's living situation (home, school, and community) that affect the child's adjustment in school
4. Mobilizing school and community resources to enable the child to receive maximum benefit from his or her educational program[3]

Courtesy National Association for Down Syndrome

Julie, a Down's syndrome child, is leading the spelling lesson. She is in a regular class at her school.

Implementation of the provisions of this law has markedly increased the numbers of school social workers in special education units, and in some states and districts social workers work only in the area of special education.

There is some commonality and so there can be some generalization in how the role of school social work has evolved. In the early decades the primary activities of school social workers were casework with individual children and youth, their families, and contact/liaison with community agencies. During the depression of the 1930s there was some decrease in the numbers of social workers based in the schools, but the pattern of slow growth was restored following World War II. In 1968 Costin found in her research that the primary emphasis of school social work was clinical casework.[4] Paula Allen-Meares replicated Costin's study in the mid-1970s and found a transition in the role from an emphasis on clinical casework to home-school-community liaison and educational counseling with the student and parents.[5] There are different models of school social work, and various authors have addressed the role of social work in education.[6] Social workers today still counsel individual students, but there is recognition and movement toward alternate delivery styles where more students can be effectively served. These include policymaking, teacher consultation, group work, program development, and systems change. Whatever the mode of service delivery, the focus is on the student(s) in the educational setting and eliminating barriers to effective learning.

THE PRACTICE OF SCHOOL SOCIAL WORK

There is great variety in the types of problems school social workers deal with and what they do, since there are vast differences in school systems. As Costin has stated, "School social work is related to a particular school system, the outside community, the characteristics of the pupils, and the social conditions they face."[7]

Most of the problems concern students who are not fulfilling expectations of the school, the family, or the community. Such problems may take the form of academic underachievement, problems in social interaction with teachers or peers, not attending school, or unacceptable behavior. The reasons for referral to a school social worker can be organized into three general categories: academic, behavior/social, and personal. Of course these overlap, and students can and often do experience difficulty in more than one area. Some of the specific problems students experience with which school social workers can help are:

Behavioral/Social	Academic	Personal
Disruption of class	Lack of organizational skills	Seeming unhappy or depressed
Poor peer relationships	Not completing assignments	Fear of going home
Demands for excessive attention	Off-task behavior	Sexuality problems
Shy and withdrawn behavior	Poor study habits	Eating disorders
Temper outbursts	Short attention span	Chemical dependency
Fear of attempting new tasks	Overdependency on teacher	Experiencing a personal loss

Behavioral/Social	*Academic*	*Personal*
Defiant behavior	Lack of motivation	Problems accepting school transitions
Fighting and aggressive behavior	Significant change in grades	Excessive anxiety and stress
School avoidance		Frequent complaints of not feeling well
Excessive lying		Suicidal tendencies
Stealing		
Impulsive behavior		
Refusal to accept responsibility		

School social workers use a variety of interventions, including individual and group counseling, parent and family counseling, parent education and support groups, consultation with teachers, serving as home-school liaison, and referral to and coordination with other agencies. In addition, school social workers become involved in program development activities, advocacy, and research.

While the school is charged with overriding socialization responsibility, the family continues to be held primarily responsible. In earlier times it was said that teachers had the child for more hours than the parents did. Now it is said the television set has the child for more hours than the school does. Yet the nexus of socialization is found in family, community, and school. The school is an institution serving its community, which in turn is comprised of the families the students come from. The social worker is the professional who spans this nexus, working at and across the boundaries. Figure 7.1 indicates the location of school social work activity vis-à-vis the child and his/her significant systems. This is a unique position. Other social workers (child welfare, juvenile court, mental health) also function at these same boundaries but enter the school as "outsiders" rather than "part of."

Generally the family, school, or community will tend to blame one of the other two institutions if things do not go well. Community members (merchants and citizens) may fault the school if they find groups of youth to be troublesome. They frequently request stricter monitoring by the school and closer supervision of young people. School personnel often attribute difficulties to the families, especially those who are different from the school or community norm or who do not meet the school's expectations in terms of home-school communication. Families fault the schools for not attending sufficiently to the wants of

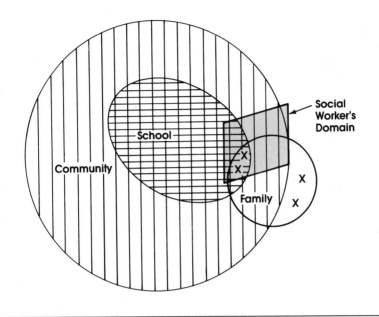

Figure 7.1 Systems Diagram of School Social Work Domain

children and parents. Social workers are committed to bringing all three institutions into better working relations around the developmental requisites of the children.

School social workers are particularly suited to intervene in situations of culture conflict.

> If the culture transmitted by the school is alien or oppositional to the culture of the child's family, the young person is in a difficult, indeed untenable, position. The technology and ways of doing things the child has become familiar with and the development of an emerging sense of self and other within has, by this time, been incorporated as a part of self. To accept a differing way may be felt as an act of betrayal of self and family. If so, efforts toward mastery may well be invested outside of the school, seeking mastery of their own culture, not that of others.[8]

An inordinate percentage of school dropouts are from minority cultures. The 1987 *Statistical Abstract of the United States* indicates that in 1980, 16 percent of blacks aged fourteen to twenty-four years dropped out of high school, compared to 11 percent of whites. In 1985 these percentages changed to approximately 12 percent for blacks and 10 percent for whites.

In the public school the significance of labeling is seen in bold relief. The school is charged with the sorting, classifying, and vocational tracking of youth. Think of the label of "school phobia" as contrasted with "truancy" or "dropout." The former arouses sympathy and understanding for the emotionally distraught while "truancy" brings to mind a bent toward delinquency. Both are avoiding school, but the labels imply both motivational and characterological attributes. "Dropout" implies volition and choice, placing the burden on the individual. It further implies giving up or quitting. Yet some of the common given reasons for leaving school are family economic need, inability to achieve, family and personal health problems, and language and cultural differences.[9]

Currently much school social work activity is devoted to the provisions of P.L. 94–142 to assure that the mandated right to education is realized for all those with handicapping conditions. This entails full and close attention to the developmental and educational needs of the individual child and family. This is a multiprofessional effort with social workers collecting the developmental history and adaptive behavior information and preparing a social history based on the information acquired, interpreting needs and recommendations to the child's parent(s), and assuring parental participation in decision making regarding an educational plan for the child.

Role Considerations

As stated earlier, there is a great variation of role definitions, deriving from variations in the educational enterprise. Some states require that school social workers also be certified teachers; others specify a certain amount of academic study in a college of education; and others require only a professional social work degree (usually a master's degree). A social worker may be assigned to only one building, a pupil personnel unit serving a number of schools, or an area special education unit. The nature of the unit of assignment is a significant determinant of role expectations.

Often the functions of social work overlap the functions of other professional disciplines found in support services, especially school psychologists and guidance counselors. Much time and effort has been devoted to clearly delineating the functions of these three overlapping disciplines. In fact most of the research and conceptual development in the field has been on the role of the school social worker. While each profession has particular areas of expertise, there remains a significant common ground based in knowledge and caring about children and their development. The expertise of social workers is acknowledged to be family and community resources, not educational technology. Therefore, one of the main roles of the school social worker continues to be serving as a liaison between school, home, and community.

Because school social workers work in a host setting and work closely with members of other professions, they must be able to do more than provide effective services to students. They must understand the setting in which they work, be able to function as part of a team, and be able to identify and interpret their role and function to others in the school. School social workers must clearly identify and describe their role to educators, yet remain flexible, so that the various and changing needs of the student, school, and community can be met.

It is essential that social workers aspiring to practice in the school understand the school as a social institution. As Robert Constable has phrased it,

> There is clearly a place and function for school social workers in the education setting but the function is inextricably tied to the education institution. The role cannot be carried out by simply using clinical skills in a school setting. School social workers need to have a thorough theoretical and practical understanding of the American education institution, curriculum and teaching methods at different levels and with different children. Social workers are finding their most profound impact is on the school institution itself.[10]

It is also essential that school social workers understand and work with the social and political nature of the school system. Laura J. Lee emphasizes, "Acknowledging that the school system is a political context enables the social worker to assess pros and cons of the work environment realistically."[11]

Educators are concerned with individual children, especially underachievers and slow learners. Teachers are frequently scapegoated for activities and attitudes mandated by society through its credentialing and certifying mechanisms. Usually social workers first enter the school scene as "outsiders" without a clear role definition or niche to occupy. Most likely, teachers have not encountered social work(ers) in their colleges of education. Thus each must get to know the other, as people and as representatives of different professions.

The social work definition contained in P.L. 94-142 establishes a clear set of expectations of social workers, which turns out to be a two-edged sword. It does serve to provide a niche or clear role expectations, but it also puts constraints on role elaboration by limiting the population served to those with suspected handicapping conditions.[12] If school social work is funded by special education monies, then school social work involvement with other students, even though they may be experiencing social or behavioral difficulties, is limited.

The following short case vignettes will give the reader a "taste" of the various ways in which school social workers provide services to students, schools, and communities.

"John"

John is a seventeen-year-old student who is entering his junior year of high school. This is John's first year at the high school, as he has spent the last three to four years in residential placements in a different community. John now lives with his father. His school file shows that ever since kindergarten John has come to the attention of his teachers because of temper outbursts and aggressive and inappropriate behavior, and was referred numerous times for psychological testing, counseling, and psychiatric evaluations. His early family life might be described as "chaotic," and his as a "multiproblem family." For a number of years John has been labeled as a student with behavior disabilities and has received special education services. He reads on a sixth grade level and has learning problems apart from the behavior disability. In addition, John has complex medical problems, including epilepsy, a drooping eyelid, and a club foot. He is on medication to control seizures. John has few friends, and his appearance is such that others sometimes tease him.

The school social worker attended John's intake staffing and began to see John on a regular basis to help him adjust to his new school and learn how to respond to remarks that might be made by other students. At one point John stopped attending school due to an increase in the number of epileptic seizures, which John's father attributed to stress. The school social worker arranged a staffing with the school nurse, counselor, psychologist, and teachers to discuss John's situation. John was also in attendance. John's schedule was changed and the counselor agreed to mediate with one of John's regular teachers who had unrealistic expectations of John.

As the year ended, John had shown no temper outbursts in school. Soon he will be eighteen and a senior. The school social worker has had regular contact with John and his teachers to monitor his progress. She has referred John to Vocational Rehabilitation, arranged a referral to an epilepsy clinic, and has taken John to see a group home where independent daily living skills are taught. John is on the waiting list to enter this group home. Close contact was maintained with other team members, especially the school counselor and school nurse.

"Amy"

Amy is three years old. Her mother called the Area Education Agency on advice from her family doctor. The mother expressed many behavioral concerns regarding Amy, including not sleeping through the night and eating problems. Amy is "always into things," "very active," and "hard to discipline."

There is a history of early medical problems including surgery involving her stomach. Amy has asthma and has been hospitalized numerous times.

Her mother indicates she has been overly protective of Amy. Amy lives with her biological parents, an older sister, and a younger sister.

The social worker and school psychologist worked together in interviewing the mother and family and in observing Amy. Information from Amy's medical doctors was obtained. Parenting information was given during the assessment process.

Amy was temporarily placed in a developmental preschool, so that her behavior could be observed out of the home. Amy's behavior in this structured setting was appropriate. This confirmed the school social worker's and psychologist's opinion that many of Amy's behaviors could be attributed to the relationship between Amy and her mother, the mother's overprotectiveness, and inappropriate expectations and parenting. (For example, Amy's mother had the same expectations of Amy as she did for her older sister who was in kindergarten.)

The school social worker continued to meet with Amy's mother and provided suggestions for discipline and information about child development. Amy's mother wanted services and was eager to make some changes. Amy is now in a regular preschool, and her mother reports significant improvement in her behavior at home.

"Justin"

Justin was a kindergarten boy who appeared to be of normal ability, but he would not talk in school. Justin talked at home and around relatives. History reveals no significant health concerns and no early traumatic events. Justin attended one year of preschool and was nonverbal in preschool. Justin gains what he wants through gestures. He is only in kindergarten and is very cute, so his teacher is very patient with him, but is concerned. His parents are extremely concerned and thought Justin would "outgrow" his not talking in school by now.

The school social worker received a referral on Justin. Justin was observed in the classroom and on the playground, and his teacher and parents were interviewed. It was learned that certain children often talked for Justin, and when Justin was asked a question or was spoken to, one of the other children would say "he can't talk" and answer for him. The teacher was concerned there were psychological reasons for his not talking and had no expectations for Justin to talk in the classroom. On the playground, Justin appeared happy and interacted with other children, although for the most part this interaction was nonverbal. Teachers noted that on occasion Justin would speak one or two words to other kindergarten children on the playground, but never in the school building and never to adults. In addition, Justin would not eat in front of others at school.

After conducting observations, interviewing teacher and parents, and consulting with the school psychologist and speech and language clinician, the school social worker met with Justin's teacher and parents. Justin was informed at the end of the meeting that he would be expected to talk in school. A behavioral plan was drawn up. This included the expectation that Justin would speak. For example, when distributing art paper and asking each child what color he or she wanted, Justin would be expected to say "blue" or "red." If he continued to only point, he would not get a paper and so not be able to participate in the activity. All other school personnel who had contact with Justin were informed of this approach. The school social worker also held four small group sessions with Justin and three of his classmates noted for "protecting" Justin from speaking. The purpose was to enable the others to see that Justin could talk and that if he did not, he did not participate. Small group sessions consisted of games, stories, and activities.

Small gains were gradually made, and at first the teacher had only the expectation of a one-word answer to a question directed toward Justin. She did not expect Justin to participate immediately in "show and tell." At the end of two weeks, Justin was no longer excluded from any activities because of not responding and was able to give one-word responses to questions asked of him. The other children also stopped answering for him and began to expect Justin to talk. As the year progressed, Justin's verbal responses increased, and he began to initiate conversations with adults and peers. Justin also began eating lunch with his classmates. Followup on a yearly basis for three years showed no relapse—Justin was a good student, had friends, and participated fully.

It should be noted the school social worker needed to do considerable "work" with the kindergarten teacher to convince her of the soundness of a behavior management plan rather than referring for psychiatric evaluation. The teacher had not encountered an elective mute child before and was concerned that more harm

than good might be done by expecting Justin to speak and ignoring his gestures. The school social worker had worked with this
teacher before, and there was a good working relationship, allowing an open dialogue to take place over the initial disagreement
on how to "treat" this child. After consultation with other team
members (who also observed Justin, but the school social worker
was the main "treatment agent") the school social worker felt a
behavioral management plan was best, but agreed that if Justin
showed no response after four or five weeks, a referral would be
made for further diagnosis and treatment. Justin responded to the
school plan and was not referred elsewhere.

These examples illustrate how school social workers become involved in counseling with students and parents, consulting with teachers, and working with teams. But school social workers do more than
casework or counseling and, as already noted, become involved in
other activities to meet the needs of students. Marlys Staudt gives a
case example of how a rural school social worker helped develop a
"Big Brother—Big Sister" program in a community, involving the
school personnel and later community members in supporting this
effort.[13] Richard Weatherley states that in addition to basic diagnostic
and intervention skills, school social workers need to have competence and knowledge in the following: (1) advocacy with regard to
pupil rights and due process procedures, (2) oral and written communication, including preparation of reports, (3) consultation, (4) data
collection and assessment of needs of a school system, neighborhood,
and community, (5) coordination of interdisciplinary efforts and collaboration with interprofessional team members, (6) determination of
priorities in managing a complex work load, and (7) activism to remedy gaps in service.[14]

Issues and Trends

One chronic issue in respect to school social work involves the
specification of educational qualifications for such work. Some argue
that any professional, except physicians and nurses, employed in the
school should have a degree in education and be eligible for certification as a teacher. This argument is firmly grounded in the belief that all
school activities are forms of education and should be planned and
carried out by educators. Another rationale for such a requirement is
that only study in education can provide a thorough understanding of
the educational enterprise.

Others firmly adhere to a position that professional education as a social worker is sufficient to practice social work in any setting. The special characteristics of any particular setting can be learned on the job.

In social work there seems to be a trend toward melding these two polarities. In this view the professional social work degree continues to be essential but is not necessarily sufficient. Social workers must have an understanding of education as well, and courses in colleges of education are one means toward that end. Work experiences may be another.

There is a related issue in social work education, not unique to school social work. Employing institutions (for example, schools, hospitals, mental health centers) want social work job applicants who have been specially trained for the work of the particular institutions. One of the strengths of the social work profession has been the versatility of its members. How can educational programs be devised that equip graduates to be both highly skilled in one specialty and at the same time competent, or potentially competent, to practice in other settings as well?

Still another recurrent problem is the definition of school social work role vis-à-vis other professions serving the schools. Territorial disputes have occurred and will continue as the various professions sort out their respective areas of competence. Role strain can result if the school social worker's ideas or perceptions in regard to what tasks to perform differs significantly from the ideas or perceptions of others in the school system. There is no overall single description of the specific tasks and functions any individual social worker might provide. School social workers at the building or district level must assess student and community needs and communicate and coordinate with other members of the team and school system. In recent years working with families has been a subject of contention. However, many have concluded there are more than enough families to go around, and this can also be a multidisciplinary activity.

As in other areas of social work practice, research and evaluation activities have become an issue in school social work practice. There are many ways in which school social workers can measure the outcome of their services to individual students or small groups of students. This type of measurement is known as client outcome.[15] School social workers can identify more than one "consumer" group, including students, parents, teachers, and principals. Program evaluation should include information from these various groups.[16]

The whole area of preschool children might be considered an emerging aspect of school social work practice.[17] On October 8, 1986, President Ronald Reagan signed P.L. 99-457, the Education of the Handicapped Amendments of 1986. P.L. 99-457 amends P.L. 94-142 to include a mandate for the provision by 1991 of educational and related services for handicapped children aged three to five years. It also provides a discretionary program to serve infants, toddlers (birth to age two), and their families. One of the components of the latter is the development and implementation of an Individualized Family Service Plan. Certainly school social workers will continue to have a role in serving infants and preschool handicapped children and their families. This includes the school social worker assisting in finding, screening, identifying, and serving young children with handicaps and their families.

Some social workers question whether the public school can be changed significantly from within. Social work values and principles center on the worth and dignity of the individual, and schools sometimes seem to violate those principles as programs are developed for masses of children and youth. Are such circumstances best rectified by advocacy from external agents or from within the schools?

With the advent of a different perception of federal responsibility for educational guarantees and continuing economic instability, the school social work job situation resembles the events of the depression of the 1930s. As fewer resources are available for education, hard choices are made about the use of those resources. Social work, being a secondary profession in schools, is particularly vulnerable to shrinkage. On the other hand, in those situations where the usefulness of these services has been demonstrated, there is strong likelihood of continuation.

Future

There is no doubt that school social work is here to stay. The importance of the total well-being of both the child and the family to the success of the school enterprise is no longer open to question. The literature of school social work of the past two decades is full of examples of role elaboration gearing services to the needs of special populations, as well as models for more effective work in school settings.

Possibilities are evident for additional social work services related to schools. In introducing a recent study of social work education commissioned by the Lois and Samuel Silberman Fund, Dr. Robert J. Havighurst of the University of Chicago stated,

A consequence of the "baby boom" is a current high rate of unemployment among young adults, but it seems clear that the demand for social workers trained at the bachelor's level will increase. The increased demand for social workers will come largely from two areas of need for human services— low income families with young children, and the growing numbers of people over seventy-five years of age. The social problems of the children of low income families in the big cities can be partially alleviated by programs in which a social worker collaborates with elementary school teachers in bringing the school and the home into cooperation, especially with children aged about three to ten.[18]

Further into the future it is conceivable that there will be fundamental changes in the school enterprise itself. Public education has been under attack on many fronts. The schools have become the battleground for almost all our social controversies. One of the most recent is AIDS (acquired immune deficiency syndrome) and the controversy around students with AIDS in school. Some schools have refused to enroll children with AIDS; others that have done so have faced an outcry from parents. Efforts to change institutionalized racism were focused in the schools through busing for integration, rather than through serious attempts to desegregate housing patterns or enrich schools serving predominately minority populations. Controversies about religion (prayer in the schools) and morality (content of textbooks) are centered in the schools.[19] The schools have become the designated agent to eliminate institutionalized sexism and discriminatory practices against the handicapped. Meanwhile the public schools are constantly criticized for not adequately preparing citizens in the "basic" skills (reading, writing, ciphering, and citizenship) that have been the central purpose of the public school since its inception.

It is unlikely that the public school (or any single institution) can continue to expand its functions, many of which are contradictory, and maintain sufficient steady state to survive. As major institutional changes do occur within the public schools, the place of social work therein will also change.

SUMMARY AND CONCLUSIONS

Social work in the schools is an established field of social work practice. It is one of the very few social work settings where primary prevention is feasible. Trite though it may sound, children are the future, and in our societal structure the school is an institution where the rights of children to develop and thrive can be realized. School social workers have an opportunity to further these purposes.

NOTES

1. *56th Report of the Board of Education*, Rochester, N.Y., 1911, 1912, 1913, as quoted in Lela Costin, "A Historical Review of School Social Work," in *Social Services and the Public Schools* (Bloomington, Ind.: The Midwest Center Consortium for Planned Change in Pupil Personnel Programs for Urban Schools, Indiana University, 1975), n. p.

2. Lela B. Costin, "A Historical Review of School Social Work," *Social Casework* 50, no. 8 (October 1969).

3. See the Education for All Handicapped Children Act of 1975 (P.L. 94–142) and rules and regulations in the *Federal Register*, December 20, 1976, 41:46977, and August 23, 1977, 42:42479–42497.

4. Lela B. Costin, "An Analysis of the Tasks in School Social Work," *Social Service Review* 43 (September 1969).

5. Paula Allen-Meares, "Analysis of Tasks in School Social Work," *Social Work* 22, no. 3 (May 1977).

6. John Brown and Al Swanson, "Reemergent Trends in School Social Work Practice," *Social Work in Education* 10, no. 2 (Winter 1988); Nancy Feyl Chavkin, "School Social Work Practice: A Reappraisal," *Social Work in Education* 8, no. 1 (Fall 1985); Robert Constable, "Toward the Construction of Role in an Emergent Social Work Specialization," *School Social Work Quarterly* 1, no. 2 (Summer 1979); Lela B. Costin, "School Social Work Practice: A New Model," *Social Work* 20, no. 2 (March 1975); Benjamin H. Gottlieb and Lois J. Gottlieb, "An Expanded Role for the School Social Worker," *Social Work* 16, (October 1971); Betty Peltier, "The Focus of School Social Work: A Discussion of Recent Viewpoints," *School Social Work Quarterly* 1, no. 2 (Summer 1979); Marlys Staudt and Scott A. Kerl, "Defining the School Social Worker's Role by Developing Service Priorities," *Social Work in Education* 1, no. 10 (Fall 1987).

7. Donald Brieland, Lela B. Costin, and Charles Atherton, *Contemporary Social Work* (New York: McGraw-Hill Book Co., 1975), p. 152.

8. Ralph Anderson and Irl Carter, *Human Behavior in the Social Environment*, 3rd ed. (New York: Aldine Publishing Co., 1984), pp. 187–188.

9. Michael L. Carl, Edward J. Pawlak, and Dan M. Dorn, "Research on Truancy," in Robert T. Constable and John P. Flynn (eds.), *School Social Work: Practice and Research Perspectives* (Homewood, Ill.: Dorsey Press, 1982), pp. 164–180; Paula Allen-Meares, Robert O. Washington, and Betty L. Welsh, "School Attendance," in *Social Work Services in Schools* (Englewood Cliffs, N.J.: Prentice-Hall, 1986), pp. 86–104; Linda Hall Harris, "Role of Trauma in the Lives of High School Dropouts," *Social Work in Education* 5. no. 2 (January 1983); and the Special Issue: Truancy and Non-Attendance, *Social Work in Education* 6, no. 3 (Spring 1984).

10. Robert Constable, "Toward the Construction of Role in an Emergent Social Work Specialization," *School Social Work Quarterly* 1, no. 2 (Summer 1979): 147.

11. Laura J. Lee, "The Social Worker in the Political Environment of a School System," *Social Work* 28, no. 4 (July–August 1983): 303.

12. See Lela Costin, "Which Children Can We Serve?" *Social Work in Education* 6, no. 2 (Winter 1984): 66–67.

13. Marlys Staudt, "School-Based Program Development in a Rural Community," *Social Work in Education* 9, no. 2 (Winter 1987).

14. Richard Weatherley, "Educating for Survival in the School Bureaucracy," *Social Work in Education* 1, no. 1 (October 1978).

15. Jeffrey L. Edleson, "Rapid-Assessment Instruments for Evaluating Practice with Children and Youth,"*Journal of Social Service Research* 8, no. 3 (Spring 1985); Linda Hall Harris, "Goal Attainment Scaling in the Treatment of Adolescents," *Social Work in Education* 5, no. 1 (October 1981); Paula Allen-Meares, "Interrupted Time Series Design and the Evaluation of School Practice," *Social Work in Education* 2, no. 3 (January 1980); Martin Bloom and Joel Fischer, *Evaluating Practice: Guidelines for the Accountable Professional* (Englewood Cliffs, N.J.: Prentice-Hall, 1982); Paula Allen-Meares, Robert O. Washington, and Betty L. Welsh, "Accountability and Evaluation of School Social Work Services," in *Social Work Services in Schools* (Englewood Cliffs, N.J.: Prentice-Hall, 1986), pp. 255–278; Nancy Kramer Banchy, "Evaluation of School Social Work in a Metropolitan School System," in *School Social Work: Practice and Research Perspectives*, ed. Robert T. Constable and John P. Flynn (Homewood, Ill.: Dorsey Press, 1982), pp. 356–362.

16. Robert T. Constable and Eldon Montgomery, "Perceptions of the School Social Worker's Role," *Social Work in Education* 7, no. (Summer 1985), Joanne Jankovic and Art Michals, "Program Evaluation and School Social Services: Issues and Problems," in *School Social Work: Practice and Research Perspectives*, ed. Robert T. Constable and John P. Flynn, (Homewood, Ill.: Dorsey Press, 1982), pp. 351–356; Marlys M. Staudt and John L. Craft, "School Staff Input in the Evaluation of School Social Work Practice," *Social Work in Education* 5, no. 2 (January 1983).

17. P. David Kurtz, "Identifying Handicapped Preschool Children," *Social Work in Education* 5, no. 4 (July 1983); and Elizabeth Floyd Gerlock, "Children with Handicaps: Transition from Preschool to School Programs," in *Achieving Educational Excellence for Children at Risk*, ed. Mable T. Hawkins (Silver Spring, Md.: National Association of Social Workers, 1986), pp. 20–32.

18. Miriam Dinerman, *Social Work Curriculum at the Baccalaureate and Masters Levels* (New York: Lois and Samuel Silberman Fund, 1981), p. xiii.

19. From the UPI published in the University of Iowa, *Daily Iowan*, July 31, 1981:

Efforts to censor books and films in the nation's public school classrooms and libraries are growing and becoming increasingly effective, a new study [reveals]. The report "Limiting What Students Shall Read," was sponsored by the Association of American Publishers, The American Library Association and the Association for Supervision and Curriculum Development. It was based on responses to a questionnaire by 1,891 elementary and secondary school superintendents, principals, librarians, and library supervisors in all fifty states and the District of Columbia.

Nearly one-fourth of those surveyed reported recent challenges to books or films used in the classroom or available in school libraries. Challenged material ran the gamut from Webster's Collegiate Dictionary to Sports Illustrated magazine and the Weekly Reader's "Our Freedom."

The study said the percentages reporting challenges were approximately equal in all sections of the country. It said that in 95 percent of the cases cited, challenges sought to limit rather than expand the information and points of view in the materials available to students.

ADDITIONAL SUGGESTED READINGS

Allen-Meares, Paula; Washington, Robert O.; and Welsh, Betty L., *Social Work Services in Schools* (Englewood Cliffs, N.J.: Prentice-Hall, Inc., 1986).

Constable, Robert, T., and Flynn, John P., *School Social Work: Practice and Research Perspectives* (Homewood, Ill.: The Dorsey Press, 1982).

Culbert, Jane F., *The Visiting Teacher at Work* (New York: The Commonwealth Fund, Division of Publications, 1930).

Dane, Elizabeth, "Professional and Lay Advocacy in the Education of Handicapped Children," *Social Work* 30, no. 6 (November-December 1985): 505–510.

Freeman, Edith M., "Analyzing the Organizational Context of Schools," *Social Work in Education* 7, (Spring 1985): 141–159.

Hancock, Betsy Ledbetter, *School Social Work* (Englewood Cliffs, N.J: Prentice-Hall, Inc., 1982).

Hawkins, Mable T., ed. *Achieving Educational Excellence for Children at Risk* (Silver Spring, Md.: National Association of Social Workers, 1986).

Hawkins, Mable T., "State Certification Standards for School Social Work Practice," *Social Work in Education* 4, no. 3 (April 1982): 41–52. Also see response to this article by Marianne Pennekamp, "State Certification of School Social Workers," *Social Work in Education* 5, no. 1 (October 1982): 66–69.

Johnson, Joy, *Use of Groups in Schools* (Lanham, Md.: University Press of America, Inc., 1977).

Osman, Betty B., *No One to Play with—The Social Side of Learning Disabilities* (New York: Random House, 1982).

Radin, Norma, and Welsh, Betty L., "Social Work, Psychology, and Counseling in the Schools," *Social Work* 29, no. 1 (January-February 1984): 28–33.

Randolph, Jerry L., "School Social Work Can Foster Educational Growth for Students," *Education* 102, (Spring 1982): 260–265.

Seipel, Michael M., "Neglecting the Educational Needs of the Disadvantaged," *Social Work in Education* 10 (Winter 1988): 77–87.

Winters, Wendy Glasgow, and Freda Easton, *The Practice of Social Work in Schools: An Ecological Perspective* (New York: Free Press, 1983).

Zischka, Pauline C., and Fox, Raymond, "Consultation as a Function of School Social Work," *Social Work in Education* 7, no. 2 (Winter 1985): 69–79.

8 Social Services and the Health Field

Katherine A. Kruse

Health, like food, clothing, and shelter, is essential to the total well-being of the individual. Health and illness influence the individual's self-image differently, in turn affecting the quality of interpersonal relationships and ability to function in the workplace and as a member of a community. One can readily see that health and illness are basic components of a person's social functioning. Hence, a person's health concerns all social work practitioners. It cuts across all fields of practice, since it is such an essential factor in psychosocial assessment, planning, and intervention. Both personal and environmental health should be of vital concern to the social work profession.

The nature of health is one of the significant issues confronting not only the professions involved in the provision of health care but also the individual person. There is increasing recognition of the complex interaction of mind and body and the specific life situation of the individual in the maintenance of health and, conversely, the development of illness. Although this understanding has existed since the development of medicine as a "healing art," only in the last two decades has scientific medicine given serious consideration to the concept of psychosomatic illness and the psychosocial implications of illness. A recent development, which incorporates the concept of stress in the etiology (cause) of illness, is the holistic perspective. A generally accepted working definition of a holistic approach is based on several beliefs:

1. All states of health and all disorders are considered to be psychosomatic.
2. Each individual is unique and represents a complex interaction of body, mind, and spirit.
3. The patient and health practitioners share the responsibility of orthodox medicine.
4. Health care is not exclusively the province or responsibility of orthodox medicine.
5. Illness [is] a creative opportunity for the individual to learn more about him/herself and his/her fundamental values.
6. The [health] practitioner must come to know him/herself as a human being.[1]

PSYCHOSOCIAL IMPLICATIONS

One can readily recognize the implications of health status, not only for the individual but also for a nation. The absence of health permeates the activities and behavior of everyone, becoming more dysfunctional for the person who does not have access to health care services. Illness may be an alienating influence, producing changes in one's self-image, functional capacities, and relationships. Families may be disrupted as a result of role reversals, confusion, and conflict. Economic breakdown is a frequent outcome of illness, as a result of both cost of needed care and unemployment. These problems are compounded by dysfunctional communication patterns between patients and health care providers as well as among the various professional disciplines and organizations involved in health care. The interdisciplinary communication problems are attributed to feelings of territoriality, lack of understanding of roles, and more important, failure of those care providers to recognize the significance of a comprehensive approach to providing care that is responsive to the total life situation of the individual.

HEALTH CARE SYSTEMS OF THE UNITED STATES

The health care system in the United States constitutes one of the largest human service "industries" in our country. It touches the lives of millions of Americans. There are various ways of describing what is actually a fragmented series of programs and policies under public and private auspices, operating at various levels of government and geographic locations. Our health care "system" has been described as levels of care: primary, secondary, and tertiary. Primary refers to early detection of dysfunction and fairly routine care; secondary care refers to acute and/or emergency care; tertiary level is highly specialized care. Still another classification one can use describes focus and duration: preventive, therapeutic, rehabilitative, and long-term. The complexity of health care is not only confusing to the "consumer" but also to the "provider." The five "A's" represent approximate goals or criteria for evaluating a system:

1. Availability to all persons regardless of age, race, ethnicity, sex, sexual preference, income level, educational level, or place of residence.
2. Acceptability to both consumer and provider.
3. Affordability for all persons.
4. Accessibility to all persons regardless of physical, mental, or civil status, or geographic location.
5. Accountability to consumers, and other sources of sanction and funding.

Special Population Groups

Within the general population, there are special population groups at risk. The term "at risk" refers to the special vulnerability of certain populations to certain diseases and/or threats of disease or availability of treatment.

Nonurban populations are at a special kind of risk. The majority of the health care system in the United States is based in urban areas. Medical research has led to discoveries that have, in turn, led to the development of highly sophisticated and technological treatment methods and equipment as well as specialized personnel. These advances in knowledge have led to changes in education for medical practice, which is far more complex, requiring complex equipment and housing for that equipment. Small rural hospitals have found it increasingly difficult to provide such facilities and as a result are finding it difficult to attract physicians to practice in rural communities. During the past twenty-five years, "physician extender" (physician's assistant and nurse practitioner) programs have been developed in both medicine and nursing as a partial solution to the problem. Since physician extenders may practice only under supervision of a licensed physician, their acceptance by the medical profession is crucial. There is continued resistance from established medical doctors to their use in many parts of the country.

Persons who are sixty-five years old or more constitute another "at-risk" population in terms of numbers, income level, health status, and health-related costs. At the present time, in the United States, people who are sixty-five and over comprise about 11 percent of the total population, and this percentage is growing. The fact that so many of the elderly are below or just above the poverty line combined with greater health care use and costs, residence in rural areas, and relative lack of medical education in care of the elderly constitutes a significant problem.

In 1981, a new disease was identified—AIDS (acquired immune deficiency syndrome). AIDS is caused by a virus that destroys the cells that combat infection.[2] Consequently, persons with AIDS are subject to illnesses that develop when the immune system does not function properly. Various pulmonary infections develop as well as infections of the renal and neurological systems.[3]

Confusion over AIDS

Jim Brown, age twenty-two, called the hospital social worker who works with people with AIDS when he was feeling like committing suicide. Jim told the social worker he had AIDS, had lost his job, had no money, and had only temporary housing. The people with whom he was staying did not know of his physical condition; the one friend who did know told him he had "better get help."

During the initial phone call, Jim expressed feelings of hopelessness because he had AIDS. After listening to Jim talk about his feelings and his situation, the social worker talked about AIDS and its symptoms. In the course of the questions and answers that followed, the social worker determined that Jim did not have AIDS, but rather had recently been told he has tested HIV positive.

Jim reported feeling much better after the AIDS education and realization that he did not have AIDS. Jim also talked about his chemical dependency. Jim agreed with the social worker to discuss treatment programs further. After the doctor's appointment, the social worker would also help Jim start planning changes in his life.[4]

It is anticipated that by 1991, the cumulative AIDS caseload in the United States will be 270,000, and the death toll 179,000. According to the Centers for Disease Control, 90 percent of the reported cases are people between ages twenty and forty-nine. The groups affected are homosexual and bisexual men, who constitute 73 percent of all AIDS patients; intravenous drug users, approximately 19 percent; and transfusion recipients including hemophiliacs, 3 percent. The remainder are heterosexuals who have had sexual contacts with a person who has, or is at risk for, AIDS and infants born to infected mothers.[5] Over half (59 percent) of these persons are white, 25 percent are black, and 14 percent are of Hispanic origin. The race/ethnicity of the remainder is unknown.[6] The World Health Organization estimates that between 5 and 10 million people in the world are already infected. They estimated that that number will increase dramatically in the next five years as a result of more accurate and expanded reporting by all countries.

Homelessness, a long-standing urban phenomenon, has become a more widespread problem that now includes all age groups—young families, women with children, young men, elderly, chronically mentally ill and adolescents (sometimes referred to as "throwaway" children). Each group has special needs and risks. However, they are all vulnerable to a variety of problems related to inadequate nutrition and maintenance of body temperature; exacerbation of chronic illnesses, especially cardiovascular, pulmonary, and metabolic diseases; exposure to pollutants; infectious diseases, constant mobility, which results in sleep deprivation and foot and leg ulcerations; and unhygienic living conditions.[7] Although it is difficult to quantify the problem, it appears that hundreds of thousands are affected.

Persons who are subject to Alzheimer's disease are a special population at risk in large part because the disease is not clearly established as a diagnostic entity. As a result, most treatment consists of maintaining a protective environment for such persons. Memory loss is an early and predominant symptom as well as lack of affect followed later by more bizarre and finally psychotic behavior. The average lag between the onset of the disease and a tentative diagnosis is two to seven years. Very approximate figures place persons who are sixty-five years and over at greatest risk (80–90 percent), with the remainder of cases occurring in persons between forty-five and sixty-four years. The total estimated number of persons affected is over 1,500,000. Currently, there are no mechanisms for insuring against direct or indirect costs.[8]

Although the number of children in the United States with some developmental disability, either physical or mental, constitutes only 12 percent of the child population, they can be considered to be at risk because of their special needs. Of these children 4 percent have serious physical disabilities that involve major health impairment or functional limitations, which in some instances are compounded by mental disabilities.[9] One study of mentally retarded persons in residential facilities showed that approximately 20 percent had one or more chronic health problems that necessitated periodic, ongoing health care. The most frequent condition was disorders of the circulatory system, followed by digestive, respiratory, and endocrine, nutrition, or metabolic disorders.[10] Although private insurance does provide some coverage for 60 percent of disabled children, needed services to maintain their day-to-day needs, such as custodial care, prostheses, limited rehabilitation, or social support services, are not covered, nor are they well covered in either Title V or Title XIX of the Social Security Act. This gap, in turn, makes more urgent the need to maintain the health of parents who are faced with twenty-four-hour care. Various kinds of respite care have been proposed, which must be funded either by the parents or voluntary sources. The Association for Retarded Citizens, a strong parent organization, has developed a range of these services for the mentally retarded, which are based primarily in urban areas.

Health Care: Costs and Coverage

Total national health care expenditures have risen from $74.7 billion in 1970 to $355.4 billion in 1983. It is projected that by 1990, national expenditures will reach $757.9 billion.[11] In 1970, 7.6 percent of the gross national product was spent on health care; in 1990 the proportion is projected to be 11.5 percent. These expenditures cover approximately 85 percent of the population, leaving some 15 percent of people in the United States without insurance coverage. This percentage represents between 31 and 37 million Americans.[12] An estimated 28 million have inadequate health insurance. Task forces in forty states are exploring the problem. Some initial responses include expanding Medicaid through a special tax earmarked for that purpose, requiring hospitals with emergency services to treat patients regardless of source of payment, and "risk pooling" to help persons with high-risk medical conditions to obtain health insurance.

Mandatory health insurance coverage at some level is also being debated in states. Massachusetts has approved legislation that would require employers who have six or more employees either to provide employee health insurance by 1992 or to pay a 12 percent surcharge on the first $14,000 of wages to help finance health insurance for employees. The state has agreed to help small employers obtain group rates and by 1989 offer incentives such as tax credits in order to encourage such business to meet the 1992 date. Those persons who still are not covered will be offered insurance from a state pool, to be paid on a sliding scale based on income. It is estimated that it will cost the state $195 million annually. There are some predictions that national health insurance may become a reality by the turn of the century.

Simultaneously, states are having to look at long-term care (for all ages) and care for persons with AIDS and AIDS-related conditions. In some states, half of the total Medicaid funds are being expended on nursing home care.[13] As a result commissions, which include representatives of the private sector, are exploring alternative ways of financing long-term care as well as rewriting standards that govern private insurance policies for such care.

Research focused on the cost of caring for persons with AIDS is expanding rapidly.[14] The results of one study indicated that state-only expenditures (not including Medicaid) increased fifteen-fold between fiscal year 1984 and 1988 to a total of $156.3 million for education, testing, and counseling. The Public Health Service in fiscal year 1988 has spent $790.7 million for research and prevention. This figure does not include Medicaid, Social Security, or other federal funds. In addition, some cities are providing funding: for example, in fiscal year 1988, San Francisco spent $17.5 million.

Another study of private health insurance focused on the regulatory activity of states relative to AIDS.[15] The majority of the fifty states have no legal constraints on insurance companies in relation to discrimination based on sexual orientation, making inquiry about HIV antibody

Table 8.1   National Health Expenditures

	1970		1983	
Total	Amount ($ billion) $74.7 billion	%	Amount ($ billion) $355.4 billion	%
Expenditures by:				
Consumers	43.1	58	195.7	55
Government	27.8	37	148.8	42
Philanthropy & industry	3.8	5	10.9	3
Expenditures for:				
Personal health care				
Hospitals	27.8	37	147.2	41
Physicians	14.3	19	69.0	19
Nursing home care	4.7	6	28.8	8
Drugs	8.0	11	23.7	7
Dental service	4.7	6	21.8	6
Other	3.7	5	16.5	5
Eyeglasses/appliances	1.9	3	6.2	2
Administration	2.7	4	15.6	4
Public health	1.4	2	11.2	3
Construction	3.4	4	9.1	3
Research	2.0	3	6.2	2

Sources: Bureau of the Census, *Statistical Abstract of the U.S., 1984*, p. 103; "Health Status and Medical Care," Economic Report of the President, House Document no. 99-19, 99th Congress, 1st Session, February 1985, p. 133.

testing, performing HIV testing, or excluding AIDS as a covered condition. These findings refer to individual rather than group health insurance policies provided for by employers. However, more large employers are self-insuring as a move to contain costs, and they are not regulated by state insurance commissions. As a result, they would be exempt from such constraints even if they had been legislated.

Expenditures for health care of the homeless do not easily lend themselves to accurate data. Much health care is provided in the emergency rooms of hospitals across the country. In 1987 Congress appropriated $50 million for an emergency food and shelter program within the Federal Emergency Management Agency.[16]

GOVERNMENT-FINANCED MEDICAL CARE

Medicare

Medicare and Medicaid are special types of programs designed to meet some part of the health care needs of specific categories of people in the United States. They are often cited as examples of "government-administered medical care," particularly the inadequacies, by opponents of a universal national health service.

Medicare consists of Part A, hospital insurance, and Part B, Supplementary Medical Insurance, which provides for coverage of physicians' services. There was a "free-enterprise" safeguard built into Title XVIII, which forbade the government "to exercise any supervision or control over the practice of medicine or the manner in which medical services are provided."[17] Medicare is financed in the following way: Part A benefits from Old Age, Survivors, Disability, and Health Insurance (OASDHI) "tax" on both employer and employee; and Part B from premiums paid by the elderly who choose to buy it. The premium amount is matched with general revenue funds. In the majority of states, Blue Cross–Blue Shield is the "carrier," the organization that processes claims of service providers. In each instance, the need for service must be established by a licensed physician and must follow a hospitalization.

Part B covers physicians' services as well as services ordinarily furnished in the doctor's office and included in the bill. Routine physical examinations are not covered, nor are eye or hearing examinations. There is a deductible that the individual must pay in both Part A and Part B. However, only 80 percent of the reasonable charges are paid during the remainder of the year. C. Carl Pegels in 1980 noted there were three types of limitations in the Medicare program: structural, inflationary, and equity. The most significant structural limitation is the result of a decision not to initiate any changes in the health care system or to control costs and promote efficiency. The second type of limitation is attributed to (1) suboptimal use of scarce medical resources; (2) provision of incentives for use of highest-cost facilities, and (3) lack of effective cost-containment measures. Equity limitations are: (1) the deductible cost of Medicare rests most heavily on low-income elderly, who must use a larger proportion of income to cover them than do higher-income persons; and (2) differences in coverage by geographic locations of both hospital and medical services. Both are in short supply in rural areas in general and in rural southern and western United States in particular.

Congress, in a 1983 amendment to the Social Security Act, instituted a prospective payment system to all hospitals serving Medicare patients, effective October 1, 1983. A classification system of 457 diagnosis-related groups (DRG's) was established, with specific fixed rates for each diagnosis. The larger private health insurance companies have instituted a companion system in an attempt to contain hospital costs. In addition, other changes made in the Medicare programs were an increase in premium for physicians' service, a freeze on the amount paid physicians for their services (for fifteen months), a requirement that employers extend health care coverage to workers' spouses over age sixty-five, and a set fee schedule for all outpatient diagnostic laboratory tests for Medicare patients.

Medicaid

Medicaid was established in 1965 as an amendment to the Social Security Act and is often referred to as the Title XIX program. It is a federal-state program that is financed from the general revenues and varies, as noted below, from state to state. The federal government pays the majority of costs. The program was to replace medical care payments previously made under public assistance programs. Persons who received Old Age Assistance, Aid to the Blind, Aid to the Permanently and Totally Disabled (now Supplemental Security Income, or SSI), and Aid to Families with Dependent Children must be included in the Medicaid program. Initially it was intended that a second group, the "medically needy," that is, people who are needy because of health problems, would also be covered. However, there is wide variation among states in that aspect of the program. Many changes have occurred in the program since 1965, as a result of the costs. Two services, inpatient hospital and nursing home care, take the major part of the available money. Emphasis is on therapeutic rather than preventive services.

Although the intent was to provide comprehensive services, soaring costs have led states to curtail services. Typically the "medically needy" are the first to be excluded, though specific services for the "needy" are also restricted.

Generally, Medicaid covers Aid to Families with Dependent Children (AFDC), medically needy (optional), aged, and disabled. However, there are fifty different programs. For example, in 1985 the annual expenditure per Medicaid recipient ranged from $821 in West Virginia to $3,384 in New York. Differences arise from who is eligible, what benefits are provided, and the level of reimbursements to providers. Social attitudes toward the poor, political variables, and the availability of tax dollars influence the nature of the differences among states.[18] In 1985 Medicaid expenditures for 1.4 million persons in nursing homes were $11.6 billion.

> Advances in medical/surgical research and procedures make possible many services that are costly, often by virtue of the equipment needed and/or technological expertise of the service provider. Low-income people are largely excluded from surgical procedures that would extend life or enhance an individual's capacity to be more independent because Medicaid programs may set a lower reimbursement cost on those procedures than the prevailing market price. Federal Medicaid rules prohibit supplementation from privately raised funds, thus also depriving a community of the opportunity to exhibit a charitable impulse. An illustration of a "Catch 22," which was reported in the press, was a four-year-old child with cerebral palsy who required immediate surgery if he was to continue to be able to walk. His mother, a single parent, appealed to the community for assistance in meeting the fee set by the hospital and physician, as a means of supplementing the Medicaid allowance. She was advised that if private funds were available, that no Medicaid funds could be used.[19]

The U.S. Public Health Service

The U.S. Public Health Service (USPHS) is a unique combination of personal and environmental services. The latter are those that are typically associated with public health, particularly at the state, regional, and local level. The first health departments were organized by city governments in the early 1800s in seaports. The primary focus was on communicable disease control, particularly those diseases "imported" from other parts of the world via sea travel. Control was attempted through the use of quarantine of the ports.

In 1975, Haven Emerson's *Local Health Units for the Nation* was published. It is based on a comprehensive study of the functions of public health agencies, which was conducted by a committee of the American Public Health Association. The basic functions of a health department are:

1. Planning: comprehensive health planning and implementation.
2. Administrative: establishing and enforcing standards for personal and environmental health; determining relationships between health needs and the economic, social, cultural, and educational factors in the community; developing legal, financial, and organization bases for health programming.
3. Health care: assuring availability of services for acute and chronic illness, maternal and child health (including nutrition and dentistry); occupational illness and injuries; all aspects of environmental health; management of governmental health programs; and evaluation of the effectiveness of health care services in the community.
4. Supportive: recruitment, training, and placement of health personnel; health information and education programs; record and reporting systems for disease control purposes.

At the federal level there are four personal service programs administered by the U.S. Public Health Service:

1. Medical care services for merchant seamen
2. Health Services for Native Americans
3. Maternal and Child Health Services
4. Crippled Children's Services

Medical care services for merchant seamen developed early in the nineteenth century, in part to protect seaport communities from diseases carried from other ports in the world as well as in recognition of the contribution of merchant seamen to the economic development of the United States.

Indian Health Services originated in the early nineteenth century as a measure to protect military posts from such contagious diseases of Indian tribes as smallpox. The federal government in 1832 was committed to such care when the Winnebago Indians were promised physician services as partial payment for property ceded to the United States government. The first hospital for the Indians was built in the late nineteenth century in Oklahoma. However, it was not until Congress transferred responsibility for Indian health from the Department of Interior to the Public Health Service in 1955 that a reasonably adequate system was developed. Public Law 98-638, the Indian Self-Determination and Education Assistance Act, enacted in 1975, provided Indian tribes and Native Alaskan groups with the opportunity to improve their capabilities to manage and operate Indian Health Service programs in their communities.[20] There are a total of fifty-one hospitals (2,286 beds) and ninety-nine health centers in the system, but they are not evenly distributed.

Both the Crippled Children's Program and Maternal and Child Health Program were developed as a part of the Social Security Act in 1935.[21] Originally both programs were administered by the Children's Bureau at the federal level. In 1969, they were transferred to the Maternal and Child Health Service of the USPHS. At the state level, Crippled Children programs are administered by any one of five state agencies: health department, public welfare department, university medical school, department of education, or as a separate agency.[22] They provide preventive services through early identification of handicapping conditions in the child population (birth to twenty-one years) of the state. Diagnostic services are provided all children regardless of financial status, race, or source of referral. States usually do have financial eligibility requirements for medical treatment. Most states accept a wide range of handicapping conditions though there are a few where services are confined to orthopedic and plastic surgery.

Maternal and Child Health programs include infant health, maternal health, child health, family planning, nutrition, and dental services. Some states have also developed specialized programs in mental retardation, genetics, teenage pregnancy, substance abuse, and child abuse. Medical care services are provided under Title V of the Social Security Act, primarily to low-income populations in both urban and rural areas through local health departments or other medical care services in the community.

During the 1960s, Congress passed legislation that expanded maternal and child health services. Special projects in maternity and infant care were set up to meet problems associated with poverty, inadequate prenatal care, and premature births. Projects were to provide comprehensive maternity care to women in low-income areas of the country and health care for their infants up to a year old. Services provided included prenatal care, hospital care for complications of pregnancy, hospital delivery, postnatal care, family planning, health care of infants, homemaker services, transportation related to medical care, and care by public health nurses, social workers, nutritionists, health educators, and other specialists as needed. The nutrition programs are popularly known as WIC, which refers to women, infants, and children. Pregnant teenagers among urban and rural poor represent a high percentage of patients served. Consequently, many projects have been involved in developing coordinated health, education, and social services as well as day care for those teenagers.

The third major project area is family planning. Major responsibility for administration of project grants was assigned to the National Center for Family Planning though locally they are administered by public health departments. This program is also a required component of state maternal and child health programs.[23]

Veterans' Administration

The Veterans' Administration (VA), long the largest independent federal agency directly responsible to the U.S. Congress, recently was provided Cabinet status as the Department of Veterans' Affairs, much like the Department of State or the Department of Health and Human Services. The VA Department of Medicine and Surgery provides care to 28 million veterans, of which 4.3 percent are women.[24] The department operates 172 medical centers, 229 outpatient clinics, 117 nursing homes, and 16 domicilliaries. In addition to patient care, the department participates in medical research and development and education of the various health related disciplines. The VA has recently developed specialty clinics in preventive health care, bone marrow transplant, diagnostic cardiovascular disease, nuclear imaging, and problems and diseases of women. In addition, recognition of the special needs of Vietnam veterans has led to the development of thirteen hospital-based programs as well as some community-based programs.

As a result of budgetary cutbacks, Congress directed that the Veterans' Administration discontinue the policy of automatic eligibility for care if the condition could be established to be service-connected.[25] Consequently, a means test is being used to reduce the number of eligible veterans and thus the need for expanding the hospital system and other health-related support facilities. It is estimated that only one-third of the patients now being cared for have health problems or disabilities that are service-related. The remainder are veterans who lack the financial resources to pay for health care who must now be cared for through other public programs.

An example of the lack of flexibility in a federally funded health care program, reported in the press, was that of a couple whose only recourse to obtaining adequate care for the quadriplegic, respirator-dependent husband, a veteran, was to divorce. The wife was employed full time and earned $22,000 a year which was above the income guidelines by the Veterans' Administration for eligibility for a medical disability pension. She had hoped that status would qualify him for additional medical benefits and a higher priority for medical services.[26]

HEALTH CARE SERVICES

The growing awareness of the general public about the importance of maintaining good health, coupled with the rising costs of health care and increasing government funding of health care—both personal and environmental—has led to an unprecedented increase in health-related legislation and subsequent development of patient service programs as well as structures designed to improve health service delivery. Such programs are subject to the ideology of the political party in power relative to the extent of the government's responsibility for the health of the nation, and more specifically those persons who are most vulnerable. During the 1950s and 1960s, the central aim of national health policy was to assure access to the best health care for all Americans. This goal was to be accomplished by "(1) remov[ing] all or most financial barriers to health care; and (2) increas[ing] health manpower, facilities, services, and biomedical research to meet the new demand."[27] By the mid-1970s, there was widespread frustration among both consumers and providers with the apparently uncontrollable costs of health services, as well as the complexity of the health service "system" that has resulted from a categorical, politically responsive accumulation of programs and services.

There are various classification systems for describing existing programs and services, none of which is adequate nor all-inclusive. Consequently, the classification of "institutional" versus "community-based" will be used. Social work services are an integral part of the majority of these programs.

Institutional Programs

Hospitals and nursing homes (used generically), public or private, are the primary service delivery systems. They may be general or specialized. Some examples of the latter are those serving only children, women, handicapped persons (rehabilitation hospitals), or military personnel. (The Veterans' Administration Department of Medicine and Surgery was described earlier.)

The second major institutional program is long-term-care facilities or nursing homes, which may be profit or nonprofit organizations. Originally, most nursing homes were sponsored and supported by churches, fraternal organizations, or philanthropic groups. There are various kinds of requirements for eligibility and payment for services.[28]

The majority of persons cared for in nursing homes are elderly. In some states, these facilities are a "dumping ground" for persons who are no longer able to care for themselves. In some instances the residents have been institutionalized for long periods of time in state mental institutions. Typically, nursing homes have not been adequately staffed to provide those services that elderly and former psychiatric patients need.

A clause in the Social Security Act provided the basis for the present "nursing home industry." It encouraged the conversion of private housing into profit-making boarding homes for the elderly, which eventually, given the medical needs of their residents, became the forerunner of today's nursing home. There are now approximately 25,000 nursing homes with a total capacity of over 1 million beds.[29] Nursing homes must meet minimum standards for licensing by the state. However, enforcement by licensing agencies may be minimal because agencies have neither the staff nor the legal "clout" to close substandard operations. In some states, care review teams comprised of volunteers from the community provide some oversight of operations.

Emergency Social Work Services

As part of the hospital-wide quality assurance effort, the Department of Social Service was asked to develop a program to evaluate emergency social work services provided to patients outside normal working hours. The director of the Department of Social Service assigned the assistant director and a supervisor the task of writing a quality assurance monitoring system that would meet the requirements set forth by the Joint Commission on Accreditation of Hospitals and would incorporate comments from the staff social workers who are directly responsible for providing after-hours emergency social work services. Two indicators (defined as a measurable dimension of the quality or appropriateness of an important aspect of care) were written. Indicators were: (1) 100 percent of the time a social worker would be available, on call, to provide emergency social work services after hours; and (2) 100 percent of the time that the on-call social worker received an after-hour request for services, that service would be provided. To collect the data necessary to measure the indicators, a simple form was developed. The form asked the on-call social worker to track the number of emergency after-hours calls received, the identity of the requester of the service, the nature of the service provided, and an indication of whether the patient required follow-up services by the daytime social worker. At the end of the first quarter, a review of the indicators revealed that there was a social worker on call for emergency after-hour services 100 percent of the time, and that 90 percent of the patients requesting services received them. Because the level of performance was not achieved in the second indicator, a follow-up assessment was completed by the Department of Social Services administrative staff.[30]

Community-based Programs

Noninstitutional or community-based services are not as well developed as institutional ones, particularly in areas of small population. Clinics to meet the needs of ambulatory patients may be "all-purpose" or specialized to meet the needs of specific population groups. Private medical practice offices may be called clinics, particularly if there is a group of physicians in practice together. Examples of large multi-specialty groups are the Mayo Clinic in Rochester, Minnesota, the Ochsner Clinic in New Orleans, and the Lahey Clinic in Boston, which provide highly specialized services on a short-term basis and are based on a fee for service. Another type of group practice is one in which various specialists are employed to provide comprehensive medical care to a group of persons who have prepaid the cost in an arrangement known as a Health Maintenance Organization (HMO). There is more emphasis on preventive services in these plans. Some of the early plans were sponsored by industry, the best known is the Kaiser Foundation Health Plan, which originated on the West Coast. The United Mine Workers Medical Plan (Ohio, West Virginia, and Pennsylvania) is the largest consumer-sponsored plan in the United States. Another well-known example is the Health Insurance Plan of Greater New York.[31] Health care services covered in these plans vary but may include inpatient hospital care, outpatient services, home health care, pharmaceutical services, physical therapy, occupational therapy, and social work services.

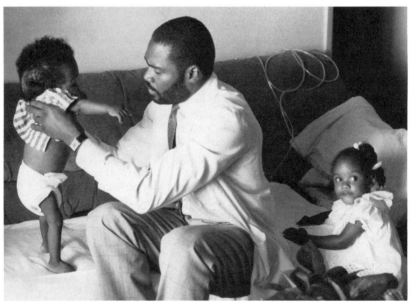

Courtesy Visiting Nurse Association of America

Visiting Nurse organizations across the nation send specialists to patients' homes to offer a wide range of services including physical therapy, occupational therapy, dialysis, I.V., and home chemotherapy. Here a visiting nurse in Los Angeles works with a medically fragile child on gross motor skills.

Another traditional community-based health service is Visiting Nurse Associations, privately funded through fees and voluntary fund-raising agencies, which provide bedside nursing services in the home. A publicly funded service that is similar and more widely developed is Public Health Nursing. The emphasis in this program is on prevention and health education of the individual and family members, primarily in the home. In some places, these two may be combined.

The mid-1960s was a particularly active period for the development of health care programs that differed markedly from the more traditional institutions. The new programs were characterized by greater outreach and concern for consumers, particularly those who were not being served adequately or served at all. Some were federally funded such as the antipoverty Neighborhood Health Clinics of the Office of Economic Opportunity (OEO). The emphasis in these clinics was outreach to people in the neighborhood—infants, children, mothers, the elderly—usually by workers who were also residents of the neighborhood. Such clinics were governed by neighborhood residents, with medical staff usually provided by the U.S. Public Health Service. In some communities, "storefront" free medical clinics were established using volunteer staff physicians, nurses, and pharmacists. Equipment and medical supplies were usually donated. Donations of money were accepted if offered by patients.

An interesting development in the private sector during the early 1980s has been the organizing of acute-care centers and surgi-centers, which offer consumers an alternative to hospitalization. In some instances, these centers are developed by hospitals as outpatient care services rather than as separate corporate entities.

Home health care programs, which were designed to enable people to remain in their own homes rather than be institutionalized for needed care, developed under various auspices, both private and public. They provide homemaker services as well as health care. Family service agencies, community nursing services, and public social service departments have administered some of these programs. The latter are usually available only to persons meeting income guidelines, at no cost to the person served.

A variation of home health care services that has been developing during the past decade is the day health care program. Its primary purpose is to enable a person who needs health services to remain at home as well as provide activities to maintain or enhance mental health.

A specialized type of care for terminally ill persons, which originated in England, is the hospice program. The first such program in the United States was founded in 1974 in New Haven, Connecticut, initially as a home-care program. The hospice concept treats the patient and family as an interrelated unit with physical, emotional, and spiritual needs. It is, in part, a response to a survey conducted for the National Cancer Institute, which showed that 57 percent of the people whose deaths were attributed to cancer between 1969 and 1971 had expressed a wish to die at home, rather than in an institution. There is growing recognition that such a program must provide inpatient facilities for those families who cannot, for medical or emotional reasons, keep the family member in the home. Preliminary studies of costs clearly establish that home care is the least expensive in actual dollars. The emotional well-being of terminally ill people and their families is also enhanced. However, communities have not provided, in sufficient volume, those supporting services necessary to a viable home-based hospice program. There is some speculation that the reluctance is based on a personal denial of death as a universal and individual experience.

In the past there were a few specialty women's hospitals in the United States, but there were few women's clinics. The women's health movement has been instrumental in the development of clinics that offer women an alternative to the more traditional programs, which often were discriminatory in philosophy, treatment approaches, and staffing patterns. The majority of women's clinics offer gynecological and obstetrical services. There are more than 1,200 women's health groups in the United States. The model for women's health centers is the Feminist Women's Health Centers, begun in Los Angeles. Those centers provide a full range of gynecological care including specialist referrals and some prenatal care with referrals for delivery. A few clinics provide primary care. There is an emphasis on a collective effort, participatory management, use of lay health workers, and active involvement or control of the health care process by the patient.[32] In some communities rape crisis centers have developed, sometimes in conjunction with a women's health clinic. These centers provide peer support services through various stages of securing medical services, reporting a rape, and prosecution of the rapist. In addition some groups provide escort services and self-defense classes, and press communities to develop preventive measures as well as other relevant services.[33]

Genetic Counseling Centers are an outgrowth of hereditary clinics (University of Michigan, 1940, and University of Minnesota, 1941).[34] There were 389 genetic clinics in the United States in 1974, an outgrowth of the medical research of genetic defects such as Down's syndrome, sickle-cell anemia, and cystic fibrosis, and evolved as a part of the medical management of patients with genetic disorders. The recent biochemical discoveries in chromosomal and genetic functioning provide the base for genetic counseling. Such centers are usually associated with medical research and teaching hospitals, are publicly funded, and are staffed by physicians, nurses, and "genetic associates." The latter are a new type of personnel who usually have a medically relevant background such as biology or nursing.

The concept of health maintenance organizations came into existence through legislative action in 1972 when Congress passed the Health Maintenance Organization Act. The legislation provided federal funding for planning and initiating prepaid group practices. Neil F. Bracht lists four major features of an HMO:

> 1) a managing organization that assumes legal, fiscal, public and professional accountability in order to 2) provide or arrange for a set of comprehensive health maintenance and treatment services, including primary care through rehabilitation; 3) enroll a defined population of individuals or groups who voluntarily join through a contract arrangement; and, 4) prepay their medical care costs on a fixed periodic payment basis.[35]

Holistic health centers have developed under various auspices and areas of the country. They emphasize the holistic nature of the person as a psycho-social-biological entity who must be treated as such. In some centers, there is less emphasis on the therapeutic use of drugs, with more attention given to less conventional therapies such as relaxation, meditation, and biofeedback. These centers usually are staffed not only by physicians and nurses but also by clergy, psychologists, and occasionally social workers.

A promising new development, both within and outside the established health care system, is the concept of wellness. The primary characteristic of wellness programs is an emphasis on prevention. Programs range from relatively simple exercise and health education to more sophisticated use of these tools as well as complex machines to monitor bodily functions in order to develop "prescription" programs for individuals or groups of individuals. Some are developed under the auspices of state health departments, and others in the private sector, both nonprofit and for-profit.

SOCIAL WORK IN HEALTH CARE

Social work practice in health care originated at Massachusetts General Hospital (Boston) in 1905 as the result of the experiences of Dr. Richard Cabot as a dispensary (clinic) physician there and as a member of the board of directors of a charitable society that cared for orphans and "unmanageable children" as defined by their parents or the school system. Dr. Cabot describes his medical practice with specific patients as useless without the intervention of the "home visitor," a term he borrowed from other sources but one that described the primary site for practice. Dr. Cabot

> established a full time, paid social worker . . . to cooperate with me and the other physicians in the dispensary, first in deepening and broadening our comprehensions of the patients and so improving our diagnoses; and second in helping to meet their needs, economic, mental, or moral, either by her own efforts, or through calling to her aid the group of allies already organized in the city for the relief of the unfortunate whenever found.[36]

The role of social work in health care has been defined by various persons and professional organizations within different conceptual frameworks. There is common definition, however, despite the fact that they represent different developmental periods and health care settings such as hospitals, public health departments, nursing homes, primary care settings, and health maintenance organizations.[37] Social workers in health care settings perform six major functions:

1. Social services to patients and families ("direct services")
2. Program planning and policy formulation
3. Participation in development and liaison with other community social and health programs
4. Consultation to other professional personnel
5. Social research
6. Social service administration

The Case of Mr. Ray

Mr. Ray was seen by the transplant team for a day of evaluation for the efficacy of a bone marrow transplant for treatment of his lymphoma, which is cancer of the lymph system. (The team emphasizes patient education as a means of assisting patients to make a decision to have a bone marrow transplant.) He was given a battery of physical tests and then was counseled by the team physician. The social worker's interview was purposely left until last, so that Mr. Ray would understand the medical plan and could share his concerns with the social worker and work toward a plan that would help him cope with transplant and the impact on his life.

Mr. Ray was a fifty-eight year-old divorced military officer who had business associates rather than close friends. His two grown sons scarcely knew him. He had a closer relationship with his sister and niece, whom he saw only once a year and talked to infrequently. Financially comfortable, Mr. Ray had an apartment to be cared for during the long upcoming hospitalization. He realized that he might die during the transplant and shared with the social worker the loneliness of his transient life. During the first meeting, they agreed to use Mr. Ray's organizational skills to increase his support system to help him cope with the transplant.

In the next few months, Mr. Ray met on a weekly basis with the social worker to identify and develop his support network and plan for his hospitalization. Mr. Ray recognized that his sister and niece did care about him, and he went to spend two weeks with them during this period. He was touched by their concern for him, and their relationship continued to improve upon his return home. He made out a will that included his sister and his sons. He called his sons to tell them about his illness, but they showed little concern. He was able to recognize honestly that his lack of involvement with them over the years had been one cause of their responses.

In addition to individual counseling, Mr. Ray regularly attended the support group for oncology patients, facilitated by the social worker, and shared the caring and support of his relatives with the group members. During the regular counseling sessions, Mr. Ray recognized his difficulties in coping with intimacy and was able to make progress in modifying these feelings. When he entered the hospital for his transplant, he felt proud of his increased connectedness to others and was able to use these relationships and new feelings to help him cope.[38]

Differentiating the Role of Social Work

Health care organizations use a wide range of personnel in the delivery of services, especially those requiring complex, high-technology diagnostic and treatment plans. Increasingly, a typical "health care team" is composed of nurses, nutritionists, pharmacists, physicians, and social workers. More complex settings may include a range of therapists: occupational, physical, recreational, respiration, speech, and vocational as well as pastoral counselors. The unique role of social work, which uses a comprehensive view of the person in the environment, is to provide the team with an understanding of the influence of the environment—physical, social, cultural, economic, spiritual—on the psychosocial functioning of the patient. In order to do so, the social worker examines the roles, relationships, resources, and responses of the individual.[39] The other significant aspect that social workers provide is making the multiplicity of experiences of receiving health care comprehensible to the patient. The social worker, as a "boundary" worker between systems, serves as a mediator and coordinator. Essentially, this is the role that Dr. Cabot described more than seventy-five years ago.

Nevertheless, there continue to be different perceptions and thus expectations among other health practitioners regarding the role of the social worker. Some of the confusion originates in the equating of social work with welfare only. In hospitals the primary social work task is often seen as planning for the discharge of patients following hospitalization, particularly if the patient has a limited income.

Medicare legislation mandates that coverage of hospitalization days for recipients be limited to the minimum necessary for adequate care of a specific medical problem. Hospital-based utilization review teams, which may include social workers, make the decisions regarding length of stay. Consequently there is pressure on social workers to develop discharge plans with patients without adequate planning.

Social Workers and Discharge Planning

Social workers are uniquely qualified to negotiate systems and are consistently called upon to develop and coordinate clinical and administrative interdisciplinary activities. A variety of professional and federal regulatory bodies mandate that hospitals develop comprehensive discharge planning programs that incorporate a determination of the patient's post-hospital-care needs, preferences, the patient's capacity for self-care, an assessment of the patient's living conditions, the identification of health, social, and financial resources needed, and counseling of the patient and caregivers to prepare them for posthospital care. Discharge planning services require expertise from a variety of health care professionals. To ensure compliance with these standards, the Social Service Department in a large tertiary health care center initiated an Interdisciplinary Discharge Planning Committee which developed hospitalwide discharge planning protocols/policies. In addition, this committee directed problem-solving activities related to recurring discharge planning problems. Due to diverse representation (ten professions in addition to physician and hospital administrators), the committee gained influence within the hospital and was reporting directly to both physician and hospital administration subcommittees. The Department of Social Service continues to be organizationally responsible for this committee.[40]

In nursing homes, confusion may arise from the way social work was introduced to the setting. That is, social work services were mandated for recipients of Medicare who are nursing home residents. These services include those functions mentioned earlier and being provided on a consultative basis, in a minimum of four hours a week, which is highly unrealistic given the preponderance of low-income elderly living in nursing homes.

The values and methods of social workers are another source of difficulty in some instances. For example, encouraging a patient to be self-determining may be seen as contradicting the patient's following medical recommendations. Traditionally nurses have been expected to implement doctors' orders, so that the social worker may be at odds with that practitioner as well. In addition, the nursing profession has expanded nursing education in the behavioral sciences, thus seeming to prepare nurses to perform functions that have been defined as social work. Nurses are becoming much more knowledgeable about individual and family dynamics as well as approaches to intervening in dysfunctional individual and family relationships. This development is often seen as a problem, creating competition rather than complementary action on behalf of patients.

Until recently, the social work profession has not seen health care as a significant practice arena. Social work education has not included content that would prepare students for future health care practice. Consequently social workers have not been prepared to function effectively in a setting that defines itself as highly scientific. The profession has, for example, permitted the Joint Commission on Accreditation of Hospitals to define social work services essential to high-quality hospital care. Nor has the profession been involved significantly in developing national health policies. Nevertheless, individual practitioners have been able to establish the unique contribution that social work can make to health care in our country.

Issues and Trends

Issues in the health care field, which ultimately affect the well-being of all individuals regardless of social class, place of residence, ethnic background, age, or sex, relate to all of the subsystems that constitute what has been described in this chapter as a health care system. The overriding issue, in the opinion of many experts in the field, is how the cost of adequate care for all Americans will be financed, as well as how costs can be controlled. National health insurance has been debated in the U.S. Congress for approximately forty years. Even middle-class Americans are concerned about the possibility of becoming impoverished in the event of a catastrophic illness. Nevertheless, in the absence of a coherent national policy of health care, it appears unlikely that adequate coverage of health care costs, using a universal mechanism, will become a reality even in the next decade. Of equal importance are such factors as:

1. lack of education of individuals relative to their own health care needs and how they can best be met;
2. a dysfunctional distribution of resources;
3. a continuing overemphasis on institutional care rather than development of health-related services in the community;
4. related to the above issue, the focus of much existing health insurance on institutional-based services only;
5. relative lack of primary care providers;
6. multiplicity and specificity of services which create residual populations that are ineligible for needed care; and
7. lack of coordination of existing services.

Specific examples include:

Cost Containment.   One attempt to control costs, which was instituted by Congress in 1983 and is popularly called DRG's (diagnostic-related groups), is basically a prospective payment system. Others instituted by the insurance industry are the funding only for outpatient surgical and diagnostic procedures, preadmission screenings, and expanded co-insurance and deductibles. The imposition of hospital-stay norms for specified diagnoses has led to the discharge of patients in the acute phase of their illness to communities that are not equipped to provide adequate care. Rural hospital rates were initially lower than urban, based on a presumption of lower operating costs. Twenty-three percent of the hospital beds in the United States are rural. Many of these hospitals are being forced to close or try to move into other service areas such as substance abuse. Since many rural patients are elderly and poor, a favorable case mix is not as feasible as it may be for their urban counterparts. The lack of a hospital not only markedly alters the quantity and quality of health care but also the economy of that community. Questions are being raised about the ethical implications of DRG's, which thus far are receiving only limited scrutiny.[41]

Home Care.   In 1982 Congress changed the Medicaid law to include a home and community-based option for care. The impetus for the change came from a Midwestern city when the case of an appealing, two-year-old child was pressed by her congressman. Only about one-fourth of the states have elected to use the waiver option thus far.

Although there has been some provision for home care through Medicare since 1966, the Omnibus Reconciliation Act of 1981 finally provided more flexibility for reimbursement. However, many home-care agencies have not applied for certification because of the added costs of implementing such a program. In 1983, reimbursement for hospice services for a maximum of six months was included for

Medicare-eligible persons. These services may be provided in home, hospital, or some form of short-term respite care. Both drugs and equipment costs are included.[42]

Long-Term Care. States that are spending half of their total health-care funds on nursing homes are establishing special bodies to explore the various aspects of long-term care. These commissions are looking at ways of financing it as well as the standards to govern long-term care insurance policies. Present policies usually are prohibitive in cost and limited in coverage.

Women. Health insurance coverage for low-income, poor, minority, and rural women remains a problem. The shift to a larger service economy, which has traditionally provided less coverage and which relies heavily on women as employees, is a part of the issue. Part-time employment, which is feasible for women with children or other responsibilities, does not provide typical fringe benefits including health insurance. Rural women are at an even greater disadvantage, as there are fewer services readily accessible to all rural persons.

A special issue of concern to women, both urban and rural, is the decreasing availability of quality obstetrical services. A 1985 survey of members of the American College of Obstetrics and Gynecology revealed that 75 percent of obstetricians have been sued at least once, and 12 percent had decided to discontinue providing that care. That decision was based on the rising costs of malpractice insurance.[43]

Homeless. In addition to physical problems, persons who are homeless are found to have mental health problems as a result of unemployment, social disconnectedness, and lack of resources, since they are usually not eligible for government programs. These are added to the special needs: care during pregnancy, care for children and the elderly, lack of immunizations, and dental care.[44]

AIDS. Persons with AIDS are of special concern to social workers. They are inevitably faced with problems of interpersonal relationships, lack of support systems, unemployment when the diagnosis becomes known, children being barred from school attendance, and the ostracism by communities of families of persons with AIDS-related diagnoses. Thus far there are few programs that provide necessary services.[45]

There is a growing consumer and corporate unrest that may ultimately lead to some changes in the field. Concomitant to that trend is a developing awareness among some health and health-related practitioners that they must take more responsibility for bringing about change in health policy rather than leaving it to the political arena.

There is increasing activity by the National Association of Social Workers in the Congress, providing testimony before committees, providing consultation on the impact of existing policies on individuals and families, as well as inclusion of social work services in health care programs that are federally funded. Another aspect of the latter activity is work for coverage of social work service in private insurance plans. The new National Center for Social Policy and Practice will strengthen such activities.

At the practitioner level, new services have been developing in hospitals such as crisis counseling in emergency rooms, anticipatory counseling for impending loss of a family member, and counseling in intensive care units. Social work services are also being developed in more primary care settings (family medicine centers, group medical practices) as well as health-related programs (home health care, day health care, child health centers). Practitioners may be employees of the organization or they may, as private practitioners, contract with an organization to provide services on a fee-for-service basis. In other words, marketing practices are spreading from the medical business world to social work, some of which appear inconsistent with social work values and practices. The basic issue is whether social workers can effectively advance social work values while effectively negotiating in the health care system.[46]

The Future

There are some indications that changes in the health care field will be incremental. However, if the goal is to reduce disparities in delivery of health care services between the "haves" and "have nots," national priorities will have to shift to defense of the general well-being of all people as well as their environment.

If the social work profession is to have a viable role in the health care system at all levels, practitioners must become more conscious of the strategic position they occupy in formulating and modifying social policy. They must become more knowledgeable and skillful in the social change process in order to intervene effectively on behalf of people at all levels—micro, messo, and macro. Concern for the individual must be extended to effective advocacy at the organizational and community levels. Dolgoff suggests that social workers do make policy in their everyday practice, that the choices and decisions they make are policy choices.[47] By making those actions more conscious, the practitioner may develop a new perspective of him or herself as a social change agent as well.

Social work education must also develop curriculum in the health care area that is relevant, sufficient, and present- and future-oriented in order to prepare practitioners for major tasks that have been minimally addressed.

SUMMARY AND CONCLUSIONS

As the health care system becomes more complex, employing more technology-intensive procedures and specialized personnel, the need for social work as an integral element of the system at all levels—direct service, planning, policy making, and administration—becomes more significant. The social worker as problem solver, coordinator, advocate, and community organizer provides the patient, the family, the health care organization, and the community with one means to a more responsive and responsible service delivery system.

If social work is to meet the challenge implicit in these roles, a much broader perspective on the cause and function of social services must continue to be developed by social work practice and education. The practitioner must have not only the specialized knowledge of the health care field but also the skills of a generalist in order to fulfill the role of a health care social worker.

Notes

1. Kenneth R. Pelletier, *Mind As Slayer, Mind As Healer: A Holistic Approach to Preventing Stress Disorders* (New York: Dell Publishing Co., 1977), pp. 318–321.
2. Lori S. Wiener, "Helping Clients with AIDS: The Role of the Worker," *Public Welfare*, Fall 1986, p. 38.
3. Daniel Gervich, "Diagnosis, Clinical Cause and Treatment," *AIDS: Iowa Information and Resource Manual*, October 1987, pp. 10–16.
4. Case Example contributed by Patricia Herring, ACSW, LSW, Medical Social Worker, University Hospitals and Clinics, Iowa City, Iowa.
5. Wiener, "Helping Clients with AIDS."
6. Joan G. Turner and Erica R. Pryor, "The AIDS Epidemic: Risk Containment for Home Health Care Providers," *Family & Community Health* 8, no. 3 (November 1985): 25–37.
7. Julian Sebastian, "Homelessness: A State of Vulnerability," *Family and Community Health* 8, no. 3 (November 1985): 14–19.
8. Joel Hay and Richard Erast, "The Economic Costs of Alzheimer's Dis-

ease," *American Journal of Public Health* 77, no. 9 (September 1977): 1169–1175.

9. Martin Nacman, "The Revolution of the 80's: Change in the Financing and Delivery of Health Care Services," *Current Issues in Health Care for Professional Leaders and Changes in Health Care Today*, Conference Proceedings, May–June 1986, p. 20. (USD, HEW, USPHS, Health Resource Administration, Bureau of Health Care Delivery and Assistance, Division of Maternal and Child Health).

10. B. Hill, R. Bruininks, and K. Lakin, "Characteristics of Mentally Retarded People in Residential Facilities," *Health and Social Work* 8, no. 2 (Spring 1983): 85–95.

11. Congressional Quarterly, *Health Policy* (Washington, D.C.: Congressional Quarterly, 1980), p. 3.

12. "The Nation's Health," American Public Health Association, March 1988, p. 10.

13. "The Nation's Health," American Public Health Association, January 1988, p. 4.

14. M. Rowe and C. Ryan, "Comparing State-Only Expenditures for AIDS," *American Journal of Public Health* 8, no. 4 (April 1988): 424.

15. R. Faden and N. Kass, "Health Insurance and AIDS: The Status of State Regulatory Activity," *American Journal of Public Health* 8, no. 4 (April 1988): 437.

16. "The Nation's Health," American Public Health Association, February 1988, p. 8.

17. James R. Kimmery, "Health Services: Public Health Programs", *Encyclopedia of Social Work*, 16th edition, (New York: National Association of Social Workers, 1971), p. 561.

18. U. S. General Accounting Office; Human Resources Division, *Medicaid Interstate Variations in Benefits and Expenditures*, May 1987.

19. Case Example: *Des Moines Register*, March 4, 1988, p. 8A.

20. "The Indian Health Program of the USPHS," DHEW Publication No. (HSA) 78-100-3, p. 19.

21. Virginia Insley, "Health Services: Maternal and Child Health," *Encyclopedia of Social Work*, 17th ed. (Washington, D.C.: National Association of Social Workers, 1977), p. 603.

22. Ibid., p. 604.

23. Ibid., p. 607.

24. "A Letter from the Administrator," Thomas K. Turvage, Administrator of Veterans' Affairs, 1988 (provided by Annie Tuttle, Staff Assistant for Community Relations, V.A. Medical Center, Iowa City, Iowa, April 15, 1988).

25. *Kiplinger Washington Letter* 65, no. 15 (April 15, 1988).

26. Case Example: *Des Moines Register*, August 27, 1986, p. 2A.

27. Anne Somers and N. Herman, *Health and Health Care: Policies in Perspective* (Germantown, Md.: Aspen Systems Corp., 1977), p. 107.

28. C. Carl Pegels, *Health Care and the Elderly* (Germantown, Md.: Aspen Systems Corp., 1980), p. 13.

29. Ibid.

30. Case Example contributed by Dan Grinstead, MSW, ACSW, Division Supervisor, Department of Social Service, University of Iowa Hospitals and Clinic.

31. Jack Kasten, "Health Care System: Group Medical Practice," *Encyclopedia of Social Work*, 17th ed. (Washington, D.C.: National Association of Social Workers, 1977), p. 581.

32. Helen I. Marieskind, *Women in the Health System: Patients, Providers and Programs* (St. Louis: C. V. Mosby Company, 1980), p. 291.

33. Ibid., p. 296.

34. Sylvia Schild, "Health Services: Genetic Counseling," *Encyclopedia of Social Work*, 17th ed. (Washington, D.C.: National Association of Social Workers, 1977), p. 591.

35. Daniel Schorr, *Don't Get Sick in America* (Nashville, Tenn.: Aurora Publishers, 1970), p. 98.

36. Richard C. Cabot, *Social Work: Essays on the Meeting Ground of Doctor and Social Worker* (New York: Houghton Mifflin, 1919), p. xxv.

37. Grace White, "Distinguishing Characteristics of Medical Social Work," *Readings in Theory and Practice of Medical Social Work*, ed. Dora Goldstine et al. (Chicago: University of Chicago Press, 1954); Beatrice Hall, "The Role of Social Service in the Public Health Program," ibid., pp. 90–99; Beatrice Phillips, "Social Workers in Health Services," *Encyclopedia of Social Work*, 16th ed., 1971; Bertram Black, Jr., "Social Work in Health and Mental Health Services," *Social Casework* 52, no. 4 (April 1971); Alice Varela, Ethel Christian, and Ann Gullian, "A Social Work Program Plan," paper presented at American Public Health Association Annual Meeting, Chicago, Illinois, October 1976; Barbara Hove, Katherine A. Kruse, and Jim L. Wilson, "The Social Worker's Role in Family Practice Education," *Journal of Family Practice* 8, no. 3 (March 1979); *Social Work in Health Care*, ed. Neil F. Bracht (New York: Haworth Press, 1978); Joan Gehrka and Shirley Wattenberg, "Assessing Social Services in Nursing Homes," *Health and Social Work* 6, no. 2 (May 1981); NASW, Inc., *Social Work: Careers in Health* (1978); American Hospital Association, *Essentials of Social Work Programs in Hospitals* (1971).

38. Case Example contributed by Jan Holland, MSW, University of Iowa Hospitals and Clinics, Iowa City, Iowa.

39. Bertha L. Doremus, "The Four R's: Social Diagnosis as Health Care," *Health and Social Work* 1, no. 4 (November 1976).

40. Case Example contributed by Greg Jensen, ACSW, LSW, University of Iowa Hospitals and Clinics, Iowa City, Iowa.

41. Stuart Spickler, ed., "Prospective Payment: DRG's and Ethics," *Journal of Medicine and Philosophy*, 12, no. 2, (May 1987).

42. Marie E. Cowart, "Policy Issues: Financial Reimbursement for Home Care," *Family and Community Health* 8, no. 2 (August 1985).

43. R. J. Gordon, G. McMullen, B. D. Weiss, and A. W. Nichols, "The Effect of Malpractice Liability on the Delivery of Rural Obstetrical Care," *Journal of Rural Health* 3, no. 1 (January 1987): 7.

44. Julian J. Sebastian, "Homelessness: A State of Vulnerability," *Family and*

Community Health 8, no. 3 (November 1985): 19–23.
45. Joan G. Turner and Erica R. Pryor, "The AIDS Epidemic: Risk Containment for Home Health Care Providers," *Family and Community Health* 8, no. 3 (November 1985): 35.
46. Kurt Reichert, "Market System Penetration of Health and Social Welfare Services: Implications for Social Work Education," Paper presented at Annual Meeting on Social Work Education, February–March 1977.
47. Ralph Dolgoff, "Clinicians as Social Policy Makers," *Social Casework* 62, no. 5 (May 1981): 292.

ADDITIONAL SUGGESTED READINGS

Azarnoff, Pat, and Carol Hardgrove, eds., *The Family in Child Health Care* (New York: John Wiley & Sons, 1981).

Burns, Eveline M., *Health Services for Tomorrow: Trends and Issues* (New York: Dunellen Publishing Co., 1973).

Cornacchia, Harold J., and Stephen Barrett, *Consumer Health: A Guide to Intelligent Decisions* (St. Louis: C. V. Mosby Co., 1980).

Ducanis, Alex J., and Anne K. Colin, *The Interdisciplinary Health Care Team* (Germantown, Md.: Aspen Systems Corp., 1979).

Field, Minna, *Patients Are People: A Medical-Social Approach to Prolonged Illness* (New York: Columbia University Press, 1953).

Frey, Louise A., ed., *Use of Groups in the Health Field* (New York: National Association of Social Workers, 1966).

Fuchs, Victor R., *Who Shall Live? Health Economics and Social Choice* (New York: Basic Books, 1974).

Germain, Carel B., *Social Work Practice in Health Care: An Ecological Perspective* (New York: Free Press, 1984).

Koff, Sandra Z., *Health Systems Agencies* (New York: Human Sciences Press, 1987).

Leukefeld, Carl G., and Manuel Fimbres, eds., *Responding to AIDS* (Silver Spring, Md.: NASW, 1987).

Lewellyn, Susan H., ed., *Encyclopedia of Social Work*, 18th ed. (Silver Spring, Md.: NASW, 1987).

Moos, Rudolph H., ed., *Coping with Physical Illness* (New York: Plenum Medical Book Co., 1979).

Silver, George A., *Child Health: America's Future* (Germantown, Md.: Aspen Systems Corp., 1978).

Woods, Nancy F., *Human Sexuality in Health and Illness* (St. Louis: C. V. Mosby Co., 1975).

9 Mental Health and Social Work

Verne R. Kelly

A view often expressed is that there is a single mental health/mental illness continuum with two opposite poles: mental health at one end and mental illness at the other. In this view much is not revealed: genetic endowment, biological conditions, nutrition, temperament, developmental stages, learned behavior, personality traits, cognitive factors, prior experiences, family communication styles, education level, socioeconomic statuses, unemployment, housing, neighborhood, race, ethnicity, gender, peer attitudes, family pressures, and other situational stresses that are unique to a particular individual. These influences act simultaneously on an individual who may have a greater or lesser array of capabilities and resources to call upon for coping with environmental stresses while attempting to lead an effective life. Actually, almost everyone can become emotionally disturbed at crucial points or crises in life.

EMOTIONAL DISTURBANCE

Because of the many influences and patterns involved in emotional disturbances, mental health literature, with good reason, seldom tries

to define such terms as "mental disorder." The definitions in the literature typically deal with classifications of types of mental disorders and
descriptions of characteristics and traits. A noted authority on the classification of mental disorders, Robert L. Spitzer, writes, "no definition
adequately specifies precise boundaries for the concept 'mental disorder' (this is also true for such concepts as physical disorder and mental
and physical health)."[1]

Thomas Szasz disputes the concept of mental illness. He claims that
it is a myth, an erroneous extrapolation from physical illness, in which
emotionally disturbed people are labeled as being "sick" inside and
needing treatment similar to those who are physically ill. The myth of
mental illness was created, Szasz asserts, out of the needs of social
human beings to scapegoat someone considered "mad," so that he
could "confirm himself as good."[2] Szasz also states that what psychotherapists are usually called upon to treat are "problems in living."[3]

Mental Health

Early attempts to define mental health began with looking at traits
exhibited by mental patients and then considering their opposite as
being characteristics of mental health. People with depression felt sad
and guilty; therefore, joyous and carefree behavior was a sign of good
mental health. Persons with neuroses were anxious and inhibited, so
that a "normal" person was gregarious and blithely self-confident. People who were "mentally healthy" seemed incapable of self-sacrifice,
which might mean they were having a depression. They did not worry
about world problems; to do so could mean that they were neurotic.[4]
Robert White prefers not to use the term "mental health" and instead
refers to "one's *confidence* of being able, when necessary, to have desired effects."[5]

In the author's view, White's suggestion leads us to think of competence in certain *capabilities*, such as:

- coping with problems of your children;
- coping with problems of your parents;
- coping with relationship problems;
- coping with conflicts at work;
- controlling spending;
- controlling use of tobacco, alcohol, and drugs;
- controlling temper;
- managing sexual behavior;
- improving rational thinking;
- improving assertiveness;
- improving racial fairness;

- improving thoughtfulness;
- improving self-understanding;
- expressing feelings constructively.

A person who is feeling confident in his or her competence in such capabilities would probably feel, and be regarded as being, in a good state of "mental health." Such capabilities also are sufficiently specific to serve as goals in psychotherapy.

Need for Services

Some of the oldest literature cites examples of persons with apparent emotional disturbances. For example, in the Old Testament, Saul, who may have suffered from manic-depressive psychosis, committed suicide.[6] Present-day studies have attempted to estimate the prevalence of emotional disturbance. It is not surprising that findings have varied considerably because they lack consensus on what is being measured and surveyed. In a Midtown Manhattan Study about 75 percent of the people surveyed had at least some degree of impairment.[7] In the Florida Health Study the prevalence of mental disorder was measured at about 28 percent.[8] The consistent finding in these surveys is that the prevalence of emotional disturbance increases with lower socioeconomic status. In another study, more schooling was found to lead to better health in general, controlling for variables of income and intelligence, and a year of schooling contributed about 1 percent to an index of health.[9] This study suggests that the relationship of schooling to mental health is an area that deserves research.

MENTAL HEALTH PROGRAMS AND SERVICES

The reaction of Western society to mental health problems is marked by ambivalence, both compassion and intolerance. The Old Testament taught social justice in temporal affairs and personal righteousness. Christians were exhorted to love and care for their families and to have compassion for their neighbors and for strangers.[10] Motivated by this ideal, mental hospitals were established. The first hospital established exclusively for treating people having mental disorders was founded in Jerusalem about A.D. 490.[11] The oldest mental hospital still operating is in Valencia, Spain; it opened in 1409.[12] In the Middle Ages, however, mental illness was also linked with witchcraft by two Dominican monks. Many people were tortured and executed as heretics based on the claim that they had freely embraced the devil as their master.[13]

This ambivalence has continued to the present day. On the side of compassion, centuries of therapeutic work, research, and advocacy have been devoted to helping people with mental illness and emotional problems. On the negative side, however, neglect, rejection, and skepticism have been simultaneously expressed, a flagrant current example being the "dumping" of mental patients out of mental hospitals into urban ghettos without adequate preparation or appropriate local services. The streets of most large American cities are now inhabited by numbers of homeless people, many of whom have chronic mental illnesses.

Many ideals have contributed to the development of mental health services. As noted by Hastings Rashdall, "Ideals pass into greater historic forces by embodying themselves in institutions."[14] Not only have the ideals of compassion and humane treatment motivated mental health services, but the ideals of professionalism (medicine, nursing, psychology, and social work), scientific research, and community care have also become established in mental health facilities. In a later section the roles of social workers in mental health facilities will be discussed.

Mental Hospitals and the First Mental Health Revolution

The first psychiatric hospital in the New World was built in Mexico in 1566. The first general hospital serving people with mental disorders was the Pennsylvania Hospital at Philadelphia, founded in 1752.[15] The first mental hospital in America was established at Williamsburg, Virginia, in 1773. The ideal of medical treatment and "moral treatment" were practiced during the colonial period. The Quaker physician, Benjamin Rush, who signed the Declaration of Independence and wrote the first American textbook on psychiatry, supported the ideal of "moral treatment." The proponents of "moral treatment" held that victims of mental illness were susceptible to morally "right" and humane influences. They taught the use of respect and courtesy with disturbed persons rather than torture and punishment. They established regimens of order and regularity and sought to develop self-respect and responsibility through work and worship. Most of the early mental hospitals did not actually deserve the name of hospital—they were merely places without treatment where people with mental illnesses were kept. Such were the institutions at London: Bethlehem ("Bedlam"), founded in 1247, and at Paris: Bicotre.[16] The emergence of hospitals with the ideals of treatment and humane care were prompted by Philippe Pinel in 1793 when he released people with mental illnesses from the chains of Bicotre and Salpetriere, the mental hospitals in Paris, an event often described as the "first mental health revolution." By 1851, "moral treatment" recovery rates were reported as high as 72 percent.[17] Many of the methods of "moral treatment" are still practiced today in concert with other methods.

Medical treatment of mentally ill persons is an ancient ideal. Insanity in the Talmud was regarded as a disease to be treated by a physician. In the fourth century B.C., Hippocrates described physical causes of "madness" and used diagnostic terms such as "melancholia" and "hysteria."[18] Medical treatment, as we know it now, had not advanced greatly by the mid-nineteenth century, but the ideal of hospital care, rather than jails and almshouses for the mentally ill, was being forcefully advocated by Dorothea Dix of Boston. She pioneered hospital care for the mentally ill in many states. In 1854 she persuaded Congress to enact a bill authorizing grants of public land for use in caring for persons who were mentally ill. President Franklin Pierce vetoed the bill, interpreting the general welfare clause of the U.S. Constitution as reserving such care to the states. This interpretation established a federal policy of nonintervention in social welfare until the various measures of the Great Depression such as the Social Security Act of 1935.[19] Fighting back from this defeat, Dix took her cause back to the individual states, and she won. By the turn of the century there were thirty-two state mental hospitals.[20]

The "success" of state mental hospitals caused them to be overused. Early in the twentieth century they started to fill up. Large, overcrowded, understaffed institutions became typical in this "snake pit" era. Average length of stay stretched out to many years, and care was almost entirely custodial. The large facilities had more negative than beneficial effects, and Dorothea Dix's ideal was shattered. While it became clear that new patterns of care were needed in local communities, many state mental hospitals improved their methods by using milieu therapy (the ideal that all aspects of the hospital, including all personnel, should be oriented to the treatment needs of patients), by instituting group methods, and by decentralization of inpatient units according to geographic areas.

Over a period of twenty-eight years, the number of people in residence in mental hospitals in the United States declined nearly 80 percent (from about 558,000 in 1955 to 117,000 in 1983).[21] This decline is dramatic, but there is still a need for state and county mental hospitals. The large decline in hospitalization is due partially to use of psychotropic drugs and increased community services. Psychiatric medications have played an important role in the community care of persons with chronic mental illnesses, but medications must be supplemented by community support services and residential and rehabilitation programs.

Most mental hospitals also provide outpatient services, which can help reduce the number of people who might otherwise need more costly inpatient care. The Veterans' Administration also operates general hospitals with psychiatric units as well as regional hospitals that provide psychiatric services exclusively. In 1985, Veterans' Administration psychiatric hospitals provided 9.4 percent of all inpatient care reported. Public and private general hospitals frequently include psychiatric units and in 1985 provided 45 percent of all inpatient care.

Dorothea Dix started the voluntary mental health movement, and her work was carried on by a recovered patient, Clifford Beers. He wrote an influential book in 1908, *The Mind That Found Itself,* and a year later he organized the National Committee for Mental Hygiene. He brought in professional and political leaders, and the movement spread. The World Federation for Mental Health (WFMH) was formed in 1948. The WFMH, a mental health coalition of individuals, professionals, and voluntary associations, is the only nongovernmental organization accredited in consultative status in mental health to all the relevant agencies of the United Nations. Another voluntary advocacy organization is the National Alliance for the Mentally Ill.

Sigmund Freud and the Second Mental Health Revolution

The ideal of understanding human motivation and behavior is probably older than the ancient Greek injunction, "Know thyself." It was not until the work of Sigmund Freud in the nineteenth and twentieth centuries that systematic knowledge and understanding began to emerge.

Freud studied the connections between the minds of children and minds of adults, and the associations between images of dreams and perceptions of reality. Freud's work is described as the "second mental health revolution" in attitudes and values regarding mental health. His work has been followed by theorists with different perceptions, such as Carl Rogers and B. F. Skinner, and the quest for understanding and knowledge continues.

Community Mental Health and the Third Mental Health Revolution

Recognizing that the resources of the federal government were needed, Congress in 1946 passed the National Mental Health Act. Its purposes were to help states to establish community mental health services and to fund research and the education of mental health professionals. The ideal motivating the community movement was that help could be delivered most effectively in the community or area where troubled people lived, where relevant concepts could be drawn from ecology, epidemiology, anthropology, public health, social systems theory, and community organization.

Mental health authorities were designated in each state to receive and allocate federal funds for the development of community mental health services. In some states the pattern of financing was that federal funds were used as "seed money" to encourage facility development with continuing operational budgets supported by local public funds and patient fees based on sliding scale of ability to pay. Elsewhere, state appropriations were authorized to match local funds on a continuing basis. Agreements or contracts were signed by local centers with the state for the provision of funds and inpatient and outpatient services. Community mental health centers operating under these origins function in many states. Social workers make up a substantial portion of the staffs of these centers, and they provide services of individual, group, and family psychotherapy, play therapy with children, after-care for former patients of mental hospitals, consultation and education, and administration. The impact of these centers and related services is strong.

In a major new development, Congress in 1955 enacted the Mental Health Study Act, setting the stage for President John F. Kennedy's "bold new approach."[22] The Mental Retardation Facilities and Community Health Centers Construction Act embodied this new concept of the federal role in community mental health delivery: development of comprehensive community mental health centers. These centers were to have a new mission to reduce dependence on state mental hospitals and to establish facilities in local communities offering a wide range of services, including inpatient, outpatient, partial hospitalization, emergency, consultation, and education services. The ideal behind this legislation was that therapeutic care in local communities should replace custodial care in mental hospitals. Key concepts were geographic responsibility, comprehensiveness, continuity, accessibility, responsiveness, community involvement, and prevention. The development of comprehensive community mental health centers has been called the third revolution in mental health, the creation of an integrated facility where everyone could find skilled help for a wide range of emotional and mental problems regardless of age, gender, race, ethnic disadvantages, color, national origin, diagnosis, or ability to pay. The goal of the program was to establish 1,500 comprehensive community mental health centers; by 1980, 789 were in place. The roles of social workers in these programs are similar to those noted in community mental health centers described above.

The community movement has been very effective in shifting the proportion of patient care from inpatient to outpatient services. In 1955, 77.4 percent of all patient services were provided by inpatient facilities, and 22.6 percent were outpatient. In 1979, only 28 percent of patient services occurred in inpatient facilities, while 72 percent were provided on an outpatient basis, almost a complete reversal of the historic reliance on institutional care. This trend is unlikely to be reversed.

Community facilities are available in most urban locations, and new ones are being developed in rural areas. The concept of community care has expanded beyond that originally established in President Kennedy's 1963 legislation. Advocacy and case management provided by community support services have grown as well as the importance of support networks. The instrumental roles that office staff play in the delivery of services are finding greater recognition, and many office staff members have developed advanced skills.

Rural mental health and other human services still lag far behind their urban counterparts.[23] The President's Commission on Mental Health Task Panel on Rural Mental Health stated that rural areas have unique mental health needs because they have higher rates of psychiatric disorders, particularly depression, severe intergenerational conflicts, an acceptance of fatalistic attitudes, and minimal belief that change is possible. Outreach programs to rural elderly are particularly needed.[24]

University Training and Research Facilities

After World War I extensive development began of university mental health facilities devoted to research, education, and service. Usually located in major research universities, these programs are typically under the auspices of medical colleges and psychology departments, in conjunction with schools of social work and nursing. Social workers in these facilities are usually employed as university staff although in some institutions they may have faculty appointments. Roles of social workers usually include research, service, and supervision of graduate practicum students.

Military Social Work

During World War II over 700 social workers participated in the armed services military social work programs. Psychiatric social work was established as a military occupational specialty in 1943, and social workers served in enlisted status in mental hygiene clinics and in psychiatric units of hospitals. Shortly after the end of the war social workers were commissioned as officers, acquiring the same professional level that had existed for lawyers and physicians.

Today, active social work programs are established in the navy, the

air force, and the army. The programs include drug and alcohol rehabilitation, hospital mental health services, community mental health
clinics, and community services for personal and family problems of
armed forces personnel.[25]

Private Practice

Private practice of social workers and other mental health professionals is growing in both urban and rural areas. Sometimes social
workers are in independent private practice, and sometimes they are
employed in a private firm with psychiatrists and psychologists. They
may work out of an office or provide services in a psychiatric unit of a
community general hospital. The most frequent type is part-time private practice, while the social worker is employed full time in a community facility or agency. The standards of the social work profession
are that practitioners in private practice should attain a Master of Social
Work degree from an educational program accredited by the Council
on Social Work Education (CSWE) and be certified by the Academy of
Certified Social Workers (ACSW). The National Association of Social
Work (NASW) maintains a register of clinical social workers in which
many private practitioners are listed. State licensure or registration of
social workers is now provided in most states, and it is often required
for social workers seeking third-party fee payments.

Alcoholism and Drug Abuse Services

Alcoholism and drug abuse services are sometimes organized in
conjunction with community mental health facilities. Such services
often include detoxification, emergency services, individual counseling, group and family therapy, referral to self-help groups, and referral to vocational guidance and occupational rehabilitation and
other needed services. This subject is discussed in greater detail in
the next chapter.

Prevention and the Fourth Mental Health Revolution

Prevention of emotional disorders has been called the fourth and
most exciting revolution in mental health. It has been a difficult service to establish, and we stand only at the threshold. Research is sorely
needed before prevention of genetic and biological determinants of
mental illness can be anticipated. In problems of interpersonal relationships, progress is being made through education and training. Interpersonal Cognitive Problem Solving (ICPS) skills, couples commu-

nication, assertiveness, and parent effectiveness training and others are prevention activities in which social workers have made an impact.

Primary prevention is proactive, seeking to build adaptive strengths and coping resources. It is concerned with the total population as well as with specific groups at risk. Its main tools are education and social engineering. It assumes that the best way to ward off maladaptive problems is to equip people with the personal and environmental resources for successful coping. The President's Commission on Mental Health noted that research had supported the efficacy of "Three main areas of primary prevention in mental health: (a) competency training and emphasizing developmental approaches, (b) the impact of social systems on individual development, and (c) the reduction and management of naturally occurring life developmental stresses."[26] While there is considerable support for primary prevention, not enough is being accomplished partly because there are few linkage institutions that have prevention as their mission and include the collection, integration, evaluation, and dissemination of prevention knowledge in their goals.[27]

Tora Kay Bikson has synthesized the literature concerning knowledge transfer and has detailed specific capabilities for linkage institutions.[28]

- Searching for, locating, and retrieving information.
- Synthesizing the retrieved information.
- Translating research into practical advice.
- Facilitating interactions among providers and users of knowledge for the purpose of implementation.

A program with potential for building positive mental health in children is called Invent America!, a program of the nonprofit United States Patent Model Foundation in Washington, D.C. This national campaign stimulates invention and creativity among children and youth by sponsoring invention contests. Many states cooperate with Invent America! with statewide programs. Invention Conventions are the idea of Marion Canedo, a Buffalo, New York, grade school administrator, who had been searching for a way to stimulate her children to think more creatively within the normal school curriculum.[29] While Invent America! was not conceived as a positive mental health program, it has that potential not only for the children involved but also for their families. It offers children another avenue besides sports and academics to build positive self-esteem. Creativity and inventiveness are not necessarily related to academic skills, and recognition of them can reach a different group of children who otherwise might go unnoticed in their schools or even by their parents.

Primary prevention of emotional disorders is a time-consuming and complex challenge. It must be approached through a concerted and integrated effort rather than through small research projects and isolated programs. While the costs are substantial, the potential reward is a more effective and healthier next generation.

Helping Disadvantaged Children

Society is discovering that an approach that works is helping poor children in their earliest months and years of life. In the 1960s, the Perry Preschool Project in Ypsilanti, Michigan, began preschool programs for three-year-old children with below average IQs from poor homes. Researchers followed 123 of these children until their nineteenth birthdays and found that they did remarkably well. They graduated from high schools and went on to higher education or to jobs at twice the rate of children who did not have preschool education. They also had fewer detentions, teenage pregnancies, and arrests. Early education enhances the children's sense of control and confidence.[30] An editorial in *The New York Times* followed:

> All the more reason not to wait until a child is 3 or 4 years old. Why not start with prenatal care for frightened mothers, often children themselves? Why not provide classes in basic skills for fathers? An array of such services could save three children at once: The teen-age mother, her baby and the child she is persuaded to defer at least until she has finished school and gained both maturity and job skills. ... Spend Where It Counts—Americans are generous about social welfare when they know it works, as with Head Start and food stamps. ... Why should they react differently to early childhood intervention? Because it is known to work. ... Imagine a baby girl born into inner-city poverty today, to a teenage mother. With an early childhood program, she's more likely to be born healthy; her mother could give her better care; and early schooling would enlarge her self-confidence. In 16 years, she'd probably be starting her last year in high school and have ambitions for the future. Without such a program, she's all too likely to have something else: a baby. And the heavy cycle will start again.[31]

A committee of top corporation executives has recommended:[32]

1. Prenatal and postnatal care for pregnant teenagers and for other high-risk mothers as well as follow-up health care for their infants.
2. Parenthood education programs for both mothers and fathers, including guidance on nutrition.
3. Quality child-care arrangements for poor working parents that stress social development and school readiness.
4. Quality preschool programs for all disadvantaged three- and four-year-olds.

Unless such programs as these are implemented, one wonders how far prevention programs can go, considering the destructive impact of poverty on so many children. The poorest segment of the nation's population is children, who are seven times more likely than those over sixty-five to be poor. Poverty is most likely for those children who live in single-parent families headed by women.[33] While two-thirds of poor children are white, both blacks and Hispanics are much more likely to live in poverty: 43 percent of black children and 40 percent of Hispanic children are poor.[34] Poor children suffer more frequently from almost every form of childhood deficiency, including infant mortality, malnutrition, recurrent and untreated health problems, psychological and physical stress, child abuse, and learning disabilities.

Another report cites savings created by investments in prevention projects.[35] Some cost-effective programs are:

1. In the Women, Infant, and Children (WIC) Supplemental Food Program and in prenatal care, a dollar can save $3.00 in short-term hospital costs and $3.38 in cost of low birthweight infants because the programs can increase birthweight and can reduce infant mortality and premature births.
2. A dollar spent on childhood immunization can save $10.00 in later medical costs because it reduces rubella, mumps, measles, polio, diphtheria, tetanus, and pertussis (whooping cough).
3. A dollar spent on preschool education can save $4.75 in later social costs because it increases school success and reduced dependence.
4. Five hundred dollars invested in compensatory education can save the $3,000 cost of repeating a grade.
5. Early educational intervention has saved school districts $1,560 per disabled pupil.
6. Youth employment and training through the Job Corps returned $7,400 per participant, compared to $5,000 in program costs.

Without early intervention of the kind recommended in these reports the volume of these disadvantaged children will continue to grow and create a permanent underclass of people lacking literacy and job skills.

Another kind of disadvantaged children are latchkey children, school-age youngsters who lack adult supervision part of the day because of divorce, unwed motherhood, and the two-career family. Of mothers whose youngest child is between six and thirteen years old, nearly three-quarters are employed. A Lou Harris poll of teachers indicated that lack of after-school supervision was the primary cause of poor school performance. Employers report that productivity drops after 3 P.M.. when parents receive calls from their children at home.[36]

Only a small portion of companies offer child care at the worksite. In California the state pays local school districts, parks departments, and nonprofit agencies to provide after-school care. San Francisco requires new companies to provide on-site care or contribute to a municipal fund that provides centers.

Nontraditional Mental Health Programs

In a variety of nontraditional mental health services social workers have carried significant responsibilities. Community support systems are organized to assist people who have major mental illnesses but who can function in the community if they have the help they need. Such help is provided by mental health professionals supplemented by case managers. A case manager may arrange for unscheduled walk-in appointments with therapists; provide assistance in locating housing, employment, and education; work with families, churches, and volunteer organizations; and engage in advocacy with bureaucracies in helping people qualify for financial aid and governmental service.

Emotional support during disasters is a service that community mental health centers can provide.[37] Services are organized to help people with the shock of tornadoes, floods, earthquakes, and other disasters. Psychosocial problems associated with disasters can include: initial numbing of senses, hysteria, intrusive thoughts (nightmares and rumination), and avoidance struggles (grieving, death anxiety, and anger). Mental health professionals can help people work through these feelings and come to "a sense of survivorship and feeling of strength," rather than "psychic numbing."[38]

Telephone and walk-in crisis centers, typically staffed by trained volunteers, offer emergency and short-term assistance for people with a variety of problems: feeling lonely, depressed, or angry, or seeking referral information. A person who has impulsively swallowed many pills may call a crisis center for help in getting emergency medical care. The staff of crisis centers often includes social workers who may administer the center and organize training for the volunteers.

Women's centers are operated in many parts of the country to provide a variety of services, such as support groups, assertiveness training, advocacy, and lobbying. In some areas women's centers have been instrumental in developing programs for rape prevention and support of rape victims, and development of spouse abuse shelters. Social workers are often prominent in these programs.

Mental Retardation Programs and Services

Social workers are active in helping mentally retarded people and their families. Most of these services are in the community because only about 4 percent of the people with mental retardation are afflicted to the extent that they need care in state hospitals, schools, or other institutions. There is a variety of community services under various stages of development in the United States, for example, special education in public and private schools, foster family homes, group homes, boarding homes, and halfway houses. The national average rate of persons with mental retardation in state-operated facilities in 1985 was 46.8 per 100,000 population, a decline to about half the rate of 1965.[39] Many mentally retarded people live in private residences, their own homes, or with their families. Many are employed, either in regular jobs or sheltered workshops, and some are eligible for Social Security benefits.

Important in the development of community services are groups of citizens who are organized for advocacy, lobbying, and volunteer services. Social workers have joined in these efforts by staffing community agencies and residential facilities, some in direct services to individuals and families, and some in program development and coordination of community services.

THE ROLE OF SOCIAL WORK IN MENTAL HEALTH

The usual professions in mental health are social work, psychiatry, psychiatric nursing, and psychology. Members of these professions usually share a commitment: the desire to help people with mental and emotional problems. Social workers often serve as a benevolent and caring arm of a mental health facility, as humanizers.

Psychiatric social work, which is simply social work practiced in psychiatric and mental health programs or setting, developed from two historical roots: hospitals and child guidance clinics. It began in 1905 at Boston's Massachusetts General Hospital, and in Bellevue Hospital and Cornell Clinic in New York City. In 1906 psychiatric social workers were hired by the Manhattan State Hospital in New York City where they visited patients' families to obtain information on background and life experiences. Later they also performed the function of preparing families and patients for their return home. The principle that treatment of the patient should be performed by a team of peers including social workers and doctors was enunciated in 1912 by Dr. Richard L. Cabot, a faculty member of the Harvard Medical

School. At the Boston Psychopathic Hospital in 1913 under the leadership of Mary G. Jarrett, psychiatric social work was given its distinctive name.

Another root in the development of psychiatric social work was in child guidance clinics. Based on early work with juvenile delinquents by Dr. William Healy, demonstration child guidance clinics were started in 1922 at Norfolk, Virginia, and St. Louis. In these facilities, the social worker treated the family, and the doctor treated the child who was the patient. Today there is considerable overlapping of these activities. The development of community facilities that are exclusively for child guidance has declined. The current trend is to establish community mental health centers providing a range of services including those for children.

The term "psychiatric social work" is in decline, and current usage tends to favor "clinical social work." The National Association of Social Workers publishes a national register of clinical social workers, which has specific professional requirements for listing. Schools of social work now prepare students along generic lines rather than graduating students who are exclusively psychiatric social workers or group workers, for example, as was the practice a few decades ago.

Courtesy Universal City Studios, Inc.

The 1989 movie "Dream Team" treated seriously, within a comedic framework, the problems of four institutionalized mental patients. Here the character of Dr. Weitzman (on left) conducts a group therapy session.

Social workers in mental health facilities typically serve on multidisciplinary teams and may provide services of individual, group, and family psychotherapy, consultation, establishing links with community services and groups, advocacy, and administration. In inpatient facilities, social workers are often the persons in contact with patients and their families to assist them in making plans for patients' return home and for referral to community services for after-care. In outpatient facilities social workers provide a variety of psychotherapeutic services, consultation, education, community organization, and administration. Typically there is much overlap and diffusion of roles with other members of the professional staff. Social workers serve as case managers and coordinators of community support systems. The role of social workers as administrators of mental health facilities is extensive. Of the 763 federally assisted comprehensive community mental health centers, more than a third have a social worker as the executive director. This person almost always has a master's degree.

Trends and Issues

Some current trends and issues are: (1) the self-help movement, (2) a balance between prevention and treatment, (3) centralization of authority, (4) private contracting, (5) accountability, (6) diagnostic labeling, (7) patients' civil rights, and (8) deinstitutionalization.

Self-help movements are growing in western Europe and the United States. Conceptually, the self-help movement appears to lie between professional mental health services and natural helper networks. Natural helpers are people who are not mental health professionals but who, by virtue of their occupation or leadership roles, are sought out by people wanting help.[40] Self-help groups allow troubled people to contact others who are like themselves. There are many kinds of self-help groups—for example, survivors of suicide attempts or families who have had a member commit suicide, bereaved parents who have had children die, and former inpatients of mental hospitals. Mental health professionals can facilitate self-help groups by providing them with consultation and referrals.

A balance is needed between prevention efforts and treatment. In most mental health facilities, prevention has received little attention in program planning and budgeting. There is no doubt that mental health facilities must try to meet current demands; yet, they need to look ahead and invest some of their funds for future generations. For example, what can a mental health facility do to aid in the development of curricula for primary grade children to teach them some concepts of family functioning and competent living?

Centralization of authority can be detrimental to the exercise of professional judgment, for example, restrictions on the number of treatment interviews allowed for patients. Yet there are broad substantive issues that are the appropriate concern of a central authority, for example, a state governing body that is responsible for a statewide or federal program. To balance the best of both central and local authority requires good teamwork between a central authority and local facilities.

Some local governments are turning over mental health services to private contractors, for example, social workers and other helping professionals in private practice, and are dissolving offices where large numbers of staff were formerly employed. While this may be bad news for public sector employment, it is part of a larger trend to view human relations and educational services as central features of modern life.[41]

Pressure has been building in recent years for an additional kind of accountability to funding bodies such as United Way and local government for private centers, and to state legislatures, federal grants, and others for public hospitals and other facilities. Traditionally, mental health facilities have accounted for the proper spending of funds to substantiate public trust. Recently, mental health facilities have also been pressured to provide evidence that their services are effective, which has raised other issues. Reliable measures of organization and treatment effectiveness are still being developed. Sometimes accountability methods jeopardize principles of patient confidentiality and professional autonomy. On the other hand, the expectation of demonstrated treatment effectiveness deserves careful attention and committed effort.

Diagnostic classification of mental disorders is a recurrent issue. Diagnoses reported to insurance companies and computer data systems have possibilities for "labeling" a person for life. Yet, charges to insurance companies need to be substantiated, and computer data systems are needed for accountability. Safeguards must be observed, and at minimum the patient's informed consent to the submission of such information should be obtained.[42] Robert Spitzer takes note of the problem of labeling and writes:

> A common misconception is that a classification of mental disorders classifies people, when actually what are being classified are disorders that people have. For this reason, the text of DSM-III-R (as did the text of DSM-III) avoids the use of such expressions as "a Schizophrenic" or "an alcoholic," and instead uses the more accurate, but admittedly more cumbersome, "a person with Schizophrenia" or "a person with Alcohol Dependence."[43]

The civil rights of patients have strengthened during the past decade. Mental disorder is an insufficient basis for involuntary hospitalization unless the person is in need of inpatient treatment and care and appears to present a danger to her or his own life or safety, or to others.

Recent court rulings have held that the inpatient has a right to treatment in the least restrictive setting available. The trend to strengthen the civil rights of mental patients is a positive contrast with a frightening practice in the Soviet Union to use mental hospitalization for political detention. Disobedience or resistance to official policies can be regarded as an "abnormal" condition requiring "psychiatric treatment." Recently, however, the United States and the Soviet Union are moving toward an agreement that would permit American psychiatrists to visit Soviet mental hospitals to determine if dissidents are being imprisoned in the hospitals.

The practice of deinstitutionalization, that is, the transfer of mental patients from hospital custodial care to community treatment, is being questioned in many places where there have been excesses and indifference. Patients had been released (dumped) upon communities that lacked the facilities to care for them. Neglect and misery have resulted for many people, reminiscent of the conditions decried by Dorothea Dix in the mid-nineteenth century. Some of the suggestions advanced have been the strengthening of local programs with the development of community support systems, and more humanitarian and judicious policies for discharge and release to community living.

Illustration of Clinical Social Work Practice

A sixteen-year-old boy was referred to a rural community mental health center because of conflicts at home and at school. The precipitating event was that in the space of one week he had "totaled" his own car in an accident and had driven his parents' pickup truck into a roadside ditch. For some time he had been associating with friends his parents disapproved of because of their use of alcohol and marijuana. He was failing at school. In contrast, his older brother was doing well in high school and was compliant at home.

The parents and their two adolescent sons lived on a farm owned by the mother's parents. All three generations of the family—the maternal grandparents, the parents, and the adolescent boys—lived together on the farm. The social worker decided to work with the three-generational family, rather than focusing only upon the youngest boy. The goal of family therapy was to help the family function better. The theoretical model followed was structural family therapy, derived from social systems theory, as developed by Salvador Minuchin.[44] One of the concepts of structural family therapy is that the maintenance of generational boundaries were deteriorating.

The grandmother appeared to be in a menopausal depression

and seemed to be disengaged from the rest of the family. The grandfather was emotionally invested in the farm, and he also sold seed corn. Both occupations kept him out of the home for long hours, and he did not seem to notice that his wife was depressed. He was also ignoring his earlier promise to his son-in-law to turn over the farm to him gradually. The father believed he was being treated like a hired hand and felt denigrated, but when he complained to his wife, she defended the grandfather. The father also seemed to be disengaging from the family and appeared to be developing a drinking problem. The mother and the oldest son were very close, and she saw him as her "good" son. She was very proud of him. She viewed the younger boy as her "bad" son and despaired of his future. He, too, was disengaging from the family. Since the parents were not working together well, he was evading their influence.

The clinical social worker's goal was to try to realign the family along generational boundaries so that it could function better. Family therapy was a partial success. The grandmother obtained treatment for her depression, and the grandfather spent more time with her. The grandfather did not release his hold on the farm. The father's dream was shattered, he drank more, he refused treatment for it, and the parents eventually divorced. The mother and the two boys stayed at the farm. She became a waitress at a truck stop on the interstate highway and met another man. The oldest boy started dating and became less enmeshed with his mother. The youngest boy dropped out of high school but later obtained a GED (General Educational Development certificate) and enrolled in a course on auto mechanics at the community college. The period of time involved in working with the family was about five years. Most of the interviews occurred in the first few months, followed by occasional follow-up contacts as requested.

Future

The future of mental health programs and services will depend considerably upon the role the federal government takes, developments in domestic and international arenas, and developments in knowledge and practices of the mental health professions. Even though the political life of the United States has shown a definite conservative trend, it seems probable that the pendulum will swing back. Federal financial support for human services has been reduced and focused toward state and local governments through decentralized block grants. It is important that the mental health professions continue in their dedication, sense of direction, and discipline to make mental health programs work better and maintain their determination to serve people in the best ways they know. With the basic strength of our economy and with the inherent resiliency of our society and its compassion and humanitarian ideals, support for human services will eventually strengthen. Teamwork through coalitions with selected groups will be needed for more effective lobbying and political action.

The shape of mental health programs could depend on events on domestic and international fronts. In the event of military crises and large-scale mobilization of armed forces, federal support would likely be channeled toward those local communities with significant military installations and to military mental health programs. In the event of major civil disturbances in metropolitan areas, the present outmigration from urban to rural localities could be hastened and create new demands on urban and rural local governments. In either military or domestic crises, it is likely that there will be insufficient numbers of mental health professionals. These events would produce great pressures on mental health professions and academic programs for innovation. The need for networks of natural helpers, volunteers, and self-help groups would grow. Mental health facilities would need to develop liaison and communication in towns and neighborhoods. Such programs would need to be well conceived and well organized, and would need provision for case managers and discretionary emergency funds and supplies in association with professional mental health consultants. A renewed role for state mental hospitals could also emerge for help in coping with increased mental and emotional problems precipitated by population dislocations.

Administration Social Work Practice in Mental Health

A community mental health center was scheduled for a site visit for its reaccreditation by a state agency. A new feature of the site visit procedure was a review of a small sample of confidential clinical records to assess compliance with accreditation standards.

There was no question that the state agency had the legal authority to review the records. The professional staff of the center, however, had made commitments of confidentiality to the people they served, which they felt they could not ethically ignore. The administrator of the center was bound by the Code of Ethics of the National Association of Social Workers regarding confidentiality. Also at issue was the possibility of lawsuits concerning invasion of privacy or breach of contract.

The administrator of the center sought a problem-solving pattern of collaboration with the state agency. Communication between the two parties led to a solution meeting the requirements of both sides. The community mental health center contacted the persons whose records might be sampled. The issue was described to them, and they were asked to sign statements either of permission or of nonpermission for their records to be in the sample. Of the people contacted 80 percent signed statements of permission. The state agency agreed to pass over those records of persons who had signed a statement of nonpermission. The site visit was smoothly and professionally managed, and the center was reaccredited. A further agreement was reached that all new persons served would be advised by the community mental health center about the procedure as a preparation step for the next reaccreditation site visit.

SUMMARY AND CONCLUSIONS

This chapter has tried to indicate the wide variety of services and programs that can be considered under the general rubric of mental health. Because of the many forces involved when people become disturbed, there are a multitude of helping services and patterns of care. The versatility of social workers as well as their skill and concern are particularly valuable in mental health programs. A person entering mental health social work should really care about disturbed people and want to help them.

NOTES

1. American Psychiatric Association, *Diagnostic and Statistical Manual of Mental Disorders*, 3rd ed., revised (Washington, D.C.: American Psychiatric Association, 1987). Used with permission.
2. Thomas Szasz, *The Manufacture of Madness* (New York: Dell Publishing Co., 1970), p. 290.
3. Thomas Szasz, *The Myth of Mental Illness: Foundations of a Theory of Personal Conduct* (New York: Harper & Row, 1961), p. 308.
4. Robert W. White, "The Concept of Healthy Personality: What Do We Really Mean?" *The Counseling Psychologist* 4, no. 2 (1973): 5–6.
5. Ibid., p. 10.
6. 1 Samuel 31.
7. Leo Srole, Thomas S. Langner, Stanley T. Michael, Price Kirkpatrick, Marvin K. Opler, and Thomas A.C. Rennie, *Mental Health in the Metropolis* (New York: New York University Press, 1978).

8. John J. Schwab, Roger A. Bell, and George J. Warheit, *Social Order and Mental Health* (New York: Brunner/Mazel, 1979).

9. Michael Grossman, "The Correlation between Health and Schooling," *Household Production and Consumption*, ed. Nestor E. Terleckyj (New York: National Bureau of Economic Research, Columbia University Press, 1975), pp. 147–223.

10. James Leiby, "Social Welfare: History of Basic Ideas," *Encyclopedia of Social Work*, 17th ed. (Washington, D.C.: NASW, 1977), p. 1513.

11. N.D.C. Lewis, *A Short History of Psychiatric Achievement* (New York: W.W. Norton, 1941).

12. J. Andriola and G. Cata, "The Oldest Mental Hospital in the World," *Hospital and Community Psychiatry*, 1969, pp. 20, 42–43.

13. Philip M. Margolis and Armando R. Favazza, "Mental Health and Illness," *Encyclopedia of Social Work*, 17th ed. (Washington, D.C.: NASW, 1977), p. 851.

14. Hastings Rashdall, *The Universities of Europe in the Middle Ages* (Oxford: Clarendon Press, 1895).

15. Paul V. Lemkau, "The Historical Background," in *Public Mental Health: Perspectives and Prospects* (Beverly Hills, Calif.: Sage Publications, 1982).

16. Gregory Zilboorg, *A History of Medical Psychology* (New York: W.W. Norton, 1941).

17. Bertram J. Black, "Milieu Therapy," *Encyclopedia of Social Work*, 17th ed. (Washington, D.C.: NASW, 1977), pp. 921–922.

18. Margolis and Favazza, "Mental Health," p. 851.

19. Chauncey A. Alexander, "History of Social Work and Social Welfare: Significant Dates," *Encyclopedia of Social Work*, 18th ed. (Silver Spring, Md.: NASW, 1987) 1:778.

20. Bernard L. Bloom, *Community Mental Health* (Monterey, Calif.: Brooks/Cole Publishing Co., 1977), p. 11.

21. Steven Greene et al., "State and County Mental Hospitals, United States, 1982–83 and 1983–1984, with Trend Analyses for 1973–74 to 1983–84," *Mental Health Statistical Note No. 176* (Washington, D.C.: U.S. Department of Health and Human Services, National Institute of Mental Health, September 1986), p. 5.

22. John F. Kennedy, "Message from the President of the United States Relative to Mental Illness and Mental Retardation," February 5, 1963 (Washington, D.C.: U.S. Government Printing Office, 1963).

23. President's Commission on Mental Health, *Task Panel on Rural Mental Health*. (Washington, D.C.: U.S. Government Printing Office, 1978), vol. 3, appendix.

24. Kathleen C. Buckwalter et al., "Mental Health of the Rural Elderly Outreach Program: A Unique Health Care Delivery System," unpublished monograph.

25. Peter J. McNalis, "Military Social Work, *Encyclopedia of Social Work*, 18th ed. (Silver Spring, Md.: NASW, 1987), 1:154–161.

26. *The President's Commission on Mental Health*, (Washington, D.C.: U.S.

Government Printing Office, 1978), vol. 4, appendix.

27. Janice Wood Wetzel, "Forging the Missing Link in Social Work," paper presented at the Council on Social Work Education Annual Program Meeting, Detroit, Michigan, March 4, 1984.

28. Tora Kay Bikson, "Getting It Together: Gerontological Research and the Real World" (Santa Monica, Calif.: Rand Corporation, March 1980).

29. Allysa A. Lappen, *Forbes*, April 6, 1987.

30. Lawrence J. Schweinhart, "Effects of the Perry Preschool Program on Youth Through Age 19: A Summary," *Early Childhood Special Education Quarterly* 5, no. 2 (1985): 26–35.

31. *The New York Times*, September 6, 1987, p. 14E

32. Committee for Economic Development, Research and Policy Committee, *Children in Need: Investment Strategies for the Educationally Disadvantaged* (New York and Washington, D.C.: Author, 1987).

33. Daniel Patrick Moynihan, *Family and Nation* (San Diego, Calif.: Harcourt Brace Jovanovich, 1986).

34. *Children and Their Families: Current Conditions and Recent Trends*, (Washington, D.C.: U.S. Government Printing Office, 1987).

35. U.S. House of Representatives, Select Committee on Children, Youth and Families, *Opportunities for Success: Cost-Effective Programs for Children* (Washington, D.C., August 14, 1985).

36. Robert Reinhold, *The New York Times*, October 4, 1987, p. 4E.

37. Trudy I. Kattner, *The Shock of Disaster* (Des Moines, Iowa: Iowa State Department of Health, Office for Health Planning and Development, 1980.

38. Ibid., p. 14.

39. U.S. Bureau of Census, *Statistical Abstract of the United States, 1988*, 108th ed. (Washington, D.C.: U.S. Government Printing Office, 1987), p. 103.

40. Verne R. Kelley, Patricia L. Kelley, Eugene F. Gauron, and Edna I. Rawlings, "Training Helpers in Rural Mental Health Delivery," *Social Work* 22, no. 3 (May 1977): 229–232.

41. *Behavior Today*, December 17, 1979, p. 5.

42. Verne R. Kelley and Hanna B. Weston, "Civil Liberties in Mental Health Facilities," *Social Work* 19, no. 1 (January 1974); idem, "Computers, Costs and Civil Liberties," *Social Work* 20, no. 1 (January 1975); idem, "Release of Confidential Information from Mental Health Records," *Administration in Mental Health* 7, no. 1 (Fall 1979).

43. Robert L. Spitzer, *Diagnostic and Statistical Manual of Mental Disorders*, 3rd ed., rev. (Washington, D.C.: American Psychiatric Association, 1987), p. xxiii.

44. Salvador Minuchin, *Families and Family Therapy* (Cambridge, Mass.: Harvard University Press, 1974).

ADDITIONAL SUGGESTED READINGS

Beers, Clifford, *A Mind That Found Itself* (New York: Longman, Green & Co., 1908).

Biegel, David E., and Arthur J. Naparstek, *Community Support Systems and Mental Health: Practice, Policy and Research* (New York: Springer Publishing Co., 1982).

Bloom, Martin, *Prevention: The Possible Science* (Englewood Cliffs, N.J.: Prentice-Hall, 1981).

Chekhov, Anton P., "Heartache," *The Portable Chekhov* (New York: The Viking Press, 1969).

Comas-Diaz, Lillian, and Griffith, Ezra E.H., *Clinical Guidelines in Cross-Cultural Mental Health* (New York: John Wiley & Sons, 1988).

Falk, Hans, "The Membership Model of Social Work," *Social Work* 29, no. 2 (March–April 1984).

Feldman, Saul, "Out of the Hospital, Onto the Streets: The Overselling of Benevolence," *The Hastings Center Report,* June 1983.

Friedman-Cohen, Nancy, and Kevin Kenwood, "Educating Social Workers about the Use of Chemotherapy and Other Treatment Modalities," *Journal of Education for Social Work* 17, no. 3 (Fall 1981).

Hartman, Ann, "The Family: A Central Focus for Practice," *Social Work* 26, no. 1 (January 1981).

Katz, Arthur J., ed., *Community Mental Health: Issues for Social Work Practice and Education* (New York: Council on Social Work Education, 1979).

Lewis, Harold, *The Intellectual Base of Social Work Practice: Tools for Thought in a Helping Profession* (New York: Haworth Press, 1982).

"Report of the Task Panel on Prevention," submitted to The President's Commission on Mental Health, (Washington, D.C.: U.S. Government Printing Office, 1978).

Rosenhan, D.L., "On Being Sane in Insane Places," *Science* 179 (January 19, 1973).

10 Social Services and Substance Abuse

Frank H. Ware

Substance abuse in the United States has become a chronic problem. Millions of individuals have access, despite a plethora of regulations, to potentially dangerous substances, and a substantial number of these individuals will develop problems as a direct result of the use of these substances.

Federal government statistics indicate that the per capita consumption of alcohol is 2.56 gallons yearly for every American over the age of fifteen.[1] There are 14 million problem drinkers, 3 million of whom are teenagers.[2] Forty billion mood-altering prescription pills are dispensed annually. Among illicit drugs, heroin is used daily by 450,000 persons, only one quarter of whom are reached by treatment. Ten million Americans have used cocaine, and 43 million have used marijuana.[3]

The social burden in economic costs is quantified by totalling the impact of substance abuse on the health care system, the general welfare and social service systems, the law enforcement and the judicial systems, and the employment market. The economic cost to the nation of alcohol abuse and alcoholism alone is estimated to be $116.7 billion.[4] Billions of dollars in goods change hands for the purchase of substances of all kinds. Substance abuse presents our society with a list of intangibles that cannot be quantified, but the tragedy of human suffering and debilitation, the destruction of families, and the disruption of communities is immense.

HUMAN NEEDS

Our perspective of substance abuse is as much shaped by political and moral forces as by scientific evidence. In the United States today, existing side by side (often in conflict), are groups of professionals who view the problem of substance use from very different perspectives: (1) as hidden within the individual and his or her attitudes toward self, others, and life in general, (2) as hidden in social conditions that create frustration and deprivations while failing to create opportunities and to control access to dangerous substances, (3) as hidden in the effects of certain substances and the biology of the user.

We do not really know why individuals abuse substances. What is evident is that such persons present a variety of problems intertwined with substance use and that there are variations in the magnitude of these problems. Substance abuse may appear to be the cause or the result of a problem. Substance abuse touches a variety of human difficulties such as intrapersonal emotional problems, interpersonal conflicts, disruptive family relations, physical disorders, work-related problems, and criminal and civil justice problems.

Many choose to use mood-altering substances for what they feel are positive reasons: curiosity, excitement, aesthetic pleasure, attempts to attain status within society, or group acceptance and attempts to experience personal or spiritual growth. For many, drugs are convenient; they dull the pain and offer elusive pleasure. If escape is the goal, the motivation is usually unhappiness, alienation, depression, or an inability to solve personal or interpersonal conflicts.

It is felt that drug addiction is caused in part by anomie, "a state of society in which normative standards of conduct and beliefs are weak or lacking; also, a similar condition in an individual characterized by disorientation, anxiety and isolation."[5] This definition applies to the condition of the ghetto dweller and the formless violence of suburban youth. The breakdown of the traditional culture of the North American Indian may be a factor in the alcohol-related problems of that social group. In general a marked discrepancy between the goals and ideals of a culture and its ability to achieve those objectives may be seen as a precipitating factor in much substance abuse. Some have promoted the idea that "addicts are the scapegoats of our modern, secular, therapeutically imbued societies."[6]

There are four basic patterns of substance abuse, as noted in the following paragraphs:

1. *Use of medically prescribed or over-the-counter drugs for therapeutic purposes.* It would be rare for an individual who uses substances under these conditions to be viewed as a drug abuser. Society in general supports both the pharmaceutical industry and the manufacturers of over-the-counter drugs in response to the large sums of money spent each year to advertise a wide variety of mood-altering substances. The public is assured that chemical remedies are available for physical and psychological problems.

   Though many benefit from this practice, many others run the risk of the misuse of prescription medication and the practice of self-medication with both prescription and over-the-counter drugs. Self-medication is a particular concern for the elderly who are generally ill informed about the potential dangers of combining drugs. Accidents and medical emergencies develop frequently when prescription medication or over-the-counter drugs are combined with the depressant drug alcohol.

2. *Occasional use of substances for moderate pleasurable effects.* This category of drug use involves a wide spectrum and large portion of the public. Persons using drugs within the medical treatment context see themselves as patients, and the drug as a way of alleviating illness. The occasional substance user picks and chooses the substance for its desired mood-altering effect, and thus pictures himself or herself as a consumer. The substances chosen may be legal or illicit. Examples of this substance use pattern are common as seen in the individual who has a few drinks after work to unwind, to the student who smokes marijuana before going to a movie.

   Such use is rarely problematic, though the use of illicit drugs raises the possibility of legal consequences. Occasional substance use can be harmful if excessive quantities or inappropriate combinations of the substances are used.

3. *Occasional use of substances for intensive psychoactive effect.* Though persons in this category are using substances in a non-compulsive manner, the intensity of the substance experience often leads to acute substance-related emergencies. These emergencies may result in medical crisis, domestic violence, and other episodes that affect the user, the family, and the community. Most substances are capable of producing the desired intensive effect with quantity, quality (purity), and method of drug intake (oral, smoking, inhalation, intramuscular, intravenous) being factors. Snorting cocaine and the taking of PCP falls into this category.

4. *Compulsive use of substances for sustained psychoactive effect and/or to avoid withdrawal symptoms.* In this category compulsive use becomes the central focus of an individual's life. Compulsive substance users often have dual or multiple addictions, switching from substance to substance depending on what is available.

SUBSTANCE CHARACTERISTICS AND TRENDS

The total list of substances abused in the United States is extensive. The following are characteristics of major substances of abuse and observable trends of use and abuse.

Alcohol and Other Depressants

Alcohol is one of a group of highly addictive drugs, the central nervous system depressants. Other depressants similar to alcohol include sedative hypnotics and tranquilizers.

Alcohol is the most commonly used psychoactive substance in the United States. More people use alcohol than all other substances combined (excluding nicotine and caffeine).

Alcoholism is also one of the most serious public health problems in the United States today. Among the 18.3 million adult heavy drinkers (defined as those consuming more than fourteen drinks per week) 12.1 million have one or more symptoms of alcoholism, an increase of 8.2 percent since 1980.[7] Alcohol abuse accounts for approximately 98,000 deaths annually, including approximately 37,000 from cirrhosis and other medical consequences, 26,000 from alcohol-related motor vehicle accidents, and 35,000 from alcohol-related homicides, suicides, and non-motor-vehicle accidents.[8] Twenty percent of national expenditures for hospital care are alcohol-related.[9]

Alcohol taken with other central nervous system depressants has a synergistic effect. One dose of alcohol combined with one dose of other depressants multiplies the effect.

Sedative hypnotics are often prescribed in the treatment of anxiety and insomnia. These drugs can cause dependence. Tolerance can develop, requiring more of the drug to produce the desired effect. Minor tranquilizers are the most frequently prescribed substances in the United States with over 90 million prescriptions filled yearly.[10] Overdose and physical addiction are possible with central nervous system depressants. Depressant addiction is severe, and withdrawal can cause death. No other drug category, including heroin or other opiate addictions, causes death during withdrawal.

Heroin and Other Narcotics

Morphine is the naturally occurring substance found in the opium poppy, producing both sedative and analgesic action. The term *opiate* refers to any natural or synthetic drug that induces morphine-like actions. Opiates include morphine; codeine, another naturally occurring opiate; heroin, a semisynthetic derived from a morphine base; and meperidine, methadone, propoxyphene, pentazocine, and other synthetic narcotics.

Heroin use can induce an intensive state of euphoria. The most common method of administration is injection, which produces the most intense reaction. Heroin and other narcotics are addictive. Heroin withdrawal is similar to a severe case of the flu, usually lasting four to seven days. Though restlessness, craving for the drug, chills, cramps, and aches and pains are common symptoms of withdrawal, it is not life-threatening.

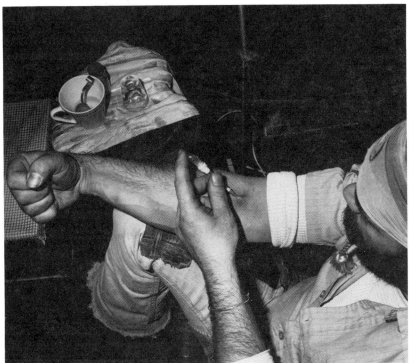

The Image Works, Inc./Charles Gatewood

Many substances are abused. A current concern, in addition to the abuse itself, is the spread of AIDS through injection by contaminated needles.

There are many myths regarding heroin use and heroin addicts. Heroin in itself does no physical damage to the body. The life-style that addicts tend to lead often results in diseases, infections, and injuries from unsterile injections and malnutrition, since the addict spends most of his or her money on procuring the drug.

Heroin purity has tended to decline, and the price of heroin has risen. This trend is generally credited to international and domestic control efforts, which have reduced the availability of the drug. Though current data suggest that the heroin problem is decreasing, there is strong support for belief that the trend will turn upward again.[11]

Methadone began to be widely used for both a detoxification and maintenance treatment of narcotic addiction in the 1970s. Currently 80,000 clients are receiving treatment in federally licensed clinics. Methadone has become a factor in illicit substance use, and in 1977 was reported to be directly attributable to 11 percent of drug-related deaths in New York City.[12]

Amphetamines and Other Stimulants

Amphetamines have a wide popularity and are used to increase the activity of many body functions. The term *stimulants* may be used to describe Dexedrine and other amphetamine drugs and nonamphetamine drugs such as Preludin®, Fastin®, and Ritalin®. Stimulants increase blood pressure, pulse, alertness, and motor and speech activity. Appetite may decrease, and agitation and sleeplessness are common. Stimulants produce euphoria that may change to anxiety, depression, and fatigue. A speed "run" or "speeding," a continuous pattern of use, can result in sleep deprivation in which hallucinations and/or irritability are common. Withdrawal from amphetamines is only emotionally serious, but the resulting depression is a high-risk time for the individual.

Trends would indicate that while amphetamines account for a small percentage of medical emergencies, their nonmedical use has been rising. While medical use of amphetamines is declining, there is much evidence to suggest that they still are improperly prescribed by some physicians.

Cocaine

Though cocaine is legally classified as a narcotic, it is usually closer to amphetamines in effect and abuse potential. Cocaine use increased in the United States steadily during the 1980s. As many as 10 million Americans are estimated to use cocaine monthly with a staggering 25 million Americans reportedly having tried cocaine at least once.[13] Despite its price, cocaine is increasingly the drug of choice of persons who have disposable income—the middle class. In a recent three-month period, 100,000 persons have called 800-COCAINE, a nationwide hotline, to ask questions about the drug.[14]

In the mid-1980s the widespread use of crack, a cocaine-based drug, increased the popularity and the availability of cocaine. By 1986 one third of all callers to the national cocaine hotline were crack users.[15] Because of the "social" nature of cocaine, its use is often promoted as harmless, a claim that is not necessarily accurate. Steady use slowly increases tolerance and, though not physically addictive, it can produce psychological dependence.

> Mike is a thirty-seven-year-old professional person who has checked into a psychiatric hospital. His wife is threatening to leave him, and his business partners have informed him that they must terminate their partnership. He experimented with drugs in college without disrupting his life. There is no family history of substance abuse, and he has a strong relationship with his parents. He began using cocaine two years ago and now has a $2,000-a-week habit. Mike reports that "this is the first time in my life things have been out of control."

Hallucinogens

Hallucinogens work by either releasing or inhibiting specific brain chemicals. Though LSD is the best-known hallucinogen, there are other laboratory-produced hallucinogens that include MDS, DOM, and DMT. Some hallucinogens come from the psilocybin mushroom, the peyote cactus button, and morning glory and other seeds. These hallucinogens differ in the intensity of physical effects, though they generally produce an extended vision-induced "trip" lasting anywhere from four to twenty-four hours. Data show that the use of hallucinogens has steadily declined. However, there has been a recent supply and demand for PCP (phencyclidine), which is classified as a "dissociative" anesthetic or as a psychedelic anesthetic.

Marijuana

The use of marijuana has been rising steadily in the past decade though there is some evidence that the trend has been leveling off. An estimated one in twenty-five adolescents between twelve and thirteen years old use marijuana monthly. In the fourteen- to fifteen-year-old group the figure rises to an estimated one out of every seven adolescents.[16]

Marijuana, once incorrectly legally identified as a narcotic, now shares the "social" status of alcohol, nicotine, and caffeine among many individuals. Marijuana use is no longer seen as an indication for substance abuse treatment.

> Joe has had no particularly disruptive or traumatic circumstances in his life with the exception of those created by substance abuse. No members of his family have had substance abuse problems, but his mother has received treatment and medication for nervous tension. As an adolescent, Joe came to experiment with inhalants such as glue; he also "ripped off" his mother's medication and participated in drinking experimentation with his peers. He has recently experienced "black outs"—periods of time that he is unable to account for once he is no longer under the influence of the substance. He has dropped out of school activities after becoming a frequent absentee from class, and his relationship with members of his family has become strained. Substance abuse has become a problem for Joe and is clearly interfering with his physical health, family life, and social well-being.

SOCIETY'S MIXED RESPONSE

The response to the use of drugs and alcohol has not always included the concept of treatment. At the time the Constitution was being drafted, a daily drink was considered necessary for good health. The problem of drunkenness and the "drunkard" was the concern of the law and the clergy.

Benjamin Rush's introduction of the concept of craving (compulsion to use alcohol) and the progressive development of a disordered pattern of drinking began to impact upon the exclusively moralistic view of excessive drinking. By the mid-1830s the notion that the desire for alcohol was a strong feeling that could overpower judgment was gaining proponents, and by 1838 Woodward, the superintendent of the asylum at Winchester, Massachusetts, described the chronic alcohol user as suffering from a "physical disease."[17]

By the middle of the nineteenth century the problems of chronic opiate use and tobacco use also came to be viewed, especially by those in the Temperance Movement, as representing moral weakness and disease. "Temperance" came to mean not temperate or moderate use, but total abstinence, and drug use outside of the medical context was seen as immoral.

Somehow the idea that alcohol was an inherently addicting substance fell into disfavor and, except in the Temperance Movement, was replaced by the view that alcohol was addicting only for those who were predisposed or vulnerable. Opium, on the other hand, came to be seen as inherently addicting. The words "alcoholic" and "inebriate" were beginning to replace the word "drunkard." Chronic opium users referred to as "opium habituates" and "opium inebriated," and the word "addict" was applied to chronic users of alcohol as well as morphine.[18]

For a brief time early in the twentieth century there was public support for treatment of opiate addiction. In a subsequent outpouring of moral fervor against the use of all drugs, the clinics that had been established to provide opiates to opiate addicts were closed in 1923.[19] Opiate addiction came to be viewed as a threat to the "fabric of society," and preventing dependence by controlling the availability of "narcotic" drugs was seen as the highest priority.

Partly in response to the growing number of opiate addicts in federal prisons, federal hospitals were established at Lexington, Kentucky, and Fort Worth, Texas. There were some sporadic efforts to treat selected opiate addicts with the newly developing techniques of psychoanalysis and psychotherapy, usually with little success.[20] For the most part, however, heroin addicts remained outside the mainstream of psychiatry and medicine, and were decidedly unwelcome at most doctors' offices and hospital emergency rooms.

A resurgence of interest in the treatment of drug dependence began after World War II and built up slowly in the decade of the 1950s as clinicians in large urban areas began to encounter many young heroin addicts. In 1966 Congress passed legislation establishing a federal civil commitment program for opiate users, but it also increased support for community-based programs. The period from 1966 to 1971 saw continued growth in the number of treatment programs funded by private solicitation and state and local governments, as well as by grants from more than half a dozen federal agencies, each operating under its own congressional mandate.

The expansion of federal support differed from previous efforts in that it was no longer specifically aimed at heroin and other narcotics, but also recognized that drug problems could be associated with a number of different drugs. It is clear from the various programmatic initiatives of the mid-1960s at the state and the local, as well as at the federal level, that concern with the "drug problem" was fueled by two distinct concerns: illicit drug use (marijuana, LSD) and nontraditional behavior among middle-class young people and a continuing belief that heroin use was linked with the rising crime rate.[21]

In 1968 a national survey conducted for the National Institute of Mental Health found 183 programs specifically focused on the treatment of drug addiction; 77 percent had been operating less than five years. Support for treatment reached its apex in June 1971 when President Richard Nixon created by executive order the Special Action Office for Drug Abuse Prevention within the Executive Office of the

President. The same presidential initiative also carried a recommendation for additional support for increased efforts to control the availability of illicit drugs and was accompanied by the dramatic labeling of drug abuse as "Public Enemy Number One."

Another policy change took place when the president, as commander-in-chief of the armed services, directed that drug use per se would no longer be a courtmartial offense. This gesture was pragmatic, given the widespread use of drugs among military personnel in Vietnam. The new push for treatment seemed not to develop from some newfound sympathy for addicts but from a belief that addicts committed crimes and created other addicts, and that the law enforcement systems needed new support to deal with a social problem that was out of control.

A strategy would develop that reflected a three-part program to reduce the negative effects of substance abuse: (1) treatment, rehabilitation, and prevention, (2) domestic drug law enforcement, (3) international narcotics control. The Drug Law Enforcement Program totaled a $435 million outlay in 1979.[22]

Though concern was expressed that not enough was being done to provide adequate treatment for alcoholism or for those who abused drugs prescribed by physicians, it was generally felt that new efforts were needed to make treatment more available to those substance abusers who had been largely excluded from the mainstream of medical care. There were a number of ironic aspects to the expansion of substance abuse treatment in 1971. Within the federal government the administrative machinery to manage the war on drug abuse was being built up just as the Office of Economic Opportunity—the machinery for the "war on poverty"—was being dismantled. Expenditures had been curtailed for community mental health programs and a general feeling developed that resources directed at specialized drug abuse treatment were being bled from resources that would have gone to more traditional programs.

Many objected to controversial programs such as the use of the synthetic opiate methadone as a substitute for other narcotics. While some felt that any focus on heroin was inappropriately narrow, others worried that the maintenance approach would place substance abuse programs under the control of the medical institutions. Some of the strongest criticism of the use of methadone came from the proponents of the therapeutic community treatment model, who felt that methadone would divert attention away from the social conditions which were believed to foster drug abuse while merely "substituting one addiction with another."[23]

Because of some of the historical developments outlined in this chapter, alcohol and drug abuse treatment developed and remain separate from each other. Ironically the National Institute on Alcohol Abuse and Alcoholism (NIAAA), established in 1970, is interested in "other drugs" as they relate to the treatment of alcoholism or dual dependency. On the other hand the National Institute on Drug Abuse (NIDA), first established as a division of the National Institute of Mental Health (NIMH), is concerned about the effects on users who combine psychoactive drugs with alcohol, or those who develop a dependency on alcohol after "licking" their drug problem.

Bureaucratic entrenchment may keep the alcohol and drug abuse fields separated on the federal level.[24] There is a growing support on the state level to develop a single state agency (SSA) for substance abuse. This movement has filtered down to the provider level, and many local programs have developed comprehensive services for all substance abusers. Simply because alcohol and drug programs have merged does not imply agreement on theories of addiction or treatment. Many substance abuse programs find themselves a house divided—not only in regard to staff differences (professional versus indigenous paraprofessional; "recovering alcoholic" versus "ex-dope-fiend")—but differences, real and imagined, also separate the client population.

Federal and state laws that delegate authority and, consequently, responsibilities to single state agencies on alcohol and drug abuse require that SSA's deal in the following services: planning, coordination, education and prevention, evaluation, training, treatment, quality assurance (licensing and certification), funding, and financial management.

In all of these functional areas of the state authority, delivery systems can be developed to provide quality services, both direct and indirect, more effectively and efficiently to clients, their families, and their communities. There would seem to be little disagreement that most of these functions lend themselves readily to a combined approach.

The following traditional and innovative approaches are found in the fabric of the substance abuse network.

TRADITIONAL APPROACHES

The Medical Model

I. Alcoholism as a Disease. The disease model, which identifies alcoholism as a progressive illness, has never caught on in regard to other areas of substance abuse. The belief in the disease model has permitted many people to seek help with less fear or being labeled as morally weak. It has permitted society to deal with alcohol-related problems as a treatment issue. The concept has also promoted a fee-for-service system for treatment in recent years as more physicians become involved in the treatment of alcoholism and as hospitals convert underused bed space to alcoholism treatment units with the support of third-party payments.

The disease model is supported by the contributions of E. M. Jellinek and his description of "gamma alcoholism," although some recent studies question the concept of set stages of alcoholism. At least part of the problem created by trying to develop a single view of alcoholism is the infusion of women, previously unstudied minority groups, and children and young adults who present few of the symptoms identified by Jellinek. One researcher states that:

> Today, after a generation of experience with the clinical intervention approach to alcoholics, and despite the proliferation of expensive alcoholism-treatment centers, alcoholics and alcohol problems persist undiminished. Doubts about the scientific foundation of the disease concept and the efficiency of the clinical intervention model are growing.[25]

II. Detoxification.   One of the first considerations in the treatment of substance abuse is the supervision of the person's withdrawal from the substance. Patients are often brought to such detoxification centers by friends, family, or the police. Residence in the detoxification facilities usually lasts from two to five days. Major withdrawal usually occurs during this period. Detoxification centers provide screening and referral services.

It has often been noted that detoxification facilities are abused by those they are designed to serve, who use the facilities to "clean up" or "dry out" in order to return to abusive patterns of use upon discharge. Physical withdrawal from addictive substances is a necessary approach to rehabilitation but is insufficient by itself. Recently there is a growing interest in the "social detox" model, which is perceived as more cost-effective than hospital treatment. In this model only patients experiencing severe withdrawal systems are transferred to a hospital setting.

III. Chemotherapy.   Chemotherapy is designed to permit substance abusers to function as socially useful individuals through the use of other chemical substances. Chemotherapy falls into three categories: (1) the use of antagonists, which block the effect of the drug or cause adverse reactions when the substance is used, (2) the use of substitutes belonging to the same family as the drug, but having fewer undesired effects, and (3) the use of symptom relievers, such as sedatives, antidepressants, and tranquilizers. Major trends in chemo-therapy are as follows.

Antagonists: Antabuse (disulfiram) is often used in alcohol treat-ment as an adjunct to other therapies. The drug offers a deterrent to re-sumption of drinking because ingestion of alcohol will, in interaction with antabuse, produce extreme nausea or vomiting. Antabuse is often used for three to twelve months following detoxification.

A major problem with antabuse treatment is that the patient may re-sume drinking within twenty-four hours after removing himself or her-self from medication. Some research indicates that less than 1 percent of all patients continue to take antabuse after discharge from treatment.[26]

Substitutes: Methadone is itself a highly addictive drug, which is used either to stabilize or to wean heroin users from their habits. (Her-oin was synthesized in Germany in 1898. It was pronounced as a "safe preparation free from addiction-forming properties" and was widely used in the treatment of morphine addiction.) Methadone in large doses may block heroin high and does not produce euphoria. Metha-done is longer lasting than heroin, and one oral dose will prevent with-drawal symptoms from developing for twenty-four hours or more.

Addicts report to clinics and receive their medication daily. Because of the lack of euphoria effect, clients maintained on methadone can hold jobs and generally function socially. These clients are, however, strongly addicted to the methadone and would suffer intense with-drawal symptoms if use were discontinued abruptly. Methadone main-tenance was pioneered by Dole and Nyswander in 1964.[27] Although administration of methadone is usually accompanied by counseling and support services, it remains a controversial treatment. According to present federal regulations persons entering methadone programs must be at least sixteen years old and must have been addicted to nar-cotics for at least two years.

While clients are maintained on methadone, they are generally able to get off heroin and lead productive lives. The relapse rate for clients as they begin to undergo detoxification from methadone is sub-stantial.[28] The clients experiencing relapse generally return to heroin or reenter regular methadone maintenance programs.

Symptom Relievers: Minor tranquilizers and antidepressants used in the treatment of substance abusers are often ineffective and perhaps counterproductive. The potential for abuse of these drugs by the ad-dict is great. Many workers in the field feel that prescriptions for minor tranquilizers and antidepressants reinforce the belief system of many addicts that they can find a "better life through chemistry." There is considerable evidence that addicts will increase the frequency of administration and the amount of dosage over time.

As many as 20 million people in the United States may be using Valium and Librium (minor tranquilizers), and these drugs themselves can be addictive and can produce withdrawal symptoms when discontinued. Used in combination with alcohol or other drugs, Valium can be lethal. Despite these concerns addicts and alcoholics will often receive prescriptions to deal with tension, anxiety, muscle spasms, insomnia, and so forth.

Nonmedical Approaches

Group and Individual Therapy. Unlike the medically oriented technologies, group and individual therapy stress the client relating to another person or persons in a therapeutic setting. Many practitioners regard group therapy as the treatment of choice for substance-dependent individuals,[29] though some researchers challenge the effectiveness of group therapy techniques.[30] The approaches to group or individual therapy are many and varied and are only being suggested here. General readings on major group therapy orientations are explored by Lieberman, Yalom, and Miles.[31]

Alcoholics Anonymous and Other Self-Help Fellowships. Alcoholics Anonymous (A.A.) and other self-help fellowships such as Narcotics Anonymous (N.A.) are an integral part of many inpatient and outpatient programs. A.A. was founded in 1935 by two alcoholics for the purpose of providing a fellowship for compulsive drinkers. A.A. has become a worldwide effort with over 16,000 autonomous groups in North America. Groups hold meetings in which personal narratives concerning the severe problems posed by alcohol consumption are shared. A.A. is unstructured but is guided by the concept of "Twelve Steps," the first of which is: "We admitted we were powerless over alcohol—that our lives had become unmanageable."[32]

Objective outcome data on A.A. are difficult to obtain, since limited research is conducted. Current data do indicate that A.A. is not as effective as the 60 percent improvement rate reported by A.A. itself.[33] A.A. as well as N.A. demands abstinence as a way of life for the "recovering person." Other offshoots of A.A. have been Al-Anon Family Groups and Alateen for children of alcoholic parents.

Mandatory Treatment. Fostered in part by the belief that the substance-dependent person had diminished capacity to control his or her own behavior, the practice has developed to order persons with "drug problems" into treatment in lieu of incarceration. In many instances the dramatic changes of social attitudes toward recreational drug use has made diversion into "treatment" an absurd parody of its original intent. At one point, in the early 1970s, 15 to 20 percent of the capacity of federally funded treatment programs was occupied by individuals who listed marijuana as their primary drug problem.[34] It is unlikely that very many of these individuals were such heavy marijuana users that impairment of health and productivity was their motive in seeking treatment.

Treatment as an alternative to punishment may be coercion into treatment. From a purely medical or scientific perspective the decision to use a drug occasionally, even if the drug is not legally available, is not in and of itself a treatable disorder.

> Sue is a thirty-five-year-old female. Her family environment had been quite dysfunctional and she had been placed in foster care and group facilities from eight years of age until she married for the first time at seventeen years. Her first husband physically abused her, and the marriage lasted a matter of months. Her second husband was an alcoholic, and she began to drink heavily with him to "keep the marriage." After the failure of the second marriage she was treated for depression through a mental health center but continues to drink heavily and misuse her medication. Norms, family dysfunction, and social factors are of great importance in Sue's substance abuse problem.

Innovative Approaches

Systems Approach. Systems theory has changed the focus of service to include the network of personal and societal factors that intertwine with the substance abuse problem. As a result of this focus supportive therapeutic approaches have been added: (1) educational and vocational counseling, (2) job placement, (3) conjoint counseling, (4) recreational counseling, (5) family counseling, (6) income maintenance, (7) public health, (8) clients' rights, (9) legal aid, and (10) prevention services. In addition, those who work from a systems theory perspective advocate social action on a community level to provide the least disruptive services for the client.

Therapeutic Communities. Maxwell Jones began the Social Rehabilitation Unit at Belmont Hospital in England in an attempt to "break away from the doctor dominated world of psychiatry." In this country the first therapeutic community (T.C.) was founded by Charles

Dederich in 1958. Named Synanon, the community found its base in a self-help model and used "recovering persons" as staff. Therapeutic communities received criticism from professionals for "dangerous confrontive techniques and for creating a small closed world."

The T.C. usually calls for a long-term "commitment" from persons who apply for services. Reflecting the elements of a primary social system, the T.C. stresses group commitment and role modeling as important aspects of treatment.[35] Impressive statistics would point to the T.C. model's success in rehabilitation.[36] Drug abuse and criminal behavior are viewed as signs of social disenfranchisement as well as family disturbance and individual maladaptation. Fundamental to the T.C. concept is the necessity for a total twenty-four-hour community impact to modify permanently lifelong destructive patterns of behavior. The base goals of treatment are somewhat overwhelming: abstinence from drugs, elimination of antisocial behavior, development of employable skills, self-reliance, and personal honesty. Nevertheless, a T.C. resident wrote:

> This is my view of the T.C. I entered after fourteen years of alcohol use and ten years of drug use. These years were filled with misery; five marriages, time spent in prison, time spent in jails, time spent in hospitals, and seven suicide attempts. It is little wonder then that I desired to change my life then. . . . I am discovering myself and my potential for the first time. I am finding honesty, tears, laughter, joy, peace, love, and most of all hope for the future. I am finding compassion and understanding within a group of people who, like myself, had found themselves lost but are now finding their way. By helping each other, we help ourselves.[37]

Controlled Drinking. The concept that alcoholics can return to a nonproblem drinking pattern is opposed by groups who see alcoholism as a disease and advocate abstinence as the only feasible choice for recovering alcoholics. Controversy was increased when the Rand Corporation in June 1976 noted that it was possible for some alcoholics to develop moderate drinking patterns. In a follow-up study published in 1980 Rand said of alcoholics free of drinking problems for four years after admission to treatment, that 61 percent had abstained from drinking and that 39 percent were able to drink socially.[38]

Perhaps the strongest precaution comes from the Rand study itself, which concludes that alcoholism is a highly unstable and chronic condition. Although remissions do happen frequently, alcoholics are subject to relapse, and any rate of remission, whether it is aimed at abstinence or nonproblem drinking, is basically unstable over the long term. The subject of nonabstinence goals for individuals is still a matter of controversy, but it is expected that this model will grow in popularity.

Genetic-Environmental Influences. The familial pattern in drug abuse is well established. That is, addicts tend to come from families where parents and siblings also have a high incidence of addiction. For example Goodwin and Erickson have estimated that, on the average, approximately 25 percent of the fathers and brothers of alcoholics will likewise be alcoholic, compared to an incidence in the general population of from 3 percent to 5 percent.[39] The relationships are not expressed to the degree that an alcoholic parent will produce an alcoholic biological child, but the statistically significant relationship is indicative of a biological-genetic predisposing condition. Of course, biological factors will interact with environmental conditions. Other biological factors that are subjects of current research include aspects of biochemistry and nutrition.

Industrial Substance Abuse Programs. Occupational alcoholism programs or Employee Assistance Programs began in the 1940s in a few major companies and have increased to approximately 4,000 in the United States today. A.A. was a strong influencing factor in the initiation of early programs and still seems to be an integral part of most industrial programs (employed addicts are often referred to N.A.). Employers and supervisors are being trained to identify substance-related problems and to intervene early.

The most effective approach in the treatment of industrial alcoholism to date has been the "broad brush" approach. Confrontation of employees becomes a legitimate management concern (job performance, absenteeism, lateness, accidents on the job, and so forth). Approximately 50 percent of the cases identified by employee assistance programs are related to substance abuse, with other problem areas such as marital, financial, psychological, or physiological making up the remainder of the identified population.

Recovery is more likely with employed persons than with unemployed or disenfranchised persons. Success rates as high as 85 percent have been claimed by some employers; on the average a recovery rate of 66 percent is still an encouraging statistic.[40]

THE ROLE OF THE SOCIAL WORKER

As many of the traditional medically oriented treatment efforts are moving toward a multidisciplinary approach, the scope of addiction studies has moved from a limited view to an interactional perspective. The social worker is uniquely qualified to view the addict or alcoholic as part of a living system which includes the subsystems of family, employer, employing organization, and in some cases the court and its legal sanctions. It is obvious that substance abuse is a problem for the individual, family, subgroups of society, and society in general.

Substance abuse as presented today will call for dedicated efforts of (1) the providers of individual, family, and small group services, (2) program administrators, and (3) planning and policymakers. Social workers find themselves encompassed in all of these efforts.

It must be noted that social workers themselves are as likely to develop substance abuse problems as is any other segment of society. For social workers who themselves are dealing with their own "recovery" there is often the need to wear "two hats"—to blend their commitment to self-preservation with adherence to their professional code of ethics. Such workers bring to the field invaluable experience and dedication.[41]

Individual, Family, and Small Group Services

The provider of individual, family, and small group services is presented with all the problems and conflicts that are presented to most front-line workers. Some social workers are initially surprised by the reaction of many clients who present the belief "you can't help me if you are not an alcoholic/addict." Statistics indicate that recovering abusers and nonabusers are equally effective in assisting clients with substance abuse problems.[42] Despite statistics, professionals have not always been welcomed in a field that had depended on indigenous paraprofessionals as care providers. Special problems sometimes arose when social workers were assigned supervision of paraprofessions, but it has been demonstrated that with sound supervision techniques these problems can be overcome.[43] Limited resources and decreased social commitment often are frustrating for the worker who is expected to provide social actualization, family reunification, job and educational capabilities, and abstinence from criminal and/or substance abuse behavior.

The number of substance abusers is far larger than the number of persons who seek treatment. Some of these users may have substance abuse problems but are able through one means or another to bring their lives under control. Many others may be addressed through other social services or the judicial system. Prejudice and skepticism are still present after years of perceiving the substance abuser as depraved and incurable. It becomes the job of the social worker to advocate for the right of the substance abuser and to demythologize society's view of the individual behind the label.

Administration

Administration of substance abuse programs must face an abundance of critical management issues. These issues may result from problems within the organization, from the local community, and from government funding. Within the program, issues of paraprofessional/professional differences, overworked staff, and facility obsolescence are often sighted. Within the community, issues of public opinion, local judicial customs and codes regarding substance abuse and substance users, and the availability of other community services are critical.

Substance abuse services have been placed under the same controls as other health facilities under the National Health Planning and Resource Development Act. All local planning for services must be approved by the local health systems agency (HSA) thus adding the additional factors of competition for local programming. Insofar as substance abuse programming can reduce the use of basic medical and health care services, continued government funding will probably continue at some level.

The social worker as administrator brings a perspective uniquely different from the management style of the business administrator, a perspective needed to handle three important categories of obligation.

1. They must create effective treatment environments.
2. They must keep the environment accountable to funders, staff, and clients.
3. They must create ways of funding and supporting that environment.

Creative and unique administrative designs have developed in substance abuse programming. Some programs have fully integrated the client population into the planning, operation, and funding of the programs,[44] and the blend of professional and "recovering" staff is a model for other human service systems.

With a reduction in social interest, and inflation and funding cutbacks, the challenging question of the future may be: Can good administrative procedures offset the demoralization of those administrators and their staffs when current funding structure puts a premium on client numbers and the cheapest possible way to provide treatment?

Planning and Policy Making

The nature of substance abuse treatment will change in accordance with changes in knowledge and shifting social priorities. The federal strategy recently has intended to provide balanced and flexible means to reduce the supply of drugs, discourage use, and make treatment available. To keep a balance between treatment and the social control aspects of substance abuse policy may be the most challenging task for planners.

Priorities once called for continued research and more specificity in treatment, prevention and planning, with increased focus on special populations, including youth, the elderly, ethnic minorities, rural population, and women. It is uncertain that these priorities will remain a prime focus of public policy in the United States.

SUMMARY AND CONCLUSIONS

Substance abuse was in the past viewed as a moral defect, a weakness of will, a view that created for many the symbol of the abuser as a social deviant in need of either salvation or incarceration. Though self-help effort and treatment programs have chiseled out dignity for the substance abuser, old views still haunt the memory of many persons who feel, "but, really, don't these people bring it upon themselves?"

To discount one's behavior entirely would be in error; to discount society's obligation would be irresponsible. Huge profits are made by those who grow crops for the production of alcoholic beverages; by brewers, distillers, distributors; by pharmaceutical companies; by the medical profession; and federal, state, and local governments receiving tax revenues through their control and distribution of alcohol.

The availability of social service programs for substance abuse is symbolic of society's view of the human condition. Views regarding substance abuse have changed from those held in the past. The question is whether new views will reflect a deeper understanding of the human condition or reestablish a standard hidden somewhere in history.

NOTES

1. White House Strategy Council on Drug Abuse, *Federal Strategy for Drug Abuse and Drug Traffic Prevention, 1979* (Washington D.C., 1979), p. 6.
2. Dario McDarby, *Drug Abuse: A Realistic Primer for Parents* (Phoenix, Ariz.: Do It Now Foundation, 1980), pp. 4–5.
3. White House Council, *Federal Strategy for Drug Abuse.*

4. Research Triangle Institute, *Economic Costs to Drug Abuse and Mental Illness: 1980*, June 1984,

5. White House Council, *Federal Strategy for Drug Abuse.*

6. Thomas Szasz, *Ceremonial Chemistry* (Garden City, N.Y.: Doubleday, 1975), p. 2.

7. National Institute on Alcohol Abuse and Alcohol, Working Paper: *Projections of Alcohol Abusers, 1980, 1985, 1990* (Department of Biometry and Epidemiology, January 1985).

8. R. T. Ravenhold, *Addiction Mortality in the U.S.* (National Institute on Drug Abuse, March 1983).

9. Office of Technology, Assessment of Medical Technology and Costs of the Medical Program, *Health Technology Case Study 22: The Effectiveness and Costs of Alcoholism Treatment* (March 1983), p. 1.

10. White House Council, *Federal Strategy for Drug Abuse*, p. 11.

11. Therapeutic Communities of America, based on observation of addiction trends in Europe, is predicting a major heroin epidemic for the United States.

12. Peter G. Bourne, *Methadone: Benefits and Shortcomings* (Washington, D.C.: Drug Abuse Council, 1975), p. 11.

13. "Crack & Crime," *Newsweek*, June 16, 1986, pp. 15–22.

14. Mark S. Gold, *800-COCAINE* (Toronto: Bantam Books, 1984), p. 1.

15. "Feeding America's Habit," *Newsweek*, February 25, 1985.

16. White House Council, *Federal Strategy for Drug Abuse*, pp. 9–10.

17. H. G. Levine, "The Discovery of Addiction," *Journal of Alcohol Studies* 39 (1978):143–147.

18. National Institute on Drug Abuse, "The Swinging Pendulum: The Treatment of Drug Abuse in America," by Jerome H. Jaffe, in *Handbook on Drug Abuse*, ed. R. DuPont, A. Goldstein, and O'Donnell (Washington, D.C.: U.S. Government Printing Office, 1979), p. 3.

19. Ibid., p. 4.

20. H. T. Conrad, "Psychiatric Treatment of Narcotic Addiction," in *Drug Addiction,* ed. W. Martin (New York: Springer, 1977).

21. DuPont, Goldstein, and O'Donnell, *Handbook on Drug Abuse*, p. 6.

22. White House Council, *Federal Strategy for Drug Abuse*, p. 61.

23. An informal "anti-methadone" develops at almost any Drug Abuse Conference. Therapeutic Communities of America is noted for its "anti-methadone" stand.

24. The list of drug abuse prevention discretionary and nondiscretionary programs is lengthy. For a breakdown consult *Federal Strategy for Drug Abuse and Drug Traffic Prevention*, Washington, D.C.

25. Harold Mulford, "'Natural' or 'Scientific' Alcohol Treatment," *The Des Moines Register*, March 15, 1988, p. 7A.

26. B. S. Labetkin, P. C. Ribers, and C. M. Rosenberg, "Difficulties of Disulfiram Therapy with Alcoholics," *Quarterly Journal of Studies on Alcohol* 32 (1971):168–171.

27. Richard C. Schroeder, *The Politics of Drugs: An American Dilemma* (Washington, D.C.: Congressional Quarterly Press, 1980), pp. 89–92.

28. Bourne, *Methadone: Benefits and Shortcomings*, p. 11; Hunter Conway, Jr., Testimony before the Senate Labor and Human Resources Subcommittee on Health and Scientific Research, September 10, 1979.
29. A. Stein and E. Friedman. "Group Therapy With Alcoholics," in H. I. Kaplan and B.J. Sadock, eds., *Comprehensive Group Psychotherapy* (Baltimore: Williams & Wilkins, 1971).
30. F. Baekland, L. Lundwall, and B. Kissin, "Methods for the Treatment of Chronic Alcoholism: A Critical Appraisal," in *Research Advances in Alcohol and Drug Problems*, Vol. 2, ed. R. Gibbins, Y. Israel, H. Kalant, R. Propham, W. Schmidt, and R. Smart (New York: John Wiley & Sons, 1975).
31. M. A. Lieberman, I. D. Yalom, and M. B. Miles, *Encounter Groups: First Facts* (New York: Basic Books, 1973).
32. Alcoholics Anonymous, *Twelve Steps and Twelve Traditions* (New York: Alcoholics Anonymous World Services, 1952), pp. 21–24.
33. Alcoholics Anonymous, *Profile of an AA Meeting* (New York: Alcoholics Anonymous World Services, 1972).
34. DuPont et al., eds., *Handbook on Drug Abuse*, p. 14.
35. Frank H. Ware, "Ideological Management in an Alternative Human Service Program: A Teaching Aid" (Master's thesis, University of Iowa School of Social Work, 1979).
36. D.D. Simpson and S.B. Sells, *Evaluation of Drug Abuse Treatment Effectiveness: Summary of the DARP Follow-up Research.* DHHS Publication (ADM) 82-1194. Washington, D.C.: U.S. Government Printing Office, 1982.
37. Anonymous, "Letter," *Pterodactyl Press* III, April 1980, p. 6.
38. Jon Newton, "Non-problem Drinking Data From Rand Tells Critics," *The Toronto Journal* 9, no. 9 (September 1, 1980), pp. 1, 4.
39. Donald Goodwin and Carlton Erickson, eds., *Alcoholism and Affective Disorders: Clinical, Genetic and Biochemical Studies with Emphasis on Alcohol-Lithium Interaction.* Spectrum, 1979.
40. U.S. Department of Health, Education and Welfare, *Occupational Alcoholism: Some Problems and Some Solutions*, National Institute on Alcohol Abuse and Alcoholism, DHEW (Washington, D.C. U.S. Government Printing Office, 1975, pp. 3–14.
41. *For Members Employed in the Alcoholism Field (those who wear "two hats")*, A. A. Guidelines, G.S.D., New York, no date.
42. U.S. Department of Health, Education and Welfare, National Institute on Drug Abuse, *Professional and Paraprofessional Drug Abuse Counselors: Three Reports* by L. Lo Sciuto, L. Aiken, and M. Ausetts (Washington, D.C.: U.S. Government Printing Office, 1979).
43. William C. Richen, "Indigenous Paraprofessional Staff," in *Issues in Human Services*, ed. Kaslow and Associates (San Francisco: Jossey-Bass, 1977).
44. Frank H. Ware, "MBO and Radical Perspective in Relation to Community Function" (paper presented at the National Drug Abuse Conference, Seattle, Washington, March 1978).

ADDITIONAL SUGGESTED READINGS

Densen-Gerber, Judianne, *We Mainline Dreams: The Odyssey House Story* (Garden City, N.Y.: Doubleday & Co., 1973).

Epstein, Edward Jay, *Agency of Fear* (New York: G.P. Putnam's Sons, 1977).

Hunt, Linda, *Alcohol Related Problems* (London: Heinemann Educational Books, 1982).

The Journal (monthly newspaper) Addiction Research Foundation, 33 Russell Street, Toronto, Ontario, Canada M5S ZS1.

Jones, M., *Therapeutic Community* (New York: Basic Books, 1953).

Kalb, M., and Propper, M. S., "The Future of Alcohology: Craft or Science?" *American Journal of Psychiatry* 133: 1976):641–645.

Kinney, Jean, and Gwen Leaton, *Loosening the Grip*, 3rd ed. (St. Louis: C.V. Mosby, 1987).

Knowles, J.H., "The Responsibility of the Individual," *Daedalus* 106, no. 1 (1977); 57–80.

Madden, J.S., et al., eds. *Alcoholism and Drug Dependence* (New York: Plenum Publishing, 1977).

Musto, D.F., *The American Disease* (New Haven, Conn.: Yale University Press, 1973).

National Institute on Drug Abuse Publications: Research Issues:
 No. 3, *Drugs and Attitude Change*, November 1974.
 No. 14, *Drugs and Personality*, July 1976.
 No. 19, *Drugs and Psychopathology*, June 1977.
Research Monographs:
 No. 6, *Effects of Labeling the "Drug Abuser," An Inquiry*, March 1976.
 No. 12, *Psychodynamics of Drug Dependence*, May 1977.

Scher, Jordan M., ed., *Drug Abuse in Industry* (Springfield, Ill.: Charles C Thomas, 1973).

Trice, H. M., and P. M. Roman, *Spirits and Demons at Work: Alcohol and Other Drugs on the Job* (Ithaca, N.Y.: Cornell University, 1972).

The U.S. Journal of Drug and Alcohol Dependence (monthly newspaper), 1721 Blount Road, Suite 1, Pompano Beach, Fl 33069.

11 Criminal and Juvenile Justice

H. Wayne Johnson

Public opinion polls in the last two decades have repeatedly found crime to be among the top concerns of Americans. By almost any standard it is a major social problem. The programs created to deal with offenders constitute a large constellation of social welfare provisions. Their limitations, both in social policy and in programs, are part of the topic of the following discussion. These limitations will be seen to characterize one of the most interesting and important, yet troubled and troubling, social welfare fields.

In this chapter we will consider the social problems of crime and delinquency, the persons accused or convicted of committing these norm violations, and the various social measures, for example, corrections, that society has devised as responses to this deviancy. The "clients" in the justice system supposedly have one thing in common—that they are in difficulty with the law. But they are anything but a homogeneous group. The illegal behaviors leading to the labeling of these persons run a wide range from the "status offenses" of youth who run away, are truant, and violate curfew or liquor laws or have trouble with their families, to public intoxication and the more serious offenses of theft, burglary, assault, embezzlement, or murder, regardless of age. Such disparate persons may have few similarities apart from their socially defined deviance. There is a world of difference among white-collar criminals, professional check writers, juvenile car thieves, and persons convicted of manslaughter, to cite some examples, and there are probably equally great differences between the individuals constituting just one of these offense categories.

In spite of the image of the offender as a menacing, dangerous creature (requiring bars and cages for containment), the fact is that the vast majority of American crime consists of property offenses rather than violent crimes against the person. As can be seen in the FBI figures in Table 11.1, the ratio of personal offenses to property offenses is about 1 to 8.

Another qualification of the often assumed homogeneity of this group of persons is that not all offenses are detected or reported; not all reported offenders are apprehended; not all of those apprehended are arrested; not all of those arrested are adjudicated; not all of those adjudicated are convicted; and not all of those convicted are penalized. There is, then, a social selection process all along the route from offense to final disposition with far fewer offenders being handled in institutions and probation offices than being committed. This process profoundly impacts upon the makeup of the group of persons under consideration in this chapter.

Within those social welfare activities constituting the justice system, some significant distinctions are made that go beyond those in almost any other social welfare field. Two of these classifications are by age and sex. Few other areas in social welfare or social work divide people according to age to the extent that we have labels like "juvenile delinquent." Urban police departments frequently have special juvenile units. Juvenile courts are set apart from those for adults. Correctional

Table 11.1 Index of Crime, United States, 1986[1]

	Offenses	Rate per 100,000 population
Murder & nonnegligent manslaughter	20,613	8.6
Forcible rape	90,434	37.5
Robbery	542,775	225.1
Aggravated assault	834,322	346.1
Burglary	3,241,410	1,344.6
Larceny-theft	7,257,153	3,010.3
Motor vehicle theft	1,224,137	507.8
Arson	*	*
Total	13,210,844	5,479.9
Violent crime	1,488,144	617.3
Property crime	11,722,700	4,862.6

*Insufficient data

services, too, are delineated by age, whether these are community-based or institutions. Similarly, there is a marked division based on the sex of the offender. In fact, probably no other social welfare field has made as great a sex distinction in its societal responses. While we do not generally have separate welfare departments, hospitals, and family agencies serving males and females, most correctional institutions are still one-sex places although training schools for delinquents are increasingly coeducational. Probation and parole caseloads are often, though not always, largely single-sex, both for children and adults. The sex barrier is changing, but it persists.

Social work as a profession has generally played a larger part with juvenile offenders than with adults, although it is active in both. Historically this activity with youth has often been seen as an aspect of "child welfare" broadly. But juvenile courts, to cite one corrections facet, not only hear delinquency cases but in some states also deal with other family-related matters such as child neglect, paternity, and nonsupport.

Our concern in this chapter is with justice—not social justice in the broader sense addressed by this book generally, that is, in housing, health, education, and other basic areas of human well-being—but justice specifically related to the accused and convicted. We need to examine the elements of the criminal and juvenile justice systems maintained by the society to provide, hopefully, "justice" for all people, including those labeled as deviant.

THE CRIMINAL JUSTICE SYSTEM

Law Enforcement

Three major subsystems constitute the criminal justice system: law enforcement, judicial, and correctional. Although social work plays the largest role in corrections, it is also related to the other subsystems, and all three must be considered to understand societal reactions to law violation and offenders. All three are involved in the treatment of these kinds of deviant persons, whether juvenile or adult. The order is significant in that, in general, first contact with suspects and the accused is usually by law enforcement personnel, whether municipal police, county sheriff's staff, state, or federal agents. In many cases this contact, alone or with others, ends the action without further activity requiring involvement of prosecution and the courts. In other situations, police work is only the first step that activates a series of events; the next phase is judicial.

One newer development in law enforcement that is especially pertinent for our purposes is police social work. Early in this century the first police social workers were policewomen. They were to provide certain social services primarily to juveniles and women. The movement then faded.[2] Starting in the 1970s, largely through the efforts of Harvey Treger at the Jane Addams College of Social Work, University of Illinois at Chicago, significant social work roles have appeared in the police departments of several Chicago suburbs and elsewhere, especially in Illinois.[3] The role of the police as commonly portrayed on television is quite distorted. It has been reported that whereas the typical police officer on TV shoots many people a year, police in the United States actually fire their guns once every twenty-seven years on average.[4] Many police personnel do not spend most of their time pursuing criminals. Rather, a large part of their job is dealing with family and neighborhood squabbles such as disputes between spouses and conflict between parents and children.[5] It is also true that this is actually among the most dangerous aspects of police work, activity for which police training is generally problematic and for which police may have little enthusiasm.[6] Based on recent FBI statistical reclassification of "disturbance calls," there is some question as to whether police work in domestic disputes is as dangerous as what had been assumed from prior records.[7] However, the new statistical results still show such work to carry a high risk for police.

In some communities, social workers employed by the police work in the juvenile unit.[8] In others, their assignments are broader, working generally with family problems. Police social work typically is team work, involving the worker, other police personnel, and community agencies and resources. Referrals and follow-up contacts are important in this context.

The acid test of innovative and experimental programs like these is what happens when the federal grants that brought them into being are exhausted. All too often the services die. This has not happened in some of the communities around Chicago and elsewhere, and the funds have become regular parts of the city and police department budget.[9] These programs can no longer be considered experimental.

Judicial

The second subsystem in criminal and juvenile justice is the judicial, the whole area of the courts, prosecution, defense, and disposition of cases by court officials. Here it is necessary to distinguish between adult criminal adjudication procedures and those of the juvenile court.

As noted, social work is more closely identified with work with juvenile offenders than adults. Nowhere is this more clear than in the juvenile court movement itself. Born in Chicago in 1899 in the Progressive

Era, the juvenile court personified a principle that is central to modern social work—individualization. Prior to this development, there was no distinction based on age among persons accused of committing offenses. Youngsters were handled the same as adults when in trouble with the legal authorities. There are records of young children even being put to death not so many decades ago for acts that today would be viewed as relatively minor. This was the way adult law violators were handled, and the same held true for youth. The juvenile court changed all of this through the assumption that each youngster could and should be treated individually toward the goal of rehabilitation. The legal principle involved here was *parens patriae*, the court acting as the ultimate parent.

As a result, the juvenile court, in appearance and procedures, became different from adult criminal court. Hearings rather than trials were conducted, and they were private and informal, aimed at determining what was best for the youth rather than simply ascertaining guilt or innocence and prescribing sentence. Bail bond was not a part of the juvenile process nor was an arraignment, a grand jury indictment, or proceedings based on the filing of a prosecutor's information as is done with adults. Until recent years, the presence of defense attorneys in juvenile hearings was the exception rather than the rule. Juries are still not part of the ordinary process for juveniles.

For the first two-thirds of the century, then, the juvenile court was a major social institution operating generally in this way. Beginning in the 1960s, profound changes began to occur with the 1966 *Kent* and 1967 *Gault* U.S. Supreme Court decisions. This grew out of growing concern nationally that the court systems designed to protect children might actually in some ways be detrimental to them. Specifically, there was (and is) reason to be concerned that in the name of helping the child and acting on his behalf, the youngster's rights may sometimes be violated. For example, there were occasions when a youth's denial of involvement in illegal acts was ignored or treated lightly because of the obvious presence of problems with the child and/or family, which were seen as requiring intervention. Or, as in the Arizona case of fifteen-year-old Gerald Gault, a youth was ordered into "treatment" that denied him his freedom until his twenty-first birthday when an adult convicted of a similar offense could have been fined between five and fifty dollars or incarcerated up to two months.[10] This sense of injustice is currently transforming the juvenile court into a more legalistic, traditional kind of judicial entity in which more attention is being paid to youngsters' constitutional and legal rights. Rules of evidence are now being followed more closely, the atmosphere in the juvenile hearing is more formal, and a defense attorney is routinely present.

The only major adult right not so far extended to juveniles in this context is a trial by jury.

Some critics of the juvenile court would take the extreme position of essentially abandoning it and making no distinction between adult offenders and at least many delinquents.[11] To do so would be to go back to the nineteenth-century practices and reject major protections for youth in the modern world. That some adolescents are violent and/or seem not to be amenable to available treatments is little justification for discarding a significant social innovation and "throwing the baby out with the bath water."

While the juvenile court is more of a "social work institution" than is the adult criminal court, the latter, too, has been influenced by legislative acts and judicial decisions. The historical direction has been generally toward devoting more attention to the individual offender as a human being and to the rights of the accused, although a more recent counter trend has been toward more severe penalties for offenses. James Q. Wilson and Ernest van den Haag are among the "new conservative" proponents of this latter thrust.[12]

Sue Markson

A victim-witness counselor talking with a rape victim in a police station. The social worker works out of the prosecutor's office or the police department on behalf of crime victims. She is supportive of and an advocate for the victim and witnesses.

Recently new attention has been devoted to victims and witnesses, often with services for such persons being provided by the prosecutor's office. Traditionally much attention was given to the accused or convicted person, and the victim might be lost in the judicial shuffle. These new programs keep victims and witnesses informed of developments throughout the often long, complex process, provide support in frequently tense situations, and provide other services as needed. Social workers could fill this role, and social work students currently have practicum placements in this setting.

Corrections: Institutions

The third criminal/juvenile justice subsystem is corrections. By the time an individual reaches this point, much has often happened at the hands of law enforcement and/or court personnel. These events have frequently left their mark on the person who has been convicted of committing an offense or, if a youth, found to be delinquent and in need of court intervention. For example, if an offender manifests bitterness, anger, defeat, resignation, or other attitudinal or behavioral attributes, part of the reason may lie within experiences he or she has had with police, judges, or other officials. Such experiences are often less than positive from the offender's view.

Corrections has two major aspects, community-based or field services, and institutions. Examples of traditional community services for both delinquents and adult offenders are probation and parole. Correctional institutions, on the other hand, run the gamut from short-term jails and juvenile detention centers to reformatories for young adults and training schools for youth to prisons mainly for adults. Various political jurisdictions are represented with jails and detention facilities tending to be city or county operated and prisons generally state or federal.

It is important to understand the difference between short-term and long-term institutional care of juvenile delinquents. Detention refers to the former. It is "temporary care of children in physically restricted facilities pending court disposition or transfer to another jurisdiction or agency."[13] When properly used, the situations for which juvenile detention may be appropriate are: (1) some runaways from other communities who it is determined present too great a risk to hold in less secure arrangements such as foster family care; (2) certain youngsters held by the police or court pending a hearing; they are held because parents could not be reached or because of the seriousness of the offense, the risk to self or others, or likelihood of subsequent illegal conduct; and (3) some youth who have had hearings and have been committed to longer-term institutions and are awaiting transportation and/or admission. Detention is often overused. While by definition it is short-term care, it all too often drags on indefinitely. The physical conditions of detention are another concern. Children should rarely, if ever, be detained in jails with adults, but all too often this is exactly what happens.[14] The distinction between detention and shelter care is that the former is physically secure and is for delinquents whereas shelter care is not secure and is for dependent/neglected youngsters. These two groups overlap, and unfortunately, some youngsters are in detention who do not require it in spite of delinquency.

While institutions are referred to frequently as "correctional," they might still today just as well be termed "penal," the traditional term, because of their typically primitive, punitive nature. All-too-frequent outbreaks of violence such as the infamous Attica (New York) riot of 1971 or the one in New Mexico State Prison in 1980 remind the public of the vastly greater potential dangers on the broader prison scene. In the latter tragedy at Santa Fe, at least thirty-three inmates died and dozens of persons were injured.[15] Among the common problems of correctional institutions contributing to their explosive potential are overcrowding; idleness; indiscriminate grouping; poorly qualified, trained, and paid staff as well as shortage of personnel; poor sanitation, food, and physical conditions; and lack of adequate educational, recreational, and treatment programs, to cite only a few. One of the fundamental attributes of prisons that is so problematic is that they tend to be physically bastille-like containing operations: they are warehouses —a place for holding people involuntarily for long periods of time under conditions that are marginal at best. Often such facilities are ancient architectural monstrosities unsuited for housing, let alone reforming, persons who have engaged in illegal conduct.

The dangers of incarceration can be summarized as follows: (1) risks of bodily injury or death for inmates and staff in such volatile environments; (2) the phenomenon of "institutionalized personality" through which the inmate becomes so accustomed to and dependent upon the highly structured environment that he or she is rendered unsuitable for living outside this narrow world; (3) the related labeling process in which one is branded by others as a convict with all that goes with this and sees oneself accordingly. Self-esteem is very much bound up in and affected by labeling; (4) correctional institutions by their very nature serve as training grounds or "schools" for crime in which techniques are shared among offenders.

It is true that today's American prison is typically not the place of open official brutality of an earlier era. But there are other often more subtle deficiencies. Idleness is its own brutality, so that the disappearance of the leather strap as a punishment instrument (to the extent that it is not as actively used as formerly) does not necessarily signify a renaissance. The problem continues to be so serious that in 1979 Sweden criticized the United States for its prison conditions by refusing to extradite a Kentucky physician who faced a sentence of fifty-nine years in America, a repugnant situation from a Swedish perspective. This reportedly was "the first time a foreign nation has refused to extradite a person in a non-political case because of American prison conditions."[16] Some of the positive changes that have taken place in American prisons have resulted from external pressures as federal courts have found conditions to be intolerable and unconstitutional, constituting cruel and unusual punishment.[17] The prisoners' rights movement has attained some significance in this context.

One response to such prison problems as overcrowding is more brick and mortar—to build new facilities. In recent years, numerous institutions have been erected by the Federal Bureau of Prisons and by state governments. But a parallel social movement in the opposite direction is epitomized by the formation by several groups in the 1970s of the National Moratorium on Prison Construction and some of the activities of organizations such as the National Council on Crime and Delinquency (NCCD). These groups contend that incarceration in American prisons is so dysfunctional (destructive, expensive, and so forth) that the solution is fewer, not more, prisons, and greater emphasis on alternatives to incarceration and on community-based correctional programs.[18] Significantly, at least part of the moratorium movement disappeared in 1987 with the demise of the National Moratorium's newsletter that had, since its start in 1975, opposed new prison construction.

There appears to be consensus that not all people locked in our prisons and penitentiaries require the high walls, guard towers, and other elements of maximum security. One of many examples is the recent statement of the director of adult corrections in a midwestern state having difficulty with its prison. He indicated that "40 percent of the people we have locked up today don't need to be in prison."[19] Some criminologists have placed the figure much higher. Clearly these architectural artifacts are extremely expensive to build and maintain (as much as $50,000 per single cell),[20] are often counterproductive, are unnecessary for many of the people on whom they are imposed, and often serve no useful purpose. Even as we continue to move to greater use of smaller medium- and minimum-security facilities, as has been done to some extent, and proportionately decreased use of maximum security, there still tends to be overuse of incarceration. As critics have often pointed out, the trouble with building more prisons is that they will be used, whether appropriately or not; whether needed or not they will fill up. An Abt Associates 1980 study found a correlation between prison population and prison capacity: "Additions are filled to rated capacity by the second year after opening," and "within five years the occupancy of the new space averages 130% of rated capacity."[21] In addition, once they exist, the state is "stuck" with them for decades to come, no matter how much lay and professional thinking may change in the meantime about the appropriateness of such treatment. Evidence of this is that institutions over a century old are still in use today in spite of the fact they are considered unacceptable by virtually everyone inside and outside the walls. Because they exist and nothing else appears available, they are used and misused. As William Nagel, an ex-warden and prison abolitionist, has said, "So long as we continue to build [prisons], we will have neither the pressures nor the will to develop more productive solutions."[22]

A current controversy has to do with privatization of prisons.[23] Some states are beginning to purchase some or all prison services from private entrepreneurs. The idea is to obtain better or cheaper (or both) prisons. Strong arguments are being made for and against privatization, and it is a significant issue for the entire social welfare field to watch.

Modern social work thinking is somewhat anti-institution and favors community-based programming in general. This is true not only in juvenile and criminal justice but up and down the social welfare line—children, the handicapped, mentally ill, elderly, and others. This is not to say that there is no place for institutions in contemporary thinking. In some fields, perhaps corrections most especially, there continues to be need for a minority of offenders to be institutionalized on a rational, purposeful basis, if for no other reason than the protection of the community and/or the offender from himself at a time when there is still much that is unknown or not fully understood about human behavior. This acknowledges, then, the social control function of corrections, which is perhaps only a more overt demonstration of an aspect of other social welfare programs going far beyond criminal justice. Control is inherent in some programs in mental health, public welfare, and retardation along with other fields.

The question then is not institutions or no institutions but their kind and quality. The dismal truth of correctional institutions generally in this country is that they are deadly, violence-prone places of defeat, apathy, and, all too frequently, suicide and homosexual rape. The latter phenomenon, rape, needs further explanation in order to understand better the "prison problem." There is reason to believe that rape in prison is not as much a sexual matter as one of power in a one-sex, macho environment.[24] Rape is a kind of ultimate degradation by people desperately attempting to hold or gain self-esteem, of others generally even more vulnerable physically and in terms of self-esteem. To speak of rehabilitation in such an environment seems somewhat unrealistic. What positive changes do occur with inmate attitudes and behaviors would appear to be often in spite of rather than because of incarceration in such settings. There is immense room to humanize such environments, but no matter what positive steps are taken to improve prisons, they always have certain inherent disadvantages, dangers, and limitations. It is important to be realistic and honest when we talk "rehabilitation" under these conditions. There tends to be more rhetoric than reality in such rehabilitation.

Community-Based Corrections

Among alternatives to institutions, "community-based corrections" is little more than a euphemism in many parts of the country. Words can be very deceiving and may mask business-as-usual practices with the appearance of change, progress, and innovation. Fortunately we know better than we do and change is possible, even in this difficult field, if there is the will to bring it about.

Alternatives run all the way through the criminal and juvenile justice systems and processes, from pretrial activities to postincarceration measures. They differ somewhat, just as do traditional services, depending upon whether the target group is juvenile delinquents or adult offenders. Another variable that has some significance in program alternatives and much in traditional programming is sex, as was noted earlier.

Early in the process of apprehending and adjudicating possible offenders there is a set of innovations in some communities aimed at streamlining and modernizing the procedures for handling adult suspects and offenders. Bail bond is an ancient practice of release from jail designed to guarantee the appearance of the accused at a later trial. By its very nature it discriminates blatantly against the poor, people unable to put up money ("make bond") to gain their release. Beginning in the 1960s with efforts of the Vera Foundation and the Vera-Manhattan Bail Project there have been a number of experiments around the country in bail bond reform.[25] It has now been conclusively demonstrated in various locations that many persons accused of committing crimes can be released on their own recognizance to await their trials without putting up money and that they will reappear later at the time of the trial. In some studies the rate of appearance for trial is even higher than with bail.[26]

The advantages are obvious: less incarceration in jail awaiting trials means less expense to the taxpayer, more productivity on the part of the suspect, who can keep or get a job and support his or her family; keeping the accused in the community or returning him there more quickly increases the likelihood of some community-based disposition such as probation being ordered for the convicted following the trial rather than more expensive and destructive incarceration. There are other virtues, one of which is the question of justice. In a system that supposedly assumes innocence until proof of guilt and one in which guilt is supposed to be demonstrated in the courtroom, not in the police station, street, media, or elsewhere, it would seem crucial to detain prior to trial only that small portion of suspects who present genuine risks of serious law violation or failure to appear for the trial. In other words, the principle of the least drastic or least restrictive alternative is operative as is individualization, an idea important to social work and one that should be important in criminal justice.

An example of this simple yet significant endeavor in one community was highlighted by an important federal agency set up in 1968 to expedite some of the nation's anticrime efforts, the Law Enforcement Assistance Administration (LEAA). Among other activities, this organization funded numerous demonstration projects around the nation in law enforcement, judicial, and correctional areas. Later a few of the most successful programs were selected by the U.S. Department of Justice as "exemplary projects" in the hope that they would be widely emulated. This designation started in 1973, and by 1981, thirty-five projects had been so designated.[27] The first such project is pertinent. In Des Moines, Iowa, the Polk County Department of Court Services was organized in 1971 just after the local county jail was condemned. This new organization consisted of four coordinated components: (1) pretrial release screening to do what has been described above; (2) pretrial community supervision of another group of persons who presented greater risks but who, it was determined, could still be released into the community if special monitoring was provided; (3) county-administered probation; and (4) a local community-centered corrections facility to house persons who otherwise would be in the jail or in a state prison. The latter was located in an army barracks building entirely different from most correctional institutions.[28]

The net result of these integrated efforts has been demonstrably better quality services at less cost to the public with no increase—and possibly a decrease—in recidivism. These services facilitate the offender's reintegration into the community without sacrificing public safety.[29] This is always one of the central concerns for the general public—protecting itself from the actions of persons perceived as a threat. People need to learn that they do not achieve security when an offender is incarcerated behind steel and stone. Incarceration is, in most cases, only a temporary measure; 95 percent of convicts will be back in the community. Hence, the appropriate question is not whether we will be exposed to him because we will be; rather it should be asked under what conditions he will return and if he will have changed for the better or for the worse as a result of his "correctional" experience. The public pays a very high cost for its *in*security, mistakenly believing it to be security.

Corrections is a bleak field filled with contradictions, paradoxes, and irony. The remainder of our account of the Des Moines community will provide an example. This very progressive "exemplary project" in Des Moines occurred at least partly as a result of abysmal conditions in the county jail and its condemnation. As a result of the project, the "jail problem" abated temporarily. Now, however, a few years later the same county has constructed a large new jail at immense cost to the taxpayer. The author has been impressed to hear, in discussing with some of the liberal backers of the jail bond issue for new construction, how humane and caring they are and how the offensiveness of the old jail motivated their efforts to replace it. But was it the most wise response? A better plan would appear to have been to build a new small jail having more relatively inexpensive army barracks-type quarters, if needed, and to use more of the alternatives which are paying off so well in the project for everyone—taxpayers, clients, and general public. The benevolent advocates of a new jail appear trapped in a value conflict in which the answer to one problem breeds another. Eternal vigilance is required in communities to assure the most positive directions for change. Without it the community may fall victim not only to reactionary forces but also to the occasional lack of vision of more progressive people.

This matter is even more complex than implied thus far, however, because of other dimensions. For example, it can be argued that a major part of the answer to the previously noted problems in state institutions such as overcrowding and violence is to incarcerate more of these offenders in local (city or county) jails and or in multicounty regional jails. There could be a number of advantages in this action including having most offenders closer to home and hence making family contacts easier to develop or maintain and strengthen. Such facilities would be or are smaller, which would generally be an improvement, since a major problem of many American prisons is their large size. More efforts could be made to involve inmates in viable employment programs in the community through work release or partial confinement measures. There are other advantages, too. Regional jails and juvenile detention facilities can be highly appropriate when two or more counties cannot or should not justify their own facilities, as in many rural areas, and can develop centralized, consolidated services cooperatively. In other words, there can be strong, sound arguments for erecting jails, if for no other reason than to reduce the need for large state prison construction. But this approach is appropriate only for the small portion of offenders who truly require incarceration.

Other noninstitutional measures are most effective and least expensive for most offenders.

Other Alternatives to Incarceration

In addition to the innovations and alternatives to institutions so far discussed, others include diversion, restitution, community service, mediation, work release, prerelease centers and halfway houses, and two large traditional services, probation and parole. Both inside institutions and in communities there also are various counseling, educational, recreational, and employment programs. The social work role in all of these developments varies from almost nil to extensive and extremely significant.

Diversion provides for the routing of the accused or convicted person away from the usual units and steps in the justice system in order to prevent the stigmatizing labeling and destructive experiences that tend to accompany the traditional process. In some programs diversion comes early and is a police function; in such cases an offender may be diverted from going to court. In other programs, diversion comes at a later stage involving prosecution and/or the court; then the person charged is diverted from some or all court or subsequent experience. When diverted, the person normally goes into a substitute program such as restitution.

There is a paradox and potential problem that has been pointed out by the critics of diversion. If the accused juvenile or adult is required to admit guilt without benefit of full legal protection in order to gain the opportunity for diversion, there is a real danger that innocent persons may be placed in diversion programs as a result.[30] This cannot be tolerated in a supposedly free society.

As is true of some other social welfare innovations, restitution as a program in the justice system is a fairly simple idea that was not entirely new in the 1970s, the time of its reemergence.[31] Restitution has the advantage of restoring the victims' losses and making amends, both tangibly and psychologically. With the increased interest in victims, victimology, and victim compensation and assistance, it can be seen that to make restitution can be valuable attitudinally and behaviorally for both the abused and the abuser. To be on the receiving end of crime is to feel intimidated and demeaned, whether as a victim of burglary, assault, or purse snatching. To be the perpetrator of such acts may be guilt or anxiety-producing. The anxiety and anger of both parties can be alleviated at least to some degree through making restitution in some form. In the new programs, restitution is often monitored by a court or administrative agency, and it may be just one aspect of a larger overall treatment plan for the offender.

In some situations, it is not an individual or group of persons who have been harmed by the offender but a collectivity or impersonal entity. An example is vandalism to public property. In such cases, the most appropriate penalty may well be community service such as painting in a courthouse, cleaning a public cemetery or park, helping in a day-care center, nursing home, or neighborhood center, or working with handicapped in a treatment facility. Although community service offers no panacea for crime and delinquency, it is appealing in several obvious respects, sharing some advantages and attributes of restitution. It is restorative both for the community or persons who suffered loss at the hands of the offender and for the norm violator. It is relatively easy and inexpensive to administer in contrast to many correctional activities. Further, it avoids the stigma and negative influences of incarceration, and it offers the possibility of facilitating changed attitudes on the part of the general public toward offenders in a more positive, useful direction. Citizens seeing their public buildings and grounds improved by law violators may acquire less harsh and punitive stances toward such persons. About one-third of the states have legislation making the judicial orders for community service an option.

An important issue with community service and some of the other related programs is whether they are actually used as alternative sanctions to institutionalization and hence reduce the number of persons who would otherwise be confined or whether they are used mainly with minor offenders who would not be incarcerated anyway. In the latter case the total number of persons in the overall criminal justice network is increased rather than decreased. In that case the net is widened, and community service would be expansionary rather than diversionary. That this net widening occurs is the conclusion of Irwin and Austin who advocate shorter prison terms as a more effective way of dealing with prison overcrowding.[32]

Work release is another option that provides some of the same positive features of other alternatives to incarceration. Grupp was one of its early advocates in 1963 although its roots date back to Wisconsin's Huber law of 1913.[33] Persons on work release experience partial confinement in that they are incarcerated in a jail or some other kind of secure institution but are released during specified time periods to obtain employment, work, or attend school or college. For example, they may work eight hours daily Monday through Friday, spending evenings, nights and weekends in jail. They may be charged for their meals and jail lodging out of their earnings, thus reducing the taxpayers' burden. Money sent home to families may make public assistance such as AFDC unnecessary or reduce the amount needed. While turning the jail into a "hotel" in this sense may complicate the life of the sheriff and staff, it has very real benefits for persons accused or convicted of offenses and for the community generally. A variation and reversal of this treatment measure is the partial confinement that takes the form of sentences to incarceration during defined times such as weekends and/or evenings. This can be useful in individual cases by breaking up or diluting such behavior patterns as problematic weekend drinking, while still allowing the person to function in the community on the job, with his or her family, in the usual environment in many contexts. These kinds of innovations also have the effect of avoiding the total institutional experience, the dependency it may create, and the danger of institutionalized personality. Encouraging, if not requiring, people to carry out their responsibilities for themselves in such day-to-day matters as meals, laundry, family, recreation, and education is encouraging people to be responsible. This alternative provides the opportunity.

A limitation on sentencing offenders to spend weekends in jail is that this tends to be a high population period for jails and may cause overcrowding. Some offenders can spend other days of the week locked up and still keep their jobs. For others partial confinement may need to be in less expensive and less restrictive facilities than jails. Many incarcerees do not require the brick and steel security features anyway.

Still another option for a judge can be sentencing a person to remain at home for specified periods. There are various "house arrest" schemes for restricting persons to their homes as they await trial or as part of the punishment following conviction. Through electronic computer devices now available and in use in some places, it is possible to monitor these people. Even with the cost of the equipment such programs are much less expensive than jails. They are probably also less damaging to the offender although it is important that the "Big Brother watching" and civil liberty aspects and potentialities of such measures be considered.[34]

Still another set of options is various mediation/conciliation programs aimed at bringing victim and offender together toward working out adjustments and making amends. The goal in such efforts is restoration. Such measures assume that the real victim in crime is the person, not the state or society, and that it is the actual victim who should be satisfied with the results of the punishment process.

All these newer community-based alternatives to institutions have their critics. People often feel that such measures are unrealistic and an easy out for offenders who are perceived as deserving severe punishment. What needs to be recognized is (1) how dysfunctional incarceration is, (2) how expensive it is, and (3) that various community-based measures can be effective and serve the need for punishment. Both the general public and the offender can experience these programs as severe constraints on the guilty parties. Furthermore, the public is not always as concerned with extracting a "pound of flesh" from offenders as is often thought. Wright notes some of the studies suggesting that in both Britain and America victims, offenders, and the public, including criminal justice personnel, favor compensation/restitution and/or community or personal service over prison terms.[35]

In the contemporary interest in more novel alternatives to incarceration, sometimes the two traditional services of probation and parole are neglected in spite of the fact that they encompass about three-fourths of all offenders under correctional supervision and continue to possess substantial potential to accomplish the multiple purposes of protection of the citizenry, conservation of public funds, and provision of useful services to those in trouble with the law. To understand what is meant by these terms, we will consider their similarities and dissimilarities. Probation and parole have in common that they are conditional releases under supervision and can be revoked. They differ in that probation is a judicial or "judge-made" decision, whereas parole is an administrative decision by a parole board, institutional authority, or some governing body. Probation is a release in lieu of incarceration, and parole comes later in the process after a period of incarceration in lieu of serving the entire sentence to its expiration.[36]

With probation more than parole, there are two aspects to the job: (1) study or investigation bringing together information used in such situations as by a judge in disposing of a case, and (2) supervision of the person who has been ordered placed on probation. In some probation organizations, one probation officer carries both responsibilities, and in others there is a separation of duties with the worker handling only one set of tasks.

Probation and parole operate with handicaps. The public often thinks of them as an easy out for pernicious people who ought to be dealt with severely rather than given a "slap on the wrist." But good-quality probation and parole are not an easy out for the offender. They place demands on him or her while presenting the opportunity and the assistance to change. Unfortunately, probation and parole are often given a bad name when a crime suspect is identified in the media as a probationer or parolee. When a suspect is not on probation or parole, this is not mentioned, of course.

Much of what is criticized is not quality probation and parole but only mediocre practices called by these terms, passing under the label. It could be argued that, in the main, the United States in all of these years has never really instituted probation and parole and given them a fair trial and that what passes for these services is destined to

fail because of such factors as (1) excessive caseloads, (2) poorly qualified and inadequately paid staff, (3) insufficient resources and support services, and (4) conflicting purposes and role ambiguity.[37]
Caseload figures alone make the point. The President's Crime Commission study in the mid-1960s found over 88 percent of all juvenile
cases, over 99 percent of all misdemeanor cases, and almost 97 percent
of all felony cases were the responsibility of probation officers having
caseloads in excess of fifty. The commission recommended an average
ratio of thirty-five offenders per officer.[38]

In recent years some states have moved to what is termed intensive
probation supervision in an effort to keep more offenders in the community and still protect the public. Caseloads are smaller, supervision of probationers is closer, contacts between staff and clients are
more frequent. Obviously it is more expensive than regular probation but still costs taxpayers less than institutionalization. Equally
important, the evidence is that it can be effective in controlling illegal behavior.[39]

THE SOCIAL WORK ROLE IN CRIMINAL/JUVENILE JUSTICE

Conflicting role expectations are problematic for probation parole "officers," "agents," "counselors," and so forth. These diverse expectations come from various external quarters and internally. Some
probation/parole staff perceive their jobs as similar to law enforcement and act accordingly. Others see the tasks as social work in nature,
and this definition determines their conduct. The position of the author is that, properly conceived, probation and parole are social work
activities. Like any social work job, they consist of multiple tasks. In
role clusters of this sort, some responsibilities are more directly and
clearly social work in nature, such as the counseling aspects, and others less so, such as some of the surveillance-type activities and the clerical duties.[40] But the overall thrust of the probation/parole job is social
work, that is, it generally includes information gathering (investigation), assessment, developing a plan of action, intervention, and evaluation. This, of course, is the social work helping or problem-solving
process, regardless of setting.

But this does not change the fact that "correctionists" and social
workers have a hard time coming together. Some corrections professionals look at social workers as impractical and idealistic, insuffi-
ciently oriented or committed to certain aspects of some jobs in
corrections, like certain perceptions of surveillance activities, and
naive about crime and criminals. Some social workers, on the other

hand, seem to see no place for social work in corrections, stressing social work's emphasis on client self-determination and noting that corrections clients are involuntary, arguing that you cannot help people who do not want help, or criticizing the confusion of corrections with law enforcement in facets of the tasks performed and punitive stances frequently held by some workers in corrections.

In light of the latter notions, the author would suggest that involuntary clients exist in many social welfare fields, not just corrections. Self-determination is not an absolute, since no one is a totally free agent and we all have constraints. People who do not want help can in fact be aided in the sense that help is relative, and the helper can and does use it selectively. The job of the helper is to enlist the client's involvement and cooperation, working through resistance and dealing with hostility.[41] If social work refuses to have a role in corrections, then it surrenders this important human service field to other, often more repressive groups. In so doing, it plays into a self-fulfilling prophecy: It criticizes punitive orientations toward offenders but relinquishes work with offenders to frequently more punitive people.

In addition to the direct service (casework and group work) activities accompanying such roles as probation, parole, institution social work, and other functions in corrections, social work is important in the other criminal/juvenile justice subsystems, as has been noted. This is particularly true in some of the innovations such as police–social work teaming. Another example is the use of volunteers. Not only may social workers as direct service workers use volunteers to help with their own caseloads, but social work may also play a significant role in community education about the need for volunteer programs and their value. Establishing such programs can be a social work task as can the recruitment, training, supervision, and evaluation of volunteers.[42] Similar relationships may develop for social work in such innovative programs as Neighborhood Justice Centers where problems that otherwise may require official court intervention are resolved through conciliation, mediation, and arbitration.[43]

A Case of Juvenile Offenders

Three sixteen- and seventeen-year-old boys were referred to the juvenile court by the police after being apprehended together for a series of burglaries, a serious offense. Adults similarly charged often face years of incarceration. The youths might very well have been institutionalized in the state training school or elsewhere. A court intake worker received the cases from the police, interviewed the boys and parents, attended the preliminary hearing, and recommended to the judge that, based on the seriousness of the offense, the youths be held temporarily in the juvenile detention center awaiting further study and information. At that point, the cases were assigned to the probation officer whose job was longer-term than that of the intake worker. It was to gather all pertinent information about the boys, their delinquency, and the total situation.

The school social worker was contacted at the school the boys had attended (all had dropped out) for information from school records. At the detention center the boys were seen individually for in-depth discussions. Detention staff gave the probation officer their observations including those having to do with the boys' attitudes and adjustment in detention. The probation officer talked separately with each set of parents.

In a few days, the probation officer decided to recommend to the judge that the boys be released from detention to their parents pending their final hearings, yet to be scheduled. Heavy caseloads generally caused more time to elapse before final hearings than was desirable, and if some youths were not released in the meantime, the population of the detention facility would be too high. Furthermore, releasing the youths made it possible to see how they would get along in the community. There was growing reason to believe that they presented few risks of further illegal activity. Throughout the probation officer's work, both before and after detention, it was learned that in spite of the delinquency and a few other weaknesses in the respective individual/family situations, there were significant strengths. All the boys and their families were concerned and cooperative with the police and the court workers. The youths appeared genuinely remorseful. They all held jobs, and one took evening classes in school.

It was the probation officer's responsibility to pull together all the material gathered into a social history or court summary and to make a recommendation to the judge for disposition of these cases. At the final hearing, the judge used the worker's information and accepted the recommendation, placing the youths on probation. In this court, the practice was for the same worker to continue with youngsters placed on probation, and this was done. There was no further delinquency although one boy married his girlfriend when she became pregnant, illustrating that in social work "success" is a relative matter. Some restitution was made. There were significant gains with regard to improved employment situations.

In this example, the taxpayer was saved the expense of unnecessary institutionalization, and three youths and their families were helped. Potentially damaging incarceration was avoided as the youths worked out their problems in the community.

Issues and Trends

The entire field of criminal and juvenile justice teems with issues, some of which have been noted in our discussion to this point. It is clearly a field of great controversy whether one is concerned with the law enforcement, judicial, or correctional realm. We will not repeat here what has already been explored. Rather, we will point out a few additional issues to increase understanding of these important areas and to illustrate further some of the kinds of problems and trends.

Major philosophical concerns in law enforcement center around the role of the police in a free society. How is one to balance individual liberty with collective order? Some famous (or notorious, depending upon one's views) U.S. Supreme Court decisions since the 1960s such as *Gideon, Escobedo,* and *Miranda* have, from certain points of view, complicated the job of law enforcement officers and worked to the advantage of offenders. On the other hand, it is also argued that the effect of such rulings is to require better quality and more professional law enforcement and that these court decisions are consistent with American ideals and principles and the civil liberties of all.

Another area of practical concern is the extent to which suspects/offenders should be pursued when there are great risks to innocent bystanders, law enforcement staff, and the suspects. For example, a number of persons each year are injured, some even killed, fleeing from the scene of a crime. Some of these injuries and deaths are inflicted by police. In some of these cases, the people injured or killed have had minimal or no involvement in illegal acts.[44] It is not uncommon for police to pursue at high speed persons who have only violated traffic laws.[45] To chase people in cars at ninety miles an hour through city streets and country roads because they have run through stop signs or lights seems unwise. It is not enough to say that police are held responsible for apprehending offenders. They should not do so *at all costs*; there must be reason and balance. Besides, many times such offenders can be safely arrested later in other places, since their identities are often already known or can be determined from auto licenses and other means.

Still another issue that affects the police but is also a larger matter is the easy availability of firearms to almost everyone in the United States. Because this presents such a great danger to peace officers and because every year so many such persons die or are seriously injured as a result of guns in the hands of other people, it is little wonder that police organizations are advocates of gun control.[46] But in spite of all such efforts, we continue to live in a nation with literally millions of guns available.[47] In many states, their availability is indiscriminate relative to some or all variables such as age, mental condition, or legal record. But powerful pressure groups and lobbies such as the National Rifle Association reflecting an older, more rural, frontier-type life-style continue to convince (or coerce) legislators that the right to possess firearms is somehow essential even to urban America. The fact that public opinion polls have found the vast majority of those surveyed favoring gun control has not so far changed this picture extensively.[48] Social workers need to be aware of such problems and participate in social action and policy development aimed at their resolution.

In the judicial arena, issues also abound. The two to be discussed here deal with trials and sentencing. A principle of American jurisprudence has long been the idea of a speedy trial following arrest. In view of this, repeated and prolonged delays often in backlogged urban courts are a matter of concern. There are many reasons for the slow pace of rendering justice such as large caseloads and frequent continuances.[49] Some of these have to do largely with prosecution, some with defense, and some with other aspects of the process. But whatever the reasons, the situation is seen by many as undesirable and problematic.

Possible remedies for this problem are on the horizon with the passage in 1975 of the Speedy Trial Act. But an important question to raise will always be, at what cost will we have swifter trials? Can this be accomplished largely through streamlining and instituting various efficiencies in established practices, or may there be more fundamental threats to due process presented? Such questions are important to many professions including social work.

Sentencing has always been problematic and in recent years has involved considerable ferment. There is a move in some states away from indeterminate sentencing toward determinate and/or mandatory sentences. A major reason for this development was growing concern over a perception of sentences as being too capricious and unequal. There is the view that similar illegal conduct should bring similar penalties. This movement then reduces the judge's discretion and options and makes sentencing more mechanical. It attacks the indeterminate sentencing idea that penalties should fit the offender rather than the offense and questions whether individualized justice (differential penalties) is not a contradiction in terms. Since individualization is a basic principle of social work, the field should give these debates thoughtful attention.

It would appear that a middle position may be appropriate in this controversy. Some limitations placed on judicial discretion could prevent the most extreme and blatant inequality and abuses in sentencing. But at the same time judges should retain some degree of discretion in order to humanize the law and make it relevant to persons and situations. For these reasons, it would be wise for legal codes to prescribe some range of possible penalties rather than a totally fixed, flat figure (x dollars fine, years incarcerated, and so forth). Convicted persons who are incarcerated could be given a clear picture of how much time they will spend locked up and hence not have to live with painful uncertainty. This can be done without rigid practices in which a prisoner's behavior has nothing at all to do with the date of release.

The whole sentencing controversy illustrates the historical evolution of social movements. Indeterminate sentencing was a reform when it was first introduced, a reaction against rigid, harsh, punitive practices. Some argue now that a new reform is needed to insure justice and equity, hence the determinate sentencing movement. Some also view indeterminate sentencing as too lenient and now are calling for mandatory sentences as a crime control measure. The resulting more certain incarceration and longer imprisonment are factors in the prison population explosion. The pendulum will undoubtedly swing again in the future.

The 1983–1984 term of the U.S. Supreme Court was noteworthy partly for the extreme positions taken by the majority on the court relative to the Bill of Rights. Now the innocent and guilty alike are to be subject to increased governmental power. Evidence produced by police searches previously held to be unconstitutional under the Fourth Amendment may now be accepted. In its decision on a jail-conditions case the cherished view of innocent until proven guilty has been ignored by the court. And prisoners' personal property may now be arbitrarily seized and destroyed.

Since future developments will be an extension of the present, it is not difficult to predict ongoing tensions and controversies. For example, there may be a decline in adult parole, even conceivably its disappearance if the movement to determinate sentences accelerates and becomes widespread. Maine abolished parole in 1976, and some other states have ended parole boards' releasing authority.[50] Federal legislation was enacted in 1984 to phase out federal parole beginning in 1987.[51] Totally eliminating parole is unfortunate in this writer's judgment because, even if one agrees with the idea of flat sentences and hence no parole decision to be made, there are important services to be provided to persons leaving correctional institutions. All persons being released, not just those leaving on parole prior to expiration of sentence, should be afforded assistance in reestablishing themselves in the community. They need help with families, housing, employment, education, recreation, counseling, and other matters to smooth the transition and maximize the chances of a positive readjustment.

Interestingly some states that have in effect abolished parole are reinstituting or retaining postrelease after-care programs that sound like parole without the name. The realities of prison overcrowding and the need to protect the community via supervising and assisting convicts returned to the community may preserve or resurrect parole. But most states now have laws establishing mandatory minimum incarceration for specific offenses, and many provide sentences of life without possibility of parole. So it seems likely that for some time to come the United States will imprison more persons for longer periods of time than was true in the past.

In the future persons in the criminal and juvenile justice systems, especially corrections, need to learn not to promise more than can reasonably be delivered. This has to do partially with claims relative to recidivism. Since recidivism is in the minds of so many the real test of effectiveness in corrections, it is tempting to make claims beyond our ability to produce. Realities must be faced—crime and delinquency are complex matters that do not easily lend themselves to our treatment activities. Given social forces and values (for example, acquisitiveness and materialism), our limited knowledge of human behavior, our unsophisticated intervention measures, conflicting community attitudes and goals, and other influences, we are not likely to be able to reduce substantially these deviancy rates in the near future.[52]

A factor that needs to be considered relative to the future of these problems and programs is the role of our leaders. Will they help to inform and enlighten the public, a much-needed service, or will they only obfuscate? A case in point is the 1988 presidential election campaign. In the late 1960s and the 1970s there was much concern about "crime in the streets" and "law and order." But early in the 1980s there were reported reductions in the crime rate. Nevertheless, both presidential contenders in the two major parties devoted attention to crime and pandered to the public's emotions. George Bush made his get-tough-with-crime stance a conspicuous part of his campaign and struck a receptive chord with Americans. But Michael Dukakis was not to be outdone. Interestingly he partially succeeded in defusing this issue by declaring his concern about crime and his intention to control it if elected. But were Americans better informed about crime and delinquency following this campaign throughout which each candidate attempted to outdo the other in his opposition to crime? These candidates could have aided millions of citizens to understand much about crime: that it is largely a youth and young adult phenomenon and the implications of this fact; that labeling itself is problematic; that it is incredibly expensive in terms of not only the losses caused by offenders but also our generally primitive, punitive, hit-and-miss ways of dealing with it that turn out not to be especially productive; that there are options and alternatives to our traditional treatment measures; that crime and criminal justice are extremely complex; that our own social structure, institutions, and values are inextricably intermeshed in our crime; that we may be expecting too much of our justice apparatus given its lack of sophistication and public support; that decriminalization in such areas as status offenders, public drunkenness, and certain drug and other offenses could go a long way toward affording a "solution";[53] and much more. But in the main this does not happen, and hence the future remains uncertain.

Finally, a consideration in future developments is how wide-ranging our mentality (information and attitudes) becomes or whether we "wear blinders." Examining the experience of other nations can be useful in assessing where we are and where we may go. This does not mean that what works well in a smaller more homogeneous country can necessarily be emulated here with equally positive results. But it is important to be informed as to the possibilities and to be imaginative in innovations and implementation. The Netherlands contrasts vividly with the United States in terms of incarceration; the former has one of the lowest rates in the world and the latter is among the highest. The Netherlands incarceration rate is 20 per 100,000 compared to 225 per 100,000 in the United States. The average sentence served in prison there has recently been reduced from 3.2 months to 1.1 months at a time when American sentences are years and are lengthening. A different conception of the prosecutor's role also characterizes the Netherlands.[54]

Sweden presents another interesting picture. In 1976, of the 10,000 persons admitted to prison in that country, 69 percent were sentenced to less than four months, 20 percent between four and twelve months, and sentences over a year were ordered for only 11 percent. The "day fine" is used in Sweden. Through this system consideration is given by the court to the seriousness of the offense and the resources of the offender so that the penalty affords more equity than the usual fine here.[55]

Denmark provides for young adult offenders alternative housing in a youth hostel half occupied by nonoffenders. Another Danish innovation is placing offenders in the homes of volunteer foster families. West Germany has come to favor for minor offenders fines over incarceration and has reduced its institutional population rather substantially.[56]

There are also differences internationally relative to the existence and use of capital punishment. In many nations, the United States included, the death penalty declined historically. Now, however, it is being resurrected in this country. While there were no executions in the United States between 1967 and 1976, the 100th since then occurred on June 14, 1988. Three-fourths of these were in Texas, Florida, Louisiana, and Georgia. Included in these executions was the first woman in twenty-two years and a retarded man.[57] Three were executed

on one day, August 28, 1987, the most on one day since executions returned in 1977. State after state has changed statutes in order to meet
U.S. Supreme Court objections, and the death penalties of many states
are apparently constitutional according to the present Court's interpretation. Since there was a record of over 2,000 persons on death rows in
May 1988 (a third in Florida, Texas, and Georgia), many more executions may take place in the 1990s in the absence of major court rulings
impeding such action.[58]

SUMMARY AND CONCLUSIONS

This chapter has examined how deviancy is socially defined and how
societal responses are made in response to crime and delinquency.
Just as traditional programs (for example, probation, institutions)
were social provisions, so modifications in these and the addition of
innovative services are social measures and reactions. The criminal
and juvenile justice subsystems have been analyzed, shortcomings
noted, and reforms such as deinstitutionalization described. Alternatives to incarceration have been stressed. The social work role in the
spectrum of services has been explored. In this connection corrections has been seen as a very difficult field generally and a problematic
one for social work, but one badly needing social work knowledge,
skills, and values. Criminal and juvenile justice have been found to be
fields ripe with conflict and controversy and with an uncertain future
but substantial potential for positive productivity. Which way these
fields go depends to a considerable extent on the ability of professionals and the public to be rational in an often irrational climate. And
which way they go is important for, in the words of Dostoevski,

> The degree of civilization in a society can be judged by entering its
> prisons.

NOTES

1. *Crime in the United States, 1986: FBI Uniform Crime Reports* (Washington, D.C.: U.S. Government Printing Office, 1987), p. 42.
2. Albert R. Roberts, "The History and Role of Social Work in Law Enforcement," in A. R. Roberts, *Social Work in Juvenile and Criminal Justice Settings* (Springfield, Ill.: Charles C Thomas Publisher, 1983), p. 91.
3. Harvey Treger, "Police-Social Work Cooperation: Problems and Issues,"
   Social Casework 62, no. 7 (September 1981): 426-433.

4. Dave Rhein, "Violence on TV Goes Down the Tube," *Des Moines Register*, January 8, 1988, pp. 1T, 5T.

5. Edward M. Colbach and Charles D. Fosterling, *Police Social Work* (Springfield, Ill.: Charles C Thomas, 1976).

6. Ibid. Also see the selected bibliography, *Police Stress* (Washington, D.C.: National Criminal Justice Reference Service, 1979).

7. U.S. Department of Justice, "Danger to Police in Domestic Disturbances —A New Look," by Joel Garner and Elizabeth Clemmer (Washington, D.C.: U.S. Government Printing Office, 1986).

8. For example, Bettendorf, Iowa.

9. Treger, "Social Service Projects," p. 39; another example is John J. Carr, "An Administrative Retrospective on Police Crisis Teams," *Social Casework* 60, no. 7 (July 1979): 416–422.

10. Ted H. Rubin, *Juvenile Justice* (Santa Monica, Calif.: Goodyear Publishing Co., 1979), p. 149.

11. D. C. Dwyer and Roger B. McNally, "Juvenile Justice: Reform, Retain, and Reaffirm," *Federal Probation*, September 1987, pp. 47–51.

12. James Q. Wilson and Richard J. Herrnstein, *Crime and Human Nature* (New York: Simon & Schuster, 1985); Ernest van den Haag, *Punishing Criminals* (New York: Basic Books, 1975).

13. National Council on Crime and Delinquency, *Standards and Guides for the Detention of Children and Youth*, 1961.

14. Ibid, p. 3. See also Rosemary Sarri, *Under Lock and Key: Juveniles in Jails and Detention*, University of Michigan, 1974; *Children in Adult Jails* (Washington, D.C.: Children's Defense Fund, 1976); Thomas J. Cottle, *Children in Jail* (Boston: Beacon Press, 1977).

15. "The Killing Ground," *Newsweek*, February 18, 1980, pp. 66–76.

16. Colman McCarthy, "Sweden's Rebuff Highlights Cruel, Inhuman Conditions in U.S. Prisons," *Des Moines Register*, March 24, 1979, p. 12A.

17. Examples are Louisiana where an entire prison was ordered shut down and someone was appointed to plan drastic reforms, and Arkansas where the state had to increase the prison's budget 600 percent to meet court demands.

18. See, for example, *Jericho*, a quarterly newsletter of the National Moratorium on Prison Construction, Unitarian Universalist Service Committee, Washington, D.C.; and Board of Directors, National Council on Crime and Delinquency, "The Nondangerous Offender Should Not Be Imprisoned: A Policy Statement," *Crime and Delinquency* 21, no. 4 (October 1975): 315–322.

19. *Des Moines Register*, June 23, 1980, p. 4A.

20. *Jericho*, quarterly newsletter of the National Moratorium, no. 34 (Winter 1984), p. 12.

21. Carol Bergman, "Criminal Justice Reforms: The Struggle Continues," *Jericho*, no. 44 (Fall 1987), p. 14.

22. William G. Nagel, *The New Red Barn: A Critical Look at the Modern*

American Prison (New York: Walker & Co., for The American Foundation Inc., Institute of Corrections, 1973), p. 148.

23. Charles H. Logan, "The Propriety of Proprietary Prisons," *Federal Probation*, September 1987, pp. 35–40. See also U.S. Department of Justice, "Private Prisons," by John J. Dilulio, Jr. (Washington, D.C.: U.S. Government Printing Office, 1988).

24. Wilbert Rideau and Billy Linclair, "Sex Power, Enslavement in Jails and State Prisons," *Des Moines Register*, June 22, 1980, p. 1C and 3C; ibid, p. 2C, Ray Cornell, "It Does Happen Here; Rape in Iowa Prisons." See also P. L. Nacci and T. R. Kane, "Sex and Sexual Aggression in Federal Prisons," *Federal Probation*, March 1984, pp. 46–53.

25. J. S. Goldkamp, *Two Classes of Accused—A Study of Bail and Detention in American Justice* (Cambridge, Mass.: Ballinger Publishing Co., 1979).

26. U.S. Department of Justice, *An Exemplary Project: Community Based Corrections in Des Moines* by David Boorkman, Ernest J. Fazio, Jr., Noel Day, and David Weinstein (Washington, D.C.: U.S. Government Printing Office, 1976), p. 8.

27. National Institute of Law Enforcement and Criminal Justice; *Exemplary Projects*, Washington, D.C., 1979.

28. Boorkman et al., *An Exemplary Project*, pp. 1–48.

29. Ibid., pp. 6–14.

30 Paul Nejelski, "Diversion: The Promise and the Danger," *Crime and Delinquency* 22, no. 4 (October 1976): 393–410; entire issue is devoted to diversion. See also Donald R. Cressey and Robert A. McDermott, *Diversion From the Juvenile Justice System* (Ann Arbor: University of Michigan, 1973).

31. See, for example, Joe Hudson and Burt Galaway, *Considering the Victim* (Springfield, Ill.: Charles C Thomas, 1975); and by the same authors, *Restitution in Criminal Justice* (Lexington, Mass.: D.C. Heath & Co., 1977).

32. John Irwin and James Austin, *It's About Time: Solving America's Prison Crowding Crisis* (San Francisco: National Council on Crime and Delinquency, 1987), p. 17.

33. Stanley Grupp, "Work Release in the United States," *The Journal of Criminal Law, Criminology and Police Science* 54, no. 3 (September 1963); 267–272.

34. U.S. Department of Justice, "House Arrest," by Joan Petersilia (Washington, D.C.: U.S. Government Printing Office, 1988).

35. Martin Wright, "What the Public Really Wants," *Jericho*, no. 44 (Fall 1987), pp. 9 and 15. See also John Doble, *Crime and Punishment: The Public's View* (N.P.: Public Agenda Foundation, 1987).

36. Charles H. Shireman, "Crime and Delinquency: Probation and Parole," *Encyclopedia of Social Work*, 17th ed. (Washington, D.C.: NASW, 1977), pp. 213–217.

37. The President's Commission on Law Enforcement and Administration of Justice, *The Challenge of Crime in a Free Society*, 1967; especially chapter 6.

38. Ibid, pp. 167–169.

39. John P. Conrad, "News of the Future: The Intensive Revolution," *Federal Probation* (June 1987), pp. 62–64.

40. Interestingly in the more professionally operated and staffed agencies there appears to have been a reduction in surveillance functions in routine cases.

41. Elizabeth D. Hutchison. "Use of Authority in Direct Social Work Practice with Mandated Clients," *Social Service Review* 61, no. 4 (December 1987): 581–598.

42. Shireman, "Crime and Delinquency," p. 217; Gordon Manser, "Volunteers," *Encyclopedia of Social Work*, 18th ed. (Silver Spring, Md.: NASW, 1987), 2:842–851.

43. *Justice Assistance News* 1, no. 5 (June/July 1980): 13.

44. National Institute of Law Enforcement and Criminal Justice, *A Community Concern: Police Use of Deadly Force*, Washington, D.C., 1979.

45. "Driver Going 160 Falls Prey to 'Silver Bullet,'" *Des Moines Register*, July 9, 1981, p. 1A. Also the television program "Sixty Minutes" dealt with this subject on November 9, 1980.

46. William H. Webster, *Crime in the United States: Uniform Crime Reports* (Washington, D.C.: Federal Bureau of Investigation, 1979), pp. 301–313. See also the selected bibliography, *Firearm Use in Violent Crime* (Washington, D.C.: Criminal Justice Reference Service, 1978).

47. "3 Million Handguns Still Hidden in N.Y.," *Des Moines Register*, August 12, 1980, p. 3B.

48. George Gallup, "Poll: Americans Want Tighter Handgun Laws," *Des Moines Register*, February 3, 1980, p. 12A.

49. *Justice Assistance News*, p. 6.

50. *State and Social Probation and Parole System* (Washington, D.C.: Law Enforcement Assistance Administration, 1978), p. 132. See also Andrew von Hirsch and Kathleen J. Hanrahan, *Abolish Parole?* (Washington, D.C.: National Institute of Law Enforcement and Criminal Justice, 1978).

51. Joseph J. Senna and Larry J. Siegel, *Introduction to Criminal Justice*, 4th ed. (St. Paul, Minn.: West Publishing, 1987), p. 528.

52. Jackson Toby. "The Prospects of Reducing Delinquency Rates in Industrial Societies," *Federal Probation*, December 1963, pp. 23–25.

53. Edwin M. Schur, *Crimes without Victims* (Englewood Cliffs, N.J.: Prentice-Hall, 1965). See also *Radical Non-Intervention*, 1973, by the same author and publisher, and President's Commission, *Challenge of Crime in a Free Society*, pp. 233–237.

54. Calvert R. Dodge, *A World without Prisons* (Lexington, Mass.: Lexington Books, 1979), pp. 133–157. At the end of 1986 there were 546,659 prisoners held by American federal and state corrections authorities, an all-time high, according to the Bureau of Justice Statistics.

55. Ibid., pp. 191–212.

56. Ibid., pp. 101–114; 159–179.

57. "Barfield Now 1st Woman Executed in U.S. in 22 Years," *Iowa City Press*

Citizen, November 2, 1984, p. 6A; "Retarded Man Executed for Rape, Slaying of Girl," *Des Moines Register,* July 31, 1987, p. 4A.
58. Robert M. Bohm, "American Death Penalty Attitudes," *Criminal Justice and Behavior* 14, no. 3 (September 1987): 380–396.

ADDITIONAL SUGGESTED READING

Coleman, James W., *The Criminal Elite* (New York: St. Martin's Press, 1985).

Currie, Elliott, *What Kind of Future?* (San Francisco: National Council on Crime and Delinquency, 1987).

Hawkins, Gordon, and Franklin E. Zimring, *The Pursuit of Criminal Justice* (Chicago: University of Chicago Press, 1984).

Morris, Norval, and Gordon Hawkins, *The Honest Politician's Guide to Crime Control* (Chicago: University of Chicago Press, 1970).

Newman, Graeme, *Just and Painful: A Case for the Corporal Punishment of Criminals* (New York: Macmillan, 1983).

Reiman, J. H., *The Rich Get Richer and the Poor Get Prison,* 2nd ed. (New York: John Wiley & Sons, 1984).

Sheehan, Susan, *A Prison and a Prisoner* (Boston: Houghton Mifflin Co., 1978).

Sherman, Michael, and Gordon Hawkins, *Imprisonment in America: Choosing the Future* (Chicago: University of Chicago Press, 1981).

Shireman, Charles, H., and Frederic G. Reamer, *Rehabilitating Juvenile Justice* (New York: Columbia University Press, 1986).

Silberman, Charles E., *Criminal Violence, Criminal Justice* (New York: Random House, 1978).

Van Voorhrs, Patricia, "Correctional Effectiveness and the High Cost of Ignoring Success," *Federal Probation,* March 1987, pp. 56–62.

von Hirsch, Andrew, *Past or Future Crimes* (New Brunswick, N.J.: Rutgers University Press, 1985).

von Hirsch, Andrew, Michael H. Terry, and Kay A. Knapp, *The Sentencing Commission and its Guidelines* (Boston: Northeastern University, 1987).

Walker, Samuel, *Sense and Nonsense about Crime: A Policy Guide* (Monterey, Calif.: Brooks/Cole Publishing Company, 1985).

Wooden, Kenneth, *Weeping in the Playtime of Others: America's Incarcerated Children* (New York: McGraw-Hill, 1976).

Zimring, Franklin E., and Gordon Hawkins, *Capital Punishment and the American Agenda* (New York: Cambridge University Press, 1986).

12 Social Work and the Elderly

Emma Jean Williams

> Old age is respectable just as long as it asserts itself,
> maintains its proper rights and is not enslaved to any-
> one. . . . The greater affairs of life are not performed
> by physical strength, activity or nimbleness of body,
> by deliberation, character, expression of opinion. Of
> these old age is not only not deprived; but, as a rule,
> has these in a greater degree. . . . Old men retain
> their intellects well enough if they keep their minds
> active and fully employed. The crowning grace of old
> age is influence.
>
> Cicero

The number of persons over sixty-five in the United States has grown since the turn of the century. According to research compiled by the American Association of Retired Persons (AARP) and the Administration on Aging (AoA) this population numbered 29.2 million in 1986, which represented 12.1 percent of the population. From 1900 to 1986 the percentage tripled. The most rapidly growing is that group over seventy-five. Projections are that this population will continue to increase in the future with some slowing during the 1990s due to the low birth rate during the Great Depression of the 1930s. There will then be a rapid acceleration between 2010 and 2030 when the baby boom generation reaches age 65.[1]

A similar increase in the older population can be noted from an international perspective. In 1950 United Nations estimates were that there were approximately 200 million persons over sixty years of age throughout the world. In 1980 there were more than 376 million people aged sixty or older in the world, including 171 million in the more developed regions and 205 million in those less developed. The projections for the world populations of those over sixty will increase at a similar rate as in the United States.[2]

This increase in the older population is significant in planning future social and medical programs. The fact that there will be increasing numbers over the age of seventy-five will mean greater frequency of chronic and debilitating conditions, which will increase the requirements for extended care.[3]

AGING AND SOCIAL PROVISION

The study of gerontology is of necessity multidisciplinary due to the nature of the aging process. It is a relatively young field; as the numbers of older persons have increased, we are learning more about the totality of the aging process. People have always been interested in and curious about longevity: why some people have a longer life span than others, searching for the "fountain of youth," and seeking some means of extending life. However, in the past three decades the United States has had a significant number of aging persons and has now identified the field of gerontology as an area of concern to numerous disciplines, including social work.

The Gerontological Society was founded in 1945 to provide attention to the field of aging and a forum for professionals along with research. It publishes two major periodicals: *The Gerontologist* and the *Journal of Gerontology*. The National Council on Aging was established in 1960 and became "a central national resource that works with and through other organizations to develop interest in work with older people and to design methods that can be used in programs that are designed to meet their varied needs."[4]

In 1961 the first White House Conference on Aging was held in Washington, D.C., which "set the tone for increasing federal involvement with the condition of the elderly population as a part of our national policy. As a result of the recommendations of this Conference, the nation could no longer ignore one tenth of its people."[5]

The theme of the second White House Conference was "Toward a National Policy on Aging." "Some of the policy resolutions of the second White House Conference in 1971 found their way into national legislation. The aged had become visible and had gained somewhat reluctant recognition as a segment of the population that was likely to increase in numbers if not yet in power."[6] Emphasis was placed on planning and coordination of services. Attention was given to the development of resources needed to sustain people in their own homes by providing them with supports to maintain independent living.

As an outgrowth of the attention they had begun to receive through their increasing numbers, the elderly began to organize themselves into groups to promote causes and point up issues that impact upon them. There has come to be an increasing awareness that the older person has power due to growing numbers. If the aged come together around those issues that affect the majority of elderly, they will have a larger voice in establishing public policy for this age group. The primary national organizations for the elderly are:

- American Association of Retired Persons
- National Retired Teachers Association
- Gray Panthers
- National Association of Retired Federal Employees
- National Caucus on the Black Aged
- National Council of Senior Citizens

There are two important national laws that have had impact on the aged: (1) the Social Security Act passed in 1935 and subsequently amended numerous times, and (2) the Older Americans Act of 1965, which also has been amended in succeeding sessions of Congress.[7]

Old-age pensions were provided by states beginning in 1915. They were means-tested, they did not provide adequate income, and only twenty-eight states provided them. The Social Security Act, passed in the midst of a severe depression, "defined the parameters of national policy and provision for the aged" for the following decades.[8]

Not until 1965 did another major piece of legislation pass that affected the elderly, the Older Americans Act. This act established a central administrative office, the Administration on Aging (AoA) and made funds available to the states to be allocated to local government and nonprofit agencies for assistance in the coordination and planning of programs. There was an emphasis on demonstration projects and providing training for personnel working with aged. Amendments in 1973 expanded the provisions including a specialized nutrition measure, which has become known as the congregate meal program.[9]

International Comparisons

The report of the World Assembly on Aging, published by the United Nations in 1982, points up many similarities among countries of the world in relation to their aging population. As has been stated previously, the international picture is similar to that in the United States. The report suggests that there needs to be a developmental plan of addressing the increasing numbers of elderly persons. There will be increasing need for appropriate and safe housing, a secure economic base, and meeting health and nutrition needs, as these are common to all cultures. Nations will have to determine how they will structure their programs. One suggestion is that in the developing countries there could be more organization of public and private resources to fill the void that may be created as families can no longer provide the care for their aging parents.[10]

The sex imbalance among older persons resulting in more women than men has certain implications that need to be taken into account in all countries of the world. The characteristics of this population include widowhood, reduced income, and increased poverty, plus greater risk of ill health and institutionalization. Many of the health problems of the elderly are those associated with older women, "and special attention should be given to the particular health conditions and health service needs of older women."[11]

Ageism

Robert Butler in 1969 used the word "ageism" in reference to prejudice against old people.[12] We tend to discriminate on the basis of stereotypes, images that we believe typify the members of certain groups. By placing people in categories, we avoid consideration of individual differences within these groups. There are many myths about older people that younger people tend to believe and that bring about discrimination. Butler summarized the stereotypes associated with old age:

> An older person thinks and moves slowly. He does not think as he used to or as creatively. He is bound to himself and can no longer change or grow. He can learn neither well nor swiftly and, even if he could, he would not wish to. Tied to his personal traditions and growing conservatism, he dislikes innovations and is not disposed to new ideas. Not only can he not move forward, he often moves backward. He enters a second childhood caught up in increasing egocentricity and demanding more from his environment than he is willing to give to it. Sometimes he becomes an intensification of himself, a caricature of a lifelong personality. He becomes irritable and cantankerous, yet shallow and enfeebled. He lives in his past; he is behind the times. He is aimless and wandering of mind, reminiscing and garrulous. Indeed, he is a study in decline, the picture of mental and physical failure. He has lost and cannot replace his friends, spouse, job, status, power, influence, and income. He is often stricken by diseases which, in turn, restrict his movement, his enjoyment of food, the pleasure of well-being. He has lost his desire and capacity for sex. His body shrinks, and so too does the flow of blood to his brain. His mind does not utilize oxygen and sugar at the same rate as formerly. Feeble, uninteresting, he awaits his death, a burden to society, to his family, and to himself.[13]

The majority of these myths or attitudes about older people are based on false generalizations. Often ignored is the fact that there are as many differences among older people as there are in the general population.

Theories of aging vary. Older people are generally viewed positively, but seen as passive and nonactive, which produces a negative view of the aging process. They are seen as leading sedentary lives, not involved in the community or with other persons. The disengagement theory of aging—that older people no longer want to be active so they withdraw into themselves by choice—has been a popular belief for some time. This is a comfortable theory to accept because, if older people withdraw by choice, we do not have to be concerned about them; after all, they do not want to be involved. They want to be left alone. A newer theory of aging, called activity theory, views the aging process in another way. The opposite of disengagement, this theory asserts that older persons continue to be involved in activities much as in earlier periods in their lives.

It is a mistake to lump all older persons under the same theory. In addition to being different from other groups of clients, the elderly constitute the most heterogeneous age grouping in the population. Differences of sex, race, religion, ethnicity, language, health conditions, social setting, economic status—and even of relative age—are but a few of the many factors that differentiate the elderly from one another. Indeed, chronological age, of and by itself, tells us no more about a person than the number of years he or she has lived or the probability that the person will be subject to certain conditions or events, such as widowhood, physical impairment, institutionalization, or death.[14]

There have been assumptions made that older people are no longer interested in or capable of sexual functioning. This is a myth that in more recent years is being dispelled. Older persons remain as sexually active as their health and other circumstances permit. This does not always mean sexual intercourse but is the broader definition of sexuality. The older person continues to respond to touch as well as caress and has a need to reciprocate these feelings. Because society has not understood that sexuality continues into the later adult years, there has been an uncertain response to meeting these needs.[15]

SOCIAL SERVICES PROGRAM PROVISIONS

Through the enactment of the Older Americans Act, a variety and range of services have come into existence to meet the needs of older persons. Emphasis has been placed on providing services to enable people to remain independent, living in their own homes as long as they are able. The decision to seek congregate or institutional housing should not be made necessary because of a lack of measures that help people to cope in their own settings.

Retirement Counseling

Retirement has an emotional and financial impact. Some retirement counseling is provided through employers, mostly having to do with financial planning. There are some educational settings such as community college and social service agencies that provide some types of counseling in preparation for retirement.

Social work is particularly suited to providing preretirement counseling because of its methodology and value system. Currently most of these programs are carried out through personnel departments.[16] At present there is little postretirement support counseling, though after retirement as well as before the day arrives, there is a greater need for emotional support. To walk away from a large portion of one's life that has been meaningful is very difficult for some people.

Retirement Income

Before the enactment of the Social Security Act most people worked their entire lives. It was an economic necessity for the great majority of the population. The Social Security Act came about in response to the Great Depression and was a way of opening up the employment market for the larger numbers of unemployed. If older workers were able to retire, it would make room for younger persons in the job market. Until that time the United States had little experience with retirement and the special problems it could bring about. When the Social Security Act was conceived, it was believed that the benefit from this source would be supplementary to other retirement programs. However, this has not been true, and today Social Security is the only or primary source of income for great numbers of older persons.

At the time of retirement it is almost a certainty that the individual will have to learn to live on a considerably reduced income. There are indications that retirement reduces expendable income by almost one-half for a large share of the population. Close to 3.5 million elderly persons were below the poverty level in 1986 ($6,630 for an older couple household or $5,255 for an older individual living alone). Another 2.3 million were classified as "near-poor."[17] The most economically disadvantaged are the black population with 35 percent, then the Hispanic with 26, Asian/Pacific Islanders at 14, and 13 percent of white elderly living below the poverty level.[18] This points up the fact that minorities are disadvantaged in two ways, minority and elderly.

There is the belief that people do not have the same kinds of needs when they retire, and therefore their income can be lower than when they were employed. "For some, the poverty of old age is a worsening of a condition that has plagued them all their lives. For others it is a new, unexpected, and frightening experience."[19] While expenses associated with employment may have disappeared, inflation has dealt the persons on fixed income a severe blow as the cost of basic necessities such as food, clothing, shelter, and medical care of all types including dental, hearing, eye problems, and drugs/medicine have increased.

Health costs are a particular concern for the elderly. Under Medicare the amount covered has decreased and the deductible has increased since the inception of the program, and "the aged now pay more out of pocket for their medical care than they did prior to enactment of Medicare in 1965."[20] It is expedient for older persons to carry a supplemental health insurance to cover those expenses that Medicare will not cover. With the advent of the shorter hospital stay, Medicare will now pay for more care given in the individual's home, such as visiting nurses and home health aides. This has brought about a more cost-effective delivery of service. The question that remains is the continued quality of care.

A variety of private pension plans have existed since before the enactment of Social Security. However, they were very limited in their coverage, and only between 3 and 4 million workers, or less than 15 percent of the work force, were covered. During the 1940s and 1950s there was considerable growth of these private pension plans, with an estimated 20 million covered in 1960. It is estimated that in 1980 approximately 30 million are covered.[21]

There have been serious problems and limitations with private pension plans related to protection of workers. Benefit rights have been lost through various plans going bankrupt, change of employment, company mergers, plant closings, and unemployment coming after numbers of years of employment. It was also discovered that monies put aside in retirement funds had been mismanaged. The Employee Retirement Income Security Act, passed by Congress in 1974, was stronger and more comprehensive in the protection of workers' benefits. There remain problems, however, with forced retirement after a worker has reached a certain age and/or numbers of years of employment. There are wide differences among employers along with differential treatment of sex and minorities. Women, nonwhite, and low-paid employees receive the least benefit from these private plans.[22] Women are further disadvantaged, as many private pension plans do not cover the wife if the spouse dies. In many instances people do not become aware of this until they retire or the spouse dies.

Transportation

The ability to get around and not be housebound is extremely important for people of all ages. People in cities need to have good, convenient, safe transportation in order to accomplish the routine tasks of everyday life. Public transit in cities is geared to getting people to work, not to the needs of the slower-moving senior citizen. Rural areas have developed publicly sponsored transportation for the elderly and handicapped who can no longer drive their cars or use the regular public transportation system. The means to get around must be safe, convenient, and affordable. Even some of the simplest routine tasks can become difficult and frustrating if one cannot negotiate getting to them.

Transportation to visit relatives who live in other parts of the country has become difficult due to the loss of many railroad lines. The only way to travel between cities (if one does not drive an automobile) is either by bus or airplane. Airports are often some distance from where the individual resides, and therefore some way must be found to negotiate that distance. It is important that older people be able to visit and stay in close contact with their families.

George W. Gardner

Transportation can be very important for the elderly who can be isolated, lonely, and unable to obtain needed goods and services. This is often particularly true for older persons in rural locations.

Housing

Good safe housing for the elderly is a prime concern. Many of the poor elderly have tended to live in the inner city where housing has been allowed to deteriorate and has become a victim of urban blight. Here conditions have not been safe either from the standpoint of physical upkeep of property or neighborhood safety. The elderly sometimes have been victims of vandals and physical abuse. They have become captives within their four walls.

Low-cost publicly subsidized housing has been slow to materialize. There are concerns about building apartment complexes that are exclusively for the elderly, as this tends to segregate them from the mainstream. There is also the possibility that these can become ghettos for the elderly. Older persons should have a choice of where they live and housing that is safe and affordable. They should be able to have a choice according to their preference of age-segregated or intergenerational housing.

There have been experimental projects with cooperative living arrangements where a group of unrelated elders has gone together to share expenses along with duties and responsibilities.[23] This type of arrangement provides support for elders, so that they don't feel as isolated and helps to stretch scarce resources.

Retirement Communities/Facilities

There are several types of retirement centers. One type is a community of homes for senior citizens of which Sun City, Arizona, is an example. Several such communities have been developed, particularly in the Sun Belt. Along with housing, these communities provide recreation, activities, and socialization. Some provide additional supportive services, including a call for help if one becomes ill or has an accident. They usually do not provide health care, but will see to it that the individual gets needed assistance. These communities have been seen as having the potential to become senior citizen ghettos. Some, like Sun City, are finding that they may have to change some of their age limits as the residents die and a younger population has not been permitted to buy into the community to fill the void.

Another type of retirement community has come with the development of condominiums. These facilities may also provide recreation activities and socialization. Maintenance of property is provided by management.

A third type of retirement center that has become popular is one that provides several levels of living. People buy into a complex that is designed to maintain independent living as long as possible and yet provides appropriate levels of care as it is needed. Some of them have apartments where the older persons continue to carry on their lives in the community as they always have done, carrying on daily living such as meal preparation and other household tasks. A second level is independent suites where individuals eat their meals in a common dining room and have other household help provided. Another level of care is often referred to as helpful living, where the older person has someone looking in on her or him regularly and providing supportive services. In connection with the retirement center is a health center which provides nursing care when it is needed. These kinds of facilities tend to be quite expensive.

Nursing Homes

The U.S. Department of Health and Human Services reported in 1978 that approximately 5 percent of older people (1.1 million) resided in institutions of all kinds. There is a tendency to believe that a much higher percentage of older people require care in nursing homes. Those requiring nursing care tend to be older and have definite health problems.

Nursing homes are either publicly owned, nonprofit, or proprietary (for profit). We have seen a growth in the number of for-profit homes in the last decade; often a company or corporation has homes in a number of communities scattered throughout the country. Nursing homes are licensed through the states for several levels of care. Skilled nursing care is extremely costly and is the only level of care that Medicare will pay for. This level of care is not long-term, and the number of months of coverage is limited. It is for a period of time between hospitalization and return to one's own home or another level of care.

A second level is intermediate care and is also costly. Intermediate care facilities receive Medicaid payments, which must be means-tested. It is not uncommon for persons requiring care over an extended period to exhaust their resources and have to apply for Medicaid. Because there is often a difference between what Medicaid will reimburse compared to what a private party will pay, many proprietary nursing homes will admit only a small percentage of their patient load that is on Medicaid.

We have seen a growth in the provision of social work in nursing homes, as this was mandated under the Medicare and Medicaid provisions. The emphasis has been on maintaining as high a level of functioning possible for each individual rather than warehousing as had occurred previously.

Elderly Abuse

There have been an increasing number of reported cases of abuse of the elderly in the homes of relatives or other caretakers. Often the spouse of the individual is the perpetrator of the abuse or neglect. There is a need for more respite care to relieve the caregivers, so that they do not become so frustrated with long hours of responsibility.

Services to Maintain Independent Living

Senior Centers.   Multipurpose senior centers have been established to provide a variety of services under one roof to facilitate the ability of older persons to use these services. Activities are also an important part of a senior center. New York City was the site of the first publicly supported senior center approximately thirty years ago. Since the enactment of the Older Americans Act there has been an expansion of centers throughout the country. Some are located in housing projects; others are provided through voluntary organizations, both sectarian and nonsectarian, while still others are publicly financed.[24] Some are located separately from other organizations, and some are housed with one or more agencies.

The senior center has the potential to coordinate services for older people, along with identifying gaps in service provision. These senior centers provide an excellent avenue for older persons to be actively involved in decision making about those programs that will benefit this population. For a senior center to be successful, the elderly need to be involved at all levels. This provides an avenue to keep the vitality and expertise of the elderly involved.

There are a number of services to help people maintain independent living, for example, handyman service, chore service, shopping service, and homemaker service. All these services are provided by volunteers recruited by an agency or offered by paid staff. Homemaker service, usually provided by personnel working for the agency, will be discussed later. Elderly persons can often remain in their own living quarters longer if help is provided with such tasks as grass cutting, snow shoveling, grocery shopping, and minor repairs to property. This is where handyman, chore, or shopping services, alone or in combination, may be extremely useful.

Peer Counseling.   A rather recent service that has been developed is peer counseling. This program uses volunteers who have been trained to be good listeners as well as role models for elderly who are experiencing adjustments problems or other crises. These volunteers provide a supportive role that can be a preventative of further deterioration of the individual.

Day Programs, Foster Care, and Shared Housing.

Day Programs, Foster Care, and Shared Housing. Two recent developments for the elderly modeled along the line of traditional children's services are day services and adult foster care. Day services for the aging are a response to the situation in which an elderly person may be living with adult family members who work away from home during the day when the person needs care and perhaps supervision, or perhaps the family caregiver needs relief to maintain her or his own well-being. By taking the aged parent or grandparent daily or periodically to a day program, the danger of leaving the elderly person alone is diminished. The relief that the caregivers receive by being able to have some time for themselves as well as taking care of other tasks may enable the family to continue to keep the elderly person in the home. This service also provides stimulation for the older person. Such facilities may be operated by nursing homes or by private or public social agencies. This type of care is much less costly than nursing or custodial care.

A service that has been developing as a complement to a day program is providing respite care in the home. The family that is providing care for a chronically ill relative needs some time away from the responsibility, ranging from a few hours to a weekend. An agency may provide a list of trained persons who will be able to provide the care.

Adult foster care makes it possible for certain elderly persons to live in family houses when unable to remain alone in their own homes. Again, the security and care required to remain out of more expensive and often less appealing institutional care is afforded through this means. An adult foster care program may be operated by a general family agency, a welfare department, or a more specialized agency for the elderly.

Shared housing is a program that provides companionship as well as services to the older person. This program can work two ways. Either a younger person comes into the home of the older person to provide some care, or it could be the other way around with a younger person or family sharing their home.

Telephone Reassurance.

Telephone Reassurance. We hear and read about incidents of elderly persons living alone who fall and cannot reach a phone to call for help. Sometimes days pass before the mishap is discovered. Sometimes it is discovered too late. The victim, in many cases, could have been saved if help had been received right away. In response to this situation volunteers in some communities are providing older people with a service, often called telephone reassurance, in which the volunteer calls every day at a specified time. If there is no answer, the caller knows something may have happened and pursues the situation further. Knowing that someone is going to be checking on them by telephone or in person reassures the older persons that they are not totally alone.

A friendly call each day provides contact with the outside world and helps combat the loneliness that many older people experience. A 1974 study conducted by the Louis Harris Associates for the National Council on Aging found that more women than men reported loneliness as the worst thing about being over sixty-five years of age. Loneliness and depression may go hand in hand.[25]

Nutrition. Congregate meals, a program funded through Title III of the Older Americans Act, came into existence in 1973. In 1969 the Department of Health, Education and Welfare commissioned a study regarding the nutritional needs of the aged, especially low-income elderly. The study reported one out of four elderly persons ate fewer than three meals per day.[26]

States are allocated monies on the basis of the proportion of elderly living in the state. The program provides a nutritional, well-balanced meal for anyone over the age of sixty who chooses to participate in the program. There is no means test, and individuals may decide for themselves how much they can afford to pay or not pay for the meal. The theory behind the congregate meal program is not just to provide a meal, but also to provide socialization to overcome some of the isolation. People have a tendency to eat better when they share mealtimes.

Another nutrition program is meals on wheels, which provides one hot meal a day to those persons who are homebound. The mobile meals are delivered by volunteers and are often prepared in the congregate meal kitchens or a hospital, for example. The major federal funding is the same as congregate meals with 10 percent of the funding going to home-delivered meals. The individual pays a small amount for the meal.

A third program that addresses nutrition is food stamps. This service is for the low-income elderly and is designed to stretch their food dollars. There are low-income guidelines that must be met to qualify for food stamps.

Home Health Care and Homemaking. This service is designed to provide health aide care in the home to enable people to remain in their own homes rather than having to turn to nursing or institutional care. There are a variety of ways in which these programs are financed and delivered, all depending upon the agency providing the service. The service provided by the health aide to individuals or families includes light housekeeping, light laundry, preparation and serving of meals, shopping, simple errands, along with a teaching function of well members of the household regarding how to accomplish these and other tasks. Some home health aide services are reimbursable through Medicare. The availability of this service depends on where people are located. It tends to be more available in cities, where there are organized public health services, than in rural areas.

Information and Referral.   The purpose of information and referral is to help people obtain the service they require. There are so many different services that it becomes difficult for people to sort out where they can get the service they need. A centralized system that provides information about services available to the elderly helps people sort out the confusion. Often this service is having someone on the other end of the telephone that is a good listener and can help the individual define what the underlying problems are along with the presenting or verbalized problem. This service also has the ability to identify gaps in community provisions, which is a tool for planning bodies.

Pets.   Authorities have come to recognize the importance of pets in the lives of older people. As the elderly lose spouses and close friends, pets can provide warmth and companionship. Pets also give back love. A pet can provide the opportunity for touching and feeling close to something that gives back affection with no questions asked. It is acceptable to talk and to share feelings with a pet.

In the last several years some nursing homes have come to accept the importance of pets. Some now allow a dog or cat to become a part of the home where all residents gain from caring for and about the animal. If the home does not have its own full-time pet, they may bring in animals from time to time. A litter of kittens or puppies gives several residents at one time an opportunity to hold and cuddle an animal. The smiles and joy that this activity brings into a nursing home are well worth the effort.

SOCIAL WORK ROLE

The role of the social worker with older persons is twofold. First, it involves direct service with the individual, small group, and family, which addresses those compelling needs that older persons present in today's world. The economic, physical, environmental, and emotional needs that confront older persons are the major areas with which social workers are involved. In working with older persons, one of the goals is to help the individual and family maintain their dignity, keeping in mind that each older person has uniqueness and value, as well as needs.

Second, the social worker's role is advocacy with and on behalf of older persons. The worker has the task of identifying issues such as poor housing, lack of transportation, health needs, economic needs, loneliness, and others that confront the elderly. The next step is to mobilize community resources to help bring about change through the development of programs that address these unmet needs. Elaine Brody writes of social work with older people:

> The vulnerability of the elderly themselves, the impact of their problems on family and society, and the comparative lack of knowledge about the needed social interventions legitimate the aging population as a prime concern of social work. Emphasis should be placed on preventive, supportive, and restorative services.[27]

The social worker who works with older people must first come to an understanding of his or her own attitudes about older people and the aging process. Does the worker believe the myths about aging and see the role as only one of maintenance? Because the elderly are more sedentary, does the worker believe that mental as well as physical involvement is impossible for them? There is also the matter of working with persons who are the age of their parents with whom they may have some unresolved conflicts. It is, therefore, necessary for the professional to have a good understanding of how his or her feelings become important and must not let these feelings intrude into the helping relationship.

Social work has been involved in working with older people over the years in the area of income maintenance and counseling. An awareness of the needs of the elderly has been emerging with the continued emphasis on the problems faced by our senior citizens. Medicare and Medicaid legislation has drawn in social work to do case planning and management around the health needs of this population. The new method of hospital care under Medicare (Diagnostic Related Groups) has placed an emphasis on discharge planning that in many hospitals is the responsibility of the social worker. Nursing homes also use the service of social workers.

Social workers have roles to play in assisting the elderly to work with feelings such as loss, guilt, and depression. A need also exists to permit the elderly to continue to enjoy the same range of opportunities enjoyed by younger age groups. The social worker can help to provide new roles and opportunities for the aged as well as caring for the fears, anxieties, and problems caused by losses.[28]

Older persons deal with many losses. They have had losses throughout their lifetime, but these accelerate as a person ages—loss of spouse, siblings, close friends, and children. Loss becomes increasingly difficult to deal with as the individual becomes more cut off from meaningful relationships. There is reluctance to reach out to establish new friends as this may lead to further losses. The individual is also confronted with loss of personal functioning. The recognition that they can no longer do some of the accustomed things brings the elderly face to face with the reality of their aging process. In the loss of both friends and functioning there is a grief process that needs to be worked through. The social worker, recognizing that this dynamic is present, can aid older individuals as they struggle with their feelings.

Most elderly are a part of a family that should be recognized by social workers in their assessment and ongoing work with people in this age group. The family is a resource for helping to solve some of the problems. Despite the fact that we are part of a mobile society, most elderly live near at least one adult child with whom they have a close relationship.[29] There also exist close ties with family even though members may be separated by distance.

The family needs services to aid them in helping their aging relative(s). They may not know what services are available and how best they can be of assistance. Further, there is the matter of their feelings in relation to the relative. They see their parent, for example, subject to change in personal functioning, which can become difficult to accept. They often feel guilt. People feel they should be able to do more for their parent(s). They fear leaving their relative in independent living, as he or she may not be able to take care of her/himself and something harmful might happen. Circumstances may prevent them from taking the aging relatives into their homes. Therefore, a question of entry into a nursing home is considered. This must be carefully worked out, so that the older person makes the decision—in cases where they are competent to do so—to enter a care facility.

Group work is another method used in work with this population. One example is support groups for widows or widowers. In the context of such a group, members can share with others in similar circumstances their sense of loss and methods for coping with the change in their way of life. Another support group is for those persons diagnosed as cancer patients to help them deal with the impact of their illness, which often has a component of dealing with body image along with what it means to have a terminal illness. There are also groups for relatives whose loved one has Alzheimer's disease with all its devastating deterioration. A different type of group work involves task-oriented groups to organize, plan, and carry out activities for the elderly.

Reality orientation is group work carried out, generally in nursing homes, to keep patients in tune with their surroundings and what is happening. It is very easy when people are in a nursing home more or less isolated from the day-to-day world to lose touch with what day it is, where they are, and so forth. Through reality orientation people have been able to maintain better functioning.

Persons going into nursing homes or other forms of institutional living are confronted with new situations, many of them difficult. They have not had experience with communal or group living requiring them to abide by decisions that are made for them.

The professional social worker has a role in bringing about social change directed at the attitudes that society holds concerning the aged. As Jordan Kosberg states "There is . . . a need for advocacy efforts that challenge currently widespread ageist values.[30]

A Case of a Retirement Home Resident

Mrs. B., an eighty-eight-year-old widow, resides in a retirement home that she moved into four years ago with her husband, who passed away two years later. They had lived in the same home for fifty-one years. She recently had a fall that reinjured her back, originally injured in an accident four years ago. Just before that she had been diagnosed as having congestive heart failure, for which she was taking medication. Mrs. B. was hospitalized for approximately a week to give her complete bed rest to help the back heal. Her biggest complaint at the time was not that her back hurt, but that she had difficulty walking and getting up from a sitting position. The doctor put her back in a girdle-type brace, which she disliked wearing.

Her two children, who lived some distance from her, were called home by the social worker, since there was concern that she was in a weakened condition and forgetful, and perhaps should be moved to the health care section where she would be supervised twenty-four hours a day. When the children arrived, they found their mother alert, very much in tune with what was going on around her, but complaining that the physician would not tell her why she had to wear that "awful" girdle that was hard to get into and out of as well as being uncomfortable.

In discussion with the children, the doctor maintained in the beginning that Mrs. B. was forgetful, that she did not remember why she was wearing the brace. In this instance the family had to interpret to the physician what reassurance his patient was asking for. Without this intervention a woman who was capable of handling herself and her medications could have had a disastrous (for her) move to a nursing care facility. This is the kind of family involvement that social workers often help to bring about.

Issues and Trends

We are beginning to witness in this country five-generation families with two generations in the over-fifty-five category. Some people, already sixty-five and at retirement age, have parents in their eighties. At a time when the fifty-five-year-old may be looking forward to a few years of freedom from responsibility along with preparing for retirement, he or she is confronted with a choice of either providing physical care, financial support, or both for parent(s). There have been instances of having two generations residing in a nursing home. There is the possibility that this will increase in the next decade.

Because of advances in health care and nutrition both dependent adult children and their parents are living longer. This means that elderly parents continue to be the caregivers for these adult children, and both will experience more of the social and medical infirmities of old age. Social workers are concerned about this trend, as it relates to planning for both populations.[31]

Social gerontologists have begun to separate the elderly into two groupings —the young-old and the old-old.[32] This is coming about because of the differences in needs between these two groups. The young-old tend to be healthier, more financially secure, better educated, and more actively involved.[33] The young-old are dealing with a changing life-style due to retirement. Separation from employment that absorbed a great share of their lives requires finding new avenues of involvement. On the other hand the old-old are more apt to have compelling health problems along with loss of spouse and friends. Their energy level is lower, often requiring an even more drastic change in life-style as they have to give up a greater share of independence. If they do not need some form of nursing, custodial, or protected living situation for themselves, they see others their age being confronted with circumstances leading to a more dependent life-style. They begin to ask "will this happen to me?"

The young-old will need services that enable people to remain active in programs for senior citizens or other community activities that use the time and the expertise of the retired person. Services that help these individuals maintain a strong sense of identity and self-worth are required. We have lost or are in danger of losing a valuable resource by not involving these people.

We need to give attention to providing affordable, suitable housing, economic security, well-elderly clinics, and a range of programs that will enable the elderly to remain as independent as possible. We need to think of a range of programs to provide alternatives depending upon individual needs. Today many older people end up in nursing homes, the most costly care, because we have not provided alternatives when a less expensive type of care would be more appropriate. Other countries such as Denmark and Sweden have been much more creative in their approach to providing for their senior citizens.

It has been estimated that the over-sixty-five population will grow during the next two decades from 25 million to 32 million.[34] This means that there will need to be an expansion of services, which implies an expanded need for workers in all the helping professions who are trained and educated in gerontology. The need is expanding for geriatric nurses, social workers, and middle-management personnel for such services as senior centers and nursing homes.[35] There is no doubt that social workers will continue to have a professional involvement with and on behalf of older persons; increased emphasis on the education in disciplines working with this population will be needed.[36]

This writer believes that we have, during the last three decades, come to a heightened awareness of the plight of the older person in this country. During the decade of the 1980s we are in the process of reexamining our priorities and financing for programs for all populations. Current thinking is that more and more will be maintained through voluntary efforts, both in money and person power. But the politicians have learned that senior citizens have become better organized and more vocal, and they also vote, which makes them a constituency to be reckoned with.

The profession of social work will need to focus on replacing the negative values we have perpetuated in keeping older people dependent. There needs to be greater opportunity for this population to have economic, physical, and emotional security with opportunities for satisfaction through vocational and leisure activities. Health care should be accessible and affordable for all persons, not just for the more affluent in our society.[37]

SUMMARY AND CONCLUSIONS

This chapter has attempted to acquaint the reader with the situation of aging people in our culture: their current numbers and projections for the future, myths and stereotyping, a definition of ageism, federal legislation, current service provisions, and the role of the social worker.

The social worker is defined as one who attends to the needs of the individual person and also acts as advocate for groups of people in order to bring about change on their behalf, working toward making the experience of aging a more positive one. Until now we have tended to view aging as a problem. With a more positive attitude it can be viewed as opportunity for human fulfillment.[38]

The field of gerontology is expanding with new knowledge in relation to the aging process. The field will be growing as the numbers of elderly increase, offering a challenge to those who choose to work in this arena to bring about creative programs.

NOTES

1. American Association of Retired Persons (AARP) and the Administration on Aging (AoA), U.S. Department of Health and Human Services, *A Profile of Older Americans*, 1987.
2. United Nations, *Report of the World Assembly on Aging* (New York: United Nations, 1982), p. 50; Sally L. Hoover and Jacob S. Siegel, "International Demographic Trends and Perspectives on Aging," *Journal of Cross-Cultural Gerontology.* 1, no. 1, (1986):5–30.
3. U.S. Census Bureau, "Demographic and Socioeconomic Aspects of Aging in the United States," by Jacob Siegel and Maria Davidson (Washington D.C.: Government Printing Office, September 1984).
4. *Encyclopedia of Social Work*, 16th ed. (New York: NASW, 1971), p. 54.
5. Louis Lowy, *Social Work with the Aging: The Challenge and Promise of the Later Years* (New York: Harper & Row, 1979), pp. 13, 14.
6. Ibid., p. 16.
7. Ibid., p. 87.
8. S. Kamerman and A. Kahn, *Social Services in the U.S.* (Philadelphia: Temple University Press, 1976) pp. 322–324.
9. Ibid.
10. United Nations, *Report of the World Assembly on Aging*, 1982, pp. 68–71.
11. Hoover and Siegel, "International Demographic Trends and Perspectives on Aging," p. 14.
12. Jack Levin and William Levin, *Ageism: Prejudice and Discrimination Against the Elderly* (Belmont, Calif.: Wadsworth Publishing Co., 1980).
13. From p. 6 in *WHY SURVIVE? Being Old in America* by Robert N. Butler, M.D. Copyright © 1975 by Robert N. Butler, M.D. By permission of Harper & Row, Publishers, Inc.
14. Jordan I. Kosberg, ed., *Working with and for the Aged* (Washington, D.C.: NASW, 1979), p. 2.
15. Thomas H. Walz and Nancee S. Blum, *Sexual Health in Later Life* (Lexington, Mass.: Lexington Books, 1987).
16. Florence Safford, "Value of Gerontology for Occupational Social Work," *Social Work* 33, no. 1 (January–February, 1988): 44.
17. American Association of Retired Persons (AARP) and the Administration on Aging (AoA), U.S. Department of Health and Human Services, *A Profile of Older Americans*, 1987.
18. "A Portrait of Older Minorities," *The AARP Minority Initiative.*

19. Georgia M. Barrows and Patricia A. Smith, *Aging, Ageism and Society* (St. Paul, Minn.: West Publishing Co., 1979), p. 186.
20. Carroll Estes, *The Aging Enterprise* (San Francisco: Jossey-Bass, 1979), p. 18.
21. James H. Schulz, *The Economics of Aging*, 2nd ed. (Belmont, Calif.: Wadsworth, 1980), pp. 124–126.
22. Ibid., pp. 124–127.
23. Kamerman and Kahn, *Social Services*, pp. 337–339.
24. Lowy, *Social Work with the Aging*, p. 144.
25. *The Myth and Reality of Aging in America*, conducted for the National Council on the Aging, by Louis Harris and Associates, 1975.
26. Kamerman and Kahn, *Social Services*, pp. 324–328.
27. Elaine Brody, "Aging," *Encyclopedia of Social Work*, 16th ed. (New York: NASW, 1971), p. 67.
28. Kosberg, *Working with the Aged*.
29. Ibid.
30. Jordan I. Kosberg and Audrey P. Harris, "Attitudes Toward Elderly Clients," NASW reprint from *Health and Social Work* 3, no. 3 (August 1978): 18.
31. Jeanette Jennings, "Elderly Parents as Caregivers for Their Adult Dependent Children," *Social Work*, 32, no. 5 (September–October 1987): 433.
32. Bernice Neugarten, "Age Groups in American Society and the Rise of the Young-Old," in *Annuals of the American Academy of Political and Social Sciences, Political Consequences of Aging*, September 1974.
33. James F. Keller and George A. Hughston, *Counseling the Elderly: A Systems Approach* (New York: Harper & Row, 1981), p. 15.
34. The National Council on the Aging, *NCOA Public Policy Agenda, 1980–81*, Washington, D.C., p. 15.
35. Ibid.
36. Kosberg, *Working with the Aged*, p. 6.
37. Kosberg and Harris, "Attitudes Toward Elderly Clients," p. 19.
38. Lowy, *Social Work with the Aging*, p. xiii.

ADDITIONAL SUGGESTED READINGS

Binstock, Robert H., and Ethel Shanas, eds., *Handbook of Aging and the Social Sciences* (New York: Van Nostrand Reinhold Co., 1985).
Blackwell, David L., and Sara S. Hunt, "Mental Health Services Reaching Out to Older Persons," *Journal of Gerontological Social Work* 2 no. 4 (Summer 1980): 281.
Brody, Elaine M., and Contributors, *A Social Work Guide for Long Term Care Facilities* (Rockville, Md.: National Institute of Mental Health, 1974).
Coward, Raymond, and Gary Lee, eds., *The Elderly in Rural Society* (New York: Springer Publishing Co., 1984).

de Beauvoir, Simone, *The Coming of Age* (New York: G. P. Putnam & Sons, 1972).

Dreher, Barbara Bender, *Communication Skills for Working with Elders* (New York: Springer Publishing Co., 1987).

Gelfand, Donald E., and Charles M. Barresi, eds., *Ethnic Dimensions of Aging* (New York: Springer Publishing Co., 1987).

Hickey, Tom, and Richard L. Douglas, "Neglect and Abuse of Older Family Members: Professional's Perspectives and Case Experiences," *The Gerontologist* 21, no. 2 (April 1981): 171.

Hooyman, Nancy R., and Wendy Lustbader, *Taking Care: Supporting Older People and Their Families* (New York: Free Press 1986).

Huttman, Elizabeth D., *Social Services for the Elderly* (New York: Free Press, 1985).

Jorm, Anthony F., *A Guide to Understanding Alzheimer's Disease and Related Disorders* (New York: New York University Press, 1987).

Krout, John A., *The Aged in Rural America* (Westport, Conn.: Greenwood Press, 1986).

Olsen, Tillie, *Tell Me a Riddle* (New York: Dell Publishing Co., 1961).

Quinn, Joan, Joan Segal, Helen Raisz, and Christine Johnson, eds., *Coordinating Community Services for the Elderly: The Triage Experience* (New York: Springer Publishing Co., 1982).

Salamon, Michael J., *A Basic Guide to Working with Elders* (New York: Springer, 1986).

13 Occupational Social Work*

Nancy J. Johnston
Irl Carter

Occupational (or industrial) social work is a significant arena for the delivery of preventive and intervention services to workers. Even though business and industry is perhaps the sector of our society that makes least use of them, social services at the work site have dramatically increased during the past twenty years. Occupational social work existed in the United States a century ago, and in fact social work took its name from industry.[1] It faded from industry by the 1920s just as it was becoming established in Europe. If the European experience is predictive, occupational social services will continue to expand rapidly both in the United States and around the world.[2]

Social workers have contributed to the humanizing of the workplace through the provision of counseling at or near the work site, administration of affirmative action or other personnel programs, consultation with management and labor unions concerning the effect of company policies on employees, and working with medical and personnel departments to improve fringe benefits and working conditions. Industries have discovered the profitability of such services, both in their

*The authors acknowledge the contributions of case materials and other suggestions by Clinton Berg and Elizabeth Ferron.

finances and in their public relations with employees and communities. Corporations have increasingly adopted such programs, and now approximately half of the "*Fortune* 500" (the nation's largest) corporations have employee assistance programs (EAPs). In reduction of employee turnover alone, industries recover the cost of occupational social services and alcoholism programs. These services have been called "the human contract"[3] or "the human face of industry."

HUMAN NEEDS AND SOCIAL PROBLEMS

Beginning in fourteenth-century England, industrial societies have been shaped by the factory system. Before that, both men and women worked in the fields (as they still do in many underdeveloped countries), or in "cottage industries" during the early stages of mercantilism. Factories drew workers out of their homes and villages, segregating adults, who spent most of their waking hours in the factory, and children, who were left unattended or with extended family. This segregation has been the basis of the dynamics of family and society as we know them, including detachment of workers from their families, lack of opportunity for children to observe parental work role models, and alienation of workers from community life.

Mechanization and automation routinized workers' jobs and made much of their work seem trivial. Often workers, whether blue-collar or white-collar, feel temporary and insignificant. Seasonal layoffs, changes in technology, declines in particular industries (such as steel, automobiles, or computers), and plant closings often reinforce these feelings. Workers who feel useless or powerless at the workplace often transfer these feelings to their homes and communities.[4] The major effects may be summarized as the "5 A's":

- *Alienation* from oneself, family, and other social groups; results may be apathy, anger and anxiety;
- *Alcoholism* or *addiction*, major problems that result in massive losses in productivity and damage to personal and social life;
- *Absenteeism*, which is notorious in some industries such as automobile manufacturing, as in "Don't buy a car made on Monday!"
- *Accidents*, many of which can be traced to workers upset with work or personal problems; and
- *Abuse* of spouses and children, some of which may be attributed to frustrations and alienation originating on the job.

There also are other needs. Some employees may be victims of discrimination, neglect, or unfair treatment: women, minorities of color, new immigrants, youths, older workers, and those who are physically,

emotionally, or mentally handicapped. Some businesses and industries may have detrimental effects upon their employees or their communities due to toxic chemicals, pollution, or physical or emotional
damage to workers. The social worker in industry may assist the business to assess and to bear its share of the resulting social costs.

Social services in the workplace existed in the Middle Ages.[5] The
medieval guilds provided payments in case of disability, poverty, old
age, and death, and provided dowries for some families. They assured
observation of holidays and Sundays. Eventually, laws replaced the
guilds' activities, including regulation of hours of work, length of apprenticeship, wages, provision of education, and almshouses.

About 1800 in Scotland, industrialist Robert Owen provided athletic
fields, education for children, "moral supervision," a village store,
housing, sick benefits, unemployment insurance, and child labor regulations at his factories. Other British factory owners followed these
practices. Later, some large British industries created new towns for
their workers. Manufacturers in Germany (for example, Krupp muni-
tions) and textile mills in the United States provided a wide array of social services.

At a subsequent stage, some owners hired "welfare secretaries,"
"welfare workers in industry," "social secretaries," *consul de famille* or
conseillères du travail (France), and *arbeiter sozial* (Germany).
These persons were hired as early as 1890 in England, Germany, and
the United States, and about 1920 in France. In the United States, such
early social workers were employed by southern textile mills, International Harvester, and National Cash Register, among others, and
provided a wide variety of services, establishing restrooms and wash-
rooms, improving sanitation, employing medical personnel, and providing schools, housing, and meals. They administered benefit
programs, supervised safety, created libraries, arranged cooking and
sewing classes, and administered first aid. One social worker secured a
swimming pool for employees and persuaded the railroad to change
its schedule for workers who commuted. Eventually, these duties were
"spun off" to new specialists such as industrial nurses, personnel officers, or administrators. Most of these were men, replacing the women
welfare secretaries. As with the guilds, the broader welfare functions
were eventually assumed by government, in the forms of public
health, schools, and programs such as unemployment insurance and
Social Security. In developing countries, the earlier pattern continues;
for example, India and Peru require that industries provide trained social workers.

Until the 1970s, there were few social workers in industry in the
United States, except during World War II to provide services to
women workers in defense industries and to merchant marine and mil-

itary personnel. After the war, the AFL-CIO started its union counselors program, through which union members receive training and are provided information and referral services. The union continues to operate about twenty labor agencies, similar to other social agencies.

Schools of social work have originated innovative social services in industry. In 1964, Hyman Weiner of the Columbia University School of Social Work founded a rehabilitation service jointly operated by the school and an outpatient service for garment workers. Weiner's work evolved into the Industrial Social Welfare Center at Columbia. Another pioneer, Dr. Dale Masi, while at the Boston College School of Social Work, originated several innovative industrial social work projects and later served as the first director of employee counseling services of the Department of Health and Human Services in Washington, D.C. Approximately thirty graduate schools of social work and some undergraduate programs offer occupational social work curricula and field placements.

The Council on Social Work Education and the National Association of Social Workers entered this new field in 1975, establishing a joint committee to study the field and make new recommendations. This led to the first national conference for industrial social work practitioners in 1978. In addition, industrial social workers themselves, as well as social work faculty members, have added to a substantial and growing body of studies of the field. Student field placements in EAPs and other settings in business and industry continue to increase.[6]

WHAT DOES THE OCCUPATIONAL SOCIAL WORKER DO?

There are approximately 5,500 EAPs in work organizations in the United States.[7] In addition, nearly 1,000 specialists, including social workers, provide services to employees away from the workplace. Social workers make up a significant portion of the professionals working in EAPs, although psychiatrists, psychologists, and drug counselors have been present longer. The Association of Labor-Management Administrators and Consultants in Alcoholism (ALMACA), the major organization for EAPs and related programs, reported that almost half its members have master's degrees; most have studied in a health-related field (for example, social work, psychology, counseling, nursing, or medicine) and most (73 percent) have some specialized training in chemical dependency, mental health, and/or employee assistance programming.[8]

Occupational social work comprises traditional social work skills and knowledge. The NASW National Occupational Social Work Task Force described three categories of occupational social work practice:

Policy, planning and administration, which involve no direct counseling; examples are coordination of employee assistance programs, functions within corporate responsibility departments,[9] training, the formulation of policies for career-path advancement, and the administration of affirmative action programs.

Direct practice with individuals, families, and special populations, such as crisis intervention, the assessment of personal problems, and the referral for treatment, alcohol and drug counseling, child care work in a company or union program, and retirement counseling.

Practice that combines direct service and administration/policy formulation.[10]

Most practitioners in occupational social work are involved in direct service, providing assistance to employees with personal and interpersonal problems.[11] Programs are commonly called EAPs; other names are occupational alcoholism programs, personnel assistance programs, and special health programs. EAPs focus primarily on employees who have difficulties that interfere with job performance, such as chemical dependency, personal or family problems, or difficulties with other employees or the job itself.[12] Growing out of the occupational alcoholism programs of the 1930s and 1940s, EAPs were traditionally staffed by medical personnel or an employee who was a recovered alcoholic. The focus was on identification and treatment of employees afflicted with alcoholism and drug addiction, which are considered medical problems by most drug treatment counselors. The first such program was the alcoholism program begun in 1942 by the Du Pont corporation.[13] Today, most EAPs take a "broad brush" approach, including social services to employees' families and significant others that might be part of the employee's problems.

In the first attempt at formulation of national standards, it was stated that:

EAPs are primarily designed to help all employees and their families who are alcohol abusers or who are affected by the disease of alcoholism. . . . In addition, most programs also offer assistance in other important areas such as other drug dependencies, mental, interpersonal, legal, occupational, financial, etc.[14]

A less developed focus for occupational social workers is on organizational issues which may indirectly affect workers—that is, issues about systems rather than individuals. Some occupational programs have evolved in which social workers consult with management and unions on the work environment, preventive physical and health programs (for example, workshops on stress, smoking, nutrition, and making exercise or meditation time available to workers), or advice on corporate donations or corporate positions on welfare legislation. The social worker may also represent the company in relations with outside groups. Chase Manhattan Bank employed social workers in some New York City locations to work with neighborhood groups. Boise Cascade in Idaho used a social worker to evaluate and recommend ways to disburse the company's charitable funds.

Social Workers in the Workplace

A female clerical employee in a large corporation contacted the employee assistance counselor saying she was feeling depressed and fearful. She had decided to divorce her husband who she described as verbally and physically abusive. She said the situation had been continuing three years, and that they had received counseling, but nothing had changed. By the end of the first session, the employee and counselor identified three distinct needs: emotional support, housing, and legal advice. At the second meeting, the counselor referred her to a support group for women in abusive relationships, presented a list of low- to moderate-income housing, and referred her to a legal assistance service at a women's center. Followup indicated that the employee had legal assistance and had received help from the support group.

A manager in a small manufacturing division of a major corporation phoned the employee assistance counselor with concerns about a valued employee who feared he was an alcoholic and needed help. The counselor met with the employee and, after an assessment, referred him to an alcoholism treatment center. The center recommended outpatient treatment. The employee and his family participated in treatment during evenings for six weeks, after which the counselor arranged a meeting between the employee, his treatment counselor, the manager, and the counselor to discuss the outcome. This gave the employee the opportunity to ask for support he needed at the workplace and to educate the manager about alcoholism. Followup showed the employee was doing well on the job and in his personal life.

In an automobile parts plant, the head of a department of technicians was a tyrant, arbitrary and unfair to his highly skilled employees. Management had threatened him with dismissal, but not wanting to lose a valuable employee, referred him to the social worker. Counseling revealed the heavy pressures he was under, receiving demands for delivery of new products within forty-eight to seventy-two hours, and little sympathy from the "front office." The social worker set up a "dialogue" between the department head and his boss; the outcome was better communication, more advance notice of orders, and recognition of his importance to the company. Within a week the social worker heard that the employee "became a different person," more considerate of his staff and willing to listen.

Auspices and Service Delivery

The auspices for social services in the workplace are trade unions and employing organizations, both for-profit and nonprofit (such as hospitals, governmental units, and universities). The U.S. Navy instituted a "Spouse EAP" for family members of naval personnel.[15] One company operates EAPs for more than ninety U.S. corporations, including Ford Motor Company, Dow Jones, and *Newsweek*, Inc.[16] The target population is the 110 million Americans who are in the labor force, and this number is multiplied in those programs that also offer services to family members and others who impact upon an employee's problem. In reality, the "population at risk" is people who need help in maintaining job performance or general well-being; the number of employees using EAPs ranges from 5 to 20 percent of the employees of an enterprise.

Delivery of services to employees may be in an office at the work site or an accessible off-site location. Most labor union and management sponsors establish their own "in-house" programs and employ professionals to staff them. An increasing number of employers are purchasing services from mental health centers,[17] family service agencies, or specialized employee assistance services. Hazelden Foundation in Minnesota, for example, contracts with private industry (including the National Football League), nonprofit organizations, and government units to provide both on-site and off-site consultation, training, assessment and referral, and short-term counseling throughout the United States. Some of these services are initially provided through a "help-line" telephone to counselors in Minnesota.

There is considerable variance among programs in services offered, ranging from information and referral only, to a full range of outpatient services (such as long-term counseling). The range of services provided depends upon the number of employees, location of the workplace, insurance or other third-party coverage available to employees, and, most important, the commitment by the union or employer to provide the services.[18] In addition to mental health services, EAPs provide consultation and training to both employees and management.

Because of the range of services provided, social workers and other professionals who are the first point of contact for employees must be knowledgeable about resources, such as long-term counseling, inpatient treatment, medical care, or child care. Important tasks for occupational social workers are identification, evaluation, and followup on services to which employees are referred. Management and labor unions regard such information as essential to the provision of social services.

Issues

The most significant issues in occupational social services are:[19]

- The potential conflict between profit and the welfare of employees, equity, and social justice.
- Confidentiality: Who is the client, the business (or union) or the employee, and what right does management (or labor) have to personal information about the employee?[20]
- The social worker's responsibility to advocate for employees versus the social worker's obligation to observe "neutrality" between management and employees.[21]
- The definition of the worker as "troublesome" or "troubled": in part, the issue is the social worker's responsibility to act as an agent of social control.
- The isolation of the social worker in a secondary or host setting, as the only human service professional, and the importance, therefore, that occupational social workers understand their roles as distinct from the personnel, medical, benefits, or employee relations departments of the company, or from that of the union.

THE FUTURE

During a period of political conservatism in which government services will decrease or remain steady rather than increase, the demand for services from business and industry seems likely to increase, despite what many see as a decline in the power of labor unions. Contemporary experience in Europe and elsewhere indicates that enterprises' exclusive attention to task achievement must be modified by concern for employees' physical, emotional, and social well-being, and for the social costs and effects upon the communities and societies within which employees and employer exist. As labor unions, businesses, and industries play larger and more direct roles in social services, they will increasingly recruit social workers and other human services professionals to provide social services to employees.

Social work education must provide knowledge about the work lives of clients and the interpersonal dynamics of the workplace, including a greater awareness of the industrial dynamics of our society and, in particular, the social, environmental, and political roles played by corporations.[22] Social work must examine its historical antipathy toward business and industry and acknowledge its responsibility to assist industry to practice social responsibility and social justice. In this, it can look to the pioneers on the "industrial frontier" a century ago, the "welfare secretaries" and social reformers who challenged businesses and industries, and the society in which they existed, to meet their social responsibilities to workers and their families.[23]

NOTES

1. Irl E. Carter, *Industrial Social Work: Historical Parallels in Five Western Countries* (doctoral dissertation, University of Iowa, 1975).
2. "EAPs International" issue, *EAP Digest* 3, no. 3 (March–April 1983).
3. Leo Perlis, "The Human Contract in the Organized Workplace," *Social Thought* 3, no. 1 (Winter 1977): 29–35.
4. Studs Terkel, *Working* (New York: Pantheon Books, 1974); Lillian Breslow Rubin, *Worlds of Pain* (New York: Basic Books, 1976); and Richard Sennett and Jonathan Cobb, *Hidden Injuries of Class* (New York: Vintage Books, 1973).
5. Carter, *Industrial Social Work*, p. 24.
6. Mei Morgenbesser, "Students Look to Business: Using EAPs as Student Training Sites Gains in Popularity," *EAP Digest* 3, no. 1 (November–December 1982): 25–26.
7. Norman L. Wyers, and Malina Kaulukukuli, "Social Services in the Workplace: Rhetoric vs. Reality," *Social Work* 29 (March–April 1984): 167–172.
8. Andrea Foote, John C. Erfurt, and Rowland Austin, "Staffing Occupational Employee Assistance Programs: The General Motors Experience," *Alcohol Health and Research World* 4 (Spring 1980): 23.
9. Pamela S. London and Marvin D. Feit, "Isn't This a Terrible Time?: Reconceptualization of EAP Contributions to Corporate Social Responsibilities in Hard Times," *EAP Digest* 3, no. 1 (November–December 1982): 31–33.
10. NASW National Occupational Social Work Task Force, *NASW News* 19, no. 5 (May 1984): 21.
11. Sheila H. Akabas and Paul A. Kurzman, *Work, Workers and Work Organizations: A View from Social Work* (Englewood Cliffs, N.J.: Prentice-Hall, 1982), p. 201.
12. See James T. Wrich, *The Employee Assistance Program: Updated for the 1980s* (Minneapolis, Minn.: Hazelden Press, 1980); and Martha N. Ozawa, "Social Work Practice in Employee Assistance Programs," *Social Casework* 64, no. 4 (April 1983): 243–246.
13. Walter Scanlon, "Trends in EAPs: Then and Now," *EAP Digest* 3, no. 4 (May–June 1983): 38–41.

14. "Standards for Employee Alcoholism and/or Assistance Programs," *EAP Digest* 3, no. 4 (May–June 1983): 42.
15. "Social Worker Carves Niche at Pentagon," *NASW News* 33, no. 4 (April 1988): 5.
16. Stephen West et al., "Social Work's New Deal: Doing Good, Doing Well," *Newsweek on Campus*, May 1988, p. 40.
17. *EAP Digest* 4, no. 3 (March–April 1984): 10.
18. Sheila H. Akabas, Paul A. Kurzman, and Nancy S. Kolben, eds., *Labor and Industrial Settings: Sites for Social Work Practice* (New York: Council on Social Work Education, Columbia University School of Social Work, and Hunter College School of Social Work, 1979).
19. Paul A. Kurzman, "Ethical Issues in Industrial Social Work Practice," *Social Casework* 64, no. 2 (February 1983): 105–111; Norman L. Wyers and Malina Kaulukukui, "Social Services in the Workplace: Rhetoric vs. Reality," *Social Work* 29, no. 2 (March–April 1984): 167–172.
20. Frank B. Wolfe, III, and Marthanda J. Beckworth, "Confidentiality of Employee Records in Employee Assistance Programs," *EAP Digest* 3, no. 1 (November–December 1982): 34–35.
21. Henry L. Hudson, "The Function of Neutrality in Employee Assistance Programs," *EAP Digest* 3, no. 6 (September–October 1983): 32–37.
22. See, e.g., J.K. Galbraith's *The New Industrial State*, 3rd ed. (Boston: Houghton Mifflin, 1978); and Richard Barnet and Ronald E. Muller's *Global Reach* (New York: Simon & Schuster, 1974).
23. See Bertha C. Reynolds, *Social Work and Social Living* (Washington, D.C.: National Association of Social Workers, 1951).

ADDITIONAL SUGGESTED READINGS

Abramovitz, Mimi, and Irwin Epstein, "The Politics of Privatization: Industrial Social Work and Private Enterprise," *Urban and Social Change Review* 16, no. 1 (Winter 1983): 13–19.

Alexander, L. B., "Unions: Social Work," in Anne Minahan, ed., *Encyclopedia of Social Work*, 18th ed. (Silver Spring, Md.: NASW, 1987).

Carter, Irl E., "Social Work in Industry: A History and a Viewpoint," *Social Thought* 3, no. 1 (Winter 1977): 7–17.

Feinstein, Barbara B., and Frank Okrasinski, "Employee Assistance Programs: New Roles and Directions for Human Relations Professionals," *Urban and Social Change Review* 16, no. 1 (Winter 1983): 3–8.

Googins, Bradley, *Occupational Social Work* (Englewood Cliffs, N.J.: Prentice-Hall, 1987).

Googins, Bradley, *Occupational Social Work: An Annotated Bibliography* (Silver Spring, Md.: Commission on Employment and Economic Support, National Association of Social Workers, 1987).

Gould, Gary M., and Michael L. Smith, *Social Work in the Workplace* (New York: Springer Publishing Co., 1988).

Kurzman, Paul A., "Industrial Social Work," in Anne Minahan, ed., *Encyclopedia of Social Work*, 18th ed. (Silver Spring, Md.: NASW, 1987).

Masi, Dale A., *Human Services in Industry* (Lexington, Mass.: Lexington Books, 1982).

Popple, Philip R., "Social Work Practice in Business and Industry, 1875–1930," *Social Service Review* 55, no. 2 (June 1981): 257–269.

Social Work 33 No. 1 (January–February 1988). This issue focuses on social work in an industrial setting.

Social Work Papers: Industrial Social Work 18, 19, and 20 (Los Angeles: The School of Social Work, University of Southern California, 1984, 1985, 1987).

Weiner, Hyman, et al., *Mental Health Care in the World of Work* (New York: Association Press, 1973).

14 Emerging and Less Traditional Settings of Social Work Practice

H. Wayne Johnson

So far in this section we have examined what may be regarded as the traditional or usual contexts for social work practice. Now we turn our attention to some innovations, both because they represent further uses of social work currently and also because they may suggest something about the future. We will look at nontraditional services, both actual and potential. Some of these were discussed earlier, but they are sufficiently important to mention again.

First, a word about the use of the term "nontraditional." Obviously there would not be consensus among social workers as to what constitutes traditional social work practice and its opposite. Each would speak from his or her own context. What is nontraditional is relative. Variables are the part of the country and the community concerned, among many others. What is commonplace in one region may be rare in another part of the country. The preceding chapter dealt with industry, which many would see as an unusual setting for social work. But as was pointed out, it is considered unusual, though now less so, for the United States whereas in some nations such as England, social work has been present in business and industry for a long time. Recently the author learned of a social work administrator of an urban family service agency who has left this position to take a job managing a large law firm. He is not an attorney. So the use of social work is not even and consistent but is a matter of degree. Dichotomous-sounding terms like "traditional" are admittedly problematic, given this unevenness, but they do serve a purpose in differentiating the generally ordinary from uncommon settings.

Still a further aspect of the relativity is seen if we ask just how new a service needs to be in order to be termed nontraditional—one year, ten years, or what? Generally, programs that have originated since the 1960s or at least the 1970s probably should be considered nontraditional because they are so much more recent than programs like medical, psychiatric, or school social work; foster care or adoption, and probation or parole, all of which date back at least half a century and in some cases much longer. The newer the program generally, the greater the likelihood that its presence will not be universal in society.

It also should be acknowledged again that in most of the fields of service discussed in previous chapters, there is a mix of traditional and newer, creative kinds of activities. Schools, for example, are clearly a traditional setting (although in parts of the nation social work is not operative or has only recently appeared), but there are certain programs involving school social workers that are innovative and perhaps experimental. In other words, it is necessary to go beyond the setting itself and to consider the diverse endeavors and roles of the social worker when discussing the nontraditional aspects of this field. Not everything to be explored here is totally new; sometimes the activities represent a changed emphasis or a different thrust but are, at any rate, worth consideration.

DEATH, DYING, AND GRIEF

One area of significant new developments in recent years is in dealing with death and dying. This subject has become somewhat less taboo, and there is more openness about it. One measure of the interest in this topic is the appearance of a syndicated newspaper column entitled "A Time for Living" by Jory Graham, who was terminally ill with cancer.[1] The column ran from 1978 until Graham died in 1983. A literature on the subject has appeared, and services are being created. While much of this is focused on the elderly, of course, it cuts across age lines to include all terminal illness and injury situations and death. This interest includes the dying patient as well as the family of the dying and significant others. Therefore, a major concern is the grief process. Human service staff members in a variety of agencies encounter persons experiencing grief who need assistance in coping.

A 1988 announcement of a conference on grief suggests how multifaceted this subject is.[2] The intended conference audience includes social workers, nurses, clergy and church school teachers, school personnel, psychologists, counselors, other mental health workers, personnel officers, and funeral home staff. Included in the topics for group discussion are:

1. Alcohol and grief: a dangerous combination
2. When babies die: help for parents
3. When children grieve
4. A support group program for grieving teenagers
5. Grief after suicide: mourning
6. Grief after suicide: reentry
7. Dangerous grief
8. Grief and high-risk professionals
9. Organ donations: a gift from and to mourners
10. Grief: sudden death (SIDS)
11. Grief among the living (loved ones of Alzheimer's patients)
12. Self-esteem and grief
13. Puppeting/clowning (working with children on grief)
14. Grief and AIDS victims/families
15. Grief after abortion

Clearly death, dying, and grief are complex phenomena.

A recent appearance on the scene holding promise for social work is the hospice movement, which was discussed earlier. Hospice is a "comprehensive program of care and support for terminally ill patients and their families."[3] Services differ from unit to unit, but the trend is toward services that are both inpatient and home-based, or a combination. These services supplement and work with those provided by physicians, nurses, ministers, and other professionals. Hospice care begins with patient admission and continues throughout the mourning period. The purpose is twofold: "(1) to help the terminal patient remain comfortable, alert and able to participate in life as fully as possible for as long as possible until death occurs naturally and peacefully, and (2) to enable the family to remain lovingly attentive to the dying person throughout the dying process."[4]

The social work role relative to hospice is multifaceted. One social work student has gone through hospice training and is a volunteer. Social workers, along with others, may help to plan and organize new hospices, work in administration, train volunteers and staff, raise funds, evaluate services and function in many other capacities. Fitting hospice into the network of services in a community and working for maximum use of these services can be an important activity. A primary role for social work is serving on the hospice team along with other specialists.[5]

The funeral director may represent a new setting for social work practice. Thus far, such arrangements are not common, but they seem to afford an obvious means of meeting needs and a way of providing service at a critical point. Helping survivors deal with pain, anxiety, depression, possible guilt, and a melange of other potential feelings along with assisting in the reorganizing of lives after a loss and all that may entail can be the job of a social worker.

CRISIS INTERVENTION CENTERS

Crisis intervention centers and suicide prevention programs were alluded to earlier in the mental health chapter. These have come into being since the 1960s and early 1970s, and in this sense may be thought of as less traditional services. Some crisis centers operate only telephone services whereas others also maintain walk-in programs. Services included are counseling, other intervention, and information and referral. Among the calls received are those from distraught or depressed persons who consider or threaten to take their own lives. Hence, suicide prevention becomes one of the problems such centers deal with. In one midwestern center, the most common types of calls in order received in 1987 were: financial/employment, relations with spouse/lover, depression, housing, social/interpersonal relations, parent/child relations, suicide, loneliness, sex, domestic violence, alcohol, and medical.[6]

When crisis centers were started in the 1960s and 1970s, one of the concerns was drug abuse and help for persons involved with drugs. Hence "hot lines" came into being.[7] Some services have been established as specialized suicide prevention per se beginning with efforts particularly in Los Angeles.

One characteristic of crisis intervention is its time-limited nature and short-term duration. Some centers are finding that callers are of two types, the true crisis caller and the regular, repeat, or chronic callers. Different needs may be manifested in these two groups, and they may call for divergent responses. The situation is complicated somewhat with the telephone callers in that in many centers, neither the volunteer nor the caller reveals their identities but use first names only to maintain anonymity.

An interesting feature of crisis centers is their use of small paid administrative staffs and relatively large volunteer staffs. Social work students are often heavily represented among the volunteers in crisis centers located in or near college or university communities. In one university community, for example, the Crisis Intervention Center has a pool of approximately 120 volunteers. Of these, about one-third are undergraduate or graduate social work students or fairly recent graduates of these programs.[8]

Often students, alone or in concert with practitioners and others, have initiated such programs. Social workers frequently are employed as administrators or staff members. In this case, major functions typically are related to obtaining community support and funding, recruiting and training volunteers, and general administrative tasks.

HEALTH

Previous chapters dealt with health and mental health. A good example of the difficulty of differentiating traditional and nontraditional settings is illustrated by nursing homes, a topic alluded to in earlier chapters. Some American nursing homes have employed social workers for years, but in others this profession is still not represented. Much has depended on federal and state policies and requirements. Practices of nursing homes and extended-care facilities reflect changes in these external regulations. The trend does seem clear toward use of social work in this setting. Interestingly, when social workers are employed in nursing homes, they are used in a variety of ways.

Recently, for example, in one midwestern state, nursing homes in communities in close proximity to each other demonstrated the following patterns:

- Full-time combined social worker/activities director in a single nursing home.
- Full-time social worker serving one facility.
- Part-time social worker serving one nursing home.
- Social worker whose services are purchased by four or five nursing homes for a few hours in each facility weekly.

In one convalescent facility, the social worker prepares social histories on all residents, does ongoing work with a few residents individually, and conducts reality orientation groups and remotivation sessions with small groups.

An example of innovations in organizations that were themselves innovations just a few years ago is seen in free medical clinics that are now providing AIDS (acquired immune deficiency syndrome) counseling and HIV (human immunodeficiency virus) antibody testing. This is a critically important service today. The author works with social work practicum students who are engaged in HIV counseling in a free clinic. The clinic is determined by the state Department of Public Health to be an alternate site for such testing. Patients may remain anonymous by using fictitious names in most cases. The director of the clinic, a social worker, refers to AIDS-related activity as, sadly, a "growth industry" for social work.

Physicians in private practice are potentially large employers of social workers. Family doctors typically see many patients a day, spending only a few minutes with each on average. Many patients need to talk with someone more than they need any medical procedure or medication. They need to ventilate pent-up feelings, or have someone objectively discuss options in problematic situations, or any one of many other possibilities. The physician is unlikely to be able to do this for all persons needing it. Therefore, the social worker provides a likely resource. Although this has not yet happened on a large scale, there are precedents.[9]

In one medical clinic comprised of twenty-one physicians, a social worker was added. One hundred cases referred by the physicians to the social worker were classified as follows: in twenty there was a diagnosis of organic disease that was accompanied by emotional stress; with sixty cases there were physical symptoms of psychogenic origin; the other twenty cases there were no physical complaints but there were individual problems such as anxiety or depression or family problems.[10]

A more common arrangement is for social workers to be employed by psychiatrists who are in private practice. These are generally experienced workers with graduate degrees who, along with other professionals, engage in psychotherapy. With considerable variations, they work with individuals, couples, and families.

As dental practice changes from emphasis on restorative work to preventive and specialized care, another new role for social work may appear. Fields such as orthodontia sometimes present situations of patient or family expectations for patient transformation that exceed the constraints of reality. This may call for social work intervention. Another aspect has to do with pain and its alleviation in this era of "pain clinics" and related measures. Dentists are increasingly interested in the phenomenon of pain because of the association of dental care and pain in negative ways. Since social work addresses the whole patient including the psychosocial realm, this may be an area for natural expansion.

Social workers have also been used in university student health services and counseling programs. Because of the struggle that certain students experience in "finding themselves" vocationally and in other ways, the stresses of academic success and other problems of the student role, it is not uncommon for them to seek professional assistance. To request such help is to be considered a strength on the student's part.

Some practitioners from helping disciplines such as social work and psychology have moved (part-time or full-time) into the field carrying such labels as "sports medicine." The broader idea is to provide various services to athletes to enhance their athletic ability/performance and to facilitate their development and functioning in a holistic way.

Social workers are sometimes employed in university health complexes to teach medical students and/or other personnel such as nurses. The content of such teaching may aim at sensitizing health care professionals to the whole spectrum of needs of patients as bio-psycho-social beings and to the importance of humanizing the medical environment. This environment with all its technical paraphernalia, which physicians and others may take for granted, is often extremely threatening to the patient. Part of the job is to demystify such a setting for patients. Helping to make patients and their families informed consumers can pay large dividends in the well-being of the patient. Patient advocacy, not in an adversarial sense but in the sense of family support for patients, can make it much easier for the medical staff to get its job done.[11] In other words, there are good pragmatic reasons for this enabling function.

An example of work with medical students is a midwestern medical school and hospital in which workshops on interpersonal skills were conducted by a social worker. These were funded in part with a mental health grant and partially by a chapter of the American Medical Student Association and other student groups. It is significant that the request came from medical students themselves, probably out of realization of the importance of communication for physicians and the difficulties frequently present in communication.

A new development in mental health is the Veterans' Administration Readjustment Counseling Service for veterans experiencing posttraumatic stress disorders (PTSD).[12] Veterans, especially of Vietnam, and others sometimes face difficulty in adjustment even years following the experience. Inpatient and outpatient programs can be useful in helping people cope in these situations.

Developmentally disabled and handicapped people are an expanding group being served by both traditional and innovative settings. As greater numbers survive into adulthood, the need for service increases. Socialization programs, special housing, and sheltered workshops are among the needs and services cutting across health and mental health lines and into education for certain subgroups of these "differently abled" people. Important social work functions are assessment, planning, and intervention. These activities require discernment of strengths and limitations, with particular emphasis on enhancement of strengths for people with disabilities.

EDUCATION

The preceding discussion overlaps with education although it has been treated under health. Social workers have been used in other parts of colleges and universities beyond those already noted. One university psychology department, for example, operates a research and training clinic, which employed a social worker to teach graduate students interviewing skills and to supervise some of their work.

Another way social workers are sometimes involved in higher education is to staff student personnel units, counseling/advising services, or in residence halls. Others work with foreign students in international programs or in special support units with minority, handicapped, and otherwise disadvantaged students or those with special needs. Some people with social work training have been employed in college/university admissions, orientation, family housing for married students, placement services, student union administration, affirmative action offices, and women's centers. The author has had contact with all these in at least one university.

As far as teaching is concerned, traditionally social work faculty were in graduate schools of social work. More recently, the major growth has been in undergraduate programs and even in two-year community and junior colleges. The expansion of social work education on all levels has necessitated drawing more people into teaching and educational administration. Generally, at least the master's degree is required as the base educational requirement for such assignments and, as more programs offer doctorates, increasingly the doctorate is called for, especially in graduate schools.[13]

School social workers are moving more and more from direct service to such activities as consultation and education. This approach enables them to educate the educators and hence to impact on greater numbers of children and youth. That this trend goes beyond the United States was observed in 1984 by the author in Australia.

FAMILIES

As was noted in Chapters 5 and 6, working with families and children constitutes a large part of social work. We want to consider now only those aspects of this field that are recent arrivals in the social services. Among these is divorce counseling. Marriage counseling is a long-established practice, but divorce on a massive scale has come into general societal awareness only more recently. In spite of the growing acceptance of divorce, it is still often traumatic for the persons involved. Hence, help for people in such circumstances may be useful before, during, and following the divorce. Some agencies are providing much more service in relation to marital and family breakdown than formerly. Developments such as joint custody of children following marriage dissolution is an example of innovations in traditional legal practices holding significance for the human services.

Another modern development is cohabiting couples. Interestingly there is reason to believe that such couples experience some of the same kinds of problems often accompanying marriage. Thus, another service need and opportunity appears.

Starting first with child abuse, there has come to be major attention devoted to various aspects of family violence. Spouse abuse is now in the national spotlight as a social problem. Another concern is physical and emotional abuse of the elderly, often by adult children. None of these problems are new, obviously. What is new is their discovery and such community responses as spouse abuse shelters. It is estimated by a national coalition that there are over 1,000 shelters in the United States for battered women.[14] Social workers play a significant role in establishing and operating these facilities. This is not the only service available, but it is a significant one. Protective services is a substantial traditional social provision but is being expanded and diversified with new measures.

New programs for the elderly are sometimes variations of established ones for other age groups, now being adapted to the aged. Examples are day services and foster care. With day care, an elderly person who should not be left alone and who is living with relatives who are occupied goes to a special facility that will meet her/his needs and provide stimulation. This kind of care can be reassuring for everyone concerned, the aged and the family. Other elderly persons are able to live in family homes, but since no family members are available, substitute family care may be arranged. Still another arrangement for some elderly is house sharing.[15] Social workers may carry a variety of roles in such measures, from direct service to planning, organizing, and administration.

Day care for children can hardly be considered new; what is nontraditional is incorporating social work into this setting. Brennan suggests some possible roles for the social worker by delineating the following children in a normal day-care population: the hyperactive, depressed, angry, fearful, loner, the "child who has a difficult time separating," and the "child who is highly sensitive to criticism."[16] All of these require individualization and understanding and may call for work with the child, parents, and day-care staff.

A newly developing field is family caregivers. In 1988 the school of social work at Case Western Reserve University established a project aimed at this problem, defining the term as "families who provide care for a disabled family member." The project is concerned with addressing the needs of such caregivers as these may be served by human service agencies. Various physical and mental disabilities may necessitate extensive family involvement such as providing care for disabled children and youth, people in frail health, stroke patients, and elderly parents with Alzheimer's disease.[17]

Very recently an interesting development has occurred that is hard to classify under the groupings being used in this chapter, so we are placing it here, arbitrarily, with families. It has to do with veterinary medicine and social work. The pioneers in this effort are at the University of Pennsylvania.[18] In the United States millions of people have pets, and in many cases these animals become a very real psychological part of the family. When pets become ill or injured and require professional attention, it is often a difficult time for their human "family" members of all ages as well as for the animal.

In 1978 a graduate social work student began a practicum placement at the University of Pennsylvania Small Animal Hospital. She began by

> donning a white coat and moving about the hospital talking to doctors, students, and pet owners; making herself available to provide support services to *Homo sapiens* in a hospital designed to treat many other species, but not that one. By the end of her first five months, she had developed a list of twenty-eight different kinds of problems referred to her—problems of communication in which the owner could not seem to understand the physician, or could not follow directions; problems of anger that represented displaced fear or guilt; problems of finances, human health, pet abuse, and/or animal behavior that were affecting family life.

The most difficult problems, or at least the ones with which veterinarians most frequently sought her help, were those involving owners who were reacting with strong emotion to the serious illness or death of an animal. The decision concerning euthanasia, for example, is one which is rarely countenanced in relation to humans. Many veterinarians are "uncomfortable in the presence of tears or guilt or anger . . . and feel they have neither the time nor the skill to deal with clients' emotional outbursts. In these situations, the assistance of a social worker is valued."[19]

How far this innovation may be institutionalized in the future may be suggested by the studies designed to explore the biological, psychological, and social aspects of the interactions between people and their pets. Other studies are exploring the therapeutic and life-enhancing possibilities of the use of companion animals with special population groups.[20] There is now an interdisciplinary Center for the Interaction of Animals and Society. In 1981 in Philadelphia an International Conference on the Human/Companion Animal Bond was held.

JUSTICE

This topic is a mix of various needs and programs in which legal rights and protections are a common core. In modern societies with complex legal and court systems, human well-being is greatly affected by the structure and functioning of these systems. The relationship between law and social work is not entirely new in that some of the early figures in social work were people with legal training. More recently, however, greater attention has been paid to linkages between these two fields. For example, a growing number of universities have developed joint programs between law schools and schools of social work.

Social work students, both graduate and undergraduate, sometimes have field experience or practicum placements in legal settings such as antipoverty legal services. The social worker may assist the legal staff in client advocacy on government benefit matters pending before administrative agencies such as the Social Security Administration, public welfare department, or public employment service. An additional significant role is working with clients and staff in seeking nonlegal solutions to client problems such as locating housing or child care. While these problems are peripheral to the legal ones, they are important. Another social work activity is community outreach. In other words, legal services may be a kind of parallel to the medical field in presenting an array of opportunities for the provision of social services as adjuncts to the central purpose of the organization.

The human rights movement that has taken place in the United States since the civil rights developments of the mid-1950s has had major impact. On the other hand, much unfinished work remains in providing equality of opportunity to racial and ethnic groups and to women. At this writing, activities of the Ku Klux Klan, American Nazi party, and other far-right and fanatical groups appear to be increasing and present a serious threat to further assuring the rights of all people. It is not just in extreme groups such as these that the danger resides, however, it is to a considerable degree in the apathy of millions of Americans. Social service professionals alone are not enough to alter this situation, but they do have responsibilities in it and opportunities to contribute to its resolution.

The consumer movement is another context of activity for social work and related professions. Some aspects of this movement have roots going back for decades, but there has been a recent impetus with the efforts of Ralph Nader and others. One example is the work in various states of the Public Interest Research Groups (PIRG) engaging in a variety of consumer-oriented efforts, environmental protection, and other activities designed to lend visibility to these needs and to institute and support social action and necessary legislation in the public interest.[21]

It has become increasingly clear that social work must be active politically if the human service system is to be well designed, adequately funded, and effective. This calls for coalitions with a variety of organizations and professions, for education of the public, and for lobbying, among other endeavors. Some social workers have operated as lobbyists and have provided information to legislators, which can be crucial in the legislative process.

Among the important areas to the social services are the various ways that law impinges on the family. In this country, family law is a state rather than federal matter, and there is lack of uniformity among the states, making for confusion. Some of the aspects of family law that are of concern to social work are those dealing with marriage, divorce, child support and custody, abortion, illegitimacy, adoption, guardianship, and child abuse.

Others have to do with crime and delinquency and were discussed in an earlier chapter. The juvenile court is especially noteworthy as a changing force in social work practice. As the rights of youth are further defined and extended, new social roles may be created and old ones modified. The whole thrust toward community-based corrections and to alternatives to institutions is promising for reforms in a traditionally difficult field. Special treatment efforts are being directed to sex offenders both within institutions and in the community. A new development, albeit controversial, is private corrections in which certain tasks such as preparation of presentence reports may be contracted out to profit-making enterprises.[22] Social workers may be employed by such organizations. The appearance of social work in some police departments is encouraging from the point of view of a different kind of intervention and, hence, providing a more preventive service to people. Finally, the addition of various arbitration and mediation programs to resolve intra- and interpersonal, family, and neighborhood issues of both criminal and civil nature is significant.

REFUGEES

While refugee movements have been part of the human scene for centuries, the groups involved have varied. Generally refugees are fleeing repressive totalitarian regimes, persecution, civil wars, and natural disasters. Forbes indicates that basically there are three solutions for refugees, which, in order of desirability, are: (1) repatriation to their own country, (2) settling in a neighboring country in which they find themselves, and (3) resettling in a third country.[23] Since so much of the

Stock, Boston/Budd Gray

Refugees and immigrants often have many problems. Social services,
legal assistance, and other help may be required.

present world disruption is taking place in poor, developing nations,
the first two options are often not feasible.

A major new wave of refugees from Southeast Asia came to this
country starting in 1975 as a result of warfare there. This group constituted about three-fourths of the million refugee arrivals in the United
States between 1975 and 1985 and was made up mainly of Vietnamese,
Laotians, and Cambodians. Other groups are from the Soviet Union,
Eastern Europe, Latin America, and Africa. Refugees tend to differ
demographically from Americans in being, on the average, younger,
and proportionately more are male.

Refugees from Southeast Asia are hindered in adapting to the
United States by major cultural differences, the absence of an established ethnic community that would aid their adjustment, and this
country's weak economy when they arrived.[24] It is important to realize
that this is not a single homogeneous group of people but a collection
of diverse groups in terms of history, language, and culture.

Some of the organizations serving refugees are old established family and/or youth agencies and community centers that expand their

programs to serve this population. Others are new and were developed specifically in response to the needs and problems of this group. Some are under the auspices of religious organizations that have become concerned about the well-being of refugees, although some private services are nonsectarian. In addition to all the physical survival needs, people from other countries often experience adjustment problems and emotional difficulties, sometimes requiring mental health services. Enabling clients to see emotional problems as normal reactions to stress that is abnormal can be useful.[25]

Southeast Asian refugees often resist using mental health services. Factors contributing to this resistance are: (1) language and communication problems, (2) cultural diversity, (3) diversity in migration and resettlement experiences, (4) stigma attached to mental illness, and (5) a tradition of reliance on kinship and community support networks.[26] Programs to meet the needs of this client population must consider their reluctance to use services and attempt to respond to these factors.

Cultural and value differences and conflict between American mental health professionals and Indochinese Asian patients are presented by Kinzie as follows:[27]

Indochinese Asian patient values	*American psychotherapist values*
Interdependence and traditional family values	Autonomy and independence
"Correct" social relationships	Relativity in values; situational ethics; rejection of authority
Holistic culture; i.e., people living in harmony with nature	People versus nature; the need to master or control nature
View of mental illness as imbalance of cosmic forces or supernatural events	View of mental illness as result of psychological and biological factors
No cultural analogy of extended psychological therapy	Belief that psychotherapy is valuable and promotes "growth"
Belief that cure should be rapid, healer active; little history of maintenance therapy	Awareness that cure will be extended and time-consuming, and therapist will often be passive
Fear of mental illness	Comfortable attitude about handling mental illness and symptoms
"Refugee" status—insecure in language, vocation, position in society	Secure status in "society," language, vocation, and position

Kinzie indicates that the subjects that need to be dealt with in working therapeutically with people who arrive from Southeast Asia are life in the homeland, the escape process, life in the refugee camp, adjustment in this country, and current problems/worries about the future.[28]

At this writing people from Central American nations are fleeing persecution and totalitarianism and entering the United States, sometimes illegally. Large numbers of Mexicans enter the country, often illegally, for employment and present somewhat different situations from that of actual refugees.

Social workers were involved with immigrants at the turn of the century and are again today active with refugees. It is an immense task to help people make the transition and settle into new lives in a strange and foreign land. The adjustment to a new environment with problems of language/communication, education, employment, housing, health, and a hundred other considerations presents a major challenge to refugees and to those working with them. Some Americans as individuals or group members are presently committed publicly to assist Central Americans (illegally in the United States) who are fleeing oppression. At the risk of arrest and punishment for such acts of civil disobedience, these people act on the basis of their humanitarian convictions. Complex challenges face social workers who may be called on to work with such people, and value conflicts abound for any who may consider participating in illegally assisting refugees.[29]

A recent special situation that deserves mention can be discussed within the context of refugees. Late in 1987 and 1988 the Orderly Departure Program brought to the United States from Southeast Asia numbers of children and youth who were fathered by American soldiers during the Vietnam War. The program had been suspended two years earlier and was reopened. Relatives of the Amerasians as well as other Vietnamese joining family members in this country were included in this group.[30]

HOMELESSNESS

Another concern currently is the homeless. While homelessness is not a new social problem, it has compounded in recent years and is receiving renewed attention. Estimates of the number of homeless in this country range from 250,000 to 3 million.[31] More exact figures are impossible to obtain, given the nature of the problem. It appears that this highly heterogeneous group tends to be largely young, male, and representative of ethnicity in the local area. On the other hand the number of women who are homeless is believed to be on the increase. Included in the homeless are individuals and families, adolescents, adults, and elderly. Alcoholism and other substance abuse are common as is mental illness. Among youth are runaways.

According to Connell the causative factors contributing to homelessness include the recession and high unemployment of the early 1980s, a dearth of low-cost housing, deinstitutionalization of the mentally ill, and an effort by the federal administration to reduce the number of Social Security disability insurance recipients.[32] With regard to the recession/unemployment factor, it is important to note that the impact was long-term for some people. The fact that unemployment declined later in the decade did not benefit all people. Some appear to have become a part of the more or less permanent underclass, and some of these are now without homes.

There is a marked shortage of affordable housing. Some such housing is actually declining in numbers and additional needed units have not been provided. An example of the former is the loss of single-room occupancy (SRO) units on a large scale. Many of the old hotels and other buildings that were being used for this purpose have been razed or converted to other uses. In addition thousands of people lost Social Security disability benefits as a result of administrative action from 1981 to 1984, and this undoubtedly contributed to loss of housing for some.

Deinstitutionalization of the mentally ill is widely thought to be a causative factor in homelessness. Patient population in state and county mental hospitals dropped 77 percent between 1955 and 1981 in the national move to replace long-term custodial care with community-based programs.[33] Unfortunately, no well-organized system for meeting the needs of mental patients on the community level has been funded. The fact that some chronically mentally ill persons are street people without homes is not an argument against deinstitutionalization but the reason for providing comprehensive supportive services in the community to help these people.

Late in 1987 it was reported that in New York City, disturbed street people were being picked up and hospitalized, a new development. Apparently the plan is that after evaluation they are to be placed in long-term care facilities or supervised housing.[34] It remains to be seen whether these programs will be progressive and forward-looking or a move backwards.

A common denominator in much homelessness is poverty (at least temporary) and, in some cases, rootlessness. While Travelers Aid and various temporary lodging provisions of the Salvation Army, missions, and others have been traditional resources, more recently other shelters have appeared. There is now a National Coalition for the Homeless. Shelters are needed in many communities as temporary measures, but they do not provide a permanent solution. What is needed is a range of housing options. As Prock and Taber have noted, the reason for homelessness is irrelevant to the affected person's need for shelter.[35]

HUNGER

Within the larger context of poverty, the problems of hunger and malnutrition persist in a developed nation of surplus agricultural products and general affluence. In the mid-1980s 20 million Americans were reportedly going hungry, and the problem was worsening. The president in May 1986 responded to critics of his administration's inaction on hunger by indicating that people who were hungry lacked knowledge about how to obtain food, the implication being that there actually was no problem.

Brown states, "Between 1982 and 1987, a total of 77 studies documented the widespread and serious impact of the increasing hunger in America" and "the evidence shows that there is hunger of dimensions not seen in years."[36] Brown attributes the reasons why one in ten Americans do not have enough to eat to three factors: (1) the national "safety net" was weak to begin with; (2) in the early 1980s the economy soured; and (3) the federal administration made the most severe cutbacks ever in nutrition programs. School meals and food stamps alone were cut over $12 billion. High unemployment, more low-paying jobs, and a tax system that results in more income for the wealthy and less for everyone else add up to poverty and hence to hunger.

Some social workers practice within the context of the newer food and nutrition programs as well as those programs that have been in existence for decades. Both aim at reducing the ravages of hunger, regardless of its causes.

SUMMARY AND CONCLUSIONS

In this chapter we have considered some of the less typical social services. A few of these were alluded to in earlier chapters but it is useful to bring them together in one place and examine them collectively. Here we have attempted also to illustrate and extend what was presented earlier.

Several points must be made in this connection. People employed to work in these nontraditional settings are not always termed "social workers." Various role titles are found. Some people are employed in these contexts because they are social workers, while others are used with less regard to that fact. Also, not all of what has been described here are actually "settings" as the chapter title suggests. Some are activities or roles of the worker. Furthermore, a distinction should be made between actual and potential social work use, as has been noted. Mention has been made of practicum placements of social work students in a few uncommon contexts. These innovative kinds of arrangements may, on occasion, be indicative of developing fields. Predictions of specific coming professional developments are not being made at this juncture because the future is so uncertain and what these various human service activities mean for tomorrow is unknown. In some cases, however, the trends appear rather clear.

NOTES

1. For example, this column was carried by the *Des Moines Register.*
2. Brochure received in March 1988 from Burlington Medical Center, Burlington, Iowa: "Good Grief . . . A Second Look."
3. From "Hospice of Central Iowa," a brochure distributed by Hospice of Central Iowa, Des Moines, undated.
4. Ibid.
5. William M. Markel and Virginia B. Simon, "The Hospice Concept," *CA-A Cancer Journal for Clinicians* 28, no. 4 (July/August 1978): 231.
6. Iowa City Crisis Intervention Center, "Quarterly Program Report: Fiscal Year 1987," Iowa City, Iowa.
7. Leon Brill, "Addiction: Drug," *Encyclopedia of Social Work,* 17th ed. (Washington, D.C.: NASW, 1977), pp. 39–40.
8. Iowa City Crisis Intervention Center, Personal communication with Ken Kauppi, Director, February 15, 1988.
9. Theresa W. Barkan, "Private Casework Practice in a Medical Clinic," *Social Work,* July 1973, pp. 5–9. See also Louis H. Forman, "The Physician and the Social Worker," *American Family Physician* 13, no. 1 (January 1976): 90–93; Ruth L. Goldberg, "The Social Worker and the Family Physician," *Social Casework,* October 1973, pp. 489–495.
10. Barkan, "Private Casework Practice," p. 7.
11. Based on discussion with Nina Hamilton, professor of social work at the University of Iowa.
12. *NASW News,* Classifieds, March 1988, p. 15.
13. According to the Council of Social Work Education, forty-six graduate schools of social work offered doctoral programs in 1987.
14. Domestic Violence Project, Personal communication with Pat Meyer, Director, Iowa City, February 15, 1988.
15. Carolyn E. Usher and Stephen R. McConnell, "House Sharing: A Way to Intimacy," *Alternative Lifestyles* 3, no. 2 (May 1980): 149–166.

16. Elaine C. Brennan, "Meeting the Affective Needs of Young Children," *Children Today*, July–August 1974, pp. 22–25.

17. Letter dated April 27, 1988, from Mandel School of Applied Social Sciences, Case Western Reserve University, Cleveland.

18. "Social Work and Veterinary Medicine," *Sociolog*, Spring 1981. Eleanor L. Ryder, Professor of Social Work, University of Pennsylvania School of Social Work, Author.

19. Ibid.

20. Ibid.

21. There were thirty-six main PIRG offices listed in 1980 by their national clearinghouse in New York City.

22. Chester J. Kulis, "Profit in the Private Presentence Report," *Federal Probation*, December 1983, pp. 11–16.

23. Susan S. Forbes, "Refugees," *Encyclopedia of Social Work*, 18th ed. (Silver Spring, Md.: NASW, 1987), 2: 468.

24. Harry H. L. Kitano, "Asian Americans," *Encyclopedia of Social Work*, 18th ed. (Silver Spring, Md.: NASW, 1987), 1:168.

25. Hideka A. Ishisaka, Quynh T. Nguyen, and Joseph T. Ikimoto, "The Role of Culture in the Mental Health Treatment of Indochinese Refugees," in *Southeast Asian Mental Health*, ed. Tom Chokin Owan (Washington, D.C.: U.S. Department of Health and Human Services, 1985), p. 54.

26. Reico Homma True, "An Indochinese Mental Health Service Model in San Francisco," in *Southeast Asian Mental Health*, pp. 332–333.

27. J. David Kinzie, "Overview of Clinical Issues in the Treatment of Southeast Asian Refugees," in *Southeast Asian Mental Health*, p. 119.

28. Ibid., pp. 120–121.

29. Sherry Ricchiardi, "Iowans Help Refugees on Underground Railroad," *Des Moines Register*, July 29, 1984, pp. 1A, 6A. See also "Social Work in the Sanctuary Movement for Central American Refugees," *Social Work*, January–February 1985, pp. 74–76.

30. "Dozens of Children Fathered by U.S. GIs Head for America," *Iowa City Press Citizen*, January 1, 1988, p. 3D

31. Milan J. Dluhy, "Housing," *Encyclopedia of Social Work*, 18th ed. (Silver Spring, Md.: NASW, 1987), 1:831.

32. Sarah Connell, "Homelessness," *Encyclopedia of Social Work*, 18th ed. (Silver Spring, Md.: NASW, 1987), 1:790.

33. Stevan P. Segal, "Deinstitutionalization," *Encyclopedia of Social Work*, 18th ed. (Silver Spring, Md.: NASW, 1987), 1:377.

34. "Mentally Ill Homeless Moved into Hospitals in New York City," *Des Moines Register*, October 30, 1987, p. 3A.

35. Kathleen Prock and Merlin A. Taber, "Helping the Homeless," *Public Welfare* 45, no. 2 (Spring 1987): 5–9.

36. J. Larry Brown, "Domestic Hunger Is No Accident," editorial, *Social Work* 32, no. 2 (March–April 1988): 99.

ADDITIONAL SUGGESTED READINGS

Breton, Margot, "Resocialization of Abusive Parents," *Social Work* 26, no. 2 (March 1981): 119–122

Disabled U.S.A., a 1978 periodical addition to the growing literature on the handicapped, published by the President's Committee on the Employment of the Handicapped, Washington, D.C.

Dore, Martha M., and Karen Guberman Kennedy, "Two Decades of Turmoil: Child Welfare Services 1960–1980," *Child Welfare* 60, no. 6 (June 1981): 371–382.

First, Richard J., Dee Roth, and Bobbie Darden Arewa, "Homelessness: Understanding the Dimensions of the Problem for Minorities," *Social Work* 33, no. 2 (March–April 1988): 120–124.

Fulmer, Richard H., "The Prison Ombudsman," *Social Service Review* 55, no. 2 (June 1981): 300–313.

Haney, Patrick, "Providing Empowerment to the Person with AIDS," *Social Work* 33, no. 3 (May–June 1988): 251–253.

Haynes, John M., *Divorce Mediation* (New York: Springer Publishing Co., 1981).

Klass, Dennis, *Parental Grief* (New York: Springer Publishing Co., 1988).

Kübler-Ross, Elisabeth, *Living with Death and Dying* (New York: Macmillan, 1981).

Oneglia, Steward, and Malinda Orlin, "A Model for Combined Private Practice: Attorneys and Social Workers in Domestic Relations," *Journal of Applied Social Services* 3, no. 1 (1978): 37–46.

Pill, Cynthia J., "A Family Life Education Group for Working with Stepparents," *Social Casework* 62, no. 3 (March 1981): 159–166.

Puryear, Douglas A., *Helping People in Crisis* (San Francisco: Jossey-Bass, 1979).

Rappaport, Bruce M., "Family Planning: Helping Men Ask for Help," *Public Welfare* 39, no. 2 (Spring 1981): 22–27.

Ropers, Richard, *The Invisible Homeless* (New York: Human Sciences Press, Inc., 1988).

Shernoff, Michael J., "Family Therapy for Lesbian and Gay Clients," *Social Work* 29, no. 4 (July–August, 1984): 393–396.

Tillema, Richard G., "Starting Over in a New Land: Resettling a Refugee Family," *Public Welfare* 39, no. 1 (Winter 1981): pp. 35–41.

Part Three

Methods of Social Work Practice

Now that the various major settings or fields of service, that is, agency and organization contexts, have been covered, we are ready to examine the principal methods of social work practice. We do so not to learn "how-to-do-its" as much as simply to gain an overview of approaches to working with people in helping capacities in a variety of situations.

Therefore, we first consider the idea of the social work generalist practitioner. This is the recently emerged way of conceptualizing much of what social workers do, especially in baccalaureate-level practice. Related to this we will examine social systems; the helping process; social work roles, skills, and competencies; case management; prevention; and rural practice.

We will explore working with individuals and families, other groups, and communities. We will also take a look at social work administration and social welfare research.

It should be noted once again that this section may be read prior to Part Two, reversing the order of the two parts. In this case the reader should keep in mind that the practice methods being described are used in a number of diverse agency settings—hospitals, schools, counseling programs, and so forth, and these organizational contexts influence the professional activity therein, just as the reverse is also true.

333

15 Newer Approaches in Social Work Practice: The Generalist

H. Wayne Johnson

In the chapters in this section we will consider what traditionally were generally referred to as social work methods, the primary ones being casework, group work, and community organization. Whether these are best conceptualized as "methods" is a valid question. They refer to service units or numbers of persons served (case, group, or community) and hence are not really methods in the usual sense of this term in that they do not suggest much about a plan of action.

Another limitation of this traditional way of thinking about social work practice is that the commonly encountered characterization of casework as working one-to-one does not allow for the vast amount of work done with families. One response is to define casework as activity with individuals *and* families, but the problem here is that the family is a group, a special kind of group, granted, but a group nonetheless. This is one of the reasons for the attention now being given to the notion of the social worker generalist and generic methods.

You may have noticed that chapters in this section are not entitled "social casework," "social group work," and "community organization." The chapter titles chosen are intended to reflect better the nature of social work practice as it is evolving, particularly the generalist thrust. The latter development was alluded to in Chapter 1, and we return to it here for further examination.

The term "generic" is used here to mean general as opposed to specific. Generic social work has had two connotations over the years. Earlier in the century (1920s and 1930s) most social work education was in casework. Graduate students (social work education then was largely graduate-level) working toward a master's degree in the one-year programs then in existence selected a specialty having to do with a field of service or setting such as psychiatric, medical, or child welfare. One's educational program was tied to this choice of setting specialization. Then because people often moved from one field of practice to another and because of a common knowledge base in all the "specialties," social work educational programs were revamped. One change was that the master's degree came to require two years. The other change had to do with the options for students. No longer did one choose a specialty such as psychiatric social work (meaning formerly casework), but now the student selected a "method" (casework, group work or, in some schools, community organization). If the choice was casework, the idea was (and still is) that the knowledge and skill gained in this area would be transferable across the various settings or fields of service and that one could engage in the helping process in a variety of agency or problem contexts. This was the first use of the generic social work term, that is, generic relative to setting or field.

More recently, the term generic social work has taken on a second meaning, that is, generic relative to method, or what is now often referred to as the social worker generalist. With the recent conception of the generalist, the lines between casework, group work, and community organization are blurred. There is the recognition that many contemporary workers must possess knowledge and skill in all these areas. Assessing individuals, understanding group dynamics, engaging in community planning all may be within one workday of a social worker; hence, the term generalist may be particularly appropriate. One may think then of integrated methods or what the worker does as a totality.

Examining some of the common social work skills helps to carry this idea further. Take interviewing, for example. Perhaps no skill is more basic in the social services. It is not just caseworkers in a variety of agency contexts who use the interview. Group workers and community organizers do, too. The common denominator in all these approaches is working with people. How does one work with communities, for example, except through people? It is not possible to deal with the community in the abstract but only by activity with individuals and, most especially, groups. In fact, a community may be thought of as a group of groups. Community organizers spend large amounts of time and energy developing and intervening with committees, task forces, and other kinds of groups toward attaining community objectives and goals.

The increased attention to the generalist practitioner model has been both a cause and result of changes in education and practice. Baccalaureate social work programs arrived on the scene in more recent years and are preparing students for entry-level generalist practice. This is consistent with the Council on Social Work Education (CSWE) accreditation standards. On the graduate level, a variety of educational models exist. One is the master's (MSW) program, which has as its objective preparation of the advanced generalist. Another is one with two or more tracks, one of which is the generalist. Still another approach in a two-year graduate program is the first year as a generalist base and a second year of specialization. The specialization may center around a particular social problem, field of service, or population.

On the graduate level the term "advanced generalist" is coming to be used by some schools of social work. What this social worker should be and do is not yet entirely clear, nor is there an adequate differentiation between a baccalaureate generalist and the MSW advanced generalist at this time. There are unanswered questions both in education and in practice on these issues.

The generalist approach in social work practice is based on the dual nature of the profession, concern with both person and environment. This focus on person-in-environment or person and situation is integral to the generalist way of thinking. Generalists consider the transactions between people and their environments or how people cope with the various life stresses confronting them. In other words the generalist way of thinking is holistic and unitary. As Goldstein points out, the preferred orientation for the generalist is an "adaptational rather than a pathological concept of behavior."[1] From this view a "problems-of-living" perspective is more useful than the medical model of pathology. Among its other advantages, this problems-of-living conception of behavior reflects a systems way of thinking.

In contrast to the traditional orientation regarding methods of social work practice that tended to be seen as separate and distinct, the generalist approach is one of integrated methods. Drawing from Ripple, Sheafor, and Landon are two conceptions of the generalist, the multimethod worker and the utility worker. They note that the latter is characterized by greater versatility, and they favor this model. The idea of the utility worker fits the realities of social work that deals with such a diversity of problems, using a variety of skills and drawing from a multiplicity of resources.[2]

Goldstein delineates from the literature seven types of generalist practice roles with some overlapping because of common goals:[3]

1. Combined-methods generalist—integrates from casework, group work, and community organization a hybrid role.
2. Case manager generalist—concerned with making service more available in an integrated and coherent way.
3. Generalist as a composite of practitioner roles. Combines case management and direct service; has a variety of competencies.
4. Problem-focused generalist—problem assessment focus and knowledge about a particular problem.
5. Human services generalist—builds coalitions within delivery systems.
6. Ideological generalist—presence of a strong belief about social work practice's valued objectives.
7. Systems-oriented generalist—uses concept of client's "system" to organize practice.

SYSTEMS

Another development in social work practice is the greater attention being paid to viewing the institution of social welfare, the profession of social work, helping activity, and client situations from a *systems* perspective. The essence of this way of thinking is to view the elements of the social welfare institution and human service professions as interrelated components within a larger network. These interdependent parts are linked to each other and affect one another. They tend toward a state of balance. Impact in one area has influence far beyond the immediate localized point just as a pebble dropped in water creates ripples moving out in all directions. For social welfare the broader system includes economic and political institutions. Similarly, social work as a profession within the social welfare institution is related to other helping disciplines such as those within education (another social institution) and health, to mention only two. In a systems view social work is seen as boundary work, that is, "at the boundary between the system and its environment."[4]

A much-noted contribution in this systems conceptualization and one that helps to bring together the helping professions and their social institution context is that of Pincus and Minahan, who delineate four systems present in helping endeavors generally.[5]

1. Change agent system: the change agent and the people who are part of his agency or employing organization.
2. Client system: people who sanction or ask for the change agent's

services, who are the expected beneficiaries of services, and who have a working agreement or contract with the change agent.
3. Target system: people who need to be changed to accomplish the goals of the change agent.
4. Action system: the change agent and the people he works with and through to accomplish his goals and influence the target system.

A particularly utilitarian feature of this conceptual scheme is that it fits and incorporates any and all "methods" in social work. It is as applicable to working with organizations and communities as it is to one-to-one work with individuals. It is then well suited for the generalist.

Related to systems theory is what has come to be termed the "life model" of social work practice, a contribution of Germain and Gitterman.[6] It uses concepts from ecology, which concerns itself with the interactions between living organisms. As with systems theory this "eco" approach is more a framework for organizing phenomena than an actual theory per se. The key concepts are those having to do with (1) "transactions" between environments and people, (2) the human attributes of "identity, competence, autonomy, and relatedness," and (3) the "layers and textures" of environment.[7]

Helping Process

It is well to spend at least a little time with the notion of the helping *process*. The idea of process is not new, but new attention has been given to it recently. Traditionally social work education taught a "medical model" of helping. The process consisted of three steps, according to this way of thinking: *study, diagnosis,* and *treatment.* Of course, the study or information gathering was particularly directed to social phenomena, just as the diagnosis and treatment were social.[8] But the terms suggest a medical orientation and a "sickness" model for the consumer of services that some social work scholars and practitioners would prefer now to deemphasize in favor of a broader, more general, and neutral conceptualization.

One such is the notion of *beginning, middle*, and *ending* stages in helping or problem solving. Whatever labels are used, the helping process inevitably in some way is initiated, continued, and terminated. This is true whether we are speaking of a single interview contact or work with an individual, group, or community over a period of years. "Clients," to use the word generically, one way or another become involved with workers (usually in agencies) or vice versa, perhaps because the client has sought help or the reverse has happened and the worker has reached out. Once engaged, the two parties work together and, ultimately, separate. Even if the terms are not used, the activities transpire. The more professionals can be consciously thoughtful and purposeful about their part in the process, the more productive and effective the work is likely to be. This is one reason self-awareness is stressed so much for social service workers.

Most scholar/writers who analyze social work practice, including generalist practice, find it necessary to consider what is variously termed the problem-solving, change, or helping process. For Compton and Galaway there are three primary phases in problem solving: contact, contract, and action.[9] The first of these, contact, encompasses problem identification, initial goal setting, data collection, and initial assessment. Within the contract part of the process is found joint assessment, goal setting, and planning. In the action phase comes implementation of the plan, endings, and evaluation. These authors point out that in implementing a plan, various worker roles are required. Endings entail such possibilities as referral, transfer, and termination.

O'Neil, in stressing that the process is a purposeful procedure, sees the components as engagement, data collection, assessment, intervention, evaluation, and termination.[10] Data collection considers all aspects—problems, persons, and environment. Assessment includes problem prioritization and contracting. Intervention often entails teamwork, and evaluation includes reviewing and possibly reformulating the contract.

In writing about the health field, Germaine, like Compton and Galaway discussed above, speaks of "phases" in the process. After some preliminary activities, the phases are the initial, the ongoing, and the ending. Encompassed in the initial part are such important activities as engagement, exploration, problem definition and assessment, contracting, goal setting, and planning.[11]

For Johnson the process consists of assessment, planning, action with clients, action with others on behalf of clients, and termination.[12] Siporin's construct is similar to the others: engagement, intake and contract; assessment; planning; intervention, evaluation and termination.[13] The change process as formulated by Shaefor and the Horejsis is similar to that of Siporin.[14]

The current way of expressing the process, then, is some variation of this formulation: study, assessment, plan of action, intervention (or action or implementation), evaluation. As indicated above, this way of thinking is less bound to the medical orientation. It suggests that in attempting to help people, initially there is a need to obtain information followed by an examination of the information, a tying of pieces together toward an understanding of dynamics, cause/effect, and other relationships. From this assessment evolves a plan. At this point, there may be contracting with a client as to what he, she, or they will do and what the worker's responsibilities will be. The plan is then implemented, action is taken, and there is intervention in whatever directions are indicated. Finally, worker and client analyze in an evaluative way what has transpired and determine what, if anything, to do next. They may decide to repeat the action, to expand or reduce it, or take some other tack.

We are speaking in the abstract thus far and obviously in the real world of helping, these steps are related to specific problems, people, and activity. Perhaps less obviously it should be noted that any discussion of steps in the helping process has inherent within it the danger of making it appear that the stages are more neat, discrete, and sequential than they are in fact. They are fluid and flow together concurrently as a two-way street. One is often intervening at the beginning contact just as assessment is ongoing and still occurring all the way through the process. One point in all of this is that, regardless of nomenclature, there is a systematic, planful approach in helping and problem solving.

ROLES, SKILLS, AND COMPETENCIES

Recent social work literature has tended to consider the diversity of skills, roles, and activities assumed by the contemporary worker. Federico suggests that six "basic skills" are essential for social work practice.[15]

1. communication
2. assessment
3. relating to others
4. planning
5. carrying out plans
6. evaluating oneself and one's plans and activities

Examination of these skills confirms that they are indeed fundamental to all social work functioning regardless of setting or method; in other words, they are generalist in nature. They further refine the process previously discussed.

It is nearly impossible to think of social work activity that does not in some way require relating to people. We relate to others through communication in its several forms. And in relating and communicating we engage in problem solving in an organized way as these skills in totality suggest and as was noted earlier.

Emphasis must be given to the fact that these are generic skills used in working one-to-one, with families and other groups, as well as with organizations and communities. Communication, relating, and systematic helping are vital in all "methods" and approaches in the human services.

Although no single list or classification may be entirely satisfactory, some breaking down of helper tasks is useful in understanding the nature of the social work job broadly. Teare and McPheeters identify twelve roles, each of which actually encompasses a constellation of tasks.[16]

1. Outreach worker—identification of need in the community by reaching out and by helping people meet identified needs.
2. Broker—helping people through establishing linkages between people and services within the community.
3. Advocate—advocate entails "going to bat" for clients individually or as a group or class; obtaining needed services from an agency and acting on behalf of a category of persons in need with a city council, legislature, or other decision makers.
4. Evaluator—evaluation of program effectiveness, assessment of needs and resources, considering alternatives, weighing possible outcomes.
5. Teacher—provision of needed information and skills through instruction.
6. Behavior changer—a whole array of activities aimed at modifying behavior through changing, expanding, or reducing specific behavior clusters.
7. Mobilizer—enlisting existing resources and creating new ones, directed toward problem resolution.
8. Consultant—consultation is working with other agencies, organizations or persons, who possess expertise on a relevant subject.
9. Community planner—planning on the community level toward enhancing human well-being.
10. Care giver—provision of needed supportive services.
11. Data manager—data processing including collection and analysis to provide a basis for improved decision making.
12. Administrator—the administrative role in program direction and management encompassing planning and other activities essential to operating a program or organization.

This list points up some of the complexity of social work and demonstrates how broad and diverse are the tasks involved in working with people in a helping capacity. Some of these have to do with *counseling* responsibilities that accompany much social work, especially that having to do with what is variously termed direct, personal, or micro services, those concerned mainly with individuals, families, and other small groups. In some settings, these are now sometimes labeled clinical.

Another set of skills and tasks are *educational* in nature. Social workers of all three traditional major methods orientations are frequently called upon to engage in instructional roles. These run the gamut through such situations as working with a group of parents who have children in day care, family members and patients who need to learn about living with a particular disease or injury, a group of youth who want to learn a new game, introducing a craft to a small nursing home group, orienting some volunteers to techniques to be used in a neighborhood survey, and teaching a man or woman different responses that may be made to a spouse, child, or employer. Part of this education activity is the provision of consultation as needed and assisting in evaluation of plans, programs, and intervention.

A third set of actions is encompassed under the concept of *community user.* This is intended to cover such diverse work as planning, organizing, mobilizing, referral, and linkage activity or what is often now described as *brokerage*.

That these three groups of tasks are seldom unmixed and never mutually exclusive is evident if we recognize that evaluation is as much a responsibility of the community user as it is of the educator. Case finding and outreach constitute other aspects of community use as it is here considered.

The social service worker has an opportunity and responsibility to serve as an *advocate* whether as direct service worker going to bat for a youngster who is being threatened with expulsion from school, a neighborhood center staff member confronting local government leaders over municipal failure to enforce the housing code, or a community worker speaking out for a whole class of persons in need, such as the elderly or handicapped. Obviously this is a role borrowed from the legal field. Just as social work identified with the medical model earlier and came to emphasize various psychotherapeutic approaches, so more recently it has rediscovered one of its roots in advocacy. At the turn of the century, settlement house workers not only provided friendly counsel, they also were activists in representing their constituents.

Finally, a group of persons in the social services work partially or largely in *organizational maintenance.* They are administrators of agencies and programs, developing new services, and redirecting existing provisions. Overlaps with previously delineated categories are seen in the importance of organizing and evaluating here. These specialists are faced with multifaceted requirements. They are managers in a broad sense including handling data and management of personnel. Public relations, supervision, and fund raising may be among their jobs. But, again it is important to avoid thinking in all-or-none ways. Many administrative tasks are and should be spread broadly in human service organizations. For example, everyone in the agency must be public relations conscious; the most elaborate and sophisticated "PR" campaign conducted by the administrator or a hired professional is no substitute for the direct service staff doing a consistently good job with their responsibilities and making their work known.

Within these broad role categories are numerous skills. Examples are interviewing and recording. These basic kinds of skills are essential to virtually all practice. They are necessary in both "micro" and "macro" realms and found in both traditional and innovative settings and approaches.

Partly because of fairly recent stress on competency-based education and in approaches emphasizing specific skills for helping professionals, there is now considerable interest in social work "competencies."[17] This is somewhat related to the "goal oriented social services" (GOSS) and "management by objective" (MBO) thrust that came into social service administrative staff development and practice largely from business and other fields. A factor contributing to the rise of such activity in the human services is the growing demand for accountability and quality control, both in education and in practice. One of the most influential publications to appear on the competency subject directed specifically toward baccalaureate-level staff is that of Baer and Federico. They propose ten competencies for the baccalaureate social worker.[18]

1. Identify and assess situations where the relationship between people and social institutions needs to be initiated, enhanced, restored, protected, or terminated.
2. Develop and implement a plan for improving the well-being of people based on problem assessment and the exploration of obtainable goals and available options.
3. Enhance the problem-solving, coping, and developmental capacities of people.
4. Link people with systems that provide them with resources, services, and opportunities.
5. Intervene effectively on behalf of populations most vulnerable and discriminated against.
6. Promote the effective and humane operation of the systems that provide people with services, resources, and opportunities.
7. Actively participate with others in creating new, modified, or improved service, resource, opportunity systems that are more equi-

table, just, and responsive to consumers of services, and work with others to eliminate those systems that are unjust.

8. Evaluate the extent to which the objectives of the intervention plan were achieved.
9. Continually evaluate one's own professional growth and development through assessment of practice behavior and skill.
10. Contribute to the improvement of service delivery by adding to the knowledge base of the profession as appropriate and by supporting and upholding the standards and ethics of the profession.

The authors of this list have acknowledged that it does not constitute the last word on baccalaureate competencies.[19] But, in spite of the fact that it has been criticized as being so broad that it does not differentiate between levels of practitioners such as BSW and MSW,[20] it is a significant milestone in the ongoing effort to describe and delineate social work practice skills.

A final thought on the matters we have just been examining—social work process, roles, skills, competencies. Attention in this text is of necessity focused on the social worker and on the mechanics of the different aspects of the profession. But social work is about helping people and, in the real world, that is where the focus should be. To go back once again to the value base of the profession, the human is at the center of our concern. People are of worth and possess dignity and integrity. And helping must be appropriate to the human needs the people present. The various processes, roles, skills, and competencies are simply devices to be used and applied in helping others.

Case Management

As noted earlier, Goldstein has suggested that one of the several forms generalist social work may take is "case management." This concept of case manager activity has received considerable attention in recent years and deserves further discussion here. With this managerial role the worker assists the client in determining what services are needed. Then the worker helps locate required resources and facilitates their use. The fragmented social service world is complex and may appear even more so from the client's perspective. Clients are often unaware of what programs are available and/or how to use a service of which they are aware. The worker can provide important assistance in coordinating services on behalf of the client/consumer. In doing so the worker often needs to be involved with the interaction between client and service(s) and between two or more programs providing service to the client. Through this means the client has greater access to service and the help provided by the service providers is more likely to be appropriate and relevant for the client's needs. Facilitating communication, then, is a central activity, both between client and organization and among the various service providers.

The case management approach is aimed at avoiding service duplication and at filling gaps in service. In some agencies a worker engages in both direct service activities and case management for a client, whereas in other organizations these functions are separated. Either way the case management role is likely at points to entail acting as advocate, mediator, linker, facilitator, and broker.[21] Providing referrals is important in case management, so that knowledge of community resources is essential.

Networking

A currently popular term is "networking," which refers to communication, informal support, and working together within a group or community or between groups. As often occurs, a new idea (or a new label for old phenomena) may be treated by some as a panacea for many issues, needs, and problems. That networking is not always an answer is confirmed by a recently published study finding that the poor have fewer network resources than have persons from more affluent groups. These researchers caution social workers not to depend only on such networks and to plan with care interventions that use this approach, so that effectiveness is enhanced.[22]

Nonetheless, networking is important and can be extremely useful. This is true both with regard to maximum service for client consumers of social services and for enhancing the strengths and effectiveness of service providers. Potential gains from networking are pointed up in a U.S. Department of Justice research report focusing on activities of police in twelve communities relative to the mentally ill, public inebriates, and homeless. Police must often deal with such persons and can do so more effectively by establishing and maintaining networks with social service agencies, according to this report.[23]

Information and Referral

Related to case management and networking is the activity known as *information and referral* (I & R). As noted earlier, the social services system is involved, complex, and fragmented. The development of information and referral services is a response to the complexity and an effort to make services more understandable and accessible to potential users.

Ours is an information society, and as Levinson notes, "Being 'information poor' is a handicap in obtaining services; being 'information rich' enables one to reap the benefits of a service society."[24] I & Rs offer advice, make referrals, and provide followup. They "steer" clients to appropriate resources and make links. The idea of I & R is organizational; it provides an interagency system or network.

Some I & Rs are independent entities separate from other organizations. Others are part of an existent agency. At this time many social agencies include I & R in their services. Some communities have centralized I & Rs serving an entire county or state, for example. In others two or more I & Rs function in one city. Some provide certain kinds of counseling and many afford advocacy. Whatever the arrangement, this "door-opening" activity is important in a complex society.

Prevention

A renewed interest in *prevention* has appeared recently on the social problems/social welfare scene. Professional journals[25] on this subject have emerged, and a significant text[26] became available in 1981. Numerous books and articles appeared in the 1980s. Every year since 1981 there have been major presentations on prevention at the Annual Program Meeting of the CSWE. Finally, the *1983–84 Supplement to the Encyclopedia of Social Work* carried a separate topic on prevention.[27] All indicate the increased attention being devoted to prevention.

Bloom uses the 1979 Public Health Service definition of prevention: "Primary prevention refers to those scientific practices aimed at simultaneously *preventing* predictable physical, psychological or socio-cultural problems for individuals or populations at risk; maintaining or *protecting* current strengths, competencies, or levels of health; and *promoting* desired goals and the fulfillment or enhancement of human potentials."[28]

Social work has long been concerned with prevention, though not always by this name. The present thrust is interdisciplinary in nature, involving professionals from a variety of helping fields. For these disciplines, including social work, there are prevention connotations both in reforming social conditions broadly and in direct services.

Prevention holds different meanings for different people. For some it is an absolute activity aimed at totally averting the appearance or emergence of a problem condition from the outset. For others it means intervention directed toward discouraging repetition or continuation of a condition or problem that has already been present. The focus also varies; for some the health field is the context for prevention, whereas for others it is crime and delinquency and still others are more drawn to families and children when thinking of prevention. Certainly social work with its family orientation would argue that whatever supports and strengthens families tends to be generally preventive of social pathology, at least in a broad sense.

The prevention model provided by the public health field includes activities of *primary, secondary,* and *tertiary* treatment/prevention. These refer to levels of care in the health field. Suffice it to say that in translating from public health to the social services, there are actual and potential activities in which social work engages or could engage that can be useful and productive on all three levels. Friedlander and Apte make the point that public health services have been directed more to the community while those of social work are pointed more to the individual.[29]

In his discussion, Wittman identifies four prevalent themes that are useful in understanding prevention and what is happening currently on this matter:[30]

1. the recognition of the importance of strengthening the natural interacting systems in which people live.
2. the reaffirmation of the importance of infancy and childhood as a focus.
3. crisis intervention (useful in early detection and treatment of problems) is closely related to prevention.
4. many approaches are necessary if services are to be truly preventive.

There are tremendous opportunities for wiser use of funds and greater economy as well as the furtherance of human well-being if priorities emphasize prevention of social problems.

Prevention is an extremely important goal in the human services, but we must be realistic about what is possible, given our present state of knowledge, and must avoid simplistic notions. For example, it is easy to assert that certain youth programs "prevent delinquency." But can this be demonstrated and documented? Often it may be easier, more accurate, and more honest to claim, sticking with the illustration, that a particular provision is useful for youth in general. It is important not to claim more than can be delivered. Social problems such as delinquency are typically too complex to lend themselves to simple solutions. There are no panaceas and therefore prevention too, appealing and attractive as it is, must be put into perspective and dealt with realistically.

Social Work and the Arts

In recent years interest has developed in using the arts in social work and other helping disciplines. This may be done as part of a therapeutic approach with individuals or in the context of recreation/leisure activities, usually of a group nature. A particular theoretical/

treatment orientation (e.g., Gestalt) is sometimes inherent in the use of the arts. This approach is used to facilitate diagnosis and assessment on one hand as well as to provide an aspect of treatment intervention on the other. Just as play therapy is often effective with children diagnostically, it is also useful for ventilation and emotional release. The same may be true of music, painting, sculpting, and dramatics. They provide means of expression for persons who may have greater need for such outlets than most people as well as presenting an option for working with social work clientele generally.

RURAL SOCIAL WORK

An area for which the generalist model of social work practice is particularly appropriate is the rural community. In the 1970s new interest emerged in nonmetropolitan human services.[31] A national rural social work caucus came into being, and national institutes on social work and human services in rural areas are now held annually. The thirteenth such conference was held in 1988.

So often both social problems and services are equated with the urban way of life. In a similar vein, the rural environment is frequently thought of as relatively problem free, static, and quiescent. This is hardly a correct image of what is transpiring currently in nonmetropolitan America. Change is pervasive, and the rural community is often in dynamic flux. Two examples of this are "impact" communities or boom towns a few years ago in western states mushrooming with coal mining or extraction of petroleum, gas, or minerals in an energy crisis era, and some towns in all regions of the country experiencing rural industrialization.[32] Such developments often transform the affected communities, and immense problems may result such as shortages of housing, schools, and recreation facilities and increases in child abuse, alcoholism, and family dysfunction. This is not to deny the many rural communities withering and declining, which presents still further problems. The farm crisis of the 1980s impacted negatively on towns and cities that are economically tied to agriculture, as well as on farms.

Rural dwellers experience many of the same needs and problems as those of their city cousins: poverty, physical and mental health, education, crime, family relations, and others. Resources for dealing with these problems in small communities may be scarce, although the author has noted elsewhere that it is often not as much a dearth of resources as a different kind and arrangement.[33] For example, rural law enforcement persons, clergy, school staff, and service clubs often perform functions informally that in a metropolitan environment may be handled in a more elaborate, formal network of social welfare agencies and organizations. There is a public welfare agency in virtually every county in the nation, although it is probably small in size and staff in a rural area. This agency is the hub of social work activity. Small-town libraries and librarians are another organization/person that may be at the center of human services provision in a rural area.

There are problems that are specific to rural communities. Examples are programs in sparsely populated areas for specialized needs such as services for the chemically dependent, developmentally disabled, or for child day care. People with these needs do exist in rural sections, but their limited numbers deny them visibility and power and make the provision of service difficult. Transportation is a particular concern in nonmetropolitan regions, especially when we consider groups such as the elderly. One problem for aged people is isolation, and lack of transportation may make this even worse. Not only does this mean absence of human interaction and contacts for stimulation and enjoyment, but it may also mean difficulty in meeting basic human needs such as obtaining medical care and groceries.

A disproportionately large part of the rural population is elderly. Five of the ten states possessing the highest percent of the elderly in 1970 were in the Midwest, a principal rural part of the United States. In all of these, the percentage of the population of persons sixty-five and over exceeded by far the national figure of approximately 12 percent.[34]

In view of the importance of transportation for rural dwellers, the elderly and others, planners in recent years have devoted attention to either or both of two aspects: how to transport people to services and how to bring services to people. Both are being done successfully in increasing numbers of communities. Examples of taking services to people are mobile libraries, meals, and certain health programs. Transporting people to resources, even in rural communities, is occurring now through scheduling of regular routes using a variety of vans, buses, and other vehicles. Social workers are often among the first persons to become aware of the need for such programs and frequently play important roles in planning, establishing, and administering them.

The energy crisis of the 1970s with high costs and shortages raises questions about the future of transportation programs like these. But an energy crisis may provide reason for increasing rather than decreasing such approaches because they may be more energy efficient than the alternatives, assuming there is to be at least a modicum of service provided.

When a social worker is one of only a few persons in an agency or perhaps the only one, as may be the case in a rural environment, he or she must be versatile and able to function independently and autonomously.[35] Ability to provide direct service, such as counseling, is important as is skill in serving as an advocate. But at the same time, the worker may need to sensitize the community to its needs and help to establish a needed resource such as a day-care center or program for the elderly. Organizing a self-help group and publicizing its availability could be another concurrent activity of this generalist. In other words, helping approaches in rural communities include both direct services and program/community development and organizing.

Another aspect of rural practice could be commented upon. In a community where it may be quite literally true that "everybody knows everybody," a new professional such as a social worker is highly visible. To gain and maintain acceptance in such places, which are often rather conservative, the worker needs to be conventional and make an effort to fit into the community. An interesting feature of working in nonmetropolitan areas is that the worker is likely to encounter his or her "clients" most anywhere outside the agency, in a supermarket, shop, restaurant, church, or to find one's children in the same school class as the client or the client's child.[36] These kinds of relationships and contacts along with the usual rural informality may present both obstacles and opportunities in the helping process.

SUMMARY AND CONCLUSIONS

In this chapter we have considered some of the newer approaches to and developments within social work practice. Included have been the generalist model, a systems perspective, increased interest in the helping process, concern with roles/skills/competencies, and a new thrust around prevention. Finally, rural social work has been examined as an important kind of generalist practice. Not everything discussed represents what the chapter title may suggest to some readers—distinct approaches. Instead, collectively we have examined varying degrees of new directions in professional social work activities.

NOTES

1. Howard Goldstein, in *Handbook of the Social Services*, Neil Gilbert and Harry Specht, eds. (Englewood Cliffs, N.J. Prentice-Hall, 1981), p. 414.
2. Bradford W. Sheafor and Pamela S. Landon, "Generalist Perspective," *En-*

cyclopedia of Social Work, 18th ed. (Silver Spring, Md.: NASW, 1987), 1: 660–667.

3. Goldstein, *Handbook of the Social Services,* pp. 420–424.
4. Gordon Hearn, "General Systems Theory and Social Work," in *Social Work Treatment,* 2nd ed. by Francis J. Turner, ed. (New York: Free Press, 1979), pp. 333–359.
5. Allen Pincus and Anne Minahan, *Social Work Practice: Model and Method* (Itasca, Il.: F. E. Peacock Publishers, 1973), p. 63.
6. Carel Germain and Alex Gitterman, "The Life Model of Social Work Practice," pp. 361–384 in *Social Work Treatment.* See also a textbook with the same title and authors (New York: Columbia University Press, 1980).
7. Ibid., pp. 362–367.
8. This point is reflected in the titles of two significant books, one a pioneer and the other modern: *Social Diagnosis* by Mary Richmond (1917) and *Social Treatment* by James K. Whittaker (1974).
9. Beulah Compton and Burt Galaway, *Social Work Processes,* 3rd ed. (Chicago: Dorsey Press, 1984), pp. 320–324.
10. Maria J. O'Neil, *The General Method of Social Work Practice* (Englewood Cliffs, N.J.: Prentice-Hall, 1984).
11. Carel B. Germain, *Social Work Practice in Health Care* (New York: Free Press, 1984), pp. 70–72.
12. Louise C. Johnson, *Social Work Practice: A Generalist Approach* (Newton, Mass.: Allyn and Bacon, 1983).
13. Max Siporin, *Introduction to Social Work Practice* (New York: Macmillan, 1975).
14. Bradford W. Sheafor, Charles R. Horejsi, and Gloria A. Horejsi, *Techniques and Guidelines for Social Work Practice* (Boston: Allyn and Bacon, 1988), p. 76.
15. Ronald C. Federico, *The Social Welfare Institution,* 3rd ed. (Lexington, Mass.: D. C. Heath & Co., 1980), p. 247.
16. Robert J. Teare and Harold L. McPheeters, *Manpower Utilization in Social Welfare* (Atlanta: Southern Regional Education Board, 1970, pp. 34–35.
17. For example see Morton L. Arkava and E. Clifford Brennen, eds. *Competency-Based Education for Social Work* (New York: Council on Social Work Education, 1976).
18. Betty L. Baer and Ronald Federico, *Educating the Baccalaureate Social Worker* (Cambridge, Mass.: Ballinger Publishing Co., 1978), pp. 86–89.
19. Federico, *Social Welfare Institution,* p. 233.
20. Shirley M. Ehrenkranz. "Report of the Committee on Articulation of Graduate and Undergraduate Social Work Education," March 7, 1981 (to Deans and Directors of Graduate Schools of Social Work), p. 2.
21. Dean H. Hepworth and Jo Ann Larew, *Direct Social Work Practice,* 2nd ed. (Chicago: Dorsey Press, 1986), pp. 563–564. See also Gerald G. O'Connor, "Case Management: System and Practice," *Social Casework* 69, no. 2 (February 1988): 97–106.
22. Gail K. Auslander and Howard Litwin, "Social Networks and the Poor: To-

ward Effective Policy and Practice," *Social Work* 33, no. 6 (May–June 1988): 234–238.

23. Peter E. Finn and Monique Sullivan, "Police Response to Special Populations," U.S. Department of Justice, January 1988.

24. Risha W. Levinson, "Information and Referral Services," in *Encyclopedia of Social Work*, 18th ed. (Silver Spring, Md.: NASW, 1987) 1:919.

25. *Journal of Prevention* (New York: Human Sciences Press) Also NASW's first reprint collection, published in 1974, dealt with *Preventive Intervention in Social Work*, Carol H. Meyer, ed.

26. Martin Bloom, *Primary Prevention: The Possible Science* (Englewood Cliffs, N.J.: Prentice-Hall, 1981).

27. Martin Bloom, "Prevention," in *1983–84 Supplement to the Encyclopedia of Social Work*, 17th ed. (Silver Spring, Md.: NASW, 1983), pp. 112–119.

28. Martin Bloom, "Prevention," in *Encyclopedia of Social Work*, 18th ed. (Silver Spring, Md.: NASW, 1987), 2:303.

29. Walter A. Friedlander and Robert Z. Apte, *Introduction to Social Welfare*, 5th ed. (Englewood Cliffs, N.J.: Prentice-Hall, 1980), p. 371.

30. Milton Wittman, "Preventive Social Work," *Encyclopedia of Social Work*, 17th ed. (Washington, D.C.: NASW, 1977), pp. 1051–1052.

31. See, for example, Leon H. Ginsberg, ed., *Social Work in Rural Communities* (New York: Council on Social Work Education, 1976), and H. Wayne Johnson, ed., *Rural Human Services* (Itasca, Ill.: F. E. Peacock Publishers, 1980).

32. Judith A. Davenport and Joseph Davenport III, eds. *Boom Towns and Human Services* (Laramie: University of Wyoming, 1979).

33. Johnson, *Rural Human Services*, p. 49.

34. "A Profile of Older Americans 1987," American Association of Retired Persons.

35. Johnson, *Rural Human Services*, pp. 147–148.

36. Barbara Lou Fenby, "Social Work in a Rural Setting," pp. 149–152 in Johnson, *Rural Human Services*.

ADDITIONAL SUGGESTED READINGS

All the practice texts listed here use a more generalist integrated methods approach than is true of the traditional or single-method texts. Traditional methods texts are listed separately after each appropriate chapter.

Anderson, Joseph D., *Foundations of Social Work Practice* (New York: Springer Publishing, 1988).

Brieland, Donald, "Definition, Specialization and Domain in Social Work," *Social Work* 26, no. 1 (January 1981): 79–83.

Brill, Naomi I., *Working with People*, 3rd ed. (New York: Longman, 1984).

Davenport, Joseph, III, and Judith A. Davenport, *The Boom Town: Problems and Promises in the Energy Vortex* (Laramie: University of Wyoming, 1980).

Day, P.J., H. J. Macy, and E. C. Jackson, *Social Working* (Englewood Cliffs, N.J.: Prentice-Hall, 1984).

Epstein, Laura, *Helping People: The Task-Centered Approach*, 2nd ed. (Columbus, Ohio: Merrill Publishing, 1988).

Germain, Carel B., ed., *Social Work Practice* (New York: Columbia University Press, 1979).

Gilbert, Neil, Henry Miller, and Harry Specht, *An Introduction to Social Work Practice* (Englewood Cliffs, N.J.: Prentice-Hall, 1980).

Goldstein, Howard, *Social Work Practice* (Columbia: University of South Carolina Press, 1973).

Gordon, William E., "Basic Constructs for an Integrative and Generative Conception of Social Work," in Gordon Hearn, ed., *The General Systems Approach: Contributions Toward an Holistic Conception of Social Work* (New York: Council on Social Work Education, 1969).

Hartman, Ann, *Family Centered Social Work Practice* (New York: Free Press, 1983).

Loewenberg, F. M., *Fundamentals of Social Intervention*, 2nd ed. (New York: Columbia University Press, 1983).

Meyer, Carol H., *Social Work Practice*, 2nd ed. (New York: Free Press, 1976).

Sundet, Paul, and Joanne Mermelstein, "Helping the New Rural Poor," *Public Welfare* 45, no. 3 (Summer 1987): 14–19.

Teaching for Competence in the Delivery of Direct Services (New York: Council on Social Work Education, 1976).

Zastrow, Charles, *The Practice of Social Work*, 3rd ed. (Chicago: Dorsey Press, 1989).

16 Working with Individuals and Families

Janet Johnson Laube

Social work with individuals and families was the earliest form of social work practice, and its traditional classification was "casework." Practitioners of this approach have historically held the professional title of "social caseworker," and more recently some have used the title of "clinical social worker." These labels indicate that their specialty is problem solving with persons experiencing personal, interpersonal, or situational stresses. While the goal of balanced social functioning is shared with other methods, caseworkers are primarily engaged with individual or family units and systems that impinge on or interact with these units. The focus is on the "person-in-the-situation," which means that both internal, psychological forces and external, social forces receive consideration in the helping process. Of course, social workers whose practice is with larger client systems often interact and intervene with individuals and families, too, so they must be familiar with the knowledge and skill base for this kind of practice. Probably the largest number of generalist social workers with bachelor's degrees work with individuals and families. The same is true of MSW workers, whether they are thought of as "advanced generalists" or specialists.

The information that the practitioner working with individuals and families must use concerns a fundamental struggle that all human beings experience; that is, the struggle between the inclination toward independence (autonomy, differentiation, mastery) and the tendency toward dependence (symbiosis, relationship, belonging). Beginning at the point of earliest development, individuals experience the vulnerability of relying on other persons for their sustenance and protection. Survival is at stake. Individuals learn to feel trust or mistrust of their environments as embodied in other persons. Even this early, individuals learn that, however responsive the family and environment may be, there is always a separateness or aloneness inherent in life. The memory of physical connectedness or symbiosis before birth contributes to the desire for reunion, touch, belonging, for eliminating the aloneness. This longing for closeness is met with affection or rejection or indifference, and individuals early develop an expectation of how well their needs will be met. Competing with the longing for closeness is the biological and psychological push toward differentiation and identity. The individual strives for mastery of physical skills and a sense of self that is distinct from other persons.

As individuals develop through the life cycle, they perform an ongoing dance of steps toward and away from independence and dependence. Their physical development and their culture's imperatives present demands for particular expressions of one drive or the other at specific periods.[1] For example, the physical stage of adolescence is characterized by an intense psychological desire for belonging and acceptance and physical touching with peers; but it also is a time when there is a need for differentiation from family and development of an adult identity that is exacerbated by cultural demands for decisions about careers and values.

Problem solving, which is the aim of any social worker, becomes centered on achieving balance for individuals and families in their relationships—with themselves and with others between aloneness and connectedness, between demands for personal expression and social survival. In order to realize this balance successfully, individuals and families must accomplish four tasks, defined by Talcott Parsons: adaptation, or changing and growing to meet internal and external demands; integration, or organizing an identity and relating to other systems; pattern maintenance, or maintaining stability, autonomy, and boundaries; and goal attainment, or self-realization and productivity.[2] Each of the tasks contains an individual and a social mandate for successful accomplishment. Social workers assist in the achievement of these tasks by encouraging individuals and families in their independent functioning and also in their transactions with their environments. For example, they may be educators when helping people to adapt, or liaisons to services when aiding integration, or therapists when facilitating identity development, or advocates when promoting goal attainment. This flexibility on the part of the professionals require knowledge of life cycle development and cultural contexts.

Social workers who assist individuals and families with personal, relationship, or environment problems make use of the independence/dependence paradox within the professional relationship. They recognize that the authority of the helper offers clients protection and guidance but also challenges their inclination for self-direction. The skill with which the professionals can use that authority to direct the course of intervention, while at the same time mobilizing the clients' initiative, determines the effectiveness of the problem-solving alliance.[3]

HISTORICAL EVOLUTION

Social work with individuals and families has a long history. It first emerged as a method of preventing or reducing pauperism in the 1880s, when "cases" were investigated to identify the "worthy" poor. The Charity Organization Society's "friendly visitors" (discussed in Chapter 3) who conducted these investigations soon recognized that forces other than "morality" contributed to individual and family dysfunction. They could see that strong social forces, as well as individual abilities and characteristics, shaped people's living conditions. Mary Richmond was a pioneer in investigating the causes for and effective ways of resolving people's problems in living.[4]

Social workers began to seek professional knowledge and skill training for improving their ways of dealing with people. While this professionalization resulted in some moving away from the morality model, it tended to keep the focus primarily on problems inside persons and used a study, diagnosis, and treatment paradigm adopted from the field of medicine. This paradigm served to organize the activities of the workers and to unite practitioners in the many fields of social casework practice (medicine, mental health, corrections, child welfare, schools, and so forth). It was limited by its focus on "symptoms," on defects rather than strengths, on labeling, and on the authority role of professionals. Freudian psychology served to enhance the knowledge base but reinforced this individualist perspective. The depression in the 1930s and World War II in the 1940s offered some contrasting evidence of the significance of social forces, so that there was always a counterpoint to the individualist theme.

Not until the 1960s did the developing profession adopt a theoretical perspective that permitted integration of practice wisdom about individual capacities and environmental demands. The social systems model has enabled social workers to articulate what they knew about the interactional influences of individuals and their environments. Social workers now know that systems not only have to organize the energy within them, but also exchange energy with the network of systems to which they are related. This enables an approach to people that takes into account their individual intelligence, values, coping skills, and communication expertise, as well as their social models, comforts, opportunities, and stressors.

In social work with individuals and families, the *relationship* between client and professional has always been considered a significant aspect of the intervention process.[5] Social systems theory is an umbrella theory that accounts for the significance of the interaction of the helper with the organisms to be helped.

WHAT THIS APPROACH IS AND DOES

Social work with individuals and families consists of helping people confront the day-to-day realities of living alone and together. This means, first, *physical coping*—the quantity, quality, and accessibility of food, clothing, sleep, and medical care; the availability of physical supports, rehabilitation, institutional care; the safety and spaciousness and financial assurance of housing; the regularity and motivation for recreation, relaxation, and exercise; the use or abuse of stimulants, tranquilizers, inhibitors. Thus, the social worker may be actively engaged with a client in trying to obtain basic food and shelter, as does the worker for the public department of social services. On the other hand, the worker may verbally investigate the influences of physical conditions on psychosocial functioning as does the individual or family therapist at a mental health center. Example:

> In obtaining data about Marie that might reveal some reasons why she is feeling depressed, the social worker asked her about her diet—what she ate on a typical day, whether her diet had shown any recent changes in amount or schedule or quality, whether there were any times in the past when Marie had had unusual eating patterns (starving, gorging, and so forth), whether she used coffee, tea, alcohol, cigarettes, drugs of any sort including birth control medication.

Along with physical well-being, and certainly related to it, is people's *economic coping*. Social workers working primarily with individuals and families may simply assess the influence of or act to alter their clients' economic standard. The drive toward independence may be frustrated by economic hardship, or congenial interdependence may be jeopardized by economic uncertainties. Example:

> Sam had had appointments that morning with two clients whose financial situations inhibited them in far different ways. The first, Jim, was frightened by the deepening recession that meant he was not likely to be called back to work by his company for many months. His eligibility for unemployment benefits might not last through his period of lay-off, and his wife's job alone was not enough for them to support their family. Jerry, the second, had a well-paying job in a company where his future was secure, but he had long wanted to start his own art gallery. He was afraid to risk loss of financial assurance by starting his own creative and personally expressive business.

Part of economic coping is educational well-being. Social workers assess and intervene in relation to schooling. Example:

> This school social worker was contacted by the third grade teacher who was worried about Kevin's self-image as failure-prone. The teacher wanted consultation about behavioral incentives for the classroom, as well as a referral for Kevin to the peer group therapy program run by the social worker. They jointly decided that Kevin's parent needed to be invited to the school for a discussion of the boy's progress and the resources available to him. One of the outcomes of that meeting was a referral for Kevin's mother to the department of social services. She wanted to enroll in college classes, so that she could improve her job-finding possibilities and improve her own self-image. She was eligible for public assistance in this educational effort.

Social work with individuals and families includes attention to social coping. *Social coping* consists of relating the individual self to other persons and organizations, or relating the family to other social systems. It includes the satisfactory negotiation of role relationships, as of student to teacher, employer to employee, parent to child, family to church, parents to schools. Social workers help individuals to develop their own interpretations of role requirements, but they often also translate social standards for individuals. Thus, they teach communication skills, parenting skills, organizational skills, assertiveness skills, budgeting skills. Social workers serve as negotiators between individuals and other groups, or between families and organizations to facilitate understanding and exchange. Example:

> John is employed by the department of social services as an outreach worker to abusing parents. He helps Darla and Dave Jensen change their expectations of their young child and also improve their own self-images as individuals and parents. He shows them how to communicate their feelings and desires to each other and how to show affection and tolerance to their child. He is helping them to modify the patterns of discipline that they learned from their own parents so that they better meet the society's standards for acceptable parenting. As he does so, he helps them distinguish those aspects of their parenting and marital styles that are unique because of their ethnic and cultural backgrounds. John also helps a group of abusing parents start a support system, a Parents Anonymous group, to give them encouragement and understanding in their growth toward better parenting.

Social work with individuals and families also is concerned with psychological coping. *Psychological coping* is developing and maintaining a sense of *self.* This evolves through viewing oneself as reflected by others and then organizing an internally defined and directed self-image. Psychological coping requires that this sense of self grow and adapt to changing physical development and the resultant changing demands of the environment upon the ego. In order to cope emotionally, individuals must be able to (1) distinguish the boundary between their perceptions and the impinging environment; (2) differentiate sensory data from internal symbols; (3) separate thoughts and feelings; and (4) develop a sense of self as having influence on the environment. Social workers aid individuals in clarifying a sense of identity and modifying maladaptive defensive stratagems. Perceptions, interpretations, feelings, and wants are identified. Then individuals are taught effective skills for communicating this self-awareness. Example:

> In her work with adolescents, Anna was quite confrontive of inconsistencies. She knew these inconsistencies were typical of this development stage, but she also knew that her comments challenged the teenagers to distinguish what was important to them, what their beliefs and feelings were, what they wanted. They used

this increased awareness in their efforts to define themselves as individuals.

In summary, social work with individuals and families requires attention to their physical, economic, social, and psychological coping. For optimum coping on each of these levels, there needs to be a balance between the drive toward independent expression of the self and the drive toward dependence or union. The social worker aids in the supply of energy or supports to effect such a balance. These provisions may be tangible or intangible. Tangible supports for independent functioning may include money, prosthetic devices, education, and physical rehabilitation. Intangible supports for independent functioning may include hope, faith, assertiveness skills, rational thinking skills, psychotherapy for ego development, and growth of self-esteem. Tangible supports for interdependent functioning may include adoption services, child care arrangements, Parents Without Partners meetings, or residential treatment for adolescents. Intangible supports for interdependent functioning may include trust, communication skills, family therapy, and marital counseling.

How It's Done

Social work with individuals and families proceeds through an orderly process despite the varying theoretical orientations about change that are held by practitioners. The process begins with establishment of a *relationship* between clients and social worker. This relationship is defined as a collaborative one, where the clients and professional are partners working for change. This arrangement is clarified in the *contract*, that is, the agreement about roles, timing, objectives, confidentiality, grievances, and fees. Information about the problem, the desired outcome, and previous problem-solving attempts is discussed so that an *assessment* may be made jointly between client and professional. Alternative problem-solving steps are reviewed, a *plan* for intervention into the situation is negotiated, and a means for *evaluating* the results is developed. The *intervention* process then proceeds toward a jointly planned *termination* of services. As described earlier, the particular intervention devised for an individual client or client family may be tangible, intangible, or a combination. The interventive services selected will be a function of the particular agency (psychotherapy at a mental health center, parenting services from a family services agency, and so on) and the theoretical predilection of the individual social worker.

The primary theoretical orientations of individual and family social workers may be classified as psychodynamic, sociobehavioral, cognitive, and existential-interactional. When using a psychodynamic (or ego psychology) approach, social workers as therapists help individuals modify their personality structures with the aim of strengthening ego functioning. This takes place within an open-ended relationship in which the professional offers interpretations of the client's conscious and unconscious needs and motives.[6] When using a sociobehavioral approach, social workers and clients identify maladaptive behaviors and environment reinforcers. They then organize new systems of reinforcement for desirable behaviors.[7] From a cognitive framework, the social worker helps clients to distinguish between rational and irrational thinking, between thinking and feeling. Clients are taught to alter their catastrophic expectations and to develop rational problem-solving skills.[8] Within an existential-interactional framework, the social worker helps clients develop authentic relationships in which their self-concepts are strengthened by clear communication.[9] This last approach often occurs in a group or family setting, because of the opportunity for relationship development. When it occurs in a family setting, special subtheories about family therapy are often employed. These include theories about differentiation of individual members from the family's emotional patterns,[10] clear communication of perceptions and events,[11] clarification of family boundaries and subsystems,[12] and identification of family functional rules.[13]

Who Does This Method?

Services to individuals and families are offered by social workers in a number of settings. The most prevalent is the family service agency, which may belong to Family Service America; it may be a voluntary, sectarian agency like Lutheran Social Services, Catholic Charities, or Jewish Family Services; it may be a private, nonsectarian agency like a child guidance or a child placement agency; or it may be a department of a government-funded social service center. Social workers at agencies of this sort usually provide family therapy, individual therapy, pregnancy and child-placement counseling of unwed parents, adolescent therapy, play therapy for children, group therapy, and even financial planning and debt adjustment services. Social workers at community mental health centers provide many of the same services to individuals and families, usually in a psychotherapeutic mode, although they also offer educational programs for such skills as assertiveness, parenting, and communication. Within mental health settings, social workers often serve individuals suffering from long-term psychological disability through day treatment or community support programs.

Services to individuals and families are offered by social workers located in several other settings. These professionals may facilitate hospital adjustment, posthospital placement, and rehabilitation when working in medical centers. They help bridge the relationship of families with schools. They conduct orientation and therapy sessions for families of residents in institutions and group homes. They also are increasingly setting up their own practices in private offices and are offering a whole gamut of psychotherapeutic, educational, and advocacy services.

The special knowledge that practitioners offer individuals and families includes personality development through the life cycle, personality dynamics, family structure, family communication process, and resources for problem solving. The special skills that practitioners offer individuals and families includes case-finding, relationship building, communication assessment and change, personality assessment, problem assessment, problem solving, and environmental manipulation.

The Position of the Approach in Social Work

Services to individuals and families have always been a cornerstone in the social work edifice, and they will continue to be demanded by our society in its "pursuit of happiness." The social work profession itself gave short shrift to the fundamental necessity for these services during the 1960s and 1970s when it experienced a much-needed surge of interest in social policy. Direct services to persons were devalued when it seemed that they were only piecemeal attacks against a vast network of destructive social forces. The profession seemed to support the redirection of social workers' energies into social activism and social policy reform. However, individual and family problems persisted in the present, and they often were controlled only partly by external forces. There continued to be a need for direct services, both tangible and intangible. Most recently, the social work profession has returned to the position that social workers must be knowledgeable about effecting change with both individuals and their social environments, although they may choose to specialize in one or the other sphere.

Issues and Trends

The major issue in provision of services to individuals and families is the same as that underlying all social work practice: Is the change effort directed to altering people's behavior and expectations so that they can function in a more adaptive way, or is it directed toward altering the demands and supports in the environment? As with all social work practice, the answer is "both." The effort is directed toward achieving balance, an integration of individual and social functioning. However, in each individual case there will be a choice of emphasis and there must be a selection of where to begin. Working with individuals and families requires the social worker to be adept at locating persons in their unique developmental and relationship contexts. This has traditionally been described as "beginning where the client is." The success of the intervention rests on how well the professional can mobilize reciprocal, interacting powers of individuals *and* environment.

Identifying supports for individuals and families became an increasingly important social work activity during the 1980s, when conservative trends altered the human service delivery system. A "social deficit" occurred when government economic supports for social programs were drastically reduced.[14] This "social disinvestment" took place during the same period in which the huge "baby boom" cohort reached adulthood; traditional family structures reached an apex of transformation through divorce, blending, and unmarried parenthood; and recession dislocated vast numbers of farmers and industrial workers. Social workers rediscovered traditional roles of locating and developing social networks, volunteers, and self-help groups to aid the victims of this social disinvestment. In many instances, they became case managers, helping to organize nonprofessional supports for farm families, homeless persons, victims of violence, persons with addictions, single mothers, the chronically physically and mentally ill, and so forth.

An outcome of reduced public funding and limitations in service provision has been the downgrading and declassifying of professional social work positions. The caseworker in the public agency increasingly has had an indirect role in assisting client functioning, as purchase-of-service arrangements have restricted service activity to problem identification, resource location, and monitoring services. Very often, case managers have been stripped of direct helping roles.[15] In contrast, clinical social workers working in private agencies, mental health centers, and private practice have organized effective drives in many states for professional licensure to clarify their practice qualifications.

There is a continuing need within the profession for a unified theory of practice, supported by evidence of effectiveness.[16] Social workers practice in a broad spectrum of settings, and individual professionals function across various practice strata. General systems theory has provided a language to describe the interrelation of individual, family, community, and societal processes, but it is insufficient in articulating direct practice applications. Thus, social work practitioners too often fashion numerous techniques of practice into an "eclectic" point of view, techniques frequently derived from the work of professionals in other disciplines. As social workers become better trained in the scientific method, practitioner-guided research will contribute to development of a testable theoretical approach.[17] The trend in the profession is toward much more rigorous evaluation of service provision, which will enable more specific education for practice and more confident practice.[18]

THE FUTURE

Social work with individuals and families in the 1990s will continue to be preoccupied with the outcomes of social structure change and social disinvestment of the last decade. Problems that clients present will continue their recent trend toward the very difficult ones of relationship abuse, substance abuse, inadequate and unsupported parenting, chronic and complex health problems due to AIDS, mental breakdown, aging, employment difficulties, and poverty. Social workers will have to arm themselves with information about intricate connections between economics and psychosocial functioning, so that they can more effectively advocate for public policy changes. Social workers who work with individuals and families are particularly suited to addressing the social costs of inadequate investment in human development.

Trends toward privatization of many public services will maintain their momentum into the next decade. The social work profession itself has paralleled this trend in the growing numbers of practitioners who are developing their own private practices. Cost-effectiveness is the byword for the decade. Private organizations will propose that they can run public institutions in a more cost-effective, but not necessarily socially just, manner. Third-party payers will determine whether it is more cost-effective to reimburse private social workers for services usually provided by more costly professionals, or less so because social work services are more widely available.

SUMMARY AND CONCLUSIONS

Social work with individuals and families has a prominent history within the profession, having long been known as "social casework." The professional helper aids individuals and families to balance their inclinations toward both dependence on and independence from their environments. The areas of physical, economic, social, and psychological coping are attended to in assessing and intervening with these clients. The process of helping is a collaborative one between client and social worker and proceeds through the phases of relationship establishment, contract clarification, assessment, planning, intervention, evaluation, and termination. A variety of theoretical approaches are used by social workers found in a variety of settings, including public and private family service agencies, mental health centers, hospitals, schools, institutions, and in private practice.

Social workers have long recognized the significance of the family for human functioning, and they are being joined by other professions in developing practice theory that takes family interaction into account. The social work profession and other professions, as well as lay persons, are currently calling for a greater national recognition of the importance of the family to societal integration. National social policies for family protection and nurturance have been recommended by many groups as vital for our society's continuing health and growth.

NOTES

1. Erik Erikson, *Identity: Youth and Crisis* (New York: Norton, 1968). See also Carol Gilligan, *In a Different Voice: Psychological Theory and Women's Development* (Cambridge, Mass.: Harvard University Press, 1982).
2. Talcott Parsons and E. A. Shils, *Toward a General Theory of Action* (Cambridge, Mass.: Harvard University Press, 1967).
3. Ronald Simons, "Strategies for Exercising Influence," *Social Work* 27, no. 3 (May 1982): 268–274.
4. Mary Richmond, *Social Diagnosis* (New York: Russell Sage Foundation, 1917).
5. Helen Harris Perlman, *Relationship: The Heart of Helping People* (Chicago: University of Chicago Press, 1979). See also Enola K. Proctor, "Defining the Worker-Client Relationship," *Social Work* 27, no. 5 (September 1982): 430–435.
6. Norman Polansky, *Integrated Ego Psychology* (Hawthorne, N.Y.: Aldine Publishing Co., 1982).
7. John Wodarski and Dennis Bagarozzi, *Behavioral Social Work* (New York: Human Sciences Press, 1979).
8. Sharon Berlin, "Cognitive Behavioral Interventions for Social Work Practice," *Social Work* 27, no. 3 (May 1982): 218–226.
9. Alan Keith-Lucas, *Giving and Taking Help* (Chapel Hill: University of North Carolina Press, 1972).
10. Murray Bowen, *Family Therapy in Clinical Practice* (New York: Jason

Aronson, 1978).

11. Richard Bandler, John Grinder, and Virginia Satir, *Changing with Families* (Palo Alto, Calif.: Science and Behavior Books, 1976).

12. Salvador Minuchin, *Family Therapy Techniques* (Cambridge, Mass.: Harvard University Press, 1981).

13. Cloie Madanes, *Strategic Family Therapy* (San Francisco: Jossey-Bass, 1981). See also Linda Stone Fish and Fred Piercy, "The Theory and Practice of Structural and Strategic Family Therapies: A Delphi Study," *Journal of Marital and Family Therapy* 13, no. 2 (April 1987): 113–125.

14. Demetrius Iatrides, "New Social Deficit: Neoconservatism's Policy of Social Underdevelopment," *Social Work* 33, no. 1 (January–February 1988): 11–15.

15. Robert F. Schilling, Steven Paul Schinke, and Richard Weatherley, "Service Trends in a Conservative Era: Social Workers Rediscover the Past," *Social Work* 33, no. 1 (January–February 1988): 5–9.

16. E. G. Goldstein, "Issues in Developing Systematic Research and Theory," in A. Rosenblatt and D. Waldfogel, eds., *Handbook of Clinical Social Work* (San Francisco: Jossey-Bass, 1983).

17. Bruce Thyer, "Contingency Analysis: Toward a United Theory for Social Work Practice," *Social Work* 32, no. 2 (March–April 1987): 150–157.

18. Joel Fischer, "Evaluations of Social Work Effectiveness: Is Positive Evidence Always Good Evidence?" *Social Work* 28, no. 1 (January–February 1983): 74–77. See also Ray J. Thomlinson, "Something Works: Evidence from Practice Effectiveness Studies," *Social Work* 29, no. 1 (January–February 1984): 51–56, and William Reid and Patricia Hanrahan, "Recent Evaluations of Social Work: Grounds for Optimism," *Social Work* 27 (July 1982): 328–340.

ADDITIONAL SUGGESTED READINGS

Frank, Jerome, *Persuasion and Healing* (Baltimore, Md.: Johns Hopkins University Press, 1973).

Gordon, Linda, *Heroes of Their Own Lives: The Politics and History of Family Violences, Boston, 1880–1960* (New York: Viking Penguin, 1988).

Gurman, Alan S., and David P. Kniskern, *Handbook of Family Therapy* (New York: Brunner/Mazel, 1981).

Hartmann, A., and J. Laird, *Family-Centered Social Work Practice* (New York: Free Press, 1983).

Hollis, Florence, *Casework: A Psychosocial Therapy,* 3rd ed. (New York: Random House, 1981).

Kahn, Alfred J., and Sheila B. Kamerman, *Helping America's Families* (Philadelphia: Temple University Press, 1982).

Lister, Larry, "Contemporary Direct Practice Roles," *Social Work* 32, no. 5

(September–October 1987): 384–391.

Maluccio, Anthony, ed., *Promoting Competence in Clients: A New/Old Approach to Social Work Practice* (New York: Free Press, 1981).

Mayeroff, Milton, *On Caring* (New York: Harper & Row, 1971).

Shulman, Lawrence, *The Skills of Helping Individuals and Groups*, 2nd ed. (Itasca, Ill.: F. E. Peacock, 1984).

Siporin, Max, "The Therapeutic Process in Clinical Social Work," *Social Work* 28 (May–June 1983): 193–198.

Walsh, Froma, ed., *Normal Family Processes* (New York: Guilford Press, 1982).

Weissman, Harold, Irwin Epstein, and Andrea Savage, *Agency-Based Social Work: Neglected Aspects of Clinical Practice* (Philadelphia: Temple University Press, 1983).

17   Social Work with Groups

Patricia Kelley

As noted earlier, "social group work" was traditionally considered to be a "method" of social work. Whether one today is oriented to the idea of a baccalaureate generalist worker, an MSW advanced generalist, or a specialist, the skills and knowledge of working with groups are basic to all social work. No matter what field of practice a social worker may be in and no matter what approach is used, knowledge of group dynamics is important. Think of the many situations in which social workers work with people in groups. Social workers attend meetings of formal organizations, they work in teams or units in agencies, they serve on committees, and they work with communities, families, or individuals. In all these situations it is important to understand people in interaction with other people.

DEFINITIONS AND CRITERIA OF GROUPS

First of all, one asks, what is a group? A group is more than a collection of individuals; the group is itself a social system. There are many definitions of the term "group," with a fair degree of consensus.[1] There are some elements common to most definitions of a group. First, there is the idea of plurality; that is a group must be two or more people. A second element is that there needs to be contact or interaction among these persons. A collection of individuals walking down a busy street in a city, then, would not be a group. If an accident occurs, and those people stop to observe the accident, then those individuals might be considered a group. If those people worked together to aid the accident victims and began to talk together about it, then it more clearly becomes a group. A third facet in defining *group* is "some significant commonality." People join a group for a purpose, and those purposes are sometimes called "goals" or "rewards." People have always bonded together for common good. In early times persons joined together to protect themselves or to find food. In today's more complex society, where an individual may feel isolated, the group can serve as a mediator between the individual and the larger society. Persons still join together to work for a common good; examples might be a trade union, a professional organization, or a political group. Through these groups people believe that they can have more impact on their lives and control over their destinies.

When we talk about people joining groups for a reward, those rewards may be tangible or intangible. For example, people may join together in a neighborhood group for something very tangible such as sidewalks, so that their children can walk to school more safely. On the other hand, people in that same neighborhood may join together for conversation and coffee, and the reward might be social interaction and finding friends. People may join a group to have a particular problem solved, such as a task force in an organization. Generally persons can be considered as being in a group if any of these criteria are met: they engage in frequent interaction with the other people; they define themselves as members of the group; they share norms or values concerning certain matters; they find some group rewards; and they pursue an interdependent goal.

Types of Groups

Groups are often classified as either primary or secondary. A primary group is one where there are primary and lasting ties; the family is considered a primary group. A secondary group is one in which the ties are not primary or permanent. Anderson and Carter distinguish between the two types of groups in the following way: "If members react to each other more as role occupants than as persons, it is a secondary group."[2] An elected city council would be an example of a secondary group.

Groups may be classified as formal or informal.[3] A formal group usually has rules, official members, and stated goals, whereas informal groups are more loosely organized. For example, look at different kinds of women's groups. The League of Women Voters has local, state, and national officers, bylaws and procedures, specific meeting times, stated goals, a membership list, and dues. However, since their meetings are open to nonmembers, there may be a more open structure than some formal groups. In a formal organizational structure, then, meetings are set and planned, agendas are prepared, and officers are elected. The goals and purposes are clearly stated, membership is defined, and members plan specific actions. On the other hand, a women's support group might be an example of an informal group, such as a group of career mothers who meet once a week for social purposes and for mutual support in the difficult job of raising children. In such a group there are no formal agendas, no membership lists, no dues; people may or may not attend according to the needs of the day.

Now, let us look at formal and informal groups in the context of social work. A parent educator group led by a social worker would be an example of a formal group in that it would be announced in advance, the social worker would be seen as the professional group leader, specific rules would be made explicit, and there might be an intake procedure for membership in that group. The number of sessions would be spelled out in advance, as would the goals. On the other hand, a youth worker in a neighborhood house might be available during after-school hours for adolescents to "drop in and chat." There would be no membership lists or rules of order, but simply a notice that there is popcorn and that the worker is available. Different people might attend on different days, and there is no official agenda. The worker here assumes the role of facilitator more than leader.

In social work settings, groups can be classified by objective or goal, by the setting, by the people in them, and by the methods involved. Examples of groups classified by objective or goal are recreational groups, educational groups, therapy groups, support groups, and political action groups. Examples of groups classified by setting would be the "inpatient group" in a hospital, or the "Smith Street Group" in a neighborhood center. A social worker talking about the high school group or the golden-age group is classifying the group on the basis of the persons in it. When social workers talk about a "TA" (Transactional Analysis) group or an "Assertiveness Training Group," they are classifying the groups by the methods of helping approach used.

Historical Antecedents of Group Work

Why do social workers deal with people in groups? Historically, there have been several ways in which these professionals have become interested in working with groups. Traditional social group work in our country can be traced back to the settlement house movement in the late nineteenth century. Grace Coyle, a pioneer in group work, wrote, "Social work as a defined method developed first in settlements and community centers in low income areas and in the youth serving agencies."[4] Settlement houses served new immigrants to this country, mainly in the large cities. An early and famous example is Hull House in Chicago, founded by Jane Addams. It was hoped that these new immigrants could assimilate better if they were educated to the norms and ways of our country. Settlement house workers aimed to educate and encourage these new immigrants in their own neighborhoods, and it was thought that this could help relieve them of their disadvantages. At the same time, social workers aimed to change the social conditions and the inequality that oppressed the immigrants who were caught in the sweat shops and squalid poverty produced by the Industrial Revolution. Main thrusts of the settlement house movement, then, were citizen education and social reform. Neighbors joined together to work on projects for the betterment of all, such as improved conditions in the neighborhood. These settlement houses did provide a haven for the immigrants; they provided an opportunity for people to learn about their new country with their friends and neighbors from their old country and to work together for social change. These themes in early social group work of social participation, social action, and democratic process remain today as important values in the social work profession.

Another historical antecedent of today's group work theory and practice is the group dynamics movement. Social psychologist Kurt Lewin coined the term "group dynamics." After escaping to this country from Nazi Germany in the 1930s, he became interested in the effects of social climate on individual attitudes. His students Ronald Lippit and R. K. White became interested in studying leadership style. Other social psychologists, adult educators, sociologists, and organizational theorists became attracted to this movement.[5] These researchers studied the behavior of the group as a developmental system itself. They viewed the group behavior as more than and different from the summation of individual behaviors of the people in the group, believing that the group develops its own values, goals, set of behaviors, and developmental cycle. They became interested in looking at the application of these groups dynamics to specific settings, especially organizations. These adherents of applied group dynamics set up the National Training Laboratories in Bethel, Maine, in the 1940s to study further the practical applications of group dynamics theory. This laboratory was established to train leaders in business, labor, government, and education, and to study group dynamics. The focus of this training

University of Illinois at Chicago, The University Library, Jane Addams Memorial Collection

Jane Addams at Chicago's Hull House in the early twentieth century.
Settlement houses were then, as neighborhood centers are today,
the scene of many group activities.

and research was for people to become more aware of their own roles, functions, and patterns of behavior in groups, and also to become aware of the effects of other group members' behavior on the group and on the individuals. Awareness of self and the development of new behaviors and skills were emphasized, and styles of leadership and decision making were examined.

The third historical antecedent to present-day group work was the group psychotherapy movement, which began early in this century but became "vastly accelerated" by World War II.[6] The term "group therapy" was coined in 1925 by J. L. Moreno, who also developed psychodrama, but not until World War II did the movement receive much attention. During the war there were not enough trained therapists to help all the individuals needing psychotherapy, so persons were treated in groups. While the initial use of group therapy was for efficiency, other benefits quickly became apparent. Therapists discovered that the patients in group therapy were often learning and changing faster than those in individual therapy. These patients learned not only from the therapist but from the others in the group as well. They began to see themselves in relation to significant others, and their social and interpersonal behavior could be examined more easily in groups. The cohesiveness of the group and the support of others with similar problems were also helpful, and it was discovered that people could learn new and more appropriate social behaviors in a group setting.

The group psychotherapists, mainly clinical practitioners, and the group dynamics people, mainly researchers, did not have much interaction or cross-fertilization of ideas until the 1960s when the "sensitivity" movement became popular. The sensitivity training movement was an outgrowth of the National Training Laboratory and its branches and focused on self-awareness through interpersonal feedback. Personal responsibility and focus on the here and now were key elements of this training, and group psychotherapists, moving away from the traditional psychodynamic view, began to incorporate these concepts into their work. The lines between these movements have become less clear, and today group work theory is pulled together from all three historical sources. While many disciplines study group phenomena and many professionals work with groups, this integration of group theory is especially important for social workers because of their wide sphere of practice—from group counseling to community change.[7]

MODELS OF SOCIAL WORK WITH GROUPS

In the 1960s, Catherine Papell and Beulah Rothman conceptualized three "models" of social group work practice, and their models roughly corresponded to the historical antecedents.[8] What Papell and Rothman called the "social goals model" is a direct descendant of the settlement house movement. The purpose of these groups is to teach social responsibility and to raise social consciousness; the role of the worker is seen as an enabler. This kind of group work is carried out in such organizations as Girl Scouts, Boy Scouts, Boys Clubs of America, YWCA, the settlement houses, and community centers. The second model of social group work practice Papell and Rothman called the "remedial model," and this is a direct descendant of the psychotherapy movement. Many social workers now are involved in group psychotherapy, where the purpose is treatment of individuals involved for personal or social adjustment. The worker here assumes the role of therapist, healer, or change agent. Such work is carried out in psychiatric hospitals, mental health centers, and youth group homes. The third model of social group work practice Papell and Rothman called the "reciprocal model." Here the individuals work together to help each other. Examples might be support groups, task forces, and peer supervision groups. The worker here is less a leader and more a facilitator, mediator, or resource person; sometimes the groups are leaderless. The purpose is mutual help; personal growth and self-actualization are stressed, rather than treatment of problems. These groups may not have specific goals other than the growth and mutuality of the people as a group and as individuals. The reciprocal model of today's group work practice is a direct outgrowth of the group dynamics laboratory, and theory is heavily drawn from Lewin's field theory, which views an individual's behavior as a function of one's "life space" or "field," and sociological systems theory.[9]

Papell and Rothman defined "model" as "a conceptual design to solve a problem that exists in reality."[10] They cautioned that models are theoretical formulations, not discrete categories, and that other writers would classify groups differently. In fact, more recently Papell and Rothman have distilled common elements from all three models into a more generic "mainstream model."[11] Indeed, what Emanuel Tropp calls the "developmental approach" to group work encompasses both the social goals and the reciprocal models.[12] Tropp distinguishes the developmental approach from the group therapy approach, and even there he sees some overlap. He believes that the sensitivity-encounter movement is basically developmental because it emphasizes human growth rather than treatment. However, the movement's intent to change people through "unfreezing, changing, and refreezing" brings it closer to the psychotherapy movement.[13] Gisela Konopka, a major theoretician in the field of social group work, has been identified with both the social goals model and the remedial model, and has worked in and written in both areas.[14]

Assertiveness training can be viewed as an example of how these theoretical models mix in practice. Assertiveness training is usually conducted in groups; its members are not usually considered patients, and the goal is growth rather than treatment. Differentiating assertive communication and behavior from aggressiveness is taught and practiced. The outcome of substituting assertive behavior (stating your own wants and needs so that negotiating can occur) from aggressive behavior (trying to push your demands onto others) is the aim of such training. While its growth goals would place it in the reciprocal category, its emphasis on change would place it in the remedial category. Such training is carried out in industries, agencies, and schools as communication and conflict management tools (reciprocal) and in mental health centers and other treatment agencies (remedial); its leaders may be clinicians (remedial) or teachers (reciprocal).[15] Thus, these models of group work should be viewed as relative, not fixed, categories, and Papell and Rothman's newer "mainstream model" more clearly represents practice today.

Social Work Practice with Groups

Social workers practice with groups in almost any field of social work. There are many self-help groups (for example Alcoholics Anonymous or Parents Anonymous, a group of persons who have abused their children) that do not require or want professional leadership, but often look to the professional social work community for consultation or help in getting started. There are groups in the human potential movement, and the facilitators of such groups are usually trained in one of the helping professions, often social work. Social workers frequently become involved in problem-solving groups. An example here might be parents of retarded children organizing a group to work for better services; the social worker might serve as consultant or group leader. Medical social workers often organize or facilitate support groups, such as in hospitals where patients or relatives of patients with life-threatening illnesses meet together for mutual emotional support. In fact, the literature on the use of groups in medical social work has increased greatly in the last decade.[16] Sometimes these groups have educational purposes, too, such as learning to live with new restrictions. Social workers often lead educational groups, such as parent education training, foster parent training, or marriage communication training, as part of their agency functions.

Social workers also become involved in developmental groups, such as inservice training or peer consultation groups. There are many kinds of therapy and treatment groups, using many different methods, that social workers may conduct within agencies and hospitals. Some group therapists conduct individual therapy in the context of a group; that is, the therapist helps individuals on individual problems while the group participates and observes. The assumption here is that the individual benefits from having more points of view, while the other group members benefit by identification with and observation of the helping process. Other group therapists use the group interaction itself as the medium of change and the issues dealt with are the here-and-now interactions of group members. The assumption behind this method is that people's problems outside the group are likely to surface in the group situation, and these problems can be observed and dealt with on the spot. This model also assumes that behavior is learned and that learning will transfer from one situation to another.

Social workers also frequently become involved in recreational groups, as in nursing homes, neighborhood houses, and in clubs such as those mentioned above under the "social goals" model. Usually in such situations recreational activities are the means to achieve ends, not the ends themselves. The ends might be educational (such as learning new skills), therapeutic (such as increasing self-esteem), or social improvement (such as decreasing delinquency). Social workers are also involved in community groups, neighborhood groups, social action, and political groups. Often "task groups," where specific tasks are undertaken, are used in community work.[17] As social workers strive toward changing the social environment as well as helping the individuals within, they become active in working for social change. To work for social change and to work in the political sphere involve sensitivity to and awareness of group process. As social workers are involved in agency meetings and in these communities, the understanding of group process is important.

A Community Support Program Group[18]

The community support (CSP) group meets for one and a half hours weekly at a community mental health center. It is designed to offer support for persons who have returned to the community after hospitalization in a mental institution. It was begun several years ago and is open-ended in that the membership changes. A few members have been with it since its beginning while others are new members. The group size is usually about eight people.

At the beginning of this particular session, the focus of the conversation was on who they knew who was a patient or employee of the Mental Health Institute. The group leader inquired why the members were focusing on past hospitalizations. The newer members then talked about their fears of living away from the hospital, their difficulties with managing money, and their problems in their jobs. When they feel afraid, the hospital seems secure and consistent. There they knew the rules.

The group leader encouraged them to share their feelings and then directed the focus of the group on specific, individual goals. Since finances were a major concern for most of the members, the leader, using a chalkboard, had a group member, Joe, plan a monthly budget. Group members were active in helping him budget for food, rent, transportation, and other expenses. The budget was then broken down to a weekly plan, and Joe was to report back to the group on how this plan worked.

The meeting ended with the leader asking each member to share thoughts and feelings about the meeting and to choose a goal they would work on during the following week. The members left, several of them getting together for coffee at a nearby restaurant.

Aspects of Group Dynamics

Social workers, then, are involved in groups at many levels of their work, in numerous fields, and using many methods. Since social workers are so frequently involved in groups, it is imperative that they have some understanding of and some skills in management of group process. Furthermore, one criterion for social group work is attention to group dynamics.[19]

There are *natural stages* or sequences of group development, just as there are stages of individual growth and development, that the worker needs to understand. Theorists vary in the number and names of stages of group development, but there is agreement as to the general progression.[20] In the early stages, most theorists would recognize that there is no real group, only a collection of individuals who must progress through certain stages before they become a group. Furthermore, sometimes individuals can meet together and never really become a group. As the individuals together come to feel more like a group, issues of power and control begin to surface. It is important for leaders here to be aware of these issues. Often subgrouping occurs as some people try to assume more power than others. As power struggles surface, the leader may be the target of attack.

If the group progresses, the next stage of development involves a closeness or intimacy. At this stage there is a strong sense of group cohesion; people support and care about each other, and there is a striving for satisfaction and dependency needs to be met. At this stage the group plans and carries out projects with more awareness and with more cooperation; thus it is often called the "working phase." There is more personal involvement and more willingness to discuss feelings at this stage. As the group continues to develop, members begin to accept one another as distinct individuals and the leader as a separate person. While the individuals may continue to function as a group, more individualization is allowed. The separation or termination phase brings various reactions. Sometimes group members regress to an earlier phase as a way of avoiding separation; sometimes members have a "flight" reaction—they say the group isn't necessary and leave prematurely; and other times separation anxiety feelings are denied. When things go well, group members reevaluate where they are, how they want to proceed with termination, and what kind of followup they want. Strong leadership is especially important in this stage. As in phases of individual development, there are no clear-cut, distinct phases; they overlap, but most groups progress through them. Emanuel Tropp writes to this point, "While all groups go through a beginning stage, a termination stage, and various experiences that occupy a middle stage, it is unlikely that any more elaborate stages can be described that would be generally applicable to a wide range of variations in purpose, function, and structure."²¹

Another aspect of group dynamics that the leader needs to be aware of is *participation and influence* of various members. It is important to be aware of the level of participation, verbal and nonverbal, of all the members. Are there some people who do not seem to be involved at all? Are there some people who seem to be highly involved? Are there some people who seem involved so highly that others' rights are usurped? Influence is not the same as participation. Some people may talk a great deal and have very little influence while others speak rarely but have influence when they do speak. It is important to note which members have influence, how they use that influence, and what style of influence is predominant. It is important for the leaders and members of groups to be aware of their struggles for leadership and rivalry for power, and to be aware of participation in subgroupings.

How *decisions* are made, conflicts resolved, and problems solved are also important group dynamics issues. Sometimes decisions are made by one or more people in the group with others agreeing; sometimes decisions are made democratically with input from all; and sometimes the group takes the path of least resistance and goes along with whatever suggestion comes up. Sometimes groups make decisions through formal vote, sometimes through informal consensus, and sometimes they evaluate and prioritize the courses of action.

It is also important to be aware of *roles* that various members play and functions that they serve in the group. Just as we all need to assume various roles in our everyday life, roles have very important functions in group development. Some group members serve roles relating to the task functions of the group. They may keep the group interested in the topic, they may suggest alternatives, and they may be the people who summarize, or call for a vote or consensus. They ask for ideas, opinions, and facts from others, and they keep the group focused. Sometimes this role is decided officially through election of a chairperson or a sergeant-at-arms at a formal meeting. In more informal groups, however, these functions are often served by someone who is either assigned or ascribed a particular role.

If a person steps in to fill the role, it can be said that that person *assumed* that role. If others ask a person to do it or if they look to that person for certain kinds of leadership, that role can be said to be *ascribed* to him or her by others. While some roles keep the group on task and are called "task" roles, others serve maintenance functions. These roles maintain the feelings and sense of the group and keep things going. Thus, we have people who bring others into the discussion; they are often called "gate-openers." When you have group members who cut off, are sarcastic to, or interrupt others, they are often called "gate-closers." Some people listen well; some seem preoccupied with other matters and seem not to be listening at all. How well the group keeps going depends upon how these maintenance tasks are attended.

Membership and subgroupings are aspects of group dynamics, also. Who seems in, partially in, or out of this group? Are these patterns consistent, or do they vary from time to time? Do the people who are out seem to have chosen that position, or does it appear that they have been shut out? Are there subgroups and do they contribute to somebody being out? Do these smaller units support or subvert the goals of the larger group?

It is also important to be aware of the *atmosphere and feelings* in the group. Is the atmosphere friendly and congenial, is there hidden conflict and disagreement, or is there open conflict and disagreement? Do the people seem interested and involved in the tasks at hand or bored by them? Are there signs of anger, warmth, excitement, competitiveness? It is important to be aware of the affective nature of the group.

Another element that is important to look for is the development of *group norms or standards*. Corey and Corey have stated that norms are "the shared beliefs about expected behaviors that are aimed at making groups function effectively."[22] Norms express beliefs or desires of the majority of the group members as to what behaviors should or should not take place in a group. Sometimes these rules are very clear, such as when guidelines are voted upon or when group standards or rules are discussed. Sometimes these group norms are not so clear and are not made explicit. If they are only known or expressed by a few, they are called *implicit norms*, which operate below the level of awareness of some of the group members. An example might be avoidance of certain areas or topics. For example, a group might have an implicit norm to avoid conflict. Thus a person serving a peacemaker function or role will jump into a discussion and try to smooth things over between the two people who disagree. How people act, whether it is all right to be late, whether the meeting should start on time, whether the group should stick to the agenda or be more open, are examples of group norms. When these norms are formalized and made more explicit, they are called *rules*.

The social worker working with groups is aware not only of the individual, where the individual is developmentally, and how that individual communicates, but the worker is also aware of the interactions among those individuals, the *communication patterns* between individuals in the group, and ways those communication patterns differ among different individuals and subgroups. The worker is aware of development of the group as a group and of norms and rules that evolve.

The *leader's role* in a group will vary according to the purpose and kind of group. For example, in a community group, the leader's goal is to develop leadership from within the people in that community, so that the group can function after the leader leaves. In a therapy group, on the other hand, the leader will continue that function until the group is terminated.

Leadership styles and the *size of groups* also affect the group. Both of these variables are heavily reviewed in the literature.[23] There is no "right" style for the leader to have; the choice would depend on the leader, the members, and the purpose of the group. Likewise, the "correct" size varies. As Vinter says, "The size of a group tends to affect members. The worker must determine the appropriate group size for the desired effects for clients as defined by their treatment goals."[24] In general it can be said that smaller groups (under ten, for example) tend to have more participation of members, more consensus, and a greater degree of cohesiveness. Larger groups can be broken into smaller subgroups when necessary. For some situations, like certain educational or community settings, a larger group, with its increased anonymity and reduced intensity, is preferable.

SUMMARY AND CONCLUSIONS

People learn, unlearn, and relearn behavior patterns from interaction with others. Self-concept is developed in large part from interactions with other people. Since social work deals with persons in interaction with other people, knowledge of group dynamics and group development is important at all levels of intervention. In addition to providing a base for social work generally, group work is also an important method of social work practice and is sometimes viewed as a field of practice.

Assertiveness Training Group[25]

Mary, a twenty-three-year-old office assistant, is in her fourth week of a ten-week Assertiveness Training program. She joined because of her difficulty in saying no, particularly on her job. She works with several assistants. One of them, Ann, often asks her to do her typing and filing, and cover for her when she is late returning from lunch. She tells Mary what a nice person she is and how they can't get along without her. Mary told the A.T. group that she leaves the office with a headache and thinks of things she wishes she had said to Ann. The A.T. leader had Mary examine what she was thinking and feeling when she didn't say no, and she replied that it was always better to help someone if you could. The group challenged these beliefs, and Mary agreed to try a new behavior. She didn't like feeling knotted up, tense, and headachy. The group leader then asked Mary to do a role-play to practice saying no. Mary chose a group member to play Ann and described her and the office environment. Another client helped Mary with saying no, and the other group members looked at the verbal and nonverbal components of Mary's behavior. The role rehearsal was also videotaped and played back for Mary and the group. The group suggested that Mary look more at Ann, increase her voice volume and be more succinct in saying no. The role play was repeated with Mary trying the group's suggestions. Mary decided to say no to Ann two times during the following week. She would share this experience at the next meeting. The group leader then discussed different techniques in saying no, the consequences of saying no, and why this can be difficult behavior to attempt. During the following week the group members were to be attentive to how they and their families and friends say no. They were also to write down when they said no or wished they had. The next meeting would start with a discussion of the assignment.

NOTES

1. Tom Douglas, *Group Process in Social Work: A Theoretical Synthesis* (New York: John Wiley & Sons, 1979), pp. 11–14.
2. Ralph Anderson and Irl Carter, *Human Behavior in the Social Environment*, 3rd ed. (New York: Aldine Publishing Co., 1984), p. 118.
3. For further discussion of this distinction, see Stephen Wilson, *Informal Groups: An Introduction* (Englewood Cliffs, N.J.: Prentice-Hall, 1978).
4. Grace Coyle, "Some Basic Assumptions about Social Group Work," in *The Social Group Work Method in Social Work Education XI*, Curriculum Study, ed. Marjorie Murphy (New York: Council on Social Work Education, 1959), p. 88.
5. For further discussion of this subject refer to Irvin Yalom, *The Theory and Practice of Group Psychotherapy*, 3rd ed. (New York: Basic Books, 1985), pp. 489–495.
6. Ibid., p. 504.
7. Anne Gero and Patricia Kelley, "The Group as a 'Wild Card' in Social Work Education," *Journal of Education for Social Work* 19, no. 1 (Winter 1983): 47–54.
8. Catherine Papell and Beulah Rothman, "Social Group Work Models: Possession and Heritage," *Education for Social Work*, Fall 1966, pp. 66–77.
9. Ibid., p. 66.
10. Ibid.

11. Papell and Rothman, "Relating the Mainstream Model of Social Work with Groups to Group Psychotherapy and the Structured Group Approach," *Social Work with Groups* 3, no. 2 (1980): 5–23.
12. Emanuel Tropp, "Social Group Work: The Developmental Approach," *Encyclopedia of Social Work*, 17th ed. (Washington, D.C.: NASW, 1977), pp. 1321–1327.
13. Ibid., p. 1326.
14. Papell and Rothman, "Social Group Work Models," pp. 66–77.
15. For further discussion of assertiveness training see Robert Alberti and Michael Emmons, *Your Perfect Right*, 4th ed. (San Luis Obispo, Calif.: Impact Publishers, 1982).
16. Thomas Carlton, "Group Process and Group Work in Health Social Work Practice," *Social Work with Groups* 9 no. 2 (Summer 1986): 6.
17. For fuller discussion and comparison of several theories of development, see Eileen Guthrie and Warren Sam Miller, *Making Change: A Guide to Effectiveness in Groups* (Minneapolis, Minn.: Interpersonal Communication Programs, 1978).
18. Case provided by Veronica Wieland, R.N., M.A.
19. Gale Goldberg and Ruth Middleman, "Social Work Practice with Groups," *Encyclopedia of Social Work*, 18th ed. (Silver Spring, Md.: 1987), 2:721.
20. For a discussion and comparison of several theories of developmental stages, see James Whittaker, "Models of Group Development: Implications for Social Group Work Practice," *Social Service Review* 44 (September 1970): 308–322.
21. Tropp, "Social Group Work," p. 1324.
22. G. Corey and M. Corey, *Groups: Process and Practice*, 3rd ed. (Monterey, Calif.: Brooks/Cole, 1987), p. 119.
23. For example the Yalom and the Corey and Corey texts cited above deal with both issues very thoroughly.
24. Robert Vinter, "The Essential Component of Social Group Work Practice," in Albert Alissi, ed., *Perspective on Social Group Work Practice* (New York: Free Press, 1980), p. 259.
25. Case provided by Veronica Wieland, R.N., M.A.

ADDITIONAL SUGGESTED READINGS

Alissi, Albert, ed., *Perspective on Social Group Work Practice* (New York: Free Press, 1980).
Balgopal, Pallassana R., and Thomas V. Vassil, *Groups in Social Work: An Ecological Perspective* (New York: Macmillan Publishing Co., 1983).
Cartwright, Dorwin, and Alvin Zander, eds., *Group Dynamics: Research and Theory*, 3rd ed. (New York: Harper & Row, 1968).

Ephross, Paul H., and Thomas V. Vassil, *Groups that Work* (New York: Columbia University Press, 1988).

Garvin, Charles, *Contemporary Group Work*, 2nd ed. (Englewood Cliffs, N.J.: Prentice-Hall, 1987).

Gitterman, Alex, and Lawrence Shulman, eds., *Mutual Aid Groups and the Life Cycle* (Itasca, Ill.: F. E. Peacock, 1986).

Johnson, David W., and Frank P. Johnson, *Joining Together Group Theory and Group Skills* (Englewood Cliffs, N.J.: Prentice-Hall, 1982).

Konopka, Gisela, *Social Group Work: A Helping Process*, 3rd ed. (Englewood Cliffs, N.J.: Prentice-Hall, 1983).

Luft, Joseph, *An Introduction to Group Dynamics*, 3rd ed. (Palo Alto, Calif.: Mayfield Publishing Company, 1984).

Napier, Rodney W., and Matti K. Gershenfeld, *Groups, Theory and Experience*, 2nd ed. (Boston: Houghton Mifflin, 1981).

Northen, Helen, *Social Work with Groups*, 2nd ed. (New York: Columbia University Press, 1988).

Shaw, Marvin E., *Group Dynamics: The Psychology of Small Group Behavior*, 3rd ed. (New York: McGraw-Hill Book Co., 1981).

Shulman, Lawrence, *The Skills of Helping Individuals and Groups*, 2nd ed. (Itasca, Ill., F.E. Peacock, 1984).

Toseland, Ronald, and Robert Rivas, *An Introduction to Group Work Practice* (New York: Macmillan Publishing Co., 1984).

18 Working with Communities

Michael Jacobsen

Social work practice with communities can be approached as one of a variety of specialized social work processes much like casework with individuals and families, social group work, administration, or as a level of intervention within the broad spectrum of generalist social work practice. The author prefers to view community practice within the latter tradition. William Gordon suggests that social work practice is concerned with the interaction between client systems and their significant environments.[1] The client system may vary from an individual, a married couple, family, small group, organization, community, to a set of communities or regions. The significant environment varies with the identified client system. For an individual returning home from a stay in a mental hospital the significant environment might include the workplace, family, neighborhood, available after-care services in the community—those portions of the environment affecting the client's situation as a returning mental patient. For a small group organized to address inadequate housing conditions and increased rent in an apartment complex, the significant environment might include the physical environment of the housing complex, all their neighbors, the landlord, and city housing ordinances.

Not only does the significant environment vary with the identified client, but as the helping process proceeds with the initial client or client group, the worker is often called upon to shift attention from one

portion of the environment to another. For example, as the worker assists an ex-mental patient with adjustment to an altered family situation, the worker may become aware of stereotypes and prejudices
concerning mental illness that are preventing that client from becoming employed. If the worker has several clients experiencing similar
difficulties, the worker might consider a community-level intervention
focused on altering the attitudes of employers regarding mental illness. In this situation the caseworker responsible for after-care services with the emotionally disabled might become a community worker
concerned with the attitudes and beliefs of the community toward the
mentally ill.

Such a shift in the focus of intervention is quite common in social
work practice. While it is likely that a caseworker, group worker, or
community practitioner may remain primarily at that level of intervention, it is also usual that in order to respond to the demands of the client situation or complex of situations, the worker must combine a
number of levels of intervention for truly effective practice. Particularly where a smaller employing organization has many functional responsibilities in its service community or where the organization must
respond to a wide range of needs of its client population, all dimensions of that organization from direct service worker to administrator
may be involved in multilevel generalist practice.

In many respects community change activities are also organizational
change or development activities. Most social work practitioners operate within the contexts of employing organizations that provide sanction for their activities, establish the possibilities and limitations of their
practice, direct their efforts, and expect accountability. People in communities commonly meet their needs through involvement with organizations such as schools, medical care facilities, retail businesses,
churches, and so forth. Human services as need-meeting mechanisms
are typically delivered through organizations. Community-based institutions and organizations such as police departments, city councils,
planning and zoning commissions, and probation and parole departments all share responsibilities for providing social order and control
within the community. As these organizations were created and are
maintained by humans, are dynamic, may make errors or fail to serve
their functional responsibilities, they are often the focus of change activities. Many community change efforts, then, require the development
of new organizational forms in communities or the revision of existing
organizations.

Community work is that portion of generalist social work practice
where the worker focuses on the community as a dimension of the significant environment of the worker's clientele and where a dimension
of the community or the community itself is the client. An example of

a portion of the community as the identified client emerges from consideration of a community group concerned with the need for sheltered workshops for the developmentally disabled in the community. The group might require assistance from a social worker to secure funding for a workshop, to help develop appropriate community support for the facility, or to seek assistance with the selection of the appropriate type of workshop for their needs and resources. Another example emerges from the contemporary example of community-based "farm crisis groups" emerging in many rural regions of America. In those situations workers are often asked to serve as resources in linking human services to the community, as consultants toward effective engagement of local natural helper systems, or as members and facilitators of the initial development group.

Since community practice may be viewed as a dimension of generalist practice, it follows that the abilities necessary for that level of intervention develop from basic values, skills, and knowledge required for generalist practice. Value considerations often include a belief in the right of access to services, of people's right to choose and participate in helping processes, citizen rights to participate in decision making, and a commitment to making social institutions more humane and responsive to people. Community practice activities include such basic social work skills as interviewing, relational abilities such as group leadership, application of the problem-solving process, and so on. For effective community-level interventions, however, it is also necessary to go beyond basic skills into more advanced activities such as power analyses, budget preparation, program evaluation, issue analyses, community studies, and needs assessments. The knowledge necessary for effective community practice includes basic understanding of human behavior and development, ethnic or cultural diversity, group dynamics, and an understanding of the relationship of social programs to social policies. It also includes knowledge of community and organizational behavior, administrative law, and federal and state regulations concerning human services, among others.

Social workers may also practice with a range of different types of communities. A common understanding of community is defined by geographic boundaries—the neighborhood, city, small rural town and outlying agricultural area, the county, region, and so forth. However, social workers also practice with "nonplace" communities where geographical identification or location is not of major concern.[2] Examples of this conceptualization include professional communities such as social workers, lawyers, and health or mental health service providers. Other examples would include "client communities" such as Native Americans, the elderly, the handicapped, or developmentally disabled.

Within communities, neighborhood meetings help develop support for issues of common concern.

Community work as the author understands it also goes under a variety of other names. Included would be community organization (the most commonly used), social planning, community development, social action, and in some instances social services administration Community organization—as a practice subspecialty—is the most recently recognized practice specialty within the field of social work.[3] Despite its rather recent official recognition, community social work dates back to the beginnings of social work practice in this country.[4] A recent formulation is "social development" particularly on the international level, the subject of Chapter 24. Historical antecedents of contemporary practice include some of the functions of the overseer of the poor and administrators of Charity Organization Societies, as well as the activities of early settlement house workers.

Social work is not the only group or profession concerned with the community as the client or in effecting community change. The planning profession has long concerned itself with purposive change at the community level. A number of universities offer advanced degrees in the fields of urban and regional planning or public administration.

While this field has historically concerned itself with the design and use of public facilities—the physical environment, transportation systems, and urban growth—it also has begun to concern itself with human and social problems such as inadequate housing and effective delivery of medical and mental health services. Agricultural extension workers have a long history of community involvement in rural America. The legal profession has also been intimately involved in community change. Historically we have had reforms in education—for example, school desegregation, the public school movement of the 1800s; in the political sector—voters and civil rights movements, anti-slavery movements predating the Revolution; and a variety of other special interest or population-specific causes and movements such as the women's movement, black and brown power groups, welfare rights groups, and advocacy groups for the elderly or handicapped citizens.

THREE APPROACHES TO COMMUNITY PRACTICE

While community practice can certainly be viewed as an integral portion of generalist practice or as related to specific types of practice such as human services administration, it is also important to recognize it as a legitimate form of specialized social work practice. Jack Rothman has developed a particularly useful conception of three types of community practice: (1) locality or community development, (2) social planning, and (3) social action.[5] This paradigm was developed for the purpose of bringing together three major themes of traditional social work involvement with communities, so that practitioners might have a device for comparison and contrast of those approaches. Rothman has used an "ideal type" format in their development, so that the three approaches are intended simply for conceptual and analytic purposes. They are not intended as descriptions of ways that community work *should* be practiced nor as three separate "pure form" approaches to practice—precise descriptions of the work of any particular practitioner.

More commonly community workers blend various components of all three approaches into an appropriate response to particular practice situations. The three types of community practice presented also to some degree represent personal orientations to community work. Some workers simply are more skilled or comfortable with particular approaches. Other workers might find that a particular approach is more "appropriate" to their particular context or organizational setting.[6] The three models are presented in Tables 18.1 and 18.2.

Table 18.1   Three Models of Community Organization Practice According to Selected Practice Variables

	Model A (Locality Development)	Model B (Social Planning)	Model C (Social Action)
1. Goal categories of community action	Self-help; community capacity and integration (process goals)	Problem-solving with regard to substantive community problems (task goals)	Shifting of power relationships and resources; basic institutional change (task or process goals)
2. Assumptions concerning community structure and problem conditions	Community eclipsed, anomie; lack of relationships and democratic problem-solving capacities; static traditional community	Substantive social problems: mental and physical health, housing, recreation	Disadvantaged populations, social injustice, deprivation, inequity
3. Basic change strategy	Broad cross section of people involved in determining and solving their own problems	Fact-gathering about problems and decisions on the most rational course of action	Crystallization of issues and organization of people to take action against enemy targets
4. Characteristic change tactics and techniques	Consensus communication among community groups and interests: group discussion	Consensus or conflict	Conflict or contest confrontation, direct action negotiation
5. Salient practitioner roles	Enabler catalyst, coordinator, teacher of problem-solving skills and ethical values	Fact-gatherer and analyst, program implementer, facilitator	Activist advocate agitator, broker, negotiator, partisan
6. Medium of change	Manipulation of small task-oriented groups	Manipulation formal organizations and of data	Manipulation of mass organizations and political processes
7. Orientation toward power structures	Members of power structure as collaborators in a common venture	Power structures employees and sponsors	Power structure as external target of action, oppressors to be coerced or overturned
8. Boundary definition to the community client system or constituency	Total geographic community	Total community or community segment (including "functional community")	Community segment

Table 18.1   Three Models of Community Organization Practice According to Selected Practice Variables (*Continued*)

	Model A (Locality Development)	Model B (Social Planning)	Model C (Social Action)
9. Assumptions regarding interests of community subparts	Common interests or reconcilable differences	Interests reconcilable or in conflict	Conflicting interests which are not easily reconcilable; scarce recources
10. Conception of the public interest	Rationalist-unitary	Idealist-unitary	Realist-individualist
11. Conception of the client population or constitutency	Citizens	Consumers	Victims
12. Conception of client role	Participants in interactional problem solving process	Consumers or recipients	Employers, constituents members

Source: Jack Rofman, "Models of Community Organization and Macro Practice Perspectives:Their Mixing and Phasing," in Fred M. Cox et al., eds., *Strategies of Community Organization*, 4th ed. (Itasca, Ill.: F. E. Peacock, 1987), p. 10.

Locality or Community Development

The origins of community development in this country can be traced to the neighborhood work of settlement house workers in the late 1800s as well as the beginnings of Agricultural Extension in the early 1900s. Since that time community development has been practiced in settlement houses and community centers, in developing countries, through the activities of adult educators, extension workers in rural America, and by social workers in public and private settings in rural areas.[7]

In community or locality development the entire community—typically a geographic entity such as a city, neighborhood, county, or village—is seen as the client system. Community residents tend to be viewed as normal citizens who have considerable potential as community members but whose potential has not been fully developed or used. They may need the services of a practitioner to help them fully realize, develop, and focus those abilities. The community developer sees each community member as unique, capable of growth, and potentially a valuable contributor to the community. It is assumed that potentially every community member may become a responsible leader in the area of their interest.

Table 18.2   Some Personal Aspects of Community Organization Models

	Model A (Locality Development)	Model B (Social Planning)	Model C (Social Action)
Agency type	Settlement houses, overseas community development: Peace Corps, Friends Service Committee, Model Cities, health associations, consumers' groups	Welfare council, city planning board, federal bureaucracy, environmental planning bodies, regional planning groups	Alinsky, black and brown power, welfare rights councils, cause and social movement groups, women's movement, trade union insurgent movements, consumer's movements, radical political groups, radical groups in the professions
Practice positions	Village worker, neighborhood worker, consultant to community development team, agricultural extension worker	Planning division head, planner	Local organizer
Professional analogues	Adult educator, nonclinical group worker, group dynamics professional, agricultural extension worker	Demographer, social survey specialist, public administrator, hospital planning specialist	Labor organizer, minority group organizer, welfare rights organizer, tenants' association worker

Sources: Jack Rothman, "Three Models of Community Organization Practice," in Fred M. Cox et al., eds., *Strategies of Community Organization,* 3rd ed. (Itasca, Ill.: F. E. Peacock, 1979), p. 31.

Community development has been defined as "a process designed to create conditions of economic and social progress for the whole community with its active participation and the fullest possible reliance on the community's initiative."[8] Community development practioners tend to assume that social change can best be pursued through broad participation of a wide range of people at the local community level. The involved community members are seen as acting in their own interest as well as being representative of the entire community's interests as a group. The community members are responsible for both determination of goals and selection of strategies to achieve these goals. Process goals—those concerned with the community's ability to function over time—tend to take precedence over task goals, those related to specific problem-solving accomplishments. Of particular concern to the community developer is the community's ability to function in cooperative forms, its ability to help itself, and the degree to which it uses democratic procedures in problem solving. Other goals of community development work include development of indigenous leadership, self-help strategies, the development of an informed and involved citizenry, enhanced communication between various subparts of the community, and the relationship of personal or family growth to community growth.

The process of community development is seen as an interactive process between community members that is at least initially facilitated by the practitioner. Community members participate in a variety of task and discussion groups to determine community needs, establish goals and priorities, and to determine "action plans" to establish those goals and priorities. Of great concern to the practitioner is the fullest possible participation of all community members in the process—both sexes and all racial, ethnic, age, and religious groups as well as people from all socioeconomic strata within the community.

The community developer sees the interests of community subparts as reconcilable. The practitioner tends to place emphasis on the unity and commonalities of community life. It is believed that rational persuasion, democratic processes, mutual understanding and communication, and a focused concern for the welfare of the entire community will bring divergent community groups together. Cooperative strategies and techniques are generally preferred over those encouraging community conflict. Some community developers see community conflict as a natural (but temporary) process that is to be experienced, so that a later consensus can be achieved. Community power actors are viewed as collaborators in the process of community problem solving.

The local community identifies problems that the community developer addresses, and therefore these issues tend to vary considerably with the local situation. Given this inherent characteristic of community development, it is quite difficult to summarize the range of problems addressed by this approach.

The community might be seen as tradition-bound and ruled by a small power elite who are very interested in controlling change. Accompanying this situation may be a large group of residents who have been inactive in community decision making because of their own limitations in education, resources, or leadership skills. In this situation the practitioner might be interested in developing leadership skills as well as the opportunity to use them in the larger populace. The practitioner would certainly be interested in beginning communication and ultimately shared decision making between the two groups.

The community may also be seen as dominated or isolated by the larger society. The community may be perceived as being unable to control its own destiny and make its own decisions. In this situation the practitioner might attempt to help groups develop and retain local decision-making capacities. The practitioner might also attempt to minimize the influence that the larger society has on the community through influencing the direction of resource exchange between the community and the larger society. The common goal of these efforts is to develop autonomy and self-sufficiency for the local community.

A third area of concern to community developers focuses on the loss of a sense of "community" in contemporary life. This loss is attributed to the effects of industrialization, technological change, and urbanization. The effects of these changes are experienced at the community level as loss of pride and sense of belonging, alienation of residents from one another, isolation, and general loss in community decision-making capabilities. It is further believed that such a situation erodes democracy in America, makes for unresponsive institutions and local organizations, and impedes personal and family development.

In community development the practitioner is seen as an enabler, encourager, teacher, and facilitator of the process of problem solving. Throughout the process the practitioner helps people express felt needs and dissatisfactions, encourages and sustains communication and interpersonal relationships among community members, helps to organize to act upon needs, and helps to identify and emphasize commonalities in the community. The practitioner may be seen as the catalyst for change, but the responsibility for change rests with the community. The practitioner tends to work within the medium of small task-oriented groups and must be skilled in guiding processes of collaborative problem identification and problem solving.

Those small task-oriented groups often emerge from within local organizations, are sanctioned by those organizations, or form the basis of a new community-based organization as one outcome of the community development process. Biddle and Biddle, for example, suggest the development of a "steering group" that becomes responsible for the initiation and development of all change efforts.[9] As that steering group matures, achieves some success, and begins to broaden its scope or discover new opportunities, it may decide to formalize as an independent organization or as a dimension of an existing organization. In some cases in the field of human services that steering group becomes the board of directors or advisory group of one product of the steering group's activities: a newly created human service organization in the community.

Social work processes have their detractors and critics. With each of the three community processes considered are major difficulties each of the other two processes may have with the process under consideration.[10] Social planners often see portions of community development as basically an "uninformed" approach to community change, an approach that may ignore more efficient solutions to problems simply because they are developed by "experts" or "outsiders." Social action practitioners have suggested that an emphasis upon cooperation and consensus is, at the least, naive, and at the worst, amenable to cooptation by power actors in communities and society. Development efforts may be easily directed to noncontroversial problems with little real substance. Both approaches might criticize community development for spending countless hours in discussion that yield few true solutions to the problem and do not speak directly to the need for fundamental change in the community. Finally, they might suggest that much of the initiative for community development actually originates from outside the community, which is a clear violation of the principles of community development.

Social Planning

The origins of social work involvement in social planning in this country can be traced to attempts at social welfare planning on the community level in the early Charity Organization Societies. Since that time, development in the early 1900s of community chests, in the federalization of social welfare during the 1930s through New Deal legislation and further legislation during the 1960s through the "War of Poverty" have had a considerable impact on furthering social work involvement in social planning. Currently social planners with a professional affiliation with social work can be found in a wide range of human service organizations from the local to the national level and in both the public and private sectors.[11]

As many of the employers of social planners are public organizations that are mandated to address specific social problems such as mental illness, unemployment, delinquency, or dependency, the field of social planning tends to be oriented to the prevention, control, or resolution of those social problems. Task goals seem to take general precedence over process goals (as discussed earlier), for example, the tangible improvement of the outcomes of a state mental health delivery system, the controlling of costs associated with administering regional AFDC programs, the development of a more efficient child protective system in a county, or tangible improvement of community coordination and referral among health agencies in an urban area.

The client system of the social planner may be seen as the residents of a geographic area. The client system may also be seen as some portion of that geographic region such as the elderly, mentally ill, disabled individuals, or other specific group. When the clients are seen as a particular population, the social planner may generally view them as consumers or recipients of services. Consumers or recipients are not necessarily active determinants of policy, procedures, or goals. Ultimate control of the activities of planners is often located in legislatures, the courts, officials within public welfare organizations, or community leaders active in welfare planning at the local level. Many social planners operate within direct legislative, administrative and judicial mandates. While representatives of client groups may be involved in advisory capacities or in some cases some limited actual decision-making roles, much of the decision making is left to formal "representatives" of the citizenry that are selected through political processes.

In this approach social problems are seen as amenable to control and resolution through the process of rational analysis, which leads to deliberately planned and controlled change. Technical or expert roles are emphasized in social planning. The planner is often seen as a technical fact finder, program implementor, and program evaluator. As a technical analyst, the social planner is expected to have expertise in empirical research methods, community analysis techniques such as needs assessments, program evaluation methods, and familiarity with fiscal decision making and control. The planner is expected to have knowledge of organizational and community behavior as well as a range of human service programs. Since much of the work of the planner is done in a formal organizational context within legal parameters and in conjunction with other professions, the planner is expected to be able to perform effectively within formal organizations and with a variety of professionals from other disciplines.

Planning seems to be essentially pragmatic in its approach to community problems. The basic strategy seems to encourage fact finding about a situation—the nature and incidence of the problem, how it affects the citizenry, its general effect upon the larger community and society, the financial and social costs associated with the problem—and then follow with logical steps intended to resolve the problem as efficiently as possible. The solution must necessarily be oriented to the particular context in which it occurs—the actors and organizations involved, legislative mandates, monies involved, the political realities of the situation—but the social planning process itself is fairly consistent. One studies a problematic situation, discovers alternative programmatic solutions, determines the most efficient solution, implements the program, and evaluates its outcomes.

Advocates for social action or community development might suggest that social planning is by definition a "top-down" approach to community problem solving. The entire problem-solving approach is seen as being dominated by politicians, technicians, bureaucrats, or elites who have little understanding of the situation as experienced by those immediately living with the problem. Social action practitioners might also suggest that planners have a long history of failure in their efforts to resolve or control social problems effectively. The social problems remain (some get larger); the "expert" solutions change. More conservative members of the community might suggest that social planning efforts have had the actual effects of only increasing costs associated with the delivery of human services or discovering new problems with no apparent solutions. This "big government" or "free spending" approach to social problems necessitates more government intrusion into private life and increases the tax burden of the average citizen. Community development practitioners may reject the formal attempt to solve community problems through technical processes removed from immediate community life. They suggest instead that local individuals acting through community groups must determine and develop their own solutions; these responses to local situations do not have to be either sophisticated or tied to formal authority to be successful. Finally, they may suggest that many of the results of social planning are actually experienced at the local level as "unrealistic" or too bound up in "red tape" to be responsive to the local situation.

Social Action

This country has a long tradition of social action and social reform. The country itself was founded as a result of a social reform—the American Revolution. Since that time, as indicated earlier, attempts at social reform have always been with us—the public education movement and its reform, the women's movement beginning in the middle 1800s, the abolition movement which contributed to the outbreak of the Civil War, and so on. Beginning in the 1870s, social workers in settlement houses in urban areas were involved with social change activities in the inner city, such as labor reform, more adequate protection for tenants, legal advocacy for neighborhood residents, better treatment of children as well as other areas of involvement. Continuing to this time the profession has involvement with labor unions, civil groups, welfare rights organizations, black and brown power groups, the women's movement, "cause" organizations of various types as well as a variety of political action organizations.[12]

The overriding goal of these involvements in social action has been basic, fundamental change in organizations, communities, and society. This process generally attempts to redistribute power, resources, and decision making fundamentally in every aspect of our environment. Most social change efforts of this nature also include intentions of bringing about societal changes in values, beliefs, and attitudes regarding the phenomena of concern. In order to effect such change, social action practitioners often attempt to secure change in large formal organizations such as state departments of social services, city councils, educational institutions, professional associations, or state and national legislatures.

The social action practitioner may stress either task or process goals. Common task goals include changes in the law such as enactment of the Equal Rights Amendment, the modification of hiring practices so that more people of color and women are hired by a particular industry, changes in bureaucratic procedures so that more low-income people may obtain their entitlements, or the political empowerment of unrepresented people by securing their election and appointment to positions in city administration. Common process goals would include a series of "open forum" discussions around the need for change in city government, identification and organization of people of color or women in a professional organization to identify and articulate their needs within that organization, or the development of a representative and articulate group of consumers of services in a rural county. A common technique of the social action practitioner is to relate the attainment of a specific goal (either task or process) to the real possibility of making fundamental change in a community, organization, and society generally. Smaller-scale goals or activities may be pursued because they are achievable, do make a difference (task), and help to build the organization (process).

The social action practitioner tends to see society as being structured through power and privilege. Decision making and control of resources are viewed as being dominated by a group of power actors who are typically the political and economic elite of the community. The clients or constituents of the social action practitioner are seen as "victims" of a system of "oppression"; they are the "underdogs" or the "have-nots" of the community. The practitioner tends to assume that the interests of the two groups are at fundamental variance and are not reconcilable. Those in positions of power and privilege do not easily give up their influence and will attempt to regain their advantage if it is removed.

The power structure is seen as the target for action—an external force that is opposed to the client, in many respects the "enemy." That power structure is often viewed as having considerable influence over community institutions and organizations that directly affect the lives of the clientele. The power structure is to be coerced or overturned, so that the interests of the client population may be furthered. In accord with their understandings of social justice and democracy, social action practitioners tend to see large numbers of disadvantaged or disenfranchised people in society who need opportunities for organization so that they may place demands on the community for just treatment, more input into decision making, or an increased share of societal resources. Social action practitioners attempt to assist the powerless in that organization so that they can independently pursue and defend their own interests.

The basic strategy of social action practitioners is to bring together their clientele and organize them to take direct action against the power structure. It is then often necessary to facilitate discussion and education within the client group regarding the issues at hand and the possibility of change. The practitioner must have an understanding of the local issues, be adept at group- or organization-building activities, and be able to lead discussions focused on the concerns of the clientele. The social action practitioner often employs both the advocate and activist roles and attempts to organize client groups, so that they may better pursue their own interests independent of the practitioner. The practitioner also may become involved as a member of the client group in a partisan social conflict intended to serve only client interests. Social action activities tend to be characterized by confrontation and conflict between the client group and the power structure. Where the practitioner is interested in attitude change in the general community regarding the identified client group, the practitioner may use broadcast and print media for those purposes. Consensus tactics are are commonly stressed within the client group. Other social action tactics include direct action such as boycotts or pickets and mass-education or mass-involvement campaigns such as voter registration drives.

As with the other two processes, social action has its critics. The community development practitioner might contend that the social action orientation to conflict and confrontation is too disruptive to the community, that rapid changes that are forced on a community are invariably resented and susceptible to retaliatory measures. They might also suggest that many of the issue formulations "imported" by the social action practitioner are developed "outside" the community and are "forced" on residents. As such they are not accurate representations of either their needs or their interests. The social planner might express displeasure with the implicit hostility of the social action practitioner toward formal human service organization and the "expert" role on decision making. The planner may express impatience with a view that suggests that the planner is not equally as concerned and knowledgeable about the conditions of people in communities. Both might combine to attack a view of community that they see as focusing on the "negatives" and ignoring many of the positive changes and features in society. Finally, both are made uncomfortable by a position that "the wars must continue," that client and other community group interests are not basically reconcilable and that communities will continue to be ordered through oppressive use of power and privilege.

SUMMARY AND CONCLUSIONS

We have outlined the historical and contemporary involvements of a range of social work practitioners with communities. The relation of community interventions to generalist practice were discussed. Three model "specialist" approaches to community practice were described along with a brief critique of each approach. Social work practice with communities is seen as an integral process within the profession that will continue.

Blending the Three Approaches

As indicated previously, it is quite common for practitioners to blend all three approaches into responses to particular situations. The following description of a practice situation is intended to demonstrate the blending of elements of the three approaches to one neighborhood setting.

Several years ago the author served as director of a new neighborhood center in a low-income housing project on the edge of a rural university community. At the beginning of the project the community, housing over 1,000 residents—many of whom were elderly, single-parent families with young children, or handicapped adults—was not served by public transportation. Additionally, many of the residents were concerned about the "quality of life" in the area, the vandalism, few recreation services for children, tenant/landlord disputes, and disagreements between neighbors.

In response to the general concerns of the residents, the center and a few tenants encouraged the development of a Tenants Association. The initial activities of the association centered on expanding membership, identifying specific needs and concerns of residents, and developing local leadership to respond to those concerns. The major focus was to develop a group of people who could begin to identify and act upon solutions to the problems present in the neighborhood. The tactics and goals of this phase seem most similar to both locality development and social action.

As both the specific problems and leaders were identified, it became quite clear that many problems were associated with difficulties with city officials, management of the housing complex, and disagreements among residents of the neighborhood. Simultaneously three projects were developed in various combinations of center staff Tenants Association leadership, residents, and management staff.

The first project was directed toward securing public transportation facilities for neighborhood residents. After failing to persuade city officials to extend services, Tenants Association members, with center consultation, began to circulate petitions and make their needs known to City Council members through telephone calls, letters, and other means. The project culminated with two direct confrontations of the council by neighborhood residents at City Council meetings. The confrontations were covered by local media and included the picketing of City Hall. Ultimately, public transportation services were extended to the neighborhood. The majority of strategies, tactics, and techniques used in this project are consistent with the social action approach.

The second project involved improving recreational and child care services to neighborhood residents. Essentially a planning process was undertaken with the management, center, and city staff to develop a comprehensive summer recreation program for the neighborhood. Residents were involved primarily as consultants and participants in a neighborhood "child care needs" survey developed by the planners. The general goal of the project was to identify and meet the needs of residents through the efficient use of center, city, and management resources. Additionally, this project helped develop the beginnings of an application for United Way Funding of the neighborhood center.

The third project entailed a "clean-up and beautification" campaign in the housing complex involving the association, center, management, and neighborhood residents. Several "clean-up days" were developed where residents and center staff picked up garbage and trash around the complex. Staff provided equipment for this project and also promised to improve maintenance practices in the "spirit of cooperation " that developed out of the campaign. Management staff also purchased some seed, plants and young trees that were promised to residents as a part of the "beautification" campaign. Neighborhood residents—particularly young people—became involved in planning the location and actual planting of the flowers and trees. Finally, participants in this project developed a community garden in a weedy lot adjoining the complex. Management provided the space and seeds, residents provided the labor, and the center staff coordinated plot acquisition and technical assistance for the garden. This third project had strong elements of cooperation among concerned parties, self-help, and the development of the capacity to work together to solve problems. All are major characteristics of the community/locality development approach to community practice.

NOTES

1. William E. Gordon, "Basic Constructs for an Integrative and Generative Conception of Social Work," *The General Systems Approach: Contributions Toward an Holistic Conception of Social Work* (New York: Council on Social Work Education, 1969), p. 7.
2. For further amplification see Ralph Anderson and Irl Carter, "Community" in *Human Behavior in the Social Environment* (New York: Aldine, 1984), pp. 61–86.
3. Recognized as a practice subspecialty by NASW in 1957.
4. See, for example, Frank Bruno, *Trends in Social Work* (New York: Columbia University Press, 1948), p. 194.
5. Jack Rothman, "Three Models of Community Organization Practice," from National Conference on Social Work, *Social Work Practice, 1968*, National Conference on Social Welfare, 1968.
6. See, for example, the author's argument for community development in rural areas in H. Wayne Johnson, ed., *Rural Human Services* (Itasca, Ill.: F. E. Peacock Publishers, 1980), p. 196.
7. William W. Biddle and Loureide J. Biddle. *The Community Development Process: The Rediscovery of Local Initiative* (New York: Holt, Rinehart & Winston, 1965).
8. United Nations, *Social Progress through Community Development*, 1955, p. 6.
9. Biddle and Biddle, *The Community Development Process.*
10. One will find very little clear and direct indictment of other processes in the social work literature. The "debates" captured here have been encountered in discussions among the practice community.
11. For further amplification of social planning involvements see Robert Morris and Robert H. Binstock, *Feasible Planning for Social Change* (New York: Columbia University Press, 1961), and Harvey Perloff, ed., *Planning and the Urban Community* (Pittsburgh: Carnegie Institute of Technology, 1961).
12. For further amplification of involvements and an example of a very influential force within the process of social action see Saul Alinsky, *Reveille for Radicals* (Chicago: University of Chicago Press, 1946); Idem., *Rules for Radicals* (New York: Vintage Books, 1972); and Steve Burghardt, *Organizing for Community Action*, Sage Human Services Guide, Vol. 27 (Beverly Hills, Calif.: Sage Publications 1982).

ADDITIONAL SUGGESTED READINGS

Burghardt, Steve, *The Other Side of Organizing: Resolving the Personal Dilemmas and Political Demands of Daily Practice* (Cambridge, Mass.: Schenkman Publishing, 1982).

Cary, Lee J., ed., *Community Development as a Process* (Columbia: University of Missouri Press, 1970).

Cox, F. M., J. L. Erlich, J. Rothman, and J. E. Tropman, eds., *Community Action, Planning Development: A Casebook* (Itasca, Ill.: F. E. Peacock, 1974).

Cox, F. M., J. L. Erlich, J. Rothman, and J. E. Tropman, eds., *Tactics and Techniques of Community Practice*, 2nd ed. (Itasca, Ill.: F. E. Peacock, 1984).

Ecklein, J. L., and Armand Lauffer, *Community Organizers and Social Planners* (New York: Jointly published by John Wiley & Sons, and Council on Social Work Education, 1972).

Fellin, Phillip, *The Community and the Social Worker* (Itasca, Ill.: F. E. Peacock, 1987).

Grosser, Charles F., *New Directions in Community Organization: From Enabling to Advocacy* (New York: Praeger Publishers, 1976).

Group Work and Community Organization, *Papers presented at the 83rd Annual Forum of the National Conference of Social Work* (New York: Columbia University Press, 1956).

Kahn, Si, *Organizing* (New York: McGraw-Hill, 1982).

Kettner, Peter, John M. Daley, and Ann Weaver Nichols, *Initiating Change in Organizations and Communities: A Macro Practice Model* (Monterey, Calif.: Brooks/Cole, 1985).

Kramer, Ralph M., and Harry Specht, eds., *Readings in Community Organization Practice*, 3rd ed. (Englewood Cliffs, N. J.: Prentice-Hall, 1983).

Mayer, Robert. R., *Social Planning and Social Change* (Englewood Cliffs, N. J.: Prentice-Hall, 1972).

Perlman, Robert, and Arnold Gurin, *Community Organization and Social Planning* (New York: Published jointly by John Wiley & Sons, and The Council for Social Work Education, 1972).

Roberts, Hayden, *Community Development: Learning and Action* (Toronto: University of Toronto Press, 1979).

Ross, Murray G., *Community Organization: Theory and Principles*, 2nd ed. (New York: Harper & Brothers, 1967).

Staples, Lee, *Roots to Power: A Manual for Grassroots Organizing* (New York: Praeger Publishers, 1984).

19 Social Work Administration

W. Stanley Good

Most social services are provided through organizations known as social agencies; having such an organization devoted to social services makes it possible for a variety of people to work together to serve many people, just as organizing a department store enables people to work together to offer a range of merchandise to a great many people (customers). All people who work in and are a part of an organization (department store) have some responsibility for making the organization function; there are specific roles and tasks assigned by the organization to make its merchandise available to the customers. Social service employees also have specific roles and responsibilities in working with other employees to make the social services available to people (often called clients or patients) needing services. Some employees of the organization are primarily engaged in the work of making the organization operate smoothly and effectively; these people are referred to as administrative staff and have titles such as supervisor, clinical supervisor or director, program director, executive director. This distinguishes their responsibilities from the direct service staff, whose titles may be social worker, case worker, group worker, child welfare worker, family service worker or family therapy team worker, to cite some examples.

The purpose of organizations in social service delivery is to enable a number of people (staff) to work together cooperatively to achieve the goals of services to people who need them. Direct service workers perform a primary function in relating to the people who need service. Administrative employees devote themselves to building the organization and creating a milieu or climate in which work of the many employees is coordinated to function smoothly in offering services needed by families or individuals to help them function more effectively in society.

The employees identified thus far comprise the "professionally trained" social work staff; in addition there are other employees, often referred to as "support staff" and including people with titles such as receptionist, secretary, typist, bookkeeper, and janitor. Beyond this range of employees some agencies will also have foster families, homemakers, home health aides, and others whose skills and knowledge are important in meeting needs of persons using the service.

Social service organizations are often complex in terms of number and variety of staff, range of services offered, funding sources, and range of persons served. Therefore the administrative work of coordinating, developing, funding, and evaluating is also complex. Thus, staff who do the administrative work need to be educated for and competent in the areas of administrative theory and practice and organizational development, as well as to be grounded in social work theory and practice, values, and ethics. One author recently stated:

> The social agency administrator is confronted by innumerable blocks, by countless limits, and by negative attitudes. The ability to perform well and wisely, to steer the social agency constructively for humane purposes, is best acquired by professional social work education and experience, combined with powerful identification with social work values and ethics. The ability to pull it all together is to be sought in the professional social worker rather than in the professional administrator.[1]

DEFINITIONS AND FUNCTIONS

A basic definition of administration is "a cooperative and coordinated endeavor, involving all members of an organization, each of whom contributes variously to the processes of goal formulation, planning, implementation, change and evaluation. In this sense, 'administration' includes the totality of activities in a social welfare organization that are necessary to 'transforming social policy into social services.'"[2] In any week's schedule an executive director may engage in some or all of these activities:

1. meeting with administrative staff to review organizational goals, quality of services, activities of staff, and/or policies relating to services.
2. reviewing financial reports and checking with financial officer the state of the budget.
3. meeting with board president and Executive Committee (private agency with this structure) to inform them about progress of agency toward goals; need to establish long-range planning committee to reassess agency goals and services and community needs.
4. meet with agency personnel committee (consisting of agency board members and representatives of staff) to discuss need for changes in the compensation plan.
5. meet with community welfare council (consists of agency board and staff representatives, representatives of business, civic, labor, and religious organizations) for sharing of information about the community, its problems, services, and goals.
6. meet with agency public relations staff person and representatives of a television station to explore public information program on needs for foster family homes.
7. meet with National Association of Social Workers program committee to plan a spring conference, which would provide good staff development opportunities, as well as to stimulate improved social services in the region.
8. meet with supervisory staff within the agency to consider problems of internal communication; also how to coordinate services better with other human service agencies in the community.
9. meet with all agency staff members (general staff meeting) to discuss problems, outline a change in procedures, solicit concerns about present operations and means of improvement.

As can be seen from these activities, much of the work of an executive director (administrator) takes place with groups of people. Thus, it is important for the administrator to have knowledge and skills to work with and provide leadership for groups. It is also necessary to have and to exercise leadership for the agency staff and board, for the professional organization, for the community, and statewide groups in terms of developing and maintaining effective social services. Some recent writings identify serious problems for some staff members of public welfare agencies, and comment as follows:

> We feel strongly that a caring Agency must be fully human in its operation, and must communicate warmth and humanity, as well as efficiency. The fact that it is identified more for its bureaucratic character than its service orientation is perhaps the saddest thing that can be said about welfare. Why should the environment in the welfare office be so much like that of the Internal Revenue Service? Turning the welfare system around, conse-

quently, requires sensitive attention to and repair of the work place and work process. Ultimately, our product is as much how we deliver dollars or services as it is the dollars or services as it is the dollars or services themselves.[3]

Within the agency the administrator sets the general tone and should create a milieu in which staff can work creatively in providing effective services. As a professional social worker, the administrator will use knowledge, skills, and professional values to guide personal and organizational relationships to clients, staff, and community. Personal characteristics important to this leadership role include integrity, openness, maturity, human warmth, respect for others, self-respect, and self-discipline.

Educational programs in business and public administration deal with theories and practice of these same administrative activities, but social welfare administration has distinctive characteristics that make it important that it be taught and practiced in the context of professional social work values and ethics. Some authors point out such characteristics that require special attention:

1. Human beings, the focus of human services, are complex; they need to be understood and served on an individual basis, and still regarded from a holistic view.
2. Services for persons are community-based and require continuous interaction among and interrelationship with many other local, state, and national services, both private and public; interaction is also required among a variety of professions, all contributing both to understanding of person and problem and to needed services and changes.
3. The human service administrator must be aware of and respond to changes in knowledge and to social/economic/political forces that impact the environment of persons served and the community.

Summarizing these discussions, Weiner states, "The extraordinary character and contribution of human services management necessitates a dynamic approach to management. And having to deal with such a continuously interactive environment of human and organizational relationships sets up a corollary: the need to have a creative approach to management."[4]

In a 1981 text, the authors comment,

Central to our viewpoint is the notion that social administration must simultaneously be concerned with ideological commitment and technological competence. Although social administration is a technical activity, it is not a neutral activity: the executive is always involved in decision-making which reflects an ideological orientation. The concern with ethics and val-

ues, fundamental to the social work profession not only provides the base-
line for executive behavior but also sets the stage for the administrative advocacy which we view as a core function of administration.[5]

Social work administrators are expected to be leaders in the profession and in the community and to take a responsible role in development of social policy at local, state, and national levels. While all social
workers are expected to be spokespersons and advocates for the people who use the services, administrators have a crucial role through
their own advocacy, as well as encouraging staff people to be active in
developing positive community attitudes about the social services.

The following sketch will help to illustrate the key role of the social
work administrator in leading and coordinating the agency's service
and program.

HISTORICAL ANTECEDENTS

History tells us that there was administration and organization at least
as early as 2000 B.C.. The pyramids of Egypt are evidence that people
planned, organized, and exercised leadership in order to build an edifice covering as much as thirteen acres, with nearly 2½ million stone
blocks, each weighing an average of 2½ tons. Construction is estimated to have taken a labor force of over 100,000 men over a period of
twenty years. This achievement is the equivalent of administering an
organization three times the size of Shell Oil Company.[6] The leading,
governing, provisioning of the people of Israel as recorded in the
book of Exodus during their trek through the wilderness on the way to
the Promised Land is another evidence of organizing and administering at a significant level.[7] Moses' father-in-law, Jethro, is likely the first
recorded consultant on administration and organization.[8]

The Industrial Revolution moved production from home to factories, which meant bringing workers together in one place to work cooperatively in mass production. This in turn led to more organizing
and to management activities. In the early years of the twentieth century, pioneer managers of business analyzed their experiences and observations and began to write about the science of management. In
this country an organizer and manager, Frederick Taylor, and in
France, Henri Fayol, were representatives of this developing interest in
the activities of managers as distinct areas of knowledge and theory.
Stimulated by these early writers, others in such fields as behavioral
sciences, human relations, organizational development, and social
systems theory have contributed to developing theory and practice
skills in further refining the theory and practice of administration.[9]

The Work of an Administrator

About 8:15 one morning, the agency director received a call from the police saying they had arrested a man on neighbors' reports that he had severely beaten his eight-year-old son. The man told the police that he was receiving services from the agency because of previous reports of severe punishment of his children, and asked that the agency be notified. The director told the police that he would be right over to talk with the man. First he talked to the caseworker who had been working with the family and who expressed great surprise, as the whole family was cooperative and had been making good use of service to develop better communication and interrelationships within the family. It was decided that the caseworker would visit the mother and son at home to gather information, the director would inform the board president of these developments, make a visit to the father in jail, and be prepared to talk with the media representatives later in the morning.

At the home the caseworker learned from the son that he had returned from his paper route to find that his mother had taken a younger child to the hospital emergency room for care of a fever. So he started out to make collections, assuming he would be home before other family members returned. However, mother and sister returned shortly, expecting to find him at home, and not finding him, became alarmed. The father was notified at an agency where he was seeking work, and he came home to search the neighborhood, as this behavior was unusual for the son. The parents had been concerned for some time that the children might get involved in some of the vandalism and pilfering in the neighborhood. When the son returned home, the father was so upset that he whipped the boy with his belt. Then the police came and took the father to jail.

The director met the father in the jail; the father expressed great regret about punishing the boy so severely. He still remembers his own boyhood during which he was punished when he disobeyed; also he is fearful that his continued unemployment and loss of income will lead to problems for the family. When the director asked the father if he would like to have his son visit, the father was eager to see all his family.

The director phoned the caseworker at the family home to find out what the worker had learned in talking to mother and son and also asked if the son had any fears about the father returning home; the social worker discussed this with the family and was assured that all family members wanted him to come home. The director then talked with the police chief, and the two of them discussed the whole incident with the county attorney who stated that if the director and agency would take responsibility for the fa-

ther's behavior, he would not file charges and would allow the father to be released from police custody. Since the news media
were carrying the story and telling of the agency's role, the director phoned the board president to inform him of the events and
the plan to reunite the family. The board president discussed with
the director whether he and the social worker felt sure that the
boy would not be harmed further if he were returned home, and
was assured they felt it was safe for the boy. He agreed the plan
was sound. He offered to ask a friend, the editor of the paper, to
assign a reporter to do a feature article about the services of the
agency in helping families deal with problems of stress arising
from the high unemployment. This would enable the agency to
focus particularly on family worry and stress and agency services
geared to helping families find ways to deal with the stress without harming the family or its members.

The director then arranged for the release of the father to the
custody of the agency and took him home. The caseworker and director spent some further time with the family discussing this situation, and helping family members to think through ways in
which such crises could be met. There was further discussion also
of ways the father and the agency could do other things that
would help in his search for employment. The director told of a
new work training program at a local community college, which
might help the father develop new work skills.

Here we see the caseworker and director working together to
help the family and to interpret the agency to public officials.
Through the board president, they could also get some good
community education about the stresses and strains of unemployment that create problems in the family, and the role of family
service agencies in helping families.

In the 1940s Harleigh Trecker, a social work administrator, wrote a
seminal text on social agency administration; later, as dean of the
School of Social Work at the University of Connecticut, he revised the
text several times based on his experience in teaching social welfare
administration.[10] In 1970 a task force of social work faculty who were
teachers of administration, under the sponsorship of the Council of Social Work Education, worked with Harry Schatz, who edited a reader in
social work administration and a book of case materials to supplement
and apply the theory. During the 1970s many graduate schools developed curricula on administration, or at least had some courses, and
there was a growing volume of good textbooks. National conferences
in social welfare and social work were sponsoring regular programs on
aspects of organizing and administering the social welfare services.
There is a journal, first produced in 1977, titled *Administration in So-*

cial Work as well as journals in related fields such as health, mental health, and education.

Previous to these developments in colleges and universities, social work administrators were largely people who began as direct service workers, with experience were promoted to supervisor, and if successful in that role were able to become administrators of agencies.[11] These people learned by experience, and some studied in public or business administration to increase their knowledge and improve their practice as administrators. As social welfare services grew in response to increasing problems and needs of individuals and families, there was and is a public awareness of growing demand for competent social welfare administrators. Some schools of social work have joined with business or public administration schools to develop a management curriculum, or have developed joint degree programs. By 1980 most of the more than eighty accredited U.S. schools of social work provided educational opportunities to learn organizational and administrative theory and apply it through practicums in social service agencies.

SOCIAL WORK ADMINISTRATORS

Within a well-staffed social agency, administrative work is a primary role and activity for persons with titles such as director, executive director, supervisor, consultant, clinical director, program director, and program developer. It is worth noting that every social worker in an organization does many administrative tasks—reporting their work, planning, coordinating with other staff and/or staff of other agencies. Knowledge of the organization structure and administrative process, including job descriptions for the various employees, will enable the social worker to be a more effective and productive part of this cooperative effort.

Social work administrative activity is most obvious within the social work agencies; in addition, many social work services are provided in "host agencies"—a social service department in a hospital will likely be administered by a social worker, though the overall hospital will be administered by a hospital administrator or a physician. A social work department in a court will typically have a social worker as administrator while a person of legal training may well be the overall administrator of the court; other host agencies for social services include schools, health departments, and business corporations.

Position of Administrative Method in Social Work

Relatively small numbers of social workers choose to prepare for a career in administration, preferring instead to devote themselves to direct service to people with problems. This is even more true for women than men. A major problem is the inadequate number of persons equipped with necessary education and training for the challenges of developing and administering the organizations through which social policy emerges and services are made available. Data from the Council on Social Work Education for November 1986 show that 5.3 percent of the graduate student population chose to concentrate in the field of administration/management. It is encouraging to note that additional students make combinations of their concentrations, and another 5.5 percent combine direct practice with community organization and planning or with administration/management; 1.6 percent combine community organization/planning with administration /management; also 14.5 percent choose the generic concentration which includes some course work and practicum experiences in all methods. Thus, this larger number of students has been introduced to basic concepts in administration/management.[12]

Despite the low numbers of students doing primary study in administrative areas, experience shows that significant numbers of MSW graduates tend to move into supervisory or other administrative work within five years of their graduation. Many of these people have taken minimal course work in administrative theory and knowledge during their graduate study. As they progress in their administrative work, they make use of inservice training and special workshops to develop their knowledge and competence.[13]

The field of administration of social services needs persons grounded in the ethics of the profession, who are immediately aware of the opportunities of developing organizations that truly respond to the human needs of persons and families with problems. The effective social work administrator will be able to develop an organization geared to the needs of the clientele to be served, and also to the needs of the professional staff to enable them to give their best, creative service to persons coming for service. The nurture of a professional staff is basic to effective services and good administration.

Trends and Issues

The need for better prepared social service administrators is made more evident by the continuing political/economic/social changes of the 1980s. Schools of social work are responding to these challenges by modifying curricula to provide better integration of basic concepts in fields of practice, especially administration/management and community organization/social development. Also, special practica are being developed to provide opportunities for application and testing of theory from these fields.

As colleges and universities familiarize students with computers and other technology for data collection and analysis, social work students and staff entering practice are readily using these tools. Accurate data are essential for good administration decision making, planning, and financial control. The goal is to make use of technology to create an environment in which concern for the client service is paramount and the technology supports staff and administration efforts at creative helpful service to the client.[14] There is debate also about the best goal statements as a basis for evaluating achievements. One author argues, "management responsibilities such as resource allocation, performance measurement, productivity enhancement and the like are more purposefully and coherently carried out if they are tied to the overriding purpose of maximizing service effectiveness."[15]

Social work administrators who have had the benefit of course work including concepts of community change, social planning, and citizen participation can provide leadership in developing services to deal with problems arising from changes in the workplace that create disruption in families and in the community. Some social/economic trends include reduced income as workers lose factory jobs and the only work is in "service occupations" at much lower pay, often part time with few, if any, fringe benefits. Many of the workers caught in this trend are female single parents unable to find or afford adequate child care. Loss of well-paying jobs also causes both parents to take employment out of the home, placing many families under severe strain for the same reasons of low income, lack of child care, or health protection. These economic patterns lead to increased social disruption including divorce, alcoholism, battered spouses and children, runaway children, and significant numbers of homeless children and families. Social work administrators are providing leadership by joining volunteers and legislators in formulating legislative proposals to mandate services at the workplace, such as increase in minimum wages, adequate child care, health services, and maternity leave.

Another role for social work administrators is joining volunteers to establish new services to meet needs of newly recognized groups, such as homeless persons, runaway children, battered spouses and children, and the hungry and ill. These conditions present both individual and community problems and require community action to find new resources and means of responding to the individual needs. A volunteer group may set up a hot meal program in a church, a free clinic, or a peer counseling program such as Alternative Service Organizations. These grass-roots agencies benefit from the involvement of the social work administrator (sometimes as a volunteer, or as paid staff member) who is knowledgeable in working with volunteers, organizing a service, and establishing ties to the existing social/health/economic structure of the community. These Alternative Service Organizations make "their contribution toward creating a more complete, responsive, and effective service delivery system."[16]

The need for broadly trained, experienced administrators continues and is the basis for some proposals for recruiting interested persons from among the clinical staff persons. As noted earlier, many of these staff do go into various administrative responsibilities within five years of their beginning employment. There are suggestions that employers recruit among their staff, provide opportunities for counseling those who exhibit interest, and provide inservice training and opportunities to test interest in specific administrative jobs by carrying such responsibilities on a part-time assignment. The agency could set up arrangements with a university or college enabling the individual to take needed course work to prepare for administration. Their experience in clinical work would be valuable preparation for many of the challenges in administration, community organization, social action, policy development, personnel administration, and other areas basic to the development of a strong community service agency.

SUMMARY AND CONCLUSIONS

Direct services tend to be the visible, overt activities emanating from a social agency, but behind the scenes, perhaps inconspicuous to outsiders, are the person or persons responsible for the organization and administration of the agency itself. Humanizing the agency and making the services responsive to human needs are the challenges to the administrative staff. Many people in administration have "worked up" into this level or area whereas others have studied management and entered such a role directly. Either way administration is important to consumers, workers, and the community.

NOTES

1. Morton I. Teicher, "Who Should Manage a Social Agency?" *Administration in Social Work* 4, no. 1 (Spring 1980): 99–103.

2. Patti, Rino J., *Social Welfare Administration: Managing Social Programs in a Developmental Context* (Englewood Cliffs, N.J.: Prentice-Hall, 1983), p. 24.
3. John Horejsi, Thomas Walz, and Patrick Connolly, *Working in Welfare: Survival Through Positive Action* (Iowa City: University of Iowa, School of Social Work, 1977), p. 13.
4. Myron E. Weiner, *Human Service Management, Analysis and Applications* (Homewood, Ill.: Dorsey Press, 1982), p. 7.
5. Felice Perlmutter and Simon Slavin, eds., *Leadership in Social Administration: Perspectives for the 1980's* (Philadelphia: Temple University Press, 1981), p. 11.
6. Stephen P. Robbins, *The Administrative Process* (Englewood Cliffs, N.J.: Prentice-Hall, 1981), p. 34.
7. Herbert May and Bruce Metzger, eds., *The New Oxford Annotated Bible* (New York: Oxford University Press, 1973), Book of Exodus, chapters 14–40.
8. Ibid., Exodus 18:13–27.
9. Stephen L. White, *Managing Health and Human Service Programs: A Guide for Managers* (New York: Free Press, 1981), p. 17.
10. Harleigh Trecker, *Social Work Administration Principles and Practices* (New York: Association Press, 1977).
11. Margaret Elbow, "On Becoming an Executive Director," *Social Casework* 9 (1975): 526–530. An interesting account of the experiences of a social worker being promoted to head the agency in which she worked.
12. *Statistics, Social Work Education in the United States*, Council on Social Work Education, 1983.
13. For a listing of special opportunities for training see Perlmutter and Slavin, *Leadership*, p. 139–144.
14. Murray L. Gruber, ed., *Management Systems in the Human Services* (Philadelphia: Temple University Press, 1981), p. 236.
15. Patti, Rino J., "Advancing Administration in Social Work: Two Views," *Administration in Social Work* 10, no. 3 (Fall 1986): 26.
16. Powell, David E., "Managing Organizational Problems, in Alternative Service Organizations," *Administration in Social Work* 10, no. 3 (Fall 1986): 57.

ADDITIONAL SUGGESTED READINGS

Bennett, A. C., "Administrators Must Share Power with Frustrated Middle Managers," *Modern Healthcare* 11, no. 10 (1981): 126, 128.
Clifton, Robert, and Alan Dahms, *Grassroots Administration* (Monterey, Calif.: Brooks/Cole Publishing Co., 1980).
Cohn, H. M., "The Executive as Integrator," *Child Welfare* 62, no. 3 (1983): 221–223.

Limburg, D.J., "The Executive in a Period of Change," *Child Welfare* 62, no. 3 (1983): 225–231.

Lowry, L., "Social Work Supervision: From Models Toward Theory," *Journal of Education for Social Work* 19, no. 2 (1983): 55–62.

Reamer, F. G., "Social Services in a Conservative Era," *Social Casework* 64, no. 3 (1983): 451–458.

Resnick, Herman, and Rino Patti, eds., *Change from Within: Humanizing Social Welfare Organizations* (Philadelphia: Temple University Press, 1980); Chapter 1 has an excellent overview of a pattern through which all staff in an organization can participate in keeping the organization dynamic and in tune with the changing needs of the community.

Sarri, Rosemary C., "Management Trends in the Human Services in the 1980's," *Administration in Social Work* 6, nos. 2 and 3 (Summer–Fall 1982).

Atkins, Jacqueline M., and Kenneth R. Greenhall, eds. *Encyclopedia of Social Work*, 18th ed. (Silver Spring, Md.: NASW, 1987). Specifically the following articles:

"Administration in Social Welfare," 1: 27–40

"Administration: Environmental Aspects," 1:8–17

"Administration: Interpersonal Aspects," 1:17–27

"Information Utilization for Management Decision Making," 1:937–944

"Citizen Participation," 1:275–280

"Community-Based Social Action," 1:292–299

"Organizations: Impact on Employees and Community," 2:217–228

"Program Evaluation," 2:366–379

"Supervision in Social Work," 2:748–756

"Macro Practice: Current Trends and Issues," 2:82–89

"Social Planning," 2:593–602

"Social Planning and Community Organization," 2:602–619

Weinbach, Robert W., "Implementing Change: Insights and Strategies for the Supervisor," *Social Work* 29, no. 3 (May–June 1984): 282–286.

20 Social Work Research

John L. Craft

Social work practice involves decision making, as does the process of making social policy. Quality decision making requires that judgments be formed on the basis of sound information. Social work research is concerned with the systematic collection, analysis, and interpretation of information for input into the decision-making process. Social work research can be considered a tool to aid the practitioner and policymaker in making the best informed decision(s) possible. The methods of social work research guide the production of practice-relevant information; the methods of social work practice determine how the information is used.

There has been a marked increase in interest in and support for social work research in recent years. This growth is evident in the continued support of social agencies for research concerned with improving service effectiveness and/or the efficiency of service delivery systems. Social work research reports have increased in both number and diversity in social work–related journals. Increased commitment by the profession and educational institutions is indicated by the recent emergence of a large number of university-based social work research centers.[1] In recent years there has been a marked improvement in the quantity and quality of social work research and a growing interest in research on the part of practitioners and students (some of whom become practitioners, of course).

Social work research, like all social research, is carried out to obtain information pertinent to the endeavors of description, explanation, and prediction.[2]

Description.   The purpose of descriptive social (and social work) research is to depict the subject(s) under study accurately. This exploratory phase of research is used to describe phenomena in detail, to describe *what* happened or *where* something happens. This is in contrast to the *explanatory* phase of social research which attempts to explain a phenomenon by specifying why or how it happened.[3]

For example, before trying to explain why children are abused, we may want to ascertain how many children are abused, what the ages of these children are, what kind of family situation these children come from, who the perpetrators are, and so on. Once we have a reasonable understanding of the characteristics of abused children and their families, we can then proceed to our next phase of knowledge building, that of explanation.

Explanation.   Providing an explanation for a given phenomenon involves specifying its causes. *Why* are reports of child abuse increasing? *How* do stress and low self-esteem relate to a person's tendency to be abusive? *What* factors affect caseworkers' decisions in foster care cases? We must bear in mind that the answers to these questions are not simple and complete at this time. Research skills enable us systematically to search for and validate these and the multitude of other relationships that exist in the social work practice arena.

Prediction.   Once we have adequately described and provided at least tentative explanations for a phenomenon, we can then use this information in an attempt to forecast or predict future instances of the phenomenon. The better job we have done in cause finding, the better job we can do in predicting. For example, if through our research efforts we can clearly establish how a variety of environmental and individual characteristics are related to abusive behavior, then we may be able to do a reasonable job in predicting the occurrence of this behavior, given a particular set of circumstances. It should be clear that strengthening our ability to be better forecasters strengthens our ability to do better social work of a preventative nature. We can then use this information to design or redesign an appropriate service for dealing with the problem.

Describing, explaining, and predicting phenomena related to social work practice and policy are not merely knowledge-building activities carried out for knowledge building's sake. Social work practice involves intervention strategies applied at various levels of social systems; that is individual, family, group, and institutional. The primary goal of social work research is the improvement of social work practice and policy. Our increased knowledge about human behavior, social processes, and social systems enables the social worker practitioner to apply intervention strategies more adequately in order to ameliorate some of the problems facing our society.

A HISTORICAL PERSPECTIVE

Social work and social welfare research has been in existence the full span of organized social work in the United States—over a hundred years. Research in social work was not differentiated from other social research for several decades.[4] Not until the 1930s was the umbilical cord between research in social work and that in sociology cut.[5] In a chronology of the development of social work research, Zimbalist notes that over the years the differentiation between the two fields of research has been made on the basis of auspices and functions of the research.[6] He notes that the more useful and meaningful criterion is the function of the research, that is, the "production of knowledge that can be utilized in planning and carrying out social work programs."[7]

Zimbalist contends that a 1948 workshop on "Research in Social Work" may have served to launch the modern era in social work research by bringing together leading social work researchers around the major issues of that time.[8] The workshop spawned the first formal structure within which social work researchers could carry out common interests. This was the Social Work Research Group, which in 1951 stated a definition of social work research as "research of the type that is or should be carried on under social work auspices and which deals directly with the materials of social work—its concepts, operation, personnel, and clientele."[9]

Mary E. Macdonald sharpened this functional definition in 1960 and stated, "Social work research begins with practical problems, and its objective is to produce knowledge that can be put to use in planning and carrying out social work programs."[10] Thus, we do social work research by concentrating on those things that social workers do. Macdonald further states that this knowledge may range widely from highly specific factual information to information of very general nature and should be in a form that is communicable and verifiable.[11] In her conception, social work research involves both general theory building and finding solutions to applied problems. This approach to the research enterprise is still valid today, although it can be argued that emphasis is still placed more on "applied" research than on more theoretical, basic research.

Social work research has involved investigation of a plethora of problems over the years of its existence. Zimbalist has identified and analyzed several major themes or emphases in research interest and activity over the years:

1. research on the causes of poverty
2. research of the prevalence of poverty
3. the social survey movement
4. quantification and indexes in social work
5. evaluative research on social service effectiveness
6. study of the multiproblem family[12]

While the research pursuits on poverty have been largely given up to other disciplines such as economics, the others are still viable and active areas of research interest today. In addition, there is increased emphasis on issues and problems involving children, families, the elderly, and minorities.

SOCIAL WORK RESEARCH METHODS

Social work practitioners (including researchers) use a variety of information generated within the discipline itself, other helping professions such as psychiatry, and the social sciences. There is a growing concern that the profession increase its own research capacity and capabilities rather than relegating these activities to other groups.[13] There is increased emphasis being placed on social workers *producing* research-based information as well as using research-based information.

The research conducted in social work can be characterized by its diversity in both methods used and the investigators who use them. Other disciplines such as sociology and psychology typically rely on one general method for carrying out their inquiries. Social work research, however, is noted for its eclectic nature in choosing a method or methods to investigate a particular problem. As Fanshel states:

> No single methodological approach to the conduct of social work research is adequate; the needs of the profession dictate that a pluralism prevails. Scholars' willingness to live with differences in investigative procedures will create the best yield for social work.[14]

Some of the many research methods used by social work research are surveys, experiments, single-subject studies, case studies, naturalistic observation, and document research. This rich diversity of methodologies applicable to social work research requires that students and practitioner/researchers become facile in using these methods and interpreting results obtained from using them. This places an added burden in the training of social workers to consume and produce research relevant to social work practice and policy.

The Research Process

Doing social work research involves carrying out several interrelated steps of the research process. It should be pointed out that the decision of what to study is not made in a vacuum, nor are other research process decisions. Research decisions are influenced by community sanctions, professional norms, ethical considerations, the sponsor of the research, and so forth.[15]

Social work practitioners are generally not accustomed to the notion that knowledge of and application of social work research methods can be useful to their work. This conception has been fostered by the view that social work research and social work practice are antagonistic pursuits carried out for different purposes. However, if one conceives of both social work practice and social work research as problem-solving approaches, then the two processes can be seen as involving analogous components.[16]

Since our focus in this chapter is on social work research as an important practice-related tool, it is important to note the similarities between the components of practice and research. The interrelated components of the problem-solving practice approach are assessment, formulation of intervention plans, implementation of intervention, evaluation of program, and termination. The components of the process of research are problem formulation, research strategy and sampling, implementation of research strategy and data collection, analyses of data, and data interpretation and conclusions. Tripodi presents a framework for comparing the two processes. The following discussion is based in part on his analysis.[17]

Assessment and *problem formulation* focus on specifying problems that need to be solved. These first steps in practice and research are similar in that concepts must be specified and defined, related information is obtained and used to articulate the problem, and a set of questions or hypotheses are derived. Both are asking, "Exactly what is it we are trying to find out and why?" The next step is deciding what to do to answer the identified question(s).

The practitioner selects and *formulates intervention* plans based on knowledge of similar problems and situations and the particular problems identified in the assessment stage. The researcher *selects a research strategy* considered to be appropriate and feasible for providing reliable and valid information relevant to the identified problem. Thus we see that both practitioners and researchers devise strategies for solving the problems they have identified. In general, in a practice situation one has to be more flexible in choosing strategies, and usually two or more strategies must be considered.

The next phase of these problem-solving approaches is to carry out the research/intervention strategies and make observations, that is, collect data. Both practitioners and researchers are collectors of information. Both collect quantitative as well as qualitative data. Both use similar sources of their information: case files, other agency-related data, community surveys, client interviews, and so forth. One major difference is the scope of the utility of the obtained information. Practitioners are first of all interested in information directly relevant to their immediate practice situation. However, social work researchers, while also interested in the direct applicability of their obtained data, are very much concerned with collecting data in such a manner that generalizations are possible beyond the situation in which their research was carried out. In addition, social work researchers typically collect more extensive data over longer periods of time.

The social work practitioner must next form a judgment about whether or not the selected intervention plan is workable. This evaluation of program is necessary to determine if an alternate strategy should be used, client contact should be terminated, or perhaps a referral to another agency should be made. These evaluations are based on the data (observations) collected by the practitioners during the course of the implementation of the interventions. The researcher analyzes data (observations) collected during the implementation of a particular strategy. While the researcher is more likely to use statistical types of data analysis, the practitioner can and does use this type of analysis to a limited extent.

Both the researcher and the practitioner then interpret their respective data and reach conclusions. These interpretations and conclusions are then potentially used in continued practice interventions or research endeavors.

This discussion has highlighted some of the similarities between problem-solving social work practice models and social work research. A discussion like this might lead one to conclude that these processes, though similar, are necessarily carried out in an independent fashion by different professionals. Nothing could be further from the truth. The social work practitioner today is becoming more sophisticated not only in using the findings of research studies (done by others) but also in conducting research in their own practice setting. As the relationship between research and practice becomes more clearly defined, the separation of the two activities becomes less visible.

Who Does Social Work Research?

As the preceding discussion has indicated, social work research is being done more and more by practitioners as well as those traditionally garbed in clothes of the "researcher." University-based research has grown over several decades and has increased our knowledge base in the form of books, monographs, articles, BSW and MSW research projects and theses, and doctoral dissertations. These research activities are conducted by both faculty and students. Some of the research done in the academic setting is directly related to practice concerns and some only in a tangential manner. The image of schools of social work as "nonacademic" schools is changing gradually to include the characteristics of a community of scholars whose purpose is to expand the knowledge base upon which the profession bases its existence.

University researchers (including students) often work hand in hand with caseworkers, supervisors, planners, and administrators within agency settings in investigating and obtaining solutions to both short-range and long-range problems faced by these practicing professionals. These cooperative efforts are important, as they serve to close even further the artificial gap that has existed between practice and research.

A great deal of what we consider as social work research is carried out in the practice setting by practitioners themselves. These information-gathering and analyzing activities are often applied in nature and sometimes limited in scope. Others are more extensive investigations either in terms of time and effort invested in the study or in terms of the particular research design and data analysis techniques employed. An example of the latter approach is a study involving an eleven-year-old boy in a residential treatment center for emotionally disturbed children.[18] The study illustrates the use of what is called the "practitioner-research" form of social work research. This kind of research involves (1) generating a set of principles relating to the interaction between worker and client, (2) systematically investigating these principles, and (3) using research techniques to test these principles as they are used in the interaction between worker and client.[19] In this research, then, the practitioner is the researcher, and research techniques are adapted to the problem. The investigator in this study first examined the client's aggressive and destructive behavior, his response to the client's behavior, and the client's response in turn to his response. The investigator then tested a proposition that limit-setting would help control these acting out behaviors and found support for this hypothesis. The type of research design used in this study is termed a single-subject design and relies on observations made of behavior of individual subjects. There is increased emphasis on the use of the single-subject design and its variants by social workers for the expressed purpose of assessing their own practice behavior and skill development. This includes social workers from the individual casework level to administrators of large agencies. Systematic self-reflection and analysis are considered necessary ingredients for the continual improvement of one's own practice.

The following is a brief description of a research enterprise that directly concerns caseworkers and agency administrators.[20] The research setting is an agency that provides intensive, in-home treatment to troubled families. The research process involves workers and families determining a set of problems (called tracks) that need to be solved by working with the family. Over the course of treatment (usually several weeks), the worker systematically records progress on each identified problem and notes the particular mode of treatment or therapy used to work on a particular problem. Each worker records this service data for each family. After a period of time these data are aggregated and analyzed to see which and how many problems are either being solved or reduced in severity over a given length of time. In addition, which treatments are most effective for certain problems is determined. Service recording systems of this type provide a rich source of information for practice-related decisions and for administrative decision making, as well as for basic knowledge building.

Another study illustrates one type of social work research carried out in a university setting by social work faculty and students.[21] The subjects for the study were child protective service workers employed by a state department of social services. These workers have the responsibility to investigate suspected cases of physical abuse, sexual abuse, and/or neglect of children. At some point in their investigation, they must decide what disposition of the case to recommend. Their primary choices are to drop the case, to offer voluntary services, or to file a petition for some sort of court action. The court action itself can be for mandated services, removal of the child, or in some cases, criminal proceedings. What information does the worker use to make these difficult decisions? This study used an experimental design to investigate the relative importance of several factors thought to influence a worker's decision to recommend court action in cases involving physical injury. The factors studied were severity of the injury, whether or not there had been a previous report, the reaction of the parent to the worker, and the consistency of the explanation regarding nature and location of injury. The findings revealed that the first two of these factors had a more pronounced effect on decisions to recommend court actions. Another important finding was a substantial disagreement among workers as to the appropriate disposition of certain types of cases. One potential impact of research of this kind is in development of training programs for child protective service workers. A goal of such training could be to clarify decision-making criteria in child abuse cases. This in turn should produce more uniformity and equity in the way these cases are investigated, serviced, and terminated.

The preceding examples of social work research were conducted in different settings using differing research strategies. However, all were concerned with the same objective, designing of appropriate research to produce sound information for improved service delivery. What knowledge and skills must be acquired in order for social workers to be capable of utilizing and producing research?

Most research training for social workers begins with an undergraduate course or two in research methods. Such a course includes general research methods such as experimental and quasi-experimental design, survey research, naturalistic observation, document research, single-subject research, and case study approaches. Sampling strategies and techniques are also typically covered. Some programs expose students to statistical analyses and computerized data-processing techniques. Increased use of computers in social service agencies, especially micro or personal computers, and the use of packaged statistical analysis programs enable social workers to process and analyze large sets of data without having to have a degree in computer science. Students also find computers very beneficial for word processing for class papers and reports. The tools of research are becoming easier and easier to use.

Students also learn to design questionnaires and interview schedules and develop new measurement devices. In addition, most courses have the student design a research project on a topic of interest. In some cases, the projects are completed and a research report written. Then, by the end of the first course in research, the student is somewhat proficient at reading and evaluating research studies and perhaps even at conducting a study.

Graduate problem courses are intended to build upon the first course(s) and further hone the skills of the researcher in social work. Often, courses provide more in-depth treatment of topics covered in the first course(s) as well as providing coverage of additional research-related topics. Topical coverage of such areas as operational research and program evaluation are found in many graduate programs. Upon completion of a graduate program, it is expected that the social work student is much more adept at *producing* research as well as *consuming* research of others.

Finally, research training and experience is increased by on-the-job experience in the field. Inservice programs and professional seminars on research-related topics are becoming more frequent.

Learning to do social work research involves the acquisition of a somewhat unique set of skills. We learn best by doing, so we learn to do research by doing research. And most students, after having completed a piece of research, contend that they found it fun to do and felt a profound sense of accomplishment.

SUMMARY AND CONCLUSIONS

This chapter is based on the premise that social work practice involves continual decision making and that research skills are an important and integral part of social work practice. It is further contended that the artificial schism between practice and research serves no useful purpose and is not a true reflection of the practice arena. Social workers are curious people and have an investigative bent. Sometimes the playing of hunches or reacting on the basis of limited information is appropriate and necessary; some questions require answers derived by intuition. But at other times social workers need to have consistent, reliable answers to questions that can be generalized beyond the immediate situation. To do this means we must apply a more systematic, rigorous approach to our inquiries and information-gathering activities. In this way in the long run we will increase our knowledge base and thus provide better services to our clients.

NOTES

1. Richard J. Estes, "Social Work Research Centers," *Social Work Research and Abstracts* 15, no. 2 (Summer 1979); 3–16.
2. Susan Philliber, Mary Schwab, and G. Sam Sloss, *Social Research: Guides to a Decision Making Process* (Itasca, Ill.: F. E. Peacock, 1980), pp. 8–9.
3. Kenneth D. Bailey, *Methods of Social Research* (New York: Free Press, 1978), p. 32.
4. Sidney E. Zimbalist, *Historic Themes and Landmarks in Social Welfare Research* (New York: Harper & Row, 1977), p. 6.
5. Ibid., p. 21.
6. Ibid.
7. Ibid., p. 24.
8. Ibid., p. 22.
9. Ibid., p. 23.

10. Mary E. Macdonald, "Social Work Research: A Perspective," in Norman A. Polansky, *Social Work Research* (Chicago: University of Chicago Press, 1960), p. 1.
11. Ibid., p. 2.
12. Zimbalist, *Historic Themes*, p. 8.
13. David Fanshel, "The Future of Social Work Research: Strategies for the Coming Years," in David Fanshel, *Future in Social Work Research* (Washington, D.C.: NASW, 1980), p. 7.
14. Ibid., p. 8.
15. Tony Tripodi, *Uses and Abuses of Social Research in Social Work* (New York: Columbia University Press, 1974), p. 11.
16. Ibid., p. 123.
17. Ibid.
18. Neal Broxmeyer, "Practitioner-Research in Treating a Borderline Child," *Social Work Research and Abstracts* 14, no. 4 (Winter 1978): 5–10.
19. Ibid., p. 5.
20. Michael Ryan, "Flexible Input—Response Service Tracking" (Manuscript, Families, Inc., West Branch, Iowa, 1981).
21. John L. Craft, Stephen W. Epley, and Cheryl A. Clarkson, "Factors Influencing Legal Disposition in Child Abuse Investigations," *Journal of Social Service Research* 4, no. 1 (Fall 1980): 31–46.

ADDITIONAL SUGGESTED READINGS

Babbie, Earl R., *Survey Research Methods*, 3rd ed. (Belmont, Calif.: Wadsworth, 1983).

Craft, John L., *Statistics and Data Analysis for Social Workers*, 2nd ed. (Itasca, Ill.: F. E. Peacock, 1989).

Grinnell, Richard, *Social Work Research and Evaluation*, 3rd ed. (Itasca, Ill.: F. E. Peacock, 1988).

Kerlinger, Fred N., *Foundation of Behavioral Research*, 2nd ed. (New York: Holt, Rinehart & Winston, 1973).

Mass, Henry S., ed., *Social Service Research: Reviews of Studies* (Washington, D.C.: NASW, 1978).

Mayer, Robert R., and Ernest Greenwood, *The Design of Social Policy Research* (Englewood Cliffs, N.J.: Prentice-Hall, 1980).

Miller, Delbert C., *Handbook of Research Design and Social Measurement*, 4th ed. (New York: McKay, 1983).

Tripodi, Tom, and Irwin Epstein, *Research Techniques for Clinical Social Workers* (New York: Columbia University Press, 1980).

Part Four

Special Groups, Issues, and Trends

W e approach the final section of this book having come a consider-able distance. We have covered background information, the major so-cial service settings and the social problems to which they relate as well as some nontraditional settings, and the principal social work practice methods including some innovative approaches.

In the remaining section we take up a few special considerations and trends such as human diversity and oppression, women's issues, and housing, a basic human need but not a large area of employment for social workers until now.

We examine a special newer focus in the human services termed so-cial development that has particular significance internationally. We also discuss the subject of educational preparation of social service personnel and their organization and professionalization in the field. Finally, we conclude with a chapter on the future that projects beyond the reach of most such commentary and leads us to look ahead, just as early in the text we looked back historically.

21 Human Diversity and Oppression

Gary R. Lowe

> Our son grew up with a Siamese cat and when he was about three the only other cat in his limited world was also Siamese. Both had blue eyes, like all their breed. One day he saw a Persian cat padding toward him, and in the manner of three-year-olds he squatted down on the sidewalk to get a better look. The Persian also sat, wrapped her tail around her feet and regarded the boy. Suddenly he jumped up and ran into the house shouting, "I saw a cat with yellow eyes, Mommy! A cat with yellow eyes!"
>
> In the moment when our small son and the Persian cat were face to face, two things had occurred to the boy: he became aware that all cats do not have blue eyes and he also became aware that until that moment he had believed that they did![1]

The discovery that all the world is not Siamese cats with blue eyes is the boy's first step toward encountering diversity on a larger scale. The cat incident puts the experience into nonthreatening form with the boy and cat assumed neutral toward each other, but encounters between humans may involve more complex attitudes.

This benign childhood experience exemplifies a discovery: an experience of diversity. The account of this incident of discovering diversity does not tell what the child did with the new insight. However, when we are confronted with difference, whether it be skin color, language, ethnicity, or sexual orientation, we all too often reject the difference and quickly assume a judgmental perspective. That is, rather than first attempting to understand the "difference," people react and begin to judge, usually concluding that the one who is different is "wrong" or "inferior." With this perspective in mind, the question presents itself: Is it the same with our own collective selves, that is, communities and society in general?

The term diversity is an encompassing idea meaning difference and variety. As a word, it has a generally positive, or at least neutral, connotation. Diversity is a quality of the United States, and with our societal milieu of space, relative abundance, and mobility, opportunities for experiencing diversity abound. Further, noting the U.S. historical experience of emerging from the gathering of peoples from all over the globe, diversity is supported in census data and the existence of numerous ethnic/cultural and racial communities within the United States. But related to these facts is the issue of the nation's subjective and social experience within this milieu of diversity: Is the United States really what its national slogan asserts, "*E Pluribus Unum*"— From Many, One?

THE CHALLENGE OF DIVERSITY

Diversity is at the very heart of social work as an activity. Social work and its representatives are most often found at those points in our society where differences have created stress. This chapter will address the reality of diversity as it takes various forms in our current society, from racial/ethnic issues to the more recent challenges such as those of sexual orientations. We will not treat diversity as a wonderful word of optimism but as a difficult challenge that grows each day in our society. We will also try to look at diversity as it represents a challenge to the reader as a would-be social worker or student of social work.

> Man [sic] who lives in a world of hazards is compelled to seek security. Perfect certainty is what man wants.[2]

While Dewey's words were a preface to a discussion of the historical separation within philosophy of fact and experience, they are also cogent for our discussion of diversity and social work. Diversity in the United States is a source of stress; it is a reality with hazards. When it clashes with our need for security and certainty, the pluralism of our society becomes an area of crucial social concern.

William L. O'Neill, in his informal history of the United States during the 1960s titled *Coming Apart*, sets the theme echoed in his title by observing that during the decade of the 1960s, "A feeling grew that events were slipping out of control."[3] The decade of the 1960s stands as a period when societal strains emerged, first in the area of the civil rights struggles, initially in the South, and by the later years of the decade spreading throughout the nation. But the issue of diversity and its challenge emerged in the United States long before that. A brief historical look is necessary, focusing primarily on the areas of race/ethnicity in order to set the stage. Later, we will return to a contemporary example of diversity as manifested in the area of sexual orientation.

Due to limitations of space, we will use the term *ethnic group* to cover *racial groups* as well. Though there is a distinction between the two, we will follow the reduction developed by Luhman and Gilman in their book *Race and Ethnic Relations: The Social and Political Experience of Minority Groups*:

> We shall employ the term "ethnic group" in a general sense to cover those groups now defined as "racial groups." . . . we find that groups of people who are said to differ racially invariably also differ ethnically from whoever is doing the labeling. Thus, racial groups are also ethnic groups. This is true for a remarkably simple reason. The term race is usually used to justify doing something unpleasant to someone else.[4]

A Brief History: It Didn't All Start Yesterday

In 1619, the first Africans were brought to Virginia as servants; that is, these Africans filled roles as indentured servants, gaining their freedom after a specific term of service, a tradition well established by other immigrants.[5] In less than fifty years, the Africans' circumstances changed from that of the relatively benign state of servant to one of legalized chattel slavery. By the time of the American Revolution, greatly diverse populations including Scotch-Irish, Germans, Huguenots, Jews, and Scandinavians had been established in the young country, and within this diversity a significant pattern of stratification was also developing, following ethnic lines. There were also native populations that were either pushed west or still negotiating coexistence through open fighting or other less violent means.

Prior to the mid-nineteenth-century cataclysm of the Civil War, the nation expanded and filled the "unlimited" spaces west from the Atlantic. While the flow of English immigrants continued, the African population was still bound in virulent slavery, and Native Americans were being steadily pushed west of the Mississippi. Also, during the first half of the nineteenth century, Catholic Irish began to arrive in the United States as a result of the Irish potato famine. The immigration reached its peak between 1846–1850.[6]

During the first fifty years of the nineteenth century signs began to appear of a growing perspective and sensitivity toward numerous elements of the ever-complex society. Dorothea Dix, the Rev. Thomas H.

Gallaudet, and Dr. Samuel Gridley Howe were but three from this period who began to speak to the national community's need to serve those who were different. In 1843, Dix documented and presented her findings showing the deplorable conditions in which the insane were kept. Dr. Gallaudet and Dr. Howe between 1815 and 1831 addressed the need to serve and educate the deaf and the blind respectively. Allied with these initial efforts toward such special populations was an emerging pressure, particularly outside the South, toward ending the institution of slavery.[7]

The American Civil War tragically bisects the nineteenth century. Numerous interpretations of how this conflict erupted fill graduate and undergraduate history classes. Aside from all the economic, political, and agricultural interpretations, the inescapable fact of slavery always asserts itself. It is not accidental that the accepted and relatively humane custom of indentured servants which began with Scotch-Irish immigrants should take an ugly twist to chattel slavery for Africans. Africans were different: linguistically, socially, and in pigmentation. The institution of chattel slavery can be traced to an institution designed to serve a particular set of economic-agricultural-geographical factors. The practice of chattel slavery institutionalized the inherent fear of difference; this fear would grow during the latter half of the nineteenth century and continues to the present. One should not overlook the accompanying factor of regional difference as a source of stress contributing to the Civil War. Even today, one can identify strong regional loyalties and attitudes that exist in the North, the South, and more recently the West.

Following the Civil War, the internal politics of the country were dominated by the arrival of the Industrial Revolution and its need for cheap labor, as well as the surge to the West and the Indian wars, supported by government policy, to assure the opening of the lands west of the Mississippi River. These often genocidal wars against Native Americans emerged as the legacy of the Civil War. Within this very complex internal history of the pain of growing awareness of our true differences was the introduction of yet another community into the patchwork of the still-emerging national society, the Mexican-American.

While internally the nation was exploding, the historical trend of the immigrant influx continued, though by the 1900s the pattern had significantly shifted. In the eastern United States the immigrant sources shifted from northwestern European to southeastern Europe, primarily Italians and East European Jews. The new immigrants were Europeans that were ethnically, linguistically, and religiously distinct from the earlier European immigrants. The still-settling West witnessed the arrival of first the Chinese and later Japanese.[8] The new waves of immigrants were also ethnically, linguistically, and religiously distinct from the earlier immigrants. They became a transitional group between the early "majority" groups and the "minority" native elements and the special group of African descendants.

With the coming of the twentieth century, the still-forming society rapidly expanded. Seeds of internal stress, pain, and possibly revolution would symptomatically appear, like a worrisome fever, from 1900 until the 1950s. Hindsight reveals the blithe unconsciousness of our society to the challenges of its own complexity. Just as the authors of the Declaration of Independence and framers of the Constitution, reflecting eighteenth-century attitudes, could simultaneously be slave owners, the nation could also enter the twentieth century deluding itself that utopia was, if not realized, then certainly close at hand. A crucial detail in all of this was overlooked by many Americans at the turn of the century as Henry Steele Commager points out in his classic, *The American Mind*:

> Nothing in all history had ever succeeded like America, and every American knew it. Nowhere else on the globe had nature been at once so rich and so generous, and her riches were available to all who had the enterprise to take them and *the good fortune to be white*.[9] (Italics added.)

The root of America had been diversity. The dawn of the twentieth century witnessed the emergence of large urban centers and the closing of the western frontier. With the new European immigration of non-English, white, Anglo-Saxon Protestants (WASPS) as labor for the rapidly emerging factories, the new century began with yet-to-be-understood dynamics of reaction to difference that were to reach into the second half of the century.

Commager effectively speaks to the evolution of the ambivalence toward diversity that marked the mid-twentieth-century America and the onset of the conservative/reactionary tendency to look to the past rather than to the future:

> As [the] mid-twentieth-century American was less zealous for the future, he [sic] became more concerned with the past, he seemed more conscious of his own history than at any time since the Civil War and, after a brief interval of cynicism and disillusionment in the decade of the twenties, found more satisfaction in its contemplation. . . . The tendency to trust the past rather than the future and the familiar rather than the original reflected an instinct for conformity. The new intolerance was distinguished not only by its quasi-official character but by a certain moral flabbiness. The intolerance of the thirties and the forties had not even the dignity of intelligence or accuracy, or of a moral purpose. Intolerance was displayed most aggressively in the realm of race relations. Intolerance sprang not only from insecurity but from mounting, though still hesitant, class consciousness.[10]

Nawrocki Stock Photo/Jeffry W. Myers

A school class with ethnic and social diversity. The school is an important means of socialization. These children are growing up with the idea of diversity.

Commager leaves his discussion and description with still-to-be-answered questions. With the perspective of four decades of hindsight, it is both impressive and frightening how his profile has emerged as a challenge facing America in the second half of the twentieth century.

The Melting Pot?

My grandparents, I am sure, never guessed what it would cost them and their children to become "Americanized." They were injured, to be sure, by nativist American prejudices against foreigners, by a white Anglo-Saxon Protestant culture and even by an Irish church. (Any Catholic church not otherwise specified by nationality they experienced and described as the Irish church). What price is exacted by America when into its maw it sucks other cultures of the world and processes them? What do people have to lose before they can qualify as true Americans?[11]

The explosion of the "melting pot" myth is perhaps the most significant communal/cultural legacy of the domestic change during the 1950s and 1960s. The United States was a unique place in its history and its heterogeneous formation. This heterogeneity created the need to absorb members into, or define others out of, the boundary of acceptable community membership. In order for this inclusion/ exclusion process to occur, a common definition was needed. This historical process was the dynamic to which Michael Novak alluded. The supporting ideology became the "melting pot" myth.

American histories available in public education prior to the mid-1960s developed and perpetuated the myth that the twentieth-century national sociological experience of the United States had been the melting pot: the melding together of great diverse peoples from around the globe into a new, unique identity group. Accompanying this idea was the dogma that here in the United States all people were transformed by the abundance of wealth, space, and opportunity, and the ambience of justice and egalitarianism. This was the stuff of the popular myth.

Now, either because of an increasing national maturity or simply because the passage of time gives greater clarity, the underlying reality of this "melting pot" has emerged. During the first half of the twentieth century, lynchings of black Americans and open oppression by such groups as the Ku Klux Klan in the South were fact. In the northern industrial cities, the creation of racial, ethnic, and religious ghettos effectively isolated southern Europeans, Jews, and southern blacks. In the still-growing West, the Mexican-American, Chinese, and Native Americans all experienced something in the social realm not totally consistent with the promise of the melting pot.

Jane Addams emerged in the first half of this century as a giant figure who attempted to capture both the uniqueness and excitement of the diversity while also trying to create a new national American character resilient enough to encompass the widest possible spectrum. Her work in Chicago and the entire settlement movement in urban American was an effort, not to level the heterogeneity of this still new society to a mediocre sameness, but to integrate the diversity while still creating a new national community.

Juxtaposed against this mighty and subtle effort at nation building were such events as the Palmer raids (1920) against so-called radicals, communists, and aliens.[12] The infamous Palmer raids seem to represent a crucial beginning of a period of hysteria against those who seemed too different, those who were not WASPS.

The underlying causes of the Palmer raids were growing political and industrial unrest as the cracks in the "promised land" began to appear. The rhetoric surrounding the Palmer raids, identifying "outside agitators" and unsavory aliens and bolsheviks, was to become a familiar theme of justification for reaction and oppression of those seen as different. Explicit in this rhetoric was the ethnocentrism and fear of difference that still accompanies outbreaks of genuine societal conflict and tension.

Individuals often have difficulty responding to large amounts of stimuli, so it seems logical that societies might also exhibit a similar problem. Diversity creates the need for an individual or a community to work diligently to understand and then work even harder to accept, or simply accommodate, the new understanding. Perhaps the numerous explosions in this society during the current century are proof that the myth of unity and homogeneity is just that, a myth, but they may also be a signal that growth may well emerge.

Currently, it would seem that the United States has outgrown the practice of overtly destroying its diversity in the way Novak describes. A current attitude toward diversity is described by James Oliver Robertson in his book, *American Myth, American Reality*:

> For Americans today, the ideal of the melting pot and the belief that it was working seem to be part of the past. The ideal still lives in the vision of a homogenous community, but more and more Americans now agree . . . that it is not unity which explains urban life or makes its realities but rather the ethnic groups with all their differences.[13]

The Facts

Diversity, as we have pointed out so far, is a social variable of great significance with a major impact on the nation; it encompasses an individual's daily life as well as a massive process such as taking the national census. Each decade the nation counts its population. The task of census tasking, straightforward enough in theory, becomes complex when one is counting a richly mixed society. A brief look at the 1980 census offers a case in point of diversity as a variable. Beyond counting the population, the census process also needs to identify whom the population represents. In this latter dimension, the census often becomes a combined political, sociological, and generally subjective process.

The 1980 census form, item no. 4, contained a "race question." (See Figure 21-1.) In Figure 21-1 notice the absence of a category for Spanish origin. In the 1980 census, in order to be identified as "Spanish origin," the respondent had to check "Other" and then fill in the particular identity in the blank space, for example, "Mexican, Latino, Venezuelan."[14] Reflecting upon the power of ethnic identity, one might be able to appreciate that this extra step could easily be seen as a "slight" or given some other negative connotation. However, in the 1970 census, if a respondent checked "Other" and filled in a Spanish-origin designation, the procedure for tabulation almost always placed the person into the "White" category.[15] Therefore, not only did the

---

The Population by States: 1980

(Facsimile of questionnaire item 4.)

| **4.** Is this person —

(Fill one circle) | ○ White
○ Black or Negro
○ Japanese
○ Chinese
○ Filipino
○ Korean
○ Vietnamese
○ Indian (Amer.)
    Print
    tribe ⟶ _____ | ○ Asian Indian
○ Hawaiian
○ Guamanian
○ Samoan
○ Eskimo
○ Aleut
○ Other — Specify ↘ |

Instructions to the respondent for questionnaire item 4.

> **4.** Fill the circle for the category with which the person most closely identifies. If you fill the Indian (American) or Other circle, be sure to print the name of the specific Indian tribe or specific group.

Figure 21.1   1980 Census Form
Source: U.S. Department of Commerce, Bureau of the Census, "Race and the Population by States: 1980," PC80-S1-3, Supplementary Reports, issued July 1981, p. 5.

process deny a portion of the population its ethnic identity; in effect it also defined them out of existence. Since 1970, there has been a growth in the Hispanic communities' political power resulting in more influence being brought to bear on numerous aspects of the nation's life. The procedural change in the 1980 census of not automatically re-classifying "Other—Spanish origin" respondents as "White" can be seen as a possible result of this new power.

Primarily, though, this example shows that the facts are not always the facts, particularly in the subjective and crucial areas of personal and group identity. The apparent factual result of the 1980 procedural change in the census has been a large proportional increase of Spanish-origin persons between 1970 to 1980 from 1 percent to 40 percent; in other words, in 1970 only 1 percent of the Spanish-origin persons remained classified as "Other," while in 1980, 40 percent were maintained in the "Other" category and not moved to "White."[16] The Spanish-origin population in the United States was real and alive in 1970, though the census did not reflect this fact. The sudden "growth" in a ten-year period turns out to be, in the final analysis, a procedural matter. Persons of Spanish origin probably do not take the matter lightly or feel neutral toward the phenomenon. This very limited look at the census hopefully provides further insight into the many nuances and challenges of racial and ethnic difference.

Within the caveats implicit in this discussion, it may be useful to cite recent U.S. Census information about the major minorities and "people of color" as these groups are now termed. These minorities constitute approximately 20 percent of the U.S. population, divided among 12 percent black, 6 percent Hispanic, and 2 percent distributed among American Indian, Asian American, and other nonwhites.[17] Recent immigrants (such as Southeast Asians, Cubans, and Haitians) are not included in these figures. It is expected that such groups will continue to increase in number more rapidly than the general population because of their younger age structure and rate of immigration.[18]

An Ambivalent Society

A cliché of growth holds that with age and maturity, one's illusions of perfection alter significantly or even slip away altogether. Such a process may result in fatalistic cynicism, or it may bring a realism that produces new growth and renewed challenge.

Now, in the latter part of the twentieth century, the United States may be facing the challenge of its maturity. Like the child discovering that all cats' eyes are not blue, the United States has, particularly since the end of World War II, discovered that as a society it is truly heterogeneous, and with this recognition of diversity has come tension and conflict. The challenge is whether U.S. society will successfully redefine *community* in a realistic way, since its earlier illusions have faded.

The current period provides us with a disturbing panorama. Refugees from Cuba and Haiti risk their lives to come to the United States; the government allows the Cubans in but turns back the Haitians. The Ku Klux Klan openly battles black Americans not only in the South but in the Northeast and Midwest.

SEXUAL ORIENTATION: LESBIAN AND GAY ISSUES

Americans have always been proud of their country as both a nation of immigrants and a home for individual liberty. But along with our recognition of diversity and individual rights, we have a strong concern for conformity.[19] Up to this point, we have focused on the more "traditional" aspects of diversity and oppression involving issues of ethnicity and race. While these areas of historical concern remain important as evidenced by incidents like Howard Beach, New York, in 1987–1988 and a resurgence during the 1980s of the Ku Klux Klan and other white supremacist groups such as those in the West, the mosaic of diversity has expanded to include other populations. One such population of current relevance for social work are those individuals and groups with different sexual orientation,[20] more specifically homosexuals (lesbian and gay).

Anthropologist Marvin Harris notes, "There is a lot of evidence that men and women acquire their aversion to homosexual sex in the course of growing up and being molded by social customs and conditions."[21] Harris cites researchers Ford and Beach who "concluded after studying the incidence of homosexuality around the world, 'Human homosexuality is not basically a product of hormonal imbalance or 'perverted' heredity. It is the product of the fundamental mammalian heritage of general sexual responsiveness as modified under the impact of experience."[22] Throughout world history, there are numerous incidents of societies and cultures in which sexual practices encompassed and even demanded homosexual relationships, for example, in ancient Greece, the Azande of southern Sudan, and the Etoro of New Guinea. Given the historical and anthropological evidence supporting the prevalence of homosexuality as a sexual orientation throughout history, Harris states that the "appropriate question to be asked about societies that instill an aversion to all forms of homosexuality and force their gays into the closet is not why homosexual behavior sometimes occurs, but why it doesn't occur more often."[23] Space limitations and the focus of this chapter do not permit a full treatment of these underlying issues, but the area of lesbian and gay issues is not simply something in vogue currently, but a long-standing issue in the overall area of social oppression.

Though now changed, as recently as the 1970s, the American Psychiatric Association's (APA) *Diagnostic and Statistical Manual of Mental Disorders* (DSM) listed homosexuality as sexually "deviant." As such, the DSM linked homosexuals with people diagnosed as perpetrators of antisocial crimes like child molestors, voyeurs, and exhibitionists. A position such as that previously held by the APA is an expression of *homophobia*, "the irrational fear of and hostility toward lesbian and gay people."[24]

In 1977, the National Association of Social Workers (NASW) supported "the right of all persons to define and express their own sexuality."[25] Further, NASW committed the social work profession to "combat[ing] archaic laws and other forms of discrimination which serve to impose something less than equal status upon the homosexually-oriented members of the human family."[26]

Sexuality is a powerful dimension of all of our lives even when being considered in the so-called "normal" aspects of social life. With the introduction of a socially and culturally defined aspect of "homophobia" into the equation, the difficulty of understanding becomes even greater. Further, the emergence of AIDS and the initial hysteria and incorrect causal linkage exclusively to the homosexual community exacerbate the challenge of prejudice and discrimination confronted by the social work profession. Our focus in this chapter has been diversity and the accompanying dynamic of oppression. Lesbian and gay issues represent the most current manifestation of these concerns. In 1981, Nancy Humphreys (NASW president in 1979–1981) articulated social work's necessary position:

> Knowledge of and sensitivity to gay and lesbian issues are a necessary part of the social worker's practice repertoire for at least three good reasons. First, gays and lesbians who receive social services from social workers are becoming an increasingly larger constituent group of the profession. Second, many social workers are gay or lesbian, some of whom are out of the closet, but quite a few of whom still choose to hide themselves in order to evade the stigma society attaches to the gay person. Third, and perhaps most importantly, gay and lesbian people represent an oppressed population, the protection of whose rights, as those of all oppressed populations, should be of primary concern to the profession of social work.[27]

Implications for Social Work

Within this social milieu of diversity and oppression, social work endeavors to find its most effective role. Social work is concerned with the individual, the larger society, and the institutions that affect its people. Prior to the mid-1960s, the social worker focused primary attention on the individual. The social upheaval of the 1960s, both national and international, forced a new awareness and challenge to social work to define its charge and responsibility. This new challenge paralleled the larger society's loss of innocence and debunking of the melting pot myth as well as the emergence of other pressing issues of diversity. By their own code of ethics, social workers are charged to be concerned with issues of diversity in a socioeconomically heterogeneous society such as ours.

SUMMARY AND CONCLUSIONS

The ultimate question that is raised by this brief chapter is the one with which Luhman and Gilman conclude their book: "How much diversity can a major industrial nation like the United States absorb and still function?"[28] This question is also one of global significance.

In countries like India, Lebanon, Australia, and South Africa one can observe the challenge of diversity. Much of their conflict has its origins in diversity and the society's ability or willingness to face these challenges. This brief discussion does not provide the opportunity to explore fully the international dimensions of diversity. Suffice it to say that in most "trouble" areas of the world, regardless of whether the presenting difficulties are economic or political, one can be fairly sure that communal factors of diversity are also present, making the dilemmas even more complex and intractable.

A final related question is what, if anything, social work can do. Roy Lubove in his critical history of social work, *The Professional Altruist*, concludes:

> if social work could claim any distinctive function in an atomized urban society with serious problems of group communication and mass deprivation, it was not individual therapy but liaison between groups and the simulation of social legislation and institutional change.[29]

Lubove's assessment is both an indictment of and a challenge to social work. The diversity of our society is real, not an illusion. The need to coexist is absolute. The place of social work should be in the midst of this reality providing leadership.

NOTES

1. Snell Putney and Gail J. Putney, *Normal Neuroses: The Adjusted American* (New York: Harper & Row, 1964), p. 1–11.
2. John Dewey, *The Quest for Certainty: A Study of the Relation of Knowledge and Action* (New York: Minton, Balch & Co., 1929), p. 3.
3. William L. O'Neill, *Coming Apart: An Informal History of America in the 1960's* (Chicago: Quadrangle Books, 1971), p. 17.
4. Reid Luhman and Stuart Gilman, *Race and Ethnic Relations: The Social and Political Experience of Minority Groups* (Belmont, Calif.: Wadsworth Publishing Co., 1980), p. 6.
5. Ibid., p. 12.
6. Ibid., p. 14.
7. Daniel J. Boorstin, *The Americans: The National Experience* (New York: Random House, 1963), pp. 44–45.
8. Luhman and Gilman, *Race and Ethnic Relations*, p. 15.
9. Henry Steele Commager, *The American Mind: An Interpretation of American Thought and Character Since the 1880's* (New Haven, Conn.: Yale University Press, 1950), p. 5.
10. Ibid., pp. 412–414.
11. Michael Novak, *The Rise of the Unmeltable Ethnics—The New Political*

Force of the Seventies (New York: Macmillan Co., 1972), p. xxi.

12. Samuel Eliot Morison, *The Oxford History of the American People* (New York: Oxford University Press, 1965), p. 884. A. Mitchell Palmer, President Woodrow Wilson's third attorney general, had aspirations toward the presidency, and he selected the so-called "Reds" to crack down on as a means to fame. He planned and condoned a series of illegal raids across the country on homes and labor offices during a January evening in 1920, arresting over 4,000 alleged communists. As Samuel Eliot Morison points out, "The raids yielded almost nothing." Strong tones of nativism and anti-Semitism undergirded such activities as the Palmer raids.

13. James Oliver Robertson, *American Myth, American Reality* (New York: Hill and Wang, 1980), p. 233.

14. U.S. Department of Commerce, Bureau of the Census, "Race and the Population by States: 1980," PC80-S1-3, Supplementary Reports, issued July, 1981, p. 3.

15. Ibid.

16. Ibid.

17. U.S. Department of Commerce, Bureau of the Census, *Statistical Abstract of the U.S. 1984* p. 36.

18. June Gary Hopps, "Minorities: People of Color," in *1983-84 Supplement to the Encyclopedia of Social Work*, 17th ed. (Silver Spring, Md.: NASW, 1983), pp. 77–78.

19. Luhman and Gilman, *Race and Ethnic Relations*, p. 281.

20. The terminology "sexual orientation" is the encompassing term suggested by the "Glossary" in Hilda Hildalgo, Travis L. Peterson, and Natalie Jan Woodman, eds., *Lesbian and Gay Issues: A Resource Manual for Social Workers* (Silver Spring, Md.: NASW, 1985), p. 7.

21. Marvin Harris, *America Now: The Anthropology of a Changing Culture* (New York: Simon and Schuster, 1981), p. 103.

22. Ibid.

23. Ibid., p. 107.

24. Hidalgo, Peterson, and Woodman, *Lesbian and Gay Issues*, p. 60.

25. Ibid., p. 1.

26. Ibid.

27. Ibid., p. 167.

28. Luhman and Gilman, *Race and Ethnic Relations*, p. 287.

29. Roy Lubove, *The Professional Activist, The Emergence of Social Work as a Career, 1880–1930* (New York: Atheneum, 1965), pp. 220–221.

ADDITIONAL SUGGESTED READINGS

Acuña, Rudolf, *Occupied America: The Chicano's Struggle for Liberation* (New York: Canfield Press, 1972).

Allen, Irving Lewis, *The Language of Ethnic Conflict* (New York: Columbia University Press, 1984).

deTocqueville, Alexis, *Democracy in America* (Garden City, N.Y.: Anchor Books-Doubleday, 1969).

Feagin, Joe R., and Clairece Booher Feagin, *Discrimination American Style—Institutional Racism and Sexism* (Englewood Cliffs, N.J.: Spectrum Book, Prentice-Hall, 1978).

Gibson, Guadalupe, *Our Kingdom Stands on Brittle Glass* (Silver Spring, Md.: NASW, 1983).

Goodman, James A., *Dynamics of Racism in Social Work Practice* (Washington, D.C.: NASW, 1973).

Hessel, Dieter, *Maggie Kuhn on Aging* (Philadelphia: Westminster Press, 1977).

Irons, Peter, *Justice at War* (New York: Oxford University Press, 1983).

Kitano, Harry H. L., *Japanese American: The Evolution of a Subculture* (Englewood Cliffs, N.J.: Prentice-Hall, 1976).

Marden, Charles F., and Gladys Meyer, *Minorities in American Society* (New York: D. Van Nostrand Co., 1978).

Maupin, Armistead, *Tales of the City*, 1978, *More Tales of the City*, 1980, *Further Tales of the City*, 1982, *Baby Cakes*, 1984 (New York: Harper & Row Publishers).

Morales, Armando, and Bradford W. Sheafor, *Social Work: A Profession of Many Faces*, 4th ed. (Boston: Allyn & Bacon, 1986).

Teal, Donn, *The Gay Militants* (New York: Stein and Day, 1971).

Webb, Sheyan, and Rachel West Nelson, *Selma, Lord, Selma* (New York: William Morrow & Co., 1980).

22 Women's Issues and Social Work

Eleanor Anstey
Marilyn Southard

Sisterhood is global. Women represent half the global population and one-third of the labor force; they receive only one-tenth of world income and own less than 1 percent of world property. They are responsible for two-thirds of all working hours.[1] The women's movement is personal and political. Women are both clients and providers of social work services. A knowledge of the issues facing contemporary women as well as the contributions of women in the past is crucial information. In this chapter we begin to explore the meanings for those social workers involved in policy and practical action affecting women. A critical examination of the large volume of empirical evidence amassed throughout the United Nations Decade (1976–1985) focused attention on the related problems of poverty and inequality. The research points out how the empowerment of women can provide new possibilities for moving beyond current economic dilemmas.

Women's contributions as workers and as managers of human welfare are central to the ability of households, communities, and nations to tackle the current crisis of survival. Even as resources to strengthen poor women's economic opportunities are shrinking, women have begun to mobilize themselves, both individually and collectively, in creative ways.

According to Sen and Grown, as part of this process of empowerment, we need to reaffirm and clarify our understanding of feminism.[2] The authors state that over the past twenty years the women's movement has debated the links between the eradication of gender subordination and of other forms of social and economic oppression based on nation, class, or ethnicity. They strongly support the position in this debate that feminism cannot be monolithic in its issues, goals, and strategies, since it constitutes the political expression of the concerns and interests of women from different regions, classes, nationalities, and ethnic backgrounds. While gender subordination has universal elements, feminism cannot be based on a rigid concept of universality that negates the wide variation in women's experience. There is and must be a diversity of feminisms, responsive to the different needs and concerns of different women and defined by them for themselves. This diversity builds on a common opposition to gender oppression and hierarchy. This heterogeneity gives feminism its dynamism and makes it the most potentially powerful challenge to the status quo. Sen and Grown state that their position allows the struggle against subordination to be waged in all arenas—from relations in the home to relations between nations—and it necessitates substantial change in cultural, economic, and political formations.

Robin Morgan in her planetary view of the situations that confront women speaks of their responsibility for children, world health, work, and an ecological balance. "The abuse of children is a women's problem because it is mostly female children who are abused nutritionally, educationally, sexually and physiologically."[3] Referring to the crisis in world health as a crisis of women, Morgan states:

> Toxic pesticides, chemical warfare, leakage from nuclear wastes, acid rain, and other deadly pollutants usually take their first toll as a rise in cancers of the female reproductive system, and in miscarriages, stillbirths, and congenital deformities.[4]

Further, she writes, it is women's work that must compensate for the destruction of ecological balance; the cash benefits accrue to "Big Brothers":

> Deforestation results in a lowering of the water table which in turn causes parched grasslands and erosion of topsoil; women, especially in developing countries, as the world's principal water haulers and fuel gathers, must walk farther to find water, to find fodder for animals and to find cooking-fire fuel.[5]

This land loss combined with the careless application of advanced technology has created a major worldwide trend: rural migration to the cities. That in turn has a doubly devasting effect on women:

Either they remain behind trying to support their children on unworkable land while men go to urban centers in search of jobs, or they also migrate—only to find that they are considered less educable and less employable than men, their survival options being mainly domestic servitude, factory work or prostitution.[6]

Since women everywhere bear the double job burden of housework in addition to outside work, they are most gravely affected by the acknowledged world crisis in housing. Within this global context, the role of women in the United States is discussed.

THE WOMEN'S MOVEMENT IN THE UNITED STATES

The last decade was not the beginning of women's concern about relationships and empowerment. In the middle of the nineteenth century, Lucretia Mott and Elizabeth Cady Stanton had attended the World Anti-Slavery Society convention in London and were denied official seats. Consequently, upon their return to the United States, they planned for women to come together to address their grievances. The first women's rights meeting in America took place in a Methodist church in Seneca Falls, New York, on July 19 and 20, 1848. A highlight of the convention was Elizabeth Cady Stanton's proclamation of a "Declaration of Sentiments" which, using the Declaration of Independence as a model, addressed the grievances of women and proclaimed eighteen rights:

> in the universities, in the trades, and professions; the right to vote; to share in all political offices, honors. . . . equality in marriage, to personal freedom, property, wages, children; to make contracts; to sue, and be sued; and to testify in courts of justice.[7]

One consequence of the women's rights meeting was the movement of women from the singular role of homemaker to participation in cultural, educational, and political activities. The most radical political activity of women was the call for enfranchisement. Other women chose to become activists in the area of social reform.

Black women and some white women viewed the abolition of slavery as the all-important issue of the era, since the slavery system had become a greater contradiction in the nineteenth century with growing industrialization. Sarah and Angelina Grimké, among the first women to speak out for women's rights, demanded that women be allowed to participate in the abolitionist movement on an equal basis with men. Born into slavery on a Maryland farm, Harriet Tubman made her escape in 1849, guided only by the North Star. She returned South nineteen times and led more than 200 slaves to freedom.[8] Sojourner

Truth, a former slave from the state of New York who could neither read nor write, traveled extensively across the country speaking not only for the abolition of slavery, but of the need for recognition of women's rights.[9]

The Civil War forced women to take jobs in factories, manage farms, serve as nurses, and do relief work. Less privileged women worked in factories in conditions that were unhealthy, required long hours, and provided little pay. Trade unions developed as women banded together to protest these poor working conditions. Whenever workers struck for their rights, "Mother Jones," an organizer for the United Mine Workers, was likely to show up and take charge of the situation. In Pennsylvania, at her bidding, miners' wives drove off scabs with mops and brooms. Once she marched a band of factory children 145 miles to confront President Theodore Roosevelt with the evils of child labor.[10] A capsule history of women in the American labor movement, from the organization of the New York City tailoresses, as early as 1825, through the garment workers' strikes and the formation of the Women's Trade Union League in 1903, reveals alliances among women workers in all industries.[11] Women were forming alliances to achieve equality in the educational realm as well as in industry.

In education, a frequent question raised was whether "'female minds' are as susceptible of intellectual culture as those that reside in a stronger wrought tenement of bone and sinew."[12] Edward Fenelon used women's assumed inferiority to show their need for education: "Women in general have feebler minds than men; the weaker the mind, the more important to fortify it."[13] In the early 1820s Emma Willard had argued fruitlessly before the New York legislature that facilities should be provided for girls' education as they were provided for boys.[14] In 1837, some 200 years after Harvard was founded for men, Mary Lyon founded Mount Holyoke Female Seminary, the first independent institution of higher learning for women in the United States. In Lyon's day, college for women was unheard of; medical opinion gravely insisted that the intellectual strain would damage girls' delicate brains. M. Carey Thomas, the woman who was to serve Bryn Mawr's Women's College with distinction, was admitted to Johns Hopkins University, a male institution for postgraduate work, "on certain conditions." She learned that the "certain conditions" were "without class, tutorial or seminary attendance."[15] She was required to sit behind a curtain and to refrain from participating in discussions. In frustration, she left that university to get her doctoral degree in Germany. Her mother never mentioned her name to friends again, since an educated woman was a disgrace.

In the area of health care, women fared no better. During times of war, women had served on the battlefields caring for maimed and dying soldiers; yet, they were refused admittance into medical schools. This exclusion was justified by the belief of school administrators that women's constitutions were too frail to endure the sight of surgical and medical procedures. The outlandish claim that women could be just as qualified as men to heal the sick was first proved by Elizabeth Blackwell. In the face of constant male ridicule, she devoted her life to fighting for the education and acceptance of women doctors. She was rejected by twenty-nine American medical schools before New York's Geneva College admitted her in 1847. The student body took a vote and agreed that "the application of Elizabeth Blackwell to become a member of our class meets our entire approbation."[16] Blackwell graduated at the head of her class, but even so the public was not prepared to be treated by the first woman M.D. in the United States. Barred from practicing in city hospitals, she opened a one-room dispensary in a New York slum and later enlarged it into her own hospital.[17]

The social roots for activists such as Blackwell, Mother Jones, Stanton, Mott, and Sojourner Truth had stemmed from issues of temperance, anti-slavery, religious revivalism, and moral reform encompassed under the umbrella of "women's rights." Eventually, women's rights was translated in the minds of many to mean only "women's suffrage." Finally, seventy-two years after the Seneca Falls Conference, women won the right to vote in 1920. This evolution from rights to suffrage was one reason that the women's rights movement did not regain momentum until the 1970s. Historically, the social work profession and the women's movement both arose from the sociopolitical turbulence of the mid-nineteenth century.

WOMEN IN EARLY SOCIAL WORK HISTORY

Another group of women involved in the antebellum social reform movement were those instrumental in the development of the social work profession. Thousands of women who were involved in the welfare activities of the Civil War period accomplished their reform functions within the limits of women's traditional role. Nevertheless, that role had become greatly expanded beyond the home to include the well-being of the community. Many women emerged from the war with a different concept of themselves and their duty to society. The United States was entering an age of science and industry, and both had a conclusive effect on the rise of a new profession—social work.[18]

Historians often characterize the post–Civil War period as a time of exploitation, corruption, and economic selfishness, but the era was also a time of proliferation of charity organizations that gave rise to a generation of reformers. While there was a definite relationship between social work and social reform, there was a difference in emphasis that was constantly debated but never fully resolved by the leading women theorists. The issue revolved around the purpose of social work: Was it the promotion of the well-being of the individual or the good of society in general? The leaders for theoretical methods of social work included Mary Richmond, Josephine Shaw Lowell, and Zilpha Drew Smith. Jane Addams was regarded as the leading proponent for social reform.

Josephine Shaw Lowell reflected the changes that were occurring in the Charity Organization Societies (COS) as they gradually developed into social work. Her influence was felt for two reasons: (1) her theoretical formulation of principles and goals and her demands that public philanthropy be professionally and efficiently managed were important factors in attracting talented people to charity work and in establishing the precedent for a scientific basis for social work; and (2) her gradual recognition of the underlying economic causes of poverty reflected the important new social reform movement that was to merge into the Progressive movement of the twentieth century.[19] COS used friendly visitors, almost exclusively women, to visit the poor and help them find their own means of overcoming problems. Lowell's methods, "scientific charity," established some of the earliest underpinnings of social work theory. Zilpha Drew Smith, another leader in the Charity Organization Societies, emphasized method and education as a basis for the professionalization of social work.[20] Mary Richmond, as director of the Charity Organization Department of the Russell Sage Foundation, devoted her energy to raising the standards of casework practice. She laid the basis for differential casework as the foundation of social work skill and technique.[21] According to Richmond, social work by definition is "the art of doing different things for and with different people by cooperating with them to achieve at one and the same time their own and society's betterment."[22]

Jane Addams was viewed as the forebear of a whole new generation of humanitarians: those women, usually wealthy, who devoted their lives to modern reform to improve the lives of the needy. Addams, twenty-nine, took over the shabby Hull Mansion in Chicago. In 1889, she opened its doors to the oppressed and underprivileged, providing services to 2,000 people daily, offering entertainment, job training, and education. These services improved the lot and shaped the lives of throngs of immigrants who swelled the United States at the turn of the century. Hull House, in West Side Chicago, became the prototype of the settlement house, and Addams became the model for those who felt they could serve the needy best by living and working among them. She fought for legal protection of the immigrants, for regulation of child labor, and for women's suffrage, and was a deeply committed pacifist.[23] In 1931, she was cowinner of the Nobel Peace Prize.[24]

CURRENT CHALLENGES FOR
UNDERSTANDING WOMEN'S ROLES

Social workers, recognizing the value and worth of each human being, seek to empower clients with basic rights, which take on special significance for women. More than thirty years ago, Biestek identified the following client rights: (1) to be treated as an individual, (2) to express feelings, (3) to get sympathetic response to problems, (4) to be recognized as a person, (5) not to be judged, (6) to make one's own choices and decisions, and (7) to keep secrets about onself.[25]

The right to individualized treatment is basic to all social work philosophy, and yet society's subtle message to women demands conformity to roles that threaten or challenge the established order. A lesbian woman, with superb professional credentials, who chooses to be open about her sexual preference may find herself in unemployment lines as a direct result of expressing her individuality.

The right to express feelings and be assured of confidentiality is vital for the client to establish a relationship with the social worker. A woman feeling shame, guilt, and fear at the thought of revealing incest, AIDS, or domestic violence will be further inhibited unless she feels secure that her integrity will be respected.

In every woman the image of the idealized mother lies barely beneath the surface.[26] Mothering is seen not as a role, task, or occupation, but rather as a set of intrinsic characteristics and dispositions that we inadvertently come to expect of all females. Social workers who do not confront this image in themselves and in their clients perpetuate a judgmental atmosphere. An angry client, verbally hostile and uncooperative, deserves validation and affirmation that she has suffered. When the professional judges her "unworkable," the client has no chance to attain independence, autonomy, or a sense of mastery over her own life.

Betty is a forty-four-year-old farm wife whose husband is alcoholic and physically abusive to her. Betty came to a mental health counselor feeling depressed, hopeless, and powerless to change her situation. The mother of three children, she felt the need to keep the family intact. Upon the marriage of her youngest son, Betty and the counselor arranged a meeting with a career adviser at a nearby college. With the assistance of the counselor, Betty began exploring the possibility of obtaining her lifelong dream of becoming a kindergarten teacher. Citing her wish to help others, Betty is now enthusiastically pursuing the requirements for a college degree.

Betty's needs were affirmed and validated through counseling and educational planning, resulting in her empowerment—in control of her own destiny.

If the concept of an individual's right to self-determination is expanded to a wider, global sisterhood, one questions how an individual woman might realize her basic rights when living in refugee camps, in political prisons, or under the rule of apartheid. Social workers active in policy arenas are under the same mandate to respect the uniqueness of the individual as those in direct service.

Empowerment of women can be viewed as using strategies that focus on building self-confidence, skills, and access to resources. Relationships that allow each person to be heard and validated provide an alternative definition of power.[27] Feeling connected to and in relationship with others is crucial to women's identity of self. The traditional model of power, being in control over others, is in obvious conflict for women's needs to grow within relationships.

Rather than the traditional diagram of power with one person at the top, this alternative describes a horizontal model with people connected together in a chain. Not only does this view recognize women as powerful, but it allows men to be much less defensive, more appreciated, and less threatened. Men, in order to maintain a masculine identity that focuses on independence and self-sufficiency, have had to forego qualities that enable close relationships.

Contemporary Issues for Providers and Clients

Some 140 years after the first Women's Rights Convention at Seneca Falls, New York, some of the same issues confront women: education, equality, health, and employment, with the difference being in expression of these needs, both in industrialized and developing countries.

Women play a unique role in the health care field, and that role will expand as we reach the next century. One million women reside in nursing homes in this country, composing three-fourths of the entire nursing home population. As health technology improves, women's dominance in the over-eighty age group will surely increase. Meanwhile, 70 percent of unpaid caregivers for the elderly are women, usually daughters or wives of the older person.[28]

The Bureau of Labor Statistics reports that the number of part-time workers in the United States has more than doubled since 1963 and that two-thirds of those workers are women. Of permanent part-time workers only 33 percent are covered by health insurance compared to 80 percent of full-time workers.[29]

Women's earnings in 1987 averaged 70 percent of men's. Compared to the 1979 figure of 62.5 percent, this is a step toward equality. The average woman worker earns $286 a week, and Hispanic women actually had a drop in their average income to $253.[30] The woman who waits tables, cleans rooms, or sits at a keyboard eight hours a day does not experience much economic relief even if her sisters on Wall Street are now competing with their male counterparts for six-figure incomes.

Pink-collar workers, nearly exclusively female, see the few men entering their field earning more than the veteran women in these positions. Secretaries and typists continue to be 98.5 per cent female, yet earn only 89 percent of male salaries.[31]

The lack of affordable child care, heretofore considered a "women's issue" in the United States, is beginning to be addressed by the federal government. More than half of all preschool children have mothers who are employed outside the home. In 1987 two-thirds of those mothers were the sole provider or had a spouse earning less than $15,000 a year; few women find themselves in a situation with the resources for the $3,000 per year per child average cost of care.[32]

Birth technology is changing the ordinary "mother role." These new technologies of reproduction, including prenatal testing, artificial insemination, in-vitro fertilization, and embryo transfer offer a wide range of possibilities for a growing number of infertile couples. However, women are the primary persons affected by these new technologies, which raise moral, legal, and ethical questions. Ethicists, feminists, and advocates for the disabled worry that the technologies will breed undesirable offspring of their own, namely new ways to wrest control and life from women, minorities, and the disabled, and eugenics, the practice of improving the species through selective breeding. Already, seventy-five clinics in the United States help couples conceive a boy or a girl, charging $600 for a male and $500 for a female.[33] Artificial birth methods can result in a child whose biological mother and father have never met. New technologies wreak havoc with laws governing adoption, inheritance, child support, and custody. Further, who should have access to expensive, controversial methods? Should in-vitro fertilization and artificial insemination be available to single women? Should homosexuals use surrogate mothers? Should infertile poor women also have access to the costly new technologies? Will women in developing countries be introduced to surrogate motherhood as a way of alleviating their poverty?

Women bear responsibility for children in almost every culture, so that problems of the homeless, acquired immune deficiency syndrome (AIDS), and incest impinge upon women in particular ways. Of the estimated 2 to 3 million homeless in America, about 500,000 are children. Small children have become the fastest growing sector of the homeless caused by the lack of housing.[34]

The global epidemic of AIDS is posing one of the greatest challenges to public health in fifty years. Cases of AIDS have now been reported in seventy-four countries, and it has been estimated that several million people worldwide have been infected with the causative virus. AIDS is a disease that attacks the body's immune system, rendering a person incapable of fighting off almost any infection—by another virus, a bacterium, a fungus, or a parasite. It has proven fatal in 85 percent of all cases within two to three years after symptoms appear, and hope for a vaccine is still years in the future.[35] The emergence of AIDS in new populations with transmission through sexual contact, transfusion-related AIDS, and infants connected with risk groups is especially significant for women's reproductive roles. An infected woman can give the AIDS virus to her baby during pregnancy or birth. If a woman is infected, her child has about one chance in two of being born with the virus. Since 1980, close to 1,000 infants have been born with AIDS in the United States, and some experts predict that by 1991 the number will be 25,000.[36] Women in developing countries suffer from lack of educational opportunities, exploitation by multinational corporations in electronics and textile industries, and in the agricultural sector. According to Ehrenreich and Fuentes, an assembly-line worker in the United States is likely to earn, depending on her length of employment, between $3.10 and $5 an hour. In many developing countries, a woman doing the same work will earn $3 to $5 a day. The great majority of the women in the new developing countries' work force live at or near the subsistence level for one person whether they work for a multinational corporation or a locally owned factory. A Coke might cost a half-day's wages, and lodging is shared in a room occupied by four or more other women.[37]

The electronics industry is generally thought to be the safest and cleanest of the exported industries. There is air conditioning (not for the workers' comfort, but to protect the delicate semiconductor parts with which they work). The United States National Institute on Occupational Safety and Health has placed electronics on its select list of "high health-risk" industries because of the high number of toxic substances.

Women do about 67 percent of the farming in many developing countries but do not receive the benefit of new technology, which is given only to men, even though women are responsible for growing the food. Agribusiness exploits the labor of women. Depending on the crop and the area of the world, women are employed in planting, growing, and harvesting. They are often hired as cheap seasonal labor for some of the most monotonous and difficult jobs such as weeding and picking.[38]

Social workers, whether providers or clients, are responsible to keep informed about the political, social, and economic factors that impact the lives of women, for this population is often affected in ways peculiar to their gender. Are any people free as long as the global society covertly supports daily murders of Brazilian women at the hands of their husbands, bride-burnings in India, the lack of potable water for a Kikuyu woman and her family, and the plight of the homeless in the United States? The horizons for social workers have been expanded.

SUMMARY AND CONCLUSIONS

Social work as a profession has its roots in the early movements of social reform in this country. Challenging the existing social order has been the role of social workers throughout history. The changing role of women in this country can be augmented by social workers who are willing once again to expand existing societal boundaries. Through work with women, social workers have an opportunity not only to promote the well-being of individuals but also to work for the betterment of all society. By challenging policies within an agency that are repressive to women and by developing a practice sensitive to women's issues, the social work tenets of individual worth and self-determination will be enhanced. Every woman who calls herself a social worker is a role model not only for clients but for all women with whom she has contact. The task of both men and women in the field of social work is to live actively as individuals unwilling to accept the powerless role society offers its female members.

NOTES

1. United Nations Development Project, *Development Issue Paper* No. 12 (New York: United Nations, n.d.).
2. Gita Sen and Caren Grown, *Development, Crises and Alternative Visions: Third World Women's Perspectives* (New York: Monthly Review Press, 1987), pp. 18–19.
3. Robin Morgan, *Sisterhood Is Global* (Garden City, N.Y.: Anchor Press, Doubleday, 1984), p. 2.
4. Ibid.
5. Ibid.
6. Ibid.
7. Elizabeth C. Stanton, Susan B. Anthony, and Matilda J. Gage, eds., *History of Woman's Suffrage* (Rochester, N.Y.: Charle Mann Publishers, 1981), 1: 67–74, 88–94, 111–117.

8. Hedley Donovan, ed., *Life Special Report: Remarkable American Women, 1776–1976* (New York: Time, Inc., 1976), p. 40.

9. Alice Rossi, ed., "The Akron Convention," *The Feminist Papers* (New York: Columbia University Press, Bantam Books ed., 1976), pp. 426–429.

10. Mother Jones, *The Autobiography of Mother Jones* (Chicago: Charles H. Kerr Publishing Company, 1977), pp. 71–83.

11. Joyce Maupin, *Labor Heroines: Ten Women Who Led the Struggle* (New York: New York Times Co., 1978), p. 33.

12. *The Lady's Pearl* 2, no. 4 (October 1841): 76–79.

13. *Godey's Lady's Book* 45, no. 3 (September 1852): 273.

14. Willystine Goodsell, *The Education of Women* (New York: Macmillan Co., 1923), p. 18.

15. Elaine Kendall, *Peculiar Institutions: An Informal History of the Seven Sister Colleges* (New York: G.P. Putnam's Sons, 1976), p. 88.

16. Ernest Rhys, ed., *Elizabeth Blackwell: Pioneer Work in Opening the Medical Profession to Women* (London: J. M. Dent & Sons Ltd., 1860), p. 53.

17. Ibid., pp. 168–169.

18. Winifred. D. W. Bolin, "Feminism, Reform and Social Service; A History of Women in Social Work," The Minnesota Resource Center for Social Work Education, Minneapolis (July 1973), p. 3.

19. Edward T. James, Ed., *Notable American Women, 1607–1950*, 3 vols. (Cambridge, Mass.: Belknap Press of Harvard University Press, 1971), 3:437–439.

20. Roy Lubove, *The Professional Altruist: The Emergence of Social Work as a Career, 1880–1930* (Cambridge, Mass.: Harvard University Press, 1965), p. 138.

21. Mary E. Richmond, "The Social Case Worker in a Changing World," in *Proceedings of the National Conference of Charities and Corrections* (Chicago, 1915).

22. Ibid.

23. Rex A. Skidmore, Milton G. Thackeray, and O. William Farley, *Introduction to Social Work*, 4th ed. (Englewood Cliffs, N.J.: Prentice-Hall, 1988), pp. 44, 78.

24. Donovan, *Life Special Report*, p. 113.

25. Felix P. Biestek, *The Casework Relationship* (Chicago: Loyola University Press, 1957), p. 17.

26. Teresa Bernardez, "Gender Based Countertransference of Female Therapists in the Psychotherapy of Women," *Women and Therapy* 6, no. 2 (Spring/Summer 1987): 29.

27. Jean Baker Miller, "Women and Power," *Women and Therapy* 6, no. 2 (Spring/Summer 1987): 1–10.

28. U.S. Congress, House of Representatives, "Exploding the Myths: Caregiving in America," Subcommittee on Human Services of the Select Committee on Aging, 100th Congress, First Session, Com. Pub. 99–611 (Washington, D.C.: U.S. Government Printing Office, 1987).

29. U.S. Bureau of Labor Statistics, Bulletin 2217 (Washington, D.C.: U.S. Government Printing Office, June 1985).

30. Rick Jost, ed., "Women Narrowing Pay Gap," *Des Moines Register*, February 2, 1988, p. 5 S.

31. U.S. Bureau of Census, Current Population Reports, *Money Income and Poverty Status of Families and Persons in the United States: 1986*, Series P-60, no. 157 (advance data from the March 1987 Current Population Survey) (Washington, D.C.: U.S. Government Printing Office, 1987), pp. 15–16.

32. Institute for Social Research Monitoring, "Panel Study of Income Dynamics" (Ann Arbor, Mich., 1987).

33. Melinda Voss, "Birth Technology: Crib Full of Moral Questions," *Des Moines Register*, May 10, 17, and 24, 1987, Home and Family, Section E.

34. Jennet Conant, "Advocate for the Homeless," *Newsweek on Campus*, March 1988, p. 41.

.35 David Sassoon, "AIDS: Its Impact on Mothers and Children," *Action for Children* 11, no. 1 (1987):1.

36. C. Everett Koop, M.D., "Understanding Aids," Health and Human Service Publication No. (CDC) HHS-88-8404 (Washington, D.C.: U.S. Government Printing Office, 1988), p. 6.

37. Barbara Ehrenreich and Annette Fuentes, "Life on the Global Assembly Line," *MS*, January 1981, pp. 53–59, 71.

38. Marilee Karl, "Integrating Women into Multinational Development?" *ISIS Women in Development: A Resource Guide for Organization and Action* (Geneva, Switzerland: Women's International Information and Communication Service, 1983), pp. 25–34.

ADDITIONAL SUGGESTED READINGS

Anstey, Eleanor, "Pesticide Poisoning: Payment of Women in Developing Countries," *Canadian Woman Studies* 7, nos. 1&2 (Spring/Summer 1986).

Braude, Marjorie, *Women and Therapy* 6, nos. 1&2 (Spring/Summer 1987).

Fraser, Arvonne S, Marsha A. Freeman, and Clarice Wilson, eds., *The Women's Watch* (Minneapolis: International Women's Rights Action Watch, Humphrey Institute of Public Affairs, 1988).

Lapierre, Dominique, *The City of Joy* (Garden City, N.Y.: Doubleday, 1985).

Mackinnon. Catherine A., *Feminism: Unmodified Discourses on Life and Law* (Cambridge, Mass.: Harvard University Press, 1987).

Miller, Jean Baker, *Toward a New Psychology of Women*, 2nd ed. (Boston: Beacon Press, 1987).

Moser, Caroline O.N., and Linda Peake, *Women, Human Settlements and Housing* (London: Tavistock, 1987).

Signs: A Journal of Women in Culture and Society 13, no. 2 (Winter 1988).

Spake, Amanda, "A New American Nightmare," *MS*, 14, no. 9 (March 1986): 35–42, 93–95.

Women and Politics 7, no. 4 (Winter 1987).
"Women in the Boardroom," AB-1595, "Sexual Harassment on the Job," AB-1168, 'Women and Money,' HB 1582 "Day Care Solutions," AB-1530. Films for the Humanities & Sciences (Princeton, N.J., 1988).

23 Housing and the Social Services

Gary Askerooth

Housing seems to be of such obvious importance in everyone's life that no justification for including it in a social service text should be required. Yet a brief explanation of its importance may be helpful, since other major areas of life requiring large-scale physical investment, such as transportation, are usually not closely tied to the social services.

Housing is of concern to the social welfare profession because at a fundamental level housing conditions are a major determinant of mental and physical health. Historically the fight for better housing conditions was the leading "cause" for social reformers who saw whole generations of immigrants to U.S. cities forced into degradation and disease by deplorable housing conditions.

Housing is *the* primary environment for a majority of the world's inhabitants. This is especially true for the citizens of northern climates with cold seasons because they spend substantial periods of time in the shelter of their homes. Experience and social research emphasizes the impact of the housing environment on human development. Populations at risk, such as children, frail elderly, disabled, and other dependent groups are particularly exposed to the influence of housing conditions. Adequate space, temperature, food preparation, and toilet facilities are crucial to their basic welfare.

At the level of social and economic policy housing is again of primary concern to all societies. In the United States it is estimated that one-third of all fixed capital is invested in housing—an incredible amount.[1] Ownership of housing on an individual unit scale by the occupants and a multiple scale by investors is perhaps the most significant source of income and expense in most people's lives.

Where we house ourselves or where others house us is probably as important as anything we do, including our chosen occupation. Along with housing comes a combination of neighborhood-related keys to our lives, including schooling for children, recreation, crime, many job opportunities, transportation, and social status in general. Ownership by choice of one's housing is often the means by which people stake out the territory of their dream for the good life—certainly the goal of much of social welfare policy. Poor housing owned and mismanaged by others is likewise often the outline of a nightmare for the less fortunate.

Except in the rare case of a nomadic tribe, to be homeless is the worst condition of all. Homelessness is often equated with personal worthlessness, no matter what the cause. Social policy, programs, and services are entangled in an unending struggle to turn housing into a positive, active influence in people's lives, regardless of their social or financial strength.

THE BASIC HOUSING NEEDS

Abraham Maslow's well-known "hierarchy of human needs" comes easily to mind when we think of housing.[2] For the refugee from war or natural disaster a simple shelter provided by a relief organization is satisfaction enough. But the complexity of human nature soon requires higher levels of satisfaction of need. The simple roof over one's head can become a prison if there is no safety in leaving to seek employment, food, and other necessities. This, indeed, is what occurs with refugee camps such as those in Kampuchea (Cambodia).[3] Housing ourselves can be thought of as a hierarchy that progresses from the most basic need, territorial security, to the most advanced, self-expression.

Territorial Security

On February 26, 1972, 132 million gallons of mud and water roared through the Buffalo Creek in West Virginia, killing 125 and leaving 4,000 of the area's 5,000 people homeless. Kai T. Erikson's book, *Everything in Its Path*, describes the results: "The loss of communality on Buffalo Creek has meant that people are alone and without very much in the way of emotional shelter."[4]

> Nearly everyone left in the community has recurring fears of future invasions of their homes by unexpected forces. Psychosomatic illnesses have dramatically increased, families, friendships and neighborhoods are no longer close-knit, as if the loss of their homes required new personalities. One resident's concerns are typical:
>> I have noticed that people do not visit each other as they did before the disaster, they don't seem to establish lasting friendships. Most people keep pretty much to themselves. You can drive through the trailer camps and see that most people stay inside with the doors closed. I do it myself. It is as though we have lost our own identity.[5]

Buffalo Creek residents received psychosocial counseling along with grants and loans for new housing. Such emergency assistance works best if disaster victims are helped to participate in rebuilding their communities.

People who lose territorial security due to social and economic disasters have a tougher time. Shelters for women abused by their husbands began only in 1974 as an emergency response to an endemic social problem. Although many have operated successfully since then, few have secure permanent sources of funding.

Shelters for the homeless are also almost universally viewed as temporary responses to emergency situations. The conventional wisdom defines the causes as mental illness and laziness. A closer look often reveals the reverse. Homelessness, a loss of nearly all territorial security, impairs most people's psychosocial functioning.

Equal Access

As an individual need and an important social value, equal access to housing ranks high among the factors that influence social welfare. Numerous laws resulting in social programs have been adopted in the last forty years to deal with discrimination in housing, a problem that interacts with all other housing needs to make housing more critical for minorities and low-income people than for the majority.

Until recently equal access to or equal opportunity in housing was hardly considered a problem. Reformers in the housing field were so concerned with the adequacy and affordability of housing for white people in the United States that the housing needs of minorities were an afterthought. The Federal Housing Authority began America's first public housing projects in the late 1930s after extended pressure from social welfare reformers, providing thousands of units of housing in most large cities. But minority groups across the country soon discovered that local prejudice and discrimination were as negatively effective in federally funded housing as in private. While nationally there were 92,476 dwelling units housing blacks in 1944, over 83,000 of these were in projects that were either totally segregated or had quotas for percentages of blacks.[6] The city of Buffalo, New York, built a 172-unit project for blacks despite having a waiting list of 1,100 eligible applicants. Discrimination was so blatant there that the city refused to move blacks into temporary housing although 4,085 of Buffalo's 5,343 units were empty.[7]

Immediately after World War II civil rights in general and equal access to housing in particular were reexamined in many parts of the country. The NAACP won its case in 1948 when the Supreme Court ruled that "restrictive covenants were unconstitutional, ending nearly a century of post-slavery abuse."[8] The glaring examples of such covenants were described by a governor's commission in Minnesota in 1947: 25 percent of the Twin Cities area was found to be covered by restrictions, while 63 percent of the white people surveyed would not sell to a black even if they received a better price than by selling to a white! One covenant read: "No lot shall ever be sold, conveyed, leased or rented to any person other than of white or caucasian race."[9]

The National Housing Act of 1949 set as a standard "The realization as soon as feasible of the goal of a decent home and a suitable living environment for every American family." Soon after this lofty goal was set, a national movement for "open housing" began. The newly formed National Committee Against Discrimination in Housing successfully organized to demand city-by-city changes in all agencies that received public funds for housing.[10] By 1964 the U.S. Congress was pressured into adding open housing to its civil rights law, and in 1968 the Fair Housing Act opened 80 percent of all U.S. housing to all races, despite opposition of the National Association of Real Estate Boards.

Fair Housing Councils throughout the country continue to grapple with racial and other forms of discrimination in housing. These private, nonprofit agencies act on a case-by-case basis with considerable success. On a larger level most major cities are still obviously segregated by race and national origin, primarily due to the large number of low-income minority households.

Equal access by the handicapped followed belatedly. Since 1964 federally funded housing projects and programs were required to make accessibility to the handicapped a high priority. As the accessibility issue became the focus of more research, demonstration projects, and organizing by handicapped people, the scale of the problem became clear. Nearly all units of subsidized housing had been built with steps as access.[11] Similar barriers were found in thousands of public buildings, such as libraries, schools, and offices of public agencies.

The Housing and Community Development Act of 1974 required that high priority be given to removing "architectural barriers" to the handicapped, an expensive but necessary policy.[12]

Adequacy

"A decent home and a suitable environment." An admirable goal, of course, but how does a society or its housing agencies and service providers know what is decent and suitable? Most would agree that the standards would change from one culture to another. Dirt floors are considered decent in many Third World homes. Outdoor plumbing is standard for most as well. Standards such as these change over time as much as by distance and culture. Abraham Lincoln's respected log-cabin birthplace would be condemned by every modern government and private agency involved in housing.

Standards of adequacy in housing are commonly expressed in "housing codes," which are enforced by city and county governments. These codes include minimum standards for a healthy and safe environment. Inspectors look for immediate hazards to the inhabitants, such as wiring with damaged insulation, a furnace or stove close to flamable materials, damaged gas supply piping, and so forth. Enforcement of housing codes is often controversial, since violations must be repaired under legal penalty. Tenants often expect the city to force landlords to improve their property, while homeowners often resist opening their homes to inspectors. Resistance to applying these standards is often based on misconceptions. Most professionals argue that minimum housing codes are an essential feature of a reasonable housing rehabilitation program.[13] When applied in a sensitive manner along with a social service or housing service program (such as those discussed below), housing codes are generally beneficial. They must not be confused with building codes, which are only applied in new construction or housing rehabilitation involving more than 50 percent change in the structure or the value of the building.[14]

From a 1901 housing inspection:[15]

- Tenements in "the worst areas," Jewish, Italian, Polish, and Bohemian, are a "destruction to morals and health."
- "Private ownership of the rays of the sun and the health-giving properties of the air."
- "Babies, almost like blind fish inhabiting sunless caves, suffer opthalmia."
- 41.9 percent of the people have less than 250 cubic feet of air space per occupant, which is 150 cubic feet less than is required by state law for each homeless and vagrant man.
- "The density of population per acre in the Polish quarter in Chicago is

three times that of the most crowded portions of Tokyo, Calcutta and many other Asiatic Cities."

From a 1981 Housing Inspection Report, St. Paul, Minnesota:[16]

Report on one house owned by a single-parent family with a $300 a month income:
Front porch—the roof is in very bad condition—large sags in the roof covering indicating rotted roof boards. The flooring and rim joists are deteriorating—recommend removal; Garage—repair or remove; Eastside: the wood porch is very hazardous and must be removed; missing sills and broken glass in several windows; Gas lites pipes still connected, can be turned on by simple hand lever—must be plugged; chimney opening covered with a paper plate; plumbing throughout building in poor repair, many fixtures leaking or cracked and badly worn. Filthy stool in 2nd floor. The whole house must be rewired. No insulation in attic; large holes in plaster in several rooms. No furniture in children's rooms. Sandbox in one bedroom used as a toilet by children.

Forty percent of some central cities' housing stock still contains lead-based paint which has poisoned hundreds of thousands of children.[17]

Adequate housing is so vital to well-being that poor people consistently rank it number one in their personal concerns.[18]

After the urban riots in the 1960s ghetto residents cited poor housing as the primary cause of their frustration. The U.S. census provides much of the housing data for public and private users. Census standards regard any dwellings lacking either toilet or bathing facilities to be "substandard."

By 1980 only 2 percent of all U.S. housing units were considered to be substandard. Improvement has been dramatic in many areas. In New Mexico 19,960 homes or 6.2 percent of the total were without hot water in 1970. By 1980 this number had dropped to 10,212 or 2.3 percent.[19]

The bureau dropped most housing condition items in 1970. City departments of community development now quite often perform their own surveys of conditions, which usually reveal major improvement needs in at least 10 percent of the housing stock.[20]

Overcrowding is another basic concern for housing and social service agencies. Horror stories of a dozen destitute children crowded into one or two dark, dirty rooms, common throughout the U. S. history, have been revived in the 1980s as millions of new immigrants are crowded into new slums. A typical view of the negative effects of overcrowding includes frustration and irritability, violence, decreased individuality and self-sufficiency, disillusionment with adult examples too closely observed, debasement of sexual interaction, loss of sleep, and constant interruptions of normal tasks.[21] The U.S. census standards consider a ratio of more than one person per room to be overcrowded; one and a half persons per room is considered to be severe overcrowding.

Evidence continues to accumulate on the influence of crowding, much of it suggesting that other factors may be more important than density in determining a family's adequacy of housing. Jonathan Freedman's extensive review on crowding and social behavior leads him to conclude that high density does not have a generally negative effect on humans.[22] The key factor proved to be income, not housing density.[23] Poor people in poor neighborhoods experience more stress, crime, and so forth, than the rich regardless of the density of housing.

Affordability and control over one's home environment are generally more important than physical conditions in housing. There are great variations among cultures. In Hong Kong public housing, thirty-five square feet per person is considered adequate. U.S. standards are often four times as spacious. In the semitropical Central American country of Belize a family is often considered disadvantaged if they do not have adequate space under their houses: space to hide from the sun. Houses built on the ground are also easy targets for frequent floods that follow tropical storms.[24]

Affordability

Sabotage on the part of property-owning and mortgage-holding interests has nearly wrecked the modest program for low-cost housing which the United States Government projected as a minor part of the national reconstruction program.[25]

A decent dwelling is not a reward withheld for the successful, but a fundamental right to which every citizen is entitled, the provision of which becomes a responsibility of government. Almost every intelligent technical or social worker would agree with these premises.[26]

Families wait in line five days at Housing Sale. The Associated Press reported that the interest rates are so high in California that a whole street has been blocked for several days with families camping out in front of model homes set to go on sale for $200,000 at 13 ⅞ percent interest. Although fewer than 5 percent of Californians can afford such housing the deals are considered bargains. One waiting buyer noted that for the same price he could buy a palace in Costa Rica.[27]

As with standards of adequacy, individuals and cultures vary widely in their ideas about how much of their income ought to go to housing. In socialist countries such as Cuba and China, a few dollars equivalent a month is the standard. In urban America on the other hand 40 percent of a family's gross income is not uncommon. Adequacy, equal access, and other basic housing needs are closely connected with cost, of course. Racial segregation still traps many people in slum housing for which they pay as much or more than whites pay for decent housing.[28]

A mythical housing market has been the basis of much public policy. Supply was said to increase for all income levels. As investors responded to demand for new middle- and upper-income housing, upwardly mobile families left older but adequate housing behind for the poor. Recent economics has made a mockery of this formula. Interest rates that varied from 2 to 6 percent in the 1950s and 1960s have remained over 10 percent through much of the 1980s.

Public agencies struggle against nearly insurmountable odds in the marketplace. In Los Angeles over 1,000 units of low-income housing has been built for families displaced by a new freeway. At a staggering cost of $125,000 per unit 40 percent of these houses and apartments sit vacant.[29] Crime and deterioration in the surrounding area discourage many eligible families from applying.

When we buy or rent our home, we also get a whole bundle of neighborhood-related services and problems. The quality of our schools, streets, parks, shopping, and police protection are only the most obvious aspects of our neighborhoods. Crime and crime prevention have an increasingly significant effect on housing in many cities. Those who can afford it install expensive security systems, hire additional police, or move to isolated, walled-in suburbs.

Few completely escape the costs of this deterioration, since taxes, insurance, and social service costs are rising dramatically to pay for the vandalism, arson, drug addiction, and family breakdown that plague many neighborhoods. The author recently found nearly 300 abandoned, vandalized homes in a suburban city, many of which were only a few years old.[30]

Nor do local authorities always do their part to provide housing opportunities for a range of incomes, even when subsidies are available. DuPage County, Illinois, an affluent suburban county of Chicago, recently refused to help a developer build subsidized housing despite a district court order to do so. The U.S. Department of Housing and Urban Development (HUD) forced a change by freezing the county's community development funds.[31]

Land cost is the other housing-related factor that has risen sharply. In 1949 land costs accounted for 11 percent of housing sales price. Today they account for 30 percent of the price.[32] These increased costs, when added to increased real estate taxes, have slowed new housing construction to only 60 percent of that expected. To create an adequate market, the National Housing Goals endorsed by HUD are set at 2.6 million units per year. Present construction rates are averaging 1.6 million units.

A tight housing market for purchasers leads directly to a squeeze on renters. Twenty thousand units are abandoned every year in New York City alone, increasing the competition for those remaining.[33]

One New York study found that while only 3.3 percent of post-1930s apartments are occupied by welfare recipients, 16 percent of the pre-1920 apartments were welfare occupied.[34] Rent levels were higher for these tenants; yet, the quality was actually lower. Buildings with greater than one-third welfare tenancy averaged 10.6 code violations, far more than others. Ninety-one percent of Spanish-speaking welfare tenants were forced to pay security deposits on these older buildings while only 45 percent of the white tenants faced this requirement.

Control over Housing

"Our culture places a high value on consumer sovereignty, and most of our national housing legislation inplicitly assumes that free residential mobility contributed to individual well-being."[35] Control over housing varies with a society's political economy. In the socialist-managed city of Bologna, Italy, the government deliberately uses taxes to force real estate investors to sell their property to the city, which then takes over the control of housing and its cost on behalf of working-class tenants. In this country, on the other hand, control is generally a function of capitalist economics. Whoever can compete for ownership or tenancy by paying the price will control as many dwellings as he or she desires. Involuntary displacement as a result of rent increases, landlords' disinvestment (allowing deterioration of property), or government development projects is estimated to be 2.5 million persons per year.[36]

The most vulnerable to being forced out of their homes by the recent trend of "gentrification" are lower-income persons, the elderly, female-headed households, and minority persons. A wave of condominium conversions is sweeping the United States, giving a new look to many inner cities. When "Condomania" hits a neighborhood, the traditional solutions used by tenants and government don't work. Rent control has often been used in large eastern cities to protect tenants from displacement, but condominium conversion allows a developer to transfer completely remodeled buildings to a new, wealthier population, replacing tenants with owners for a more profitable, short-term return on investment.

Rural Americans and many people in rural and urban areas in Third World countries have maintained a measure of independence and quality of life through control over their housing. Owner building of housing is an ancient tradition among rural peoples. In the United States it is associated with homesteading of land for farming, ranching, and perhaps logging. Turner and Fichter argue that modern Americans have been led by government and industry to see housing as a commodity provided by someone else, when it should more accurately be called a process.[37] Their research shows that a steady 17 to 20 percent of all single-family dwellings are built by people for themselves at a substantial savings of 22 to 53 percent. Very few owner builders are assisted by government programs. Only 6 percent received VA or FHA financing, for example, as compared with 33 percent of all developer-built single-family homes.[38]

In Third World cities control over housing and land by urban squatters who are desperate for a bit of shelter is seen as a major problem by planners and policymakers around the world. Brasília, Brazil, is notorious for having been planned as a major government and employment center without consideration of housing for the masses. Squatters were able to set up housing overnight in the shadow of urban skyscrapers. Social workers who tried to get these poor families to move voluntarily met with total failure. Only one family out of 4,000 in a neighborhood was willing to move to remote "satellite" settlements.[39]

The author has seen squatters organize so well in Mexico and Guatemala that overnight an entire village can be created out of salvage materials, complete with street names, numbered houses, and connected utilities. Governments usually move in rapidly to remove these squatments, under pressure from developers, landowners, and the utility companies from whom the squatters illegally "borrow" electricity and water.[40]

HOMELESSNESS

Rather suddenly in the early 1980s a wave of homelessness has seemed to spread across the country. Large numbers of destitute, discouraged people, mostly single men, were discovered sleeping in parks, huddling over heating exhaust grates, or hiding in trash bins. At first the housing authorities, especially HUD officials, were mainly concerned with minimizing the problem. HUD claimed in 1984 that there were only about 300,000 homeless in the United States. Local shelter providers believed the number was more like 3 million.[41]

In the early 1980s shelter was provided to the homeless mainly on an emergency basis. Very reluctantly, a small amount of support was provided through the Federal Emergency Management Agency. The principal causes of homelessness were soon found to be:

1. Transient unemployed people in search of work;
2. Mental patients discharged from institutions without community-based alternatives;
3. Evictions due to loss of economic or familial support. More recently, it has become generally recognized among shelter providers and local governments that there may be another underlying cause;
4. Drastic reductions in federal government support for low-income housing.

Short-term shelter is still the main focus of housing for the homeless. Usually run by private social agencies with considerable public financial support, the shelters are often forced to limit stays to a few days or at most a few weeks. Despite the growing numbers of homeless and the increasing percentage that are families, not single men, governments at all levels continue to regard the problem as temporary. Of the more than $500 million for federal homeless programs in 1987 only $15 million went to permanent housing.

In Los Angeles County, where there are approximately 35,000 homeless people, there are only 5,000 beds for the homeless, all in short-term shelters. This represents a doubling of short-term beds in the three years from 1984 to 1987.[42] Many of the 114 shelter agencies provide only fifteen to twenty beds, although one downtown center has 528. These agencies have sought to serve special populations as the need escalates. Among these Los Angeles shelter beds, 429 are set aside in twenty separate locations for homeless victims of domestic violence.

Long-term solutions will require major new efforts with federal and state support. Currently the most success is in saving and restoring single-room-occupancy hotels. Examples are the SRO Corporation in Los Angeles which has renovated five hotels downtown for homeless people and the eighty-two-unit rehabilitated hotel managed by the Chinese Community Housing Corporation in San Francisco.

HISTORICAL HOUSING POLICIES AND PROGRAMS

Historically, housing policies and programs in the United States have gone through several stages of increasing sophistication in recognizing the various factors in problem causation, with several subsequent belated stages in levels of government involvement in response to these problems. As each stage adds a new program, along with social services in some instances, problems and programs left over from earlier periods do not disappear but are instead carried over into the present.

We can divide this history into roughly four periods.

1. From the 1890s to the 1930s, a period of slum identification, code legislation, and voluntary social services.
2. From 1937 to the early 1960s, an era of home ownership subsidies for the middle class, slum clearance for the cities, and growing public services for investors and developers.
3. From about 1964 to 1981, a short, rapidly changing period of diversified subsidy programs, neighborhood-focused redevelopment, and increasing demands for services and supports to many different and diverse groups including renters.
4. 1981 to the present, rapid increase in homelessness associated with major reduction in federal government programs, except for tax incentives.

Slums and Slumlords

Nineteenth-century social reformers and social service workers agreed that slum housing was a major problem in American cities. The solutions they proposed often differed, however, as reformers focused on the "slumlords" as the cause, which required tough laws involving codes, while traditional social workers regarded lack of education and poor earning power of the workers as primary causes of slums. These attitudes and methods remain as part of our current housing policies.

The nation's first housing code was passed in New York City in 1867. Slums were then seen as physical problems requiring identification and technical prescriptions. Code programs were ineffective in stemming the tide of crowding and deterioration. A new wave of indignation followed the reformers' house-by-house inspections of the 1890s. Social workers played a prominent role in exposing deplorable conditions. New York's 1901 law was much more specific in detailing proper environment for living. By 1920, after the Russell Sage Foundation and the National Housing Association sponsored a national drive to force housing codes into law, the slumlord became a national symbol of disgrace.

Tenants' associations and social service agencies continue to demand stiff penalties for violations of housing codes. The high cost of maintenance and taxation, however, as well as the potentially profitable use of land upon which slum buildings often sit, make code enforcement without proper replacement housing and tenant relocation an unhappy experience for slum housing occupants.

In 1954, when housing codes were first required by the Housing and Home Finance Agency (HHFA), only fifty-six cities had such laws. By 1963, 736 had adopted them, mostly because the HHFA withheld federal housing dollars from cities without adequate housing codes.[43] Codes are now usually applied selectively, allowing city housing authorities and welfare departments to withhold payments, grants, and loans to induce housing rehabilitation. Most of these "creative" uses of codes were developed in the 1960s as a result of rent strikes. Some states now allow tenants or welfare departments to deposit part of the rent in an escrow account for vital housing repairs. Despite all these innovations, there remains a widespread belief that tenant and landlord education in maintenance for health and safety is as useful as code enforcement. Many housing programs still emphasize this individualized social service approach.[44]

Home Ownership Support

Before the New Deal period of the 1930s federal government support of housing was extremely limited. Public housing was limited to military employees. Mortgages were insured by private companies only. Through the Home Loan Act of 1932, the National Housing Act of 1934, and the Housing Act of 1937 a new social policy for housing was clearly established. The primary purpose of the new policy was to save a large group of middle- and upper-income Americans from losing their homes from default on mortgage loans. There is some evidence that the policy worked to the advantage of working-class families as well, since continual movement upward (socially) and outward (to the suburbs) left a large, decent housing stock to "filter down" to the less wealthy.[45]

Most of the housing programs on the 1940s and 1950s worked through a two-level insurance program. FHA, or Farmer's Home Administration in rural areas, or the Veterans' Administration insures the loan so that a bank or a savings and loan organization can lend a large percentage of the value of a home, in some cases up to 100 percent, to the borrower. The government added other "secondary mortgage" agencies with names such as "Fannie Mae" and "Freddie Mac" (Federal National Mortgage Association and Federal Home Loan Mortgage Corporation) since 1934 to allow private lenders to recycle their funds by selling loans. Until the government began to subsidize interest rates for developers, there was little obvious benefit to individuals in the mortgage guarantee system. The main subsidy that encouraged home ownership was a tax law that allowed a homeowner in the 50 percent tax bracket a deduction worth one-tenth of the house cost.[46]

Passed in a post–World War II climate, the 1949 Housing Act added several varied subsidy programs. Assistance was provided to developers by lowering the interest rate (usually to 3 percent) and guaranteeing a "fair market value" for sale or rent of structures. These new programs produced subsidized housing for college students in dormitories, to veterans by direct loan if they lived too far from a lending institution, and for housing cooperatives, among others. By the 1970s, the bewildering array of below-market interest rate programs had attracted many critics.

"Redlining" is a common complaint of neighborhood-based housing critics. After the Fair Housing Act of 1968, FHA was required to make loans in inner-city neighborhoods. Research by citizens' groups showed a glaring pattern of refusal to make regular mortgage loans in these neighborhoods at the same time that there were quick foreclosures on FHA-insured loans. The practice is called redlining because it is argued that lenders were drawing red lines around poor and racially mixed neighborhoods and refusing loans within them. Chicago's largest bank was returning sixteen times as much of depositors' money in home loans to suburban residents as to city dwellers.[47] The Federal Home Loan Disclosure Act passed in 1975 requiring reporting by ZIP Code, along with the Community Reinvestment Act of 1978, have allowed community organizers to expose unequal treatment in this fundamental housing support system.

From Urban Renewal to Community Development

Urban renewal holds the distinction of being the most expensive, most criticized, yet one of the longest-lived housing-related programs in recent history. In 1954, when the program began, many cities were enthusiastic about its goals of combined slum clearance, housing development, and "prevention of blight." By the early 1960s critics had discovered that most cities had used their grants to revitalize downtown shopping areas and industrial parks. The worst slums were not removed, nor was low-income housing increased by most urban renewal projects. Indeed, the cities used their money to build middle-income housing and businesses to build up their tax base. Low-income and minority housing units numbering 243,000 were destroyed by the federal bulldozer, to be replaced by only 20,000 low-income units.[48]

Urban renewal came to be called "Negro removal" among its critics. The poor learned to fear the double-barreled combination of this clearance program and the wide swaths cut through cities by interstate freeway construction. Although families were supposed to be "relocated" by workers who would provide counseling and adequate funds to move to a better environment, local governments were reluctant to comply with the rules. Less than 1 percent of the program funds went to relocation expenses until Congress passed the Uniform Relocation Act of 1966.

Public housing is another small but long-lasting component of the

U.S. housing strategy, but it is a major item in some countries with large low-income populations. Hong Kong, for example, houses nearly half of its people in large-scale public buildings. The U.S. government entered the field in 1937 with a modest program. The federal government provides grants to local housing authorities (LHA), which are generally made up of conservative business, real estate, and political representatives. The LHA contracts for the construction of buildings with local developers and manages the projects when completed. Contrary to some people's perceptions, public housing accounts for only 1.5 percent of all the nation's housing. Fewer than 4 million Americans live in these units. Nearly one-half are elderly. The majority are not not welfare recipients.[49]

Severe criticism of public housing has kept the allocation by Congress small throughout history. The recent trend is for local authorities to request funds for elderly high-rise apartments which require less maintenance, fewer square feet per person, and create less controversy in the community. Housing to be built publicly for younger families is now likely to be at "scattered sites" throughout the city. Complaining neighbors cannot so easily organize opposition, compliance with school integration laws is made easier, and the poor are less visible.

Current publicly managed housing is more likely to be leased or rented from private owners under Section 8 of the Housing Act. Renters find their own apartments once they are on the eligibility list, and the city inspects and sets a fair rent level, after which the renter's income is used to determine what amount of the rent must be subsidized by the government. A variety of incentives, including low-interest loans, is available to owners of Section 8 housing if they are willing to construct new units or rehabilitate old ones for low-income tenants.

Community Development Block Grants (CDBG), initiated in 1974, provide cities over 50,000 in population an "entitlement" grant. Like the Model Cities program of the 1960s, neighborhood areas are chosen by the local government for concentrated efforts. Local citizens are appointed to advisory committees, which funnel requests for social services, street repairs, parks, housing rehabilitation, and related improvements to the city for final approval of a comprehensive program.

Large cities tend to have long-drawn-out citizen participation processes during which social service workers, community organizers, and city planners jockey for support. The primary focus of the program for many local governments is the improvement of streets, utilities, and other public works, including commercial developments. Community representatives usually demand social or housing services from the program.[50] Small cities, rural areas, and Indian reservations, which contain some of the poorest people and the worst housing, must compete for only 20 percent of the total fund. A study of small cities' CDBG programs showed that they spent only 17 percent for housing compared to 46 percent for large cities.[51]

Dismantling the System

Ronald Reagan was elected on a platform of reducing the burdens of big government. In the housing and social service fields this meant a concerted effort to reduce government expenditures and dismantle government programs, The results have been dramatic. Federal support for low- and moderate-income housing was cut 70 percent during the 1980s, while homelessness increased rapidly.

The strategies behind this federal approach have been wide-ranging and complex, since they are often tied to financial sector problems such as persistent high interest rates or bank and savings and loan failures. An outline would include:

1. Attempt to force abandonment or sale of public housing projects by cutting maintenance of existing units;[52]
2. Deregulation of financial institutions, resulting in shortage of affordable loans for housing;
3. Restriction of tax-exempt bond authority of cities and states, reducing financing to builders of affordable housing;[53]
4. Allowing rent restrictions on existing subsidized projects to expire, resulting in the conversion of hundreds of thousands of units to market-rate rents;
5. Severe cuts in nearly all direct government support for low-income housing;
6. Replacement of direct with indirect support, such as substituting vouchers for certificates in the Section 8 rental program, which encourages low-income renters to pay more than 30 percent of their income for rent;
7. Greatly reducing the incentives for investors in low-income rental housing by reducing depreciation and other deductions from taxes.

These and other strategic decisions in our housing system will, according to recent research, result in the loss of 7.8 million *more* lower-income housing units in the next fifteen years; 18.7 million more Americans will either become homeless or, if they can, cut out other essentials to pay more than they can afford to for rent.[54]

DIRECT SOCIAL SERVICES IN HOUSING

Social work involvement in housing has historically been in the roles of social reformer or community organizer. Housing has been seen as a social provision, a commodity that should be provided for all groups. When direct services are made available, the usual pattern is for public agencies to have a few social workers for thousands of families. They function primarily as information and referral persons who connect clients with available services from other agencies once an initial problem identification is made.

Social workers are also found in planning and program evaluation positions in Public Housing and Redevelopment Authorities. The services to residents in this role are indirect, as they usually use computerized social research tools to formulate housing assistance plans for CDBG purposes or to determine which groups of people in need of housing assistance should receive scarce housing first.

Relocation workers may in some cases be social workers. HUD regulations require that each person or family that is forced to move due to a federally assisted project be given a comprehensive social service diagnosis in addition to just financial compensation. HUD estimates that 10,000 persons are involuntarily relocated as a result of CDBG projects. A few direct services such as employment counseling and housing budgeting assistance are sometimes provided along with relocation. Generally, however, clients are referred to a number of other existing social services.

In public housing projects and some large publicly subsidized, privately managed projects community service coordinators are employed in an office on site. In some projects this office becomes the catalyst for tenant organizing and advocacy on behalf of the low-income residents. Residents' councils are often formed to deal with common problems such as crime, lack of recreation facilities, poor maintenance, and so forth.

Often these offices are understaffed and short on funds. Tenants usually complain that the councils do not solve basic problems, and community organizers seize the legitimate issues of the tenants to confront the local housing authority. Tenants have been more successful when they could find a local, nonprofit group, often a legal aid foundation, legal services corporation, or affiliate of tenant support groups such as the National Housing Institute to help confront authorities, to provide support on individual and collective issues such as rats, roaches, broken utilities, and other problems.[55]

Specialized housing and social services are often provided to specific groups such as the disabled. One innovative example is Carbon Creek Shores, a forty-unit apartment complex in Orange County, California, that was built and staffed by and for the disabled. The sponsor, Dayle Macintosh Center, also operates an emergency shelter for the disabled homeless.[56]

Health and Human Services Departments and many other agencies fund joint programs of housing and social services that are managed by private, nonprofit groups. Many of these groups also operate matching services, especially for elderly people who have low incomes and special needs. Shared living can also be designed into multiple-unit construction to cut costs and improve the living environment. One of the leaders in this field is the Shared Housing Resource Center in Philadelphia.[57]

Self-help strategies provide another set of financial and social benefits to participants, especially if a nonprofit group is the organizer of cooperative efforts. The Delta Housing Corporation in Mississippi has long been a leader in building low-cost housing jointly with employment programs with CETA (now JTPA) workers and residents. Self Help Enterprises of Visalia, California, has used FmHA funds and private support to help over 3,000 families build their own homes, through more than twenty years of service.[58]

Other self-help services related to housing include apartment maintenance and rehab programs with unskilled tenants, urban homesteading in which vacant buildings are completely redone by individuals or groups of low-income people, and community policing actions to control the recent surge in drug dealing and gang violence in many poor neighborhoods.

Organized housing services often begin independently in local areas, sponsored by such national organizations as the Catholic Campaign for Human Development, the Ford Foundation, Center for Community Change, and others. By the early 1970s many of the local groups became tied together in a national movement for neighborhood preservation. A key leader in this movement is National People's Action, which supports the network in the Midwest and eastern United States from its Chicago office. Other networks soon developed in other or in overlapping regions. The Enterprise Foundation and Local Initiatives Support Corporation have both been very strong supporters of local groups by providing training, loan funds, and planning help to package low-income housing deals, sometimes including wealthy community-oriented investors.

The largest national network is supported by the congressional corporation, Neighborhood Reinvestment (NR), which was begun in 1978 to create public-private partnerships for revitalization. NR has developed these groups in 140 cities in ten years, serving over 200 neighborhoods through Neighborhood Housing Services (NHS) and Mutual Housing Associations (MHA). These are resident-controlled service centers that began by upgrading old houses for lower-income home-owners but soon learned to organize forces throughout their neighborhoods for crime prevention, clean-up campaigns, parks, and other public improvements.

In Salt Lake City the NHS organizes neighborhood youth into housing construction crews to keep them out of gangs. In Boise, Idaho, the NHS purchased thirty housing units to rent to homeless families. Comprehensive social services are provided to the families along with the housing, with the aims of keeping the families intact and reducing the demand on emergency shelters.

Rural and small city NHS's often organize groups of ten or more families to build their own housing, while big city MHA's such as in Baltimore, finance, build, and manage a cooperative form of rental housing. The keys to the success of all these various local efforts are the balance between solid government funding for housing construction, strong business sector or private foundation contributions to the operating budget, and the continued training and technical assistance from an outside support network.

The Future

The 1990s will doubtless see some increase in federal government funding of housing and related social services, although it is hard to imagine reconstructing the entire system of programmatic and financing support that was dismantled during the Reagan years. Public-private partnerships will continue to grow in scale and significance, probably with a simultaneous growth of sophistication among the national support networks.

Home ownership will continue to decline unless by some miracle the U.S. deficit disappears and property values stop rising. California and New York City are signposts to the future, pointing to housing prices that are as much as 50 percent above the national average. High costs will drive more millions into less desirable but passable alternatives of shared living and smaller shelter. Cities, counties, and states will become much more involved in housing and related services, hopefully in creative ways such as tax-increment financing and the use of public reserves to back bonds and other forms of credit. Combinations of public welfare and housing, such as the proposal to use AFDC grants in California for homeless families to make security deposits (rejected in 1988 by the federal authorities) should reemerge.

Other local initiatives that may survive include the plan to charge housing code violators fines that would go directly to creative affordable housing, to the sale of homeless housing bonds similar to savings bonds. The affordability gap will, however, continue to grow, as more households pay 40 or 50 percent of their income for housing.

Numerous local housing services will, of course, continue to provide housing and social services. They will become much more competitive with government and business-sector approaches and will likely specialize as in housing for the homeless female mentally ill low-income person and other very specific groups.

National social policy initiatives may be somewhat influential, depending upon the political environment and the defense department budget, of course. One remarkable approach is "A Progressive Housing Program for America" published by the Institute for Policy Studies,[59] which argues for housing to be defined as a social provision through public and private nonprofits only, along with protected occupancy for renters by a sort of national rent control system.

The majority of Americans will continue to house themselves in a variety of creative ways that provide territorial security, adequate quality, and individual or family control over the process. Unfortunately an ever-larger number of us will experience hardship in housing. A sign of this is the millions who are already homeless, the unknown numbers who live in unsafe, deplorable spaces such as garages in Los Angeles and Oakland.

Local governments will be forced to create more efficient housing delivery and maintenance systems probably by more direct support of the strongest private nonprofits. Small, unsophisticated local groups will either grow, merge, or die, similar to the trends in the financial industry.

With the disappearance of the Reagan administration, we can expect some movement toward reregulation in the housing and social services field. The Supreme Court upheld in February 1988 a San Jose rent control law limiting rent increases for low-income tenants, the first national support for income-based rent control in the private market. The boom years are no doubt gone forever, but a renewed focus of public and private sectors on the need for comprehensive policies and programs in housing and social services seems likely as the latest cycle of laissez-faire strategies fades.

SUMMARY AND CONCLUSIONS

Housing is of primary concern to social policy because of its great economic costs and wide impacts on everyone's psychological and social development. Housing in capitalist societies is seen as simply another commodity. This works fairly well for most people until market forces push the cost of shelter to burdensome levels for many. In a social development perspective housing is a community process organized to meet a hierarchy of needs, including security, equal access for all, adequate quality at an affordable cost, and individual or family control over their living space.

U.S. housing policies and programs have evolved slowly away from the idea that the private market would provide decent housing for all citizens eventually. Government intervention was limited to code enforcement until 1934, when a pattern of loan guarantees, tax subsidies, and other supports began to assist middle-class consumers and builders of single-family houses. Public housing and low-cost rental housing have never been a main focus of our public programs.

Long-term bonds, public-private investment syndicates, various tax incentives, and "creative financing" mechanisms will continue to have more influence on the commodities of shelter. Social workers and other human service professionals can play very important roles as advocates, organizers, and planners of housing through involvement with groups of constituents such as the homeless, public housing tenants, and the working poor. Nonprofit community-based organizations, especially those with skilled management and national networks are the most likely places to look for creative approaches to the growing challenges.

Housing is the most complex social provision imaginable, since it creates an environment, expresses and controls our quality of life, drains our pocketbook, and supports our financial institutions.

NOTES

1. Michael Stegman, *Housing and Economics: The American Dilemma* (Cambridge, Mass.: MIT Press, 1971).
2. Abraham Maslow, *Toward a Psychology of Being* (New York: Van Nostrand, 1962).
3. Examples abound in Southeast Asia where thousands escape from the shelter of camps to seek work or freedom.
4. From *Everything in Its Path*. Copyright 1976 by Kai T. Erickson. Reprinted by permission of Simon and Schuster, Inc.
5. Ibid., p. 226
6. William L. Evans, *Race Fear and Housing in a Typical American Community* (New York: National Urban League, 1946), p. 40.
7. Ibid., pp. 32–33.
8. *Shelly v. Kramer*, 334 U.S. 1 (1948).
9. Minnesota, Governor's Interracial Commission, *The Negro and His Home*

in Minnesota, a report to Governor Luther W. Youngdahl, 1947, p. 66.

10. Juliet Saltman, *Open Housing* (New York: Praeger 1978), p. 44. The majority of large U.S. cities are still overwhelmingly segregated in housing patterns. See Karl Taeuber, "Racial Residential Segregation 1980" (University of Wisconsin).

11. Edward Steinfield, *Adaptable Dwellings* (Washington, D.C.: National Association of Housing and Rehabilitation Officials, 1977).

12. Housing and Community Development Act of 1974, 570. 606.

13. Roger S. Ahlbrandt, Jr., *Flexible Code Enforcement* (Washington, D.C.: National Association of Housing and Redevelopment Officials, 1976).

14. *Uniform Building Code*, International Conference of Building Officials, issued yearly since 1927.

15. Robert Hunter, *Tenement Condition in Chicago: A Report by the Investigating Committee of the City Homes Association*, 1901, pp. 18, 52, 79.

16. West Side Neighborhood Housing Services, files of city inspection reports, St. Paul, Minnesota, 1981.

17. Despite this evidence, HUD provides no funds to test or remove this paint.

18. Chester Hartman, *Housing and Social Policy* (Englewood Cliffs, N.J.: Prentice-Hall, 1975).

19. U.S. Department of Commerce, Bureau of the Census, Census of Population and Housing, 1970; and Metropolitan Housing Characteristics 1980, Summary 1984.

20. This is based on personal experience in several cities and the NAHRO publication cited above.

21. Walter A. Friedlander and Robert Z. Apte, *Introduction to Social Welfare* (Englewood Cliffs, N.J.: Prentice-Hall, 1980), pp. 339–340.

22. Jonathan Freedman, *Crowding and Behavior* (New York: Viking Press, 1975), p. 104.

23. Ibid., p. 69.

24. Personal observation and discussion with social development personnel of the government of Belize.

25. Carol Aronovici, *America Can't Have Housing*, edited by Carol Aronovici, page 69, Copyright 1934 The Museum of Modern Art, New York. All rights reserved. Reprinted by permission.

26. Catherine Bauer, *America Can't Have Housing*, edited by Carol Aronovici, page 21. Copyright 1934 The Museum of Modern Art, New York. All rights reserved. Reprinted by permission.

27. *Los Angeles Times*, 1983. By permission of The Associated Press.

28. U.S. Department of Housing and Urban Development, *Blacks Pay More*, cited in Hartman, *Housing and Social Policy*, p. 12.

29. *Los Angeles Times*, December 28, 1987, Section I, p. 3.

30. The Pomona Valley NAACP brought this issue to the surface. At their request I discovered that at least 265 single-family homes were repossessed and held vacant by HUD, nearly all in small, segregated black neighborhoods.

31. *Chicago Tribune*. April 25, 1984.

32. This formula, as with real estate values in general, varies greatly from one market to another.

33. U.S. Department of Housing and Urban Development, *Displacement Report*, 1979.

34. George Sternlief, *The Ecology of Welfare: Housing and the Welcome Crisis in New York City* (New Brunswick, N.J.: Transaction Books, 1973), pp. 59, 79, 91.

35. Arthur P. Solomon, *Housing the Poor* (Cambridge, Mass.: MIT Press, 1974), p. 173.

36. Richard LeGates and Chester Hartman, *Displacement* (Berkeley, Calif.: National Housing Law Project, 1981), p. 38.

37. J.F.C. Turner and Robert Fichter, *Freedom to Build* (New York: Macmillan, 1972), p. 243.

38. Ibid., p. 5.

39. David G. Epstein, *Brasilia, Plan and Reality* (Berkeley: University of California, 1973.

40. The squatter population numbers in the millions in cities like Manila and Mexico City where these "illegal" towns eventually become legalized due to the lack of alternatives.

41. The 3 million figure is almost universally accepted by all but HUD. Contact the National Coalition for the Homeless for current figures.

42. The Shelter Partnership, *Short Term Housing Directory of L.A. County,*. May 1987, 1010 S. Flower St., Los Angeles, CA 90015.

43. Lawrence M. Friedman, *The Government and Slum Housing: A Century of Frustration* (Chicago: Rand McNally, 1968), p. 50.

44. Rent strikes were a popular means of educating landlords in the 1960s and 1970s. Ironically they seem to survive in high-income communities such as Santa Monica, California, not among the poor.

45. Henry J. Aaron, *Shelter and Subsidies: Who Benefits from Federal Housing Policies?* (Washington, D.C.: The Brookings Institution, 1972).

46. Rates were reduced in 1986, but 100 percent of the interest is still deductable, even for those who buy million dollar homes.

47. National Training and Information Center, *Lending Policies Exposed: Prime Factor in Neighborhood Decay,* Chicago, 1976, p. 7.

48. Bernard J. Friedman and Marshall Kaplan, *The Politics of Neglect: Urban Aid from Model Cities to Revenue Sharing* (Cambridge, Mass.: MIT Press, 1975), p. 24.

49. Hartman, *Housing and Social Policy,* p. 123.

50. People's Resource Committee, *CDBG Action Manual,* School of Social Development, University of Minnesota-Duluth, 1981.

51. Terry E. Ball and Leonard F. Heumann, "An Analysis of the HUD Nonmetropolitan Community Program," *Journal of the Community Development Society* 10, no. 1 (Spring 1979), p. 56.

52. The 1988 budget for public housing modernization included enough for approximately $1,100 per unit across the country. LHA directors the author has talked to say they need at least ten times as much.

53. Congress became disillusioned with the use of mortgage revenue bond programs by many localities, where housing was overbuilt for middle-

income people through this method. The 1986 tax reform law, as a result, severely limited the bond programs.

54. Philip L. Clay, *At the Risk of Loss: The Endangered Future of Low-Income Rental Housing Resources*, (Washington, D.C.: Neighborhood Reinvestment Corporation, 1987, p. 4.

55. NHI publishes *Shelterforce*, a tenant advocacy journal, at P.O. Box 2518, East Orange, NJ 07018.

56. Personal visits to the center's facilities, December 1987.

57. Leah Dobkin, *Shared Housing for Older People*, Philadelphia, SHRC, 1983. (6344 Greene St., Philadelphia, PA 19144).

58. Self Help Enterprises, *Working Together: Twenty Years of Self Help Enterprises*, Visalia, Calif., 1985.

59. IPS Working Group on Housing, 1901 Q, St., N.W., Washington, D.C. 20009, July 1987.

ADDITIONAL SUGGESTED READINGS

Blumberg, Richard E., and James R. Grow, *The Rights of Tenants* (New York: Avon, 1978). A complete handbook including sample legal forms.

Civic Action Institute, *Neighborhood Action Guides*, Washington, D.C., 1980, short booklets on housing rehabilitation, crime prevention, co-ops, and so forth.

Disclosure, monthly news from NPA and NTIC, Chicago. Timely social action perspectives on housing issues.

Downs, Anthony, *Neighborhood and Urban Development* (Washington, D.C.: The Brookings Institution, 1981).

Greer, Nora Richter, *The Search for Shelter* (Washington, D.C.: American Institute of Architects, 1986). Policy arguments and experimental examples of shelter for homeless people.

Kozol, Johnathan, *Rachel and Her Children: Homeless Families in America* (New York: Crown, 1986).

Mayer, Neil S., *Neighborhood Organizations and Community Development: Making Revitalization Work* (Washington, D.C.: The Urban Institute Press, 1984).

Low Income Housing Information Service, "Low Income Housing Roundup," 1012 14th St., N.W., Washington, D.C. 20005.

National Housing Law Project, "The Subsidized Housing Handbook, 1982."

Pickman, James, et al., *Producing Lower Income Housing: Local Initiatives* (Washington, D.C.: Bureau of National Affairs, 1986).

24 Social Development: An International Perspective

Judith Lee Burke

In some countries, social development refers to the central government's plan for a unified set of activities ranging from social services to organized efforts for people to help themselves. These latter efforts have commonly gone under the name of community development, although other labels are also used for programs aimed at broad-scale participation. The United States does not have any such comprehensive plan or program efforts.[1] Here, social development as an approach to social work emerged out of discontent. Criticisms of both narrow worker-client relationships and the overgrown welfare state have led to a new social development perspective. The community development programs in the United States, sometimes called community resource development, emphasize a holistic approach with a strong component of self-help. However, these programs are local in nature even though they may have federal or state support.

Many social workers who operate within a social development framework spent years working with people in the traditional human services agencies. They learned firsthand the limitations and frustrations of trying to provide services within systems unequipped to attack the roots of social problems. Social development agents work to establish alternative forms of institutions. They often challenge the very systems that a country has designed to solve its social problems.

Nawrocki Stock Photo/Jim Wright

A UNICEF-initiated self-help program for mothers in the Philippines.

One of the key differences between social work and social development is the greater emphasis upon psychological forces in the former. Social development workers insist that "the individual is affected by ... social circumstances and that the political and economic forces have a great impact in shaping the social circumstances of individuals and groups."[2] Social development workers differ from social treatment workers mainly in their efforts to change circumstances, through reforming institutions, policies, and procedures. While clinical social workers act as advocates for clients, individuals, and families, they are less likely to work on behalf of larger units of people like communities or local organizations.[3] Social development workers take a broad systems view of the structural inequities that create people's problems. For instance, David Gil, Ira Sharkansky, Jeffrey Galper, and others view America as underdeveloped in social (if not economic) terms because of its great number of poor people among the more affluent and its erratic provision of services.[4]

Social development spans a vast range of human needs. It is both an outlook and a process. As a discipline social development is based on core values. Social development workers prize participation, respect for human dignity, global awareness, collective action, and economic redistribution. Their highest priority is to fulfill basic human needs through equalizing means, or the access to opportunities.[5] These values differ from mainstream social work in the emphasis upon global awareness, collective action, and economic redistribution. As Falk points out, most U.S. workplaces put people in hierarchical, production-oriented competition, rather than in a situation where group action could be encouraged.[6]

SOCIAL DEVELOPMENT DEFINED

As more and more applications of social science emerge, the problem of defining and clearly separating one from the other becomes more acute. Social development is one of the more recent practice fields to emerge where a problem of definition is difficult. Different writers define it differently. In order to understand what is meant by social development, it will be useful to consider some conflicting definitions. After this examination, we can return to the issue of how to define social development, with an awareness that controversy exists for good reasons.

In the United States conceptualizations of social work have lacked the breadth and depth of social work concerns in many other countries. Hollister, Paiva, and others have criticized U.S. social work practice for restricting itself to a narrow range of interventions.[7] Many countries, collectively known today as the South, have traditionally been regarded as "developing," or "less-developed countries (LDCs)," because they have low per capita incomes and few services.[8] Social workers from these nations often define their roles in broad and ambitious terms. In some cases these professionals have studied social work in Western universities; yet, they have found many models of clinical, social welfare, and technical practices unsuitable for application in their home countries. Their ideas about their work often refer to both Western and non-Western societies and will be included in this chapter. It is imperative that we in the Western industrial world understand that social development requires an interdisciplinary, international perspective. Indeed, this comparative view can enhance understanding of our own social development process and of our own social service systems.[9]

Ralph Pieris, an Asian scholar, defined social development as "the greater capacity of the social system, social structure, institutions, and policy to utilize resources to generate favorable changes in levels of living interpreted in the broad sense as related to *accepted social values*, and a better distribution of income, wealth and opportunities."[10] This statement has many facets. Each facet has received attention as policymakers here and abroad have planned social change. Pieris's emphasis upon income and opportunity distribution typifies social development views of many professionals with experience in developing countries. His definition contains the judgment that human needs will be better met by the redistribution of wealth. Many social workers see poverty in their countries as perhaps the greatest problem. Yet if we compare Pieris's definition with other definitions of social development, a variety of meanings emerges.

First, there are differences of meaning based on ideological positions. People's perspectives on social development are rooted in their ideology. Ideology affects the conceptualization of both the means of social development and the ends. Two ideologies—socialism and capitalism—have dominated the debates over these means and ends. As Western countries became more "modern" through industrialization, "development" began to appear as a concept.[11] Early users of the term "development" often spoke as if becoming industrialized like Western Europe or the United States should be a common goal. The means of development for less developed societies was thought to be accomplished by encouraging private enterprise; this kind of thinking was circular because underdevelopment was also viewed in profit-making terms. The models of economic and social development we have generally accepted in the West are actually based on specific philosophical assumptions. That is, the poor were regarded as people who had to be taught how to produce. This led to practices in which the prime actors of development were economists and technical consultants. Social gains were assumed to accompany economic gains. To produce work for subsistence and purchasing power beyond subsistence was the major social reality that the free-enterprise model accepted. Economic gains were the desired ends, the goals of all change.

The other ideology that shaped many theories of social development was predicated on egalitarianism, an equal distribution of the wealth among all. Much of this ideology is derived from the economic and social rationale of Marxism. These social activists or reformers also describe their goals in terms of improving human life and eliminating the obstacles to the satisfaction of basic needs. The means proposed to reach these goals have varied. Often the means involved putting people back in touch with the products of their own labor, making decisions about production, and then sharing the benefits for the general good. In this system, services and benefits should be available to those who produce or contribute to production and to their dependents.

Until recently, many proponents of social development have sided with free enterprise or cooperative models of development, as if a choice had to be made and were clear-cut.[12]

Social workers reflecting on the thorny issues of social welfare and development in the United States and elsewhere have struggled with these poles of thought. They have not, as a group, achieved much resolution or consensus. It is vital that students of social work learn to appreciate how ideology affects their thinking about the economic and social welfare of people with whom they may work. David Gil, an American policy analyst, has written about conditions in the United States that preclude social development. Gil has repeatedly advocated for a cooperative egalitarian model of social development to replace a failed welfare system.[13] He has argued that social policy based on profit motives must be unraveled and redirected to provide employment, to develop resources, and to distribute rights and services more equitably. In *Unraveling Social Policy*, he used a system of policy and service revisions to support mothers' wages to show his method of social development.[14] Gil's emphasis upon changing social policy and the institutions that implement policy has been influential by stimulating social workers to see the conditions that restrict people's growth. However, his work has been criticized for failing to describe realistic methods of achieving equality and cooperation.[15]

A fresh perspective on social development has emerged, which goes beyond both the models of growth through private enterprise and of development which demands people to sacrifice to cooperatives for a long-range reward. Berger has argued that neither model of development, when imposed by people in authority, gives people informed choices about the problems entailed. Berger described how at least one generation sacrifices for no immediate gain as they undergo development under systems as different as, for example, Brazil's model or China's comprehensive socialism.[16] The point is that both systems were imperfect and imposed from national governments downward. Both Berger and Denis Goulet gave high priority to the meaning of development for its intended recipients. Many people perceive their needs in terms other than economic.

In his *Defining Development*, Lackey argued that the objectives of development are an admixture of all cultural values and that the means employed are of equal importance to the ends sought.[17] In *The Cruel Choice*, Goulet observed that in order for people to be motivated to take part in development, they personally have to face the "shock" of recognizing that they are "less developed."[18] Goulet noted that there are people who have the power and knowledge to depict others as less developed, and there are people who, to improve their lot, must first accept that they are less developed. Facing this choicepoint may mean loss of security, social and economic self-esteem. These costs of movement from a valued position in a known order of things in society to an unknown may be greater than the gains that clients or change agents of development can imagine.

What do these international examples have to do with social development in the United States? There are many parallels. Pieris described social development as aimed at changing levels of living in accordance with *accepted social values*. The food stamp program in the United States was designed especially to help older adults, but the elderly have made relatively little use of food stamps. In part this was due to older people's reluctance to define themselves as poor enough to need public assistance.[19] While the incomes of many older people are substandard, most apparently did not see themselves as using a government program in its original form. The Gray Panthers, National Council of Senior Citizens, and other activist groups for older adults, however, found common needs among the elderly and organized them to change policy and programs.[20] A major difference in the two approaches—federal food stamps program versus a citizen's movement —lies in the appeal of self-help and dignity participation of the latter.

National Programs or Local Community?

For a period between roughly 1950 and 1975, the major models of development that the Agency for International Development and the World Bank promoted were economic approaches to raise the gross national product (GNP) of less developed countries.[21] This model was one that many social workers did not embrace, because of disagreements with growth economists.[22] Growth-oriented economists believed that overall economic gains for developing countries would "trickle down" to poorer citizens. However, the "trickle-down" theory of development simply did not work. The benefits that were supposed to reach the poor were "carried in a leaky bucket."[23] Poor people never received the products of growth. Instead, what they often gained was heightened awareness of what is meant for *some* local people to benefit from development.

One of the more puzzling and difficult tasks for developers has been to find effective ways to reach such population groups as small farmers, small traders, domestic workers, and the unemployed. Failure to reach such groups has not been limited to large-scale capital-intensive programs. Programs aimed at forming local cooperative efforts when mandated from above have also been unsuccessful. Both types of programs have suffered from various forms of corruption resulting in the misuse of funds.[24]

E. F. Schumacher has criticized large-scale models of economic development, proposing instead an intermediate technology. Schumacher was referring to exaggerated means of production that created unemployment by requiring less direct human labor. He recommended "methods and equipment which are cheap enough so that they are accessible to virtually everyone."[25] While concerned with technology, Schumacher might have added that we need *social* solutions that give people access to the means for improvement.

Unit of Participation and Social Development

Schumacher strongly favors local control and input, to keep efforts small and responsive so that people can meet their needs. Bruce Stokes and Sugata Dasgupta agree that self-help is vital for people to solve their own problems, as they cannot depend upon national or international government. Stokes believes that centralized initiative is necessary to lead a program thrust in an area, but that local people should supply the services.[26] Dasgupta has proposed that a regional unit of organization be formed for development, small enough to permit individual participation, yet large enough to transcend local politics.[27] Dasgupta based his idea on a comparison between Indian villages, which differed in the extent to which communities adopted new practices.

Developers' thinking has gone full circle since the 1950s, returning to a reliance on community development. Small projects where people participate fully to manage the operation are receiving renewed emphasis. Instead of trickle-down, trickle-up programs now receive centralized agency funding, but operate on a small scale.[28] These programs stress people's ability to define their problems on a local level and achieve some solutions. However, if local participation and small-scale planning were all that was needed for development, problems would take care of themselves. Within social development some prefer a decentralized approach, which develops a locality so that people can build or reform their own institutions. Local people must be able to participate at the level of formulating policy, which a centralized agency will honor and implement.[29]

Probably no magical units of organization exist to facilitate development. Yet, a principle emerges from the social development "case" literature: successes have attained commitments from the projects' intended beneficiaries. In practice, social development encompasses a variety of methods. These range from small-scale interventions that organize community members, to nationwide programs that provide policy, capital, and models for local people to follow. Hyman and Miller have synthesized six models of community engagement, planning, and management, ranging from the consensus-based, rational planning, locality development approaches to the conflict-based, advocacy planning, social action approaches.[30] These variations of approach will continue to exist, given the great diversity of settings in which people strive to meet their needs.

We have reviewed some critical issues of which social workers must be aware. Many practitioners of social development have reached consensus about some issues, but are polarized about others. On the issue of participation, for example, most respect people's experience of their own needs, and have realized that external plans for improvement may miss citizens' concerns. The dilemma is how to raise consciousness about changes that could be helpful, yet preserve clients' dignity. Goulet described this as the "cruel choice" for people who may lose meaningful traditions. Practitioners agree that the scale of human development and service institutions is inappropriate and inefficient. At the same time, services personalized as casework are regarded, from a social development perspective, as a drop in the bucket. Proposals to promote development include gearing the technical solutions to a level that can enhance (not engulf) people's livelihoods and planning policies that integrate and improve institutions.

Social development also implies more than a collection of projects or single-problem focused activities. These may be vital as starting points, to show people that they can have the power to create changes in their lives. Yet, the roots of poverty and underdevelopment go deep into institutional elitism.[31] The structure of major institutions that affect local opportunities for growth must be changed. The emphasis in the United States has been on modifying institutions except where few existed as in new boom towns.[32] Here, the goal is institutional reform or, as a growing number of critics contend, to change institutions into a manageable scale.[33] By contrast in developing countries, the goal has often been to *build* institutions where few existed.[34]

PLANNED INSTITUTIONAL CHANGE

One model of social development has been proposed by a social worker to fit the case of development through existing institutions. Hollister has described social development as "planned institutional change to bring about a better fit between human needs and social policies and programs."[35] Hollister sees social development as a process in which the institutional mechanisms or organization for the delivery of services are improved in order to serve people better. Hollister developed a model to depict the parts and processes of social development (see Figure 24.1).

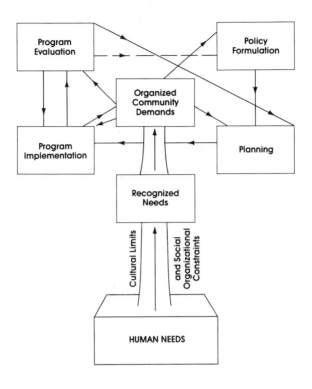

Figure 24.1 A General Model of the Social Development Process
Source: Hollister models reproduced by permission of *Social Development Issues.*

Human needs, at the base of the model, is a concept worth examining. Hollister stressed that when workers try to meet human needs through social development planning and policy, they should not assume that they know what people need. Needs should be self-defined. Although the people should define their own needs, professionals can aid the process of need definition through community development. Butler and Howell have provided a manual for professionals to use in working with community groups for helping them to define their needs.[36]

Cultural limits (see the "trunk" of the model) determine which needs a people recognize and put forth as legitimate concerns for social action. As an example, consider the possible dilemma on those social workers who believe that women should have control over their own bodies. These social workers may see a society without family planning as lacking the means to meet a basic human need for self-determination over reproductive processes. The people themselves may not view birth control as a felt need. In several parts of the world strong values are placed on having children, and large families are linked with women's status or the security of a family labor supply.[37] These values regarding family life also differ within subcultures of the United States. During the War on Poverty under the Johnson administration, the Office of Economic Opportunity offered family planning programs through Planned Parenthood and other agencies. The services were intended to give choices about birth control, but program outreach efforts were viewed as genocidal by some black Americans.[38] Right-to-life groups believe that they advocate for unborn children. The needs of the people to be served by social programs cannot and should not be taken for granted. Social developers must grasp the quality of life as people see it and respect those values.

Value conflicts require analysis and education to bring about change. Mandating solutions and programs does not work. Lackey has described a process of development which involves the optimization of conflicting values rather than the maximization of one.[39]

Political forces affect each part of the social development process. Hollister urged social workers to recognize political influences upon policy formulation, planning, and program implementation. Political processes characteristic of the region in which social development is attempted have an important role in the strategies employed, and success attained, in every step of social development. Perhaps you have taken part in community groups that had decisions of mutual interest to make. While the larger group met around a community problem of wide concern, this awareness and organization did not mean problems were easily resolved. Political factions probably emerged as groups formed among people who have unequal amounts of power, funds, and visibility. (If no factions appeared, perhaps this was a planning elite, and other people could not be represented.)

Hollister's emphasis upon political process is well taken. Workers have sometimes failed because they underestimated this factor. When Western workers from countries like England and the United States first tried to apply principles of democratic community development overseas, they found that local elites posed obstacles.[40] More disturbing, many community development workers, especially in rural areas, worked comfortably with these elites, perhaps because of common bonds like education. These tendencies detracted from reaching development goals. Many social workers involved in social action expect and learn to handle conflict. Khinduka and Coughlin (1975) have pointed out that all societies encompass two worlds—integration-coercion, and consensus and conflict; and social action uses both strategies—norm adhering and norm testing.[41] It is partly because of political influence that people's situations are dynamic and capable of change. Without this premise that change is possible and an egalitarian process can occur, social development workers should seek employment "elsewhere."

Social Development Links Systems

Perhaps where social development departs most from other forms of social work is in its multiple linkages between systems. In order for this to succeed, workers must transcend the boundaries of traditional agencies and institutions. This is a challenge when human service agencies divide into separate empires, with few incentives to work jointly. One of the tasks of social development workers is to administer systems that are broad enough in scope to avoid artificial problem definitions and solutions; at the same time, management must attend to detail, so that the systems can respond.

Paiva has identified four features of social development: "structural change, socioeconomic integration, institutional development, and institutional renewal."[42] To attain these, the relations between dominant decision makers and the people will have to change to permit a more democratic decision-making process. Intermediate institutions at the community or regional level provide a measure of popular control although the stimulus may be a national, or international, plan.

The following account describes an example of social development. As you read, you may want to evaluate it against your own model of development efforts that attempt to give poor people control over their work and other aspects of their lives.

Women of Ahmedabad[43]

Those who took part in the program were women of Ahmedabad, India, and their families. The women were mostly self-employed, although the movement attracted some already poorly served by unions. The women's occupations ranged from street vendors to headloaders, who carried cloth bundles for local garment industries. These women perceived needs, which became a basis for organizing. As working women with families, they needed to make a profit. They faced obstacles including: (1) limited access to credit through moneylenders, who charged high rates; (2) lack of basic tools of their trade like pushcarts, forcing them to rent; (3) lack of outside child care, no accommodation for children in the workplace; (4) harassment by local authorities while working, and for some, sexual harassment by male employers; (5) failure of unions and employers to recognize their problems; (6) inequitable wages. Jain described how the Self-Employed Women's Association (SEWA) grew out of a textile workers union, which already existed.

Social development efforts thus began as a trade union effort to extend support and union staff to workers not then part of the union. There were some preconditions for this movement. First, some "headloaders" who were familiar with unions, asked the textile workers to help with their demands for a pay standard.[44] The textile union women's branch was already in place. Other groups of working women who were victims of arbitrary treatment became interested. The next condition was that the union's leaders of the women's wing knew how to organize their communities. In the accepted style, they went through the "dominant women of (each) trade group,"[45] held many sessions, and heard the complaints that expressed the group's basic concerns. The next step was critical, as it brought about a change in policy that had broad implications for social development. These self-employed women who plied many trades had more diverse problems than the textile union organizers could handle. Their leaders felt that autonomy and self-help were necessary, but could be boosted with the legitimacy and formal union status. Under Indian law, workers without a specific identifiable employer could not form a union. Despite this policy, self-employed women had organized, made visible gains, and shown collective force. SEWA then "challenged this narrow interpretation" and "argued that a union could be formed for the workers 'development,' that is, freedom from exploitation, assurance of regular work, and access to opportunities for advancement."[46] They won this interpretation, and SEWA became a registered trade union. This was a very significant change in policy. It strengthened SEWA's ability to offer many kinds of support for its members. Individuals' small dues were combined to hire social workers who worked with the women and their families. They assisted women in meeting their loan repayments and did crisis intervention. These workers, Jain notes, got "closer to members and assured them of (SEWA's) financial and moral support in all cases of genuine distress."[47] Credit was established at local banks interested in development. SEWA generated too many activities to cover fully here. Some examples were: (1) teaching workers about basic banking; (2) changing bank procedures to aid illiterate customers; (3) developing self-ownership of tools and improving them. SEWA bought and rented its own handcarts at less than middleman rates. The carts were redesigned with brakes to relieve strain, and with seats for children's safety. This technological side of social development has received less attention from social workers, but it is a practical and helpful approach. The difference between SEWA's technology and Hess's Community Technology (below) may have been that SEWA's women shared in the problem statement and the solution. Also, SEWA offered immediate relief for pressing problems. SEWA provided maternity, widowhood, and death benefits for women's families, day care to supplement poor government facilities, and occupational training and health education for workers. Leadership training was available to women who displayed interest in extending SEWA's work and their own skills. This, of course, helped ensure participation and continuity as professionals turned it back to members.

SEWA shows how the processes of social development intertwine. The basic needs of the women were evoked in a series of organizational meetings which brought together women with common interests. Cultural and social institutions, including existing trade unions, informal networks of street workers, and development-oriented (risk-taking) banks, were used to guide expression of these needs in a form society was able to accept. Planning led to a major federal labor policy change and many local changes, for example, those in bank loan policies and procedures. SEWA maintained an ongoing evaluation of workers' complaints, and satisfactions with its programs. In this way the structure formed to meet one set of initial needs tried to remain responsive to its constituency.

Appropriate Technology

In both international and U.S. development, the term "appropriate technology" describes an ideal application of technological solutions to human problems. Appropriate technology refers to technical aids that a community can use to assist in meeting its goals. Two examples might show what planners of appropriate technology hope to accomplish. The first is in the area of nutrition, and literally involves the life or death of infants in underdeveloped areas of the world where infant mortality is high. Global plans to alleviate world hunger by increasing food production and redistribution still fall far short. In countries where sanitary conditions are lacking, infants are likely to die from bottle feeding. The technology of bottle feeding, which appeals to many mothers for convenience and provides sufficient diet in the right conditions, is highly inappropriate, *given the context.* The bottle babies debate was won recently: U.S. churches have pressured our government and the formula-producing companies to stop exporting, and two high-ranked A.I.D. officials quit in protest over our ethics in supporting this bit of free enterprise.[48] One of the major multinational companies involved in distributing infant formula to Third World countries agreed to take steps to reduce the dangers of their product.

In a less dramatic and life-threatening example, social workers from developing countries often complain that the macromethods of social work practice, based on computer information systems, simply do not fit their practice settings. Critics like Schumacher contend that they do not fit ours either.

Social workers are attuned to social solutions and can contribute greatly to development by assessing all the factors influencing the use of new "tools." They know that on a local level, the status and meaning of a new program—and who accepts or uses it—will make a difference.[49] This is true in several sectors of services: health, nutrition, welfare, and mental health services. Yet social workers, even at high administrative levels, are plagued themselves with technology that they might improve. A balance must be struck between social scientists' attention to cultural, historical, and political factors affecting problem solution and potential technical improvements.

The emphasis on appropriate technology replaced the notion that transfer of technology was automatic. It implied that once a problem was found that resembled a problem elsewhere, the solution would be the same. While this thinking sometimes worked, often it did not.

Another reason why transfer of technology changed into a concern for appropriate technology is that "transfer" suggested a one-way process. The image was of experts (often outsiders) transferring their knowledge and tools to receivers who had everything to gain. It is hoped something will be seen to be wrong with this thinking even on the face of it. It is reminiscent of Goulet's point that people on the verge of development face a loss of self-image. This loss can be small if workers are talented at adapting people's resources to the problems posed by development.

Transferring technology, in its early form, overlooked the contributions that clients could make. For example, U.S. mental health planners are now learning from indigenous folk healers the skills that they use to treat people. In parts of Africa and in North America these local helpers were practicing long before our discovery of community healing in America. So transfer of skills and solutions is a two-way transaction.

Appropriate technology also implies an emphasis on small-scale projects that people can maintain themselves. The impetus for small-scale development came from two very different sources: rural areas of countries where there was little infrastructure or resources to maintain larger systems, and Western postindustrial societies like ours, where the energy waste and scale of institutions has gotten out of hand. Neither the underdeveloped nor the overblown situation promises much support for people. There are limits for growth in natural resources, energy costs, and people's capacity to be taxed.[50]

With the issues of appropriate technology in mind, a project that tried to improve urban life through the introduction of technical devices will be examined.

Adams-Morgan and Community Technology

In the 1970s many people in the United States turned to a focus on self-production, rather than consumerism, in a search for alternative ways to meet their needs.[51] During this time, Adams-Morgan, a predominantly black and Hispanic neighborhood in the heart of Washington, D.C., became the target for the introduction of technology that planners hoped would fit such a city neighborhood. The kinds of technical improvements were described by Karl Hess in *Community Technology.*[52] They included rooftop gardens, basement fish tanks, neighborhood tool shops, bacteriological toilets, and other innovations. Efforts to make these tools part of people's lives were based on beliefs about the value of self-sufficiency from outside controls—over food supply for instance, or city sewage systems. In the long run, however, the projects that were so enthusiastically promoted failed to gain acceptance by the people of Adams-Morgan.

Not long after the Community Technology group started to apply "appropriate technology" in Adams-Morgan, the movement lost its force. What happened? Hess, who was part of the Community Technology (C.T.) organization, wrote an account giving his view. David Morris, an associate of Hess and resident of Adams-Morgan, countered Hess with an analysis of his own.[53]

How did appropriate technology become inappropriate? First, nowhere in Hess's book is there evidence that community residents were asked about their priorities. Hess was vague about the means of obtaining participation. C.T.'s failure to consider the history and values of residents caused the enterprise to fall far short of social development. Self-sufficiency was an overall value of the C.T. leaders. Morris, however, pointed out that Adams-Morgan had already been organized and had only recently won some political power when C.T. proposed its projects. Morris said that neighborhood ownership of housing (which was owned by absentee landlords) was the community's primary concern, and that "solar collectors, trout farms, community gardens, even credit unions, or self-managed businesses, mean little until one controls the land."[54] There were other signs that Hess and C.T. misread community values and tastes (literally), as when the children were said to regard garden vegetables as "underclass" food. The conception of a unified program which, on the face of it, would include changes in people's attitude toward nutrition, food production, and property use, was lacking. Technical ideas, while creative, were apparently offered in a piecemeal fashion, by people convinced that positive demonstration and explanations would encourage residents to adopt them.[55]

The saga of C.T. suggests that developers must share with clients a holistic plan of what they are trying to achieve. Increased production is meaningless for people who have not agreed that the products are useful. A demonstration by outside proponents of new ways often does not have its desired effect. Apparently, C.T. missed the critical first step of social development planning, which is to base programs on people's felt needs. People are not thinking in terms of offbeat solutions. Leaders hoping to have people adopt new methods must be able to show their potential to meet residents' needs. In Adams-Morgan the gap between C.T. efforts and the larger community seemed due in part to the fact that C.T. had preconceived plans for problems that community residents saw quite differently.

Participation is a core value of social development, a means and an end of development. Projects are not participatory when workers predefine both the problems and the solutions. Similarly Morris observed: "many people in D.C., blacks as well as whites, chided [Hess] for . . . ignoring power and concentrating on what they perceived as interesting backyard hobbies and inventions."[56]

Let us return to Hollister's model, while we probe further into the failure of Community Technology in Adams-Morgan. The politicized climates in which social development takes place almost guarantees that different parties will interpret the process differently. Development planners and policymakers may promote the tools of self-reliance; yet, local citizens may mistrust self-help as a poor substitute for power or for influence over government.

The people of Adams-Morgan in the 1970s were gaining some influence and feeling an impact on their institutions. Morris argued that "the strength of the appropriate technology movement—the focus on small communities—can also be its major failing." He urged developers to recognize the great institutional forces which impinge on people and also to "reach out, to build coalitions with labor unions, city governments, professional organizations, state legislatures, machine tool shops, so that the movement can link scientific knowledge to political power."[57] In short, Morris advocated for social development.

SKILLS NEEDED FOR SOCIAL DEVELOPMENT

Most social workers are taught to do some community organization and planning. These skills are also required for workers in social development. The critical difference is that social development combines community organization and planning with "knowledge of economic, political, and social structures into strategies for social development."[58]

Certain social work skills stand out as most immediately useful to practice social development. They include the analysis and reform of social policy, research and evaluation, and group work and community organization. With these, social workers can facilitate social development and measure both its process and outcome. Basic relationship-building techniques, in which workers "facilitate patterns of social relationships . . . helpful to clients or constituents" are as vital to social development as to social work in general. Yet in their attempts to exert influence at organizational and community levels, workers in social development need special skills. Will Dodge summarized principles that he learned in many years of working in community development.[59] He urged development workers to recognize self-interest, negotiate compromises, and endure being disliked or unappreciated for their efforts.

Social development, after all, demands change. Tradition-loving people may find change difficult for reasons we have already discussed. Powerful people are likely to resist those changes which they view as eroding their power, including ownership reforms, credit reallocations, income redistribution, and the expansion of opportunities. Indeed, the other side of the Cruel Choice that Goulet depicted as necessary for development was the "voluntary" sacrifices that the privileged must make.

Preparation for an International Perspective

We noted earlier that social development requires comparative knowledge of the structures of social welfare and of alternative ways of meeting human needs. Anders has charged that international study is a weak component of U.S. social work education.[60] He pointed out the irony of having social work students take supportive course work in anthropology and sociology, which increases sensitivity to cultural variations, then entering a curriculum which may restrict itself to one nation's practices. He showed how internationalism can apply to social work in a pluralistic society such as ours.

Students interested in comparing social development and welfare programs can get an overview of postindustrial countries in Kahn and Kamerman's *Social Services in International Perspective*,[61] or the new *Journal of International and Comparative Social Welfare* and *Community Development Journal: An International Forum*.

Associations of social workers practicing social development publish journals and convene at meetings; they form a network of members here and abroad. The International Association of Social Welfare meets yearly and publishes the journal *International Social Work*. The Inter-university Consortium for International Social Development (I.U.C.I.S.D.), another such organization, exchanges its views through sessions at the Annual Program Meetings of the Council for Social Work Education, and in proceedings of its international meetings. Following Schumacher's model, many associations exchange information and practical manuals for intermediate and appropriate technologies to help people become self-sufficient in meeting their basic needs. VITA, an organization for Volunteers In Technical Assistance, publishes materials on appropriate technology.[62]

SUMMARY AND CONCLUSIONS

Social development is an order of social work that spans policy analysis and change, social service systems modification, and the enabling of people to help themselves by establishing alternative institutions. Its goals are to provide conditions in which people can meet basic needs and, beyond that, improve the quality of their lives in ways that they select. Workers in social development place great value on collective action and economic redistribution to make opportunities more accessible to those who want and need them. Another value held by social workers is that of global awareness. Practitioners of social development are able to see linkages between problems of people in developing countries who are vulnerable in the existing economies and welfare systems, and similar problems faced by people in the United States. Social development programs are carried on both in this country and internationally. Some social development workers have gained experience in the Peace Corps, Vista, or in agencies and found that they were committed to helping solve human problems by innovative means. Many social development professionals work within institutions or coordinate functions which involve more than one sector of human services, while still other workers serve outside of human services agencies, as traditionally conceived, wherever they can help people meet their needs.

NOTES

1. Irving A. Spergel, "Social Development and Social Work," in S. Slavin, *Social Administration* (New York: Council for Social Work Education, 1978), pp. 24–35.
2. Salima Omer, "Social Development," *International Social Work* (Bombay: International Council on Social Welfare, 1979).
3. Spergel, "Social Development."
4. David Gil, *Unravelling Social Policy* (Cambridge, Mass.: Schenkman, 1975); Jeffrey Galper, *Social Work Practice: A Radical Perspective* (Englewood Cliffs, N.J.: Prentice-Hall, 1980); Ira Sharkansky, *The United States: A Study of Developing Country* (New York: David McKay, 1975).
5. These social development values appear in J.F.X. Paiva, "A Conception of Social Development," *Social Service Review* 51, no. 2 (Chicago: University of Chicago Press, 1977): 327–336, and Dennis R. Falk, "Social Development Values," *Social Development Issues* 5 (1981): 67–83.
6. Falk, "Social Development Values"; Falk reported these values from a survey of practitioners of social development.
7. See Paiva, "Conception of Social Development," and David C. Hollister, "Social Work Skills for Social Development," *Social Development Issues* 1 (1977): 9–20.
8. Terms from international social development that refer to the countries to be developed include South, underdeveloped, developing countries, hosts and less-developed countries ("LDCs"). "LDCs" lost favor because, to many Third World people, the term implied cultural or social inferiority. In the United States similar sensitivities occurred around terms like the "culture of poverty." Charles Valentine argued that we ought to distinguish between the indicators of poverty and the cultural heritage of people who are poor (C. Valentine, *The Culture of Poverty*).
9. J. R. Anders, "Internationalism in Social Work Education," *Journal of Education for Social Work* 11, no. 2 (1975): 16–21.
10. Ralph Pieris, *Social Development and Planning in Asia* (New Delhi: Abhinav Publications, 1976), p. 97.
11. Dan A. Chekki, Prologue, in D.A. Chekki, ed., *Community Development: Theory and Method of Planned Change* (New Delhi, India: Vikas, 1979).
12. Peter L. Berger, *Pyramids of Sacrifice* (Garden City, N.Y.: Doubleday & Co., 1976).
13. David G. Gil, *The Challenge of Equality* (Cambridge, Mass.: Schenkman, 1977).
14. Gil, *Unravelling Social Policy*.
15. Bruce H. Lagay, review of *The Challenge of Equality, International Social Work* 20 (1977): 58–59.
16. Berger, in *Pyramids of Sacrifice*, has made the point that revolutionary socialism has failed to benefit people in their lifetime, no less than growth models of development; see Denis Goulet's *The Cruel Choice*

(New York: Atheneum, 1975), for a discussion of the sacrifices "haves" and "have-nots" must make to foster development.

17. Alvin S. Lackey, "Defining Development," *Development Praxis*, special issue, no. 2 (May 1984): 1–10.

18. Goulet, *The Cruel Choice.*

19. Susan Welch et al., "Where Have All the Clients Gone? An Examination of the Food Stamp Program," *Public Welfare* 31 (1973): 48–54; see also Elizabeth Moen, "The Reluctance of the Elderly to Accept Help," *Social Problems* 25 (1978): 293–303.

20. Harry C. Boyte, *The Backyard Revolution: Understanding the New Citizen Movement* (Philadelphia: Temple University Press, 1980).

21. Lane E. Holdcroft, *The Rise and Fall of Community Development in Developing Countries, 1950–65*, MSU Rural Development Paper No. 2 (East Lansing: Michigan State University, 1978).

22. Stephen M. Aigner and Ronald L. Simons, "Social Work and Economics: Strange Bedfellows," *Social Work*, July 1977, pp. 305–308.

23. Arthur Okum, *Equality and Efficiency: The Big Tradeoff* (Washington, D.C.: The Brookings Institution, 1975), p. 91.

24. Lackey, Alvin S., *Why Development Projects Don't Work as Planned: Pitfalls and "Solutions,"* Special Studies Series on Global Development No. 5 (College Park, Md.: World Academy of Development and Cooperation, 1987).

25. E. F. Schumacher, *Small Is Beautiful: Economics as if People Mattered* (New York: Harper & Row, 1973).

26. Bruce Stokes, *Helping Ourselves—Local Solutions to Global Problems* (New York: Norton & Co., 1981).

27. Sugata Dasgupta, "Three Models of Community Development," in D. A. Chekki, ed., *Community Development.*

28. Glen Leet, "Trickle-up Development," *Social Development Issues* 3, no. 3 (1979): 22–36.

29. Lackey, *Why Projects Don't Work.*

30. Drew Hyman and Joe A. Miller, *Community Systems and Human Services: An Ecological Approach to Policy Planning and Management* (Dubuque, Iowa: Kendall-Hunt Publishing, 1984); see also Spergel, "Social Development."

31. Paiva has made this point, especially regarding the U.S. social welfare institutions, in Paiva, "Conception of Social Development."

32. Elizabeth Moen et al., *Women and Social Costs of Economic Development* (Boulder, Colo.: Westview Press, 1981).

33. These have been Schumacher's and Galper's criticisms in works already cited; see also Karl Hess, *Community Technology* (New York: Harper & Row, 1979).

34. Melvin G. Blase, *Institution Building: A Source Book* (Washington, D.C.: A.I.D., 1973) (Final Report AID/CSP—3392).

35. Hollister, "Social Work Skills," p. 10.

36. Lorna Michael Butler and Robert E. Howell, *Coping with Growth Commu-*

nity Needs Assessment Techniques, WREP 44 (Corvallis, Ore.: Western Rural Development Center, 1980).

37. Fred Arnold et al., *The Value of Children: A Cross-National Study* (Honolulu: East West Center Population Institute, 1975), vol. 1.
38. The author traveled nationwide as an evaluator of the local family planning clinics, learning firsthand of these attitudes.
39. Lackey, "Defining Development."
40. Holdcroft, in *Rise and Fall*, stated that community development leaders' failure to handle conflicts and factions of local elites led to the decline of community development programs abroad by the late 1960s.
41. S. K. Khinduka and Bernard J. Coughlin, "A Conceptualization of Social Action," *Social Service Review* 49 (1975): 13.
42. Paiva, "Conception of Social Development," p. 327.
43. Devaki Jain, *Women's Quest for Power* (Sahibabad, India: Vikas House, 1980).
44. Note that the only thing the headloaders wanted initially was a standard, or scale for pay, as the rates fluctuated and were arbitrary; not even a raise was involved (Ibid., p. 523).
45. Ibid., p. 25.
46. Ibid., p. 24.
47. Ibid., p. 39. Both relationship skills for counseling women and advocacy skills for establishing credit were vital components of the SEWA program.
48. Front Lines, *Agency for International Development*, Washington, D.C..
49. Herbert Lionberger, *Speeding Adoption of New Techniques*, University of Missouri Extension Guide Sheet, 1979.
50. William H. Matthews, ed., *Outer Limits and Human Needs* (Uppsala, Sweden: The Dag Hammarskjold Foundation, 1976).
51. David Moberg in J. Case and R. C. R. Taylor, eds., *Co-ops, Communes, and Collectives* (New York: Pantheon, 1979).
52. Hess, *Community Technology.*
53. David Morris, "Adams-Morgan Revisited: Lessons from Community Technology" (Washington, D.C.: The Institute for Self-Reliance, May–June 1979), pp. 3, 10–11, but see also D. Morris and K. Hess, *Neighborhood Local Power* (Washington, D.C.: Beacon Press, 1975).
54. Morris, "Adams-Morgan Revisited," p. 10.
55. Hess, *Community Technology*, p. 43.
56. Morris, "Adams-Morgan Revisited," p. 11.
57. Ibid.
58. Hollister, "Social Work Skills," p. 11.
59. Willard K. Dodge, "Ten Commandments of Community Development of One Middle Aged Graduate's Advice to New Graduates," *Journal of Community Development* 11 (1980): 49–57.
60. Anders, "Internationalism in Social Work Education."
61. Alfred J. Kahn and Sheila B. Kamerman, *Social Services in International Perspective* (New Brunswick, N.J.: Transaction Books, 1980).
62. Volunteers In Technical Assistance, 3706 Rhode Island Avenue, Mt. Rainier, MD 20822.

ADDITIONAL SUGGESTED READINGS

Caplow, Theodore, *Toward Social Hope* (New York: Basic Books, 1975).

Chodak, Szymon. *Societal Development: Five Approaches with Conclusions from Comparative Analysis* (New York: Oxford University, 1973).

Coombs, Phillip H., *Meeting the Basic Needs of the Rural Poor: The Integrated Community Based Approach* (New York: Pergamon Press, 1980).

The Community Development Journal, published at 22 Kingston Road, Didsbury, Manchester 20, England.

Himmelstrand, Ulf, ed., *Spontaneity and Planning in Social Development*, Sage Studies in International Sociology, vol. 24 (Beverly Hills, Calif.: Sage Publications, 1981).

Honadle, George, and Rudi Klauss, eds., *International Development and Administration: Implementation Analysis for Development Projects* (New York: Praeger, 1979).

Illich, Ivan, *Tools for Conviviality* (New York: Harper & Row, 1973).

Journal of the Community Development Society (Athens, Ga.: University of Georgia).

Korten, David C. "Community Organization and Rural Development: A Learning Process Approach," *Public Administration Review*, September/October 1980, pp. 480–511.

Moris, Jon R. *Managing Induced Rural Development* (Bloomington, Ind.: International Development Institute, 1981.)

Social Welfare, Social Planning, Policy and Social Development: An International Data Base, *Sociological Abstracts*, two issues yearly.

Todaro, Michael, *Economic Development in the Third World*, 2nd ed. (New York: Longman, 1981).

Warren, Roland L., *Social Change and Human Purposes: Toward Understanding and Action* (Chicago: Rand McNally, 1977).

Wilber, Charles K., ed., *The Political Economy of Development and Underdevelopment*, 4th ed. (New York: Random House, 1988).

25 Professionalization, Education, and Personnel in the Social Services

H. Wayne Johnson

Not surprisingly, at a time of pervasive ferment in American society and the world, social work, like many other professions, is undergoing major changes. It is experiencing change in educational preparation, in personnel standards, and in a number of aspects of professionalization.

Whether or not social work is actually a profession or the extent to which it is constitutes a long-standing question. Abraham Flexner, an educator, speaking to the 1915 National Conference of Charities and Corrections, advanced criteria for a profession and contended that on some of these measures social work did not qualify.[1] Greenwood, in 1957, noted that professions possess five attributes: a knowledge base, authority, sanction of the community, regulative codes of ethics, and a professional culture.[2] Based on these, Greenwood found social work to be a profession.

The issue was also dealt with by Etzioni (1969) in his work on what he called "semi-professions" that dealt with teachers, nurses, and social workers.[3] All three are fields in which women outnumber men in contrast to most of the older, more established and recognized professions in which males predominate.

In the Etzioni book, Goode predicted that, "These semi-professions will achieve professionalism over the next generation: social work, marital counseling, and perhaps city planning."[4] Interestingly, in a reference to this statement he writes:

> Perhaps it should be emphasized that we are referring to the social worker, who has undergone professional training which culminates in the M.S.W. or the doctorate in social work. By contrast, the welfare or case worker in urban departments of welfare is much less likely to have been trained in a formal curriculum and, of course, does not fall into this category.[5]

It should be stressed that while in some respects Goode's comment is still applicable today, recent undergraduate social work education developments and expansion have, to some degree, transformed the picture. This does not change the fact, however, that considerable numbers of persons without social work education are employed to staff the human services.

One essay in Etzioni is based entirely on a sample of social workers from one county welfare department.[6] In view of this, it should be pointed out that public welfare agencies nationally do not constitute a uniform homogeneous entity and that they are probably more bureaucratic than at least some other fields of service in the extremely broad, diverse, and complex field of social work totally. The author of the essay acknowledged that the group was not presented as representative or typical of social work generally.[7]

THE PROFESSION OF SOCIAL WORK

Understandably, the reader may have difficulty appreciating the significance of this whole professionalization subject. The point is that questions, debates, and struggles over whether or not a particular field, in this case social work, is or is not a profession are indicative of the professionalization process itself.[8] Some occupations obviously developed much earlier as professions whereas others such as social work did so later or are still emerging now.

Regardless of how social work is perceived relative to its position as a profession, clearly it is in the process of professionalization. Just as clearly it has come a long way in the twentieth century, the time of most of its maturing, but it still has a distance to go.

Characteristics of the Profession

The Bureau of Labor Statistics counts 380,000 to 390,000 social workers in the United States. Of these over 100,000 are members of the National Association of Social Workers. NASW estimates that, in addition, an equal number of nonmembers are employed in the field who have social work degrees, a requirement for membership. Hence, totally about half of those in the Labor Department's figures are "trained" social workers.[9]

A 1982 survey of NASW membership produced some interesting findings from the 57,000 responses. In terms of setting, 27 percent of the respondents worked in social service agencies, 19 percent in hospitals, 16 percent in outpatient clinics or mental health centers, 9 percent in colleges/universities, and 8 percent in private practice.[10] About 42 percent worked in local or state public service, approximately 34 percent in nonsectarian private, 12 percent in private for profit, 9 percent in sectarian private, and about 3 percent in the federal public sector.[11] With regard to function, over 57 percent of the respondents were in direct service, 18 percent in management/administration, 6 percent in supervision, and 5 percent in education/training. The balance was scattered over several other functions.[12]

These social workers' major practice areas were also tabulated as follows (in round numbers):[13]

NASW Members by Practice Area, Shown in Percentage

Mental health	29	School social work	4
Medical/health care	15	Developmental disabilities	3
Children & youth	15	Substance abuse	3
Family services	12	Community organizing	2
Combined areas	5	Criminal justice	2
Aged services	4	Public assistance	1

Organizations for the Profession and for Education

The National Association of Social Workers (NASW) is the principal professional organization in this field today. It emerged in 1955 as a consolidation of seven previously separate organizations: the American Association of Group Workers, American Association of Medical Social Workers, American Association of Psychiatric Social Workers, American Association of Social Workers, Association for the Study of Community Organization, National Association of School Social Workers and Social Work Research Group. In 1987, the NASW membership was 108,000, compared to 22,500 in 1955. There are fifty-five state chapters in the United States, Virgin Islands, Puerto Rico, and Europe. Another example of marked growth during the twentieth-century push toward professionalization was in the old American Association of Psychiatric Social Workers that started out with 99 charter members in 1926 and had grown to 2,200 in 1955 when it combined into NASW.[14]

Like many organizations of professionals, NASW engages in activities having to do with (1) standards, (2) professional development, and (3) social action as well as (4) providing services to individual members. Standards include such endeavors as personnel classification and protection. Development includes continuing education, conferences, publications, and other related pursuits. Action encompasses lobbying and political activities. Member services range from insurance programs to travel plans.[15]

Originally NASW membership was restricted to persons holding the graduate Master of Social Work (MSW) or equivalent degree. As a result of the recognition of the facts that (1) large numbers of people occupying social work positions did not hold graduate degrees in this or any other field, and (2) undergraduate social work educational programs were growing rapidly in number and enrollment, membership in NASW was opened in 1970 to people with social work baccalaureate degrees from programs approved by the Council on Social Work Education (CSWE). In 1974, this program approval evolved into accreditation paralleling the existent CSWE accreditation of graduate programs.

As of 1987 there were 349 accredited undergraduate programs in American colleges and universities.[16] At the same time there were ninety-three master's level programs.[17] Over fifty schools offer postmaster's and doctoral programs. For most of the latter, offerings beyond the master's are relatively new. These have expanded to the extent that it is debatable whether the MSW should continue to be referred to as the "terminal degree" as was the case traditionally in staffing faculties of college and university social work programs. Schools that just a few years ago may have had mostly MSWs on the faculty now often employ more persons holding the doctorate. This appears to be more true of graduate schools and combined graduate/undergraduate programs than in those exclusively undergraduate. Student memberships are available in both NASW and CSWE.

There are still social workers who believe that either or both the inclusion of BSW workers in the national organization and/or the accreditation of undergraduate programs were mistaken actions. Some contend that this reduces the viability of the profession. The opposite view argues that such actions merely recognize the realities of the social services work force and attempt to build in some basic guarantees of quality social work practice and protection for the service consumer. The recency of many of the issues under discussion should be kept in mind. If we remember that neither admission of baccalaureate level workers to the national professional organization nor accreditation of undergraduate programs appeared until as recently as the 1970s, it is not surprising that some issues and controversies are still present.

For an undergraduate program to be accredited, it must have as its objective preparing students for entry-level practice. An exposure to social work/social welfare is not sufficient, but there must be at least 400 hours of field experience as well as classroom instruction aimed at preparing people to enter the profession. The curriculum must include content on social work practice, social welfare policy and services, human behavior and social environment, and social research.[18] In other words such a program may be very different in content today than just a few years earlier or than another nonaccredited social work program today with differing objectives.

Differentiating Levels of Personnel

It is noteworthy that the traditional NASW definition of the professional social worker identified the master's degree as the base educational level. Now that this has been expanded to include the baccalaureate practitioner, the idea is that undergraduate education prepares one for the entry level, for beginning professional practice, increasingly seen as a generalist. This development, along with others, presents questions as to the proper role for the MSW worker. So far, this matter is unresolved, but it appears that in general it is thought that the graduate degree worker moves ahead in one or both of two directions: specialization and advanced practice. Examples are supervision, administration, psychotherapy, or teaching/research. Another way of organizing specialization/advanced practice is around fields of service such as certain roles in the health field, for example, alcoholism.

Two attempts to come to grips with the problem of differential use of personnel in the social services will be examined briefly. In the early 1960s, before some of the major changes we have just described occurred, Richan proposed that the roles of "professional" and "nonprofessional" workers be delineated based on two factors: (1) client vulnerability, and (2) worker autonomy.[19] From this base he classified four levels of workers: (1) the professional, (2) the specialist, (3) the subprofessional, and (4) the aide. When Richan equated high client vulnerability and high worker autonomy with his professional, he seemed to be calling for the MSW. The specialist, according to Richan, may serve very vulnerable clients but does so in narrower, more technical ways. Hence, the specialist's training could come from "agency-operated schools or community college settings."[20] Richan's subprofessional worker appears to be one with a baccalaureate degree who handles the same kinds of responsibilities as the professional but with clients who are less vulnerable. Finally, the aide deals with the least vulnerable clientele and has only limited responsibilities. Training would be "brief in-service orientation courses."[21] It is important to recognize that this proposal is dated partly because of the NASW and

CSWE developments related to undergraduates. But the idea of client vulnerability and worker autonomy as determinants of worker roles and qualifications still seems significant today.

NASW offered a classification plan more recently consisting of two preprofessional and four professional levels as follows:

Preprofessional

Social service aide. Entry is based on an assessment of the individual's maturity, appropriate life experiences, motivation, and skills required by the specific task or function.

Social service technician. Entry is based on completion of (1) a two-year education program in one of the social services, usually granting an associate of arts degree, or (2) a baccalaureate degree in another field.[22]

Professional

Basic Professional Level. Requires a baccalaureate degree from a CSWE accredited social work program.

Specialized (expert) Professional Level. Requires a master's degree from a CSWE accredited social work program.

Independent Professional Level. Requires two years of appropriately supervised postmaster's experience following receipt of an accredited MSW degree.

Advanced Professional Level. Requires proficiency in special areas or ability to conduct advanced social welfare research; usually requires possession of a doctoral degree in social work or a related field.[23]

No matter what the proposal is regarding levels of personnel, the inescapable conclusion must be that the situation is still open and unfinished. A great range and variety of persons are employed in the social services, and a refined, consistent system for using people with certain qualifications exclusively or even primarily for particular responsibilities does not, in fact, exist at this time. Research thus far has not very convincingly demonstrated differential functioning and competencies.[24]

Since the designation ACSW has been used, further explanation is warranted. These letters stand for Academy of Certified Social Workers. Practitioners holding MSW degrees may qualify for ACSW by passing a written examination after completing 3,000 hours of experience under the supervision of a worker who is an ACSW. This is another example of the credentialing that tends to accompany professionalization in a field.

Licensing, Certification, and Declassification

Another development is the nationwide appearance on a state-by-state basis of some form of licensing or certification for social workers. NASW and other groups are promoting this development for a number of reasons having to do with protection of the service consumer from quacks and unscrupulous persons, assuring base levels of qualifications/competence, and enabling practitioners to receive "third-party payments" (for example, an insurance company or program paying a professional on behalf of an insured client) for services provided. As of 1987 social work was legally regulated in forty-two states.[25] In some states workers are licensed, and in others there is provision for registration or title protection. Some state laws cover both registration and licensing.

While the trend would appear to be toward more licensing in social work, the future on this matter is difficult to predict in view of the Carter and Reagan administrations' push for governmental deregulation generally. Another potentially complicating factor is the presence in some states of so-called "sunset" laws that require legislatures periodically to reconfirm the existence of state governmental regulations, provisions, or programs or, failing to do so, their automatic termination at specified times. This system has not been significant for social work licensing so far, but the potential to impact negatively upon it would seem to be real. In 1980 Kansas became the first state to conduct a "sunset" review of an existing social work licensing law; another licensing law was enacted.[26]

A related issue is the advent in some states of "declassification," that is, state merit or civil service systems modifying the requirements for employment of staff in the public social services. This modification may take the form of reducing, diluting, or dropping the requirements that must be met to obtain positions in the system; hence, the term *declassification* is used. The concern of some professionals is that this will mean poorer quality services for the consumer. This is another area where hard data and solid documentation would be most useful but generally do not exist.

THE SOCIAL SERVICE WORK FORCE AND SPECIAL PERSONNEL

A group of developments having to do with the helping disciplines revolves around the diversity of people who staff the social services. This personnel matter has been alluded to earlier but warrants special attention here. There is a tendency when discussing social welfare to consider only the profession of social work and within that to focus narrowly on "mainstream" professionals, ignoring many closely related occupations and different levels within broad employment groupings. The lines between some of these occupational categories are often unclear, and there are gray areas as to who does what. For purposes of discussion, we will divide this topic into four interrelated and overlapping parts: self-help, indigenous workers, paraprofessionals, and volunteers. They represent four special groups in the work force. They are in addition to those staff that carry the title of social worker. The latter are largely baccalaureate and master's level workers whose titles, too, are multiple and hence part of the ambiguity in this field as to who does what.

Self-Help

The modern self-help movement is a striking development of recent decades although its roots date back through centuries of mutual-aid endeavors. Katz and Bender characterize self-help groups as

> voluntary, small group structures for mutual aid and the accomplishment of a special purpose. They are usually formed by peers who have come together for mutual assistance in satisfying a common need, overcoming a common handicap or life-disrupting problem and bringing about desired social and/or personal change. The initiators and members of such groups perceive that their needs are not, or cannot be, met by or through existing social institutions. Self-help groups emphasize face-to-face social interactions and the assumption of personal responsibility by members.[27]

In earlier years, there were few such groups formalized, and Alcoholics Anonymous, which was founded in the 1930s, is generally viewed as one of the first. More recently, the number and kind of self-help groups has grown rapidly. The central idea of these is reciprocal relationships and interaction toward the benefit of all involved in the group. It has been estimated that there may be 500,000 of these mutual support groups in the nation involving 15 million people.[28]

Currently, there are self-help groups of the "anonymous" nature such as alcoholics, gamblers, overeaters, and others, groups with various physical or mental health problems or histories, dieters, addicts, ex-prisoners, homosexuals, persons with certain family characteristics such as parents of handicapped children, single parents, and many others.

Among the values noted in this kind of helping approach is the phenomenon of everyone "being in the same boat" and being able to identify with and support each other because of shared experiences and feelings, past, present, or both. This can be a powerfully supportive force and help to alleviate anger, anxiety, guilt, and other dysfunctional feelings. Another advantage points up the overlap between self-help and indigenous workers, a category to be discussed next. When a poor person who is a welfare recipient helps another poor person with meal planning, budgeting, child care, or whatever, there can be a tremendous psychological boost for that person in being a "giver" instead of a receiver. The same is true of an ex-offender working with offenders.

In the past social workers have not generally played a large direct role in self-help groups. They may help to organize them, refer others to them, and provide consultation. An article based on the experience of a large family service agency makes a strong case for the consultation role. Defining self-help as "the process whereby people with similar problems come together to alleviate their distress, independent of professional intervention," this agency employed a self-help coordinator whose job was to provide consultation service to self-help units in the agency's catchment area. This service was for both people wishing to start a group and for existing groups. Important among the worker's activities were assessment and linking the groups with the agency and community[29].

Indigenous Workers

A distinction is being made here that is not always made in the literature. Paraprofessionals and indigenous workers are being differentiated because of the formalized (for example, community college) training programs that often exist for the former and may not for the latter. The two groups may be combined, however. During the 1960s, particularly within the context of the antipoverty movement, considerable attention came to be given to involving people in the human services who knew from experience the hardships of being "clients" or potential clients. An example is employing welfare recipients or former recipients to work with the poor. Hiring unemployed or underemployed persons to work in income maintenance programs or in any one of a variety of social welfare areas has two major potential benefits: it is helpful to those persons requiring service, and it is also useful to the person wanting to move into or up within the labor force. Many of these so-called "indigenous" workers (that is, people from client groups served by social work) were at points employed in fields other than social welfare either as an employment end in itself or as a means toward stable work. But often various roles within the helping service systems themselves were occupied by such people.

With the passage of time in the 1970s and 1980s, there appears to have been diminishing enthusiasm in certain quarters for such approaches, and some critics are asking whether social work has lost its commitment to this effort.[30] To the extent that this activity has declined, a number of factors are undoubtedly present. One of these is the current concern within the social work profession over "declassification" of professional social work positions in state merit and civil service systems. There is now the desire to protect the earlier gains made by the professionals and to argue that quality service to the consumer requires fully qualified professional staff. There is a dilemma in this.

In one state, the merit system developed a plan in which a person with an undifferentiated baccalaureate degree qualified for employment at the Social Worker I level, whereas persons with bachelor's degrees from accredited social work programs were hired at the Social Worker II level. This arrangement later was changed, in the name of affirmative action, so that Social Worker II was opened to others. Experience and education are often equated, so that a job applicant may count specified amounts of experience toward educational requirements. But this raises a question as to the qualifications of the persons employed at this level and whether, for example, minority clientele are well served by movements in this direction. Whatever the outcome of such issues and controversies, it is likely that there will continue to be a diversity of persons working in the human services.

Somewhat related to these personnel issues is the use of so-called "natural helpers," particularly in rural areas.[31] Bartenders, beauticians, barbers, ministers, school personnel, law enforcement persons, and others are often cast into helping roles in communities. Social workers in some communities have established programs to enhance the knowledge and skills of such persons to make them more effective helpers.

Paraprofessionals

Although it is difficult to generalize on social work credentials, it can be said that, from the point of view of the National Association of Social Workers and the Council on Social Work Education, the four-year college degree in social work is now viewed as the base educational requirement for beginning professional practice. The content of that undergraduate education presents another set of issues dealt with earlier in this chapter. In spite of this consensus, there are many people in social work–type positions with less formal education, often persons who meet a state's merit system or civil service experience alternative requirements or persons with a college education but not in social work.

Beneath the baccalaureate degree there are various levels of workers employed in the social services, often under the collective rubric "human services." One group is persons with two-year degrees from junior or community colleges. In general, these are relatively new arrivals on the social welfare scene. In the main, such persons fall into one of two situations. They either have rather undifferentiated degrees such as Associate of Arts (AA) or something similar, which tend to be made up of basic arts and sciences or liberal arts content, or they are somewhat specialized along a certain vocational line. Often the latter lead to some sort of certificate in human services or a related area. One such program illustrates the latter phenomenon. The community college offering this "Human Service Associate" program describes it in its bulletin:[32]

> The Human Services program prepares students for entry level jobs or for transfer to a four-year degree program. By the end of the program students will be able to interact effectively with clients in a human services agency.
>
> The program emphasizes skills needed in working with clients such as interviewing, determining eligibility for services, making appropriate referrals, and assisting with counseling. A supervised field experience allows students to apply their skills in a work setting.
>
> Specializations are offered in chemical dependency counseling, eating disorders, mental health and social services.
>
> When the program is completed, students may find employment in a wide variety of settings including public and private social service agencies, treatment centers, group homes, institutions, hospitals, community centers and state or county departments of social services.

Some agencies and organizations require personnel with the specific educational backgrounds just described. Others with say, one, two, or three years of college but less than a baccalaureate degree, end up in human service positions in either a planned or unplanned way. It is common practice for certain kinds of social welfare organizations to employ college students on either a part-time or full-time basis in specified roles, depending upon the personnel needs of the agency. Here, again, the result is sometimes a mix with the same job title in an agency being held by college students, persons with some college training, and people with undergraduate degrees who may qualify for higher-level positions but, for varying reasons, hold the lower-level jobs.

Use of so-called "paraprofessionals" results from many factors, chief of which is the fact that not all social welfare jobs working directly with people require a high level of formal education. Even if this were not the case, there are not enough professionals to fill all of these job slots nor are there sufficient funds to employ the higher-paid persons.

A concern with this paraprofessional category of workers has to do with their somewhat marginal status. Few people want to be thought of or think of themselves as subprofessional, and to be in a nonprofessional category may be equated with being lesser. Yet, the responsibilities of such persons are often immense and of critical importance to the well-being of the people with whom they work. Child care workers or youth workers in group homes or children's residential centers may be, in important respects, the most significant persons in the lives of the youngsters. They work closely with them many hours a day, every day, in contrast to the professional therapists (social workers, psychologists, psychiatrists) who may see the child once a week or less often for an hour or so. The same is true of a worker in a mental hospital whose job is on the ward with the patients on an ongoing basis. In the latter situation, we are referring to essentially nursing-type personnel rather than social work, but the point about time and responsibility is valid.

The role of the social worker in relation to these paraprofessionals is noteworthy. Often social workers have partial or total responsibility for orientation and supervision of paraprofessionals. Inservice training and staff development may be significant social work roles with a variety of personnel.

Volunteers

Volunteers have been defined as "individuals who freely contribute their services, without remuneration, to public or voluntary organizations engaged in all types of social welfare activities."[33] Typically, in the complex and challenging social services there is more work to do than there are people to do it. Added to this is the fact that some of the tasks to be done do not require special educational backgrounds. Since most social services are governmental or nonprofit, funds are not sufficient to employ personnel to cover all tasks. Volunteers are a partial response to this situation. Among other contributions, they can free the time of professionals and other staff from assignments not requiring professional skills. Other volunteers shoulder such significant responsibilities as serving on agency boards and making policy.

Sieder and Kirshbaum have suggested the following possible roles for volunteers: (1) identifying problematic conditions requiring services, (2) policy making, (3) providing direct services, (4) fund raising, (5) acting as spokespersons for an organization, interpreting its programs and the problems with which they are concerned, (6) reporting and evaluating community reactions to programs, (7) community planning activities, (8) developing new service-delivery systems, (9) advocacy for the poor and disenfranchised, and (10) protest and public action.[34]

Youth volunteers care for children whose mothers attend an English-as-a-Second-Language class. Social workers may have responsibility for recruiting and working with volunteers.

One of the largest users of volunteers is hospitals. In a hospital, volunteers often perform a range of more or less routine activities that may greatly improve the quality of the hospitalization experience for the patient and family. Volunteers also have a large role in nursing homes and often in programs for the elderly. They are also used as "friendly visitors" in some public welfare departments, where they may help to humanize the large bureaucracy and provide some personal individual attention in an otherwise mass system. Other contexts in which volunteers are even more essential to the total operation are crisis intervention centers and big brother/big sister organizations that provide adult companions for children and youth. In these, the volunteer is the person who delivers the service. Similarly, volunteer leadership is conspicuous in scouting, YMCA/YWCA, church groups and similar activities, and in United Way fund raising and community organization.

Social workers often constitute the paid professional staff in some of these programs that depend on volunteers for staffing. In such cases, the worker's job may include recruitment of volunteers, orientation and training, program planning and evaluation of volunteers, and program. Training of volunteers takes on added importance where the volunteer becomes the service deliverer because the quality of the program hinges directly on his or her knowledge, skill, and ability.

While volunteers make major but undetermined contributions to social welfare, social work as a profession has a somewhat ambivalent position relative to them. NASW did, in 1977, approve a policy statement on "Volunteers and the Social Service System." This organization, along with CSWE, the Association of Junior Leagues,[35] and other groups are working together in a project "to enhance the effectiveness of volunteers and to improve the means of preparing social work students to work with volunteers."[36] With the cuts in human service budgets, there is some fear that volunteers might replace professionals. On the other hand, there is an important place for volunteers in social welfare, and they should be made an integral part of the whole.

Volunteerism has an uncertain future partially because a major source of volunteers in the past has been women. As more and more women take paid employment, there may be fewer available as volunteers. On the other hand, the growing number of elderly and retired persons may provide a major new source of volunteers at least in some social service areas.[37]

From this discussion of special social welfare personnel, which has been somewhat arbitrarily divided into self-help, indigenous workers, paraprofessionals, and volunteers, it is apparent that there is considerable confusion in the field. It is useful, therefore, to keep in mind that social work is a relative newcomer to the professions and that some students of the subject see it as a semiprofession.[38] However it is viewed, clearly it is still evolving and is in transition.

Burnout

In recent years there has been growing attention to and concern about what has come to be called "burnout." The term is used in reference to a condition, actual or potential, of workers in the social services. One definition of burnout is that of Maslach: "a syndrome of emotional exhaustion, depersonalization, and reduced personal accomplishment that [occurs] in response to . . . the chronic emotional strain of dealing extensively with other human beings, particularly when they are troubled or having problems."[39] Social work is a challenging and often stressful occupation. Dealing with human and social problems in heavy doses over prolonged periods of time can, and sometimes does, take a toll on employees in helping professions.

A study of counselor burnout in seventeen family agencies found a relatively small incidence. What there was appeared to be associated with such factors as work pressures, job dissatisfaction, lack of support, authoritarian administration, and personal vulnerabilities.[40] There may be more burnout than characterized these private agency findings in public agencies that so often have heavier workloads.

Burnout can be prevented, reduced, or treated through various measures that tend to enhance the workers' coping abilities. Included are assuring adequate rest, nutrition, diversion, and exercise for individuals. Reorganizing the workday to include such things as mini-breaks can be useful. A positive self-image for professionals is important, so that support groups of peers in and out of the agency and supervisory support are helpful. Improved communication within organizations is important as is identifying sources of stress and taking appropriate action. An example of the latter might be for a worker to take assertiveness training. Also it is often essential to help workers maintain detached concern for clients with reduced personal involvement in clients' problems and more emphasis on client self-responsibility.[41]

SUMMARY AND CONCLUSIONS

In this chapter the phenomenon of professionalization has been examined. As with any field this has included such considerations as professional organizations and education. In this particular field it has also been important to examine the various levels of existing personnel and issues around regulations. Special work-force developments included the use of volunteers, paraprofessionals, indigenous workers, and the self-help movement. It should also be noted that most of the chapters in this book deal with professionalization in the social services without necessarily expressing the matter specifically.

NOTES

1. Abraham Flexner, "Is Social Work a Profession?" *Proceedings of the National Conference of Charities and Corrections* (Chicago, 1915), pp. 576–590.

2. Ernest Greenwood, "Attributes of a Profession," *Social Work* 2, no. 3 (July 1957): 45–55.
3. Amitai Etzioni, ed., *The Semi-Professions and Their Organization* (New York: Free Press, 1969).
4. William J. Goode, "The Theoretical Units of Professionalization," in Etzioni, *Semi-Professions*, p. 280.
5. Ibid., p. 310.
6. W. Richard Scott, "Professional Employees in a Bureaucratic Structure: Social Work," in Etzioni, *Semi-Professions*, pp. 82–140.
7. Ibid., pp. 83–84.
8. An example from another field, pharmacy, was reported in the June 6, 1981, *Des Moines Register*, p. 1A, "Iowa Druggists Debate Using the Title of 'Doctor.'"
9. *NASW News*, September 1983, p. 9.
10. "NASW Data Bank, Selected Tables" (Silver Springs, Md.: National Association of Social Workers, May 1985), Table E, p. 3.
11. Ibid., Table B, p. 2.
12. Ibid., Table E, p. 3.
13. Ibid., Table C, p. 2.
14. *Encyclopedia of Social Work*, 17th ed. (Washington, D.C.: NASW, 1977), pp. 1501–1502.
15. "Program Highlights" (Washington, D.C.: National Association of Social Workers, August 1980).
16. "Colleges and Universities with Accredited Social Work Degree Programs," (Washington, D.C.: Council on Social Work Education, July 1987).
17. Ibid.
18. *Handbook of Accreditation Standards and Procedures* (Washington, D.C.: Council on Social Work Education, 1988).
19. Willard C. Richan, "Determining Roles of Professional and Nonprofessional Workers," *Social Work*, October 1961, p. 27.
20. Ibid.
21. Ibid., pp. 27–28.
22. NASW Policy Statement 4, "Standards for Social Service Manpower" (Washington, D.C.: NASW, undated), p. 6–11. According to personal communication with Myles Johnson of NASW on September 9, 1984, the preprofessional classification is still seen as viable.
23. "NASW Standards for the Classification of Social Work Practice" (Silver Spring, Md.: NASW, 1981), p. 9.
24. Patricia L. Kelley, "The Relationship between Education and Socialization into the Profession of Social Work" (Doctoral dissertation, The University of Iowa, 1981), pp. 39–49. An exception to the inconclusiveness and mixture of findings in studies is the doctoral dissertation of Walter H. Baily, "A Comparison of Performance Levels between BSW and BA Social Workers," Catholic University of America, 1978. He found higher performance on the part of BSW graduates than undifferentiated BA persons.
25. "State Boards Regulating Social Work" (Silver Spring, Md: NASW, June 1988).

26. *NASW News* 25, no. 6 (June 1980): 19.
27. Alfred Katz and Eugene Bender, quoted in "Self Help Groups," by Alfred Katz, *Encyclopedia of Social Work*, 17th ed. (Washington, D.C.: NASW, 1977), p. 1257.
28. Gordon Manser, "Volunteers," in 1983–1984 *Supplement to the Encyclopedia of Social Work* (Silver Spring, Md.: NASW, 1983), p. 172.
29. Brian A. Auslander and Gail K. Auslander, "Self-Help Groups and the Family Service Agency," *Social Casework* 69, No. 2 (February 1988): 74–80.
30. Edward A. Brawley, "Social Work's Diminished Commitment to the Paraprofessional," *Journal of Sociology and Social Welfare* 7, no. 5 (September 1980): 773–788.
31. Patricia Kelley and Verne Kelley, "Training Natural Helpers in Rural Communities," in H. Wayne Johnson, *Rural Human Services* (Itasca, Ill.: F. E. Peacock Publishers, 1980), pp. 130–139.
32. Des Moines Area Community College Catalog, 1987–88, Ankeny, Iowa, p. 46.
33. Violet Sieder and Doric C. Kirshbaum, "Volunteers," *Encylopedia of Social Work*, 17th ed., (Washington, D.C.: NASW, 1977), p. 1582.
34. Ibid., pp. 1582–1583.
35. "Voluntarism and Social Work Practice," an announcement from the Association of Junior Leagues, New York, February 1981.
36. Manser, "Volunteers," p. 173.
37. Ibid., pp. 169–170.
38. Etzioni. *Semi-Professions.*
39. As quoted by Dorothy Fahs Beck, "Counselor Burnout in Family Service Agencies," *Social Casework* 68, no. 1 (January 1987): 3.
40. Ibid., pp. 5–15.
41. Ibid.

ADDITIONAL SUGGESTED READINGS

Approaches to Innovation in Social Work Education (New York: Council on Social Work Education, 1974).

Baer, Betty L., and Ronald G. Federico, eds. *Educating the Baccalaureate Social Worker: A Curriculum Development Resource Guide II* (Cambridge, Mass.: Ballinger Publishing Co., 1979).

Career Development, a periodical initiated in 1971 as a publication "for professionals and paraprofessionals," by the Human Service Press, Washington, D.C.

The Community Services Technician: Guide for Associate Degree Programs in the Community and Social Services (New York: Council on Social Work Education, 1970).

Gartner, Alan, and Frank Riessman, *Help: A Working Guide to Self-help Groups* (New York: New Viewpoints, 1980).

Katz, Alfred H., and Eugene I. Bender, *The Strength in US: Self-Help Groups in the Modern World* (New York: New Viewpoints, 1976).

Leighninger, Robert D., and Leslie Leighninger, "Hail and Farewell— Undergraduate Social Work and the Social Sciences. 1974–1979," *Journal of Education for Social Work* 16, no. 3 (Fall 1980): 110–118.

McPheeters, Harold L., *A Core of Competence for Baccalaureate Social Welfare* (Atlanta: Southern Regional Education Board, 1971).

"Network Helps AIDS Caregivers to Cope," *NASW News* 33, no. 5 (May 1988): 3.

Ratliff, Nancy, "Stress and Burnout in the Helping Professions," *Social Casework* 69, no. 3 (March 1988): 147–154.

Richan, Willard C., and Allan R. Mendelsohn, *Social Work: The Unloved Profession* (New York: New Viewpoints, 1973).

Sherman, Susan R., Russell A. Ward, and Mark LaGory, "Women as Caregivers of the Elderly: Instrumental and Expressive Support," *Social Work* 33, no. 2 (March–April 1988): 164–167.

26 Social Services: The Future

Thomas H. Walz
Nancee S. Blum

We are living in the midst of an unprecedented social revolution. All social institutions in society are experiencing great change, including two institutions of foremost concern to the social work profession— the family and social welfare. The accelerated rate of change in our society is related to the phenomenon of high technology—its rapid introduction and application to our daily lives.

The so-called high technology era has its beginning around 1950. The pressures of World War II, coupled with the cumulative advancement of science, produced the conditions for the remarkable spurt in technological innovation.[1] Inventions like the interdigital computer, nuclear energy, video communications, and laser technology formed a set of powerful tools that would eventually produce a new cultural orientation in America.[2] Accommodating the demands of the high-technology age has led to the continuous redesign and reshaping of our social institutions.

Wilensky and Lebeaux argued that institutional welfare was an expected outcome of an industrial society.[3] Similarly, we shall argue that a new "advanced welfare state" is a predictable outcome of a high-technology-driven (postindustrial) society. Every new model of society, however, comes with its own imperfections. The high-technology era can be expected to produce its own unique range of "human casualties." Social change comes with a price, and unfortunately, some segments of the population end up paying a higher price for change than others. Typically these are persons marginalized or oppressed by changes taking place in the economic and social structure.

SOCIETY IN THE NEXT CENTURY

As new social problems present themselves, society must organize some institutional response to the new (and old) needs. In postindustrial societies the sum of these responses forms the basis of what we will refer to as the advanced welfare state. In this chapter we will explore (1) the nature and type of human casualties—social welfare needs—that result from living in a high technology society, and (2) the probable responses to these emerging needs that can be expected by the twenty-first century.

The shape of the probable welfare state in the twenty-first century can best be understood through an analysis of present societal conditions and current trends. Yet we need to be prepared for surprises. Predicting the future is always a risky business, particularly in times of rapid and heavy change.

While we can speak about high technology as the overall agent of change, high technology masks a number of factors that act interdependently in shaping our future. Each of the following is closely related to the high-technology movement, but each can also be viewed independently as a force or catalyst of social change:

- The development of a high-technology-driven global economy that operates through large national and multinational corporations.
- The growth of the national (and international) indebtedness of many nation-states, including the United States, which is the largest debtor nation in the world today.[4]
- The changing demographics of the world population, especially the aging of the population and the marked decrease in the birth rate.[5]
- The changing structure and function of the family, especially in the postindustrial nations.[6]
- The omnipresence of the cold war and the use of international terrorism as factors in the expanding defense budgets of both industrial and developing nations.
- The changing communication and transportation technologies that have altered our sense of space and time.
- The rising dominance of urban centers as the decision-making locus for the modern world.

- The rapid deterioration of the quality of the world environment and the severe crisis this imposes on the world's water supply, air supply, and natural resources.[7]
- The emergence of new diseases such as AIDS.

These are only a few of the developments linked to the high-technology revolution that can be used in our analysis of social welfare needs and responses. They are listed to alert us to the power and magnitude of the change factors at work in the modern era. While the social change developments are worldwide in scope, we shall restrict our focus to changes anticipated in our own society in the coming years.

The Family

The family is perhaps the best place to begin to explore the issue of human casualties that result from life in a high-technology society. Structurally the family has been reduced in size. The nuclear family that once consisted of two parents and children is now often a subnuclear family headed by a single parent. The fertility rate in the United States has dropped from 3.6 per white woman to 1.75 children since mid-century.[8] Family size is not only a function of the number of children produced, but of family stability. During the current decade the number of divorces have equalled the number of marriages, producing a situation where the single-parent family is now a prominent form of family life in America. Teenage pregnancies outside marriage occur at an unprecedented rate. The number of children living in broken homes is the largest in history.[9] Marital unhappiness and discord are omnipresent as the divorce rates would suggest.

In effect, the family today is an institution involved in a great social experiment, seeking to make the transition from industrial to post-industrial conditions, particularly in the work patterns of its adult members. Especially remarkable is the vast increase in the numbers of women entering the work force and the consequent rise of dual-career families. This development produces a demand for substitute child care and results in a greater dependency on other institutions (such as schools) to provide for the socialization of the young.

The family must also cope with the emergence of four generations of active membership. Families are still expected to provide long-term care to the greatly expanded number of aged members. These families are expected to share in the full range of social economic and health security needs that an enlarged and aging group membership presents. Yet the reduced size and stability of the family reduces the support it is able to provide, placing pressure on the state to share in this responsibility.

A further long-term care development is the number of developmentally disabled children surviving childbirth. The mentally retarded and physically disabled present a serious burden to families, even when and where assisted by government. An added long-term care issue soon to be experienced within the family is the rapid increase of AIDS victims.

Keeping the overview of the changing family system in mind, what changes and/or trends in social welfare responses to existing and emerging needs can be expected by the twenty-first century? What are the implications of these trends and developments for the social work profession?

Income Security and Employment Programs

The cornerstone of income security in modern society historically has been wage labor. While there are nearly 110 million adults in the work force, the pattern and nature of employment is dramatically changing. More people are working fewer hours per week over a greatly compressed work life. In the employment area, public policy initiatives that support expanded employment opportunities through direct government measures have largely been withdrawn. The private market has been allowed to seek its own level and arrangements of employment. Even affirmative action measures designed to redress discrimination in employment have been allowed to languish. Government supports for various manpower programs (Job Partnership Training Act, Comprehensive Employment Training Act) have been severely cut back. Only unemployment insurance has continued to be used to cushion the blow of the traditional work marketplace. In many states with high unemployment, trying to support unemployment insurance has been a factor in the growing fiscal crisis of state governments.

Other factors that complicate the traditional wage labor system have been the declining birth rates that could auger a labor shortage in the twenty-first century and the future policy decisions regarding international immigration. Labor shortages have often been addressed through a flexible immigration policy.

The real issue, however, is the nature and availability of work opportunity itself in a high-technology society. While we see figures indicating more jobs than ever before, the reality is that most of these jobs are new service-connected, low-wage jobs, often part-time and without fringe benefits. Other available jobs may fail to address the needs of many unemployed persons (such as single parents or black youth) because of high entry requirements or physical inaccessibility.

The coming decade will see profound advances in technology,

among them a rapid growth in quantity and sophistication of robots, major developments in artificial intelligence, and further advances in computer capabilities. As technological capacity expands, what effect does it have on the labor pool?

As a trend, it would appear that public policy in the United States is increasingly accepting a notion of "worklessness" as a way of life, allowing the welfare state to grow through expanding transfer payments to the unemployed and the unemployable. This acknowledges the reality that a high technology society comes to depend more heavily upon technology (machines) than labor to produce needed goods and services.[10]

Such a trend also helps to explain the current difficulties of a patched-up 1935 Social Security system in meeting the income needs of an aging population. Nowhere is this more evident than in the case of the Social Security retirement program. Throughout much of the 1980s, the Social Security trust fund was in crisis, that is, on the verge of bankruptcy. As large numbers of people retired and became beneficiaries, the revenues flowing into the program were disrupted by economic stagnation. Since Social Security retirement and unemployment insurance are based upon a tax on the wages of those currently employed, the presence of unemployment and underemployment greatly reduced tax dollars needed to pay beneficiaries. With Social Security trust funds depleted, the system fell into trouble. While changes in Social Security benefits were quickly enacted and the crisis, for the moment, weathered, the fundamental issue still remained. Could a Social Security system based on taxes on the labor of the current work force support the volume of beneficiaries expected during the first quarter of the twenty-first century? Given the smaller number of babies being born today, there will be fewer working-age people to bear the burden of the retired aged. Even an anticipated buildup of resources in the Old Age Retirement Trust Fund may not be enough to ensure retirement security for the aging baby boomers by 2025.[11]

In light of this analysis, it would seem that government will slowly move away from social insurance income schemes toward acceptance of a straightforward means-tested income transfer program. We can expect only a modest growth of Social Security retirement insurance but a far greater growth of Supplemental Security Income (SSI) and Aid to Families with Dependent Children (AFDC). We suspect that the concept of a guaranteed minimum income plan, popularly discussed in the 1960s, which today would integrate the AFDC and SSI programs, is a distinct possibility. It would federalize all the basic income transfer programs and standardize benefits across various categories. Such a plan would fit an efficiency-oriented welfare bureaucracy with conservative political leanings. We could also anticipate such a "guaranteed minimum income" plan would be truly "minimal" (mean and lean), since a high technology society will seek to reinvest its surplusses in further technological developments rather than expand its welfare state base.

In-Kind Assistance

In addition to direct cash supports, our social welfare system provides various noncash supplements to selected categories of people. Most notable of the noncash supports are health care financing, food stamps, and housing assistance.

The basis of government health care financing is contained in Title XVIII (Medicare) and XIX (Medicaid) of the Social Security Act. Medicare provides partial financing of health care for the elderly, some disabled persons, and those needing renal dialysis. Medicaid provides payment of health care for the poor and, in some states, the medically needy. Both programs have experienced substantial growth since their passage in 1965. Expanded use, along with greater-than-average increases in health care costs, have resulted in new public policy efforts to control and, where possible, reduce costs. Health care cost containment has taken many forms. Recipients are asked to pay deductible and co-payments for using health care. Access to health care by hospital admission and length of stay have been made more stringent. Many optional services are no longer covered. Medicare and Medicaid policies, however, have also been expanded in a few areas, such as additional coverage for home health and hospice services.

These are current developments. What future changes can be anticipated with respect to Medicare and Medicaid coverage? With the marked increase of frail elderly and functionally compromised individuals in society, medical costs will continue to rise at an alarming rate even with cost containment measures in place. It is anticipated that the Medicare trust fund could be bankrupt by the mid-1990s if new measures are not taken.[12] Medicare, unfortunately, suffers from the same problem as Social Security retirement. It depends heavily upon a tax on the wages of currently employed workers for its revenues (Part A, hospital insurance). In a world with diminishing work opportunities and an effectively smaller labor force, this creates serious difficulties in financing the program. Either Medicare will be greatly restricted by redefining the age of eligibility, such as from sixty-five to seventy years, or limiting the insurance to only part of the old-age cycle. Other anticipated restrictions will probably include limiting coverage to only certain types of care or procedures. For example, Medicare could refuse to pay for certain types of surgery for those of advanced age or for those who are terminally ill. It is doubtful that further increases in co-payments can be added, since the Medicare recipients are already sharing costs to the limit of their financial ability.

Medicaid, on the other hand, being directed toward the poor, cannot really employ cost-sharing strategies. Modest co-payments by recipients are already permitted at the discretion of the states that co-finance and administer the program. States have also been given discretionary authority to seek co-payments from families of Medicaid recipients, although few have taken steps to take advantage of this authority. As for the future, we can expect Medicaid to remain the principal means of providing access to health care for the poor. However, we can also expect that such health care in the future will be carefully rationed, will have fewer optional coverages (dentistry, eyeglasses, and the like), and will require greater family co-payments when families have the resources. In addition, fewer assets of the poor, such as equity in a home or car, will be protected under the current means-test arrangements.

The current trend in both Medicare and Medicaid to require recipients to use health maintenance organizations (HMO) and other prepaid group health plans will definitely continue. It is very likely that capitation payment plans (fixed amounts per year for care) will replace the more open-ended care-as-needed financing arrangements. The capitation payment system could replace the current DRG's (diagnostic related groups) as a mode of cost containment and cost stabilization for hospital care as well.[13]

With the government health financing system in fiscal trouble, there could be experiments with more dramatic changes in the future. Some partial forms of a national or state health service could be implemented. Here direct care would be provided by government-salaried health personnel to groups such as the poor, the elderly, the disabled, or those with AIDS.

Government could enter the health care market as a provider to insure tight competition in the health care system and to moderate costs by direct control of care for select groups.[14] We only need to remember that government has been a direct provider of care to merchant seamen, veterans, and Native Americans living on reservations. Other industrial societies (such as Great Britain) have long been active in providing a national health service.

The future for social work practitioners in health care settings will be greatly influenced by changes in health care financing policies. The current use of DRG's to control admissions and length of stay has turned hospital social workers into mainly discharge planners. Patient therapy, patient education, and family counseling activities are restricted by the fact that social workers are ineligible for third-party reimbursement. It is unlikely that the social work role in hospitals and health care will increase because the attention of government and private health insurers is so heavily focused on cost containment. The oversupply of doctors and the versatility of nurses will encourage these groups to take over more of the social work diagnostic and treatment functions.

The future is brighter for social work opportunities in home health, hospice, primary care, and AIDS programs. The nature of care in these settings follows a less medical model and a more social care model. Less high technology is involved in care provided outside the hospital, which favors a greater role for social workers.[15]

Another growth area for social work practice is long-term care facilities. Social work currently plays a very modest and limited role in nursing homes. Government requirements typically demand that nursing homes provide only a few hours of social work per week. However, the number of nursing home beds is expected to double by the twenty-first century to accommodate the needs of the growing numbers of severely compromised chronically ill elderly. Consequently there will be additional opportunities for social work practice. Gerontological social work is considered one of the principal occupational growth areas today.

Before leaving the health arena, there are several new developments of interest to social work. The expanded interest in health maintenance, illness prevention, and holistic health taps into an existing orientation of many social workers. These are low-technology approaches to health that theoretically open up new opportunities for appropriately trained social workers. Another development is the increased concern and attention given to AIDS as a public health concern. While AIDS patients require intensive medical care at times, the incidence and progressive nature of the disease makes it more of a long-term-care rather than an acute-care problem. The psychological effects of AIDS on the patient and the family are also a major factor in the way the disease is experienced. Social workers definitely have a role to play in AIDS education, prevention, and long-term care of the AIDS patient. The social work profession has been a leader in the outreach to the gay community, which is particularly threatened by the AIDS virus.

As is evident from this cursory look to the future, health care remains a major field of practice for the social work profession.

THE SOCIAL SERVICES

The social work profession in many ways has been the central profession in the provision of social services to the American family. As defined in this text, social services consist of the range of hands-on and support activities designed to enhance social functioning of individuals, couples, and families. These services cover the gamut from counseling to residential care to both the troubled individual and family, as well as those seeking to enrich their personal and family lives. While social services historically have been provided through private sectarian and philanthropic interests, government at all levels has greatly increased its provision and financing of social services. Nearly $3 billion per year is expended to the states as part of the social service block grant program. But what about the future? Can substantial increases of social services be expected in the twenty-first century?

This question can really be answered only from the experience of the high-technology-based economic gamble in which we are currently engaged. Should it produce significant surplus wealth, as it did in the late 1950s, the public might well support a substantial growth of social services. However, at each step, policymakers will weigh the relative merits of further investing in technological innovations and expansion against investing in an enlarged welfare state.

One trend does appear to govern how resources available for social services will be allocated. Those human social needs that tend to "pollute" the general environment will receive more attention than services needed only by marginal groups in society. Services that cut across social classes such as chemical dependency, family violence, AIDS, long-term care, and care of the mentally disabled and physically handicapped will be competitive for scarce dollars because people with such needs are able to command powerful advocates. This serves to remind us of the reality of a class bias in what services we fund and for whom.

The state will continue to assume substantial responsibility for those who are obviously dependent—children, the handicapped, and the elderly. The government, however, will expect families to participate more actively in financing and providing care. In child welfare, for example, we have seen how family-based approaches have replaced many traditional foster care and residential care approaches. Indications are that this trend will not only expand, but will be increasingly employed in long-term care for the elderly and other functionally compromised individuals. Hospice, respite care, and day-care programs for young and old will continue to command public support, assuming they remain cost-effective.

There are other social services such as child day care and counseling the individual and family that may not experience increased public support. Government efforts to remove welfare families from transfer payments have been more rhetoric than real action. Experience has shown that many such efforts are not cost-effective. Subsidized child care for AFDC parents may consume much of their earned income. Job training and placement activities have, in fact, contracted in recent years. The outlook is for limited growth in these areas, at least in terms of public support.

For those who are employed in the larger corporate world, employee assistance services could well expand. However, these private enterprise social services are largely directed at more privileged members of society. They have limited impact on the needs of the poor or marginalized families. Alongside the employee assistance programs is the documented growth of private marketplace social services. More social workers enter private practice today than ever before. This trend will clearly continue into the twenty-first century.

Many persons entering social work education and training espouse a career in private practice. Again this portends an interesting class-biased trend. Those who are economically better off will have increasing access to social services, while those who are less well off will make do with what the welfare state chooses to provide. As we indicated earlier, the state will respond to problems that disrupt the general well-being of society.

The private sectarian and nonprofit social services have been sustained in recent years through purchase-of-service contracts with government. Only a few of these service agencies are so richly endowed that they can be self-supporting. Thus the private social work sector will rise and fall with the policy choices that make money available for social services. Overall, the picture we see today is unlikely to be expanded in the decades to come.

We are still living in a period of social welfare austerity. The public mood is to hold back further expansion of the welfare state including social services.

Professionally, social work has developed technologies that could enrich the lives of many persons. The expanded range of social services for the mentally retarded is a case in point. We have moved away from institutional care to a rich range of community and family-based alternatives. There are group homes, assisted living apartments, day activity centers, work and training programs with job coaches, respite care services, special education programs, and others. Yet, each of these alternatives requires funding. Will funds continue to be available?

There is a paradox in professional enrichment. Each new service, more elaborately delivered, costs more. If additional funds are not available, then access to such services becomes more restricted. The more affluent are able to take advantage of this development, since they can buy the new technologies without the benefit of public subsidies. For other families, only the willingness of the public sector can make them available.

Ironically, the twenty-first century in all phases of life seems to be moving toward a two-class structure: those who live in the mainstream of the high-tech world and those who are shifted into the welfare state addendum of such societies. Different levels of access to social services depend on one's social class position.

This raises the final point to be made in this chapter. What role will the social work profession play in advocating for fairer, more expanded access to social services? Currently there is limited interest in schools of social work for community organization, social development, and advocacy careers. The majority of students desire to pursue careers in therapy and counseling. Unless this is reversed, these students will go where the market for counseling and therapy is, that is, in the corporate and private practice world.

Beyond this, there is the reality that our world is becoming a global village. The problem of the human family in the developing portion of the world also calls for added social services, as well as social justice. Who will give leadership to these concerns: the many homeless children of the world, displaced and refugee families, and those whose poverty cripples the spirit? Where does North American social work fit into this scenario? Should a troubled marriage in an urban suburb in the United States command more resources than a hungry child in a developing country?

The twenty-first century may well witness the rise of an international welfare state. The reality is that the global technology-based economy must accept responsibility for the changes it creates. One way or another, the world that benefits from economic change must pay for its human costs. Social workers could do well to be the watch dogs of this development. Leadership is needed to prevent and reduce such human costs and when they do occur, advocate for responsible action to remedy such tragedies.

This is a time of great change. The 1990s will witness the rise of biomedical technologies, robotics, advanced cybernetics, and a host of other technological developments. Social workers must understand the dynamics of technologically induced social change and enter into the policymaking arena at all levels.

Much is demanded of the social work profession. The question remains, will it respond? Much depends on the quality and concern of those entering the profession today, for they will be the practitioners that bring social work into the twenty-first century.

NOTES

1. D. Bell, *The Coming of Post Industrial Society* (New York: Basic Books, 1976), p. 21.

2. F. E. Emery, *The Emergence of a New Paradigm of Work* (Canberra: Centre for Continuing Education, Australian National University, 1978).
3. H. Wilensky and C. Lebeaux, *Industrial Society and Social Welfare* (New York: Free Press, 1965).
4. P. G. Peterson, "The Morning After," *The Atlantic Monthly* 260, no. 44 (October 1987).
5. F. White, "The Environment of Medicine in the 21st Century: Implications for Preventive and Community Approaches," *Canadian Medical Association Journal* 136 (March 15, 1987): 571–575.
6. J. Naisbitt, *Megatrends* (New York: Warner Books, 1982).
7. R. K. Turner, "Sustainable Global Futures," *Futures* 19 (October 1987): 574–582.
8. A. Thornton and D. Freedman, *The Changing American Family* (Washington, D. C.: Population Reference Bureau, Inc., October 1983).
9. A. Cherlin and F. F. Furstenberg, Jr., "The American Family in the Year 2000," *The Futurist* 17 (June 1983): 7–14.
10. G. Thernborn and J. Roebroek, "The Irreversible Welfare State: Its Recent Maturation, Its Encounter with the Economic Crisis, and Its Future Prospects," *International Journal of Health Services* 16 (1986): 319–338.
11. M. J. Baskin, "The Coming Social Security Surplus," *Fortune*, March 30, 1987, pp. 111–112.
12. Health Care Financing Administration, "National Health Expenditures, 1986–2000," *Health Care Financing Review* 8 (Summer 1987): 1–37.
13. J. C. Goldsmith, "The U.S. Health Care System in the Year 2000," *Journal of the American Medical Association* 256 (December 26, 1987): 3371–3375.
14. K. D. Yordy, "Current and Future Developments in Health Care," *Bulletin of the New York Academy of Medicine* 62 (January–February 1986): 27–38.
15. R. A. Kane, "Health Policy and Social Workers in Health: Past, Present, and Future," *Health and Social Work* 10 (Fall 1985); 258–270.

ADDITIONAL SUGGESTED READINGS

Theobald, Robert, *The Rapids of Change* (Indianapolis: Knowledge Systems, Inc., 1987).
DiNitto, Dianna M., and Thomas R. Dye, *Social Welfare, Politics and Public Policy* (Englewood Cliffs, N.J.: Prentice-Hall, 1987).
Costello, Manuel, *High Technology, Space and Society* (Beverly Hills, Calif.: Sage Publications, 1985).
Teich, Albert H., ed., *Technology and the Future*, 4th ed. (New York: St. Martin's Press, 1986).
Gil, David G., and Eva A. Gil, *Toward Social and Economic Justice* (Cambridge, Mass.: Schenkman Publishing Co., 1985).

Epilogue

H. Wayne Johnson

We have come to the end of a journey that I hope has been instructive and enjoyable. The contents of this book have been arbitrarily organized as is true to some degree of an introductory text in almost any field. There is some overlap among topics but, when the same subject has been dealt with in two or more places, we have attempted to emphasize aspects appropriately in relation to their context. In other words a topic has not been given equal and similar attention in two places but has an emphasis in one.

Starting with basic principles, concepts, and historical resumé, we spent considerable time on social services as community and societal responses to an array of social problems. Both traditional and nontraditional programs were studied as we saw that a multiplicity of responses occur to conditions perceived as problematic, themselves numerous. We saw the "3 Ps" construct at work, of problem-policy-program, intermeshed and reciprocally influential. Many measures for assisting people to cope with change and stress were examined as these exist on all levels from micro through macro.

Social work as practice was also considered through discussion of generalist social work practice and newer helping approaches. Attention was given to working with individuals and families, groups, and communities. Research and administration in a social work/welfare context were also examined. Finally, in the last section we introduced content on racism, sexism, diversity and discrimination, and the social services. Housing as a unique field and social development, particularly international, as a special practice area were explored. Matters related to professionalization in social work constituted one chapter as did likely future developments in this field. What the future holds for the social services is uncertain, yet is partially predictable. Clearly change will continue to be pervasive and ever present. Change has been a continuous theme throughout this entire text as it has been historically and inevitably will be in the future.

Although our voyage is over, we have really just begun. The need is for an enlightened, informed, rational citizenry as voters, taxpayers, committee and task force members, and decision makers. This is actually a greater need than for more and better social workers, although the latter is not insignificant. Especially is this true at this time when there are people in high office around the country providing stimulus and leadership to a national mentality that is not conducive to general widespread human well-being.

You can make a difference; we all can. So, in the words of Horace Mann,

Be ashamed to die until you have won some victory for mankind.

Index

THE SOCIAL SERVICES: An Introduction
Third Edition

Composed by *Compositors Corporation*, Cedar Rapids, Iowa

The text is set in ITC Garamond with display lines
in ITC Avant Garde

Printed and bound by *Braun–Brumfield, Inc.*,
Ann Arbor, Michigan

Designed by *Willis Proudfoot*, Mt. Prospect, Illinois